From Reading to Neurons

From Reading to Neurons

edited by Albert M. Galaburda

A Bradford Book
The MIT Press
Cambridge, Massachusetts
London, England

The illustrations for chapter 6 are copyrighted by Ursula Bellugi and the Salk Institute.

This book was set in Palatino by Graphic Composition, Inc. and printed and bound in the United States of America.

Library of Congress Cataloging-in-Publication Data

From reading to neurons / edited by Albert M. Galaburda.

p.   cm.—(Issues in the biology of language and cognition)
   Contains papers given at a conference held in Florence, Italy, June 8–12, 1987, sponsored by Emily Landau and the Fisher-Landau Foundation of New York City.
   "A Bradford Book."
   Includes bibliographies and index.
   ISBN 0-262-07115-0
   1. Dyslexia—Congresses. I. Galaburda, Albert M., 1948–   . II. Landau, Emily.
III. Fisher-Landau Foundation.   IV. Series.
[DNLM: 1. Dyslexia—physiopathology—congresses.   2. Neurons—physiology—congresses.   3. Reading—congresses.   WL 340.6 F931 1987]
RC394.W6F76 1989
616.85′53—dc 19
DNLM/DLC
for Library of Congress   88-23134
                                                                                        CIP

To the memory of Norman Geschwind, my teacher, colleague, and friend

Contents

Series Foreword

The MIT Press series on Issues in the Biology of Language and Cognition brings new approaches, concepts, techniques, and results to bear on our understanding of the biological foundations of human cognitive capacities. The series will include theoretical, experimental, and clinical work that range from the basic neurosciences, clinical neuropsychology, and neurolinguistics to formal modeling of biological systems. Studies in which the architecture of the mind is illuminated by the fractionation of cognition after brain damage or by formal theories of normal performance are especially encouraged.

John C. Marshall

Preface

This book contains most of the papers given at the conference From Neurons to Reading, which took place in Florence, Italy, from June 8 to 12, 1987. The conference was sponsored by Mrs. Emily Landau and the Fisher-Landau Foundation of New York City to encourage thinking and research on developmental dyslexia; it was organized by Albert M. Galaburda of Harvard Medical School and the Beth Israel Hospital in Boston with the help of Massimo Piattelli-Palmarini, then at the Florence Center for the History and Philosophy of Science and now at the Center for Cognitive Science, Massachusetts Institute of Technology.

The choice of speakers reflected the main motivation of the conference, to gather together researchers whose work was deemed by me to be relevant but by and large not yet applied to research on developmental cognitive disorders, particularly developmental dyslexia. A great deal of past and present work seeks to classify dyslexia into functionally determined subtypes; less of the ongoing research aims to look at medical and neurological underpinnings; still less work has taken full advantage of the remarkable theoretical and methodological advances made in fields such as developmental molecular, cellular, and systems neurobiology, clinical and experimental developmental neuropathology, neurology of behavior, developmental cognitive science and linguistics, and computational modeling of learning and cognition. It is my strong wish that such observations, theories, and methodologies now begin to be incorporated into research on developmental dyslexia and related disorders of brain and cognitive development and my conviction that they will be. Not only will this development eventually help children and adults affected with learning difficulties, but also research on disorders of brain and cognitive development will help advance neuroscience and cognitive science as a whole, as it already has in the study of the acquired aphasias. The conference and these proceedings thus represent an attempt to set up a starting point.

The work of many other distinguished researchers, some of whom have long been involved actively in dyslexia research, was also deemed to be of great importance to the goals of the conference, but unfortunately inability to attend, on the one hand, and time constraints, on the other, prevented their inclusion in the program of delivered papers; such work, however, was repeatedly cited by conference participants, and we were fortunate to have some of these people present in the audience as our guests.

Some of the basic fields relevant to dyslexia research, e.g., neurophysiology, basic immunology and neuroimmunology, genetics, the neurobiology of learning and memory, neuroimaging, and visual cognition, were not specifically represented for reasons similar to the above, but by and large relevant issues were informally raised in papers and during discussions.

I discussed with Harry and Betty Stanton, of Bradford Books, The MIT Press, the potential difficulties for a reader of this book due to the wide range of fields represented: from neurophilosophy and computational psychology, through behavioral neurology and developmental experimental neuropathology, to systems, cellular, and molecular neurobiology, each with its specialized lexicon and set of ideas. Together we decided that I would write brief editorial comments at the end of each chapter for the purpose of attempting to link the material in the chapter to that of other chapters and to the central theme of the book: the growth of research on disorders of brain and cognitive development. The editorial addenda are not meant to be commentaries on the individual chapters per se but rather are provided as guidelines to additional reflection and discussion. I trust that the reader will continue this process well beyond this book.

Conference Participants

Ursula Bellugi
The Salk Institute for Biological
Studies
La Jolla, California

Paul Bertelson
Université libre de Bruxelles

Verne S. Caviness, Jr.
Massachusetts General Hospital,
Boston
Harvard Medical School

Patricia Smith Churchland
University of California, San
Diego

Kathryn L. Crossin
Rockefeller University

Antonio R. Damasio
College of Medicine
University of Iowa

Hanna Damasio
College of Medicine
University of Iowa

Béatrice De Gelder
Tilburg University
Netherlands

Yadin Dudai
The Weizmann Institute of
Science
Rehovot, Israel

Albert M. Galaburda
Beth Israel Hospital, Boston
Harvard Medical School

Lila Gleitman
University of Pennsylvania

Patricia S. Goldman-Rakic
Yale University

Mary Louise Kean
University of California, Irvine

Norman A. Krasnegor
National Institute of Child
Health and Human
Development
Bethesda, Maryland

André Roch Lecours
Université de Montréal

John C. Marshall
Radcliff Infirmary
Oxford

James McClelland
Carnegie-Mellon University

Bruce S. McEwen
Rockefeller University

Jacques Mehler
Laboratoire de science et
psycholinguistique

Centre d'études des processus
cognitifs et du langage
Paris

John Morton
Cognitive Development Unit
Medical Research Council
London

Laura Pettito
McGill University

Massimo Piattelli-Palmarini
Masachusetts Institute of
Technology

Pasko Rakic
Yale University School of
Medicine

Glenn D. Rosen
Beth Israel Hospital, Boston
Harvard Medical School

Mark S. Seidenberg
McGill University

Gordon F. Sherman
Beth Israel Hospital, Boston
Harvard Medical School

Acknowledgments

The conference came about as a result of the warm generosity of Emily Landau and the personal involvement and support of Caryl Frankenberger of the Fisher-Landau Foundation of New York. The hard work and dedication of Loraine Karol, administrative assistant to our Neurological Unit at the Beth Israel Hospital, guaranteed a flawlessly organized conference, comfortable travel, and a pleasant stay for all speakers and guests in Florence, Italy. William Baker, director of the Research Division of the Orton Dyslexia Society, videotaped all lectures and discussions, and he and his wife, Deborah, were responsible for several of the conference's amenities. Lilli Piattelli and Hilaria Martin ensured that travel and local arrangements went smoothly from Rome to Florence and back. Speakers and guests alike made the conference succeed beyond all expectations. My colleagues Gordon Sherman and Glenn Rosen offered helpful advice during the editing stages, and Lisa Bennett's help was invaluable during the preparation of the typescript. Finally, Harry Stanton and Betty Stanton of The MIT Press made my job of editor almost pleasurable. To each I offer my grateful appreciation.

Introduction

The topic of dyslexia may seem at first to be esoteric and of concern to only a few people, mainly educators and educational psychologists. However, it does not take deep reflection to realize that it is in fact part of the larger topic of brain and cognitive development and, as such, carries implications for one of the central questions of neurobiology, the relationship between brain and mind and their development from the time of conception. Moreover, and perhaps more down to earth, the formal study of this topic offers a potential for opening new doors to the understanding of a set of particularly debilitating conditions, those in which children and adults are deprived of their full intellectual power.

Developmental dyslexia is a pretheoretical, operationally defined condition or group of conditions characterized mainly by difficulty with learning to read and with achieving expected reading levels. The diagnosis is often made on the basis of reading-history questionnaires and standardized tests. In the restricted definition of the disorder, the reading difficulty need not be part of a more generalized disturbance of sensorimotor function, intellectual capacity, thought or affective processes, or cultural opportunity. Studies continue to show that both dyslexic children and adults exhibit abnormalities in spoken language as well as written language consisting predominantly of problems with oral comprehension of syntactically complex sentences, problems of awareness of the phonological structure of words, and problems with working memory for linguistic objects. Most experts agree that dyslexia represents a true behavioral anomaly rather than simply an extreme example of a normal variation in reading competence, but this question too needs further study.

As dyslexia is currently defined, figures of its prevalence cannot possibly help us discover the frequency in the population of anomalous cognitive structures involved in reading acqusition and achievement; rather we can use them to discover only those individuals that fail to find innate and environmental processes that enable them to compensate. Moreover, as dyslexia is usually defined, a diagnosis can be made only in children of at least eight or nine years in the second or third year of school, who must be able to demonstrate a reading age equal to or greater than two years below the expected level. Earlier behavioral markers of the disorder capable of being detected in the preschool years are currently not available, although they are a focus of active research. Also not available are markers of the disorder in dyslexic adults, who may have achieved an adequate reading capacity after a period of childhood difficulties.

On the basis of these considerations dyslexia is perhaps diagnosed in approximately five percent of the school-age population; diagnosis in older individuals falls off because of diminished screening and the arrival of compensatory strategies that hide, but do not correct, the underlying abnormalities. Most studies show that dyslexia tends to run in families and is diagnosed more commonly in males, and some studies report an increased frequency among left-handed and ambidextrous individuals, and increased left-handedness and ambidexterity among dyslexics. Other disorders of learning are more commonly diagnosed in dyslexics (e.g., stuttering and attention-deficit disorders), and ailments that implicate a dysfunction of the immune system, such as allergies and autoimmunity, are reported more commonly in dyslexics and their families.

Until recently dyslexia has been viewed principally as an educational problem. Early biological characterizations at most suggested an arrest of brain maturation, but without observational or experimental support. The level of ignorance has not substantially changed. At a recent conference on the general topic of developmental neuropathology and developmental behavioral disorders organized by Martha B. Denckla, then of the National Institutes of Health in Bethesda, several experts from the fields of developmental neurobiology and neuropathology agreed that we do not know the causes and mechanisms underlying the great majority of developmental neurologic and cognitive disorders. Yet observations in autopsies, observations of experimental animal brains, and theories, methods, and observations in neurobiology and cognitive science permit a fresh look at these developmental problems.

The normal steps involved in the formation of the human cerebral cortex, its architectonic organization into connectionally functional assemblies, can be surmised from observations of human brains and by extrapolating from comparative studies of experimental animals. This normal process involves the induction of neural tissue from the neural ectoderm, the generation of neurons and glia, their migration to their mature locations in the cortical laminae, their maturation and differentiation *in situ* (which includes the establishment of long and short circuit networks followed by synaptogenesis and the expression of specific chemical properties). At each appropriate developmental stage there is overproduction followed by a removal of cells, axons, synapses and molecules that are not selected for survival. Interfering with the normal steps of generation, maturation, and selection can lead to brain malformation. Depending on the date, severity, and type of interference, different types of anomalies emerge, some of which can kill the fetus. A rich literature, both descriptive and experimental, has recently grown around the issue that genetic determinants like trisomies and mutations in mice and early epigenetic events like viral infections, x-irradiation, exposure to toxins, trauma, and immunogenic injury can lead to congenital brain anomalies that vary in type, severity, localization, and behavioral consequences. In this volume we deal with several of these aspects of the normal and abnormal development of the brain substrates of cognitive structures relevant to the language and reading disorder in dyslexia.

Since extraordinary inheritable characteristics and perturbations in the fetal environment can result in peculiar neuroanatomical characteristics, it is important to ask whether changes in the anatomical characteristics of the brain can lead to behavioral changes. In other words, does a variation in brain architecture inevitably lead to a variation in cognitive capacity? If so, what is the nature of the cognitive change, that is, can it be documented at the level of cognitive potential or cognitive strategy?

Recent research in dyslexia has opened new connections to observations in developmental neural and cognitive science. This research suggests additional descriptive and experimental research to test hypotheses already proposed and to help generate new hypotheses for study in suitable experimental animals and on living human subjects. It now appears likely that the problem of developmental dyslexia has its roots in fetal brain development and is not significantly related to the brain's postnatal growth and interaction with the postnatal environment. This is not to say that an unusually configured brain will not respond better to one or worse to another type of environment, and therefore that the environment has no role to play in the expression of dyslexia after birth. Yet the nature of the anatomical changes in the brains of dyslexics points to events that take place from the middle of pregnancy to at most shortly after birth, that are related to the architectonic and connectional development of at least the cerebral cortex at a time when biologically determined maternal-fetal interactions are more important than psychosocial effects, and that occur before birth injury can play a role. Elucidating maternal-fetal interactions capable of subtly restructuring the developing brain will be likely to greatly enhance our understanding of developmental learning and other congenital disorders. An understanding of the initial state of brain and cognitive structures brought forth by the newborn infant just prior to exposure to the psychosocial environment provides a starting point for our understanding of an individual's learning and acquisition of mature behavior. This volume is an attempt to consider some of the steps involved in the production of the initial brain, the initial behavioral state, and the course the brain takes in acquiring cognitive structures in the normal and deviant environment. Our emphasis is on the cerebral cortex and the development of language. Yet the concepts advanced here may also apply to the rest of the nervous system and to other cognitive capacities as well.

From Reading to Neurons

Chapter 1

Learning about Reading from Illiterates

Paul Bertelson and Béatrice De Gelder

Introduction

Reading research derives both an important practical incentive and a major theoretical challenge from the consideration that acquisition of literacy is difficult compared to the earlier acquisition of speech. Specific difficulties are apparent at two different levels.

First, acquiring literacy is difficult to the extent that it seems to require instruction of the kind generally provided by schools. The capacities to speak and understand speech develop independently of any deliberate effort on the part of adults in all children allowed a minimum of linguistic input. But for written communication, all societies that have considered it important have developed instructional facilities in the form of either schools or individual tuition. There is in fact no convincing evidence that sheer exposure to written material can lead to advanced reading and writing. Many children for instance spontaneously develop a sometimes extended capacity to identify words in brand names and road signs. Yet this capacity greatly depends on the usual appearance of the symbols and suffers markedly when they are represented in ordinary print (Masonheimer et al., 1984). And there is no suggestion that it allows children to acquire independent deciphering capacities that can be applied productively to unknown words.

At the second level we have the phenomena on which the present conference is focused, developmental dyslexias. Even when provided with school instruction, a non-negligible minority of children with normal intelligence and motivation for school achievement display strong and specific difficulties in acquiring literacy. These difficulties are not necessarily homogeneous. Recent work based mainly on the single-case methodology has provided rather good evidence for the existence of at least two different forms of developmental dyslexia (Coltheart et al., 1983; Temple and Marshall 1983; Seymour 1986). No similarly widespread anomalies have been reported for speech acquisition.

Phonological Awareness

Among the several proposals that have been offered about the origin of reading-acquisition difficulties (see Bertelson 1986 for a selective review), one has exerted a dominant influence on research during the last fifteen years or so. It is that the acquisition of reading and writing, at least in a submorphemic orthography (one that maps characters onto submorphemic units), requires a form of explicit knowledge of the phonological structure of the language, which is not required for acquiring speech. That knowledge has been called *phonological awareness*.

That notion, as originally formulated in the early 1970s (Liberman 1971; Liberman et al. 1977; Rozin 1978), had its roots in the Chomskyan preformist conception of language acquisition (see the discussion in De Gelder 1985 and also Levelt et al. 1978). The primary linguistic activities (Mattingly 1972) of speaking and listening are served by a specific machinery whose development is to all important extents under endogenous control. These activities function automatically without conscious reflection. A hearer normally becomes aware only of the intention, the meaning of an utterance, and not of the more superficial syntactic and phonological aspects.

The speech machinery is not available for visual inputs and, hence, does not by itself permit reading and writing. The latter are secondary linguistic activities, which must be constructed in deliberate, willful fashion in the same way as other artificial skills, like piano playing or counting. In particular, they require an awareness of those aspects of phonology that are relevant to the orthography at hand. As generally used, the concept of phonological awareness involves awareness both that speech is sound and that it can be represented as a concatenation of particular units. These units can be at different levels: words, morphemes, syllables, or segments. It has generally been assumed that awareness of segments represents a more advanced level of phonological awareness than awareness of syllables, which in turn is more advanced than awareness of morphemes or words. Different writing systems which map different units onto characters would thus require different levels of phonological awareness.

In early formulations, the exact role of phonological awareness in reading acquisition was generally left implicit, but there can be little doubt that what theorists had in mind was the kind of rule-governed assembly of phonology postulated for the indirect procedure in dual-route models of lexical access (Coltheart 1978). The link was made explicit by Liberman et al. (1977), who explained that the strategy of "relating the orthographic components of the written word to the segmental structure of the spoken work" allows the child to exploit advantages of the alphabetic representation: "Given a word that is already in his lexicon, the child can read it without specific instruction, although he has never before seen it in print; or given a new word which he has never before heard or seen, the child can closely approximate its spoken form and hold that until its meaning can be inferred from the context or discovered later by his asking someone about it" (p. 209). This notion of phonological assembly as a self-teaching device, which allows reading to take advantage of existing speech recognition facilities, has been further elaborated by other theorists (most explicitly by Jorm and Share 1983) and incorporated in systematic models of reading development (Frith 1985).

It must be noted here that the question of the role of assembled phonology in reading acquisition is a different one from that of its role in fluent adult reading. It is quite conceivable that phonological reading is important or even necessary at some stage of reading development, as the conception of an "alphabetic stage" implies (Frith, 1985), but that it is restricted to a secondary backup role later on. As a matter of fact, the situation at the adult stage is still the focus of much debate, while there seems to be some kind of consensus regarding development.

There is little doubt that the acceptance of the phonological awareness notion owes much to the fact that it has generally been considered an integral part of the concept of indirect reading and has thus benefitted from the strong intuitive appeal of the latter. For expository purposes it nevertheless remains necessary to keep the general notion that phonological awareness is an important condition of reading acquisition separate from the more specific one of its role in indirect reading. The first shall be called here the hypothesis of phonological awareness.

Empirical Evidence for the Hypothesis of Phonological Awareness

Several arguments have been offered in support of the hypothesis of phonological awareness. One line of argumentation that has commanded much attention is based on the history of writing systems. In their persuasive 1977 paper Gleitman and Rozin adopted Gelb's (1952) conception of that history as an evolution from costly logographies through syllabaries to the parsimonious alphabet. They theorized that what made that evolution slow was the difficulty of accessing the linguistic units that submorphemic systems represent ("phonographic" systems in Sampson's [1985] classification). The same factor, the low accessibility of phonemes, was thus supposed to explain both the late discovery of the alphabet and the difficulty of learning alphabetic reading and writing. Gelb's evolutionary views, and in particular the critical assumption that the representation of segments was a late discovery, have recently come under severe criticism (Sampson 1985; Mattingly 1985; Holender 1987). So arguments based on historical evidence might need some reassessment.

Among arguments of an observational or experimental nature, some apply in a general way to the role of indirect reading in acquiring literacy but not specifically to that of phonological awareness. There is for instance the well-documented fact that reading nonsense is one of the capacities that best predict ability to comprehend text (see the review by Stanovich, 1982). Such data support the hypothesis of phonological awareness only indirectly and to the extent that deciphering is considered to depend on phonological awareness. Here we shall concentrate on the more direct evidence.

The empirical evidence first brought to bear on the hypothesis did not directly address the issue of the direction of influence. Some studies showed that the capacity to manipulate submorphemic strings of speech is poor in prereaders (Calfee et al. 1972) and also that they find phonetic segments more difficult to deal with than syllables (Liberman et al. 1974). These were important findings, as they showed that phonological awareness should be considered not as an all-or-none state but as having several levels. On the other hand, several studies demonstrated some correlation between capacity at analyzing speech into submorphemic units and reading ability: speech analysis improves in tandem with the acquisition of reading (Liberman et al., 1974) and poor readers do not perform as well in speech-analysis tasks as better readers (e.g., Rosner and Simon 1971; Liberman et al. 1974; Fox and Routh 1976). Yet such correlations, as Liberman et al. (1977) noted, can result as well from effects of reading instruction on speech-analysis capacity as from the reverse type of influence.[1] Later work has untangled the knot to some extent.

Direct evidence in favor of the basic hypothesis of phonological awareness, i.e., evidence that higher phonological awareness promotes progress in reading, has only become available recently. As late as 1982 Henderson could conclude his review of the then available evidence with the remark that "the central role of phonological awareness remains as yet no more than a plausible hypothesis" (p. 63). One new line of evidence is based on training experiments; another on correlational studies.

Several authors (e.g., Williams 1980; Bradley and Bryant 1983; Fox and Routh 1984; Torneus 1984; Olofsson and Lundberg 1985) have shown that training children on tasks designed to promote various forms of phonological awareness can improve their later reading achievements. One problem is that in some of these studies some form of additional reading instruction has been administered together with training in phonological awareness. Bradley and Bryant (1983), for example, obtained a significant increase of reading performance in a group of subjects trained both in phonological awareness and in letter-sound correspondences, but in a group trained in phonological awareness only the increase fell short of significance. On the other hand, these real-life training studies have often involved rather complex training procedures and have thus left the nature of the particular manipulations responsible for the effects in doubt. Fortunately more analytic information has been provided by simulation experiments in which subjects have been trained on specific forms of speech analysis and effects on particular reading capacities have been measured (Treiman and Baron 1983; Fox and Routh 1984). Thus, although none of these studies is completely conclusive by itself, taken together they definitely point to an influence of training in phonological awareness on reading achievement.

The correlational evidence comes from longitudinal studies in which phonological awareness measured at one stage has been shown to predict later reading achievement. The problem with this kind of study is, of course, to control for the possible contaminating effect of the reading experience itself on initial phonological awareness. One must distinguish here between two cases. There is first the case of those studies where phonological awareness is measured before the beginning of reading instruction, both formal instruction at school and the various forms of tuition that some children may receive at home shortly before being sent to school. There are a few studies in which these conditions were probably met. The best known is the monumental investigation carried out by Bradley and Bryant (1983) with more than four hundred children. Correlations that survived controls for general intelligence and memory span showed up between a test of the ability to categorize words on the basis of sound similarities, administered at four or five years of age, and performance on standard reading and writing tests three years later. In the second case phonological awareness is measured after the start of instruction. To obtain evidence on the direction of causation, it is then necessary to resort to special statistical devices like partial correlation and multivariate methods to isolate the specific effect phonological awareness at one stage has on later reading achievement. Using that approach, Perfetti et al. (1987) have provided what looks like convincing evidence that the ability to delete and add phones at one stage has a causal effect on subsequent progress in word decoding and spelling.

One can thus conclude that although none of the studies we have considered is free of criticism, taken together they provide convincing support for the hypothesis that phonological awareness is important for progress in reading. Yet they do not allow the extreme conclusion that it is *necessary* for progress in reading. Some observations, like the description by Campbell and Butterworth (1985) of an adult subject who is a fluent reader in spite of a history of severe inability to deal with the phonological aspects of speech, suggest that there might be alternative routes to reading ability.

The Development of Phonological Awareness

In much of the early literature the focus has been on the role of phonological awareness in reading acquisition, and the conditions under which phonological awareness itself develops have not been much considered. The emphasis on the distinction between primary and secondary linguistic activities might be one reason for that relative neglect. In the second category reading and writing were lumped together with achievements such as appreciating and producing puns and verse, judging grammaticality, effecting speech repairs, and playing word games, many of which appear not to depend on specific learning opportunities. The possibility that these activities might be heterogeneous from the point of view of developmental history has not been raised until relatively recently.

There is now rather good evidence that the emergence of at least some forms of phonological awareness requires specific instruction. The main argument is that phonological awareness improves in lockstep with reading instruction. It can be shifted on the age axis as a result of variations in national educational practices (Skjelford 1976) or of individual differences in age at the start of the school year (Alegria and Morais 1979). On the other hand, in one of the rare studies in which effects of different teaching methods have been considered, three months of phonics instruction resulted in a stronger ability to invert initial and final consonants of a syllable (54 percent correct) than the same time under a strict whole-word method (15 percent correct) (see also Bruce 1964; Perfetti et al. 1987). However, the more demonstrative data are provided by comparisons of adults with different literacy situations: illiterates, literates of varying degrees, and also readers of different writing systems. The rest of the paper will be focused on these data.

Morais et al. (1979) got access to an agricultural area of Portugal where illiteracy was the norm but some people had had reading instruction at an adult age, either during their military service or at a literacy class run by a local factory. One could thus find living side by side under similar economic and cultural conditions people of comparable ages who had not been to normal school but some of whom had attended literacy classes as adults while others had not. Subjects from both groups were administered tests that involved either deletion of the initial consonant of an utterance (*posa* → *osa*) or addition of a particular consonant to an utterance beginning with a vowel (*ima* → *pima*). The experimenter pronounced the test item and the subjects' task was conveyed through examples, followed by training trials in which the experimenter provided the correct response whenever the subject failed to do so. In half the experimental trials both test item and correct response were words, while in the other half both were pseudowords. The results, which appear in table 1.1, were that illiterates performed very poorly in both tasks, while ex-illiterates performed considerably better. As a matter of fact, illiterates were at the same low level as Belgian first graders tested during the third month of the school year, and ex-illiterates at a level similar to that of second graders tested in the fourth month of the year (see table 1.1 again). The pattern of results was almost exactly the same for words and pseudowords, showing that the poor performance of illiterates is not due to the low familiarity of pseudowords.

The result for consonant deletion has now been replicated in several studies, one (Morais et al. 1986) with two new groups of Portuguese adults, comparable in all relevant aspects to those of the original experiment, another one with Brazilian adults from the same environment, some of whom had learned to read at school while others could not read as a result of total or partial lack of school attendance (Bertelson et al., in press).

The Evidence from Illiterates: Implications and Limits

Before discussing the interpretation of the results, we shall first consider what their potential implications are and what they are not. In other words, we propose first to ask if in principle the results can lead to interesting conclusions and only then examine whether they really support such conclusions.

(1) The most important aspect of the results would be that adult illiterates cannot analyze speech into segments. It would imply that awareness of the segmental structure of language does not emerge spontaneously. The data from the ex-illiterates would show mainly

Table 1.1
Manipulating the initial consonant of an utterance (mean percent correct responses)

Task	Subjects		References
	Portuguese adults		
	Illiterates	Ex-illiterates	
Adding to word	46	91	Morais et al., 1979
pseudoword	19	71	
Deleting from word	26	87	ibid.
pseudoword	19	73	
Deleting from pseudoword	19	73	Morais et al., 1986
	Brazilian adults		
	Nonreaders	Readers	
Deleting from pseudoword	33	76	Bertelson et al., in press
	Chinese literates		
	Logographic	Alphabetic	
Adding to and deleting from word	27	93	Read et al., 1986
pseudoword	21	83	
	Japanese children		
	1st grade	4th grade	
Deleting from pseudoword	24	62	Mann 1986
	Belgian children		
	1st grade (mo. 3)	2d grade (mo. 4)	
Adding to pseudoword	29	79	Alegria and Morais 1979
Deleting from pseudoword	18	73	

that the inability displayed by the illiterates is not a general one in this population, due perhaps to the fact that they did not exercise their speech analysis capacities during the sort of critical period proposed by Mattingly (1984) or even to some more fundamental deficits that may be cultural, genetic, or nutritional. Awareness of segments can develop in adult illiterates as a result of some particular experience that is provided in the literacy classes.

(2) On the other hand, the nature of these critical experiences is not something that data of the present kind will readily allow us to elucidate. As a matter of fact, we know very little about the methods that were used in the classes attended by our ex-illiterate subjects. In principle, literacy training could promote phonological awareness both *directly,* because it involves explicit teaching of speech segmentation or exercises in segmentation,[2] and *indirectly,* because literate subjects can use orthographic knowledge to solve phonological awareness test questions. It is important to discriminate between these two possibilities. We shall return to the question later, but it is not one that can be answered easily.

(3) The findings would not contradict the hypothesis of phonological awareness: it is quite possible that some forms of phonological awareness appear only as a result of instruction and also constitute an essential step in the development of literacy. There has been a tendency in the literature to apply to the relation between speech analysis and reading a version of the familiar chicken-and-egg question: is the ability to segment speech a prerequisite of reading acquisition or one of its consequences? Bryant and Bradley (1985), for instance, take much pain to argue for a causal link from phonological awareness to reading achievement, and they credit us with the reverse position. Actually, we never wanted to take sides in a debate on a question that in our opinion is poorly formulated (Bertelson et al. 1985; Bertelson 1986). One cannot expect to find interesting unidirectional causal relations between entities as global as phonological awareness on one hand and reading instruction on the other. Literacy evidently results from a complex sequence of steps, some triggered by maturation and others by particular instruction. On the other hand, as we already suggested, phonological awareness probably admits of several levels or even breaks down into several heterogeneous components, which allows for the possibility that some of them may precede reading instruction and others develop during acquisition. The relation is thus in all probability an interactive one. As with other types of developmental interaction, the final goal is to analyze the total process into the sort of episodes between which unidirectional causal relations might hold.

(4) Demonstrations of awareness of phonetic segments per se in subjects who have not been taught segmental analysis would contradict the present results. We shall later discuss results reported by other authors that might have such implications (Bradley and Bryant 1983; Mann 1986).

How strong is the demonstration provided by comparing illiterates and ex-illiterates? To answer this question we must first realize the limits of the approach.

The conditions under which it is possible to test illiterate people clearly do not allow all the controls one might wish for. There can be noise, interference from neighbors and relatives, etc. Fortunately, these conditions also prevail for control literate subjects; so their main effect, if any, was probably to increase the variability of performance within each group. Another concern is the reliability of biographical data, especially data on literacy status and school attendance, which are based mainly on subjects' declarations. For instance, in the Brazilian study subjects who volunteered their services as illiterates were later found to be able to read. More reliable information was available in the Portuguese studies, in which subjects were generally recruited through local collaborators who knew them, but even there one cannot totally exclude the possibility that some subjects classified as illiterates may have had more exposure to instruction than they revealed.

These problems had to be acknowledged, but since their eventual effect would have been to mask intergroup differences, they do not compromise the interpretation of those differences that were actually observed. A more serious problem is the multiplicity of the possible sources of differences in performance between literates and illiterates. The source we are interested in is the direct effect of reading instruction. Yet we cannot assume that our ex-illiterates differ from the illiterates only in the direct effect of that specific experience on phonological awareness. At least the following additional possibilities must be considered:

(1) The two groups of subjects were perhaps different before literacy training. It is not an implausible assumption that those members of a given community who take advantage of the existence of literacy classes or who are admitted to them tend to be the more intelligent and/or better motivated ones.

(2) Training may have produced more general cognitive or attitudinal changes, which may influence test performance directly. For instance, attending a literacy class may promote communicative skills, which facilitate understanding test instructions or provide practice at inferring a rule from examples or at analyzing all sorts of things into parts. At a more general level, it has the effect of familiarizing stu-

dents with school-like activities, such as being tested. Illiterates often try to escape the testing situation on the ground that they should not be expected to succeed in such activities, and that sort of attitude may well affect the amount of effort they apply when they agree to participate.[3]

(3) Literacy gives access to a range of opportunities from printed information to jobs. As a result, the superiority of ex-illiterates may also reflect their wider life experiences.

There are in fact so many possible nonspecific differences that could explain away literacy effects that once one starts listing them, it is tempting to give up the whole enterprise as undecidable. Our position has been that although one cannot hope to gain precise control of all the relevant factors, multiplying the comparisons—different tasks, different groups of subjects—may allow some estimation of their respective contributions. The surprising result of applying that strategy has been that the influence of the various contaminating factors has turned out to be rather small.

The Specificity Issue

One prediction common to the three groups of causes considered in the preceding section is that differences should be observed across a large range of tasks, while differences due specifically to reading instruction should occur only in tasks that tap knowledge acquired from alphabetic-reading instruction, namely, awareness of phonetic segments and possibly other units of speech. So one obvious way to narrow down the range of possible interpretations was to compare illiterates with ex-illiterates on a wider range of tasks.

In a new study, we have applied tasks imposing the manipulation of different linguistic units and extending also outside of the linguistic domain, to two new groups of illiterate and ex-illiterate Portuguese adults in general similar to those of the original experiment (Morais et al. 1986). The results, reproduced in table 1.2, were rather clear. In speech manipulation tasks, illiterates gave very low performances whenever they had to deal with phonetic segments, and that irrespective of the form of the task, whether consonant deletion, detection of a target consonant in a spoken sentence, or the task of progressively segmenting a sentence into smaller units. They gave a better performance, though not equal to that of ex-illiterates, when the segments to be manipulated were syllables, that is, in the tasks of deleting the initial syllabic vowel of an utterance, detecting a syllable target in a spoken utterance, and also in a rhyme-judgment task (choosing a probe picture with a name rhyming with that of a target).

Table 1.2
Performance of Portuguese illiterates and ex-illiterates on Various Tasks

Task	Score	Illit. (N = 20)	Ex-illit. (N = 21)
Deleting initial consonant of pseudoword	% correct	19	73
Deleting initial syllabic vowel of pseudoword	% correct	55	85
Deleting initial note of melody	% correct	26	34
Detecting consonant /k/ in sentence	% correct	36	81
Detecting syllable in sentence	% correct	62	81
Progressive segmentation of utterances	% phonemic responses	7	62
Rhyme judgments	% correct	67	93

Source: Morais et al., 1986

In a nonspeech segmentation task (playing back on a simplified xylophone a short tune produced by the experimenter but leaving out the first note) both groups performed at the same low level.

More evidence concerning nonlinguistic performance has been obtained in other studies. Morais and Cary took the direct step of administering a standard intelligence test, Raven's Matrices (three first series only), to literate and illiterate Portuguese adults, and they found only a small nonsignificant difference. Kolinsky et al. (1987) examined similar groups on a visual analysis task in which the subject has to decide if a complex visual pattern contains a target component, and they observed no differences.

In our recent Brazilian study (Bertelson et al., in press), illiterate and literate subjects, generally from the same families, were tested at home on successively a rhyme-judgment task (deciding whether two words pronounced by the experimenter—*coca-mola, mito-fama*— rhyme or not), an initial-vowel deletion task (*ako* → *ko*), and an initial-consonant deletion task (*ful* → *ul*). For rhyme judgment and vowel deletion, testing continued to a criterion of six consecutive correct responses. All readers reached the criterion in both tasks, and among illiterates, 12 out of 16 reached it for rhyme judgment and 10 for vowel deletion. For the consonant-deletion test, which involved 24 trials irrespective of results, 7 out of 9 readers and only 3 out of 16 illiterates reached the criterion. Percent of correct responses were 33 percent for illiterates and 77 percent for readers (see table 1.1). These results again seem to show that rhyme judgment and analysis into syllables are not associated with analysis into consonants. Rhyme judgments and analysis into syllables are within reach of illiterates, although school experience can still bring improvement, but analysis into consonants is at floor level in illiterates, with some rare exceptions, and is substantial in readers.

An illustrative single-case observation that this study provided was that of a lady, Dona M., completely unschooled but who in a preceding study by Leda Tfouni had achieved near perfect performance on syllogisms. She is a community leader who is used to talking in public and also to giving private advice on all sorts of matters. In our testing situation her communicative skills were manifest: she did such uncommon things as to ask for repetition and clarification of instructions ("what do you mean by . . .") and impose silence on her relatives during the test. Her performance was perfect from the start in both rhyme identification and vowel deletion, but she produced only four correct responses out of 24 in consonant deleting, in spite of having had the instructions repeated all over again.

The Case of Rhymes

As we have noted, versification and appreciation of rhyme have often been offered together with learning to read as examples of secondary linguistic activities requiring metalinguistic knowledge. In the empirical literature, judgments of rhyme or sometimes of other forms of phonological similarity, like alliteration or assonance, have been used as measures of phonological awareness and were correlated with reading performance. Yet there are reasons to suspect that rhyme appreciation and possibly production as well obey developmental constraints different from those of segment analysis, as measured, for example, by phoneme-counting and phone-deletion tasks. There are illiterate poets who resort to rhyme and sometimes alliteration and assonance in their art. Illiterates appreciate and enjoy verse, just as prereading children enjoy nursery rhymes and engage in word games based on phonology (see Slobin's observations [1978] on his own three-year-old daughter, who said things like "Eggs are deggs," "Enough duff," and "More bore"). The ability of pre-reading children to appreciate rhyme has been documented also in systematic studies (Read 1978; Lenel and Cantor, 1981; Bradley and Bryant 1985). Studies mentioned in the preceding section make the same point for illiterates (Morais et al. 1986; Bertelson et al., in press).

The interpretation of the different developmental courses of rhyme judgment and segment manipulation depends very much on how one analyzes the operations involved in the appreciation of rhyme. Some authors, like Bradley and Bryant (1985), think that rhyme judgements require identification of each of the segments common to the rhyming utterances. The nonreaders' lower performance on segment manipulation tasks would be due to the additional counting or subtraction operations. This interpretation runs into difficulties once we consider that counting syllables (Liberman et al. 1974) or deleting initial syllabic vowels (Morais et al. 1986) are not equally difficult for these subjects. The alternative possibility is that rhyme decisions do not require analysis into segments proper and can be carried out at the level of syllables by appreciating some holistic sound identity or similarity.

Relevant evidence might be provided by illiterate poets. In semi-literate cultures one can find people who did not learn to read and yet who versify and have thus become expert at dealing with the sound properties of language in general. The opportunity to examine such a person arose recently in Portugal in the same rural region where the second illiterate study was conducted (Morais et al., 1986). F. J. C., a seventy-four-year-old illiterate poet, has been persuaded to take part in several testing sessions. For several decades he has created poems that he recites on festive occasions or even, in recent years, tape-records. These poems generally involve the rich rhymes typical of Portuguese poetry (identical-VCV endings) and linked to the fact that in Portuguese the penultimate vowel of polysyllabic words is nearly always stressed.

In the first two testing sessions a very clear pattern of results was obtained. F. J. C. was 100 percent correct on tasks of rhyme appreciation (choosing a picture with a name rhyming with a target, classifying pairs of words as rhyming or not) and thus superior to most illiterates we have tested so far. He performed 100 percent correctly also in rhyme production. Yet it was impossible to have him define rhyme or explain his reasons for rejecting nonrhymes. His typical response to such requests was to provide examples of rhyming words. On tests of syllable detection (identify the word in a sentence containing a target syllable) or initial-syllabic-vowel deletion, he was also superior to most illiterates. He displayed the same superiority in the task of comparing spoken words on syllabic length, in spite of an opposite contrast at the level of referents (e.g., *cauliflower* versus *oak*). However, his performance was confined within the range of other illiterate subjects on tasks involving phonetic segments (deleting the initial consonant of a pseudoword: 30 percent and 10 percent correct in two sessions; detecting a stop consonant in a spoken sentence: 10 percent correct). These results suggest that F. J. C.'s life-long involvement with the sound aspects of speech promoted his abilities to deal with syllables and phonological similarity much more than his ability to manipulate segments.

Further testing, however, has since raised the possibility that F. J. C.'s inability with consonants might be less extreme than it first appeared. After informal explorations that suggested that he was good at detecting and producing alliterations, we have now tested him on word-pair classifications (Do *filha* and *fato* begin the same way?). He was correct on 21 out of 24 trials. On a repeat of the consonant-detection task, he now scored 10/10. On the other hand, he was still completely unable to delete initial consonants (0 percent correct in two separate sessions). He still failed also to explicate his rhyme judgements and could not isolate the common part of pairs he had correctly classified as rhyming.

At this time, we have no comparative data for ordinary illiterates on judgements of alliteration or the effect of repeated testing on consonant detection. It is thus not yet possible to say to what extent F. J. C.'s good performance on alliterations and possibly his sudden success in consonant detection reflect learning during the testing sessions or some original ability, possibly a result of his practice with verse. If the case is not as clear-cut as we first thought, it still supports the notion of a dissociation between the capacities involved in syllable manipulations, rhyme appreciation, and detection of phonological similarity on the one side and segmental analysis on the other.

Evidence from Other Orthographies

Whether phonological awareness depends on the content of instruction or on the type of orthographic knowledge that is produced, the kind of phonological awareness promoted by reading instruction should depend on the principles of the writing system being taught. Subjects taught a nonalphabetic script are of interest because they possess none of the possible nonspecific characteristics of illiterates (individuals who did not want to learn to read, did not acquire the general cognitive skills promoted by schooling, nor benefited from the richer life experience that results from literacy). So they provide a purer measure of the effect of not being taught the alphabet.

Read et al. (1986) have applied our tasks of consonant addition and deletion to two groups of literate Chinese adults: a group of alphabetic readers, who could read both the traditional logographic characters and the alphabetic pinyin introduced after the revolution, and a group of logographic readers, who could read only the logographic characters. The mean results (averaged over addition and deletion, see table 1.1) are strikingly similar to those from the Portuguese ex-illiterates and literates, respectively. In spite of the fact that there was a small age difference in favor of the alphabetic group (an average of 33 years against 49), this result suggests that the major part of the literacy-related differences in segment analysis observed in the other studies is linked specifically to having been taught the alphabet rather than to more general correlates of schooling. Instruction in pin-yin was the result of an administrative decision that applied to all school children without exception and presumably resulted in neither better cognitive skills nor better opportunities. So if such factors played an important role in determining the differences between literates and illiterates, a smaller difference would have been found there.

Mann (1986) applied the syllable- and phoneme-counting tasks of Liberman et al. (1974) and the initial-consonant deletion task to Japanese first and fourth graders. As one would expect, the first-graders were inferior to American contemporaries on phonemic tasks and slightly superior on syllable counting. The surprising result is that fourth graders, who had still not been taught an alphabetic orthography, did much better on the phonemic tasks (table 1.1). That result might require that we reexamine our ideas regarding the experiences that allow the emergence of segmental awareness. One possibility that has probably received too little consideration so far is that differences in phonological structure can make the same units unequally accessible in different languages. We certainly need more interlinguistic comparisons of this sort.

From a more conservative viewpoint, one consideration that might reconcile Mann's result with the rest of the evidence is that some Japanese kana stand for phonemes, so that kana are not pure syllabaries. Perhaps having to deal with representations of phonemes in some particular cases is enough to get children started on the way to generalized phonetic analysis. As a matter of fact, in a study by Treiman and Baron (1983) in which prereaders were trained on segmentation of particular initial consonants from the rest of a syllable, the most proficient subjects gave signs of generalizing to consonants they had not been trained on.

The Critical Contribution of Instruction

As we have noted before, reading instruction whether at school or in literacy classes can promote phonological awareness either directly, by actual teaching speech analysis, or indirectly, because literacy creates new ways of representing language, which can be used to solve items in tasks of phonological awareness.

The extreme position that the effect is completely mediated by literacy can probably be excluded. A number of studies with preschool children have now shown that performance on the sort of tasks generally used to measure phonological awareness can be developed independently of reading instruction and prior to it (e.g., Olofsson and Lundberg 1983; Fox and Routh 1984; Content et al. 1986). And we have now shown that the same is true of the performance of adult illiterates on initial-consonant deletion (Morais et al. 1988).

One question that can be asked is whether the forms of phonological awareness promoted in these acceleration studies, in which subjects are often trained throughout on one particular speech-analysis task, are identical to the phonological awareness results from full reading instruction (see Content 1985 for some relevant reservations based on transfer studies; see Content et al. for a study involving more than one task). It remains possible that the phonological awareness that results from reading instruction reflects both the direct effects of teaching and the indirect effects mediated by literacy.

There are many examples of effects of literacy on the representation of spoken language. Pronunciation is often influenced by spelling, and changes in pronunciation over time sometimes go in the direction of conforming to orthography. A striking demonstration of the influence of orthography on the mental representation of speech has been provided by Seidenberg and Tanenhaus (1979), who showed that the time taken to decide that two spoken words rhyme is shorter when their spellings are similar (*pie* and *tie*) than when they are dissimilar (*pie* and *guy*), and that the opposite effect holds for negative decisions (it is faster for *hood* and *rude* than for *hood* and *mood*).

Another relevant example is provided by a phenomenon demonstrated by one of us some time ago (Bertelson 1972). In the task of judging the temporal location of an extraneous sound superimposed on a spoken sentence, the click is judged as coming earlier in the sentence when its apparent spatial origin is to the left of that of the sentence than when it is to the right. This effect, which has been found with both English and French material, appears to be related to the direction of writing typical of these languages. French and Hebrew bilingual subjects showed the same pattern of results when tested with French sentences and the mirror image one when tested with Hebrew sentences. The dependence of the effect on reading competence has been confirmed in yet unpublished studies of its development: it is not observed in children before the seventh grade.

Orthographic knowledge has been shown to affect performance on tests of phonological awareness. Ehri and Wilce (1979) found, for instance, that in the task of counting the number of phonemes in spoken words, children are sometimes influenced by the number of letters in the orthographic representations of these words: they will count one more phoneme in *pitch* than in *rich*. Mann (1986) describes similar tendencies in the mora and phoneme counting performances of her Japanese subjects.

The best available evidence on the relative contributions of direct and indirect effects to phonological awareness comes from comparisons of different teaching methods. The finding of Alegria et al. (1982) that phonic instruction promotes performance on segment manipulation much faster than whole-word instruction suggests that the direct effect is important. The authors unfortunately provide no information on the reading capacity attained by the two groups of subjects, so that some of the difference may still have been mediated through literacy. This is a case where a reading-level match would be useful. Anyway, one can note that none of the many studies reviewed by Chall (1967) have revealed effects of teaching methods on progress in reading skill comparable to those obtained here on segment manipulation. So we must conclude that the direct effect is the more important component.

Relevant also is the fact mentioned by Read et al. (1986) that some of their alphabetic subjects could not read pinyin well, yet performed well on segmental analysis. As they note, "the segmental conception acquired with alphabetic literacy may persist even when the literacy itself is dormant" (p. 41).

Phonemes in Percepts versus Processing

In the field of speech perception, some theorists have based arguments regarding the units involved in speech processing on the data showing that segmental awareness is not spontaneous. For example, Mehler et al. (1984) write that the similarities found by Morais et al. (1979) between illiterates and young prereaders "bolster the view that the syllable is the primary unit for speech perception and the phoneme is a derived one arising in conjunction with literacy" (p. 101). This conclusion involves a confusion between the level of automatic preconscious processing and that of conscious representations. As Morais (1985) has shown in a review of the whole issue, the confusion is basic to the studies, starting with the one by Savin and Bever (1970), that tried to obtain evidence about units used in speech processing from phoneme, syllable, and word detection, activities that presumably tap the level of conscious representation. Viewed from the dualist position that lies at the heart of the conception of phonological awareness, questions about processing and about representations are orthogonal. It is perfectly conceivable that some intermediate level of speech processing deals with phonemes but that in the absence of specific experience the listener is only aware of words or still larger units. There is also some evidence that this is actually what happens. Morais, Castro, et al. (1987) have obtained results that suggest the operation of phoneme-level codes during speech perception in illiterates. In a selective dichotic listening situation, illiterates had the same tendency as ex-illiterates to commit feature blendings, that is, to attribute to a phoneme of the attended utterance a feature of the corresponding phoneme in the unattended one. This type of mistake would seem to reveal extraction of information at the phonemic level.

The opposite inference, that the fact that it is possible to learn to analyze speech into segments demonstrates the existence of segment-level operations in speech perception, has also been made. The reasoning seems to rest on the principle that the only way to discover a new property of a representation is to access some stage of the perceptual processes that lead to the representation. When one thinks about it, the notion takes on a somewhat absurd tone. It would mean that when a child discovers that canaries have feathers or that automobiles have four wheels, he has accessed the outputs of, respectively, feather or wheel detectors in his visual-processing machinery. One cannot exclude the possibility that people could learn to represent speech as a sequence of segments, even if speech processing proper was starting with syllabic templates and by-passed segments altogether.

The division between perceptual processing and conscious representation is thus essentially an empirical one. For the time being, however, there are not sufficient data to see where the border lies.

Notes

The present work has been supported by the Belgian Fonds de la Recherche fondamentale collective (conventions 2.4505.80 and 2.4562.86) and the Ministry of Scientific Policy (Action de Recherche concertée "Processus cognitifs dans la lecture"). Thanks are due to José Morais, Jesus Alegria, Daniel Holender and Alain Content for critical comments on former versions of the paper. The paper was written before publication of the discussion of the same topics by Morais, Alegria, and Content (1987) and the commentaries it provoked. These important contributions are thus not taken into account.

1. It has now become customary to dismiss correlational evidence as irrelevant because it does not answer the question of the direction of causation. As a matter of fact, this position is excessive: the presence of a correlation between a and b does not allow the inference that b is caused by a, but the absence of correlation could make a causal link improbable. So correlations are still worth considering when they are available.

2. During a recent discussion John Marshall suggested that our results might be trivial in that they would simply show that teaching people to manipulate segments allows

them to do it. The answer is that the main interest of the findings does not lie in the superior performance of the ex-illiterates but in the zero-level performance of the illiterates.

3. A result obtained by Scribner and Cole (1981) in their well-known Vai Literacy Project has often been quoted as showing that effects one might at first sight be tempted to attribute to literacy may rather reflect the influence of a particular form of schooling. Among the Vai people of Liberia the authors could study users of different writing systems living in communities with complete illiterates in otherwise similar socioeconomic circumstances: users of the Vai script, a local syllabic writing system taught only through a sort of private tuition; users of Arabic writing, learned at Koranic school; and users of the Roman alphabet, learned at western-type schools. The authors found that only former students of the latter schools were superior to illiterates on syllogism-type problems. Although that is undoubtedly an interesting finding, there is no reason to expect that other literacy-related effects would show the same pattern of distribution. Unfortunately, the authors did not apply tests specifically designed to measure the abilities that might be affected by learning the different orthographies.

References

Alegria, J., and Morais, J. 1979. Le développement de l'habileté d'analyse consciente de la parole et l'apprentissage de la lecture. *Archives de Psychologie* 183:251–270.

Alegria, J., Pignot, E., and Morais, J. 1982. Phonetic analysis of speech and memory codes in beginning readers. *Memory and Cognition* 10:451–456.

Bertelson, P. 1972. Listening from left to right vs. right to left. *Perception* 1:161–165.

Bertelson, P. 1986. The onset of literacy: Liminal remarks. *Cognition* 24:1–30. Reprinted in Bertelson 1987.

Bertelson, P., ed. 1987. *The onset of literacy: Cognitive processes in reading acquisition.* Cambridge, Mass.: MIT Press.

Bertelson, P., De Gelder, B., Tfouni, L. V., and Morais, J. In press. Metaphonological abilities of adult illiterates: New evidence of heterogeneity. *European Journal of Coqnitive Psychology.*

Bertelson, P., Morais, J., Alegria, J., and Content, A. 1985. Phonetic analysis capacity and learning to read. *Nature* 313:73–74.

Bradley, L., and Bryant, P. E. 1983. Categorising sounds and learning to read: A causal connection. *Nature* 301:419–421.

Bradley, L., and Bryant, P. E. 1985. *Rhyme and reason in reading and spelling.* Ann Arbor: University of Michigan Press.

Bruce, D. J. 1964. The analysis of word sounds by young children. *British Journal of Educational Psychology* 34:158–170.

Bryant, P. E., and Bradley, L. 1985. *Children's Reading Difficulties.* Oxford: Basil Blackwell.

Calfee, R. C., Chapman, R., and Venezky, R. L. 1972. How a child needs to think to learn to read. In L. W. Gregg, ed., *Cognition in learning and memory.* New York: Wiley.

Campbell, R., and Butterworth, B. 1985. Phonological dyslexia and dysgraphia in a highly literate subject: A developmental case with associated deficits of phonemic processing and awareness. *The Quarterly Journal of Experimental Psychology* 37A:435–476.

Chall, J. 1967. *Learning to read: The great debate.* New York: McGraw Hill.

Coltheart, M. 1978. Lexical access in simple reading tasks. In G. Underwood, ed., *Strategies of information processing*. London: Academic Press.

Coltheart, M., Masterton, J., Byng, S., Prior, M., and Riddoch, J. 1983. Surface dyslexia. *The Quarterly Journal of Experimental Psychology* 35A:469–495.

Content, A. 1985. L'Analyse segmentale de la parole chez l'enfant. Unpublished doctoral dissertation, Université libre de Bruxelles.

Content, A., Kolinsky, R., Morais, J., and Bertelson, P. 1986. Phonetic segmentation in pre-readers: Effect of corrective information. *Journal of Experimental Child Psychology* 42:49–72.

Content, A., Morais, J., Alegria, J., and Bertelson, P. 1982. Accelerating the development of phonetic segmentation skills in kindergartners. *Cahiers de Psychologie Cognitive* 2:259–269.

De Gelder, B. 1985. The cognitivist conjuring trick, or How development vanished. In C. J. Bailey and R. Harris, eds., *Developmental mechanisms of language*. Oxford: Pergamon.

Ehri, L. C., and Wilce, L. S. 1979. The mnemonic value of orthography among beginning readers. *Journal of Educational Psychology* 71:26–40.

Fox, B., and Routh, D. K. 1976. Phonemic analysis and synthesis as word attack skills. *Journal of Educational Psychology* 68:70–74.

Fox, B., and Routh, D. K. 1984. Phonemic analysis and synthesis as word attack skills, revisited. *Journal of Educational Psychology* 76:1059–1064.

Frith, U. 1985. Beneath the surface of developmental dyslexia. In K. E. Patterson, J. C. Marshall, and M. Coltheart, eds., *Surface dyslexia: Neuropsychological and cognitive studies of phonological reading*. London: Lawrence Erlbaum.

Gelb, I. J. 1952. *A study of writing*. Chicago: University of Chicago Press.

Gleitman, L. R., and Rozin, P. 1977. The structure and acquisition of reading, I: Relations between orthographies and the structure of language. In A. S. Reber and D. L. Scarborough, eds., *Toward a psychology of reading*. Hillsdale: Lawrence Erlbaum.

Henderson, L. 1982. *Orthography and word recognition in reading*. London: Academic Press.

Holender, D. 1987. Synchronic description of present-day writing systems: Some implications for reading research. In O'Regan, J. K., and Levy-Schoen, A., eds., *Eye movements: From physiology to cognition*. Amsterdam: Elsevier North Holland, 397–420.

Jorm, A. F., and Share, D. L. 1983. Phonological recoding and reading acquisition. *Applied Psycholinguistics* 4:103–147.

Kavanagh, J. F., and Mattingly, I. G. 1972. *Language by ear and by eye*. Cambridge, Mass.: MIT Press.

Kolinsky, R., Morais, J., Content, A., and Cary, L. 1987. Finding parts within figures: A developmental study. *Perception* 16:399–407.

Lenel, J. C., and Cantor, J. H. 1981. Rhyme recognition and phonemic perception in young children. *Journal of Psycholinguistic Research* 10:57–67.

Levelt, W. J. M., Sinclair, A., and Jarvella, R. J. 1978. Causes and functions of linguistic awareness in language acquisition. In A. Sinclair, R. J. Jarvella, and W. J. M. Levelt, eds., *The child's conception of language*. Berlin: Springer-Verlag.

Liberman, I. Y. 1971. Basic research in speech and lateralization of language: Some implications for reading disability. *Bulletin of the Orton Society* 21:71–87.

Liberman, I. Y., and Shankweiler, D. 1985. Phonology and the problems of learning to read and write. *Remedial and Special Education*. 6:8–17.

Liberman, I. Y., Shankweiler, D., Fisher, F. W. and Carter, B. 1974. Explicit syllable and phoneme segmentation in the young child. *Journal of Experimental Child Psychology* 18:201–212.

Liberman, I. Y., Shankweiler, D., Liberman, A. M., Fowler, C., and Fisher, W. F. 1977. In A. S. Reber and D. L. Scarborough, eds., *Toward a psychology of reading*. Hillsdale: Lawrence Erlbaum.

Lundberg, I., Olofsson, A., and Wall, S. 1980. Reading and spelling skills in the first school years predicted from phonemic awareness skills in kindergarten. *Scandinavian Journal of Psychology* 21:159–173.

Mann, V. 1986. Phonological awareness: The role of reading experience. *Cognition* 24:65–92. Reprinted in Bertelson 1987.

Masonheimer, P. E., Drum, P. A., and Ehri, L. C. 1984. Does environmental print identification lead children into word reading? *Journal of Reading Behavior* 16:257–271.

Mattingly, I. G. 1972. Reading, the linguistic process, and linguistic awareness. In J. F. Kavenagh and I. G. Mattingly, eds., *Language by ear and by eye*. Cambridge, Mass.: MIT Press.

Mattingly, I. G. 1984. Reading, linguistic awareness, and language acquisition. In J. Downing and R. Valtin, eds., *Language awareness and learning to read*. New York: Springer.

Mattingly, I. G. 1985. Did orthographies evolve? *Remedial and Special Education* 6:18–23.

Mehler, J., Morton, J., and Jusczyk, P. W. 1984. On reducing language to biology. *Cognitive Neuropsychology* 1:83–116.

Morais, J. 1985. Literacy and awareness of the units of speech: Implications for research on the units of perception. *Linguistics* 23:707–721.

Morais, J., Alegria, J., and Content, A. 1987. The relationship between segmental analysis and alphabetic literacy. *Cahiers de Psychologie Cognitive*, 7:415–438.

Morais, J., Bertelson, P., Cary, L., and Alegria, J. 1986. Literacy training and speech segmentation. *Cognition* 24:45–64. Reprinted in Bertelson 1987.

Morais, J., Cary, L., Alegria, J., and Bertelson, P. 1979. Does awareness of speech as a sequence of phones arise spontaneously? *Cognition* 7:323–331.

Morais, J., Castro, S. L., Scliar-Cabral, L., Kolinsky, R., and Content, A. 1987. The effects of literacy on the recognition of dichotic words. *The Quarterly Journal of Experimental Psychology* 39A:451–465.

Morais, J., Content, A., Bertelson, P., Cary, L., and Kolinsky, R. 1988. Is there a sensitive period for the acquisition of segmental analysis? *Cognitive Neuropsychology* 5:347–352.

Olofsson, A., and Lundberg, I. 1983. Can phonemic awareness be trained in kindergarten? *Scandinavian Journal of Psychology* 24:35–44.

Olofsson, A., and Lundberg, I. 1985. Evaluation of long-term effects of phonemic training in kindergarten: Illustrations of some methodological problems in evaluation research. *Scandinavian Journal of Psychology* 26:21–34.

Perfetti, C. A., Beck, I., Bell, L., and Hughes, C. 1987. Phonemic knowledge and learning to read are reciprocal: A longitudinal study of first grade children. *Merrill-Palmer Quarterly* 33:283–320.

Read, C. A. 1978. Children's awareness of language, with emphasis on sound systems. In A. Sinclair, R. J. Jarvella, and W. J. M. Levelt eds. *The Child's Conception of Language*. Berlin: Springer.

Read, C. A., Zhang, Y., Nie, H., and Ding, B. 1986. The ability to manipulate speech sounds depends on knowing alphabetic reading. *Cognition* 24:31–44. Reprinted in Bertelson 1987.

Rosner, J., and Simon, D. P. 1971. The auditory analysis test: An initial report. *Journal of Reading Disabilities* 4:384–392.

Rozin, P. 1978. The acquisition of basic alphabetic principles: A structural approach. In C. A. Catania and T. A. Brigham, eds., *Handbook of applied behavior analysis*. New York: Irvington.

Rozin, P., and Gleitman, L. R. 1977. The structure and acquisition of reading, II: The reading process and the acquisition of the alphabetic principle. In A. S. Reber and D. L. Scarborough, eds., *Toward a Psychology of Reading*. Hillsdale: Lawrence Erlbaum.

Sampson, G. 1985. *Writing systems: A linguistic introduction*. London: Hutchinson.

Savin, H. B., and Bever, T. G. 1970. The non-perceptual reality of the phoneme. *Journal of Verbal Learning and Verbal Behavior* 9:295–302.

Scribner, S., and Cole, M. 1981. *The Psychology of Literacy*. Cambridge, Mass.: Harvard University Press.

Seidenberg, M. S., and Tanenhaus, M. K. 1979. Orthographic effects on rhyme monitoring. *Journal of Experimental Psychology: Human Learning and Memory* 5:546–554.

Seymour, P. H. K. 1986. *Cognitive analysis of dyslexia*. London: Routledge and Kegan Paul.

Skjelford, V. J. 1976. Teaching children to segment spoken words as an aid in learning to read. *Journal of Learning Disabilities* 9:297–306.

Slobin, D. I. 1978. A case study of early language awareness. In A. Sinclair, R. J. Jarvella, and W. J. M. Levelt, eds., *The Child's Conception of Language*. Berlin: Springer.

Stanovich, K. E. 1982. Individual differences in the cognitive processes of reading, I. Word decoding. *Journal of Learning Disabilities* 15:485–493.

Temple, C. M., and Marshall, J. C. 1983. A case study of phonological developmental dyslexia. *British Journal of Psychology* 74:517–533.

Torneus, M. 1984. Phonological awareness and reading: A chicken and egg problem? *Journal of Educational Psychology* 76:1346–1358.

Treiman, R., and Baron, J. 1983. Phonemic analysis training helps children benefit from spelling-sound rules. *Memory and Cognition* 11:382–389.

Williams, J. P. 1980. Teaching decoding with an emphasis on phoneme analysis and phoneme blending. *Journal of Educational Psychology* 72:1–15.

Editor's Comments

The study of reading and reading disability represents a particular challenge to scientists because as we are reminded in the present chapter, mature reading competence never develops without substantial formal instruction, in contrast to spoken language, which emerges spontaneously and therefore reflects a strong innate brain capacity. This means that a complete understanding of the processes and mechanisms involved in reading acquisition and in reading difficulties must encompass knowledge about brain development and about the culture to which that developing brain is exposed.

Reading instruction is not usually begun until there is a good amount of development in several other cognitive capacities, some of which bear directly or indirectly on the process of acquiring an ability to read. The latter capacities may spontaneously arise without any formal teaching at ages that are reasonably uniform among children (see Bellugi et al., this volume). However, as with everything else biological, there is likely to be a certain degree of variability in their developmental schedules, whose effect on reading readiness is not known. Yet the acquisition of reading ability may also depend on prerequisite capacities that do not arise spontaneously but rather depend on sociocultural matters. In that case such environmental differences would distinguish some children from others during reading instruction.

Owing to innate or cultural factors acting before children are first exposed to reading tasks, some children may thus be more ready than others. Furthermore, as a corollary of the previous argument, some children may rely on some prerequisite capacity more than others, according to what is innately or culturally available in their own individual circumstances, and these differences in strategy may result in differences in the speed and degree with which children acquire the ability to read. If the ability to read does not arise spontaneously, all other factors relating to brain and cognitive development are more likely to play more significant roles.

Dyslexic children are exposed to formal reading instruction, and yet they experience serious difficulties with reading acquisition and never quite reach ordinary levels in reading performance. The problem is to determine whether these difficulties represent antecedent problems with brain development or antecedent problems with acquisition of the prerequisite behaviors that need be in place for one to begin to learn to read. Research has shown that dyslexics also exhibit a range of language difficulties both in spoken and written tasks. Problems with acquiring the spoken language, which may be genetically determined or result from acquired brain changes, may predispose one to later reading problems, and limited reading competence may in turn limit general linguistic capacity. So researchers interested in the behavioral characteristics of dyslexics must separate those that predispose to dyslexia, those that have no relationship to the reading deficiencies, and those that result from illiteracy itself.

Chapter 2

Literacy and Acquired Aphasia

André Roch Lecours

In 1904 Ernst Weber claimed that literacy is more an environmental determinant of functional lateralization for language than the acquisition of spoken language, a bold claim and one that might have been more appropriately presented as a cautious suggestion. His belief was based on anecdotal observation of a few illiterates and semiliterates in whom left-brain damage did not disturb language behavior or else resulted in minor transient aphasia. Weber's claim did not constitute a challenge to Broca's (1865) embryologically founded hypothesis that left cerebral dominance for language is innate. Formulated in general terms, Weber's implicit assumption was rather that for the complete functional actualization of this particular genetic program to occur, there needs to be interaction between the human organism and its environment, a reasonable assumption.[1] More specifically, Weber's idea was apparently that the acquisition of reading and writing skills is the main environmental influence in this interaction.

This chapter deals with the cerebral representation of the literate language. In the first part I shall summarize the results of a research project carried out by me and my co-workers on the effects of unilateral strokes on the language of illiterates. In the second part I shall compare our results and conclusions to those of other researchers.

The Illiteracy Project

Population

A population of 296 subjects (153 men and 143 women) was studied in our illiteracy project. All of the subjects spoke only Brazilian Portuguese, were 40 years of age or older, and were absolute or preferred right-handers. Of this population 157 were totally unschooled illiterates, and 139 had received at least four years of schooling and thereafter retained writing skills and reading habits. A total of 108 were neurologically healthy, and 188 were seen within two months of and, as a rule, more than two weeks after a unilateral stroke (109 in the left

Table 2.1
Population Studied

	Controls	Left strokes	Right strokes
Illiterate subpopulation			
Number	62	48	47
Age	60.3	61.9	60.5
M/F	22/40	21/27	31/16
Literate subpopulation			
Number	46	61	32
Age	59.3	58.2	64.3
M/F	24/22	34/27	21/11
School	8.3	8.6	8.3

Controls = neurologically healthy subpopulation. Left strokes and right strokes = brain-damaged subpopulation. Number = absolute number of subjects per group. Age = average age per group, expressed in number of years. M/F = absolute number of males and females per group. School = average duration of school education in the literate subpopulation, in years.

hemisphere and 70 in the right). In a large majority of the cases the strokes were clinically diagnosed as in the Sylvian region.[2] Brain-damaged subjects reported no past history of neurological illness of any kind and were hospitalized following their single strokes (table 2.1).

The six groups were statistically homogenous with regard to age (Kruskall-Wallis test: $H = 7.7$; d.f. $= 5$; $p = .17$; Siegel 1956).

The six groups were not statistically homogenous with regard to sex (chi square $= 14.5$; d.f. $= 5$; $p = .013$). Nonetheless, the distribution of sex was comparable in the illiterate and the schooled left-stroke groups (chi square $= 1.10$; d.f. $= 1$; $p = .29$) as well as the illiterate and schooled right-stroke groups (chi square $= 0$; d.f. $= 1$; $p = 1$).

The three groups of the literate subpopulation were statistically homogenous with regard to number of years of schooling (Kruskall-Wallis test: $H = 0.18$; d.f. $= 2$; $p = .92$; Siegel 1956).

At the time of initial testing, all but four of the 188 brain-damaged subjects had hemiparesis or hemiplegia (table 2.2). In the four remaining subjects, all of them school-educated, the existence of a left Sylvian stroke was documented by computerized tomography. Examiners examining somesthesia and visual-field intactness were requested to note their observations in terms of "deficit absent," "deficit present," or "deficit impossible to assess with a reasonable degree of confidence" (table 2.2). There was an obvious bias in favor of frontal-lobe and global Sylvian lesions within the stroke subpopulations. This no doubt reflected the greater probability of admission to the wards of overcrowded public hospitals for stroke patients with hemiplegia. There was also a greater frequency of unassessables within the right-stroke illiterates than within the right-stroke, schooled patients.

Testing Procedure
Each subject in the above population was administered at least the oral components of a Portuguese adaptation of Protocol MT-86 d'Examen linguistique de l'aphasie, version alpha (Lecours et al. 1986). MT-86 Alpha is designed as an elementary bedside aphasia screening test. It is composed of a directed interview and of seven scored subtests: (1) matching pictures with spoken words or sentences, (2) matching pictures with written words or reading sentences, (3) repeating words and sentences, (4) copying words and sentences, (5) taking dictation of words and sentences, (6) copying words and sentences, and (7) naming. Only the oral subtests, (1), (3), and (7) which have been detailed elsewhere (Lecours et al. 1987a), will be systematically considered in the present chapter.

Matching   The matching tasks include a total of 11 stimuli. In word-picture matching, the subject is requested to point at the one of six line drawings that corresponds to a stimulus uttered by the examiner,

Table 2.2
Frequency of motor, somesthetic, and visual-field sided deficits among subjects of the four groups of the stroke subpopulation (percentages of subjects per group)

	Left strokes		Right strokes	
	Illit.	Lit.	Illit.	Lit.
Hemiplegia or hemiparesis				
Absent	0	7	0	0
Present	100	93	100	100
Unassessable	0	0	0	0
Hemihypesthesia or extinction				
Absent	31	38	26	31
Present	48	41	61	63
Unassessable	21	21	13	6
Hemianopsia or extinction				
Absent	73	69	65	63
Present	4	7	17	31
Unassessable	23	25	17	6

and in sentence-picture matching, at one of four line drawings. For each item the picture is presented in a single display (15 by 21 cm). A verbal stimulus may be repeated once if the subject so requests or if he fails to respond to the first presentation. Scoring bears on the first (or absent) response only.

The verbal stimuli in word-picture matching are five nouns, such as "pente" (comb) and "faca" (knife). Each picture other than the target is a semantic foil: one is a phonological foil, one is a formal foil (a drawing of an object visually similar to the target), and two are without any linguistic or visual kinship to the target whatsoever (neutral foils). For example, in the case of the comb drawing, the five foils represent a wig, a bridge ("ponte"), a rake, a carrot, and a key).

The verbal stimuli in sentence-picture matching are three simple sentences with intransitive verbs, such as "A menina anda" (The girl is walking) and three reversible complex, sentences with transitive verbs, such as "O cavalo puxa o menino" (The horse is pulling the boy). Symmetrically distributed in quadrants, the four drawings in each display share iconographic and semiotic features, like the same or related actors, the same or related actions, or the same or related accessories, so that each of the three nontarget drawings is a semantic syntactic, phonological, or formal foil. For instance, with the drawing of a girl walking are three foils representing a girl running, a boy walking, and boy running.

Repetition   The repetition subtest consists of 11 stimuli: 8 words such as "cavalo" (horse), "cruzeiros" (money), and "embarcação" (boat), and three sentences, one of which is "Nos lhe daremos que ela reclame" (literally, "We it-to-him will-give when he requires"). Scoring bears exclusively on the subject's first complete response (if any) and does not take phonetic distortions into account. Two scores are given for word repetition: the total number of inadequate behaviors (absence of response, phonemic deviations, verbal deviations, and so forth) and the total number of phonemic deviations.[3] Two scores are also given for sentence repetition: the total number of inadequate behaviors (absence of response, verbal deviations, phonemic deviations, and so forth) and the total number of verbal deviations (word substitutions, deletions, additions, and displacements).[4]

Naming   The naming subtest proceeds from a set of simple line drawings (each 15 by 21 cm). These are presented one after the other, and the subject is requested to utter the corresponding nouns (for instance, "sino" [bell], "violão" [guitar], and "cachimbo" [pipe]). Scoring bears exclusively on the subject's first complete response (if any)

Table 2.3
Error scores of control, left-stroke and right-stroke illiterates and literates in the matching, repetition, and naming tasks (percentages of inadequate responses per group)

	Controls		Left strokes		Right strokes	
	Illit.	Lit.	Illit.	Lit.	Illit.	Lit.
Matching	24.0	7.1	43.0	24.5	36.4	21.9
Repetition	25.5	6.9	44.0	27.7	24.1	13.4
Naming	14.1	4.7	32.2	27.7	20.6	10.7

within five seconds and does not take phonetic distortions and phonemic paraphasias into account. Three scores are given for naming: the total number of inadequate behaviors (absence of response, neologistic responses, verbal deviations, and so forth), the total number of failures to respond within five seconds ("anomia score"), and the total number of verbal deviations like semantic paraphasias and referential circumlocutions ("paraphasia score").[5]

Results
Whether one considers the scores of neurologically healthy controls or those of either of the two stroke subpopulations, cultural differences were obvious between the illiterate and the school-educated subgroup. Global error scores were always greater in the former group than in the latter (table 2.3). These differences were significant in all tasks: matching, repetition, and naming (Mann-Whitney test: $p < .02$ in all cases; Siegel 1956).

Matching   Absence of response in a matching task was found to be an exceptional behavior in all six subgroups (13 failures to respond altogether, versus 1,601 matches, correct or otherwise). Mismatches were frequent in illiterate controls and in all pathological subgroups, more so among left-stroke subjects than among right-stroke subjects. Two particularly frequent mismatches among illiterate controls, although not among school-educated ones, were pointing at the running girl rather than the walking girl and pointing at the boy pulling a horse rather than the horse pulling a boy. Mismatching patterns were more complex among the pathological subgroups.

My co-workers and I used a chi-square test for two independent samples on 2 by 2 contingency tables, with cut-off points defined as the smallest error scores encompassing the behavior of at least 75 percent of the controls for 11 stimuli. Significant differences between controls versus left-stroke or right-stroke subjects were found both within the illiterate and literate subpopulations (left-stroke illiterates: χ^2 = 15.8; d.f. = 1; p = .0001; right-stroke illiterates: χ^2 = 11.4; d.f. = 1; p = .0007; left-stroke, school-educated subjects: χ^2 = 12.2; d.f. = 1; p = .0005; right-stroke, school-educated subjects: χ^2 = 9.8; d.f. = 1; p = .0018).

We also restricted analyses of sentence-picture matching to halved displays and took target lateralization into account. Using a chi-square test with cut-off points defined as the smallest error scores encompassing the behavior of at least 60 percent of controls for six stimuli, we found significant differences for both left and right halves of the displays in the left-stroke groups but only for the left half of the displays in the right-stroke groups (left-stroke illiterates with left half: χ^2 = 12.1; d.f. = 1; p = .0057; left-stroke illiterates with right half: χ^2 = 5.1; d.f. = 1; p = .02; right-stroke illiterates with left-half: χ^2 = 11.8; d.f. = 1; p = .0006; right-stroke illiterates with right half: χ^2 = 3.1; d.f. = 1; p = .8; left-stroke school-educated with left half: χ^2 = 3.8; d.f. = 1; p = .05; left-stroke school-educated with right half: χ^2 = 4.8; d.f. = 1; p = .028; right-stroke school-educated with left half: χ^2 = 12.1; d.f. = 1; p = .005; right-stroke school-educated with right half: χ^2 = 0; d.f. = 1; p = 1).

These results show that there is neglect of the visual field in the right-stroke subpopulation and both impaired auditory comprehension and neglect of the right visual field in the left-stroke subpopulation, as reported in Lecours et al. 1987b. In that same publication my colleagues and I also claim that unilateral visual neglect, as shown by the M1-Alpha sentence-picture matching tasks, is quantitatively comparable in left- and right-stroke subjects, independent of schooling, unrelated to hemianopia, and in the right-stroke subjects unrelated to the syntactic or iconographic complexity of the stimuli (in left-stroke subjects there was a relation).

Repetition   Two very frequent repetition errors among illiterate controls and subjects of the two right-stroke subgroups were "prato" for "pratos" and "cruzeiro" for "cruzeiros." These two and other deviations were observed in left-stroke illiterates and literates (for instance "tem" for "trem," "ratos" for "pratos," "cruzeivinho" for "cruzeiros," "embração" for "embarcação," and so forth). On the whole, the most frequent errors in sentence repetition were deletions of attributes or functionals, more so among left-stroke illiterates and school-educated subjects.

Using a chi-square test on 2-by-2 contingency tables, with cut-off points defined as the smallest error scores encompassing the behavior of at least 75 percent of controls for eight stimuli, my colleagues and I found significant differences in word repetition within both the illiterate and the school-educated subpopulations, between control and left-stroke subjects, although not between control and right-stroke subjects (left-stroke illiterates: $\chi^2 = 20.6$; d.f. = 1; $p < .0001$; right-stroke illiterates: $\chi^2 = 0.22$; d.f. = 1; $p = .64$; left-stroke, school-educated subjects: $\chi^2 = 6.24$; d.f. = 1; $p = .013$; right-stroke, school-educated subjects: $\chi^2 = 0$; d.f. = 1; $p = 1$).

Sentence repetition generated large numbers of inadequate responses in all three groups of the illiterate subpopulation and in left-stroke literate subjects. Hence, the only significant difference was that left-stroke, school-educated subjects produced more inadequate responses than their controls ($\chi^2 = 7.85$; d.f. = 1; $p = .005$).

As discussed in Lecours et al. 1988, the repetition and matching results presented above are on the whole consistent with the tenets of classical aphasiology.

Naming Most inadequate behaviors of illiterate controls in the naming task were of the anomic type and seemed related to difficulty in visually decoding the iconographic substrate of the test (Lecours et al. 1987b). Similar behaviors were observed within the four pathological subgroups, more among the illiterates. Also observed were varying numbers of circumlocutory responses and semantic paraphasias (for instance, "dog" for "cat," "cigar" for "pipe," "man" for "pipe," "hair" for "whiskers," "fruit" for "banana," "sugar cane" for "banana," and so forth).

Using the chi-square test on 2-by-2 contingency tables, with cut-off points defined as the smallest error scores encompassing the behavior of at least 75 percent of controls for 12 target items, my colleagues and I found significant differences in overall scores for naming between controls and left-stroke illiterates, between controls and school-educated subjects, and between controls and right-stroke illiterates, but not between controls and right-stroke, school-educated subjects (left-stroke illiterates: $\chi^2 = 10.7$; d.f. = 1; $p = .001$); left-stroke, school-educated subjects: $\chi^2 = 10.7$; d.f. = 1; $p = .001$; right-stroke illiterates: $\chi^2 = 8.09$; d.f. = 1; $p = .004$; right-stroke, school-educated subjects: $\chi^2 = 1.88$; d.f. = 1; $p = .17$).

Using the same statistical procedure, we found that right-stroke illiterates differed from their controls on their paraphasia scores ($\chi^2 = 5.12$; d.f. = 1; $p = .02$), although not on their anomia scores $\chi^2 = 2.03$; d.f. = 1; $p = .15$). This naming behavior by right-stroke illiterates was not expected according to the tenets of classical aphasiology (see Lecours et al. 1988).

Discussion

Our matching and repetition results confirm classic aphasiologic teachings. This is also true for our naming results for the school-educated subpopulation, but not for our right-stroke illiterate subgroup. One might raise the possibility that the latter results are somehow linked to visual neglect and not to genuine word-finding difficulties. In my opinion, this possibility is at best improbable, since manifestations of visual neglect among our subjects were shown to be independent of literacy (Lecours et al. 1987b). If interfering at all with the M1-Alpha naming task, visual neglect should thus be apparent in both the illiterate and the school-educated right-stroke subgroups. Two other tentative hypotheses can be put forward.

One, given that a difficulty in decoding line drawings was observed among our illiterate controls (Lecours et al. 1987a), one might think that the naming results of our right-stroke illiterates show more of the same difficulty rather than anomalies in lexical access. Of course, since a difference from appropriate controls is observed in right-stroke illiterates but not in fluent readers with similar lesions, this hypothesis would entail that pathology in picture decoding occurs only in right-brain-damaged illiterates.

Two, our data on word-finding difficulties in right-stroke illiterates could also be taken to indicate a more diffuse, more ambilateral representation of the lexicon in illiterates than in fluent readers. Since even the standard form of left cerebral dominance for lexico-semantic abilities is relative (Hannequin, Goulet, and Joanette 1987) and since the paraphasia scores seem to be crucial in the difference in naming behavior between right-stroke illiterates and their controls (see above), I favor the second hypothesis, at least for the time being.

Although no one has ever revived Weber's 1904 claim as a whole, some influence by written-language acquisition on functional lateralization for language has occasionally been defended on the basis of aphasiological data or speculation (Cameron, Currier, and Haerer 1971; Critchley 1956; Eisenson 1964; von Mundy 1957; Métellus et al. 1981; Wechsler 1976). But this notion has also been rejected on the basis of aphasiologic data or speculation (Damasio, Castro-Caldas, et al. 1976; Jakobson 1964; Tikofsky 1970). Other than the work of my collaborators and me, only two published studies have gone beyond the anecdotal stage or the expression of personal beliefs: one carried out in Mississippi (Cameron et al. 1971) and the other in Lisbon (Damasio, Castro-Caldas, et al. 1976). Cameron et al. used the hospital records of 65 adults with a left Sylvian strokes and right hemiplegias. These records were of literate, semiliterate, and illiterate individuals.

The comparative incidence of aphasia within the three groups was the object of this research. After examining left-stroke adults with right hemiplegia, neurologists of the University of Mississippi Medical Center in Jackson reported that an associated aphasia occurs less frequently when patients were illiterates than when they were fluent readers.[6] It is more than likely that the criterion of aphasia in the context of this study was a nonstandardized bedside examination, without pencil-and-paper calculations of any sort. There is little doubt that any seasoned clinician testing patients for aphasia in this manner will require less from an illiterate than from a school-educated patient by referring to an implicit ideal norm (at least if he does not have the opportunity or the habit of referring to explicit and presumably reliable norms). In the conclusion to their article Cameron et al. suggested that "language is not as well 'planted' in the dominant hemisphere in illiterates as it is in literate persons" (1976, p. 163).

Damasio and his co-workers used the expertly noted aphasiologic records of 247 subjects with unilateral brain lesions. These records were those of fluent, schooled readers or of totally unschooled illiterates. As in the Mississippi study, the object of research was the comparative incidence of aphasia within the subgroups. Yet there was a vast difference between the two studies, since in the Portuguese study, attributing aphasia to a subject was no longer a matter only of clinical flair. Rather, the researchers carefully pondered various exact measures modeled on the Boston Diagnostic Aphasia Evaluation (Goodglass and Kaplan 1972). These included such measures as verbal production rate, the number and types of errors in repetition and naming, the quantitative results of tests of matching pictures and words or sentences, token-test scores, and so forth. Using this explicit methodology, Damasio, Castro-Caldas, et al. were led to conclude that aphasia is the result of left-brain damage in the illiterate as well as in the fluent reader, that it is equally frequent in both, and that "brain specialization for language does not depend on literacy" (1976, p. 300).

For some reason the Mississippi and the Lisbon studies were considered to have yielded irreconcilable results, which led to controversy (Currier, Haerer, and Farmer 1976; Damasio, Castro-Caldas, et al. 1976; Damasio, Hamsher, et al. 1976). In my opinion, this controversy was unfounded because of the methodological differences between the two studies. As a matter of fact, the results of my collaborators and me are compatible with the conclusions of both studies. On the one hand, we found no difference between illiterates and readers in the incidence of aphasia following left-brain damage (between 55 and 60 percent of cases in both subgroups according to MT-Alpha screening procedure).[7] I therefore agree that left cerebral dominance for language does not depend primarily on literacy. On the other hand, since our pathological data were in each case compared to appropriate controls, we were able to document the existence in right-stroke illiterates of a naming anomaly that would not have been apparent in neurologically healthy illiterates. I therefore agree that as a rule, left cerebral dominance for language can be less exclusive among illiterates than among school-educated individuals.

A dichotic study by Damasio et al. (1979) of functional lateralization in illiterates and school-educated readers also yielded a result that is compatible with less than absolute cerebral dominance among the illiterates: when the dichotic stimuli consisted of pairs of phonologically similar, meaningful words differing only in their initial consonants (such as "ponte" "fonte" and "caneta" "maneta"), a right-ear advantage was found in fluent readers and a left-ear advantage in illiterates. They therefore suggested that the illiterates might have "less mature dominance, calling for particular perceptual strategies in specific circumstances" (p. 337). I agree.

It is now largely accepted that the right hemisphere of school-educated, dextral adults is involved in an number of highly efficient linguistic behaviors (Bradshaw and Nettleton 1983; Hannequin et al. 1987; Joanette et al. 1983). My current view is that illiterates have a lower threshold on the left side, that is, they must resort to strategies that use the right hemisphere to access frequent, concrete nouns from simple line drawings (see above) and phonologically discriminate similar words (Damasio et al. 1979), which literate subjects can do using only left-hemisphere functions.

Since illiteracy and total absence of school education completely overlap in our population,[8] our data provide no indication as to whether a more complete picture of functional lateralization to the left should be linked to literacy per se, to school education as a whole (or some aspect of it), or to a combination of these two factors. It has been shown that learning to read and write can indeed modify certain aspects of language processing, such as syllabic versus phonemic segmentation (Morais et al., 1979; also see Bertelson and De Gelder in this volume). Yet there are also studies by Scribner and Cole on literacy without education among Liberians of the Vai community, (1981, p. 238) and by Parente, (1984) in which healthy, young, adult illiterates copying a two-dimensional cube regularly show evidence of constructional apraxia. These studies can be taken to mean that schooling as a whole, rather than the acquisition of a written language per se, is the determining parameter. In any case, it seems that although our species-specific biological tendency toward functional asymmetry for language is progressively actualized through early exposure to a spoken code, social and historical factors do have an impact on human brain function.[9]

Notes

This research was supported by the Harry Frank Guggenheim Foundation, New York.

1. The assumption would remain reasonable even if normal human neonates were proven to show evidence of early left-brain specialization in the discrimination of speech sounds (Entus 1977; also see Mehler in this volume).
2. That is, the subjects exhibited brachiofacial hemiparesis.
3. The maximal error score is 8 for each score.
4. The maximal error score is 3 for each score.
5. The maximal error score is 12 for each score.
6. Chi-square test: $p = .02$ (p. 162).
7. Blind assessment of a subset of tape-recorded interviews led an experienced speech pathologist to suspect the presence of "mild aphasia" in 9 of 20 right-stroke illiterates and in 4 of 23 neurologically healthy, illiterate controls.
8. As a matter of fact, illiteracy and personal and maternal malnutrition substantially overlap in our experimental population. Yet malnutrition does not seem to interfere substantially with the genetic program that gives rise to fundamental left dominance for language.
9. Given the general theme of this volume, one might have wished to conclude by stressing a fundamental difference between social alexia and developmental dyslexia. Genetic programming is expected to play a role in the former but probably not in the latter (see the chapters by Sherman, Rosen, and Galaburda and by Galaburda, Rosen, and Sherman in this volume). Nonetheless, one might wonder if being unable, rather than not having the opportunity, to acquire reading and writing skills might not involve similar cognitive particularities in certain circumstances (Galaburda in a personal communication, 1987).

References

Bradshaw, J. L., and Nettleton, N.C. 1983. *Human cerebral asymmetry*. Englewood Cliffs: Prentice-Hall.

Broca, P. 1865. Sur le siège de la faculté du langage articulé. *Bulletin de la Société d'Anthropologie* 6:337–393.

Cameron, R. F., Currier, R. D., and Haerer, A. F. 1971. Aphasia and literacy. *British Journal of Disorders of Communication* 6:161–163.

Castro, S. L., and Morais, J. 1987. Ear differences in illiterates. *Neuropsychologia* 25:409–418.

Critchley, M. 1956. Premorbid literacy and the pattern of subsequent aphasia. *Proceedings of the Society of Medicine* 49:335–336.

Currier, R. D., Haerer, A. F., and Farmer, L. J. 1976. Letter to the editor. *Archives of Neurology* 33:662.

Damasio, A. R., Castro-Caldas, A., Grosso, J. T., and Ferro, J. M. 1976. Brain specialization for language does not depend on literacy. *Archives of Neurology* 33:300–301.

Damasio, A. R., Hamsher, K. de S., Castro-Caldas, A., Ferro, J. M., and Grosso, J. T.
1976. Letter to the editor. *Archives of Neurology* 33:662.

Damasio, H., Damasio, A. R., Castro-Caldas, A., and Hamsher, K. de S. 1979. Reversal
of ear advantage for phonetically similar words in illiterates. *Journal of Clinical Neuropsychology* 1:331–338.

Eisenson, J. 1964. Discussion. In A. V. S. de Reuck and M. O'Connor, eds., *Disorders of
language*, p. 259. London: Churchill.

Entus, A. K. 1977. Hemispheric asymmetry in processing of dichotically presented
speech and nonspeech stimuli by infants. In S. J. Segalowitz and F. A. Gruber,
eds., *Language development and neurological theory*, pp. 63–73. New York: Academic
Press.

Goodglass, H., and Kaplan, E. 1972. *The assessment of aphasia and related disorders*. Philadelphia: Lea and Febiger.

Hannequin, D., Goulet, P., and Joanette, Y. 1987. *La contribution de l'hémisphère droit à la
communication verbale*. Paris: Masson.

Jakobson, R. Discussion. 1964. In A. V. S. de Reuck and M. O'Connor, eds., *Disorders
of language*, p. 259. London: Churchill.

Joanette, Y., Lecours, A. R., Lepage, Y., and Lamoureux, M. 1983. Language in right-
handers with right-hemisphere lesions: A preliminary study including anatomical,
genetic, and social factors. *Brain and Language* 20:217–248.

Lecours, A. R., Mehler, J., and Parente, M. A. 1987a. Illiteracy and brain damage: 1.
Aphasia testing in culturally contrasted populations (control subjects). *Neuropsychologia* 25:231–245.

Lecours, A. R., Mehler, J., and Parente, M. A. 1987b. Illiteracy and brain damage: 2.
Manifestations of unilateral neglect in testing 'auditory comprehension' with iconographic materials. *Brain and Cognition* 6:243–265.

Lecours, A. R., Mehler, J., and Parente, M. A. 1988. Illiteracy and brain damage: 3. A
contribution to the study of speech and language disorders in illiterates with unilateral brain damage (initial testing). *Neuropsychologia* 26:575–589.

Lecours, A. R., Nespoulous, J. L., Joanette, Y., Lemay, A., Puel, M., Lafond, D., Cot,
F., and Rascol, A. 1986. Protocole MT-86 d'examen linguistique de l'aphasie (version alpha). Laboratoire Théophile-Alajouanine. Montreal, 1986.

Métellus, J., Cathala, H. P., Issartier, A., and Bodak, A. 1981. Une étude d'aphasie chez
une illettrée (analphabete): Reflexions critiques sur les fonctions cérébrales con-
courant au langage. *Annales médico-psychologiques* 139:992–1001.

Morais, J., Cary, L., Alegria, J., and Bertelson, P. 1979. Does awareness of speech as a
sequence of phones arise spontaneously? *Cognition* 7:323–331.

Parente, M. A. 1984. Habilidades construtivas em analfabetos: Um estudo através de
desegnho e construção do cubo. Dissertation, Pontificia Universidale Catolica, São
Paulo.

Scribner, S., and Cole, M. 1981. *The psychology of literacy*. Cambridge: Harvard University Press.

Siegel, S. 1956. *Nonparametric statistics for the behavioral sciences*. New York: McGraw-Hill.

Tikofsky, R. 1970. Personal communication cited in Cameron et al., 1971.

Tzavaras, A., Kaprinis, G., and Gatzoyas, A. 1981. Literacy and hemispheric specialization for language: Digit dichotic listening in illiterates. *Neuropsychologia* 19:565–
570.

von Mundy, V. 1957. Zur Frage der paarig veranlagten Sprachzentren. *Der Nervenartz*
28:212–216.

Weber, E. 1904. Das Schreiben als Ursache der einseitigen Lage des Sprachzentrums. *Zentralblatt für Physiologie* 18:341–347.

Wechsler, A. F. 1976. Crossed aphasia in an illiterate dextral. *Brain and Language* 3:164–172.

Editor's Comments

When invited to participate in the conference on developmental dyslexia, from which this volume emerged, André Roch Lecours tactfully reminded me that his work on Brazilian illiterates was concerned with acquired language disorders, not developmental disorders. Yet the importance of this chapter to developmental disorders of language is quite clear. For instance, an important issue that needs to be resolved regarding developmental dyslexia and its linguistic anomalies, particularly among adult dyslexics, is whether the anomalies reflect an abnormal initial state and/or abnormal subsequent language acquisition or whether they reflect the fact that the affected individuals never acquire full literacy. In other words, does illiteracy per se affect linguistic capacity? The study of adult illiterates who are ordinary in every other way offers a unique opportunity for answering this question (see also the chapter by Bertelson and De Gelder in this volume).

A second issue raised by the study of adult illiterates without previous developmental problems is that of cerebral dominance. There is reason to believe that cerebral dominance reflects the asymmetric organization of brain circuitries subserving lateralized behaviors. Furthermore, we have learned that brain asymmetries have been demonstrated to exist before birth and so before significant language acquisition. Asymmetries in gross anatomical structures involved in language function are visible in the fetal brain soon after the middle of pregnancy, when most of the neurons have reached the cortical plate and long subcortical, intra, and interhemispheric neural connections are being established (see the chapters by Caviness et al. and by Rakic in this volume). However, short interneuronal circuitries, synaptic architectures, and neurochemical characteristics continue to be established well beyond the time of birth (see, for instance, Rakic in this volume). It appears quite likely, therefore, that the coarse organization up cerebral dominance is established early but that the more detailed characteristics of cerebral dominance can be altered later in life when the individual is exposed to the psychosocial environment by the establishment of specific patterns of local connections, synapses, and receptors. It is not surprising, therefore, to discover that the detailed pattern of aphasic disturbance differs in illiterates and readers even though illiterate subjects do not differ in their overall response to hemispheric injury (they become aphasic from lesions of the left hemisphere just as often as ordinary readers). It is intuitively satisfying that the differences between illiterates and readers mainly involve semantic aspects of language, since it makes perfect sense that the coding of the external environment in illiterate subjects would take increasing advantage of the types of experiences not reinforced by written language, namely, functions typically attributed to the right hemisphere.

Is this an important issue also in the functional organization of the brains of individuals with developmental language problems? At this early stage of research it is entirely possible that the relatively impoverished linguistic interactions between dyslexics and their social environment may lead to extraordinary coding topographies, including unusual patterns of cerebral lateralization, patterns that are different from the anatomical changes seen in dyslexic brains and attributed to prenatal perturbations (see Galaburda et al. and Sherman et al. in this volume). The several reported instances of deviant cerebral dominance among dyslexics may thus reflect both early anomalous circuitries and the effects of subsequent deviant interactions with the environment.

Chapter 3

An Information-Processing Account of Reading Acquisition

John Morton

Introduction

The dangers of structuralist simplification are amply illustrated by those who grasp at parallels between acquired and developmental disorders. Curiously, even scientists of otherwise unimpeachable mental habits have lapsed when the temptation of drawing equivalences between acquired and developmental dyslexia have presented themselves (Ellis 1984; Marshall 1984). However, a label such as *deep dyslexia* has a full definition not in terms of a precise list of symptoms (Coltheart, Patterson, and Marshall 1980 not withstanding) but by its contrastive force in a more or less agreed upon information-processing framework (Morton and Patterson 1980; Patterson 1981; Shallice 1981). One may find a group of children with symptoms that more or less correspond to those found in a prototypical acquired deep dyslexic, but what does it do to term those children "developmental dyslexics"? The similarities are spurious, arising, as they do, from the structure of the material (in this case reading material) rather than from the structure of the disorders.

There are a number of reasons for pointing forcefully to the aberration just described. The first, and one that will occupy the major part of this chapter, is that it negates the truth that "the most obvious thing about development is that there is change" (Frith 1986a, p. 70). To this one can add that the most obvious thing about developmental disorders is that they affect development. It seems to me that any intellectual stance that obscures these truths is on the wrong track. Developmental disorders must be treated in their own right, and this means separately from acquired disorders.

A second reason for separating developmental and acquired disorders is that to do otherwise can lead to errors of inference. Of particular interest is the error of the following pattern. Suppose one has a developmental theory in which it is hypothesized that a particular disorder, leading to the absence of a skill, s, results from the absence of a specific ability, *a*. Suppose one found a group of adult patients with acquired disorders such that the ability *a* was missing. Whether or not these patients had *s* preserved would tell us something about the localization of the neural substrate underpinning *s* and *a* but could have nothing to say concerning the *developmental* relationship between the two. Yet, consider the following from Ludlow (1980), who was examining the issue of whether impaired language development could be the result of auditory processing deficits. Against the proposal she adduces her own finding that patients with Huntington's disease sometimes have severe auditory-processing disorders without having any language disorder (Ludlow et al. 1979). She continues, "*Thus,* auditory processing disorders . . . are probably not the basis for the language problems" (p. 158). Of course, what may be the case for the Huntington's patients, whose language functions were established many years before they suffered a deficit of auditory processing, has no bearing on whether normal language *acquisition* depends over time on an intact auditory-processing system.

The fallacy in Ludlow's argument is fairly obvious. More dangerous, because it is more concealed, is the futility of discussions as to the reality of developmental dyslexia based on collections of test results. These become translated into "syndromes" that can look like syndromes with different etiologies. Thus, Marshall claims, "the syndromes of developmental dyslexia will accordingly be interpreted as consequent upon the selective failure of a particular adult component (or components) to develop appropriately, with relatively intact, normal (adult) functioning of the remaining components" (1984, p.46). Marshall believes that such precepts can form the basis of a "rational" taxonomy of developmental disorders. Bryant and Impey (1986) believe that such arguments can be countered by finding normal readers with the same pattern of test results as the supposed developmental deep and surface dyslexics. Both sides of the discussion ignore the developmental facts of the children in question and allow the debate to obscure the nature of the underlying psychological processes. As the debate stands, it can continue as long as one side or the other can find a dyslexic or normal reader with more and more extreme patterns of performance on particular tests. But the debate is actually about the developmental trajectory, which cannot be addressed by producing a profile of individual readers, howsoever complete, at one single moment in development.

In this article I hope to point to some relationships between acquired and developmental dyslexics by examining the information-processing implications of Frith's framework for reading acquisition.

These relationships will then be derived through comparisons of processes rather than behavior.

Frith's Framework

No serious student of developmental dyslexia can afford to be ignorant of the work of Uta Frith (e.g., 1985, 1986). In this article I can do no more than summarize the essential aspects of her thinking. What she required was a model "that can help bridge the gulf between the child who scribbles and the highly literate adult" (Frith 1986, p.72). Her proposals, therefore, are developmental. She assumes that it is sufficient to consider three basic strategies for dealing with the written word that the beginner has to master. These strategies are called *logographic, alphabetic,* and *orthographic.* Frith is concerned partly with the processing differences associated with these three strategies, but more importantly, with the fact that they follow in sequence and to a large extent are developmentally contingent (Morton 1986). By this I mean that later strategies cannot be attained unless prior ones have been achieved at a certain level of mastery. All I intend to do here is to give a brief outline of Frith's ideas. For additional evidence the reader is referred to Frith 1985. First of all, I will give an overall view of the framework. In the second part of the chapter I will take each stage in turn and give an information-processing interpretation.

Frith believes that normal reading acquisition cannot be understood fully without also taking into consideration the acquisition of spelling. The three strategies, then, are to be seen as strategies for both reading and spelling.

Logographic

In the logographic phase words seem to be recognized independently of each other. Indeed, it seems plausible to think of each word as being identified by an idiosyncratic schema. While it is the case that individual letters typically enter into the recognition, it is also the case that not all the letters in a word are crucial, and in some instances nonalphabetic information appears to be crucial. Typically, the first letter acts as a salient feature, but irrelevant detail too can be incorporated into the recognition schema. Thus, a child may only be able to read the sign ESSO when the letters are surrounded by the familiar oval (Augst 1986). Similarly, a child will respond with "Harrods" when presented with "Hrorasd" or "HaRroDs" (Coltheart 1986). The extent to which the logographic way of reading is elaborated depends upon the age at which the child is taught to read and the method by which he is taught. Such things may have consequences that are a matter only of degree. This remains to be established. In all cases the child will be able to use some of what he has learned in logographic writing. In the normal course of development logographic reading and logographic writing display equivalent peculiarities. The child who could read ESSO only with the oval around it could only write it with the oval around it. In addition, only the initial letter may be crucial; the other letters may be in any order or even omitted. This is characteristic of this phase of learning. Yet it is clear that the child has learned something of the essential features of the writing system, since it would be exceptional for them to employ signs other than letters in their constructions.

Alphabetic

Frith believes that the child's earliest alphabetic attempts are to be seen in writing. The alphabetic strategy depends on analyzing words into component letters and phonemes and devising rules for mapping the two onto each other. The main difference between alphabetic and logographic modes of operation is that in the former the order of the elements is absolutely crucial. The beginning of the alphabetic phase is characterized by the inability of children to read back what they have written. Read (1971) has given a number of examples of this. For example: 2 DADDY I EM SRY TAT U R SIC (To Daddy: I am sorry that you are sick). What seems to be happening is that the child's first efforts at decoding the writing system involve the use of two codes under the child's control: phonological representation of words and written letters. A child may say any sequence of phonemes she wishes, playing around with sets of words and matching them to letters. The child attempts an analysis of the segmental structure of her own speech, sometimes arriving at a phonetic analysis rather than a phonemic analysis (Read 1971).

The precise nature of the dependency of alphabetic reading upon alphabetic writing remains to be elaborated. That there is such a dependency, at least at the beginning of the alphabetic stage, is shown by dissociations between reading and writing. Thus, Read (1971) identified precocious writers who could not read back their own writing. And Bryant and Bradley (1980) found cases in which reading by sight coexisted with writing by sound. At this time a regular word may be spelled correctly (alphabetically) but not recognized, while an irregular word may be recognized (logographically) but not spelled correctly. As alphabetic reading ability develops, the situation changes, and the child is able to pronounce all regular words correctly, but she may lose the ability to recognize irregular words that used to be in her vocabulary.

Orthographic
The orthographic strategy is the construction of recognition units above the alphabetic level. This enables the morphemic parts of words to be recognized instantly. The resulting processing units correspond to what I have called "logogens" (Morton 1969, 1979, 1980; Morton and Patterson, 1980); they are referred to as lexical units in other models. In Frith's framework the orthographic stage occurs in reading well before it becomes established in writing. Most English children are fluent readers of quite complicated material at a time when they are habitually making regularization errors in their writing. Indeed, many adults (including the author) never completely established an orthographic writing system even for quite common words.

The Development of an Information Processing System

Mention of "stages" in what follows should not lead the unwary reader into believing I am suffering from "incipient Piagetization" (to quote Jacques Mehler at the Florence conference). In traditional, a stage models the stages themselves are times of stability when the child rests as it were, after the latest achievement. In contrast, the stages in Frith's framework and in the information processing model proposed here are identified by the elements of *maximum* change. As should already be clear, I do not suppose that once a new strategy has been set in train, there will be no more development in the old one. Rather, the contingencies in normal development are found at the level of detail. Thus, one learns to read ESSO logographically, and while one is learning to read other words logographically, the logographic writing of ESSO can proceed. The force of the contingent relationships among the stages emerges when, as in the case of dyslexics, change does not occur, and the next stage cannot be reached. Then the subsequent stage is blocked as well. Thus, if a child is incapable of segmenting his own phonological representations, he will not be able to proceed to the alphabetic stage of writing. In the strongest form of the model, then, the alphabetic stage of reading and the two orthographic stages will be forever out of reach. In practice it might be possible to adopt an idiosyncratic strategy that enables the obstacle to be bypassed, though there is not much evidence that this is possible for organic dyslexics. On the other hand, children who struggle with reading and who are either relatively slow in their development or for some reason cognitively blocked can be helped so that they overcome the obstacles (see Bryant and Bradley 1985).

On Method
The finishing point for this exercise in development is a model of the adult literate. That this model resembles the logogen model I have previously proposed is no coincidence. In the logogen model units in which morphemes are recognized give one access to not only a phonological lexicon but also semantics. The orthographic strategy depends on the existence of such units. It is natural to speculate on how the schema by which a word is recognized at the logographic level is replaced by the orthographic recognition unit. Is it, for example, that the representation, crude and lacking precise indication of the required order of the elements, is gradually refined as the child has experience with print? In this way of thinking, a logographic representation resembles minilogogens mapping in the adult way directly into the semantic organization built up in conjunction with speech. I reject this idea for a number of reasons, of which the most relevant are as follows:

· It appears to be the rule that when children who have developed a sight vocabulary begin to read, they suddenly cease to recognize words they could previously respond to appropriately. If logographic representations were simply elaborated by increasing the input specification but maintaining the same mapping semantics, we would not find such discontinuities.
· Words have a special meaning in special scripts even for adults. Thus, *Coca-Cola* may be orthographically the same as what we see on the red and white can, but it fails to exploit the special representation that the advertised script has set up.
· As we shall see later, classical developmental dyslexics make "semantic" errors in reading without any displaying the slightest suspicion of verbal semantic problems.

Accordingly, I am proposing that logographic recognition units map directly onto object semantics rather than verbal semantics. That is, words learned early resemble pictures, but later words do not. Before proceeding with my elaboration of the information-processing model, I will briefly describe what I intended by the distinction between the two kinds of semantics.

Picture Semantics and Verbal Semantics
The separation of verbal semantics from picture, object, or visual semantics is not new. It has occurred in my own work in the context of

naming disorders (Morton 1985) and in the work of Seymour (1979), Shallice (1981), Beauvois (1982), and Riddoch and Humphreys (1987).

I will make no attempt here to give a complete definition of the roles of the two kinds of semantic systems. Nor will I do more than hint at the kind of evidence available that supports the division.

At the most basic level, object semantics can be seen as mediating between the visual world and action. The functions include functions similar to what Gibson (1979) calls *affordances*. The idea here is that we can react to objects, parts of objects, or features of the environment without passing through a stage of verbalization, hypothesis formation, or other problem-solving-like activities. It is thus that we can sit upon solid surfaces without identifying them as parts of tables, windowsills, or walls. Other such visuomotor primitives for an object would be the property of being a container and the property of having something that can be used as a handle that can be picked up in an appropriate way.

One line of evidence in favor of separating the two kinds of semantics comes from analyses of the abilities of stroke patients. One of the cleanest examples is the patient M. P. reported by Beauvois (1982) and Beauvois and Saillant, (1985). Beauvois characterizes this patient as having a disturbance between her visual and verbal semantics, though her visual semantics and her verbal semantics each operated normally. Beauvois carried out verbal, visual, and visuoverbal tests in which color was the relevant feature.

The definition of verbal test was one in which the stimulus, the response, and the intervening processes required for the subject to perform the task were all verbal. There were two tests of this kind. In one of them the patient was required to answer questions of the form "Which category does the word *blush* belong to: brown, red, or yellow?" In the second verbal test the patient was asked to produce a color name from a verbal description in cases where the color name did not correspond to the color of an object. Thus, "What is the other name for *Jambon de Paris?*" elicited the reply *"Jambon blanc,"* which is a pale pink. Similarly, the color name commonly associated with envy can only be ascertained through verbal systems. M. P. performed at ceiling levels on these tests and on other purely verbal tests.

The visual tests were designed to exclude the need for verbal mediation, and for this reason M. P. had an adhesive plaster stuck on her mouth during the tests. In the first test she was presented with pairs of pieces of colored wool and had to decide simply whether they were the same or different. In the second test she had to point out the correctly colored picture of an object from among five pictures of the same object. To increase the purely visual component, the stimuli included traffic signs, of which people have poor verbal knowledge. M. P. performed at near ceiling levels on these tests. In conclusion, M. P. appeared to have normal visual color processing, as well as normal knowledge of the colors of objects. We will see whether it is reasonable to think of such knowledge as semantics.

There were two kinds of visuoverbal tests. In one set the stimulus and response came from different modalities. Thus, there was a test of color naming and a test where the patient had to name the appropriate color for a line drawing of an object. The verbovisual equivalents were pointing to a color patch in response to the name or to a request like "Show me what color a cherry is." On these tests M. P.'s performance averaged 29 percent. She could not point out the color of a cherry, made very gross errors in pointing to colors (e.g., pointing to brown instead of "bright blue" and saying that a carrot should be "green").

In the second class of tests the stimulus and response were in the same modality, but the means of mediating between the two was in the other modality. When asked questions like "Tell me what color a gherkin is," which was presumed to involve visualization, M. P. could answer only 8 of 20 correctly. There was a large decrement on a test of picking out the "correctly" colored object, in which the correct response was an inappropriate color of the correct name. In a third series of tests M. P. showed a decrement in responding to the color of "snow". Here the stimulus and response were both verbal, but she was encouraged to use a visual strategy. Purely visual tests in which verbal mediation was encouraged resulted in a similar decrement.

If one has doubts as to the felicity of the term "semantic" for the purely visual tasks, there should not be much question when one considers M. P.'s failure on the cross-modal tasks. The ability to visualize the appropriate color of an object on verbal demand certainly cannot be termed perceptual by any normal definition. The storage and retrieval of information that can be translated into the word "green" has the properties in the color domain that we are looking for. If the reader objects to "semantic," suggestions for an alternative term are welcome.

Evidence similar to that provided by Beauvois is provided by Riddoch and Humphreys (1987). They present data from the patient J. B. This patient appears to have an unimpaired verbal system, since he performs 100 percent correctly when asked to provide a name to an auditory definition. However, his naming of everyday objects fell below 50 percent correct. With knife, fork, and spoon he accessed the three names of these implements, but he performed at chance levels in deciding among them. But when asked to make an appropriate gesture at these objects, he not only makes a correctly discriminating action but also makes it with the correct hand (left hand for the fork and right hand for the spoon and knife, J. B. being British). The knowledge that enables the correct action to be performed is accessed by the object but is apparently not available in the search for the correct name. Let this do as an operational indication of the distinction between object semantics and verbal semantics.

Note that if we grant that the chimpanzee possesses semantic knowledge and hold that the species has no language, we have perhaps an equivalent, and certainly a parallel, organization to picture semantics. As to the nature of the organization of this knowledge we have only scattered clues. Suffice it for the moment to remark that we have no reason to suppose other than the roughest equivalence between the two semantic systems. It is not the case that for each node in picture semantics there is a node in visual semantics into which it projects (or the equivalent statement in the metaphor of your choice). When I am presented with a picture of Fido, while my verbal system has instructions to retrieve the basic-level term *spaniel*, my pictorial system may send it a message that is only interpretable as *dog*. The resulting reconciliation can be classified by an experimenter as an error.

Stage 1a—Logographic Reading
When a child begins to read, there are a number of processing elements already established. These are shown in Figure 3.1. In this figure and in subsequent figures the cognitive systems comprise all the cognitive apparatus not specifically mentioned elsewhere. The two shown elements of the cognitive systems are the two kinds of semantic processes: picture semantics (p) and verbal semantics (v). Picture semantics has input from systems concerned with the world of objects and has an output connection concerned with mediating action. At the beginning of the logographic-reading stage the child has already developed a speech system. This includes processes that have to do with both speech recognition and production. On the recognition side there is a categorization system, which I have called elsewhere an authority-input logogen system. This produces a phonological representation of lexical items, which can be unpacked, modified, and turned into motor instructions in the response buffer. These speech processes connect with semantic representations that are noncontroversially called verbal semantics. The child also has established a categorization system for pictures and objects, which accesses object semantics, as discussed in the preceding section. This

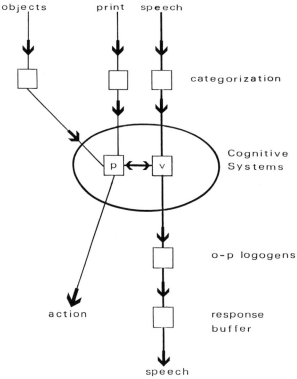

Figure 3.1

Stage 1*a*. An information-processing model of a child during Frith's (1985) logographic-reading stage. Only those processes relevant for the processing of single words and objects have been depicted. In this and subsequent figures p represents pictorial semantics and v represents verbal semantics. O-p (output) logogens contain the phonological specifications necessary for speaking individual words. The special feature of this model is that logographic reading is equated with picture recognition and accesses pictorial semantics rather than verbal semantics. This stage is characterized by growth in the categorical representations of print.

semantic system also has the facility to control action, as shown in figure 3.1.

We can imagine that a child discovers that printed words correspond to meanings and equates this correspondence to that obtaining between pictures and meaning. For this reason the result of categorizing a word should lead to access to picture semantics. When the child comes to recognize words without a simple referent, the nature of the organization of picture semantics itself is changed.

Another consequence of the child's processing words in the same way as pictures is that it makes sense of his indifference to quite major changes in the form of the word. In the same way drawings of the same cat can differ greatly from each other, since the cat itself undergoes major changes in projected form as it moves around. The picture of the cat may show four paws, but there may be only two or three visible. Similarly then, why should it be important that all the letters in a word should be represented all the time? And if a lemon has to be yellow to be a lemon, should not COCA-COLA *have* to be red and white to be Coca-Cola?

The logographic-reading stage has not been studied very extensively in normal children, largely because it lasts for such a short time and contains such a small vocabulary. One of the few studies is Seymour and Elder 1986. My colleagues and I currently conducting a study of this phase, and in table 3.1 I present the responses of Thomas, aged 4. One can see that his vocabulary is reasonable, though the response of "pull" to *yellow* might seem a little extraordinary. But it is no coincidence that both words have a double *l*, which may act as the salient feature. In table 3.2 are Thomas's responses to the same words misspelled. He almost does as well with these stimuli as with the words, and he can now read *yellow*. Particularly revealing is his response to *liltle*. The stimulus satisfied the general description of "little" but failed in some particular. Again, presumably not by co-

Table 3.1
Thomas's responses

Stimulus	Response
milk	"milk"
child	"camel"
house	"house"
blue	"blue"
grandfather	"grandfather"
little	"little"
yellow	"pull"

Table 3.2
Thomas's responses

Stimulus	Response
grodftehr	"gr . . . grandfather"
honse	"house"
mlik	"milk"
yollwo	"yellow"
chld	"cat"
bleo	"blue"
liltle	"*Little*. No that's not *little*, not two *t*s. *Lift*."

incidence, the double *t* is salient for this child, and the fact that it is now *ltl* rather than *ttl* is just a little disturbing to him. His response is rather like saying that it can't be a cat because it is wagging its tail.

Stage 1b—Logographic Writing
At some point while the child is building up a vocabulary of logographic words (what many people call a "sight vocabulary"), she begins writing. The child's own name is the most favorite word, and that is learned by copying from a sample. Later on, children try to write other words, especially ones they have learned to recognize. Most of these words are not perfect copies, and so must be based on representations that the child has herself created. The form of these representations is likely to be idiosyncratic to a certain extent, but the few children whose early written output has been studied share the feature that letter order apart from the initial letter can be varied. One imagines that the representation consists of a collection of letters (in contrast to a list, which would preserve the order) selected according to some perhaps aesthetic criteria.

   In other cases the criteria might be exhaustive sampling, as in the following examples from Scheerer-Neumann (1987): Hanno, a preschooler, wrote *papa* either correctly or as APAP. He wrote *opa* (the familiar form for grandpa) as OPA, APO, or OAP. He is reported to be equally happy with any of these forms.

   Further analysis must await more extensive data. What is clear is that at this stage there must be an accumulation of information on the set of letters. This would be used when the child is creating new written forms. In addition, there will be a set of representations of the items in the written vocabulary. In figure 3.2 I have termed the latter the lographemic store, though it is probably best to regard the term *store* as one of convenience only, rather than to think of some discrete

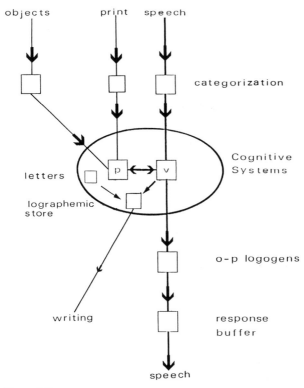

Figure 3.2
Stage 1*b*. An information-processing model of a child during the logographic-writing stage. Experience with print has led to a store of knowledge about letters. This is being used in the creation of lographemic representations, the growth of which characterizes this stage. Classic developmental dyslexics are frozen at this stage.

storage location or a system resembling a logogen system. In fact, lographemic knowledge is likely to consist of a set of discrete records.

In figure 3.2 the small arrow connecting letter knowledge with the lographemic store is intended to indicate a *source* of information over the long term, rather than short term information processing. Note also that action output from pictorial semantics has been omitted in order to simplify the figure.

Stage 2a—Alphabetic Writing
Logographic writing is eventually replaced by alphabetic writing. What is happening during this stage is that the child gains access to her own phonological representations and is able to isolate individual phonemes within them. This is an absolutely essential step, because

of the way our writing system works. Alphabetic scripts represent speech sounds at the level of the phoneme. With nonalphabetic scripts this stage would be very different.

There are a number of options available to us in accounting for how the child is able to isolate individual phonemes. These options are dependent upon the details of the model and will not be discussed further here. All of these options involve processes that follow the output lexicon in speech production. After individual phonemes are isolated, they have to be mapped onto written letters. This requires setting up phoneme-grapheme rules. These I have shown in figure 3.3 as being fed from the response buffer, though there is other processing involved. Clearly the phoneme-grapheme rules will use the letter knowledge that has been accumulating.

The process of phonemic segmentation is the most important single aspect of learning to read. Rozin and Gleitman (1977) write, "The child's insufficient access to the segmented nature of his own or another's speech . . . is the major cognitive barrier to initial progress in reading." A large proportion of backward readers are stuck at the logographic stage, though they can relatively easily be helped over the barrier by a well-directed program of remediation (Bryant and Bradley 1985; Bradley and Bryant 1985). As we will see in the final section, a class of developmental dyslexics that Frith terms *classical dyslexics* have a more serious problem in moving into the alphabetic phase.

In the early part of this stage, the child's productions are minimal. Here are some examples from Scheerer-Neumann (1987): TT for *Tante*, HS for *Haus*, LP for *Lampe*, KF for *Kaffee*. It is important to note that the child knows that he has not been able to put down all the sounds in the word. In addition, at this stage the child can rarely read the words that he has written, as I have already noted.

In the alphabetic stage of writing, words that might have been correctly written by the child in the logographic phase (as occasionally happens) may now be incorrectly written. An example from Scheerer-Neumann (1987) is her son's writing his own name. His first attempts were simply the initial letter H, which for him was a complete written representation of his name. Later he learned to write it correctly as HANNO. At the beginning of the alphabetic phase of writing, during which he produced the examples quoted in the preceding paragraph, he wrote his name as HNO. This kind of regression indicates that the lographemic representations previously set up have lost their connection with semantics. This is indicated in figure 3.3 by weakening the connections. Note that logographic writing and alphabetic writing can coexist, but so far as we know, not for the same item.

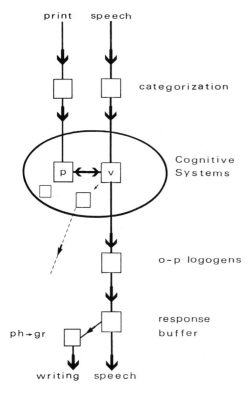

Figure 3.3
Stage 2*a*. An information-processing model of a child during the alphabetic-writing stage. (The processes involved with objects have been omitted for the sake of simplicity.) Logographic writing is dropping out and the child is concerned with learning about the relationship between the phonemic structure of her speech and the writing system. This leads to setting up phoneme-grapheme rules, which are labeled *ph-gr* in the figure.

Stage 2b-i—Alphabetic Reading

The alphabetic-reading stage is divided into two sections that are distinguished by the connections made with the semantic system. At the beginning of the alphabetic phase the child is beginning to segment words into component letters rather than recognizing them as wholes. Individual letters consolidate their representations, and a set of mapping rules are set up between them and the phonemes. Presumably, the setting up of grapheme-phoneme rules is influenced by the already existing phoneme-grapheme rules. Yet there is no simple reverse procedure to arrive at the correct rules. Such an influence is indicated in figure 3.4. Again, however, there does not appear to be sufficient information on the development of individual children to enable such hypotheses to be tested.

Alphabetic writing cannot develop without a minimum of explicit instruction. Similarly, alphabetic reading appears to require some kind of systematic approach. Such instruction consists of detailing the rules themselves, as "G is 'guh'." Certainly, explicit instruction in the knowledge that letters map onto sounds is a part of any contemporary reading instruction. This proves to be a difficulty for some theories in recent or current vogue. Analogy theories of adult reading hold that there are no grapheme-phoneme rules at all, merely mapping between input lexical representations and output lexical representations. Abilities such as being able to read nonwords are accounted for in terms of the use of principles of analogy on the lexicon (Glushko 1979; Henderson 1982; Marcel 1980). Apart from problems related to the viability and adequacy of such theories as have been specified (see Patterson and Morton 1985), it is not clear how these theories would account for children's abilities in the alphabetic-reading stage. Most notably, only regular words can be read, and nonwords can be read as accurately as words. In addition, if the child has learned an irregular word once this phase has begun, he will not attempt to use that ability in trying to read a word that differs by the initial letter (Marsh et al. 1980).

The problems for current connectionist models are different. McClelland and Seidenberg (this volume) do away with lexicons of all kinds, acknowledging only letters, phonemes, and semantic features. Such a model can not cope with the logographic phase at all and can only begin to operate at the alphabetic phase. However, their model is not currently built to allow *direct* mapping between elements such as the letter *d* and the phoneme /d/. Rather, the mapping between end elements is determined via a large number of intervening "hidden units" with connection weights. The owner of such a network (i.e.,

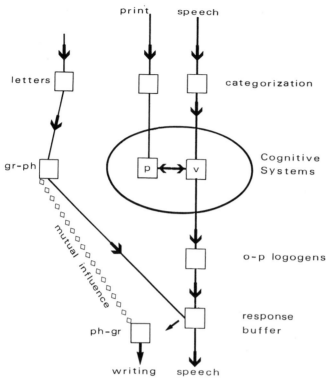

Figure 3.4
Stage *2b-i*. An information-processing model of a child during the early part of the alphabetic-reading stage. This stage is characterized by the child's increasing her understanding of the phonological equivalents of individual letters and setting up grapheme-phoneme rules (labeled *gr-ph*). These rules are context-sensitive as well as context-free and include rules relating to letter combinations, not just single letters. The nature of the emerging grapheme-phoneme rules is influenced by the nature of the already existing phoneme-grapheme rules.

the child in the alphabetic stage) would not be able to offer any insights into its mode of operation in a way that would help with establishing the networks. Such insights, like *"B* means 'buh,' " would be only incidental.

One interesting feature of the child's performance in stage 2*b-i* is that they cannot understand the words they read alphabetically. Marx (1987) reports that after his son successfully read a list of words, he said "Now you read them so that I know what they mean." Examination of figure 3.4 reveals the reason for this. When the child reads alphabetically, the letter sequence is converted into a phonemic sequence. This is sent to the response buffer, the only process capable of handling it. However, there is no feedback from the response buffer to the semantic systems. So the child can correctly read regular words, though he has no means of understanding what he has read (acoustic feedback not being a possible means for this; see Morton, 1968). This situation slowly changes. Scheerer-Neumann writes, "Gradually reading comes under lexical control." By this means the child moves to the next stage.

Stage 2b-ii—Alphabetical Reading with Understanding
The main feature of this stage are that the child now has feedback from phonology to meaning and that logographic reading drops out completely. The connection with meaning is established directly from the response buffer to verbal semantics. These features are depicted in figure 3.5.

Stage 3a—Orthographic Reading
The final stages of development are of less interest to those whose primary concern is with dyslexia. By the time a child has mastered most of the alphabetic stages, progress on to the orthographic stage is a simple consequence of the interaction of reading, linguistic knowledge, and the general processes of cognitive abstraction. Very few children fail to make the transition painlessly.

What happens is that input representations become established in which letter order is respected and morphological structure is central. The resulting recognition units map onto the verbal semantic system directly. This is shown in figure 3.6.

Stage 3b—Orthographic Writing
In the final stage, shown in figure 3.7, we approach the literate adult. All that needs to be established is a proper graphemic-lexicon system, in which each word is noted with proper acknowledgment of the morphological structure. Seventeen percent of the population fail to

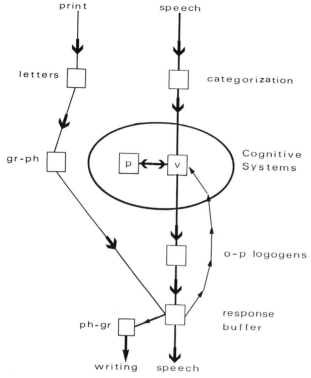

Figure 3.5
Stage *2b-ii*. An information-processing model of a child during the later part of the alphabetic-reading stage. Logographic reading has become completely suppressed. Feedback is being established from the response buffer to the cognitive systems so that the words can now be understood.

achieve this stage. They fall in the category of "type B spellers" (Frith 1985).

Frozen Cases

The very nature of the developmental process means that we get only a passing glimpse of children with only logographic reading or of children in the alphabetic stage. Most children are in the logographic phase for only a brief time before they begin to get instruction in reading. Thus, we may not be able to find many examples of logographically represented words in any child. In Frith's framework, classical developmental dyslexia results from a failure to attain the alphabetic strategy. Dyslexic children, therefore, give us a chance to

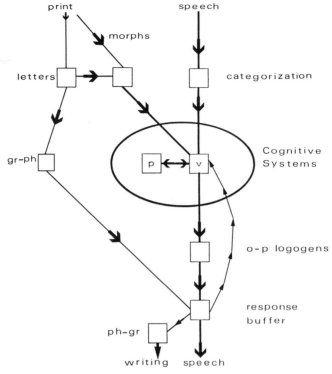

Figure 3.6
Stage 3*a*. An information-processing model of a child during the orthographic reading stage. A new input lexicon is being established that takes account of the morphology of words. This lexicon has access to the verbal semantic system.

examine in more detail the consequences of sticking at the logographic stage.

I regard logographic reading as equivalent to picture recognition. The exact visual form of lexical items is not required by the recognition system. Furthermore, there is a very strong bias towards acquiring lexical items for which there is a representation in the child's pictorial semantics.

What are the consequences of these two constraints? First, the reader should produce responses of words in his vocabulary to stimuli that physically resemble these words. The relationships between stimuli and responses will resemble those already described as typical of the logographic phase. Furthermore, the child should make similar responses to nonwords that resemble words in his vocabulary.

The second question concerns the nature of the pictorial-semantic system. Clearly, we would expect to find accurate representations of

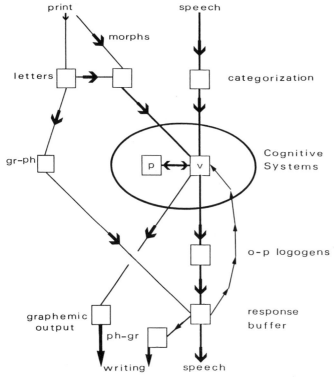

Figure 3.7
Stage 3*b*. An information-processing model of a child during the orthographic writing stage. During this final stage of development a graphemic-output system is being established within which lexical items are represented. This figure corresponds to the adult model (see Morton 1980).

the world of objects. More generally, we can expect that the more a word can be linked up to an image, the more likely that it can be read.

A good example of a logographic dyslexic is described by Johnston (1983). The case is that of C. R., a girl of between 16 and 18 years during the time of testing. She is reported to have a full WISC score of 75 and a reading age on the BAS Word Reading Test of 6.2. What of her reading? First let us look at the semantic effects. C. R. was given 60 words of high imageability and 60 of low imageability. She managed to read 9 of the high-imageability words but only 1 of the low-imageability ones. In addition, there was a part-of-speech effect with the high-imageability words: 5 out of 20 nouns were correctly read but only 3 out of 20 adjectives and 1 out of 20 verbs. As Johnston remarks, this difference could reflect an imageability effect. C. R. was also given a test in which she had to judge whether pairs of words were synonymous. With pairs of high-imageability words she was correct 58 percent of the time; with low-imageability words she was correct only 32 percent of the time.

Overall, C. R. was asked to read 382 words. Of these, 78 were correct and 219 were not attempted. The most common errors were what Johnston called "visual" errors, following Coltheart, Patterson, and Marshall (1980). In these errors the stimulus and response words had 50 percent of their letters in common. These errors are typical of the logographic phase. I should point out that Johnston presents the case as an example of a developmental deep dyslexic. She argues by analogy. Acquired deep dyslexic patients favor highly imageable words; so does C. R. They produce visual errors, like C. R. again. C. R. is also reported to produce a few semantic errors, such as saying "table" when presented with *chair*, but there are only 5 of these reported out of a total of 163 responses, and this is not a sufficient number to give us confidence that they are genuinely semantic (Ellis and Marshall 1978). More crucial in rejecting the analogy with deep dyslexia is the fact that C. R. often made word responses to nonword stimuli. Deep dyslexics hardly ever do this.

Conclusion

Frith's (1985) framework has been used as the basis of a preliminary information-processing account of reading acquisition. The stages of Frith's framework should be understood as designating the location of maximum change in the nature of the processing. A crucial aspect of the model is that in the first, logographic stage of reading, words access pictorial semantics rather than verbal semantics. This theoretical step has the advantage of providing an account of what have hitherto been called developmental deep dyslexics. I propose that we henceforth call them logographic dyslexics.

Note

Uta Frith not only has provided the starting framework for this article but has advised me throughout its writing, preventing me from making gross errors. I am also grateful to Guinevere Tufnell for comments on an earlier draft.

References

Augst, G. 1986. Descriptively and explanatorily adequate models of orthography. In *New Trends in Graphics and Orthography*, ed. G. Augst. Berlin: de Gruyther.

Beauvois, M. F. 1982. Optic aphasia: A process of interaction between vision and language. *Philosophical Transactions of the Royal Society* B298:35–47.

Beauvois, M. F., and Saillant, B. 1985. Optic aphasia for colours and colour agnosia: A distinction between visual and visuo-verbal impairments in the processing of colours. *Cognitive Neuropsychology,* 2:1–48.

Bradley, L., and Bryant, P. 1985. *Rhyme and reason in reading and spelling.* Ann Arbor: University of Michigan Press.

Bryant, P., and Bradley, L. 1980. Why children sometimes write words which they cannot read? In U. Frith, ed., *Cognitive processes in spelling.* London: Academic Press.

Bryant, P., and Bradley, L. 1985. *Children's reading problems.* Oxford: Blackwell.

Bryant, P., and Impey, L. 1986. The similarities between normal readers and developmental acquired dyslexics. *Cognition* 24 (1–2): 121–137.

Coltheart, M., Patterson, K. E., and Marshall, J. C., ed. 1980. *Deep dyslexia.* London: Routledge and Kegan Paul.

Coltheart, M. 1986. Graphemics and visual word recognition. In G. Augst ed., *New trends in graphemics and orthography,* pp. 326–340. Berlin: de Gruyter.

Ellis, A. 1984. *Reading, writing, and dyslexia.* London: Erlbaum.

Ellis, A.W., and Marshall, J.C. 1978. Semantic errors or statistical flukes? A note on Allport's "On knowing the meaning of words we are unable to report." *Quarterly Journal of Experimental Psychology* 30:569–575.

Frith, U. 1985. Beneath the surface of developmental dyslexia. In K. Patterson, J. Marshall, and M. Coltheart, eds., *Surface Dyslexia: Neuropsychological and Cognitive Studies of Phonological Reading.* London: Erlbaum.

Frith, U. 1986a. A developmental framework for developmental dyslexia. *Annals of Dyslexia* 36:69–81.

Frith, U. 1986b. Psychologische Aspekte des orthographischen Wissens: Entwicklung und Entwicklungsstörung. In G. August, ed., *New trends in graphemics and orthography research,* pp. 218–233. Berlin: de Gruyter.

Gibson, J. J. 1979. *The ecological approach to visual perception.* Boston: Houghton Mifflin.

Glushko, R J. 1979. The organization and activation of orthographic knowledge in reading aloud. *Journal of Experimental Psychology: Human Perception and Performance* 5:674–691.

Henderson, L. 1982. *Orthography and word recognition in reading.* London: Academic Press.

Johnston, R. 1983. Developmental deep dyslexia? *Cortex* 19:133–139.

Ludlow, C., Caine, E., Cudahy, E., and Nutt, J. 1979. Impaired auditory processing in Huntington's disease. Paper presented at the meeting of the International Neuropsychology Society, New York.

Ludlow, C. L. 1980. Impaired language development: Hypotheses for research. *Bulletin of the Orton Society* 30:153–169.

Marcel, T. 1980. Phonological awareness and phonological representation: Investigation of a specific spelling problem. In U. Frith, ed., *Cognitive processing in spelling,* pp. 373–404. London: Academic Press.

Marsh, G., Friedman, M., Welch, V., and Desberg, P. 1980. The development of strategies in spelling. In U. Frith, ed., *Cognitive processes in spelling,* pp. 339–354. London: Academic Press.

Marshall, J. C. 1984. Toward a rational taxonomy of the developmental dyslexias. In R. N. Malatesha and H. A. Whitaker, eds., *Dyslexia: A global issue.* The Hague: Nijhoff.

Marx, H. 1987. Paper presented at Arbeitstagung: Theorien und Probleme des Lesenlernens, Beilefeld, May 1987. Proceedings to be published.

Morton, J. 1968. Considerations of grammar and computation in language behaviour. In J. C. Catford, ed., *Studies in language and language behaviour*, CRLLB Progress Report no. 6, University of Michigan, pp. 499–545.

Morton, J. 1969. Interaction of information in word recognition. *Psychological Review* 76:165–178.

Morton, J. 1979. Facilitation in word recognition: Experiments causing change in the logogen model. In P. A. Kolers, M. E. Wrolstad, and H. Bouma, eds., *Processing of visible language*. New York: Plenum.

Morton, J. 1980. The logogen model and orthographic structure. In U. Frith, ed., *Cognitive processes in spelling*, pp. 117–133. London: Academic Press.

Morton, J., and Patterson, K. E. 1980. A new attempt at an interpretation, or an attempt at a new interpretation. In M. Coltheart, K. E. Patterson, and J. C. Marshall, eds., *Deep dyslexia*. London: Routledge and Kegan Paul.

Morton, J. 1985. Naming. In S. Newman and R. Epstein, eds., *Current perspectives in dysphasia*. Edinburgh: Churchill Livingstone.

Morton, J. 1986. Developmental contingency modelling. In P. L. C. van Geert, ed., *Theory building in developmental psychology*, pp.141–165. Elsevier Science Publishers B. V. (North-Holland).

Patterson, K. E. 1981. Neuropsychological approaches to the study of reading. *British Journal of Psychology* 72:151–174.

Read, C. 1971. Pre-school children's knowledge of English phonology. Harvard Educational Review 41:1–34.

Riddoch, M. J., and Humphreys, G. W. 1987. Visual object processing in optic aphasia: A case of semantic access agnosia. *Cognitive Neuropsychology* 4 (7): 131–185.

Rozin, P., and Gleitman, L. R. 1977. The structure and acquisition of reading. II: The reading process and the acquisition of the alphabetic principle. In A. S. Reber and D. L. Scarborough, eds., *Toward a psychology of reading*. Hillsdale, N.J.: Erlbaum.

Scheerer-Neumann, G. 1987. Paper presented at Arbeitstagnung: Tehrein und Probleme des Lesenlernens, Bielefeld, May 1987. Proceedings to be published.

Seymour, P. H. K. 1979. *Human visual cognition*. London: Collier Macmillan.

Seymour, P. H. K., and Elder, L. 1986. Beginning reading without phonology. *Cognitive neuropsychology* 3:1–36.

Shallice, T. 1981. Neurological impairment of cognitive processes. *British Medical Bulletin* 37:187–192.

Shallice T. 1987. Impairments of semantic processing: Multiple dissociations. In M. Coltheart, G. Sartori, and R. Job, eds., *The cognitive neuropsychology of language*. Hillsdale, N.J.: Erlbaum.

Editor's Comments

The initial warning in the present chapter—that one should not attempt to establish overly strong homologies between developmental and acquired disorders of language irrespective of the often great similarity in symptoms and signs—is in general worth repeating at other levels of observation. (Marshall presents his views on this subject in his chapter in this volume.) Interference at some early stage of brain development can and often does produce major alterations in subsequent stages, which do not resemble response to injury in adult brains. For example, injury to the developing cortex during neuronal migration can lead to misplacement of neurons in the cortical plate and anomalous circuitries (See Caviness et al. and Sherman et al. in this volume).

Furthermore, there is a tendency for effects to propagate across levels in unpredictable ways. For instance, a genetic lesion taking place at the molecular level is apt to propagate to higher levels, including complex behavior, in a way that just by examining the changes at the higher levels, it is difficult or impossible to reconstruct the original event (a related phenomenon is examined in the introduction to the chapter by Churchland and Sejnowski in this volume). In some cases, moreover, what would undoubtedly be called a pathological event at an earlier stage at one level may lead to advantage later. We learn from Pasko Rakic, for example, that early removal of an eye in the fetal monkey can lead to superior performance in the animal's ability to perceive Vernier deviation later in life.

The functional consequences of developmental events, whether physiologic or pathologic, depend specifically on the system under consideration. For instance, a spinal cord transection produces similar symptoms and signs in young children and adults for the same reasons, while similarities between brain injured children and adults with aphasic symptoms may turn out to be superficial. In theory, the ability to establish equivalences between children and adults depends on the developmental state of the neural system when damaged, which varies from system to system for a given chronological age, and on the ability of the particular system to reorganize, which also varies. Moreover, the cognitive consequences of injury in children and adults must have something to do with the particular relationship between structure and function in the damaged system. This gives rise to the questions of how much the anatomy can change before a new functional capacity emerges in the mechanism, and what the nature of any compensatory processes is? (For example, a certain amount of asymmetry in the length of the lower limbs can be tolerated before limping is seen. Limping emerges as a functional characteristic only after the degree of leg asymmetry surpasses a boundary, and increasing the spine curvature can no longer compensate for it. In that situation substantial anatomical change in the legs is tolerated without visible functional consequences, unless one examines the curvature of the spine.) Furthermore, how much can earlier stages of brain anatomy or language acquisition change before they affect structural characteristics at following stages? The brain and cognitive architectures of the child are in marked flux, and those of adults are much less so. One expects that child and adult differ considerably in these matters. Yet questions regarding similarity of symptoms and processes are ultimately empirical.

According to Uta Frith's theory, children pass through three developmental stages—the logographic, the alphabetic, and the orthographic—on their way to acquiring mature cognitive structures for reading and writing. Morton suggests that most developmental dyslexics become arrested at the level of logographic reading. This raises the issue of whether developmental anomaly is brought about by arrest or by branching. By "arrest" I mean that significant progress does not proceed beyond a given point; by "branching" I mean that at a given point development proceeds along a separate line. Is it indeed possible to have developmental arrest after an early injury (or even in senescence, for that matter)? In phylogenetics the issue has already been settled: no serious observer would claim that monkeys, as compared to humans, became arrested in evolution; instead, there was a branching at an earlier evolutionary period, and both monkeys and humans proceeded along different lines, acquiring specializations useful (or at least not detrimental) for survival in their own niches.

What, then, is the meaning of the logographic errors made by some developmental dyslexics? In my own view, comparing developmental dyslexics to ordinary children may be akin to comparing them to adults with acquired reading disturbances. As the starting paragraphs of the present paper rightfully warn, the similarity of the errors may be only superficial here too. For what it is worth, the anatomies of dyslexic brains thus far examined are *never* seen during earlier developmental stages. Dyslexia can thus be more easily understood as the consequence of branching during earlier ontogenetic stages *in utero* followed by individual progression. It may be advisable, therefore, to consider developmental dyslexics as an altogether separate group with unique anatomical and linguistic structures. These unique anatomical and linguistic structures should guide future research.

Chapter 4

The Description and Interpretation of Acquired and Developmental Reading Disorders

John C. Marshall

Introduction

Consider the following three conjectures: (1) Reading performance in the acquired and developmental dyslexias fractionates in strikingly similar ways (Marshall 1985). (2) The development of normal reading skills proceeds by the simple addition of components without qualitative change by stages (Marshall 1987b). (3) The basic functional components of reading competence are *preformed*, but their operation must be *triggered* from an experientially derived database (Marshall 1984).

These modest conjectures are really one hypothesis seen at three different interpretive levels. The first conjecture is a view at a level as close to pure observation as the human mind can attain. That is, the claim presupposes a common descriptive language with which to characterize patterns of impaired and preserved performance but no further theoretical baggage. The second conjecture would, if true, constitute a partial explanation of *why* acquired and developmental dyslexias manifest strictly analogous subtypes. The explanation presupposes that the correct description of the normal mature reading system is modular in the weak sense of that term: namely, that the basic components of the system are independent mechanisms with relatively minor and highly constrained interactions between components. The third conjecture would in turn provide a basis for understanding why a system of relatively independent components should have been chosen as the physical (that is, anatomophysiological) instantiation of reading capacity. The structures "tinkered" (Jacob 1977) by evolution must conform to "the principle of modular design," so that any large computation "should be split up and implemented as a collection of small sub-parts that are as nearly independent of one another as the overall task allows" (Marr 1976, 483). Marr continues: "If a process is not designed in this way, a small change in one place will have consequences in many other places. This means that the process as a whole becomes extremely difficult to debug or to improve, whether by a human designer or in the course of natural evolution, because a small change to improve one part has to be accompanied by many simultaneous compensating changes elsewhere." Preformed modules (now in the strong sense of the term: modules committed to different aspects of the reading process and coming into operation at different times) accordingly provide the basis for the additive ontogenetic development hypothesized in conjecture two.

This overall framework, uncontroversial as it might seem at first blush, has not enjoyed the unqalified support of students of reading. In general, however, the arguments against such a framework have not been based upon detailed analysis of the empirical evidence. Rather, it is claimed that the approach can be rejected on a priori grounds.

Thus, with respect to the first conjecture Morton (this volume) writes: "Curiously, even scientists of otherwise unimpeachable mental habits have lapsed when the temptation of drawing equivalences between acquired and developmental dyslexia have presented themselves" (p. 43). That the claim is a lapse arises, on Morton's account, from the notion that "the similarities are spurious, arising, as they do, from the structure of the material (in this case reading material) rather than from the structure of the disorders" (p. 43). But no evidence is provided to show that *all* such similarities are due to intrinsic, material-specific constraints. In particular, Morton fails to address the importance of *patterns* of error types and their covariance with the character of stimulus types within the individual.

The second conjecture has been attacked on the grounds that "the most obvious thing about development is that there is change" (Frith 1986, p. 70). To which Morton (this volume) adds that "the most obvious thing about developmental disorders is that they affect development" (p. 43). One can, of course, cheerfully agree with all this without feeling threatened. Conjecture two does not claim that infants can read within a few months of birth, and it does not deny that most children become progressively better at reading with experience thereof. Rather, the conjecture asserts that the processing components involved in normal, fluent adult reading become available to the child at different ages. What *is* denied is that the components undergo *qualitative* change.

Conjecture three has, perhaps, evoked the most purple prose. Ellis writes that he is "reluctant to believe that proto-reading modules exist preformed in the neonatal brain, simply requiring the right environmental stimulation to bring them into action" (1987, p. 249). But behind this mild expression of scepticism, Ellis has a developmental explanation that purports to account for erroneous belief in preformed reading modules: "Only someone whose formative years occurred in the heyday of Flower Power and extreme Chomskyan nativism could seriously contemplate such a possibility" (Ellis 1985, p. 189). Ellis's argument against preformed modules reduces to the following two true claims: the alphabet has not been around very long in the overall history of *Homo sapiens,* and most people even now are illiterate. As a refutation of preformed modules Ellis's observations are parallel to the following "arguments": Classical counterpoint is of relatively recent origin; hence, musical capacities cannot have a strong innate basis. Profoundly deaf children do not spontaneously acquire an auditory-vocal language; hence, linguistic capacities cannot have a strong innate basis.

But enough of this jocularity; let us consider the evidence. I shall outline data and theory that support my central hypothesis in the same order that I introduced the three conjectures: from observation to speculation.

Structured Parallels

The basic observation that underpins the parallel between the acquired and developmental dyslexias is this: if one takes a corpus of reading responses from a child or adult with developmental dyslexia and from an adult with an acquired dyslexia, it is impossible to tell *solely from the characteristics of the corpus* which subject is which. That is, identical types of error are manifest in both the developmental and the acquired varieties of dyslexia. Morton (this volume) argues that such similarities are spurious, because errors are determined by "similarity gradients" that arise from the intrinsic structure of the items to be read.

How, then, are written words similar to each other? First, they are often *visually* similar: If *cab* is read as "rot," stimulus and false response have the same lengths in letters and in millimeters. They also share a global configuration (two *x*-height characters followed by one with an ascender). And finally, the individual letters themselves are visually similar.

Second, they are often syntactically and semantically similar: If *girl* is read as "boy" both stimulus and false response are common concrete nouns. Furthermore, they both refer to nonadult humans.

Third, mistakes often depend on rule-governed correspondences between sublexical characters. If *pint* is read as "pint" (with a short *i*), it is because that pronunciation is appropriate to the majority of English words with the configuration of *pint* (e.g., *dint, hint, lint, mint, tint*). *Pint* is simply an unprincipled exception.

Errors of these three types are characteristic of acquired and developmental dyslexia. And if errors are made that do *not* have some obvious characteristics in common with the stimuli that provoked them, they are listed as "others" (e.g., *cat* → "whatever") and resolutely ignored.

Morton's argument is valid, as far as it goes. We see only a *limited* set of similarities between words; the dimensions of such similarities are severely constrained. But notice that this way of phrasing the matter begs the question to some extent. It is, after all, an empirical observation that the *same* set of similarities manifests itself in normal adult reading, acquired dyslexia, normal development, and developmental dyslexia. There is no a priori reason why this should be the case, and indeed, a theorist committed to metamorphosic stages (e.g., creeping Piagetianism) should be surprised to see the same dimensions appearing across the four populations.

Nonetheless, to concentrate solely on error types is to trivialize the research program within which the similarities between acquired and developmental dyslexia is embedded. The crucial issues concern the overall pattern of performance by child and adult and the interpretation of that pattern in terms of a universal functional architecture for reading capacity. Thus, current models of normal, adult reading recognize the existence of three primary routes that mediate reading aloud. These are (1) a phonic route, which assigns segmented phonological representations to sublexical graphemic units prior to semantic access and pronunciation; (2) a direct route, which assigns a pronunciation to *words* (as holistic units) in the subject's sight vocabulary without semantic mediation; (3) a lexicosemantic route, which assigns a semantic representation to sight vocabulary prior to phonological access for reading aloud. These routes are held to operate in parallel with only limited and highly constrained interaction between their component mechanisms (Marshall 1987a; Patterson, Marshall, and Coltheart 1985). Although the second and third routes take precedence in adult reading (because they are faster and more accurate modes of operation), the sublexical or phonic route remains important for reading new words not yet in sight vocabulary. This function is, of course, critical for the child learning to read, as he has not yet acquired a substantial sight vocabulary.

Researchers in the new modular research program conjecture that the developmental dyslexias can be interpreted in terms of the functional architectures of such models of adult reading. The guiding idea is that though in the normal case all three routes develop efficiently, the child with reading difficulties will show deficiencies in one or more routes and hence an overreliance upon the remaining route or routes.

What pattern of performance should we expect, then, if a child had difficulty in acquiring sight vocabulary and was thus forced to read predominantly by route one using sublexical correspondence rules? The pattern is easiest to see in a language like English, which has a notorious number of words that are exceptions to regular phoneme-grapheme correspondence rules (*dint, hint,* and *mint* are all pronounced with a short *i*, but *pint* requires a long *i*). A child who reads phonically should commit errors that consist mostly of regularizing words like *pint* to rhyme with their regular counterparts.

Holmes (1973, 1978) studied four dyslexic boys without known neurological pathology who showed a striking tendency to make such errors of regularization as *of* → "off," *shoe* → "show," and *ceiling* → "selling." They also pronounced silent consonants, reading, for example, *bristle* (with a silent *t*) as *Bristol* (the town in the southwest of England). In all these cases the meaning that was assigned was the meaning of the false responses, not the meaning of the stimulus. A similar phenomenon also occurred when the word was correctly pronounced but then understood as its homophone. For example, *mare* was read correctly but interpreted as *mayor.* One further property of the sublexical route is that it makes no distinction between regular words and nonwords (which by definition have a regular pronunciation). This constellation of symptoms, in which regular words and nonwords are read more accurately than irregular words (which tend to be regularized), has now been described in many children with developmental dyslexia (see, for example, Coltheart et al. 1983; Temple 1985). The syndrome, surface dyslexia, has an exact analogue in adult cases of acquired dyslexia in which routes (2) and (3) have been selectively impaired by relatively focal brain damage (see Marshall and Newcombe 1973; Patterson, Marshall, and Coltheart 1985). Surface dyslexia is easy to diagnose in English and French, but must be investigated in a slightly different fashion in Italian, whose orthography is fully regular at the segmental level. Yet there are in Italian multisyllabic words whose stress pattern is exceptional. The surface dyslexic should regularize at that suprasegmental level in Italian. It is likewise possible to construct homophonous pairs in which a word (e.g., *lago*) has exactly the same pronunciation as a phrase (e.g., *l'ago*). The Italian patient with surface dyslexia should be unable reliably to assign the correct meaning to such stimuli. Job, Sartori, Masterson and Coltheart (1984) describe a developmental case in which these predictions are upheld.

Let me now turn to the direct route. What evidence would indicate that the developmental dyslexic was reading aloud using direct whole-word sight-to-sound associations? The ability correctly to read irregular words aloud *without* knowing what they mean is the critical diagnostic: irregular words cannot be correctly read by the phonic route, but the lexicosemantic route involves the assignment of semantic representations to words.

A case of this nature was reported by Aram, Rose, and Horwitz (1984). Their patient was a developmental "hyperlexic" in his late thirties. The phonic route was relatively intact, since the patient could read nonwords fairly accurately. The patient must also "have established a considerable store of word-specific print to sound associations" (Aram et al., 1984): his ability to read *irregular* words aloud was good, despite being unable to indicate what these words meant.

Once again, the pattern of performance in such cases is highly similar to that found in some patients with acquired dyslexia. For example, Schwartz, Saffran, and Marin (1980) reported a patient who had presenile dementia with prominent language difficulties against a background of progressive memory impairment. Despite a severe impairment of semantic knowledge, she retained for a considerable time the ability to read single words aloud. She could accurately read aloud such irregular words as *leopard*, *climb*, and *both* (cf. *Goth*, *moth*) at a time when her poor performance on semantic classification, categorization, and matching tasks strongly suggested that she could not understand the words.

This pattern contrasts with reading that is mediated principally by the lexicosemantic route. If the phonic route is underdeveloped or otherwise inaccessible, we should see a picture in which a person can read known words relatively well but has a poor ability to read nonwords. Temple and Marshall (1983) described one such case of developmental dyslexia in a seventeen-year-old girl with an above average oral vocabulary. Her ability to read nonwords was much lower than her ability to read words. Furthermore, her responses to nonwords were frequently real words with considerable visual similarity to the stimulus (e.g., *gok* → "joke," *hib* → "hip"). There were no semantic errors and no regularizations of the type seen in surface dyslexia; words read aloud correctly were understood correctly. This form of developmental phonological dyslexia has been extensively described in many children and adolescents (see, for example, Seymour and McGregor 1984; Snowling, Stackhouse, and Rack 1986). Despite the simplicity of sublexical correspondence rules in Italian, this condition has also been found in Italian children with developmental dyslexia. The fact that these children have a reading age significantly lower than their chronological age and so are dyslexic is an indication of the importance of the phonic route during the normal acquisition process. It is nonetheless *possible* to acquire an above average sight vocabulary without having command over any of the skills that define the phonic route (Campbell and Butterworth 1985).

These cases of developmental phonological dyslexia are once again matched by adult patients who present exactly the same constellation of symptoms after acquired brain damage. Cases of acquired phonological dyslexia have been well documented in speakers of French (Beauvois and Dérouesné 1979), English (Patterson 1982), and Italian (Sartori, Barry, and Job 1984).

In other children with developmental dyslexia there appears to be more widespread impairment of the lexicosemantic route. Like the phonological dyslexics, these children too have no effective phonic skills and so cannot read nonwords. Similarly, their limited ability to read words is unaffected by whether the test words conform to sublexical sight-to-sound correspondence rules. These children differ from phonological dyslexics in that they make errors of semantic substitution even when reading single words aloud. A case of this nature was reported by Johnston (1983); this adolescent girl made semantic paralexias (*chair* → "table"), function word substitutions (*down* → "up") and morphological errors (*child* → "children"), in addition to many visual errors. Some similar cases were described by Siegel (1985). Six children between the ages of seven and nine had severe reading disorders and extremely poor phonic skills. Their semantic paralexias included *cat* → "kitten," *chicken* → "duck," *girl* → "man," and *away* → "go"; function-word substitutions included *you* → "we," *him* → "you," and *us* → "yours."

One problem with these studies is that the rate of semantic paralexias is extremely low and may indeed be well within the chance range calculated by Ellis and Marshall (1978). However, Temple (1988) recently reported a case of a nine-year-old dyslexic boy who made paralexic errors 20 percent of which had a semantic component; this value is outside the chance range. Comparable cases of acquired deep dyslexia are described in Coltheart, Patterson, and Marshall (1987).

There is also some evidence that when all three reading routes fail to develop appropriately, the dyslexic child may nonetheless acquire some very limited proficiency in reading by using the adaptive strategy of spelling aloud. If letter recognition is relatively intact, the child attempts to read by producing a sequence of letter names and letter sounds; comprehension is then based upon this combined name and sound code (Prior and McCorriston 1983). This pattern of performance is well attested in cases of acquired dyslexia (Patterson and Kay

1982; Newcombe and Marshall 1985). In some of these adult cases, cases of alexia without agraphia, writing to dictation is relatively well preserved. A similar dissociation can be seen in developmental dyslexia. Cossu and Marshall (1985), for example, have reported two mentally retarded Italian boys whose written spelling was greatly superior to their reading, despite the fact that visual acuity was within normal limits and that visual-matching tasks were well performed. This same pattern (albeit in much less extreme form) can also be found in some normal young children learning to read and write (Read 1978).

An Additive Architecture

One way to interpret the similarities outlined in the previous section is this: the common multiroute model of Patterson, Marshall, and Coltheart (1985) suffices to describe normal adult reading, acquired dyslexias, the acquisition of normal reading skills, and developmental dyslexias. Within each of these populations the primary source of variability is differential reliance upon *one* of the routes explicated in the universal reading model. Or to put the same point the other way around, differential impairment of one or more routes will lead to qualitatively and perhaps quantitatively distinct patterns of reading performance.

Baron and Strawson (1976) have demonstrated that normal adults give different relative weight to lexical and sublexical strategies in reading. They term these strategies Chinese (or ideographic) reading versus Phoenician (or alphabetic) reading. Seidenberg (1985) has shown how the time courses of these routes differ and how their utilization may be under the strategic control of task and word characteristics (see also Seidenberg et al. 1984). The extremes of variability in subject populations may be very wide indeed (see Campbell and Butterworth 1985).

These normal contrasts between lexical and sublexical reading routes become even more extreme when we compare cases of acquired dyslexia with focal deficits. In deep and phonological dyslexia, for example, we find word reading relatively intact though reading neologisms is severely impaired (Coltheart, Patterson, and Marshall 1987). In contrast, in the many varieties of surface dyslexia we see relatively good reading of sublexically regular words and nonwords along with poor reading of irregularly spelled words (Patterson, Marshall, and Coltheart 1985).

If between-route variability is found in the normal adult population, it is reasonable to expect that similar variation will be seen in the population of normal learners (children who at a particular point in time are within normal limits for acquiring reading skills). The relevant variation between reliance on lexical and reliance on sublexical strategies is indeed seen in children whose overall reading attainment is normal for their age (Baron and Treiman 1980; Treiman 1984; Bryant and Impey 1986).

We should also expect to find that when developmental discrepancies between the efficiency of the different routes are very extreme *and* persist over considerable stretches of time, the child's development will begin to lag progressively behind that of his or her peers. The child will then be diagnosed as suffering from developmental dyslexia. Within those so diagnosed we should see discrepancies in the effective utilization of reading routes that match discrepancies found in the population of acquired dyslexics. Individual case studies of developmental dyslexia reveal the predicted variation (Coltheart et al. 1983; Temple and Marshall 1983; Seymour 1986).

In sum, a close match in the qualitative variation seen in populations of normal and dyslexic children is now well established (Mitterer 1982; Treiman and Hirsh-Pasek 1985; Bryant and Impey 1986). Moreover, such variation is qualitatively if not quantitatively comparable to that seen in normal adults and in the acquired dyslexias of adult life. Developmental lag in the operation of one route will thus have behavioral consequences that are analogous to selective acquired damage to that route (Coltheart 1987; Marshall 1987b; Temple 1987).

Let us now step back a little from these empirical analogues and logically contemplate how they can and cannot arise. Consider the developmental stages in the creation of a mature butterfly by metamorphosis, and by painting by numbers.

In metamorphosis the components of the mature system do not directly match the components of the developing system. Removing a wing from a butterfly does not produce a caterpillar; lesioning a caterpillar does not give rise to a chrysalis. For such systems, the effects of development and developmental lag do not correspond with the effects of damage to the adult creature. The structures found in the immature system have been transformed and are simply no longer there in their original form in the adult. Developmental and acquired disorders cannot phenotypically coincide.

By contrast, in painting by numbers an outline is laid down in advance. "Development" consists of filling in these preexistent structures in some temporal order: first the right wing, then the body, then the left wing, for example. In any system of this general nature the effects of damage to the finished product can be matched with the configurations constructed at some prior developmental stage (see Simon 1962). The phenotypic effect of removing the left wing from the completed work leaves a state identical to one in which the left wing has not yet been filled in. Developmental and acquired disorders *do* coincide.

My contention, then, is that the observed parallels between the acquired and developmental dyslexias are far from trivial or superficial. On the contrary, they are trying to tell us that the acquisition of reading skill is more akin to painting by numbers than to metamorphosis. Or to put the point less metaphorically, "there is (as yet) no evidence that developmental failure distorts the functional architecture of the reading system in ways that cannot be accounted for by selective impairment of particular (adult) components" (Marshall 1987b, p. 25). Developmental stages in reading are more additive than interactive.

Despite their protesting to the contrary, I can see no evidence that the developmental models proposed in Frith (1985) and Morton (this volume) are anything other than additive in the sense I have outlined.

It is, however, of very considerable interest to consider the question, In what order are the components added? And in particular, we need to know "the precise extent to which the sequence is 'fixed' and the points at which it is labile (i.e. under the control of instructional variables)" (Marshall 1987b). To do so, we must consider the notion of being performed in slightly more detail.

Is Reading Special or Specialized?

The notion that there just *cannot* be a functional architecture and responsible brain areas preestablished for reading and writing is firmly entrenched in the literature. Ellis provides a clear summary of the position with respect to developmental disorders: "Whatever the deficits in developmental dyslexics are, they cannot be *specific* to reading and writing, but must affect cognitive processes which are necessary to the acquisition of literacy but not specific to it" (1987, p. 249). Such a line of argument, while not in itself unreasonable, did, however, seriously impede progress in understanding reading skill and its impairments.

The problem arose in the nineteenth century. Clinical taxonomies of acquired and developmental dyslexias rapidly came to be dominated by the notion of associations of symptoms. Relatively pure acquired dyslexia was described by Dejerine (1892); relatively pure acquired dysgraphia was described by Gordinier (1899). But it is more usual to find dyslexia with dysgraphia, although without more generalized dysphasia (Dejerine 1891). It is still more usual to find dyslexia and dysgraphia occurring with Wernicke's aphasia (Starr 1889) or Broca's aphasia (Benson 1977). Other patients may have dyslexia and dysgraphia with, say, spatial disorder, agnosia, apraxia, or acalculia (De Massary 1932). The temptation thus became to classify patients with acquired reading and/or writing disorders not on the basis of the intrinsic nature of the reading impairment but rather by the associated symptoms in other domains of cognitive functioning. The question of whether or not these associated symptoms were *causally* implicated in determining the nature of the reading disorder seemed unimportant from the standpoint of clinical classification and inference to the locus of the responsible lesion (Marshall 1982).

The notion of guilt by association was then carried over into studies of the developmental dyslexias. Mattis, French, and Rapin (1975), for example, distinguish between dyslexia with more generalized language disorder, dyslexia with articulatory and graphomotor dyscoordination, and dyslexia with visuospatial perceptual disorder. To this classification Denckla (1979) adds dyslexia with "dysphonemic sequencing difficulty" and dyslexia with "verbal memorization disorder." The most striking characteristic of most of the developmental taxonomies reviewed in Benton and Pearl 1978 is that they are *not* systematic analyses and classifications of reading impairment at all. Rather they are ad hoc groupings of children who do indeed have some reading disorder or other, but the grouping itself is determined by the associated symptomatology.

The dangers of this strategy are many and manifest. The first crucial disadvantage is that correlational taxonomies distract attention from describing what actually happens when the child is attempting to read or write. The second is that such taxonomies pay little or no attention to the question of whether the associated impairments are *causally* related to the reading or writing disorder. This is in part a theory-dependent issue. Only a reasonably detailed analysis of the mechanisms employed in reading and writing will specify which of the subcomponents of these skills can also be implicated in other tasks.

There is no sensible alternative to trying to elucidate *causal* relationships between variables. A purely correlational approach will of necessity fail to establish whether the deficits often associated with dyslexia constitute necessary and/or sufficient conditions for the manifest reading impairment. If, for example, an inability to repeat words is associated with a reading deficit, this does not in itself demonstrate either that the repetition disorder is the cause of the reading disorder or vice versa or that some more general processing deficit is the underlying cause of both disorders.

To a limited extent some preliminary constraints upon the interpretation of associations of symptoms can be obtained by using appropriate control groups. Stein and Fowler (1982), for example, reported a failure to establish ocular dominance in over 50 percent of the dyslexic children they examined. Without further thought they interpreted this instability of dominance as a *causal factor* in the reading disability. Yet Newman et al. (1985) "confirmed" their results in both a new sample of poor readers and a group of children *without* any reading difficulty. That is, comparable rates of unstable ocular dominance were found in *both* groups! Failure to establish ocular dominance is thus neither a necessary nor a sufficient condition for failure to acquire reading skills.

In an important paper Guthrie and Tyler (1976) noted that some correlations between ability in reading and ability in other tasks may be due to causal connections from reading to other skills. They accordingly suggested that an appropriate control group for retarded readers would be a group of chronologically younger children with the same reading age as the retardates (but now, of course, normal for age). If these controls matched for reading age nonetheless outperform the retarded readers on some other task, the argument that reading skill and experience is a *causal* factor in determining performance on the other task immediately collapses. It then becomes more likely that the mechanisms involved in the other task have a causal influence on success or difficulties in learning to read.

Although such controls are essential in some circumstances, the basic issue of describing the patterns of impaired and preserved performance *within* the domains of reading and writing remains crucial to any eventual theoretical understanding of the mechanisms involved. It is at best unfortunate that the question of patterns of association and dissociation *within* reading and writing skills was for so long confused by the issue of associations *between* reading or writing deficits and deficits in other areas of cognitive performance. Even in these times of more rigorous scholarship scholars who have attempted to reduce dyslexia to some more basic underlying incapacity have conspicuously failed to search for counter examples to their hypothesis. They have often not looked for cases where a subject reads perfectly adequately despite manifest problems in some domain purportedly crucial to the acquisition of literacy (see Campbell and Butterworth 1985 for one such counterexample to the claim that phonological awareness is a precondition of literacy). Likewise, little attention has been paid to the existence of individuals in a dyslexic group who perform within normal limits on a task that supposedly taps *the* cause of dyslexia. Lieberman et al. (1985) are instructive in this regard. They document significant deficiencies in phonetic speech perception in a *group* of adult developmental dyslexics. But they scrupulously note considerable variation within their population: "The mean error rate for the subgroup of dyslexic Subjects 9, 14, 16, and 17 (10.5%) does not differ significantly from that of the nondyslexic control group" (p. 485).

Are there then any aspects of reading skill that are at least more specialized for reading than the capacities for visual discrimination, phonological analysis, and syntactic organization per se? Ellis dismisses such a possibility: "Given writing's late entry onto the evolutionary stage there is no way that the genetic endowment of the *Homo sapiens* neonate can include a Language Acquisition Device containing proto-modules specifically earmarked for the processing of alphabetic scripts" (1985, p. 189). I have no doubt that Ellis's conclusion is true, but it does reflect an alarmingly parochial way of looking at the issue. Biological specifications for the acquisition of auditory-vocal language are not fine tuned for English, Turkish, or Mandarin; comparable specializations for the acquisition of sign are not fine tuned for American sign language, British sign language, or Chinese sign language. The infant does not know in advance that he or she will be born in London, Tokyo, or Cairo. By developing a universal grammar, Chomsky (1988) attempts to discover the biological constraints and parameters within which the child will be able to acquire *any* natural language to which he or she is exposed.

Likewise, if there are biological specializations for the acquisition of written language, they must apply indiscriminately to deep (English) alphabets and superficial (Italian) alphabets, to syllabaries (Japanese *kana*), and to the logographs of classical Chinese. Even phrased in these terms, a gross oversimplification has taken place: practically every modern script (with the exception of the International Phonetic Alphabet) mixes representational levels with great abandon. The bottom line of orthographic representation must lie in the capacity to assign semantic (lexical) structure to two-dimensional visual forms. Since children normally acquire spoken language before written language (or recognizably representational drawing), one expects to find parametric variation in the extent to which natural substructures of visual form map onto natural substructures of phonological form in the orthographies of the world.

We must distinguish between core reading skills, which are needed to acquire and fluently manipulate *any* evolved orthography, and a marked periphery of skills, which are only applicable to subsets of the orthographies of the world (Marshall and Newcombe 1981). Clearly, an innate bias to search the orthography of one's native language for word-, syllable-, phonemic-, and phonetic-level structure in that order would lead to fewer blind alleys than the reverse order of search. Imagine the confusion that would arise if the child first searched for sublexical grapheme-phoneme correspondences, only to discover later that he or she had been born in Peking, not Zagreb. The correct developmental bias of looking for lexical correspondences before sublexical correspondences is, of course, precisely what we find in the acquisition of reading skill (Frith 1985; Morton, this volume). The direct routes must take precedence over sublexical recoding. There is interesting preliminary work to suggest a considerable heritable component to the acquisition of the marked peripheral skills (Olson and Wise 1986). Coltheart summarizes their work as follows: "They conclude that the ability to use the sub-lexical procedure depends upon inheritable phonological skills, so propose a genetic explanation for developmental phonological dyslexia" (1987, p. 98). Little attention has been paid to the distinction between the routes of lexical and sublexical reading (and the consequent variation in pathologies) in previous attempts to specify the genetic basis of reading capacity (Smith et al. 1983; DeFries, Fulker, and Labuda 1987).

There is, however, a conceptual problem with Coltheart's analysis of the findings of Olson and Wise. In the manuscript version of 1987, Coltheart takes their work to "indicate that the ability to use the lexical procedure for reading is not inherited." Strictly, however, the results show that *variation* among subjects in the effective use of the lexical procedure is not greatly determined by heritable factors (see Marshall 1980). The results do not directly bear upon the existence (or nonexistence) of an endogenously driven module committed to the interpretation of written language.

Thus, I claim, we have not disproven that the direct route that constitutes the core mechanism used in reading any modern orthography evolved very early in the development of *Homo sapiens*. This mechanism interprets the conceptual significance of two-dimensional signs. The mechanism is modular, that is, distinct from object-recognition capacities, precisely because important constraints applicable to three-dimensional recognition are *not* relevant to important constraints applicable to two-dimensional interpretation. Texture gradients and lighting gradients provide important cues to the recognition of three-dimensional objects; they are not relevant to two-dimensional signs. A two-dimensional pictorial outline *can* impart three-dimensional information to the viewer (see Marr 1982), but the types of figures employed in the precursors of true writing (descriptive-representational signs and identifying-mnemonic signs) are not typically adapted to this function. Their two-dimensional representation suffices for recognition and interpretation. The importance of recognizing two-dimensional signs arises from their role in tracking. A hunting community that could not interpret the marks left by animals would not survive for very long. It is thus not unreasonable to suppose that such abilities can be selected by neo-Darwinian means. It is true, of course, that some tracks are significantly three dimensional. Yet even here the nature of the interpretation is quite distinct from that employed when line and shape per se are cues to a three-dimensional form. The outline and the depth of a footprint are independent cues to independent aspects of the maker. Depth does not here convey three-dimensional *shape*.

In conclusion, the direct route for reading has a biological history, although the input to that route from current orthographies has been elaborated by successive stages of cultural evolution. To this extent I can see little difference between reading and any other human capacity.

Note

Acknowledgements: I would like to thank John Morton and Andy Ellis for their provocation.

References

Aram, D. M., Rose, D. F., and Horwitz, S. J. 1984. Hyperlexia: Developmental reading without meaning. In R. N. Malatesha and H. A. Whitaker, eds., *Dyslexia: A global issue.* The Hague: Nijhoff.

Baron, J., and Strawson, C. 1976. Use of orthographic and word-specific knowledge in reading words aloud. *Journal of Experimental Psychology: Human Perception and Performance* 2:386–393.

Baron, J., and Treiman, R. 1980. Some problems in the study of differences in cognitive processes. *Memory and Cognition* 8:313–321.

Beauvois, M.-F., and Dérouesné, J. 1979. Phonological alexia: Three dissociations. *Journal of Neurology, Neurosurgery, and Psychiatry* 42:1115–1124.

Benson, D. F. 1977. The third alexia. *Archives of Neurology* 34:327–331.

Benton, A. L., and Pearl, D., eds. 1978. *Dyslexia: An appraisal of current knowledge.* New York: Oxford University Press.

Bryant, P., and Impey, L. 1986. The similarities between normal readers and developmental and acquired dyslexics. *Cognition* 24:121–137.

Campbell, R., and Butterworth, B. 1985. Phonological dyslexia and dysgraphia in a highly literate subject: A developmental case with associated deficits of phonemic processing and awareness. *Quarterly Journal of Experimental Psychology* 37A:435–475.

Chomsky, N. 1988. *Language and problems of knowledge.* Cambridge: MIT Press.

Coltheart, M. 1987. Varieties of developmental dyslexia: A comment on Bryant and Impey. *Cognition* 27:97–101.

Coltheart, M., Masterson, J., Byng, S., Prior, M., and Riddoch, J. 1983. Surface dyslexia. *Quarterly Journal of Experimental Psychology* 35A:469–495.

Coltheart, M., Patterson, K. E., and Marshall, J. C., eds. 1987. *Deep dyslexia*. 2nd ed. London: Routledge and Kegan Paul.

Cossu, G., and Marshall, J. C. 1985. Dissociation between reading and writing in two Italian children: Dyslexia without dysgraphia? *Neuropsychologia* 23:697–700.

DeFries, J. C., Fulker, D. W., and LaBuda, M. C. 1987. Evidence for a genetic aetiology in reading disability of twins. *Nature* 329:537–539.

Dejerine, J. 1891. Sur un cas de cécité verbale avec agraphie, suivi d'autopsie. *Mém. Soc. Biol.* 3:197–201.

Dejerine, J. 1892. Contribution a l'étude anatomopathologique et clinique des different variéties de cécité verbale. *C. R. Soc. Biol.* (Paris) 4:61–90.

De Massary, J. 1932. L'Alexie. *Encephale* 1:53–78.

Denckla, M. B. 1979. Childhood learning disabilities. In K. M. Heilman and E. Valenstein, eds., *Clinical neurology*. New York: Oxford University Press.

Ellis, A. W. 1985. The cognitive neuropsychology of developmental (and acquired) dyslexia: A critical survey. *Cognitive Neuropsychology* 2:169–205.

Ellis, A. W. 1987. Review: On problems in developing cognitively transmitted cognitive modules. *Mind and Language* 2:242–251.

Ellis, A. W., and Marshall, J. C. 1978. Semantic errors or statistical flukes? A note on Allport's "On knowing the meaning of words we are unable to report." *Quarterly Journal of Experimental Psychology* 30:569–575.

Frith, U. 1985. Beneath the surface of developmental dyslexia. In K. E. Patterson, J. C. Marshall, and M. Coltheart, eds., *Surface dyslexia*. London: Erlbaum.

Frith, U. 1986. A developmental framework for developmental dyslexia. *Annals of Dyslexia* 36:69–81.

Gordinier, H. C. 1899. A case of brain tumor at the base of the second frontal circonvolution. *American Journal of Medical Science* 117:526–535.

Guthrie, J. T. and Tyler, S. J. 1976. Psycholinguistic processing in reading and listening among good and poor readers. *Journal of Reading Behavior* 8:415–426.

Holmes, J. M. 1973. Dyslexia: A neurolinguistic study of traumatic and developmental disorders of reading. Ph.D. thesis, University of Edinburgh.

Holmes, J. 1978. "Regression" and reading breakdown. In A. Caramazza and E. B. Zurif, eds., *Language acquisition and breakdown: Parallels and divergencies*. Baltimore: Johns Hopkins University Press.

Jacob, F. 1977. Evolution and tinkering. *Science* 196:1161–1166.

Job, R., Sartori, G., Masterson, J., and Coltheart, M. 1984. Developmental surface dyslexia in Italian. In R. N. Malatesha and H. A. Whitaker, eds., *Dyslexia: A global issue*. The Hague: Nijoff.

Johnston, R. S. 1983. Developmental deep dyslexia? *Cortex* 19:133–139.

Lieberman, P., Meskill, R. H., Chatillon, M., and Schupack, H. 1985. Phonetic speech perception deficits in dyslexia. *Journal of Speech and Hearing Research* 25:480–486.

Marr, D. 1976. Early processing of visual information. *Phil. Trans. R. Soc. Lond.*, series B., 275:483–524.

Marr, D. 1982. *Vision*. San Francisco: Freeman.

Marshall, J. C. 1980. On the biology of language acquisition. In D. Caplan, ed., *Biological studies of mental processes*. Cambridge: MIT Press.

Marshall, J. C. 1982. What is a symptom-complex? In M. A. Arbib, D. Caplan and J. C. Marshall, eds., *Neural models of language processes*. New York: Academic Press.

Marshall, J. C. 1984. Toward a rational taxonomy of the developmental dyslexias. In R. N. Malatesha and H. A. Whitaker, eds., *Dyslexia: A global issue*. The Hague: Nijhoff.

Marshall, J. C. 1985. On some relationships between acquired and developmental dyslexias. In F. H. Duffy and N. Geschwind, eds., *Dyslexia: A neuroscientific approach to clinical evaluation*. Boston: Little, Brown, and Company.

Marshall, J. C. 1987a. Routes and representations in the processing of written language. In E. Keller and M. Gopnik, eds., *Motor and sensory processes in language*. Hillsdale, N.J.: Erlbaum.

Marshall, J. C. 1987b. The cultural and biological context of written languages: Their acquisition, deployment and breakdown. In J. Beech and A. Colley, eds., *Cognitive approaches to reading*. New York: Wiley.

Marshall, J. C. and Newcombe, F. 1973. Patterns of paralexia. *Journal of Psycholinguistic Research* 2:175–199.

Marshall, J. C. and Newcombe, F. 1981. Lexical access: A perspective from pathology. *Cognition* 10:209–214.

Mattis, S., French, J. H. and Rapin, I. 1975. Dyslexia in children and young adults: Three independent neuropsychological syndromes. *Developmental Medicine and Child Neurology* 17:150–163.

Mitterer, J. O. 1982. There are at least two kinds of poor readers: Whole-word poor readers and recoding poor readers. *Canadian Journal of Psychology* 36:445–461.

Newcombe, F., and Marshall, J. C. 1985. Reading and writing by letter sounds. In K. E. Patterson, J. C. Marshall, and M. Coltheart, eds., *Surface dyslexia*. London: Erlbaum.

Newman, S. P., Wadsworth, J. F., Archer, R., and Hockly, R. 1985. Ocular dominance, reading, and spelling ability in school children. *Journal of Ophthalmology* 69:228–232.

Olson, R., and Wise, B. 1986. Heritability of phonetic and orthographic word-decoding skills in dyslexia. Psychonomic Society Meeting, New Orleans, 1986.

Patterson, K. E. 1982. The relation between reading and phonological coding: Further neuropsychological observations. In A. W. Ellis, ed., *Normality and pathology in cognitive functions*. London: Academic Press.

Patterson, K. E., and Kay, J. 1982. Letter-by-letter reading: Psychological descriptions of a neurological syndrome. *Quarterly Journal of Experimental Psychology* 34A:411–442.

Patterson, K. E., Marshall, J. C., and Coltheart, M., eds. 1985. *Surface dyslexia*. London: Erlbaum.

Prior, M., and McCorriston, M. 1983. Acquired and developmental spelling dyslexia. *Brain and Language* 20:263–285.

Read, C. 1978. Writing is not the inverse of reading for young children. In C. H. Frederikson, M. F. Whiteman, and J. F. Dominic, eds., *Writing: The nature, development, and teaching of written communication*, vol. 1. Hillsdale, N.J.: Erlbaum.

Sartori, G., Barry, C., and Job, R. 1984. Phonological dyslexia: A review. In R. N. Malatesha and H. A. Whitaker, eds., *Dyslexia: A global issue*. The Hague: Nijhoff.

Schwartz, M. F., Saffran, E. M., and Marin, O. S. M. 1980. Fractionating the reading process in dementia: Evidence for word-specific print-to-sound association. In M. Coltheart, K. E. Patterson and J. C. Marshall, eds., *Deep dyslexia*. London: Routledge and Kegan Paul.

Seidenberg, M. S. 1985. The time course of information activation and utilization in visual word recognition. *Reading Research: Advances in Theory and Practice* 5:199–252.

Seidenberg, M. S., Waters, G., Barnes, M. A., and Tanenhaus, M. K. 1984. When does irregular spelling or pronunciation influence word recognition? *Journal of Verbal Learning and Verbal Behavior* 23:383–404.

Seymour, P. 1986. *Cognitive analysis of dyslexia*. London: Routledge and Kegan Paul.

Seymour, P., and McGregor, C. J. 1984. Developmental dyslexia: A cognitive experimental analysis of phonological, morphemic, and visual impairments. *Cognitive Neuropsychology* 1:43–82.

Siegel, L. S. 1985. Deep dyslexia in childhood? *Brain and Language* 26:16–27.

Simon, H. A. 1962. The architecture of complexity. *Proc. Amer. Phil. Soc.* 106:467–482.

Smith, S. D., Kimberling, W. J., Pennington, B. F., and Lubs, H. A. 1983. Specific reading disability: Identification of an inherited form through linkage analysis. *Science* 219:1345–1347.

Snowling, M., Stackhouse, J., and Rack, J. 1986. Phonological dyslexia and dysgraphia—A developmental analysis. *Cognitive Neuropsychology* 3:309–339.

Starr, A. 1889. The pathology of sensory aphasia. *Brain* 12:82–99.

Stein, J. F., and Fowler, S. 1982. Diagnosis of "dyslexia" by means of a new indicator of eye dominance. *British Journal of Ophthalmology* 66:332–36.

Temple, C. M. 1985. Surface dyslexia: Variations within a syndrome. In K. E. Patterson, J. C. Marshall, and M. Coltheart, eds., *Surface dyslexia*. London: Erlbaum.

Temple, C. M. 1987. The nature of normality, the deviance of dyslexia, and the recognition of rhyme: A reply to Bryant and Impey (1986). *Cognition* 27:103–108.

Temple, C. M. 1988. Red is read but eye is blue: A case study of developmental dyslexia and follow-up report. *Brain and Language* 34:13–37.

Temple, C. M., and Marshall, J. C. 1983. A case study of developmental phonological dyslexia. *British Journal of Psychology* 74:517–533.

Treiman, R. 1984. Individual differences among children in spelling and reading styles. *Journal of Experimental Child Psychology* 37:463–477.

Treiman, R., and Hirsh-Pasek, K. 1985. Are there qualitative differences in reading behavior between dyslexics and normal readers? *Memory and Cognition* 13:357–364.

Editor's Comments

This chapter constitutes, in part, a reply to the chapter by John Morton (this volume). Both raise important questions on the relationship between acquired and developmental cognitive disorders, particularly reading disorders, and they display preferences for developmental mechanisms to account for the acquisition of reading that are markedly different in principle.

The data consist of observations that both developmental and acquired dyslexics can be shown to make identical errors in reading.

Morton's interpretation is that the nature of the tasks limits the types of errors possible, and thus a variety of widely different brain and mind architectures could produce them. Moreover, this argument goes, difficulties during development change the course of development so as to give the final mature structure deep characteristics never seen in the normal course of development. If this is the case, errors do not address issues of development, and the damaged adult cognitive architecture has no resemblance to the machinery of the child with developmental dyslexia.

Marshall, on the other hand, argues that the similarity of the errors is not superficial but rather reflects the fact that the innate processing modules remaining and lost in acquired dyslexia are identical to those that develop or fail to develop in developmental dyslexia. According to Marshall, then, development proceeds by adding functional components, and the developmental stages are found preserved somewhere within the mature system. Furthermore, Marshall implies that the damaged brain in cases of acquired dyslexia returns the individual to an earlier developmental stage, since it loses the functions of a particular module, while the developmental dyslexic is arrested at an earlier stage of ordinary reading acquisition by failing to acquire the next modules.

To defend one position or the other, it is more appropriate, it seems to me, to compare the reading characteristics of adults with acquired dyslexia and those of developmental dyslexics to those of normal children learning to read, because it is not at all clear that acquired and developmental dyslexics make solely errors characteristic of earlier stages of reading acquisition. For instance, do normal children ever read *table* as "chair," as do some acquired and developmental dyslexics?

Can the study of brain development shed some light on the solution of the problem? First, the normal state: As discussed in other parts of this book (e.g., the chapters by Rakic, Caviness et al., and McEwen), the brain develops according to a genetically determined plan that is quite uniform among humans and reflects our common phylogenetic past, as well as according to epigenetic regulation dictated in part by individual ontogenetic histories. Take for instance the cerebral cortex. The same types of neurons are generated in all of us, they migrate to the cortical plate, they establish long connections, local circuits, synaptic and receptor architectures, myelin, and other features of mature neurons. (I suspect that this fact accounts for the innate and universal properties of language in all human populations.) At each step there appears to be epigenetically regulated individual variation in the exact numbers of surviving neurons, connections, synapses, and so forth, which in turn results in individualized brain architectures. This fact, I suspect, accounts for personal cognitive strategies, different spoken languages, and other similar instances of individual cognitive diversity.

It does not appear that with each developmental brain stage the old stages are altogether eliminated, although partial elimination is characteristic of brain development. At least at stages other than the very first steps of embryogenesis, the process is unlike the passage from tadpole to frog, in which tails and gills are transformed and legs and lungs are produced in their places. Yet the environment of the growing child does not change to the same degree as that of the tadpole, which must emerge from a watery environment to an atmospheric environment. A frog does not have to remember how to breathe in the water as a child has to remember the language of his mother for the rest of his life. There is to my knowledge no evidence that earlier acquired neural structures are destroyed once the more mature ones kick in. In this sense, the system appears to grow in an additive fashion.

What about the brain of the dyslexic child? The evidence thus far accumulated suggests that it is not like the brain of ordinary readers at any stage of development. In terms of numbers of neurons and axons it differs markedly from the brains of ordinary adults and children (see Galaburda et al. and Sherman et al. in this volume). Yet at this time it does not appear that ordinary brains have classes of neural elements not present in the brains of dyslexics.

What happens to the ordinary adult brain after it is injured in the adult state? It is unwarranted to assume that the injured elements become functionless and are simply removed, as when one removes a component from a radio. Instead, the lesioned elements may function partially (as in hemiparesis), not function at all (as in dense hemiplegia), or function abnormally because they have remodeled themselves through plasticity and regrowth (as when abnormal reinnervation of the face muscles after facial nerve injury causes blinking to produce contraction of the orbicularis oris muscle).

Thus, one may view a lesion of the adult brain not as simply returning it to some normal earlier stage but rather as a trigger leading to structures and functions that may be partially or wholly subtractive or otherwise unpredictably anomalous. Likewise, the dyslexic brain may be viewed not as simply arrested at an immature stage, for it has taken a novel route in development subsequent to the interference.

The similarity of errors between developmental and acquired dyslexics may, therefore, reflect not only subtraction or lack of expression of innate processing modules, although this may be true for some types of errors. For other types of errors, e.g., those never seen during ordinary development, similarity of errors may reflect the way by which the brain responds to tinkering (damage or developmental interference). The evidence suggests that the responses of immature and mature brains differ in magnitude but not in overall type.

It is reasonable to think that both addition and metamorphosis occur during abnormal development and that subtraction and metamorphosis occur during and after injury. The similarities in some of the error types may reflect the tendency of both developing and injured brains to undergo metamorphoses of their connections and synaptic architectures driven by shared mechanisms, but to different extents.

Chapter 5

Great Expectations

Lila Gleitman, Henry Gleitman, Barbara Landau, and Eric Wanner

Known writing systems are relatively straightforward derivatives of spoken languages. In almost all cases, the child who is learning to read already knows the spoken language that is encoded in these orthographies. Therefore, or so it seems, all the child has to do to learn to read is to transfer this knowledge from one physical medium to another. For instance, if the writing system is logographic, the child has to learn which squiggle on the printed page represents which already mastered word in the spoken language. If the writing system is strictly alphabetic, the skill of reading should reduce to learning a very small set of associations between the sounds of the spoken language and squiggles on the page. Yet if this analysis is correct, learning to read should be easy, for it involves little that is new. The rich structures of syntax and semantics, and the relations between patterns here and the sound patterns of language, are already known in large part to the kindergartener. To read, it appears that one must merely transfer all of this knowledge of language to a visual modality whose symbols map onto it roughly one to one.

Then considering all that must be learned in order to speak and understand, beginning (as an infant) with no language in advance, acquiring one's native tongue should be a difficult and lengthy task. In contrast, learning to read should be simple. But the facts clearly violate these expectations. Significant numbers of individuals fail to read after years of lessons at school, and success in this task varies according to intelligence (Thorndike 1971), motivational and cultural factors (Downing 1973), and internal differences in the nature of the writing system that is to be acquired (Downing 1973; Leong 1973; Gleitman 1985). Moreover, there appears to be a sizeable population afflicted with a specific disability for reading acquisition (dyslexia). Pathologies of speech and comprehension, while not unknown, are much rarer. The acquisition of spoken language proceeds successfully across broad ranges in intelligence and across vastly different cultures and child-rearing practices (see Slobin 1987 for a collection of articles that document this point). And the development of adequate spoken language is resistant to any number of oddities and apparent defects in the learning environment (see Gleitman 1986 and references therein and Curtiss 1973). Why should reading and writing, which appear to be the simpler and more derivative tasks, be so much more difficult and variable than speaking and understanding?

Of course we have no solution to this puzzle. But we want to discuss one factor that may be involved. It concerns what novices expect the environment to be like, compared with what it *is* like. Children appear to have highly constrained expectations about the nature of the oral language to which they are exposed, and, in general these expectations are fulfilled. This means that they do not have to wander down the garden path, developing and discarding a variety of hypotheses about the system to which they are being exposed. In contrast, the systematic properties of written languages often come as an unwelcome surprise to novices, and so learning often involves false starts, errors along the way, and a fair proportion of outright failures to extract the system. We shall briefly mention some evidence on the topic of early reading difficulties from this perspective; then the body of this paper will review evidence for the biologically guided process of learning a first (spoken or gestured) language.

Discovering the Level of Representation Exhibited in the Script

One of the problems for aspiring readers is that they don't quite know what to expect. Somehow there's a representation of language on the page, but novices don't know what form this will take. They aren't clear about what each written symbol stands for among the many units that are operative in the oral language. Thus many youngsters fail to understand even that for English script there is a fundamental relationship between sound and writing: that words that take longer to say are written with more letters (Rozin, Bressman, and Taft 1974). First graders often expect the orthographic units to be word meanings, in which case words (that is, the letter sequences between the white spaces) that are spelled similarly should encode related lexical items. Asked "What else sounds like *cat, rat,* and *bat?*" beginners will often respond "horse" or rhinoceros." The phrase "sounds like" is evidently interpreted as 'means like.' A more sophisticated but still false conjecture, apparently based on a small vocabulary of written items, is that each symbol represents a syllable. As one instance, a six-year-old once told us that *tomato* "can't be sounded out" because according to her this would come out "/tu/,*t,o*; /mah/,*m,a*; /tu/,*t,o*: /tumahtu/." Since English script is neither a logography nor a syllabary, these learners are at least temporarily stymied. Learning to read thus necessarily involves, among many other things, understanding the level of language design that is directly rendered in the orthography.

Not only is there a problem of discovering the level of analysis transcribed in an orthography but, of all known choices, the segmental phone level is hardest of all for children to discover (for a review of this evidence see Gleitman and Rozin 1977). Children of five can be taught the difference between the concepts 'word' and 'sentence' with little difficulty, but it is hard for them to distinguish among such concepts as 'word,' 'syllable,' and 'sound' (Downing and Oliver 1973– 74). Children of this age have some mild difficulty in segmenting speech into words (Holden and MacGinitie 1972), often failing to isolate connectives (such as *and*) and determiners (*the*) as separable words. They have greater difficulty in segmenting words into syllables (Rosner 1974; Liberman, Shankweiler, et al. 1977). And they have the greatest difficulty of all in segmenting words or syllables into phonemes (Liberman 1970; Rosner 1972; Elkonin 1973; Rosner and Simon 1971). In our own studies (Rozin, Poritsky, and Sotsky, 1967; Gletiman and Rozin 1973) we found that we could teach nonrepresentational logographies to six-year-olds whose prognosis (based on socioeconomic variables) for acquiring English orthography was poor and to older children who had failed to acquire any measurable reading facility after two years of school instruction. Their learning, using the word unit of analysis, did not differ appreciably in rate or character from that of more fortunately circumstanced middle-class children. Moreover, the difference in learning for these groups when exposed to a syllabary was rather small. But we also reproduced the well-known finding that teaching an alphabet to middle-class children was very hard, and teaching one to disadvantaged youngsters was close to impossible.

Overall, there is strong evidence that good and poor readers, as well as younger and older individuals, will respond similarly to meaning distinctions and meaningful contexts. At the other extreme, the ability to read word lists (Shankweiler and Liberman 1972) or nonsense-syllable lists (Firth 1972) aloud distinguishes very reliably between good and poor readers. That is, the ability to recruit the phonological distinctions transcribed by the script distinguishes between young and older, and poorer and better, readers (though, of course, success at the phonetic decoding skills does not immediately or fully guarantee fluency).

But why should reading, particularly reading alphabets, be difficult? All of the units transcribed in known orthographies appear in the spoken language as well, and the child—whatever his or her environmental circumstances—extracts and organizes all of them to acquire his native tongue, as we shall discuss. Rozin and Gleitman (1977), along with many other investigators of early stages of reading, have argued that decoding the visual script had to be carried out at a higher level of awareness than acoustic decoding. Reading is a comparatively new and arbitrary human ability for which specific biological adaptations do not, so far as we know, exist. One must quite consciously learn to carry out the analysis of visual symbols on the page "in the same way" one naturally analyzes speech signals without insight and without learning. The preponderance of the evidence is that the required conscious access is easier for more meaningful units such as morpheme and word, and harder for more superficial units, such as phoneme and syllable. (This may be because the decay rate for the more meaningful representations constructed at later stages of processing is slower, allowing such representations to be held in consciousness and inspected (Hirsh-Pasek, Gleitman, and Gleitman 1978). Whatever the real explanation, this generalization holds for a variety of judgmental linguistic tasks (so-called *metalinguistic* tasks), of which reading acquisition is only one (Gleitman and Gleitman 1970, 1979).

To summarize, aspiring readers face a difficult inductive task in discovering the language units symbolized in an orthography. The relevant units vary from script to script. The evidence is that the more superficial units are less likely to be conjectured by learners than the more meaningful units. This is one of the major reasons why it's hard to learn to read an alphabet. A significant subpopulation ultimately fails at this task and remains functionally illiterate. Success in reading acquisition is heavily influenced by particular environmental circumstances, with so-called disadvantaged youngsters being at particular risk of failure. As we'll now discuss, none of these generalizations hold for learning to speak and understand an oral language.

Learning a First Language

Beyond the framework principles just mentioned, we have nothing to contribute concerning the specific procedures used either by normals or dyslexics in acquiring written codes. But it may be helpful, by way of contrast and comparison, to consider what is known about the acquisition of a first spoken or signed language. This latter procedure seems to be characterized by Great Expectations: learners are in possession of a skeletal bioprogram ("Universal Grammar") that guides their learning of the specifics of the exposure language. This biological guidance accounts for the rapid and relatively errorless progress of oral-language acquisition as opposed to the slow and effortful progress of reading acquisition; for the indifference of the oral learning process to significant variations in the environment provided; and for the fact that pathologies of speech acquisition are orders of magnitude rarer than pathologies of reading acquisition.

In what follows, we focus primarily on a single aspect of the discovery procedure for spoken language: the machinery that enables a child to detect language-relevant units in the sound stream and in extralinguistic experience and to represent these appropriately. It is these units (and sequences of them) that constitute primary linguistic data, the base on which learning procedures must operate to acquire the exposure language. As Chomsky has recently put this issue, "We have to assume that there are some prelinguistic notions which can pick out pieces of the world, say elements of this meaning and of this sound" (1982, p. 119). Extracting these categories of form and of meaning is easily accomplished by all nonpathological children under widely varying circumstances of exposure. This contrasts with the case for reading, where even careful teaching under optimum conditions often fails.

The Category-Induction Problem
The child's task in learning a language is to pair the indefinitely many sounds to the indefinitely many meanings. His primary data must be samples of the sounds together with samples of the meanings. But how are the appropriate sound elements and meaning elements to be detected in the world and classified so as to constitute a representational basis for learning? If the child is free to choose among such potential elements (as he is when he faces the task of learning to read), surely we must expect variation in the rate and character of what is learned. For example, the child who happens to represent certain heard sounds as /r/ + /æbit/ and cooccurring meaningful scenes as 'undetached-rabbit-parts' ought to learn English more slowly than the child who represents the heard sound as /ræbit/ and the observed scene as 'a rabbit.' Since that variation in learning rate is hardly observed, it must be that there are biologically or environmentally inevitable constraints on which elements learners construct from the input.

Sound Units from Speech Information
Following Chomsky, the first question is how the learner picks out "pieces of the acoustic-linguistic world" from the sound stream— how he detects and represents sound. Notoriously, the phones,

words, phrases, and sentences of everyday speech run together so complexly that their proper segmentation seems very difficult to accomplish. As one example of the misanalyses that occur in the course of learning, one of our children at age six rendered (in writing) a teacher's command as "Class be smissed!" How does the learner finally come up with whole words and phrases, and so forth rather than halves of words or words-and-a-half?

One might guess that caretakers initially present category instances in isolation to improve the infant's chances of detecting them (just as they present isolated phonelike entities to aspiring readers—"buh," "ah," "tuh": "bat"). But at least in linguistic communities that have been studied carefully, this is not so. Maternal speech even to neonates is connected and intonationally natural. Moreover, it is to this connected speech that the infants are naturally responsive. Infants only one month of age will suck more on a nonnutritive nipple for the privilege of hearing intonationally natural, connected speech than for hearing speech without these intonational properties, that is, read essentially like a word list (Mehler et al. 1978). In this complex environment, infants and very young children have been shown to construct the full range of linguistic categories. In fact, so tuned in are infants to linguistic stimulation that they show significant calibration for the native tongue within 48 hours following birth (Mehler et al. 1988; also see Mehler, this volume).

We shall now discuss how the prelinguistic child represents the sound wave of speech. The nature of these representations is important to understand, for it constitutes one of the inputs to the learning procedure, which is to correlate these forms with their meanings.

Phonetic segments   Infants perform an initial segmentation of the wave form to derive phonetic segments. For example, two-month-old infants who hear the sound /ba/ contingent on their sucking at a nonnutritive nipple will increase their sucking rate, evidently for the mere pleasure of hearing /ba/ more often. But eventually the infants habituate to this stimulus (their sucking rate decreases). The infants readily dishabituate (suck faster again) if the signal is switched to /pa/ (Eimas et al. 1971). And Japanese babies will habituate to /ra/ and then dishabituate to /la/ despite the fact that their Japanese parents recognize only a single liquid consonant (Eimas 1975).

These studies have shown that a variety of phonetic distinctions are perceived categorically. That is, within a continuum of physical variation on some dimension, e.g., voice-onset time, the infants show sharp discrimination of variations that cross phonemic boundaries in human languages, but they show poor discrimination for variations of the same physical magnitude that are always within phonemic boundaries. Thus, no learning apparatus appears to be required for an initial segmentation of the acoustic wave into discrete phones. The segmentation has been provided in the nervous system.

At this level, then, an objective, highly instrumented sequence of empirical investigations shows that the language learner has relevant information in advance about the inventory of possible phonetic elements: he is biologically prepared to pick out useful pieces of the acoustic world for the sake of language learning (for a review of this literature, see Jusczyk 1986).[1] Notice, then, that while aspiring readers struggle, sometimes for years, to grasp that phonetic segments are represented on the printed page, all infants seem to be disposed to discriminate among these units for the sake of acquiring an oral language.

Stressed syllables and the word unit   The phonetic elements could not exhaust the child's inventory of acoustic linguistic primitives, for phonetic sequences woefully underdetermine the identification of words (is it *an adult* or *a nuhdult?*), word classes (is *yellow* a noun, verb, or adjective?), and phrases (e.g., *I saw a man eating fish*). The question, then, is whether there are units above and beyond the phonetic distinctive features, physically manifest in the wave form and operative in the child's induction of language structure. We discuss here one such perceptual category that the learner appears to use in extracting the unit *word:* the stressed syllable. This cannot be the only physical cue usable or used, because stress varies in informativeness over the languages of the world. The position is that there is a small number of physical cues to which the child is specially attentive in his search for the word inside the heard utterance. We concentrate attention on stress because it appears to play a major role in the languages whose acquisition has been studied extensively.

Suppose for now (we shall return to this point) that learners are predisposed to identify a conceptual unit *word.* Slobin (1973) suggested, on the basis of cross-linguistic acquisitional evidence, that they are disposed to identify this unit with particular physical aspects of the wave form, to believe that each wordlike conceptual unit has an "acoustically salient" and "isolable" surface expression. Accepting Slobin's perspective, Gleitman and Wanner (1982) proposed that the stressed syllable is this isolable physical unit that learners first identify as the linguistic repository of the word. A first supportive piece of evidence is that in languages like English words are first pronounced as their stressed syllables, e.g., "raff" for *giraffe* and "e-fant" for *elephant.* Moreover, when the unstressed syllables begin to be uttered, it is often in undifferentiated form (as the syllable schwa for all instances), for example "əportcard" for *reportcard*. That is, the unstressed syllables are at first not analyzed as fully as the stressed syllables.

Identification of stressed syllables is a useful heuristic for locating the word formative in the sound stream, but stressed syllables give no sure cue as to where the item begins or ends. Physical cues to word juncture are as likely to be found in unstressed syllables as in stressed ones. So if children are inattentive to unstressed syllables and the subtle junctural information they may contain, they should exhibit some confusion between unstressed words and the unstressed syllables of polysyllabic words. Young learners do seem to have this difficulty. Frequently they misanalyze clitic pronouns as the unstressed syllables of preceding words, e.g., "read-it" and "have-it," yielding such utterances as "Readit ə book" and "Havit ə cookie." Getting the unstressed syllables properly bound into the words is a late and lengthy task. As one example, the child mentioned earlier who at two years of age said "əportcard" and "tape əcorder" at four years of age asked "Can we go to Grandma's repartment house today?" False segmentations are often found in much older children (e.g., "Class be smissed"). Of course this does not mean that there are no physical cues to word segmentation in English (see Nakatani and Dukes 1977; Nakatani and Schaffer 1978). But these are subtle and rather unreliable; moreover, by necessity these cues sometimes appear in the relatively disfavored unstressed syllables.

Later stages of speech development lend further weight to the claim that the word and the stressed syllable are perceived by the learner as roughly coextensive. Bellugi (1967) demonstrated that when the elements of the English verb auxiliary make their first appearance in children's speech, the items are in their full (whole-syllable), rather than their contracted (subsyllabic), form, e.g., "I will go" rather than "I'll go." This is in contrast to the input corpus, in which these items were contracted in over 90 percent of the instances. Evidently, the contracted version of these words fails to be the acoustically salient element the child requires as the sound-stream reflex of *word*, if we take *stressed syllable* to be the appropriate specification of salience.

Other properties of children's speech support the stressed-syllable hypothesis. One of the most striking facts about English speakers' first utterances is that the functor words are approximately absent; hence, the speech sounds "telegraphic" (Brown and Bellugi 1964). To this extent the child's early linguistic behavior deviates systematically from the environmental model. It is particularly interesting that youngsters learning Russian omit the inflectional affixes that are the main device for marking the thematic roles in that language, adopting instead a word order strategy that has poor support in the input data, the speech of their Russian mothers (see Slobin 1966).

We have just identified the items missing from the young child's speech, in such languages as English and Russian, by a special name. These are the *functors*, a coherent and important subcomponent of the lexical stock of the language whose members are not only phonetically special (that is, unstressed in certain positions) but semantically and syntactically special as well. Things now start to get interesting: It may well be that a low-level perceptual bias toward stressed syllables is the mechanism that attracts youngsters to the *content* words and leads them to ignore the functors. But the consequence of the operation of this bias would be the extraction of a linguistically very important distinction. However, we must do more to solidify the hypothesis that it is the phonetic encoding of these items—rather than the child's prior discovery of their special syntactic-semantic functions—that delays their learning.

Consider again Slobin's finding for Russian children. It is impossible to suppose that they leave out the functors because these are semantically unimportant. Surely it is communicatively urgent to distinguish between *who did it* and *who it got done to* (between, say, *The dog bit the cat* and *The cat bit the dog*) and, as just stated, the youngest Russian learners do make this semantic distinction, but by means of word ordering rather than inflections. It is no more likely that the omission of the functors represents an initial syntactic bias in the child; namely, a bias toward word ordering rather than inflectional marking as the preferred encoding for thematic roles. Slobin (1982) has shown that Turkish children acquire Turkish inflections very early in life, unlike Russian children, who pass through an inflectionless word-order stage. The remaining hypothesis is that prosodic-phonological (ultimately physical) properties of the functors is what make them hard to learn: It is their unstressed and subsyllabic character that is hard for the children to detect.[2]

The most striking evidence comes from investigations by Slobin (1982) concerning comprehension among two- to four-year-old English, Italian, Serbo-Croatian, and Turkish learners. The Turkish children comprehend Turkish inflectional cues to thematic roles earlier in life than Serbo-Croatian learners comprehended Serbo-Croatian inflectional cues to thematic roles. According to Slobin, the relevant inflectional items in Turkish are a full syllable long, are stressed, do not deform the surrounding words phonetically, and do not cliticize. The late-comprehended Serbo-Croatian inflectional items are subsyllabic, stressless, and phonetically deformed by adjacent material. In sum, these two languages differ according to whether the inflectional cues to the thematic roles are encoded in isolable stressed syllables. This distinction predicts the differences in learning rate.

In the other two languages investigated by Slobin—English, and Italian—thematic roles are cued primarily by word order, not inflection. Thus, as with Turkish, they do not require the young learner to analyze unstressed grammatical items in order to recover the relational roles. Accordingly, there are no main-effect differences between Turkish and these other two languages in the rate at which relevant comprehension develops. Only Serbo-Croatian stands apart, showing a clear delay at each point in development.

Gleitman and Wanner's reading of this evidence was that a single principle, the advantage of stressed over unstressed material, accounts for Slobin's main findings. Evidence from the acquisition of Quiche Mayan (Pye 1983) is particularly informative in this regard, for in relevant cases Mayan—unlike the other languages just discussed—usually does not confound inflection (and hence semantic saliency) with stress. For many verbs in certain syntactic environments, this language stresses inflectional suffixes, while the verb root is unstressed. According to Pye, young learners often pronounce only one of these two syllables; that is, they are forced to make the choice between the semantically salient root and the perceptually salient suffix. They very consistently choose perceptual saliency, pronouncing the inflection and omitting the root. In fact, morpheme boundary and syllable boundary often do not coincide, providing a good testing ground for what the child is actually picking up and reproducing of a verb that she hears. According to Pye, Mayan children reproduce the syllable rather than the morpheme. They pronounce the whole syllable, including the terminal consonant of the root as well as the inflectional suffix.

To summarize, the cross-linguistic evidence supports the idea that the stressed syllable is highly salient perceptually. Materials encoded in stressed syllables thus appear in speech early. Stressed verb roots are pronounced early (English, Serbo-Croatian, Turkish, Italian) and unstressed verb roots are often omitted (Mayan). Symmetrically, stressed inflections are pronounced early (Turkish, Mayan) and the unstressed ones are often omitted (English, Serbo-Croatian). Insofar as attention to unstressed materials is crucial to recovering the argument structure of utterances, the child will show some comprehension delay (Serbo-Croatian). Insofar as the pronunciation of roots is obviously necessary to the adult's comprehension of the child's messages, children's speech in those languages that contain unstressed roots will be hard to understand (Mayan, as noted by Pye).

The best guess from this fragmentary evidence is that the distinction between stressed and unstressed syllables provides the learner with a first evidentiary source for partitioning the morphological stock in a linguistically relevant way. This partitioning (ultimately, the functor/content word distinction) is observable throughout the acquisition sequence, with the unstressed subcomponent acquired in a late and quasi-independent series of steps (Brown 1973). Moreover, chronologically late learning of a first language and features of second language learning show effects of this same distinction, with the unstressed material being forever the last and the hardest for older emigrés to acquire (Johnson and Newport 1986; Morgan, Meier, and Newport, in press). The same or a related distinction also helps to explain properties in other domains of language organization and use, including creolization (Sankoff and LaBerge 1973), speech production (Garrett 1975) and perception (Grosjean and Gee 1987), language forgetting (Dorian 1978), metalinguistic performance (Gleitman and Gleitman 1970, 1979) including reading acquisition (Rozin and Gleitman 1977), and pathological language dissolution (Kean 1979).

Summarizing, the physical realization of language categories in the sound stream affects the course of language discovery by the child. The perceptual saliency of stress is one property that supports the early discovery of the (content) word unit and delays the extraction of distinctions among the low-stress (functor) elements. This initial partitioning of the input according to stress is useful for learning because it is well correlated with the morpho-syntactic distinctions that the child must eventually make between subcomponents of the lexical stock.

The unit phrase   If Gleitman and Wanner are correct in their interpretation of the child evidence, the stressed syllable stands out from the rest of the wave form approximately as figure stands out from ground in the analysis of physical space. Although the stressed syllable is by no means equivalent to the mature word form, the evidence suggests that its acoustic correlates (fundamental frequency, intensity, and duration) are available to the child as a bootstrap into the morphological scheme of the language.

Gleitman and Wanner (1982) then proposed that prosodic properties of the wave form facilitate learning more broadly than in the identification of the (content) word unit. The phrasal and clausal organization is marked physically in the wave form by such factors as timing, pauses, syllable length, and the rise and fall of fundamental frequency; moreover, it has been shown that adults are sensitive to these acoustic markers (Klatt 1975, 1976; Streeter 1978; Klatt and Cooper 1975; and Lehiste, Olive, and Streeter 1976). More directly, Morgan, Meier and Newport's experiments on artificial-language learning (see note 3) suggest that adults can and do use this kind of physical cue to group words together and thus to induce phrasal patterns in a nonsense language. Gleitman and Wanner hypothesized that infants too were sensitive to these properties of the wave form and thus were probably recovering a phrase- and clause-bracketed representation (a parse tree) of the speech that they heard. This was even more likely, since the physical cues to phrase boundaries were known to be more reliable and to be exaggerated in the speech of caretakers to very young children.

By now there are compelling demonstrations in the literature that infants attend to these cues. Fernald (1984) removed from taped adult-to-adult speech and from maternal speech all cues to segmental content, leaving only prosodic information (the resulting signal sounds like the muffled speech heard through a wall to an adjoining hotel room). The infants still preferred the maternal version. The rhythmic and tonal information must be doing the work of differentiation. This information, in turn, is correlated with phrase and clause boundaries, as shown by Klatt and other investigators just mentioned. Hirsh-Pasek et al. (1987) have shown that disruption of the usual phrase-boundary information is noted by prelinguistic children: Infants under one year of age are more interested in (they look longer at) a loudspeaker producing maternal speech if it is doctored to contain a long half-second pause *between* the subject and predicate phrases than if it is doctored to contain a long pause *within* either the subject or predicate phrase. These studies taken together provide strong evidence that physical cues to phrase boundaries are salient to learners well before they speak at all.

If this is the case, it has important consequences for the way we should think about language learning. This is because an infant who is innately biased to treat intonationally circumscribed utterance segments as potential phrasal constituents would be at a considerable advantage in discovering the distributional patterns of the exposure language. As an easy example, the learner must discover whether specifiers (such as *the* and *a*) precede or follow nouns in noun phrases, for this property varies across languages. A pattern analysis of English speech which proceeded without prior knowledge of the noun-phrase boundary could not settle this question except with an excruciatingly cumbersome, and therefore unrealistic, manipulative procedure. This is because specifiers do follow rather than precede nouns if a phrase or clause boundary is crossed (e.g., "John gave the *boy the* book" and "Some *men the* boys liked ate tacos").

The unit clause The child seeking to discover the syntax of a language would also be aided if she could find a physical correlate of the category *clause*. Many crucial properties of a language are stateable only by reference to the clause unit, for example, the interpretation of pronouns and anaphors and the domains of movement transformations (see Lust 1986 for evidence that young children control these abstract linguistic properties). Then there also must be an antecedent procedure for establishing the category *clause*. Recent evidence suggests that there are reliable acoustic cues to clause boundaries in speech. These include longer pauses, segmental lengthening, declination of fundamental frequency, and stress marking (Garnica 1977; Cooper and Paccia-Cooper 1980; Klatt 1975, 1976; Jusczyk 1986). There is also considerable evidence that adults are sensitive to such cues (e.g., Streeter 1978; Luce and Charles-Luce 1983). This physical marking of the clause boundary can again be expected to be exaggerated in maternal speech. And again, infants have been shown to be responsive to these properties.

One admirable finding from the literature on this topic (Hirsh-Pasek et al. 1986) adapts Fernald's selective looking measure. Maternal speech by a stranger to the child was recorded and doctored by inserting half-second silent intervals either at clause boundaries or at arbitrary places within the sentence (three words before a clause boundary). Eight-month-old infants were presented with samples of both kinds of recording and their looking-time at the loudspeaker from which the speech emanated was recorded. The infants' clear preference was for the form in which the pauses appeared at the clause boundaries.

The rationale was this: It was assumed for the maternal speech, just as for ordinary speech, that a variety of acoustic cues converge at the clause boundary. The effect of the doctoring was either to maintain this convergence of cues (by inserting pauses at clause boundaries) or to dissociate them (by introducing pauses where the other cues do not ordinarily appear). The findings show that infants can and do identify these clues to clause units and expect them to converge on a point in time in input speech.

Sequence and the extraction of the sentential parse To learn a language, it is insufficient that children recognize the units in the ways just described. They must also attend to the temporal sequence in which these units appear in the sound stream. For example, one has to perceive the serial order of *p, a,* and *t* to distinguish the morphemes *pat, tap,* and *apt.* It has been demonstrated that infants are sensitive to sequential events in the sound stream. Recall that Mehler et al. (1978) found that one-month-old infants extract intonational properties over a continuous speech event. Their sucking rate increased for speech with natural prosodic and intonational qualities but not for speech that lacked these properties. Similarly, infants respond to a change of stress in a disyllable: *bà-ba* versus *ba-bà* (Spring and Dale 1977). Thus, they seem to be picking up information that is displayed across a temporal stream and is not available by analysis of the wave at single time points within that stream.

Gleitman and Wanner (1982) argued that the same attention to sequence is evident early in the development of speech. In a long line of observation beginning with Braine (1963), it has been demonstrated that even the two words of telegraphic speech are ordered, usually in accord with the canonical phrase ordering in the exposure language. For instance, Bloom (1970) showed that American children who say both "Mommy throw" and "Throw ball" usually do not say "Ball throw" to render the same propositional intent.

It is fair to ask about the essence of the units the children are ordering in their speech, but the answer to this question is not so clear. Some investigators hold that the first sequenced units are such lexical classes as noun and verb, but others believe that they are semantic-relational ones such as agent and patient. Present evidence is too weak to adjudicate these distinct claims about the labeling of word classes in the child's head. But without answering this question, we can still consider the discovery procedure by which the units that are sequenced (whatever their real essence) are derived from the data of experience.

All solutions to this problem somewhere implicate a distributional analysis à la Bloomfield (1933), which works by considering the privileges of occurrence of items in heard speech. For example, Maratsos (1982; see also Maratsos and Chalkey 1980) suggests that the noun class is derived as the items that appear after *the* and verbs are the ones that appear after *can* and *have* and before *-ed.* This solution has some difficulties. The first is that the child who is to profit from this information must be clever enough to decide that such items as *-ed* and *can* are good diagnostic environments for performing the distributional analysis. If the children decided instead to compare the distribution of *black* with respect to certain words (*coal, ink*) and *white* to others (*swan, snow*), they would extract subcategories of nouns that have little general relevance to the overall design of the language.

Notice that we have already granted the learners a basis for making the correct choices. To a good approximation, they can limit the analysis by considering solely the distribution of content words (the stressed ones) to functors (the unstressed and subsyllabic ones). In fact, Maratsos's scheme implicitly presupposes such a basis for selecting the units that figure in the distributional solution for the major lexical classes. But another difficulty for the envisaged analysis is that its critical use of functor evidence would lead to many misanalyses (misanalyses that do not characterize real learners so far as we know). For example, *hightail* and *hotfoot* do appear before *-ed* and are indeed verbs, but *high-handed, bobtailed,* and *club-footed* meet this *-ed* criterion and all the same are not verbs.

Gleitman and Wanner proposed certain extensions and revisions of Maratsos's (and, indeed, Bloomfield's) schematism for distributional learning, which may render it more workable. They did so by taking to heart the findings just reviewed, which suggest that even the youngest children have the apparatus to construct a rough phrase-structure representation of heard sentences (also see Morgan 1986 for striking experimental evidence for this hypothesis). They can bracket the clause into phrases using prosodic information. Moreover, recent formal demonstrations suggest that phrase labeling can be derived from the bracketings (Levy and Joshi, 1978). Finally, they are attentive to the temporal orders in which the units occur. Thus, there may be a rudimentary structural analysis of the whole sentence available to the learner, which he can bring to bear on disentangling the noun phrases from the verb phrases and even on the discovery of the semantic values of individual words as they appear within the sentence. For the *hightailed/high-handed* example, potential misanalyses can be avoided by attending to the global properties of the sentential parse. Appearance of *-ed* in the verb phrase identifies a verb item (so in this environment *-ed* can signal 'pastness'), but appearance of *-ed* on a morpheme that occurs after *the* and before a noun (e.g., in "the high-handed policeman") identifies a modifier, and so the interpretation of *-ed* is participial.

To summarize the argument, it is clear that sequential constraints on morphemes hold only up to the phrase boundary. Therefore, the child who is to discover these constraints by distributional analysis must have an analysis antecedently in place to set this boundary. After all, phrase-structure descriptions of language are convenient, indeed explanatory, just because they so operate as to express the domains of categorial contingencies, e.g., that *the* is limited in its relative distribution with respect to nouns up to the level of the phrase and no further. We have reviewed evidence indicating that the young learner can recover the crucial phrase and clause boundaries by observing the prosodic grouping cues in the utterances heard. The advantage conferred by phrase-structure representation is that it permits a global description of the sentence so that the values for its morphemes can be assigned in a way that is consistent with the whole sentence.[3]

Discovery of linguistic form: summary and concluding comments   Infants and youngest language learners are attentive to physical aspects of the speech stream that are well correlated with such categories as phonetic segment, word, phrase, and clause, and to sequences of such units as they occur in heard utterances. Taken at its strongest, this evidence suggests that a phrase-structure representation of heard speech is available as the child is just beginning to speak or earlier. The content words are identified and placed within the parse structure owing to their realization as perceptually salient stressed syllables (perhaps, early on, the unstressed material is represented as associated "mush"). The phrase and clause boundaries are given according to other physical grouping cues just discussed.

If the analysis just given is correct, it has important consequences for a theory of language learning. For example, it is often supposed that the learner receives input in the form of word strings, and must construct the phrases therefrom (see Wexler and Culicover 1980 and Pinker 1984 for interesting proposals taking this perspective). But it may well be that the child has information about the phrases as early as—or earlier than!—he has information about the words inside the phrases. After all, prosodic information about phrase boundaries is far more reliable and obvious than information about word boundaries. Any investigator (or mother) can adduce many child usages that are best interpreted as false word segmentations (e.g., /a nədult/ or /əplejəl iyjəns/), but it is very hard to find even anecdotes that are describable as cases of false phrase segmentation. To the extent that phrasal information is physically available and is actually recruited by the learner, the discovery procedure for phrases (given word sequences) can be weakened or dispensed with. The same weakening of a discovery procedure is possible if the child knows where the clause boundaries are when he sets about learning which phrase sequences constitute a whole sentence.

Let us return briefly to reading. Known orthographies do not physically mark phrase and clause boundaries. To be sure, there is such a thing as the comma but its use is notoriously inexact in English writing, and it certainly does not line up one-to-one with phrasal boundaries. For example, no comma is allowed between the subject and predicate phrases (though it does occasionally appear) even though this is the major and most informative phrase boundary in the clause. If phrase-boundary marking plays as crucial a role in learning as we have supposed, its absence in orthographies ought to exacerbate the learning problem. To a considerable extent clause boundaries are also unmarked in known scripts. Sentences end with a period, and some clauses are marked off with commas but most are not. For instance, owing to their intonational properties, restrictive relative clauses and many other kinds of embedded sentences are not physically marked at all (one can't write "I believe, that John is tall"). In this sense at least, the written system does not map onto the spoken system in a simple or regular way. It is an impoverished representation of the spoken language that the child knows.

Primitive Interpretive Elements
We have just suggested that the infant is well prepared prelinguistically to pick out relevant pieces of sound from the wave forms as the primitive representational basis for finding the linguistically functioning phones, words, phrases, and clauses and more generally for extracting a phrase-structural analysis of the speech stream. But since language is a pairing of sounds to their meanings, this is only half the battle. The other half of the representation problem has to do with picking out relevant "pieces of meaning" from the observation of extralinguistic context.

Here too (just as for linguistic forms), some role may be played by the special character of speech to young children. Caretakers evidently limit the topics of their conversations to those that are appropriate to the extralinguistic context. As Bruner (1974/75) and Ninio (1980) have discussed, speech to infants and young children predominantly concerns the "here and now." Usually the addressee of the speech is the child listener, and conversation focuses on the identification and manipulation of objects present. Slobin (1975) has argued from an examination of caretaker speech that it is accompanied by contextual cues so reliable as to render its interpretation unproblematical in most cases.

These properties of speech to children may have their source in the caretaker's attempt to get the everyday business of life accomplished (the juice drunk, the toys picked up) by a cognitively and linguistically inadequate listener. Still, they may well be helpful for learning. It seems more useful for learning the meaning of *rabbit* to hear this word in the presence of rabbits than in discussions of what one ate in Paris last summer. And the positions and motions of those objects in space, relative to the child, can be informative only insofar as the child is really the addressee. For example, when a child is told, "Give me the rabbit!" the source and goal positions of the rabbit, relative to the listener, are relevant to the interpretation of *give*, but these spatial interpretations would be irrelevant or misleading if the mother were referring to herself and to nonpresent events, e.g., "I gave three rabbits to the zoo last week."

But just as was the case for analysis of the wave form, this constraint from the environment does not mitigate the inductive problem for learners unless they are disposed to accept this information in the spirit in which it is given. Speaking of whole rabbits cannot really help the learner who is predisposed to inspect its pieces or to suppose that they may at the next inspection turn into pillars of salt. If learners are open minded about how the scene before them is to be represented perceptually and conceptually, surely learning the meanings of words from observation of their instances is impossible. So no one, to our knowledge, has ever assumed that the child's interpretation of the observed world is neutral. At the extreme, the child's hypothesis space could not include the exotic chimeras, disconnected parts, and capriciously transforming objects conjectured by worried philosophers. Significant perceptual and perhaps conceptual biases underlie babies' organization of the continuously varying, multiply interpretable world (MacNamara 1972; Carey 1982, 1985).

Discovery of these biases and predispositions in the infant must ultimately be relevant to understanding how young children learn the meanings of words (even though there are sure to be refinements, elaborations, and even discontinuities between infant perceptions and the concept space of one- and two-year-old language learners). To the extent that words describe the world and are uttered in appropriate real-world settings, the child at least partly "bootstraps" the meanings of words by observing what is actually going on when they are said. How this is accomplished depends on just which "little pieces of the world" it is possible to extract from the flux of external stimulation.

Infant studies during the past decade suggest that learners are quite well prepared for this task. Perhaps rich and various experiential categories are given by nature and can immediately be connected to the task of learning a language. Or perhaps the appropriate experiential categories are derived by learning, based on a very narrow initial vocabulary. But whichever of these alternatives is closer to the truth, one fact is clear: The child has a considerable armamentarium for representing the real world by the time this is required for learning a language at about age one.

Primitive (or close to primitive) perceptual categories Human infants come richly prepared with means for picking up information about what is going on in their environment—looking, listening, feeling, tasting, and smelling. In fact, these different sensory routes appear to be pre-coordinated for obtaining information from the world (Spelke 1979). Infants evidently impose a great deal of order on the gloriously confusing world that is detectable from these information sources.

To be sure, studies with infants provide only probabilistic data, and very often it is difficult to introduce enough parametric variation into experiments to be sure of exactly how to characterize the sources of these small subjects' responses. Another major problem is that there are severe limits on which neonate behaviors can be brought under control in the laboratory. Infants can systematically look at things, suck on nipples, and register observable facial and bodily surprise, and psychologists have to be content to derive whatever they can by manipulating this narrow repertoire. Finally, it is not feasible to perform experiments on neonates at the instant they emerge from the womb, and therefore have had no experience of the world. These theoretically ideal subjects are inattentive and fall asleep in the midst of even the shortest experiments. On these grounds (and some grounds of theoretical persuasion) there is controversy about how much of the infancy work is to be interpreted (see the chapters by Mehler and Krasnegor in this volume). But this literature does begin to make the case that infants from the beginning are purposive and highly constrained in their inspection of ongoing things, events, and scenes in the world, in a way that ultimately can be connected to the question of how a year or so later they acquire their first words and sentences (for a major review and discussion of the literature on perceptual development, see Gibson and Spelke 1983).

To take a few central examples, infants appear to perceive the world as populated with objects that endure over time (Spelke 1982) and that cannot occupy two positions at the same time (Baillargeon, Spelke, and Wasserman 1986). Once the infants have learned about objects, they rapidly come to distinguish among their varying properties, such as their rigidity or elasticity (Walker et al. 1980; Gibson and Walker 1984), their size (Baillargeon 1986), and even their animacy versus inanimacy (Golinkoff et al. 1984). They distinguish between moving and stationary objects in the first few months of life (Ball and Vurpillot 1976). They use the perceived layout of surfaces as information about their own position and the positions and movements of other objects relative to their own bodies (Acredolo and Evans 1980; Field 1976). Finally and most surprising of all, infants aged six to eight months are sensitive to numerosity, for they will note the difference between two- and three-item visual displays (Starkey, Gelman and Spelke 1983).

Learning word meanings, given perceptual-interpretive abilities   We have asserted that the learner roughly picks out words by relying on such physical manifestations as the distinction between the stressed and unstressed syllable. The literature on vocabulary acquisition suggests that learners map these formal units onto the world in ways that are globally consistent with findings from the infant perception laboratory. Gentner (1982) showed that learners acquire nouns before verbs (roughly, object labels before action labels), and Bloom (1973) showed that they acquired object names before property names (*dog* before *big* or *green*). Nelson (1974) showed that they first acquire names for small moving things in their environment (*duck*) as opposed to large immobile things (*sofa*). Mervis and Crisafi (1978) demonstrated that they acquire "basic level" terms (*duck*) before superordinates (*animal*) and subordinates (*mallard*).

One series of studies seems to show that these early word choices are not simply describable as responses to the word usage of the caretakers. Goldin-Meadow and Feldman (1979) and Feldman, Goldin-Meadow, and Gleitman (1978) studied deaf children of hearing parents who received little or no linguistic information. They could not learn English from their parents, because they were deaf, and they could not learn sign language from these hearing parents, who did not use or even know any sign language. Children in these circumstances spontaneously develop an iconic gestural-communication system (though they promptly trade it in for formal sign language whenever they are first exposed to the latter (see Newport and Supalla, in press). The Goldin-Meadow group showed that the isolated deaf-language inventors first devised manual equivalents for the same vocabulary items that are acquired early by children learning English or French; and the ages at which they did so were the same as those of the hearing children.

Such findings suggest that factors pertaining to the child's initial conceptions of the world help to explain the course of lexical learning. But there is orderliness in the acquisition sequence that is not wholly explained by facts about early percepts and concepts. In particular, why should object concepts be linguistically encoded earliest, since so far as we know, infants perceive actions and connected events as soon as they perceive objects? (Even more strongly, Spelke and Born (1982) contend that part of the very basis for object perception is the behavior of those bodies when in motion). And why are nouns chosen to label object concepts and verbs to label action concepts? Why not choose some word to be the label for a whole event or proposition? We shall discuss now two approaches to these issues. The first speaks to how the child parses situations so as to come up with their pertinent foci. The second asks about the contribution of language design to language learning.

Domain specificity in the interpretation of the world   The ability to perceive and categorize the observed world differently under different observational circumstances is surely critical to the acquisition of word and sentence meaning. Gelman (1986) illustrates this problem with a nice example. "On day one I point to these two (duck, pig) and say DUCK, PIG; on day two I point to these two and say YELLOW, PINK; on day three I point to these two and say ONE, TWO. Why wouldn't a beginning language learner think she should call this (duck) DUCK, YELLOW, ONE?" A learner equipped to notice objects, colors, and numerosity should be able to generate three hypotheses, all sensible, for labeling the observation of a single yellow duck. But which is the true label in the exposure language for the concept 'duck'? Perception seems to leave too much latitude for the solution to this problem.

Gelman's proposal for a solution draws on two supposed biases or strategies in the child learner. The first is a conjecture by Markman (1985) about the child's initial picture of how words map onto the world. Markman's evidence suggests that the child is biased to believe that when a novel word is presented in the context of a novel object, the word refers to that object as a whole. For example, suppose a cup (a familiar object with a known name) or a pair of tongs (an unfamiliar object with no name known by the child subjects) is presented and called "pewter." The children believe that *pewter* is the name for tongs but not a new name for cups. By default they assign the new term to the substance (the material) for the case of the cup. It is as though they believe that since the cup already has a linguistic title ("cup"), the new word used to refer to it must pertain to its other properties. Thus, in Markman's terminology, there is a principle of "mutual exclusivity" operating in acquiring word labels (a principle closely related to the uniqueness principle of linguistic and learnability theory). Each object class, however derived from experience, will have its unique, unchanging, word label. Ducks are not sometimes to be called "aardvark" (though they are sometimes called "Donald" and sometimes called "animal," a problem to which we will return). Thus the principle of mutual exclusivity would predict that the child's first guess is that *one* and *duck* are not synonyms but are likely to encode different aspects of the observed scene.

The second component of Gelman's solution to the labeling problem draws on her findings on the child's early concept of number and counting. Gelman and Gallistel (1979) have elucidated the following basic counting principles and shown that preschoolers have considerable understanding of them: "(1) One-one: Each and every item in a collection must be uniquely tagged. (2) Stable order: Whenever tags are used, they must be organized in a list that is stably ordered. (3) Cardinal order: The last tag in a tag sequence represents the cardinal value of the numerosity of the collection. (4) Item indifference: Any set of entities, no matter their attributes, can be collected together in a count trial. (5) Order indifference: The how-to-count principles can be applied to any ordering of the elements in an array."

An ordered list of words is used for counting. Children acquire the count list by memorization, a hard job. But another task the child must confront is to understand that the five principles just listed account for the observed use of these terms. The independence of this task from memorizing the verbal count sequence was shown by Gelman and Gallistel by a very striking phenomenon: Children who have the list wrong (who have idiosyncratic count lists, such as "one, two, thirteen, five") observe the count principles in using this list to refer to numerosity. For example, they will assert that all three-item arrays are collections of thirteen, correctly honoring the cardinal order principle. More generally, these investigators have shown that preschool children carry out number tasks very systematically and consistently in accordance with the five principles if the numbers are very small.

Now we are ready to reapproach the duck/one decision. Gelman points out that the use of count terms according to count principles systematically violates the principle of mutual exclusivity that (by Markman's hypothesis) applies to object naming. Two ducks are both to be called "duck," but one duck (and either one, across count trials) is to be called "one" and the other "two." Each item is given a different count term, even if each such item is a duck (the one-one principle), and the word *one* can be used to label different objects over trials (the principles of item indifference and order indifference). There are no physical attributes that are invariant for uses of the word *two* that will account for its contexts of use other than the count principles.

Summing up, it is possible to begin to think about the acquisition of such relatively tidy concepts (and terms) as *two* and *duck*, on the assumption that the child learner has some initial principles for organizing the flux of ambient stimulation that is presented to his senses; and maps words on to their meanings as they do or do not accord with these principles. The same external stimulations will be differently labeled according to which principles are invoked in using them; and different external stimulations will be labeled identically insofar as they are organized by some single principle or set of principles.

Limits on the informativeness of observation: the subset problem The principle of mutual exclusivity or uniqueness in assigning labels to objects really will not work as stated, for—even leaving aside synonyms— the same object is often (in fact, always) provided with more than one name, e.g., *animal, duck, Donald Duck.* One would expect that the adult speaker has little difficulty in selecting the level of specificity he wants to convey, and so he can choose the correct lexical item in each case. And indeed, the learner may be perceptually and conceptually equipped to interpret the scene at these various levels of abstraction and to construct conceptual taxonomies (Keil 1979). But this very latitude makes a mystery of the child's vocabulary acquisition, for how is he to know the level encoded by the as yet unknown word that he hears? The scene is always the same. For every time there is an observation that satisfies the conditions (whatever these are) for the appropriate use of *duck*, the conditions for the appropriate use of *animal* have been satisfied as well. Similarly, to mention a case to which we will return, *perceive, look, see, eye* (in the sense of "set eyes on"), *face, orient*, and so on pose the same subset problem.

Gold (1967) addressed a problem that may be analogous to this one. He showed that a learner who has to choose between two languages, one of which is a subset of the other, can get no positive evidence that he has chosen wrong if he happens to conjecture the superset (larger) language. This is because the sentences he would hear, all drawn from the subset, all are members of the superset as well. It has therefore been proposed that learners always hypothesize the smaller (subset) language, that is, they initially select the most restrictive value for a parameter on which languages vary (Wexler and Manzini 1987).

But the facts about the acquisition of a lexicon do not allow us to suppose that the child has a solution so simple as choosing the least inclusive possibility. In the end, the learners choose all of them—they learn all the words just mentioned. Moreover, they select neither the most nor the least inclusive level as their initial conjecture. The middle-sized, or so-called "basic level," categories *duck* and *see* are the actual first choices of learners (see Rosch 1978) for the clearest attempts to describe the basic-level vocabulary and its privileged role for both children and adults in various classificatory tasks).[4] These results cannot be written off as a simple consequence of the greater frequency in speech of *duck* compared to *mallard* (the subcategory) or *animal* (the superordinate category) in light of the so-called "overextention" findings for early lexical development (Rescorla 1980). Sometimes a subordinate term really is the most frequent in the child's environment, for the dog in the house is usually called "Fido," and the man in the house is usually called "Daddy." But then the young learner may interpret these words as basic level all the same, calling the dog next door "Fido" and the man on the street "Daddy."

We have nothing to contribute to the explanation of preferred levels of categorization by children (or adults for that matter). What is central to the present discussion is that on the one hand, the preferences exist and on the other hand, the word labels for the nonpreferred category levels are finally acquired also. That is, perception and conception allow the same scene to be represented and linguistically described at more than one level. The subset problem assures that different and distinguishable observations of the world when, say, *perceive* or *see* are uttered cannot account in any simple way for how the semantic values of these words are disentangled by the learner.

In sum, we have tried here to indicate that perception and conception provide too various and thus too weak a basis for matching the right words with the right meanings. These problems remain even though mothers naturally speak to their young children of pertinent objects and events in the ongoing scene (see Slobin 1975). Somehow the evidence from extralinguistic observation must be constrained. As we will now try to show, important constraints derive from the child's natural ("innate") preconceptions about language design.

Interpretative biases from language design   Almost all proposals for learning word meaning by observing the extralinguistic context implicitly or explicitly implicate additional principles that derive from language design itself. For instance, Markman's principle of mutual exclusivity, while it alludes to observation, depends as well on how experience maps onto language design in particular: i.e., for object classes at some predefined level there is to be a single label in the language. A number of findings show that the child's flexibility in interpreting the extralinguistic world is constrained by such preexisting biases about how that world is to be viewed, *given its linguistic description.*

The semantic interpretation of word classes   Earlier we discussed proposals by Maratsos (1982) and Gleitman and Wanner (1982) for how the child discovers words and their lexical classifications. Children apparently identify these formal classes with distinctive semantic values. Some supportive evidence comes from Markman and Hutchinson (1984) and Waxman and Gelman (1986). These investigators began with the observation that youngsters tend to sort objects according to thematic rather than taxonomic groupings. Shown a poodle replica and asked which other present object goes with it, two- and three-year-olds are likely to choose a bone replica rather than a terrier replica. There is nothing incoherent about such a choice: terriers are dogs, but also poodles like bones. The bias can be reversed if the task is changed to focus on the object's label. Suppose the child is told "This puppet speaks only Japanese, and he likes *this dobutso*." (the poodle is shown, and placed near the puppet). "Give him another dobutso." The children are now likely to choose the terrier. If the label is a noun, the concept pertains to a taxonomic grouping. Thus, the linguistic information acts to narrow down the hypotheses offered by the perception of objects and events.

Such language-concept mappings were investigated by Brown (1957), who showed his child subjects a picture in which, say, spaghettilike stuff was being poured into a vessel. Some subjects were asked to show "some gorp," others "a gorp," and still others "gorping." The subjects' choices were, respectively, the spaghetti, the vessel, and the action. Evidently, the semantic core of the word classes affects the conjecture about the aspect of the scene in view that is being labeled (for an experimental demonstration with younger children, see Katz, Baker, and MacNamara 1974).

The clause is the natural repository of propositions   A fascinating line of research, beginning with Bloom's (1970) groundbreaking work on children's spontaneous speech, provides evidence at another level about how children meaningfully interpret the world and map it onto linguistic categories. As mentioned earlier, from the earliest two-word utterances children's ordering of component words interpreted against their contexts of use suggests that they conceive words as playing certain thematic roles such as agent and patient within a predicate-argument structure (Bloom, Lightbown, and Hood 1975; Bowerman 1973; Brown 1973; Braine 1976). Evidence cited earlier from Golinkoff et al. (in press) suggests that even one-word speakers understand the semantic implications of phrase orderings. They realize that "Cookie Monster tickles Big Bird" means one thing, but "Big Bird tickles Cookie Monster" means something quite different. Feldman, Goldin-Meadow, and Gleitman have shown that a similar componential analysis describes the signing of the deaf isolates, for these children too differentiate their sign-order choices depending on the relational roles played by various nominal gestures. Slobin and Bever (1982) adduced cross-linguistic evidence to support a strong generalization of such findings: Learners construct a canonical sentence schema as the preliminary framework for language acquisition.

This early linguistic-conceptual organization becomes a bit easier to understand in the light of the evidence just reviewed. Infants understand the connectedness of events in which objects are seen or felt to move, relative to each other, in visual and haptic space. Whatever the precise content of the first relational categories, it seems clear that the child approaches language learning equipped with a propositional interpretation of the scenes and events in the world around him.

The question remains how much this tells us about learning a language. This depends on how the categories and forms of natural language map onto the preexisting meaning structures. From varying perspectives, a number of authors have assumed that linguistic categories and forms map transparently from meaning structures and hence that the bulk of explanatory apparatus for child learner and developmental psycholinguist alike exists when these categories are isolated and described (see for example Bates and MacWhinney 1982; Braine and Hardy 1982; Bloom 1973). This view is not unreasonable on the face of it. After all, we previously subscribed to a version of the view that the mapping between words and concepts may be quite direct. The question now is whether the relation between sentences and propositional thought is as straightforward as the relation between words and first concepts may be.

As a first pass at this issue, consider one finding from Feldman et al.'s deaf isolates. A distributional-interpretive analysis of these children's rudimentary sentences showed that they gestured a single noun in construction with such action gestures as *dance*, two nouns with *hit*, and three with *give*. Moreover, the noun items were sequenced differentially with respect to the action item, roughly according to the thematic roles these items played (patient first, recipient second). It appears that learners realize that events are to be described linguistically as a predicate-argument structure in which noun phrases playing the argument roles are ranged around the verb in systematic ways. Moreover, they realize that *give, hit,* and *dance* are concepts that by their logic require a different number of such arguments. Evidently, the mapping between argument structure and sentence structure is quite transparent for these isolated children. Perhaps the youngest learners of real languages also first approach the task by supposing that this transparency condition will hold (for a discussion see Wexler and Culicover 1980).

Semantic bootstrapping: syntactic form from meaning   One way of thinking about a discovery procedure that extracts form/meaning relations has been called "semantic bootstrapping." Its first premise is the uncontroversial idea that something about the semantics of various words and structures can be discovered by noticing the real-world contingencies for their use. No one would contest such a view. But its second and more surprising claim is that, once the meanings have been culled from observation, these meanings themselves yield conjectures about linguistic classification (e.g., a word describing an action is probably a verb; different actions imply different syntactic encodings of the verbs that express them; see Bowerman 1973, 1982; Grimshaw 1981; and Pinker 1984 for discussions that adopt this point of view). This idea has been very interestingly outlined and defended by Bowerman, who has collected children's spontaneous syntactic usages that are at variance with those of the surrounding linguistic community.

Bowerman's evidence suggests that children take a strong view of how predicate-argument structure is to be mapped onto sentences at the surface. For example, children who properly say "John moves the block," "The block moves" and "The baby eats" are sometimes also observed to say—not so properly—"Don't eat the baby!" when they evidently mean "Don't feed the baby" (cause it to eat). The analogy, false in the given case, evidently comes from words such as *move* (as in *The book moves*) which have a lexical causative variant (*John moves the book*). It seems then that using the meaning extracted from the observation of events, the child makes a conjecture about syntactic form that assumes that the relation between argument structures and subcategorization frames is transparent. Insofar as the exposure language embodies such a relation, the young learner has a productive basis in semantics (derived in turn from observation) for constructing clausal syntax. Of course, insofar as the exposure language deviates from this relation, the child makes errors, as Bowerman showed. Moreover, insofar as meaning cannot be fully derived from observation in the first place, owing—among many other things—to the subset problem, there are limits on how far the child can go by adopting this stance.

Syntactic bootstrapping: acquiring meanings from forms   In response to such problems Landau and Gleitman (1985) developed a verb-learning theory that incorporates the Bowerman-Grimshaw-Pinker insights, but capitalizes on the form-meaning relations in a further way. If there is really a strong correlation between verb syntax and verb meaning, and if Gleitman and Wanner are correct that very young learners represent input utterances as phrase-structure trees, the learner can make conjectures from form to meaning with only the same trepidation that should apply to his conjectures from meaning to form. For example, *gorp* in "John *gorps*" is unlikely to mean 'bring' because the surface structure contains too few argument positions. Such subcategorization evidence about verb meanings is particularly useful because the syntactic information from the caretakers is categorical: maternal subcategorization errors are vanishingly rare (Newport 1977; Landau and Gleitman 1985). This contrasts with the probabilistic and degenerate information available from scene inspection.

Landau and Gleitman's first basis for this hypothesis was an argument by exclusion. They showed that children whose observational conditions differed radically nevertheless achieved closely related meaning-representations for the same items: Blind learners by age three, just like sighted learners of the same age, understand that the verbs *look* and *see* describe spatial-perceptual acts and states and are distinct from the contact term *touch*. For both blind and sighted children, *look* describes the dominant perceptual means for discovering objects in the world, and *see* describes the state that results from such exploration. Thus, for the blind the terms describe haptic exploration and perception, while for the sighted they describe visual exploration and perception. Moreover, blind three-year-olds understand that these words, applied to sighted individuals, describe perception that takes place at a distance, requires line-of-sight orientation, and is blocked by barriers; that is, they understand much of how these terms apply to the visual experience of the sighted.

The view that word meanings are acquired through extralinguistic observation must be subtle enough to cope with this finding of closely related semantic conjectures from distantly related observational evidence. How does the blind child discover the spatial-perceptual interpretation of these words and correctly induce the spatial components of sighted individuals' seeing and looking? Surely not from seeing and looking, nor from literally observing the seeing and looking of others. Evidently, some word-meaning acquisition takes place despite impoverishment, or significant change, in the observational evidence.

This problem is of course quite general, extending to sighted children as much as to blind children. The blind learner's manifest competence serves only to dramatize an issue that has always been recognized but is sometimes submerged in recent thought about the usefulness of observation. Consider the acquisition of the word *know* by sighted children. What is there to observe in the world whenever an individual is said to know something? It is wildly implausible to suggest that the learner stores (in a pro-tem, hardly organized fashion) a set of relatively lengthy events and cooccurring lengthy conversations in which *know* (somewhere) appears, to discover the precise real-world contingency for the use of this word. The storage and manipulation problems appear to be hopelessly difficult, especially as one would independently have to store another detailed set of observed scenario-conversation pairs for *think, guess,* etc. Discussion of solutions solely in observational terms have certainly lacked specificity. They have usually given little attention to the proliferation of conjectured interpretations of individual scenes that will ensue if the learner is allowed great latitude in his representational vocabulary and great ingenuity in reconstructing the interpretation of events. Even a partial theory for extracting interpretation from observed scenes will require a technical and detailed research endeavor in its own right, along the lines suggested by students of perceptual and conceptual development. This problem cannot be solved simply by alluding to the fact that what is said is usually appropriate to the external circumstances in some way.

Some of the real issues that will have to be faced if an unaided observation-learning proposal is to achieve detailed support are worth at least listing here. One difficulty is that sometimes the child listener is attending to one thing (say, the cat on the mat) while the parent is speaking of something altogether different ("Time for your nap, dear"). A theory of observational learning has to state why the child makes no attempt to pair this observation to that meaning, or must have a procedure for recovering from errors made along the way. A second problem has to do with the stimulus-free character of even language use that is in some way pertinent to ongoing events; there seems no end to the pertinent things one could say in an observed situation. So how is the child to guess which of these alternatives is encoded in the utterance that accompanies the observation? As stated earlier, the problem reaches its limit for words that stand in a class-inclusion relation to each other and differ in no other way. The child who conjectures that *see* means 'perceive' will never experience scenes or events to dissuade him, for every time his caretakers appropriately speak of seeing something, there will be an event of perceiving taking place. Such problems pertain as much to everyday verbs of physical motion, for there is no running without moving, chasing without following, placing without putting, nor taking without getting (or giving).

Syntactic evidence in utterances heard ought to mitigate these problems significantly. As an example, consider the child who by perceptual and conceptual endowment (or by prior learning) is prepared to believe that there is a word in her language meaning 'perceive by eye' (or by 'hand' in case the learner is blind). The question is how that learner decides that *see*, rather than *give* or *have*, etc., is the right word in the exposure language for this notion.

To understand how this problem is solved is to bring together many of the strands already discussed. We know that the child who is learning verb meanings has already acquired word labels for many objects and persons, as many nouns are learned before verbs begin to be acquired. We know also that speech to the child is predominantly addressed to her, and overwhelmingly often concerns the locations, movements, and goals of objects, with known names, in the observable scene. If the speech is addressed to the child, the object motions relative to her own body therefore provide experiential clues to the meaning of the verb in the heard utterance. That is, she can tell if she is the source or the goal of that object motion depending (for one thing) on whether pertinent objects are moving toward or away from her. We know from the infant perception studies cited earlier that the young word learner can understand the scene as such a layout in which there are objects in motion, organized relative to the position of her own body. Thus, the learner indeed has some observational evidence about the objects that are participating in that observed event, and are being described in an utterance now heard.

The question is whether observational information alone is sufficient to discover that /siy/ means 'see' while /giv/ means 'give.' The problem, in a nutshell, is that while the child observer can notice that objects are in motion, she can also notice that she is perceiving this scenario. And the adult can appropriately refer to either of these aspects in his utterance. He can say "Do you see the apple?" and "Can you give me the apple?" in response to the same scene. Indeed, reference to perceptual acts (listening and looking) and states (hearing and seeing) as they apply to the ongoing scene are frequent in maternal usage even to blind babies.

A solution is available if the learner is equipped with a parse (that is, a phrase-bracketed representation) of the heard sentence, can identify the structural positions of the known nouns and unknown verb (*see* or *give*) in that parse, and has a conjecture about the logic of the notions 'see' and 'give.' We have already discussed some of the evidence. To repeat one theme, even the isolated deaf subjects of Goldin-Meadow know that the language encoding of 'see' and 'give' must be different. Seeing involves an observer's perception of the scene (and hence requires two noun phrases), while giving involves the transfer of an object between two parties (and hence requires three noun phrases). A linguistic object (verb) that is to mean 'give' must be one that can appear in parse trees with three argument positions, while a verb that is to mean 'see' can have only two. This is because perception is inalienable and involves no external causal agent to be expressed in a third noun phrase (barring psychokinesis, there is no way to interpret *John looked the ball to Mary*).[5] These strictures derive from the theta criterion (Chomsky 1981): Every argument is mapped onto a noun phrase and the number of noun phrases is limited by the argument structure. More generally, the logic of verb meaning is exhibited in the surface structures. Since different verbs vary in their logic, their surface structures are different too. These surface structures are available for the learner's inspection.

Landau and Gleitman discussed a number of such surface-structure derivatives of the meanings of the verbs here under discussion, and showed that the appropriate forms were used by a mother in her utterances to a young blind child. Many of their claims go well beyond the requirement of a one-to-one mapping of noun phrases to arguments. Here are some examples. Since (visual and haptic) perception is of both objects and events, a verb meaning 'see' will appear with noun phrase complements and also sentential complements, while a verb meaning 'give' cannot take sentential complements because one cannot transfer events from party to party or from place to place (*John gave Mary to come to the party* defies interpretation). A verb meaning 'see' pertains to a spatial perception and so should and does appear with a variety of locative prepositions, while 'give' concerns motion to or toward and thus should be and is restricted in the locative prepositions it can accept. Landau and Gleitman presented evidence to show that such observational and syntactic evidence provided by a mother of a blind child *taken together*, was sufficient to distinguish the interpretations of the common verbs that this child heard and learned (while neither of these data bases was sufficient by itself).

The hypothesis that children will conjecture verb meanings from subcategorization information has begun to be tested more directly. A first experiment asked whether children will conjecture new meaning components for known verbs if those verbs are used in new syntactic environments (Naigles, Gleitman, and Gleitman, in press). Notice that this question is the converse of Bowerman's question (namely, will children conjecture new syntactic properties for verbs whose meaning is already known). The answer seems to be yes. Two- to four-year-old children were asked to act out (with toys) scenes described by the experimenter, e.g., "The horse comes to the elephant." But some of the sentences were anomalous, e.g., "The horse brings to the giraffe." The known verbs were being used in structures that the child surely had not heard. The children by their actions showed that they knew that *come* in "The elephant comes the giraffe to the ark" is to be interpreted as *bring* and that *bring* in "The elephant brings to the giraffe" is to be interpreted as *come*. They understood the semantic significance of adding or subtracting a noun phrase in sentences with motion verbs. This pertains to whether the causal agent of the motion is being expressed.

Stronger demonstrations of the child's attention to syntactic structure come from studies in which the verbs are entirely new ones. For these studies we adapted the selective looking procedure of Golinkoff and Hirsh-Pasek. The subjects aged 25 to 28 months (children in the very early stages of verb acquisition) were shown two videos of two aspects of a single act, one on a screen to their left and the other on a screen to their right. For example, one screen showed a rabbit and a duck repeatedly bowing to the ground; the other screen showed a standing rabbit forcing a duck into this bowing position. Half the subjects heard *The rabbit is gorping with the duck* while the other half heard *The rabbit is gorping the duck*. The children's looking time to the two screens turned out to be a function of the linguistic stimulus: the causal scene was looked at most when the introducing stimulus was the transitive sentence and vice versa. Thus, the syntactic information acts to focus the child's attention on different aspects (causal or noncausal) of a single observed action (bowing, in the present case). Note that the intransitive stimulus mentions the two words *rabbit* and *duck* in the same sequential order as does the transitive stimulus, so it is rather remarkable that children as young as these pick up the subtle cue to intransitivity provided by *with* in this sentence (Hirsh-Pasek et al., in preparation).

Perhaps the most dramatic demonstration to date shows that young child observers (mean age 25 months) can use syntactic evidence to decide on the meaning of a new verb when the observed scene shows two utterly different acts (Naigles 1987). The children first see a single screen in which a duck and a rabbit are making wheeling motions with their left arms and with his right arm the rabbit is simultaneously forcing the duck into a squatting posture. While they see this screen, half the subjects hear "The rabbit and the duck are gorping" and the other half hear "The rabbit is gorping the duck." This scene is removed from view and then two videos are presented, one showing the two actors performing only the wheeling motion, the other showing the one actor forcing the other to squat. These videos are accompanied by the syntactically uninformative audio "Oh, look! There's gorping! Show me gorping!" The children looked primarily at the video which matched the syntax of the prior introducing sentence. In short, the syntactic information led the learners to decide which of two observed acts was encoded by the new verb *gorp*.

These studies suggest that verb learning—and indeed vocabulary acquisition in general—proceeds in two directions at once. A child provided by nature with the wherewithal to conceive of perceiving and moving and to notice instantiations of such notions in the ongoing scene has taken the first step to distinguish among such verbs as *give* and *see* (and, for that matter, *gorp*); this procedure is sometimes called semantic bootstrapping. But which verb is the adult currently uttering, pertaining to scenes in which both seeing and giving are going on? Crucial clues come from linguistic observation, that is, from observation of the sentences that are being uttered, as represented by their phrase structures. These observations have relevance to the extent that the phrase structures are reasonably straightforward reflexes of the propositions being encoded. A learning procedure that makes use of this evidence might as well be called syntactic bootstrapping (see Landau and Gleitman 1985 for one idea about how such a procedure could be realized).[6]

Both semantic and syntactic bootstrapping are perilous and errorful procedures. Bowerman's children drawing syntactic conclusions from meaningful overlap are sometimes wrong. Errors are made to the extent that the scenes are multiply interpretable, but also because the form-to-meaning mapping in the exposure language is complex and often inexact. For instance, *exit, enter, reach,* and *touch* do not require prepositional phrase complements in English even though they describe directed motion through space (see Jackendoff 1983, 1988). One outcome of this inexact mapping of form onto meaning is errorful learning (e.g., the child may say, "I touched on your arm"). Another is corrective language change (we, but evidently not Shakespeare, find it acceptable to say, "He exited from the stage"). The position we have suggested is that the child to a very satisfactory degree recovers the forms and meanings of the exposure language by playing off the two data bases (the events and the utterances) against each other to derive the best fit between them.

Final Thoughts

We have tried to describe what is known about the child's first representations of the sound wave and of the flux of external stimulation. For the wave forms of speech, current evidence suggests that the learner extracts and represents just the right acoustic properties,

those that are well-correlated with linguistically functioning forma-
tives such as phone, word, phrase, and clause. For the interpretations, the evidence suggests that the child is richly endowed with
flexible strategies for interpreting the external world as it is presented
to her sensorium.

But our major point is that the very flexibility of observation within
the broad bounds established by perception and early conception
poses a new (perhaps we should say "new new") riddle for induction
when taken together with the stimulus-free property of language use.
One can't learn the meanings solely from observation, for the child's
hypothesis space is too large, and the options open to the adult
speaker are too large. There is an almost limitless number of appropriate comments the adult can make about some scene to which her
child is attending. Worse perhaps, the conditions of use give little cue
to the level of specificity at which the speaker is describing the scene
in view. Similar problems obtain for a procedure that attempts to learn
meanings solely from inspection of the semantically relevant syntactic environments. This is because of the variability and unreliability
with which surface structures encode predicate-argument structure.

Despite these formidable barriers, the learner achieves knowledge
of language that is categorical (or close enough), hardly reflecting the
probabilistic and degenerate properties of the two data bases. This is
one more way of acknowledging that the discovery procedure for language is not, and should not be confused with, the knowledge that is
finally attained or the form in which that knowledge is represented.
The discovery procedure itself can be successful only because it ac-
cepts evidence from two imperfect sources, discovering the grammar
in their convergence. We have tried to show that children have no
aversion to learning the meanings from the forms whilst simultaneously learning the forms from the meanings, for the circularity in
this procedure is not vicious. The learners' only desideratum is the
simplest statement of these relations.

How does all this bear on the problem of learning to read? We're
not at all sure that is does. Children surely aren't evolutionarily
adapted to make an analysis of squiggles and squiggle sequences by
eye in the same way that they are adapted to make an analysis of
sounds, words, phrases, and clauses by ear. Indeed, children learning to read find it enormously difficult to note the visual analogs of
phonetic units that they aurally discriminated as neonates. Moreover,
the evidence for structure in the written forms is nowhere near as rich
and restrictive as the information in the sound wave. Written sentences are in the form of a linear string of words, while prosodic information in the speech wave as represented by learners yields a

hierarchical arrangement of the words. In sum, orthographies do not offer the same basis for recovering structure as does spoken input.

Of course, learning to read is not like learning a new language. Rather than constructing a language from the information on the printed page, the learner must conceive the written forms as a code or cipher, a new representation of the old language. Even so, a major subtask is to discover the linguistic units that are physically exhibited by the script. In the case of alphabets, the single symbols directly represent phonetic elements that are quite inaccessible to consciousness. Thus the child's expectations about the categories of a script are violated by the facts about alphabets. In the case of speech, the required analysis is carried out without awareness by an old and evolutionarily adapted system that apparently is in place in the first few days of life. The language that is heard fits the child's innate expectations about the forms, the meanings, and the relations between them.

Notes

This chapter makes significant use of material first presented in Gleitman et al. 1988. We acknowledge with thanks a grant from the University of Pennsylvania Biomedical Research Support Grants (NIH), which supported the writing of this chapter.

1. Some other animals, including macaques and chincillas, have been shown to make the same acoustic discriminations (see Kuhl and Miller 1975). This does not mitigate the usefulness of these discriminations for human language learners. It only suggests that there must be some other reason why macaques don't acquire English.
2. Another possibility has been suggested by Hyams (1986). This is that the varying learning rates are attributable to a morphological distinction among these languages. If the bare verb stem can be a whole word, the inflections are first omitted; if the bare stem does not constitute a whole word in the exposure language, the words appear with inflections from the beginning. This is a very appealing hypothesis, but unfortunately, it does not accord closely enough with the cross-linguistic acquisitional evidence to constitute the whole story. Moreover, Hyam's explanatory principle has to be amplified in terms of the stress/nonstress distinction, for even in languages in which unstressed inflections appear early, they are often not differentiated at first: a single inflected form may be uttered by the child, regardless of case and other distinctions that underlie the choices among the inflectional morphemes of the language. But Hyam's idea is so plausible that we think that it will figure in the final explanation of these phenomena.
3. Adults apparently require this prosodic information as well. Morgan and Newport (1981: see also Morgan, Meier, and Newport, in press) have shown that adults will induce a phrase structure description for a miniature language presented without interpretative cues, but only if structural cues to the phrase boundaries are supplied. In their experiments, physical cues to phrase groupings such as intonation contour (when sentences were presented orally) or physical closeness of within-phrase items (when sentences were presented visually) were necessary and sufficient for induction of the phrase structures. Infants are surely better language learners than adults; the corpora to which they are exposed are neither miniature nor artificial, and their

learning procedures may be different in part from those of adults. Still, these laboratory results indirectly suggest that physical cues to phrase boundaries may be required in the acquisition process.

4. We are using *basic level* as a term that describes a variety of classificatory and labeling preferences that have been observed both in adults and in children. But see, for example, Fodor 1981; Armstrong, Gleitman, and Gleitman 1983; and Landau and Gleitman 1985, chapter 9, for some pessimistic discussion, and queries about whether the label "basic-level term" is explanatory or simply names an unsolved and perhaps unsolvable problem.

5. In the rare case when looking is causal, of course, this structure does become available, e.g., *The shortstop looked the runner back to second base.* The rules and procedures of baseball here assign a causal role to looking. And consider the football comment *The wide receiver looked the ball into his hands.* This case does come close to a claim of psychokinesis.

6. Independent evidence is required to document how strong and refined the semantic information in surface structure may be. If the information isn't there, children can't be using it. Jackendoff (1983) has provided substantial analyses in these terms, particularly for verbs of motion. See Talmy 1983 for further analysis and some cross-language evidence. Fisher, Gleitman, and Gleitman (1988) have tried to provide some experimental demonstrations. For a limited set of verbs they were able to show that a partitioning of the set along semantic lines corresponds to syntactic (subcategorization) distinctions within the set. One group of subjects provided the subcategorization facts about the verbs, by giving judgments of grammaticality for all these items in many syntactic environments. Another group of subjects judged all triads of these verbs, presented without sentential context, for semantic relatedness by discarding the semantic outliner. The number of times two verbs remained together in the contexts of all the other verbs presented with them was taken as the measure of semantic relatedness. The semantic space so constructed (either by multidimensional scaling or cluster analysis) reflected a number of syntactic distinctions, and the factors (or clusters) derived are usually semantically interpretable (for example, as spatial-perception verbs or interpersonal cognition verbs). That is, semantic and syntactic judgments partition the verb set in closely related ways. These findings continue to hold when near synonyms are substituted for the original verb items.

References

Acredolo, L. P., and Evans, D. 1980. Developmental changes in the effects of landmarks on infant spatial behavior. *Developmental Psychology* 16:312–318.

Armstrong, S., Gleitman, L. R., and Gleitman, H. 1983. What some concepts might not be. *Cognition* 13 (3): 263–308.

Baillargeon, R. 1986. Representing the existence and the location of hidden objects: Object permanence in 6- and 8-month-old infants. *Cognition* 20:21–42.

Baillargeon, R., Spelke, E., and Wasserman, S. 1986. Object permanence in five-month-old infants. *Cognition* 20:191–208.

Ball, W. A., and Vurpillot, E. 1976. Perception of movement in depth in infancy. *L'Année psychologique* 76:383–399.

Bates, E., and MacWhinney, B. 1982. Functionalist approaches to grammar. In E. Wanner, and L. R. Gleitman, eds., *Language Acquisition: State of the Art.* New York: Cambridge Univ. Press.

Bellugi, U. 1967. The acquisition of negation. Unpublished Ph.D. thesis, Harvard University.

Bloom, L. 1970. *Language development: form and function in emerging grammars.* Cambridge: MIT Press.

Bloom, L. 1973. *One word at a time.* The Hague: Mouton.

Bloom, L., Lightbown, P., and Hood, L. 1975. Structure and variation in child language. *Monographs of the Society for Research in Child Development.* Serial no. 160.

Bloomfield, L. 1933. *Language.* New York: Holt.

Bond, Z. S. and Garnes, S. 1980. Misperceptions of fluent speech. In R. Cole, ed., *Perception and production of fluent speech.* Hillsdale, N.J.: Erlbaum.

Bowerman, M. 1973. Structural relationships in children's utterances: Syntactic or semantic? In T. E. Moore, ed., *Cognitive development and the acquisition of language.* New York: Academic Press.

Bowerman, M. 1982. Reorganizational processes in lexical and syntactic development. In E. Wanner and L. R. Gleitman, eds., *Language acquisition: The state of the art.* New York: Cambridge Univ. Press.

Braine, M. D. S. 1963. The ontogeny of English phrase structure: The first phase. *Language* 39: 1–14.

Braine, M. D. S. 1976. *Children's first word combinations.* Monographs of the Society for Research in Child Development, 41, serial no. 164.

Braine, M. D. S. and Hardy, J. A. 1982. On what case categories there are, why they are, and how they develop? An amalgam of *a priori* considerations, speculations, and evidence from children. In E. Wanner, and L. R. Gleitman, eds., *Language Acquisition: State of the Art.* New York: Cambridge Univ. Press.

Brown, R. 1957. Linguistic determinism and parts of speech. *Journal of Abnormal and Social Psychology* 55:1–5.

Brown, R. 1973. *A first language.* Cambridge: Harvard Univ. Press.

Brown, R., and Bellugi, U. 1964. Three processes in the child's acquisition of syntax. *Harvard Educational Review.* 34:133–151.

Bruner, J. S. (1974/75). From communication to language: A psychological perspective. *Cognition* 3:255–287.

Carey, S. 1982. Semantic development: The state of the art. In E. Wanner and L. R. Gleitman, ed., *Language acquisition: The state of the art.* New York: Cambridge University Press.

Carey, S. 1985. *Conceptual change in childhood.* Cambridge: MIT Press.

Chomsky, N. 1981. *Lectures on government and binding.* Dordrecht: Foris.

Chomsky, N. 1982. *The generative enterprise: A discussion with Riny Huybregts and Henk van Riemsdijk.* Dordrecht: Foris.

Cooper, W. E., and Paccia-Cooper, J. 1980. *Syntax and speech.* Cambridge: Harvard Univ. Press.

Curtiss, S. 1977. *Genie: A psycholinguistic study of a modern-day "Wild Child."* N.Y.: Academic Press.

Cutler, A., and Foss, D. J. 1977. On the role of sentence stress in sentence processing. *Language and Speech* 20:1–10.

Dorian, N. 1978. The fate of morphological complexity in language death. *Language* 54 (3): 590–609.

Downing, J., ed. 1973. *Comparative reading: Cross-national studies of behavior and processes in reading and writing.* New York: MacMillan.

Downing, J., and Oliver, P. 1973–74. The child's conception of "a word." *Reading Research Quarterly* 9:568–82.

Eimas, P. D. 1975. Auditory and phonetic coding of the cues for speech: Discrimination of the r-l distinction by young infants. *Perception and Psychophysics* 18:341–357.

Eimas, P. D., Siqueland, E. R., Jusczyk, P., and Vigorito, J. 1971. Speech perception in infants. *Science* 171:303–306.

Elkonin, D. B. 1973. In J. Downing, ed., *Cross-national studies of behavior and processes in reading and writing.* New York: MacMillan.

Field, J. 1976. Relation of young infants' reaching to stimulus distance and solidity. *Child Development* 50:698–704.

Feldman, H., Goldin-Meadow, S., and Gleitman, L. R. 1978. Beyond Herodotus: The creation of language by linguistically deprived deaf children. In A. Lock, ed., *Action, symbol, and gesture: The emergence of language.* New York: Academic Press.

Fernald, A. 1984. The perceptual and affective salience of mothers' speech to infants. In L. Feagans, C. Garvey, and R. Golinkoff, eds., *The origins and growth of communication.* New Brunswick, N.J.: Ablex Corp.

Firth, I. 1972. Components of reading disability. Unpublished doctoral dissertation, Univ. of New South Wales, Kensington, N.S.W., Australia.

Fisher, C., Gleitman, H., and Gleitman, L. R. 1988. Syntactic-semantic correlations in the organization of English verbs: An experimental investigation. Unpublished manuscript, Univ. of Pennsylvania, Philadelphia.

Fodor, J. A. 1981. The present status of the innateness controversy. In J. A. Fodor, *Representations.* Cambridge: MIT Press, Bradford Books.

Garnica, O. K. 1977. Some prosodic and paralinguistic features of speech to young children. In C. Snow and C. A. Ferguson, eds., *Talking to children: Language input and acquisition.* Cambridge: Cambridge University Press.

Garrett, M. 1975. The analysis of sentence production. In G. H. Bower, ed., *The psychology of learning and motivation,* vol. 9. New York: Academic Press.

Gelman, R. 1986. First principles for structuring acquisition. Presidential address to division 7 of the American Psychological Assn.

Gelman, R., and Gallistel, C. R. 1979. *The young child's understanding of numbers: A window on early cognitive development.* Cambridge: Harvard University Press.

Gentner, D. 1982. Why nouns are learned before verbs: Linguistic relativity vs. natural partitioning. In S. Kuczaj, ed., *Language development: Language, culture, and cognition.* Hillsdale, N.J.: Erlbaum.

Gibson, E. J., and Spelke, E. 1983. The development of perception. In J. H. Flavell and E. Markman, eds., *Cognitive Development,* vol. 3 of P. H. Mussen, ed., *Handbook of Cognitive Psychology.* New York: Wiley.

Gibson, E. J., and Walker, A. S. 1984. Intermodal perception of substance. *Child Development* 55: 453–460.

Gleitman H., and Gleitman, L. R. 1979. Language use and language judgment. In C. J. Fillmore, D. Kempler, and W. S. Wang, eds., *Individual differences in language ability and language behavior.* New York: Academic Press.

Gleitman, L. R. 1985. Orthographic resources affect reading acquisition—if they are used. *Reading and Special Education* 6 (6): 24–36.

Gleitman, L. R. 1986. Biological dispositions to learn language. In A. Marras and W. Demopoulos, eds., *Language learnability and concept acquisition.* New Brunswick, N.J.: Ablex Corp.

Gleitman, L. R., and Gleitman, H. 1970. *Phrase and paraphrase.* New York: W. W. Norton Co.

Gleitman, L. R., Gleitman, H., Landau, B., and Wanner, E. 1988. Where learning begins: Initial representations for language learning. In F. Newmeyer, ed., *The Cambridge linguistic survey.* New York: Cambridge University Press.

Gleitman, L. R., Newport, E. L., and Gleitman, H. 1984. The current status of the motherese hypothesis. *Journal of Child Language* 11 (1): 43–80.

Gleitman, L. R., and Rozin, P. 1973. Teaching reading by use of a syllabary. *Reading Research Quarterly* 8: 447–83.

Gleitman, L. R., and Rozin, P. 1977. The structure and acquisition of reading. I: Relations between orthographies and the structure of language. In A. S. Reber and D. L. Scarborough, *Toward a psychology of reading*. Hillsdale, N.J.: Erlbaum.

Gleitman, L. R., and Wanner, E. 1982. Language acquisition: The state of the state of the art. In E. Wanner and L. R. Gleitman, eds., *Language Acquisition: State of the Art*. New York: Cambridge Univ. Press.

Gold, E. M. 1967. Language identification in the limit. *Information and Control* 10: 447–474.

Goldin-Meadow, S., and Feldman, H. 1979. The development of language-like communication without a language model. *Science* 197: 401–403.

Golinkoff, R. M., Harding, C. G., Carlson, V., and Sexton, M. E. 1984. The infant's perception of causal events: The distinction between animate and inanimate objects. In L. P. Lipsitt and C. Rovee-Collier, eds., *Advances in infancy research* 3:145–165.

Golinkoff, R. M., Pasek, H. P., Cauley, K., and Gordon, L. In press. The eyes have it: Lexical and syntactic comprehension in a new paradigm. *Journal of Child Language*.

Grimshaw, J. 1981. Form, function, and the language acquisition device. In C. L. Baker and J. J. McCarthy, eds., *The logical problem of language acquisition*. Cambridge: MIT Press.

Grosjean, F., and Gee, J. P. 1987. Prosodic structure and spoken word acquisition. *Cognition* 25 (1–2): 135–56.

Hirsh-Pasek, K., Gleitman, H., Gleitman, L. R., Golinkoff, R., and Naigles, L. In preparation. Syntactic influences on scene observation.

Hirsh-Pasek, K., Gleitman, L. R., and Gleitman, H. 1978. What did the brain say to the mind? Detection and report of ambiguity by young children. In A. Sinclair, R. J. Jarvella, and W. J. M. Levelt, eds., *The child's conception of language*. Berlin: Springer-Verlag.

Hirsh-Pasek, K., Golinkoff, R., Fletcher, A., DeGaspe-Beaubien, F., and Cauley, K. 1985. In the beginning: One-word speakers comprehend word order. Paper presented at the Boston Language Conference, October 1985.

Hirsh-Pasek, K., Kemler-Nelson, D. G., Jusczyk, P. W., Cassidy, K. W., Druss, B., and Kennedy, L. 1987. Clauses are perceptual units for young infants. *Cognition* 26 (3): 269–286.

Hirsh-Pasek, K., Kemler-Nelson, D. G., Jusczyk, P. W., Woodward, A., Piwez, J., and Kennedy, L. 1987. The perception of major phrase boundaries by prelinguistic infants. Manuscript, Swarthmore College, Swarthmore, Pa.

Holden, M. H., and MacGinitie, W. H. 1972. Children's conceptions of word boundaries in speech and print. *Journal of Educational Psychology* 63: 551–557.

Hyams, N. 1986. *Language acquisition and the theory of parameters*. Dordrecht, Holland: D. Reidel Publishing Co.

Jackendoff, R. 1983. *Semantics and cognition*. Cambridge: MIT Press.

Jackendoff, R. 1988. Babe Ruth homered his way into the hearts of America. Unpublished manuscript, Brandeis Univ., Waltham, Mass.

Johnson, J., and Newport, E. 1986. Critical period effects in second language learning: The influence of maturational state on the acquisition of English as a second language. Speech delivered at the Boston Child Language Conference, October 1986.

Jusczyk, P. W. 1986. A review of speech perception work. In L. Kaufman, J. Thomas, and K. Boff, ed., *Handbook of perception and performance*. New York: Wiley.

Katz, N., Baker, E., and MacNamara, J. 1974. What's in a name? A study of how children learn common and proper names. *Child Development* 45: 469–473.

Kean, M. L. 1979. Agrammatism: A phonological deficit? *Cognition* 7 (1): 69–84.

Keil, F. 1979. *Semantic and conceptual development*. Cambridge: Harvard University Press.

Klatt, D. H. 1975. Vowel lengthening is syntactically determined in a connected discourse. *Journal of Phonetics* 3:229–240.

Klatt, D. H. 1976. Linguistic uses of segmental duration in English: Acoustic and perceptual evidence. *Journal of the Acoustic Society of America* 59:1208–1221.

Klatt, D.H., and Cooper, W. E. 1975. Perception of segment duration in sentence contexts. In A. Cohen and S. Nooteboom, eds., *Structure and process in speech perception*. Heidelberg: Springer-Verlag.

Kuhl, P. K. 1983. Perception of auditory and equivalence classes for speech by infants. *Infant Behavior and Development* 6:263–285.

Kuhl, P. K., and Miller, J. D. 1975. Speech perception by the chinchilla: Voiced-voiceless distinction in alveolar plosive consonants. *Science* 190:69–72.

Landau, B., and Gleitman, L. R. 1985. *Language and experience: Evidence from the blind child*. Cambridge: Harvard Univ. Press.

Lasky, R. E., and Gogol, W. C. 1978. The perception of relative motion by young infants. *Perception* 7:617–623.

Lehiste, I., Olive, J. P., and Streeter, L. A. 1976. The role of duration in disambiguating syntactically ambiguous sentences. *Journal of the Acoustical Society of America* 60:1199–1202.

Leong, C. K. 1973. Hong Kong. In J. Downing, ed., *Comparative reading: Cross-national studies of behavior and processes in reading and writing*. New York: MacMillan.

Levy, L. S. and Joshi, A. K. 1978. Skeletal structural descriptions. *Information and Control* 5: 3–5.

Liberman, I. Y. 1970. Segmentation of the spoken word and reading acquisition. *Bulletin of the Orton Society* 23:65–77.

Liberman, I. Y., Shankweiler, D., Liberman, A., Fowler, C., and Fischer, L. 1977. Phonetic segmentation and recoding in the beginning reader. In A. S. Reber and D. S. Scarborough, eds., *Toward a psychology of reading*. Hillsdale, N.J.: Erlbaum.

Liberman, M., and Prince, A. 1977. On stress and linguistic rhythm. *Linguistic Inquiry* 8:249–336.

Luce, P. A., and Charles-Luce, J. 1983. Contextual effects on the consonant/vowel ratio in speech production. Paper presented at the 105th meeting of the Acoustical Society of America, Cincinatti, May.

Lust, B. 1986. *Studies in the acquisition of anaphora*. Vol. 1, *Defining the constraints*. Dordrecht: Reidel.

MacNamara, J. 1972. Cognitive basis for language learning in infants. *Psychological Review* 79:1–13.

Maratsos, M. 1982. The child's construction of grammatical categories. In E. Wanner and L. R. Gleitman, eds., *Language acquisition: The state of the art*. New York: Cambridge Univ. Press.

Maratsos, M., and Chalkley, M. A. 1980. The internal language of children's syntax: The ontogenesis and representation of syntactic categories. In K. Nelson, ed., *Children's language*, vol 2. New York: Gardner Press.

Markman, E. M. 1986. How children constrain the possible meanings of words. In N. Neisser, ed., *The ecological and intellectual basis of categorization*. Cambridge: Cambridge Univ. Press.

Markman, E. M., and Hutchinson, J. E. 1984. Children's sensitivity of constraints on word meaning: Taxonomic versus thematic relations. *Cognitive Psychology* 16 (1): 1–27.

Mehler, J., Bertoncini, J., Barriere, M., and Jassik-Gerschenfeld, D. 1978. Infant recognition of mother's voice. *Perception* 7:491–497.

Mehler, J., Jusczyk, P., Lambertz, G., Halsted, N., Bertoncini, J., and Amiel-Tison, C. 1988. A precursor of language acquisition in young infants. *Cognition* 29 (2): 143–178.

Mervis, C. B., and Crisafi, M. 1978. Order of acquisition of subordinate, basic, and superordinate level categories. *Child Development* 49 (4): 988–998.

Milewski, A. E., and Genovese, C. M. 1980. The effects of stimulus movement on visual attention processes on one- and three-month infants. Paper presented at the International Conference on Infant Studies, New Haven, Conn., April.

Morgan, J. 1986. *From simple input to complex grammar.* Cambridge: MIT Press.

Morgan, J., Meier, R., and Newport, E. L. In Press. Structural packaging in the input to language learning: Contributions of intonational and morphological marking of phrases to the acquisition of language. *Cognitive Psychology.*

Morgan, J., and Newport, E. L. 1981. The role of constituent structure in the induction of an artificial language. *Journal of Verbal Learning and Verbal Behavior* 20:67–85.

Naigles, L. 1988. Syntactic bootstrapping as a procedure for verb learning. Unpublished Ph.D. dissertation, Univ. of Pennsylvania.

Naigles, L., Gleitman, H., and Gleitman, L. R. In Press. Children conjecture verb meaning components from syntactic evidence. In E. Dromi, ed., *Language and Conceptual Change.* New Brunswick, N.J.: Ablex.

Nakatani, L., and Dukes, K., 1977. Locus of segmental cues for word juncture. *Journal of the Acoustic Society of America* 62 (3): 714–724.

Nakatani, L., and Schaffer, J. 1978. Hearing "words" without words: Prosodic cues for word perception. *Journal of the Acoustic Society of America* 63 (1): 234–245.

Nelson, K. 1974. Concept, word, and sentence: Interrelations in acquisition and development. *Psychological Review* 81: 267–285.

Newport, E. L. 1977. Motherese: The speech of mothers to young children. In N. Castellan, D. Pisoni, and G. Potts, eds., *Cognitive theory,* vol. 2, Hillsdale, N.J.: Erlbaum.

Newport, E. L. 1988. Maturational constraints in language learning. Manuscript, University of Illinois.

Newport, E. L., and Supalla, T. In press. A critical period effect in the acquisition of a primary language. *Science.*

Ninio, A. 1980. Ostensive definition in vocabulary teaching. *Journal of Child Language* 7 (3): 565–574.

Pinker, S. 1984. *Language learnability and language development.* Cambridge: Harvard Univ. Press.

Pye, C. 1983. Mayan telegraphese. *Language* 59 (3): 583–604.

Rescorla, L. 1980. Overextension in early language development. *Journal of Child Language* 7 (2): 321–336.

Rosch, E. 1978. Principles of categorization. In E. Rosch and B. Lloyd, ed., *Cognition and categorization.* Hillsdale, N.J.: Erlbaum.

Rosner, J. 1971. *Phonic analysis training and beginning reading skills.* Learning Research and Development Center, University of Pittsburgh publication 1971/19.

Rosner, J. 1974. Auditory analysis training with prereaders. *The Reading Teacher* 27:379–384.

Rosner, J., and Simon, D. P. 1971. *The auditory analysis test: An initial report.* Learning Research and Development Center. University of Pittsburgh publication 1971/3.

Rozin, P., Bressman, B., and Taft, M. 1974. Do children understand the basic relationship between speech and writing? The mow/motorcycle test. *Journal of Reading Behavior* 6:327–334.

Rozin, P., and Gleitman, L. R. 1977. The structure and acquisition of reading. II: The reading process and the acquisition of the alphabetic principle. In A. S. Reber and D. Scarborough, ed., *Toward a psychology of reading*. Hillsdale, N.J.: Erlbaum.

Rozin, P., Poritsky, S., and Sotsky, R. 1967. American children with reading problems can easily learn to read English represented by Chinese characters. *Science* 171:1264–1267.

Sankoff, G., and LaBerge, S. 1973. On the acquisition of native speakers by a language. *Kivung* 6:32–47.

Shankweiler, D., and Liberman, I. Y. 1972. Misreading: A search for causes. In J. F. Kavanagh and I. G. Mattingly, ed., *Language by ear and by eye: The relationships between speech and reading*. Cambridge: MIT Press.

Slobin, D. I. 1966. The acquisition of Russian as a native language. In F. Smith and C. A. Miller, eds., *The genesis of language*. Cambridge: MIT Press.

Slobin, D. I. 1973. Cognitive prerequisites for the development of grammar. In C. A. Ferguson and D. I. Slobin, ed., *Studies of child language development*. New York: Holt, Rinehart, and Winston.

Slobin, D. I. 1975. On the nature of talk to children. In E. H. Lenneberg and E. Lenneberg, eds., *Foundations of language development*, vol. 1. New York: Academic Press.

Slobing, D. I. 1982. Universal and particular in the acquisition of language. In E. Wanner and L. R. Gleitman, ed., *Language acquisition: The state of the art*. New York: Cambridge University Press.

Slobin, D. I. 1987. *The cross-linguistic study of language acquisition*. Hillsdale, N.J.: Erlbaum.

Slobin, D. I., and Bever, T. G. 1982. Children use canonical sentence schemas: A cross-linguistic study of word order and inflections. *Cognition* 12:229–265.

Spelke, E. S. 1979. Perceiving bimodally specified events in infancy. *Developmental Psychology* 15:626–636.

Spelke, E. S. 1982. Perceptual knowledge of objects in infancy. In J. Mehler, E. C. T. Walker, and M. Garrett, ed., *Perspectives on mental representations*. Hillsdale, N.J.: Erlbaum.

Spelke, E. S., and Born, W. S. 1982. Perception of visible objects by three-month-old infants. Unpublished manuscript.

Spring, D. R., and Dale, P. S. 1977. Discrimination of linguistic stress in early infancy. *Journal of Speech and Hearing Research* 20:224–231.

Starkey, P., Gelman, R., and Spelke, E. S. 1983. Detection of 1–1 correspondences by human infants. *Science* 210:1033–1035.

Streeter, L. A. 1978. Acoustic determinants of phrase boundary perception. *Journal of the Acoustic Society of America* 64: 1582–1592.

Thorndike, R. L. 1971. Reading as reasoning: A study of mistakes in paragraph reading. *Journal of Educational Psychology* 8:323–332.

Walker, A. S., Owsley, C. J., Megaw-Nyce, J. S., Gibson, E. J., and Bahrick, L. E. 1980. Detection of elasticity as an invariant property of objects by young infants. *Perception* 9:713–718.

Waxman, S., and Gelman, R. 1986. Preschoolers' use of superordinate relations in classification. *Cognitive Development* 1:139–156.

Wexler, K., and Culicover, P. 1980. *Formal principles of language acquisition*. Cambridge: MIT Press.

Wexler, K., and Manzini, R. 1987. Parameters and learnability in binding theory. In T. Roeper and E. Williams, ed., *Parameter setting*. Dordrecht, Holland: Reidel.

Editor's Comments

It is indeed a great puzzle that human infants learn their first languages despite the fact, amply documented in this scholarly paper, that the environmental stimulus is so confusing. Researchers by and large conclude that there must be an innate capacity to approach the task in a predetermined way, a capacity that helps the infant dispense with the myriad possibilities for analyzing environmental stimuli and without which there would be no language acquisition at all. Neuroscientists cannot at the present time offer any explanations as to how this innate capacity is expressed in the brain structure or how it changes after acquiring a language.

Yet the learning of language may not be altogether different from the learning of other biological skills (others have discussed this analogy). For instance, at first exposure to the hostile extrauterine environment, the infant must manufacture antibodies against foreign chemicals for self preservation. The chemical environment is continuous, albeit inhomogenous, and for survival some of it is segmented, categorized, stressed, and recognized in very specific ways for making antibodies against it, while much of it remains uncategorized, unstressed, and even unnoticed (e.g., foodstuffs, vitamins, medicines). In fact, giving meaning to, or learning the meaning of, inappropriate segments of the chemical environment leads to trouble (allergy and autoimmunity).

The normal genome must code for the ability to know a priori which of the chemical segments and categories are likely to be meaningful and which are meaningless. This knowledge, which is present in the code, must have been established during phylogeny when distinctions between hostile and friendly chemical categories first became apparent. But the evolution of the immune system is another story that is as poorly understood as it is for language. Suffice it to say that the environment must have played a role in the establishment of innate immunological capacities and must retain the ability to continue to influence the organism for further evolutionary changes. Protochemical interactions between organism and environment determined the evolution of immunological genes, but what sort of protolanguage interactions between organism and environment might have lead to extant innate linguistic brain structures?

Antibodies must be manufactured against any foreign chemical capable of harming the organism. Moreover antibodies are even made for some synthetic chemicals that do not exist as natural products and so the organism cannot previously have been exposed to them in evolutionary time. (This is perhaps akin to our ability to learn natural languages and artificial languages.) How is this accomplished? It was once argued that the young organism did this simply by having available an antibody prototype capable of changing, adapting, and molding itself to a foreign chemical, in other words, of deriving information for the chemical that leads to changes in its configuration. As long as the offending chemical exhibited some salient feature compatible with eliciting an immunological response, e.g., natural or artificially generated sequences of amino acids, the primitive could conform to it. Clearly, the primitive cannot conform to just anything, because of its genetically predetermined chemical structure, and therein lies the innate propensities of the system.

Though this hypothesis was attractive because it was capable of handling the problem of artificial chemicals, it was wrong. It became clear not long ago that no primitives would be identified. Instead, the young organism has at its disposal a specific antibody for nearly every potentially noxious chemical, natural or artificial, with which it might come into contact. Although it seemed at first unreasonable that the body carried around copies of antibodies against imaginary antigens, it wasn't, for the antigens still needed to conform to a predetermined chemical class, a fact that limited the number of antigens to a large but manageable size. Furthermore, it was necessary to build a system that could cope with newly created noxious chemicals (such as those created by viruses, for instance).

In the latter scheme an immunogenic chemical on exposure simply selected the appropriate antibody and stimulated its replication. Immunological capability thus resulted from matching the offending chemical with one of the members of the antibody repertoire, followed by stabilization, reinforcement, and maintenance of the cells that produced that antibody. Immunogenesis takes place by matching and selection, not by instruction.

We might propose a similar process for the acquisition of language. The brain has been phylogenetically prepared for the aural environment so that potential matches between brain and salient aspects of the environmental stimulus preexist in the brain. The brain does not have to start from ground zero, so the input need not have a full set of instructions. Rather, exposure to natural languages realizes the predetermined match, and the anatomical structures are then stabilized, reinforced, and maintained. As with the immune system for the chemical environment, the nervous system must contain templates for any of the sensory stimuli that belong to the predetermined group in order to cope with new, open-class words of the native language and with other natural languages. For obvious reasons of space the number of templates in the nervous system has to be limited, although it can be very large indeed if the templates exist at the molecular level rather than the cellular or network levels. What inevitably comes from this proposal, among other things, is that even open-class words must be limited in number and are better thought of as members of a large and probably huge closed-class family.

Another important point raised by the present paper has to do with the role of the input in determining the ease or difficulty of learning a particular cognitive task. Clearly the nature of the input will partly determine how quickly and strongly a match between environmental structure and brain structure is achieved. Yet it is also clear that the match will depend in part on the state of the brain itself.

We know that already quite early in life brain architecture varies from region to region, but we do not fully know whether the innate capacity for matching linguistically relevant sensory stimuli is equivalent for all types of input, e.g., auditory, visual, somesthetic (we suspect that this is to a large extent the case on the basis of comparisons between the acquisition of sign language and oral language, but more needs to be known).

Furthermore, we do not know what happens to the brain after a first language is learned. It is possible that learning the first language changes the innate capacity of the machinery for learning a second language. This would suggest, as some researchers contend, that true bilingualism is not possible. Indeed, few would argue against the claim that bilingualism becomes progressively more difficult with age, thus suggesting chronological changes in the machinery. Certainly the richness of the stimulus does not seriously change from language to language.

Learning to read touches on both the heterogeneity of brain organization and the chronology. The areas of the brain affected by reading differ from those affected by the oral language, and in most instances reading is learned years after the oral language is acquired. Enriching the nature of the script is likely to increase the chances for a quicker and more efficient match between input and brain (a fact that is realized by methods of special reading education). In any case, the state of the brain will continue to play an important role.

Although issues about the nature of the stimulus have a tangible role to play in partially explaining differences between oral and reading language acquisition in ordinary children, they offer no explanation of the origin of developmental dyslexia. Children affected with this disorder demonstrate difficulties with oral as well as written language, difficulties that implicate the brain itself unless one can demonstrate that the stimuli are degraded in oral and written language input in these children (but such widespread sensory abnormalities have not been shown). As suggested by the findings reviewed in the present chapter, the differences in the nature of the input between oral and written language likely cause these two areas of language functioning to be affected differently in dyslexics, the oral language being functionally more intact.

Chapter 6

Dyslexia: Perspectives From Sign and Script

Ursula Bellugi, Ovid Tzeng, Edward S. Klima, and Angela Fok

1 Introduction

The term dyslexia is commonly applied to reading difficulties of two very different kinds: acquired and developmental. Generally, acquired dyslexia refers to disruption of reading performance after brain damage to an adult, who presumably was a normal fluent reader before the lesion. Depending upon the site and degree of damage, acquired dyslexic patients usually suffer other types of speech or general cognitive deficiencies in addition to their reading disorder. In contrast, developmental dyslexia is a term used for children who seem to have a specific difficulty in learning to read and spell, despite seemingly normal or above average intelligence and an adequate intellectual, social, and emotional background.

Ever since the seminal work of Marshall and Newcombe (1973), research on acquired dyslexia has attracted considerable attention. Theoretical proposals involving information processing models based on the analysis of normal adult reading have been intensively sought and vigorously tested on a small number of carefully selected patients. Similarly, work on developmental dyslexia has been equally intensive in recent years. There have been important findings of distinctive anatomic abnormalities in postmortem analysis of the brains of several male dyslexic subjects (Galaburda et al. 1985; Galaburda 1988), the 4 to 1 ratio of male versus female left-handers associated with dyslexia (Crowder 1982), and the localization of a particular gene on chromosome 15 in members of families in which there is a history of reading disorder (Vellutino 1987; Lubs et al. 1988). The diagnosis of developmental dyslexia is generally one of exclusion: the failure of an individual of normal or superior intelligence with no visual, auditory, social, or psychiatric handicaps to learn to read normally. Some posit a visuospatial deficit as a basis for developmental dyslexia (Orton 1928, 1937); others posit a deficit in auditory phonetic processing as a basis for language delay and developmental dyslexia (Tallal et al. 1988; Shankweiler and Crain 1986); and still others suggest a central linguistic deficit. Research on children with normal intelligence but impaired reading ability is currently very lively and somewhat controversial.

We propose here to examine some related issues that may in the long run cast some light on questions relevant to dyslexia by investigating groups of individuals who have difficulties in learning (or relearning) to read that stem from different sources. In recent years collaborative work in the laboratories of the Salk Institute, the University of California at Riverside, the University of California at San Diego, and the University of Hong Kong has included the study of linguistic systems that rely heavily on the visuospatial modality for their forms of expression. One set of studies focuses on the primary linguistic systems passed down from one generation to the next of deaf signers, the primary sign language (of which American Sign Language [ASL] is an example). Another set of studies focuses on visuospatial scripts exemplified by the Chinese writing system. A third set examines the deaf child's visual approach to script. In this paper, we will address issues relevant to the neural basis for primary and secondary linguistic systems in the visuospatial modality. Experimental results from such studies may broaden our understanding of reading processes and indirectly shed light on aspects of developmental dyslexia.

2   *Sign Language: A Primary Visual Language*

Until recently nearly everything learned about the human capacity for language has come from the study of spoken languages. The complex organizational properties of languages have traditionally been assumed to be intimately connected with the production and processing of vocally articulated sounds (Liberman 1982). In research over the past few decades, however, studies comparing signed languages with spoken languages have aimed at specifying the ways in which the formal properties of languages are shaped by their modalities of expression, sifting properties peculiar to a particular language mode from more general properties common to all languages (Klima and Bellugi 1979; Bellugi and Studdert-Kennedy 1980). The subject population in these studies is limited to the 5 to 10 percent of profoundly deaf people born to deaf parents who have learned a signed language as a primary linguistic system and have grown up within deaf communities. Among this special population there are primary gestural systems passed down from one generation of deaf people to the next. It thus becomes clear that the human capacity for language is not limited to the vocal, auditory mode and that in the absence of hearing, an independent visual, gestural language has developed across generations.

The Structure of American Sign Language

We have found that ASL has been forged into an autonomous language with its own internal mechanisms for relating visual form to meaning (Klima and Bellugi 1979; Bellugi, Poizner, and Klima, in press). ASL has evolved linguistic mechanisms that are not derived from those of English (or any other spoken language) and thus offers a new perspective on the determinants of language form. ASL shares underlying principles of organization with spoken languages, but the instantiation of those principles occurs in formal devices arising out of the very different possibilities offered by the visual, gestural modality (Bellugi 1980; Bellugi 1988).

Like spoken languages ASL exhibits formal structures at two levels: the internal structure of the lexical sign and the grammatical scaffolding underlying sentences. But unlike spoken languages ASL displays a marked preference for layered organization (as opposed to linear organization); grammatical mechanisms exploit the possibility of simultaneous and multidimensional articulation. In ASL morphology, root, derivational patterns, and inflectional patterns cooccur as layered in the final surface form, and forms can be spatially nested within one another (figure 6.1a). Signed languages, unlike spoken languages, make structured use of space at all linguistic levels. Many syntactic functions fulfilled in spoken languages by word order or case marking are expressed in ASL by spatial mechanisms. For example, a nominal introduced into ASL discourse may be assigned an arbitrary locus in a plane of signing space. A pronominal sign directed toward that locus clearly refers back to the previously mentioned nominal, even with many other signs intervening. The ASL system of verb agreement is also in essence spatialized (figure 1b). Verb signs for a large class of verbs move between the abstract loci in signing space, bearing grammatical markers for person and number via spatial indices and thereby specifying subject and object (Lillo-Martin and Klima, in press). This spatialized system thus allows explicit reference through pronominals and agreement markers to multiple distinct third-person referents. The use of spatial loci for referential indexing, verb agreement, and grammatical relations is most evident in complex embedded structures; this spatialized organization is clearly a unique property of visual, gestural systems.

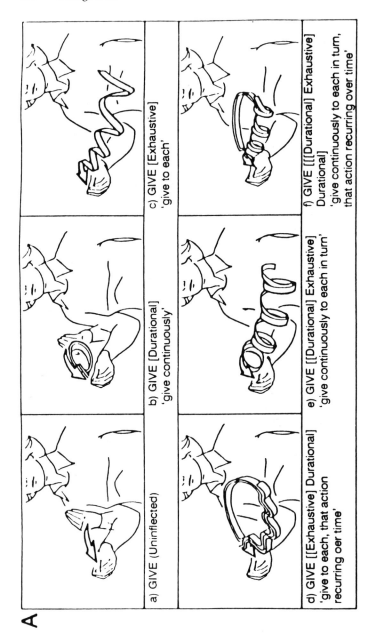

A

a) GIVE (Uninflected)

b) GIVE [Durational]
'give continuously'

c) GIVE [Exhaustive]
'give to each'

d) GIVE [[Exhaustive] Durational]
'give to each, that action
recurring oer time'

e) GIVE [[Durational] Exhaustive]
'give continuously to each in turn'

f) GIVE [[[Durational] Exhaustive]
Durational]
'give continuously to each in turn,
that action recurring over time'

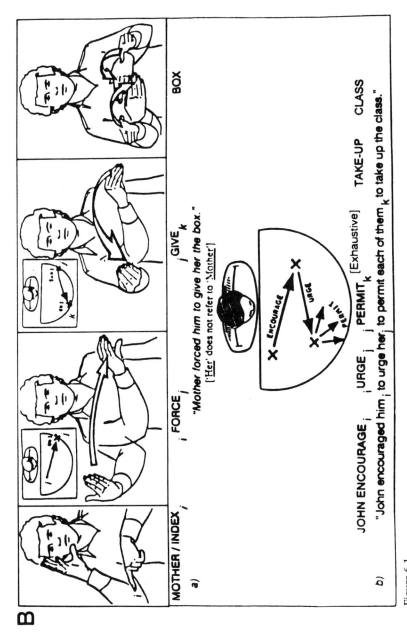

Figure 6.1
ASL layered morphology and spatially organized syntax.[1]

Properties of signed languages   Studies of Chinese Sign Language (CSL) provide a direct way of examining the independence of signed language from spoken language, and the issue of the relationship between modality of transmission and the surface form of language (Fok et al., 1988). These studies show that signs within a sign language indeed exhibit formational constraints specific to individual sign languages (Fok and Bellugi 1988). Thus, signed languages are constrained not merely by motor limitations on handshapes, locations, and movements nor by general visual constraints but also in ways that are far less predictable and language-specific. Certain handshapes, locations, and movements occur in one sign language but not in another. Furthermore, some parametric values may be common to two signed languages and yet show fine-detailed consistent differences from one sign language to another. Internal, patterned relationships of this kind within sign languages suggest that signed languages are tightly constrained, even at the level of formational elements. The systematization of language occurs anew in languages produced by the hands and perceived by eyes (Fok, Bellugi, and Lillo-Martin 1986). Moreover, studies of CSL show that it exhibits the same principles of grammatical patterning as ASL, although they are completely distinct mutually unintelligible signed languages. As in ASL the grammatical patterning that has arisen in CSL is heavily conditioned by the modality in which the language develops. Both signed languages are predominantly multilayered with respect to form with differences in levels of grammatical structure mirrored by differences in layers of form, and both have complex, spatially organized syntax.

The Acquisition of a Primary Visuospatial Language

Language acquisition in deaf children of deaf parents exposed to a signed language as a primary linguistic system has been investigated in great depth and widely reported (Bellugi and Klima 1982; Newport and Meier 1986; among others). We have been investigating the acquisition of the spatial mechanisms of the language and the separable structural systems they embody in deaf children of deaf parents who are learning sign language as a primary linguistic system. The study of the acquisition of ASL in deaf children thus brings into focus some questions about the representation of language and the representation of space in the developing brain.

Because visual, gestural languages are remarkably unlike spoken languages in their surface form, one might expect to find that sign language is acquired in ways radically different from spoken languages. In fact, the similarity in the acquisition of signed and spoken language as primary linguistic systems is remarkable. The differences that do appear may reflect the spatial nature of sign-language organization. We shall mention some developments in the acquisition of the spatial mechanisms of ASL by deaf children of deaf parents, including pronominal reference, the morphological inflections associated with verb agreement, and the syntactic system of referential spatial indexing (see also Bellugi 1988; Bellugi and Klima 1982; Lillo-Martin 1986).

Inflections: Spatial verb agreement   The function of the ASL system of verb agreement is like that of many spoken languages, but the form of verb agreement in ASL requires that the signer mark connections between spatial loci. Around the age of two deaf children begin using uninflected signs, even when imitating their mothers' inflected signs and even in cases where the adult grammar requires marking for person and number. Although they are perceiving complexly inflected forms, deaf children begin (as do hearing children learning English or any of many other spoken languages) by analyzing out the uninflected stems. By the age of three deaf children have learned the basic aspects of verb morphology in ASL (inflections for person, for temporal aspect, and for number). At this age they make overgeneralizations to uninflected verbs, analogous to "eated" and "goed" in the speech of hearing children. Such errors reveal the child's analysis of forms across the system (Bellugi 1988). Despite the difference in the form of spatial marking, the development and the age of mastery of the spatial inflection for verb agreement is the same in ASL as for comparable processes in spoken languages.

Spatially organized syntax and discourse   The integration of pronominal reference and spatial verb agreement in sentences of and discourse in ASL is highly complex. When deaf children first attempt indexing verbs to arbitrary locus points in space, they sometimes incorrectly index verbs for different referents to a single locus point. By the age of five, however, deaf children give the appropriate spatial index to nearly every nominal and pronoun that requires one, and almost all verbs show appropriate agreement. The deaf child, like his hearing counterpart, extracts discrete components of the language presented to him across a range of linguistic subsystems. Furthermore, the evidence suggests that even when the modality and the language offer possibilities that seem intuitively obvious or transparent (pointing for pronominal reference, for example), deaf children ignore this directness and analyze the language input as part of a formal linguistic system (Bellugi 1988; Petitto 1988). The young deaf child faced in sign language with the dual task of spatial perception, memory, and spatial transformations on the one hand and processing grammatical structure on the other, all in one and the same visual event (Stiles-Davis, Kritchevsky, and Bellugi 1988). Studies of the acquisition process have found that deaf and hearing children show a strikingly similar course of development if exposed to a natural language at the critical time. These data thus dramatically underscore the biological substrate of the human capacity for creating linguistic systems. Such findings powerfully show how language, independent of its means of transmission, emerges in the child in a rapid, patterned, and above all linguistically driven manner.

Brain Organization for Sign Language in Deaf Signers
ASL displays complex linguistic structure comparable to that found in spoken languages but conveys much of its structure by manipulating spatial relations. ASL thus exhibits properties for which each of the hemispheres of hearing people shows a different predominant functioning. The study of deaf signers with unilateral left or right cerebral lesions offers a particularly revealing vantage point for understanding the organization of higher cognitive functions in the brain and how modifiable that organization may be (Bellugi 1983; Poizner, Klima, and Bellugi 1987). The broad aim of these studies is to investigate the relative contributions of the cerebral hemispheres, with special reference to the interplay between linguistic functions and the spatial mechanisms that convey them in profoundly deaf people whose primary mode of communication is a visuospatial language.

The language capacities of left- versus right-lesioned deaf signers   We have intensively analyzed six deaf signers with unilateral brain damage either to the left hemisphere or to the right hemisphere (Bellugi, Klima, and Poizner 1988; Bellugi, Poizner, and Klima 1983, in press; Klima, Bellugi, and Poizner 1988; Poizner, Klima, and Bellugi 1987). The signers with left hemisphere damage showed frank sign-language aphasias and had relatively preserved nonlanguage spatial functions. One left-hemisphere damaged signer was agrammatic for ASL. Her signing was severely impaired, halting, and effortful, reduced often to single sign utterances, and completely without the syntactic and morphological markings of ASL. Her lesion was typical of those that produce agrammatic aphasia in spoken language. The other two left-hemisphere damaged signers had fluent sign aphasias but differed in the nature of their impairments. A second left-lesioned signer was completely grammatical in her poststroke signing, although she made selection errors in the formational elements of her signs, producing the equivalent of phonemic paraphasias in her sign language. Her signing, while grammatical, was sometimes vague, as she often omitted specifying who or what she was referring to. She also had a marked sign-comprehension loss. Interestingly, this marked and lasting comprehension loss would not be predicted from her lesion if she were hearing. Both major language-mediating areas (Broca's area and Wernicke's area) were intact. Her lesion was in the inferior parietal lobe, an area known to function for higher-order spatial analysis. The third left-hemisphere damaged signer had many grammatical errors; in fact, he was paragrammatical. He made selection errors and additions with ASL morphology and erred in the spatialized syntax and discourse processes of ASL. Thus, differential damage within the left hemisphere produced sign-language impairments that were not uniform but rather cleaved along lines of linguistically relevant components.

Quite remarkably, considering the spatial nature of sign language, the signers with right-hemisphere damage were not aphasic. They exhibited fluent, grammatically correct, virtually error-free signing, with a good range of grammatical forms, no agrammatism, and no signing deficits. Furthermore, left-hemisphere damaged patients, but not those with right-hemisphere damage, were impaired in tests of ASL structures at different linguistic levels. Importantly, this signing ability was preserved in the face of marked deficits shown by the right-hemisphere damaged signers in processing nonlanguage spatial relations. Across a range of tests the signers showed the classic visuospatial impairments seen in hearing patients with right-hemisphere damage.

Spatial cognition in left- versus right-lesioned deaf signers Selected tests that are sensitive distinguishers of visuospatial performance in left- versus right-hemisphere damaged hearing patients were administered, including drawing, block design, selective attention, line orientation, facial recognition, and visual closure (Poizner et al. 1984). The drawings of the right-hemisphere damaged patients tended to show severe spatial disorganization, whereas those of the left-hemisphere damaged patients did not. The right-hemisphere damaged patients were not able to indicate perspective; several neglected the left side of the drawing, and one right-hemisphere damaged patient even added unprompted verbal labels on the drawings. The drawings of the left-hemisphere damaged patients were in general superior, with overall spatial configurations preserved. The two groups of deaf, signing patients differed across the range of visuospatial tasks administered, with right-hemisphere damaged patients showing gross spatial disorganization. These nonlinguistic data show that the right hemisphere in deaf signers can develop cerebral specialization for nonlinguistic visuospatial functions. The right-hemisphere lesioned patients in general showed severe left-sided neglect and were seriously impaired in nonlinguistic visuospatial capacities, but their signing was still fluent and remarkably unimpaired. They showed no impairment in any of the grammatical aspects of their signing; however, their impairments were vividly apparent in spatial mapping, which we consider next.

The Distinction between Spatial Syntax and Spatial Mapping
The patients' impairments in the use of space differ according to whether differentiated points in space are used syntactically or are used to give relative positions in space (Poizner, Klima, and Bellugi 1987). Patients were asked to describe the physical layout of their living quarters from memory; in this task, signing space is used to describe space, and actual spatial relations are thus significant. The descriptions given by the right-lesioned signers were grossly distorted spatially. These patients were able to enumerate all the items in the room, but displaced their locations and even distorted spatial relations among them. In contrast, the left-hemisphere damaged patients' room descriptions sometimes were linguistically impaired (matching their linguistic breakdown in other domains) but without spatial distortions.

When space is used in ASL to represent syntactic relations, however, the pattern was reversed. One left-hemisphere damaged patient showed an impairment of spatial syntax: he had a disproportionately high ratio of nouns to pronouns and tended to omit verb agreement (both pronouns and verb agreement involve spatial indexing in ASL). Furthermore, when he did use spatial syntactic mechanisms, he sometimes failed to maintain the correct agreement. For all three right-lesioned signers, spatially organized syntax was correct and appropriate; indeed, all three even used the left side of signing space for syntax. Thus, even within signing, the use of space to represent syntactic relations and the use of space to represent spatial relations may be differently affected: the former is disrupted by left-hemisphere damage, and the latter by right-hemisphere damage (Bellugi, Klima, and Poizner 1988).

Analysis of the patterns of breakdown of a visuospatial language in deaf signers thus allows new perspectives on the nature and determinants of cerebral specialization for language. First, these data show that hearing and speech are not necessary for the development of hemispheric specialization: sound is not crucial. Second, the data show that in these deaf signers, it is the left hemisphere that is dominant for sign language. The patients with damage to the left hemisphere showed marked sign-language deficits but have relatively intact capacities for processing nonlinguistic visuospatial relations. The patients with damage to the right hemisphere showed much the reverse pattern. Thus, not only is there left-hemisphere specialization for language functioning, there is a complementary right-hemisphere specialization for visuospatial functioning. The fact that much of the grammatical information is conveyed via spatial manipulation appears not to alter this complementary specialization. Furthermore, the fact that components of sign language (e.g., lexicon and grammar) can be selectively impaired suggests that the functional organization of the brain for sign language may turn out to be modular.

3   The Chinese Script: A Visuospatial Orthography

Natural primary languages (spoken or signed) differ from secondary representational systems. While all human communities have natural languages, not all have writing systems. All normal hearing children acquire a natural language, but not all successfully master written language. By the age of four or five a child's primary language (spoken or signed) is very complex, but the child may be only beginning to learn to read and write. Learning a primary language requires no explicit instruction. Learning to read and write, on the contrary, requires a relatively long period and special training and depends heavily on other factors. Even so, learning to read and write is not accessible to all, and the problems of learning disabilities are severe.

All major systems of writing are based on spoken language, though they differ radically in the ways in which they map to primary spoken languages and the linguistic level at which the mapping of script unit to linguistic unit occurs. Generally, in logographic orthographies the basic script unit corresponds to the lexical unit or to the morpheme, in alphabetic orthographies it corresponds to the phoneme (Klima 1972). We have been exploiting these differences in order to investigate the processing of script and its underlying neural substrate (Tzeng, in press; Tzeng and Hung, 1988, in press; Tzeng and Wang 1983, 1984). In particular, we have been contrasting alphabetically based orthographies such as English with logographic orthographies such as Chinese characters.

There is currently an accumulation of evidence that the processing of Chinese orthography by hearing speakers of Chinese is quite different from the processing of an alphabetic orthography such as English. Visual processing seems to be the key for remembering and processing Chinese characters, and in some instances the speech recoding that accompanies the knowledge of sound and script relationships may even interfere with aspects of processing (Hung and Tzeng 1981; Hung, Tzeng, and Warrent 1981; Tzeng and Hung 1984, 1988, in press). We address issues relevant to these differences in script in the next sections; first with respect to the neural substrate for Chinese script in hearing Chinese-speaking subjects, then by examining deaf, signing childrens' approach to learning different scripts.

Brain Organization for Chinese Script in Hearing Speakers
Throughout the history of research on hemispheric specialization there has been speculation about the possibility that the functional organization of a literate brain may be related to the type of written script one has learned to read. According to Hasuike, Tzeng, and Hung (1986), before the mid-1970s, there seemed to be no disagreement about the role of the left hemisphere for processing Chinese logographs. Tzeng, Hung, Cotton, and Wang (1979) manipulated the number of logographs in two experiments and found a left-visual-field superiority for recognition of single logographs and a right-visual-field superiority for two-logograph words. Hausike et al. (1986) went a step further, carrying out an extensive comparison among all relevant experiments up until 1985. They found that when the exposure time is adequate and when the task requires linguistic analysis, the left hemisphere dominates. There is thus little evidence from either experimental or clinical studies to suggest a stronger involvement by the right hemisphere in the linguistic analysis of Chinese logographs. However, the idea persists that Chinese characters are mediated by the right hemisphere (e.g., Henderson 1982).

Spatial script and spatial representation Experiments with brain-damaged Chinese hearing patients in Taiwan has shed light on this issue and provided unequivocal evidence against the suggestion that Chinese logographs are processed primarily by the right hemisphere (Tzeng et al. 1986). Chinese hearing patients with either right- or left-hemisphere lesions took part in studies in which two types of visuospatial tasks were administered. One task involved drawing on command or from a model; the other involved writing Chinese logographs (a visuospatial script). The performance of hearing patients with right- versus left-hemisphere damage showed intriguing and important contrasts (see figure 6.2). In the nonlinguistic task of drawing, the left-brain-damaged patients produced good copies of geometric figures and well-configured (if simplified) drawings, like the house, the flower, and the teapot, whereas the right-brain-damaged patients showed signs of visual neglect in the left visual field. Their drawings are lacking in perspective and, importantly, show neglect of the left half of the figure (note the block, the house, and the flower).

When the hearing patients were asked to write Chinese characters, the performance differed, but in opposite ways. The left-brain-damaged patients made many errors of both omission and commission; the errors often involved deleting parts of a written character while maintaining the orthographic structure of the original character and using the entire space available. In contrast, the right-hemisphere damaged patients used the right side of the space available for writing, again showing a neglect of the left side this time for script, but importantly, they wrote the full and completely correct characters without any linguistic errors (Tzeng et al. 1986). Figures 6.2c and 6.3a show the responses in Chinese script by right- or left-brain-damaged patients.

Mental reconstruction of characters   In another task six hearing Chinese patients were asked to mentally reconstruct a sequence of components into a recognizable Chinese character (see figure 6.3b). Results of this visual glueing experiment are quite clear in their implication that the left hemisphere plays a critical role in processing Chinese characters. The right-hemisphere damaged patients were able mentally to glue various pieces together for almost perfect identification in their mind's eye. In sharp contrast, the left-hemisphere damaged patients had tremendous difficulty in the glueing task. In sum, the results of the visual glueing experiment by left- versus right-hemisphere damaged patients support a left-hemisphere basis for the recognition of Chinese logographs.

These studies taken together point to several interesting conclusions: First, for Chinese speakers the Chinese characters are not represented in any picture-like fashion, as has recently been claimed. Instead, they may be represented in the same way as words transcribed by alphabetic letters. Second and most importantly, these data suggest that the left hemisphere, not the right, plays a dominant role in the writing of Chinese characters. Thus, the effects of right- and left-hemisphere damage on signing and on processing Chinese script provide strong evidence for left-hemisphere processing for primary languages and writing systems based on these primary languages, even when the writing systems are visuospatial (e.g., Chinese script

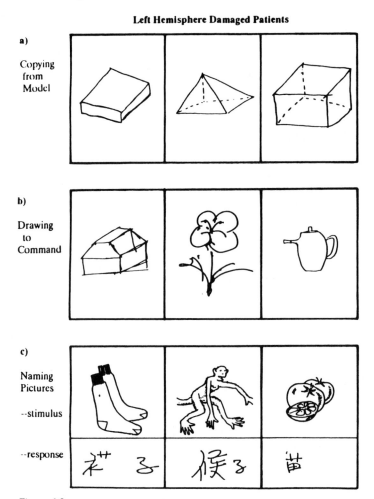

Figure 6.2
Chinese hearing patients' responses to drawing and naming tasks

Right Hemisphere Damaged Patients

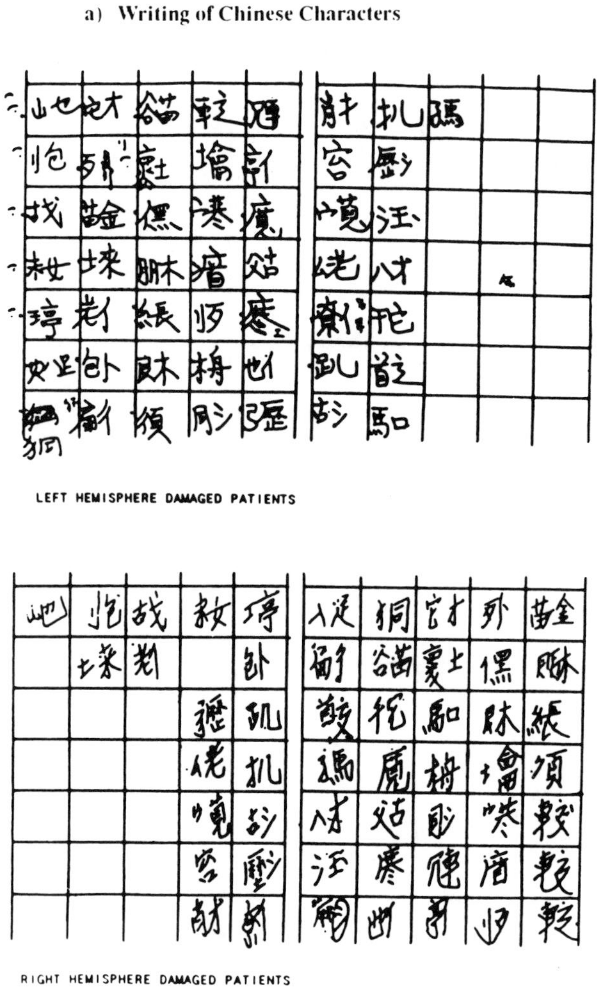

a) **Writing of Chinese Characters**

LEFT HEMISPHERE DAMAGED PATIENTS

RIGHT HEMISPHERE DAMAGED PATIENTS

Figure 6.3
Brain organization for script in Chinese hearing patients

**b) Stimulus for Mental Reconstruction
        of Chinese Character**

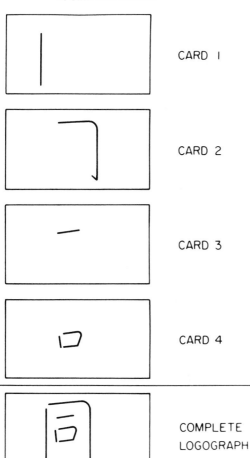

CARD I

CARD 2

CARD 3

CARD 4

COMPLETE
LOGOGRAPH

for hearing Chinese speakers; signed languages for deaf people of deaf parents).

4 Deaf Children's Approach to Different Scripts

As mentioned above, many studies have by now shown that deaf children exposed to ASL as a primary language acquire sign language with the same developmental milestones and at the same rate as the acquisition of comparable spoken languages. Some of these children, however, may have difficulty learning to read English fluently for reasons that are likely very different from those of children classified as dyslexic. There are no generally accepted orthographies for sign language itself, although there are currently several efforts to develop writing systems based on sign language, including a computer-based system (Hutchins et al. 1986). ASL and English are completely independent languages with entirely different grammars.

The primary problem is that the child who is born deaf has little or no access to the spoken language around him. How does a deaf child approach the task of learning a written representation of a spoken language he has never heard? We shall here investigate the young deaf child's beginning approach to writing with different scripts, asking how hearing and deaf children differ in their approach to script and whether Chinese and American deaf children approach their two kinds of scripts in different ways. Our goal is to examine the interplay between the primary-language modality (auditory or visuospatial) and orthographic structure (alphabetic or logographic).

Written samples were elicited systematically from hearing and deaf children just learning to read and write in the United States and in Hong Kong. In one study, American preschool deaf children's ASL signing, fingerspelling, and attempts at script were contrasted (O'Grady, van Hoek, and Bellugi, in press). In other studies, American school age deaf and hearing children's written English was contrasted with comparable deaf and hearing Chinese children's written Chinese (Fok and Bellugi 1986). The deaf children who took part in these studies were congenitally and profoundly deaf, learned a sign language as a primary form of communication, and were in schools for the deaf. Forty line drawings of common objects were presented in booklet form to the children, and they were asked to write down the word or character for each object (the same task used with Chinese brain-lesioned subjects above) We examined correct and incorrect responses given by the children that reveal aspects of their entry into writing and their knowledge of the principles of orthography (Fok and Bellugi 1986).

A Phonetically Based Script

Aspects of the interaction between ASL and other linguistic systems in the deaf child's environment (signing, fingerspelling, and script) in preschool deaf children of deaf parents have been examined by O'Grady, van Hoek, and Bellugi (in press); Padden (in press); Padden and LeMaster (1985). By the age of three all the deaf children knew the correct ASL signs for nearly all the items, performing almost at ceiling levels in their primary language. The 3-year-olds, however, were incapable of writing letters or words and often produced scribbles. By the age of four most of the deaf children wrote actual English letters, but frequently these were random combinations of letters. Some of the scribbles of the youngest children provided insight into their attempts to make connections across linguistic systems. One child volunteered that what he had scribbled for the picture of a duck and for the picture of a pie were in fact based on the forms of the corresponding ASL signs (figure 6.4a). He made the ASL sign DUCK, pointed to the handshape and then to the writing, indicating that the two were intended to be the same. For "pie" the child first drew a square and showed that he was illustrating the first handshape of the sign. He then made another drawing and indicated that he was illustrating one hand moving across the other. Thus, his written responses (or more appropriately, his graphic representations) involved invented forms for representing the handshape and/or movement of the ASL sign and provided explicit evidence that he was attempting to connect the written language with his native language, ASL (O'Grady, van Hoek, and Bellugi, in press).

We are currently examining responses from school-age children on the labeling task described above and are finding clear and consistent differences between the deaf and hearing groups (Fok, van Hoek, et al. 1988). First-grade hearing children frequently base their early attempts at spelling on phonological analysis of words. Their spellings are heavily influenced by a tendency to use letters to orthographically represent sounds of words (e.g., *n-d-n* for *indian*, *p-n-o* for *piano*, responses starting with *g* or *j* for *chair*) and otherwise to spell by ear (*n* for *knife*). Deaf children, on the other hand, are quite uninfluenced by pronunciation. By the first and second grade almost a third of the deaf children's responses were entirely correct. Yet their mistakes differed from those made by hearing children in several ways. There are systematic elements in the deaf children's spelling patterns derived from the orthographic system itself without reference to sound. The errors sometimes reflect awareness of the visual form of English words in terms of number of letters, double letters, and the shapes of the letters. Even when all the letters were correct, they sometimes got

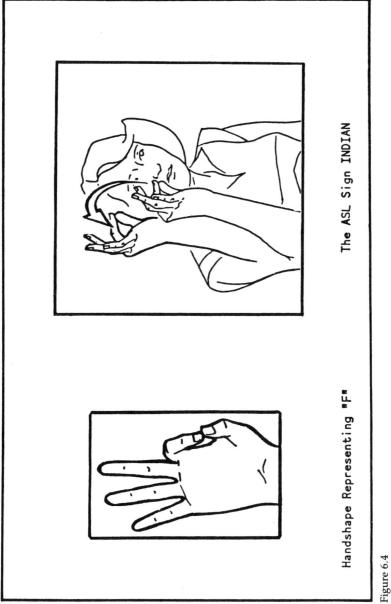

Handshape Representing "F"

The ASL Sign INDIAN

Figure 6.4
American deaf children's borrowing from ASL principles

b)

them in the wrong order (e.g., they crossed syllable boundaries as in "bota" for *boat* or "alppe" for *apple*). Deaf children were more likely to give correct silent letters at all grade levels than were hearing children (e.g. the *k* in *knife* or the *c* in *duck*), which provides evidence for their essentially nonphonological visual approach.

Although there are only very tenuous points of contact between ASL signs and English words, we did find isolated instances were school-age deaf children attempted to connect writing to their primary language, ASL. As an example, many of the incorrect written responses of the young deaf children to the picture of an Indian began with the letter *f*, and a common incorrect response to fork began with the letter *w*. Children explained their responses by showing the ASL signs INDIAN and FORK, which are made with the ASL handshapes also used for *f* and *w* in finger spelling (see figure 6.4b). These results taken together suggest that deaf children who do not have access to the phonological forms of the spoken language, bring a visual approach to their entry into written English and even at times make attempts to connect the opaque orthographic system of written English to their native sign language, ASL.

A Visuospatial Script
The Chinese writing system is opaque with respect to the relationship between script and speech and is emphatically spatial in the layout of every logographic symbol. The principles underlying the contrasting orthographies of Chinese and English are radically different in the degree of correspondence between sound and symbol, in the numbers of distinct units, and in spatial organization. Fok and Bellugi (1986) investigated the beginning stages of writing in deaf and hearing Chinese children in four Hong Kong schools using the same picture-naming task used with the American children reported on above. To provide a different perspective on the entry into writing, these studies examined the entry into a nonalphabetic script of young Chinese deaf signers and of matched young Chinese hearing nonsigners. In a recent report we focused primarily on the nature of the errors made by deaf and hearing children in their beginning approach to writing Chinese characters.

The deaf and hearing children exhibit clear differences in terms of their basic approach to learning and using the Chinese writing system. Although the opportunities for using a phonological approach to writing are less direct in Chinese than in English, the Chinese hearing children did bring their knowledge of the sound structure of the language into play in that some of their written errors were based on homophones in the spoken language and typically took the form of substitutions of one character for another having similar pronunciation but no visual similarity. The deaf Chinese children in our study made no errors of this sort; rather, their errors frequently involved substitution of characters or components of characters that were visually similar to the correct character. The most revealing types of errors were those involving invented character forms (that is, nonexisting Chinese characters). Often target and error pairs made by deaf and hearing children alike were strikingly similar in spatial architecture and spatial organization. Even when the invented characters were unrelated to the target, they were invariably well-formed characters that showed sensitivity to the implicit rules of the spatial architecture of characters.

Some of the errors the children made appeared to be based on principles of CSL, combining elements in ways appropriate in CSL sign formation devices but inappropriate in written Chinese (Fok et al., in press). Figure 6.5 presents examples of writing errors in which deaf children created nonsense compound characters, added extra movement lines to characters, and used size and shape characters to name objects, which would be appropriate in CSL but not in written Chinese. The children thus extract rules of their primary language, CSL, and apply them to another visuospatial language, written Chinese (Fok and Bellugi 1986).

The Interplay between Spatial Language and Spatial Cognition
We are investigating both visual, gestural language and visuospatial script. The young deaf child, unlike his hearing counterpart, must acquire nonlanguage spatial capacities that are prerequisites to the linguistic use of space. In our studies we examine the development of spatially organized syntax and discourse in ASL as well as the visuospatial cognitive functions underlying these linguistic systems. To examine the spatial abilities that deaf and hearing children bring to bear in learning a visuospatial script we designed a special experiment to assess their ability to analyze nonsense Chinese characters as dynamic spatial displays. Deaf and hearing children in four Hong Kong schools served as subjects for these studies. Sixty nonsense Chinese characters were presented as rapidly moving patterns of light, created by videotaping (in a darkened room) a person writing the pseudocharacters in the air with a light-emitting diode attached to the fingertip. In this way, only the dynamic pattern of movement representing the character is shown on the videoscreen. Deaf and hearing Chinese children were asked to watch each point-light display and write down the character underlying the continuous flow of movement (figure 6.6). The deaf children's responses are much more accurate than those of the hearing children, which demonstrates a superior ability to remember, analyze, and decode the complex movement in space into

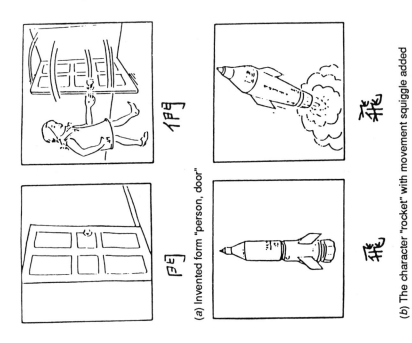

(a) Invented form "person, door"

(b) The character "rocket" with movement squiggle added

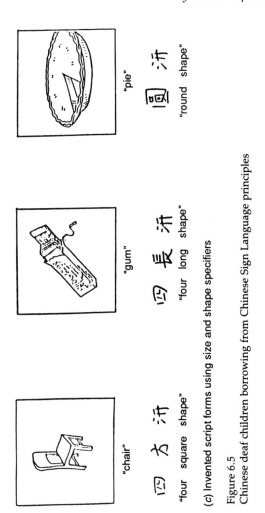

"chair"

四 方 泭
"four   square   shape"

"gum"

四 長 泭
"four   long   shape"

"pie"

圓 泭
"round   shape"

(c) Invented script forms using size and shape specifiers

Figure 6.5
Chinese deaf children borrowing from Chinese Sign Language principles

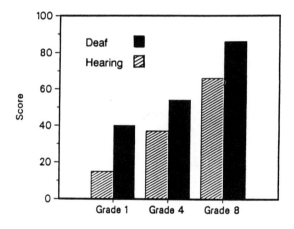

SPATIAL ANALYSIS OF HEARING AND
DEAF CHILDREN

Figure 6.6
Spatial analysis of dynamic point-light displays of Chinese nonsense characters. Figure
continued on next page

GRADE 1

HEARING CHINESE CHILDREN

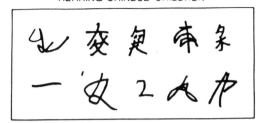

DEAF CHINESE CHILDREN

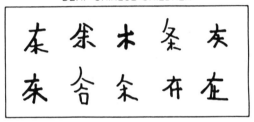

TARGET
STRUCTURE

POINT LIGHT
MOTION

its discrete components (Bellugi, O'Grady, et al., in press; Bellugi, van Hoek, et al. 1988; Fok, Bellugi, Corina, et al. 1986).

It is evident that this spatial cognitive task taps deaf children's special abilities for spatial analysis of movement. The deaf children, but not the hearing children, were able to distinguish between the movements representing strokes and transitional movements, and to remember the sequence and spatial arrangements. Thus, deaf children exposed to a visuospatial language appear to bring markedly enhanced spatial abilities to this task. These results are consistent with Neville's studies, which used correlations between electrophysiological indices and behavior to show that attention to peripheral visual space is superior in deaf signing subjects and is mediated by different neural systems than in hearing subjects (Neville 1988; Neville, Schmidt, and Kutas 1983).

5   Summary

In these studies, we have investigated both visuospatial language and visuospatial script and some aspects of the interplay between them. We have raised issues with respect to reading and its underlying neural organization from the special perspectives of the relation of sign and script and of a nonphonological route to reading.

First, the studies of sign language reveal that human primary languages are not restricted to the speech channel; sound is not crucial to either language or hemispheric specialization for language. The studies show that among deaf people of deaf parents primary linguistic systems have emerged that share central organizational principles with all spoken languages and yet differ radically from spoken languages in their surface form. Second, deaf children exposed to a signed language from birth acquire that language at the same rate and with the same milestones as those for spoken languages, despite the great differences between them. Third, signed languages, like spoken languages, display complex linguistic structure; but unlike spoken languages they convey much of this structure through manipulation of spatial relations. Thus, signed languages exhibit properties for which each of the hemispheres of normal hearing people shows a different predominant functioning. Patterns of breakdown of visuospatial language in deaf signers allow a new perspective on the nature of cerebral specialization for language, since in sign language there is interplay between visuospatial and linguistic relations. The data show that in these subjects the left hemisphere is dominant for sign language. The patients with damage to the left hemisphere showed marked sign aphasias but relatively intact capacity for processing nonlinguistic visuospatial relations. The patients with damage to the right hemisphere showed the reverse pattern. Furthermore, differential damage within the left hemisphere produces sign-language impairments that are not uniform but break down along the lines of linguistically relevant components. Taken together with other converging evidence (e.g., Damasio, et al. 1986), these data suggest that the left cerebral hemisphere in man may have an innate predisposition for language that is independent of language modality.

The studies of the functional organization of the brain for different orthographies show that in hearing Chinese patients with left- or right-hemisphere lesions, the left hemisphere again is dominant for a visuospatial script (e.g., Chinese logographs). The fact that the script relies heavily on visuospatial processing does not alter this basic complementary specialization. From these different perspectives it is clear that the primary specialization of the two cerebral hemispheres rests not on the form of the signal but rather on the linguistic function it subserves.

Studies of the beginning stages of writing in Chinese and American deaf children show that they approach script via a nonphonological route. Their errors underscore an essentially visual approach to either logographic or alphabetic representations of spoken languages they have never heard. Although the two kinds of script may present somewhat different task demands at the very early stages, they are likely to be equally difficult to master fully for those who have limited access to the spoken languages they represent. Our pilot studies of deaf children just learning to write suggest that visuospatial aspects of the organization of Chinese characters may offer some special opportunities at the early period and may be less opaque than alphabetically based systems.[2] An important finding from our studies is that deaf, signing children attempt to extract principles from their primary signed languages (American or Chinese) and map them to the process of learning to write. In these studies we examine the interplay between orthographic structure (alphabetic or logographic) and primary language modality (auditory or visuospatial).

Notes

This research was supported in part by the National Institutes of Health, grants no. NS 15175, NS 19096, and HD 13249, as well as by the National Science Foundation grant no. BNS86-09085 to the Salk Institute for Biological Studies. We thank Karen van Hoek, Daisy Hung, and Lucinda O'Grady for their help in these studies. We also thank the subjects and their families who participated in these studies, as well as faculty, staff, and students at the California School for the Deaf in Fremont, the Riverside School for the Deaf, the Hong Kong School for the Deaf, and the Canossa School in Hong Kong.

1. Notational conventions used in this chapter are as follows. Words in capital letters (SIGN) represent English glosses for ASL signs. The gloss represents the meaning of the unmarked, unmodulated, basic form of a sign out of context. Morphological processes may be indicated by specifying the grammatical category of change or by the meaning of the inflected form in brackets (e.g., SIGN [Exhaustive]). As part of the spatialized syntax of ASL, a horizontal plane in signing space is used for abstract spatial loci. Nouns, indexable verbs, pronouns, classifiers, size and shape specifiers can be associated with abstract spatial loci, and these are indicated by subscripts. Subscripts from the alphabet are used to indicate spatial loci ($_iSIGN_j$). Nouns, pronouns, and verbs of location are marked with a subscript to indicate the locus at which they are signed in planes of signing space (INDEX$_a$, BOY$_a$, AT-X$_a$). Inflected verbs are marked with an initial subscript to mark origin location and/or a final subscript to indicate the endpoint location ($_aGIVE_b$). Subscripts indicate abstract reference as well as coreference.

2. This is not, of course, to suggest that deaf children should be taught English through Chinese script. In an interesting experimental approach some schools for the deaf in Denmark are using a notation system representing Danish Sign Language to allow

deaf children to learn a writing system based on their primary language that is then used to teach written Danish by means of systematic comparison of the two languages.

References

Bellugi, U. 1988. The acquisition of a spatial language. In F. Kessell, ed., *The development of language and language researchers: Essays in honor of Roger Brown.* Hillsdale, N.J.: Erlbaum Press.

Bellugi, U. 1983. Language structure and language breakdown in American Sign Language. In M. Studdert-Kennedy, ed., *Psychobiology of language.* Cambridge: MIT Press.

Bellugi, U. 1980. The structuring of language: Clues from the similarities between signed and spoken language. In U. Bellugi and M. Studdert-Kennedy, eds., *Signed and spoken language: Biological constraints on linguistic form.* Dahlem Konferenzen Weinheim/Deerfield Beach, Fla.: Verlag Chemie.

Bellugi, U., and Klima, E. S. 1982. The acquisition of three morphological systems in American Sign Language. Keynote address, Child Language Research Forum. *Papers and reports on child language development* (Stanford University) 21:1–35.

Bellugi, U., Klima, E. S., and Poizner, H. 1988. Sign language and the brain. In F. Plum, ed., *Language, communication, and the brain.* New York: Raven Press.

Bellugi, U., O'Grady, L., Lillo-Martin, D,. O'Grady, M., van Hoek, K., and Corina, D. In press. Enhancement of spatial cognition in deaf children. In V. Volterra and C. Erting, eds., *The transition from gesture to language.* New York: Springer-Verlag.

Bellugi, U., Poizner, H., and Klima, E. S. 1983. Brain organization for language: Clues from sign aphasia. *Human Neurobiology* 2:155–170.

Bellugi, U., Poizner, H., and Klima, E. S. In press. Mapping brain function for language: Evidence from sign language. In G. Edelman, W. E. Gall, and M. Cowan, eds., *Signal and sense: Local and global order in perceptual maps.* New York: Wiley.

Bellugi, U., and Studdert-Kennedy, M., eds. 1980. *Signed and spoken language: Biological constraints on linguistic form.* Dahlem Konferenzen. Weinheim/Deerfield Beach, Fla.: Verlag Chemie.

Bellugi, U., van Hoek, K., Lillo-Martin, D., and O'Grady, L. 1988. The acquisition of syntax and space in young deaf signers. In D. Bishop and K. Mogford, eds., *Language development in exceptional circumstances.* Edinburgh: Churchill Livingstone.

Crowder, R. G. 1982. *The psychology of reading: An introduction.* New York: Oxford University Press.

Damasio, A,. Bellugi, U., Damasio, H., Poizner, H., and Van Gilder., J. 1986. Sign language aphasia during left hemisphere amytal injection. *Nature* 322:363–365.

Fok, Y. Y. A., and Bellugi, U. 1986. The acquisition of visual-spatial script. In H. Kao, G. van Galen, and R. Hoosain, eds., *Graphonomics: Contemporary research in handwriting.* Amsterdam: North Holland.

Fok, Y. Y. A., and Bellugi, U. 1988. Sign and script processing in Chinese. International Congress of Psychology, Sydney, Australia.

Fok, Y. Y. A., Bellugi, U., Corina, D., and Tzeng, O. J. L. 1986. The perception of Chinese characters. First Asian-Pacific Regional Conference of Deafness, Hong Kong.

Fok, Y. Y. A., Bellugi, U., and Lillo-Martin, D. 1986. Remembering in Chinese signs and characters. In H. Kao and R. Hoosain, eds., *Linguistics, psychology, and the Chinese languages.* Hong Kong: University of Hong Kong.

Fok, Y. Y. A., Bellugi, U., van Hoek, K., and Klima, E. S. 1988. The formal properties of Chinese languages in space. In M. Liu, H. C. Chen, and M. J. Chen, eds., *Cognitive aspects of the Chinese language.* Hong Kong: Asian Research Service.

Fok, Y. Y. A., van Hoek, K., Tzeng, O. J. L., Klima, E. S., and Bellugi, U. 1988. Deaf children's entry into writìng: Comparison between English and Chinese script. Manuscript, the Salk Institute.

Galaburda, A. M. 1988. The pathogenesis of childhood dyslexia. In F. Plum, ed., *Language, communication, and the brain.* New York: Raven Press.

Galaburda, A. M., Corsiglia, J., Rosen, G. D., and Sherman, G. F. 1987. Planum temporale asymmetry: Reappraisal since Geschwind and Levtisdy. *Neuropsychologia* 25:853–868.

Galaburda, A. M., Sherman, G. F., Rosen, G. D., et al. 1985. Developmental dyslexia: Four consecutive cases with cortical anomalies. *Annals of Neurology* 18:222–233.

Hasuike, R., Tzeng, O. J. L., and Hung D. L. 1986. Script effects and cerebral lateralization: The case of Chinese characters. In J. Vaid, ed., *Language processing in bilinguals: Psycholinguistic and neuropsychological perspectives.* Hillsdale, N.J.: Erlbaum Press.

Henderson, L. 1982. *Orthography and word recognition in reading.* New York: Academic Press.

Hung D. L., and Tzeng, O. J. L. 1981. Orthographic variations and visual information processing. *Psychological Bulletin* 90:377–414.

Hung D. L., Tzeng, O. J. L., and Warren, D. H. 1981. A chronometric study of sentence processing in deaf children. *Cognitive Psychology* 13:583–610.

Hutchins, S., Poizner, H., McIntire, M., Newkirk, D., and Zimmerman, J., 1986. A computerized written form of sign language as an aid to language learning. *Proceedings of the Annual Congress of the Italian Computing Society (AICA)* (Palermo, Italy) 141–151.

Klima, E. S. 1972. How alphabets might reflect language. In J. F. Kavanaugh and I. Mattingly, eds., *Language by eye and by ear.* Cambridge: Harvard University Press.

Klima, E. S., and Bellugi, U. 1979. *The signs of language.* Cambridge: Harvard University Press.

Klima, E. S., Bellugi, U., and Poizner, H. 1988. The neurolinguistic substrate for sign language. In L. M. Hyman and C. N. Li, eds., *Language, speech, and mind.* London: Rutledge.

Liberman, A. M. 1982. On finding that speech is special. *American Psychologist* 37 (2): 148–167.

Lillo-Martin, D. 1986. Parameter setting: Evidence from use, acquisition, and breakdown in American Sign Language. Ph.D. dissertation, University of California, San Diego.

Lillo-Martin, D., and Klima, E. S. In press. Pointing out differences: American Sign Language pronouns in syntactic theory. In P. Siple, ed., *Theoretical issues in sign language research.* New York: Springer-Verlag.

Lubs, H. A., Smith, S., Kimberling, W., Pennington, B., Gross-Glenn, K., and Duara, R. 1988. Dyslexia subtypes: Genetics, behavior, and brain imaging. In F. Plum, ed., *Language, communication, and the brain.* New York: Raven Press.

Marshall, J. C., and Newcombe, F. 1973. Patterns of paralexia: A psycholinguistic approach. *Journal of Psycholinguistic Research* 2:175–199.

Neville, H. J. 1988. Cerebral organization for spatial attention. In J. Stiles-Davis, M. Kritchevsky, and U. Bellugi, eds., *Spatial cognition: Brain bases and development.* Hillsdale, N.J.: Erlbaum Press.

Neville, H. J., Schmidt, A., and Kutas, M. 1983. Altered visual evoked potentials in congenitally deaf adults. *Brain Research* 266:127–132.

Newport, E., and Meier, R. 1986. Acquisition of American Sign Language. In D. I.

Slobin, ed., *The crosslinguistic study of language acquisition.* Hillsdale, N.J.: Erlbaum Press.

O'Grady, L., van Hoek, K., and Bellugi, U. In press. The intersection of signing, spelling, and script. In F. Karlsson, ed., *Fourth International Symposium on Sign Language Research.*

Orton, S. T. 1928. Specific reading disability-strephosymbolia. *Journal of American Medical Association* 90:1095–1099.

Orton, S. T. 1937. *Reading, writing, and speech problems in children.* New York: Norton.

Padden, C. A. In press. The acquisition of fingerspelling in deaf children. In P. Siple, ed., *Theoretical issues in sign language research.* New York: Springer-Verlag.

Padden, C. A., and LeMaster, B. 1985. An alphabet on hand: The acquisition of fingerspelling in deaf children. *Sign Language Studies* 47:161–172.

Petitto, L. A. 1988. Language in the prelinguistic child. In F. Kessel, ed., *The development of language and language researchers.* Hillsdale, N.J.: Erlbaum Press.

Poizner, H., Kaplan, E., Bellugi, U., and Padden, C. 1984. Visuospatial processing in deaf brain-damaged signers. *Brain and Cognition* 3:281–306.

Poizner, H., Klima, E. S., and Bellugi, U. 1987. *What the hands reveal about the brain.* Cambridge: MIT Press.

Shankweiler, D., and Crain, S. 1986. Language mechanisms and reading disorder: A modular approach. *Cognition* 24:139–168.

Stiles-Davis, J., Kritchevsky, M., and Bellugi, U., eds. 1988. *Spatial cognition: Brain bases and development.* Hillsdale, N.J.: Erlbaum Press.

Tallal, P., Curtiss, S., Shear, P., Jernigan, T., and Bellugi U. 1988. Neuroanatomical, neuropsychological, and neurolinguistic studies of specific developmental language/reading impairment. International Neuropsychology Society, New Orleans.

Tzeng, O. J. L. 1988. Neurolinguistics: Writing systems and cerebral lateralization. In *Oxford international encyclopedia.* Oxford: Oxford University Press.

Tzeng, O. J. L., and Hung D. L. 1984. Orthography, reading, and cerebral lateralization. In H. W. Stevenson and Q. Jing, eds., *Issues in cognition: Proceedings of a joint conference in psychology.* Washington, D.C.: National Academy of Sciences and American Psychological Association.

Tzeng, O. J. L., and Hung D. L. 1988. Cerebral organization: Clues from scriptal effects on lateralization. In M. Liu, H. C. Chen, and M. J. Chen, eds., *Cognitive aspects of the Chinese language.* Hong Kong: Asian Research Service.

Tzeng, O. J. L., and Hung D. L. In press. *The origin of cerebral lateralization of language: A psycholinguistic perspective.* Cambridge: MIT Press.

Tzeng, O. J. L., Hung D. L., Chen, S., Wu, J., and Hsi, M. S. 1986. Processing Chinese logographs by Chinese brain-damaged patients. In H. Kao, G. van Galen, and R. Hoosain, eds., *Graphonomics: Contemporary research in handwriting.* Amsterdam: North Holland.

Tzeng, O. J. L., Hung D. L., Cotton, B., and Wang, W. S.-Y. 1979. Visual lateralization effect in reading Chinese characters. *Nature* 282:499–501.

Tzeng, O. J. L., and Wang, W. S.-Y. 1983. The First Two Rs. *American Scientist* 71:238–243.

Tzeng, O. J. L., and Wang, W. S.-Y. 1984. In search for a common neuro-cognitive mechanism for language and movement. *American Journal of Physiology: Regulatory, Integrative, and Comparative Physiology* 246:R904–R911.

Vellutino, F. R. 1987. Dyslexia. *Scientific American* 256:34–41.

Editor's Comments

There are several issues in the research presented here that can be linked to outstanding questions about developmental dyslexia on the one hand and a general theory of brain and language on the other. It appears that information gathered over the past century showing that linguistic modules are organized in part around perisylvian auditory representations may have accidentally arisen out of the fact that most individuals have an auditory language as their first language. Therefore, acquired lesions involving the auditory association cortices of the left hemisphere in most people lead to aphasic disturbances in many, because their primary language was learned through auditory inputs, not because the language center resides in that posterior temporal region. There is support for this hypothesis in the present chapter and in a recent study involving positron emission tomography. The latter technique has found that linguistic activities employing visual and auditory inputs are associated with separate sensory-related areas of the cortex, which in turn access outputs independent of each other. In other words, reading seems not to require passage through the classical Wernicke's area in the temporal lobe. Moreover, the multiple language areas converge on the same frontal lobe output center, which I suspect would not be the case if the subjects were asked to vary their output among sign language, writing, and spoken language.

Thus, researchers may have been mistaken to think that there is a language center, Wernicke's area, a particular region of the brain innately capable of supporting language to the exclusion of other areas. Instead, innate linguistic capacities, encoded in and transferred from generation to generation through genes, may have something to do with a predetermined tendency for neural networks surrounding the known sensory representations in the human cerebral cortex to achieve a particular anatomical architecture related not to any specific sensory modality, but instead to the sensory modality employed during critical early periods of exposure to language. In the case of hearing subjects, the most common case, this architecture is related to the auditory cortical representation. In nonhearing humans, parieto-occipital cortical areas appear to play the pivotal role, because of sign language. One would presume that congenitally deaf-blind individuals might achieve this architecture in sensory-association areas related to braille input.

It is not known what the anatomical and physiological properties of such networks might be nor how late in life the appropriate architectures can be achieved. The essential characteristics of a language network, whether auditory, visual, or other, can perhaps be demonstrated in the patterns of interhemispheric, intrahemispheric, and cortical-subcortical connections, in the patterns of their short interneuronal circuits, in the synaptic architecture, in the architecture of specific receptors, or in other molecular characteristics. Since the basic connectional architecture of the neural substrates in question is already established long before the individual is exposed to any particular language through any particular sensory modality, my hunch is that the ultimate plasticity of the cortex for establishing linguisitc modules rests with genetic regulation of synaptic, receptor, and other molecular characteristics of the networks, which indeed can continue to take place long after the connections are established.

The molecular architecture of neural networks capable of language might give rise to specific antigens not seen in brain substrates for other, nonlinguistic cognitive functions. (This type of antigen sharing by the components of a neural network has been demonstrated for the Papez circuit of the limbic system.) If linguistic modules have unique antigens, the findings of this chapter would suggest that it might be possible to demonstrate the presence of such antigens in auditory cortices of hearing subjects and in parieto-occipital cortices of congenitally deaf individuals. Moreover, perhaps literacy would give rise to language-related antigens in secondary areas, e.g., in parieto-occipital cortices of hearing individuals and in somesthetically related cortices of braille readers.

Developmental dyslexics display difficulties with language in both the visual and auditory modalities, which supports the hypothesis that there is an alteration in the expression of language genes rather than a defect involving a specific sensory modality. If so, does this failure reflect anomalies in the genes themselves, or do other genes and additional environmental factors interfere with their expression? Findings of nonlinguistic as well as linguistic deficiencies in dyslexics would show either that the language-related genes are shared among several cognitive capacities or that the factors interfering with their expression also interfere with genes related to other cognitive capacities. The latter seems the most likely possibility from our current neurobiological perspective.

What do dyslexics borrow when making spelling errors? It is illuminating to learn that some deaf children initially tend to think that the words *indian* and *earring* are written in English beginning with the letter *f*. We learn that in ASL the signs for both words begin with the handshape for the letter *f* in fingerspelling. The children borrow from principles for ASL and apply this loan to written English. Clearly, there would be no way of understanding the spelling error in English without the prior knowledge about signing in ASL. In fact, it is fruitless to try to interpret the error on the basis of what is known about rules of written English. This is related to the tendency of Japanese to substitute *r* sounds for *l* sounds in English words containing an *l* sound. A crucial part of the explanation is the knowledge that *l* sounds are not expressed in Japanese.

Researchers in dyslexia often attempt to explain dyslexic spelling errors intuitively on the basis of some phonological or morphological characteristic of English. We learn from the present research on deaf children who learn to read and write English as a second language that dyslexics may also be borrowing from structures entirely outside of ordinary English and that understanding the errors made by dyslexics depends on the discovery of the rules and parameters that characterize their unique understanding and associations, and not vice versa.

Chapter 7

Measurement of Learning, Sensory, and Linguistic Capacity Early in Life: A Selective Overview of Recent Research

Norman A. Krasnegor

Reading is a skill. The acquisition of reading skills depends at a minimum upon abilities to learn, perceive, remember, and integrate the auditory and visual information that relates to language. Developmental dyslexia, the condition in which an otherwise normal child does not become a competent reader, may be etiologically related to impairments in any or all of the capacities listed.

Research seeking the necessary and sufficient conditions for becoming a competent reader and research seeking to uncover reasons for failure to read typically focus upon school-age children. Measures of hearing, vision, language and other brain functions are employed to ascertain how different biological factors and their interaction create conditions sufficient for reading skills to operate properly or to be impaired.

This chapter employs a somewhat nontraditional approach in that the overview begins at a time in development not previously considered when asking questions about dyslexia. My strategy involves presenting recent, selected findings on processes that may serve as preconditions for the reading capacities expressed later in life. The overview focuses upon the questions of what capacities emerge when. The rationale for a strategy is that it may help to elucidate how to study the fundamental underpinnings of the capacities listed above.

Research on dyslexia is moving in new directions as a result of the new research tools becoming available. For example, genetic markers for subtypes of dyslexia (Smith et al. 1983) may allow researchers to identify specific mechanisms associated with the condition. The earlier and more precisely such children are identified, the more likely that help given them will indeed enable them to compensate for their learning difficulties. Also, the more that is known about mechanisms involved in specific subtypes of dyslexia, the more likely that effective treatment approaches can be developed.

I hope that this review may foster a useful perspective for posing questions that will lead to a deeper understanding of the mechanisms that underlie developmental dyslexia. Basic knowledge of this type may ultimately aid clinicians in reliably identifying and diagnosing dyslexic individuals much earlier in development.

Included in this overview are: (1) a review of some of the latest findings on animal models of early learning, (2) a selected review of findings and methods for measuring capacities for perceiving and reacting to speech in the perinatal period of development, (3) an analysis of selected methods for measuring hearing early in life, (4) a selected overview of methods for measuring which perceptual capacities the human infant possesses for differentiating and detecting operationally relevant linguistic stimuli, and (5) the implications of these findings for future research.

1   An Animal Model of Fetal Learning and Behavioral Development

During the early part of this century there was considerable scientific interest in prenatal behavioral development. A question thought to be important by developmentalists was, *when* during life can learning first be demonstrated? More specifically, is there a prenatal capacity for learning? (The term *learning* is defined for the purposes of this discussion as associative or Pavlovian conditioning.)

During the 1930s scientists undertook to answer the above question. Ray (1934) attempted classical conditioning in a human fetus. In his study he paired a neutral, vibrotactile stimulus with an unconditioned stimulus that was known to produce fetal movement. If made suddenly in the present of a fetus, the unconditioned stimulus, a loud noise is reliably followed by a startle movement. This response can be detected by placing one's hand on the abdomen of a pregnant woman. Ray paired the unconditioned stimulus with the neutral stimulus for a number of trials presumed sufficient, but he was unsuccessful in demonstrating classical conditioning.

A decade and a half later Spelt (1948), who employed procedures similar to those used by Ray, claimed success in demonstrating classical conditioning in the human fetus during the last trimester. He also claimed that his data demonstrated the fetus's capacity for extinction and retention of the classically conditioned response. However, other scientists sharply criticized these findings on methodological grounds (Sameroff and Cavanaugh 1979), thus leaving open the question of prenatal learning.

Significant progress had to await methodological innovations and research at the start of this decade (see Krasnegor et al. 1987). The studies of interest employed fetal rats. Blass and Pedersen (1980) and Strickrod (1981), for example, developed procedures for externalizing the uterus of pregnant rats late in gestation and injecting substances into the amniotic sac containing the fetus. These were important advances, because they provided researchers with the opportunity for direct observation and manipulation of a mammalian fetus. Furthermore, these techniques allowed the rat fetus to complete its development, to be born at term by normal vaginal delivery or Cesarean section, and to be cross-fostered to recently delivered mothers.

Kolata (1984) summarized these and other techniques for viewing and manipulating the mammalian fetus after a workshop sponsored by the National Institute of Child Health and Human Development. Attending that workshop was William Smotherman. He and his co-workers have carried out a number of studies that demonstrate the capacity of the fetus for learning. In the first of a series of investigations of prenatal learning (Stickrod, Kimble, and Smotherman 1982a), they demonstrated that rat fetuses have the capacity for associative learning. On day 20 of gestation they injected apple juice into the amniotic fluid surrounding the externalized fetuses and the irritant lithium chloride into the fetal peritoneum. The pairing of an aversive stimulus such as lithium chloride with a novel taste or odor causes normal adult rats after a single trial to avoid that taste or odor on subsequent presentations. The externalized uterus of the dam was reinserted, the abdomen was sutured, and the fetuses were delivered at term and tested at various times subsequently. When the pups were allowed to suckle from their anesthetized mother, they preferred to attach to some nipples rather than others as a result of their prenatal experience. Those pups exposed to the aversive conditioning trial attached less often to nipples painted with apple juice than control pups (Smotherman and Robinson 1987). In a second study it was demonstrated that conditioned pups showed delays in crossing a runway to gain access to their mother if the air contained the odor of apple juice. And in a variant of the experiment the pups preferred instead to stay at the end of a box containing a low concentration of the same odor (Stickrod, Kimble, and Smotherman 1982b). These findings are important because they indicate both that conditioning took place before birth and that the learned response was retained for more than two weeks after birth.

Smotherman and his co-workers continued their studies along two fronts. First, they developed new procedures for the direct observation of fetuses: they worked out techniques for delivering the fetus into a warm saline bath while still connected to its mother anesthetized by chemomyelotomy. They also conducted a number of studies from days 16 to 19 of gestation to characterize the ontogenesis of movement in the fetus. By combining the new observation techniques with the knowledge gained of the ontogenesis of fetal movement patterns, these researchers were able to study the fetus's capacity for conditioning during gestation. In a series of elegant experiments, which included rigorous control procedures, Smotherman and Robinson (1987) demonstrated that rat fetuses exposed on day 17 of gestation to a single trial pairing of a neutral stimulus (mint) and an intraperitoneal injection of lithium chloride are conditioned as of day 19. The mint solution alone does not suppress endogenous movements on day 17 or 19 of gestation. But when paired with the lithiumchloride injection on day 17, it markedly suppresses movement by itself in 19-day-old fetuses that had received the conditioning.

In additional experiments undertaken in the same series, researchers manipulated the concentration of the mint solution. They found that conditioned fetuses could discriminate varying concentrations of the conditioned stimulus by measuring the amount of spontaneous movement suppressed on day 19 (Smotherman and Robinson 1985a, 1985b). This finding may provide a method for measuring sensory thresholds in fetuses (Smotherman and Robinson 1987).

The results described above provide reliable evidence that learning in the rat can take place prior to birth. Moreover, the extensive work of Smotherman and his co-workers substantiates the claim that prenatal behavioral development can be studied and systematically characterized. There is also evidence that the mammalian fetus is responsive to the sensory stimuli it encounters during gestation. Such stimulation may prenatally alter postnatal behavior. (Smotherman and Robinson 1987). These observations have served as the basis for another series of experimental questions concerning auditory and speech perception by the human fetus.

2   *The Human Fetus's and Neonate's Preference for the Maternal Voice and Capacity for the Perception of Linguistic Stimuli*

Questions about auditory stimulation of the human fetus and the capacity of the fetus to benefit from that experience and employ the information after birth became the focus of scientific inquiry at the beginning of this decade. Interest was raised on this subject by a study of DeCasper and Fifer (1980). They demonstrated that on the first day of life a human baby of either gender shows a preference for its mother's voice over that of another woman. Within hours after birth human infants given the opportunity to listen to a tape recording of their mother reading a Dr. Seuss story preferred that tape recording to one of the same story read by another woman (also see Mehler in this volume).

In their experiment DeCasper and Fifer used a nonnutritive nipple. They conditioned for two different sucking patterns, and babies were randomly assigned to one or the other condition. Eight of the ten babies studied learned the pattern of sucking that initiated their mothers' taped voices. A subsample of these babies (four of the eight successful learners) were given the opportunity to repeat the task 24 hours later. This time they were required to suck using the pattern that had turned on the tape of the other female voice the day before. All four were successful at learning the new pattern. These results demonstrated a remarkable capacity in the one-day-old infant to recognize and show a preference for its mother's voice.

DeCasper and Prescott (1984) next questioned whether paternal voices were preferred in the same manner as maternal voices. They conducted studies that had two surprising results. They utilized a similar testing procedure: they required a newborn to learn a sucking pattern on a nonnutritive nipple to listen to its father's voice or to that of another man reading a Dr. Seuss story. The babies showed no preference for their fathers' voices over those of other men. The experimenters then wondered whether the babies could tell the difference between the two male voices. A second experiment clearly demonstrated that the neonates could indeed make that discrimination. In sum, these two sets of studies revealed that the newborn baby prefers its mother's voice but is impartial about its father's. These results suggest that the neonates' preferences may be linked to prenatal experience (Kolata 1984).

DeCasper and Spence (1986) addressed this hypothesis by asking pregnant women to read a passage of text aloud each day during the last six weeks of pregnancy. The stories read were "The Cat in the Hat," "The King," "The Mice and the Cheese," and "The Dog in the Fog." The newborn babies were subsequently tested to determine whether the sounds to which they had been prenatally exposed were more reinforcing than those from a novel passage. The newborn's task was to learn a sucking pattern that would allow it to listen to the prenatally presented story or to a novel one. The results, which are quite complex to interpret because of the many control conditions, revealed that sounds associated with the stories to which the babies had been exposed *in utero* were more reinforcing than those that were novel.

Two recent papers add to the body of data on this topic. Lecanuet and co-workers (1986) report on a study of fetal perception and discrimination of speech stimuli. Their investigations employed women in their last trimester of pregnancy (between the thirty-fifth and thirty-eighth week). Every three seconds for three minutes a loudspeaker delivered repeated pairs of tape recorded syllables ("babi' or "biba") using female voices. The speaker was placed over the pregnant woman's abdomen and played at 90 decibels. Half of the subjects received the stimulus "babi" followed by "biba"; in the other half the order was reversed. Fetal heart rate was recorded, and stimulation was given only during periods of low variability. The data indicated a significant decrease in the heart rate during the first 30 seconds of stimulation in comparison with prestimulation control rates. Change in the order of the syllables had a similar effect. The preliminary conclusion from these experiments is that fetuses have the capacity to perceive and discriminate some acoustical aspects of speech stimuli.

DeCasper et al. (1986) have also collected data indicating that familiar and unfamiliar speech stimuli elicit different cardiac responses in human fetuses. Most researchers studying fetal perception associated with acoustic stimulation believe that the mother's heartbeat, speech, and voice sounds are aspects of the fetus's endogenous acoustic environment. Querleu, Renard, and Crepin (1981) and DeCasper, Maugais, et al. (1986) have pointed out fetal reactions to sound depend upon the behavioral state of the fetus at the time it is being stimulated (in addition see Lecanuet et al. 1986). Also, as stated above, newborns appear to prefer sounds and voices experienced *in utero,* over those that are novel (DeCasper and Spence 1986).

The above findings suggested to DeCasper, Maugais, et al. (1986) that previous experience with specific sounds, particularly speech, can have an effect on the fetus's reaction to those stimuli later. They reasoned that a fetus should be particularly sensitive to the speech of its mother in comparison with the speech of others. In this study 13 pregnant women in the thirty-fourth postmenstrual week were told how to read brief children's stories aloud. Eight of the women were assigned one of two French stories (*"Le poulet"* or *"Le petit crapaud"*); the other five were assigned the other. Each woman read her assigned story three times per day for the next four weeks. At the end of that period each woman came to the laboratory to have fetal heart rate monitored while the fetus was stimulated by a tape recording of the familiar and unfamiliar stories. The latter were read aloud by a female graduate student and broadcast by a speaker placed on the mother's abdomen. The fetuses exhibited different heart-rate patterns to the different stories. Specifically, during periods when they were exposed to familiar passages, heart rates decreased, but when they were exposed to unfamiliar passages, they showed an increase in heart rates. These findings strongly suggest that the fetuses heard and remembered aspects of what their mothers read.

Similar heart-rate findings in fetuses and newborns (Fifer 1987) provide additional evidence that prenatal auditory exposure to speech sounds may be important for the development of speech and language. However, as the investigators note, one should not generalize too broadly from these findings.

Taken together, these findings suggest that both prior to birth and just after it human babies are familiar with aspects of auditory stimuli and speech that could be important for developing the attachment between a baby and its mother. Clearly, those infants whose sensory systems are intact will have the best chance to take advantage of such stimulation and to utilize the information adaptively in the postnatal environment. That is, the infant's recognizing and expressing a preference for aspects of the mother help to strengthen the attachment between mother and offspring. Those infants who have impaired sensory capacities may be at a distinct disadvantage here. Reported research has recently begun to focus on how to assess auditory capacity soon after birth.

3 A New Method for Measuring Audition in the Neonate

One of the most difficult tasks faced by researchers and clinicians alike is the measurement of a newborn's auditory capacity. Researchers have good methods for presenting and controling for independent variables (e.g., amplitude and frequency of auditory stimuli), but there is no comparable ability on the side of dependent measures (e.g., conditioned head turning, button pressing, talking). This is particularly true for babies just after they are born. Recent research by Howard Hoffman and his colleagues has led to a new method for measuring hearing within hours of birth.

During the last two decades Hoffman has been studying the startle response and its development. When looking at the startle response in animals he discovered that it can be modified. Then in experiments carried out on human adults, he found that when an exteroceptive stimulus precedes by 100 to 200 milliseconds a stimulus that elicits the glabella response, the resulting eye blink is reduced in amplitude (Hoffman and Ison 1980). When the same stimulus is presented simultaneously with the eliciting stimulus, the eye blink amplitude is instead enhanced (Hoffman and Stitt 1980a; Hoffman, Cohen, and Stitt 1981).

In a developmental study Hoffman and co-workers next compared these reduced and augmented responses in adults and newborns. They found that as in adults, newborns (16 to 65 hours old) exhibited augmented reflexes to the simultaneous pairing of an exteroceptive stimulus and a gentle, calibrated tap between the eyes. However, they did not show a reduced eye-blink response when the exteroceptive stimulus was presented prior to the eliciting tap (Hoffman, Cohen, and English 1985).

The researchers recognized that they had found significant developmental differences; they also realized that they may have uncovered a method for testing hearing in the newborn. They reasoned that if they could show an augmented reflex when they simultaneously presented a variable tone with a gentle tap on the glabella, an audiogram might be constructed. Results from two studies indicated that this approach was successful in achieving the intended effect. Hoffman, Cohen, and English (1985) thus demonstrated reflex augmentation with a 1000-hertz tone at either 90 decibels or 70 decibels. Cohen, Hoffman, and Anday (1986) demonstrated that an augmented reflex could be obtained in human neonates using tones of 1000, 2000, and 4000 hertz presented at 90 decibels. Also of interest is the observation that the babies could be asleep during the procedure.

4   Measurement of Language-Related Discrimination Behavior during the First Year of Life

Assessment of the capacity for discriminating aspects of speech has been more thoroughly pursued for the postneonate period (Aslin, Pisoni, and Jusczyk 1983; Gottlieb and Krasnegor 1985). Two methods for investigating speech discrimination during infancy (2 to 10 months of age), high amplitude sucking (HAS) and auditory, visual speech perception (AVSP), have recently been reviewed by Jusczyk (1985) and Kuhl (1985), respectively.

Eimas and colleagues (1971) spurred research in the field of speech perception in infants by adapting the HAS procedure to questions of what aspects of speech infants can distinguish when. Though it is not my intent here to describe the many findings obtained using this method (see Aslin, Pisoni, and Jusczyk 1983), it is worthy of note that users of this methodology were the first able to demonstrate categorical perception of speech in infants (Eimas et al. 1971). Moreover, related later work indicated that categorical perception is not restricted to speech (Jusczyk et al. 1983).

Other workers using HAS have asked what the basic units of infant speech perception are. For example, Miller and Eimas (1979) asked whether infants are sensitive to the speech sound characteristics of a single consonant but failed to demonstrate this capacity. Other studies were carried out to determine whether the syllable is the basic unit of perception. However, interpretation of the results has been hampered by lack of adequate measures of perceptual categorization (Aslin, Pisoni, and Jusczyk 1983). Suffice it to say that HAS, with all its variants, continues to be employed by researchers to determine when and how infants first come to perceive speech.

The fruitful productivity of HAS led to other questions concerning infant speech perception. Answers to these questions required the development of new methods which also turned out to be particularly germane to dyslexia, since they address cross-modal (auditory and visual) sensory integration. One such method of interest is known as audio, visual speech perception (AVSP).

The idea behind ASVP was to study cross modality speech perception in 6-to-10-month-old infants (Kuhl and Meltzoff, 1982). The investigators wished to observe whether babies could correlate what they had heard with what they saw. In the experimental protocol infants were placed facing two identical filmed faces each of which silently articulated a different vowel sound. The infants had to discriminate between the vowel sounds /a/ and /i/. A single sound that matched only one of the faces emanated from a loudspeaker at a point midway between the faces. The sound and film tracks were arranged to ensure that the auditory stimuli were temporally synchronized with both the matching and unmatching faces.

The investigators reasoned that an infant that could match the auditory and visual aspects of the speech sound would look longer at the face articulating the vowel sound being broadcast. Kuhl and Meltzoff (1982) found that 24 of the 32 babies studied looked longer at the matching face and vowel sound. The results obtained supported the hypothesis of a cross-modality integration of speech sounds.

They followed this study with a second one (Kuhl and Meltzoff 1984). The testing situation was the same, except for changes in the auditory signals to remove spectral information. The investigators thought that if the infants were matching on the basis of the spectral information of the vowel sounds, in the new testing situation they would not be able to match sound with image. The results confirmed the hypothesis: only 17 out of 32 babies matched the stimuli, a result not above chance. Kuhl (1985) is continuing to use this method to gain an understanding of what other speech characteristics 6-to-10-month-old infants can discriminate.

5   *Summary and Implications for Future Research*

The goal of this chapter is to direct attention toward the earliest appearance of some of the sensory and perceptual processes thought to be important to the development of speech and language. I deem this useful for the study of dyslexia and its mechanisms. Let me summarize this overview.

The work on fetal learning in rats demonstrates that such learning can occur early and be retained at least until after birth. Moreover, reports on the ontogeny of behavior during gestation provide important information indicating that conditioning is possible in the rat fetus as early as day 17 of gestation and the consolidation of that learning can be demonstrated on day 19 of gestation (the gestation of rats lasts 21 days).

The findings on prenatal speech perception in humans indicate that fetuses are able to remember acoustic patterns to which they were previously exposed, which is shown by changes in heart rates; already on the first day of life neonates prefer their mothers' voices to those of other females; they do not prefer their fathers' voices to those of other males; and they remember aspects of stories read to them prenatally.

New methods are being developed for assessing hearing in human neonates. At the same time reliable techniques for measuring what aspects of speech infants can perceive when are providing valuable information on this aspect of perceptual development. Methods for assessing cross-modal matching are addressing the infant's capacity for integrating auditory and visual experience, especially as these modalities apply to speech.

What are the implications for future research? One of the most interesting new hypotheses about the etiology of dyslexia is that put forth by Geschwind and Behan (1982). They postulated that immune disorders associated with high levels or elevated sensitivity to testosterone during gestation may also be pathogenetically related to the observed learning problems.

New Zealand Black mice that suffer from spontaneous autoimmune disease (see Sherman et al. in this volume) show greater immune abnormality when they are castrated males and less abnormality if they are females that have been administered testosterone. Sherman, Galaburda, and Geschwind (1983, 1985) have also demonstrated that these mice show asymmetrical neuroanatomical anomalies in their cortices consisting of dysplasias and ectopias identical to those observed in the brains of humans diagnosed as having dyslexia (Galaburda et al. in this volume). Indeed, Galaburda is attempting to develop an animal model for dyslexia by showing brain anomalies and learning deficits in mice with spontaneous and experimentally induced immune defects.

The work on fetal learning in rodents may offer an additional methodological approach. For example, testosterone could be administered directly to developing male and female fetuses in strains known not to show immunological, anatomical, or behavioral deficits. *In utero* behavioral development could be measured along with the capacity for learning. To determine whether there are changes in brain architecture and cerebral asymmetries, neuroanatomical studies could be carried out at points in gestation after the administration of testosterone and at other points during postnatal development. Using this approach, researchers may be able more precisely to test the implications of the proposed hypothesis by comparing results with those obtained in immune-deficient rodents.

Studies involving analyses of the capacity of fetuses and newborns to perceive aspects of speech and linguistically relevant stimuli are provocative. They strongly suggest that during the third trimester the human fetus is capable of hearing aspects of human speech and of reacting later on to those with which it is familiar. They also indicate that the newborn shows a preference for speech stimuli heard earlier, including the voice of its mother.

While research on this topic is only in its early stages, it may represent an important approach for identifying early in life the perceptual, learning, and memory capacities of infants and for describing individual differences at this stage in development (Fifer 1987). The methods described may also be able to pick out infants who are prone to learning disabilities and to provide clues about mechanisms of normal and abnormal development of language abilities. For example, research now under way (Fifer 1987) is comparing the preference for the maternal voice in full-term and premature infants. Any detected differences could add new knowledge about the behavioral risks associated with premature birth.

Studies of perinatal audition and those of the capacities of more mature infants to perceive aspects of speech are important in that they provide, on the one hand, a methodology for early detection of auditory deficiencies and, on the other, sophisticated strategies for research on development from the perinatal period through infancy. A research focus upon the continuity of speech and language perception from the prenatal period through birth to infancy would be helpful for determining how well perinatal measures predict subsequent developmental achievements (Bornstein and Krasnegor 1989).

I hope that the developmental research on early learning, speech perception, and audition described above will help to deepen our understanding of how these processes may relate to the acquisition of reading skills and will stimulate new questions on the processes underlying dyslexia.

References

Aslin, R. N., Pisoni, D. B., and Jusczyk, P. W. 1983. Auditory development and speech perception in infancy. In Paul H. Mussen, ed., *Handbook of child psychology*, vol. 2. New York: Wiley.

Blass, E. M., and Pedersen, P. E. 1980. Surgical manipulation of the uterine environment of rat fetuses. *Physiology and Behavior* 25: 993–995.

Bornstein, M., and Krasnegor, N. A., eds. 1989. *Stability and continuity in mental development*. Hillside, N.J.: Erlbaum.

Cohen, M. E., Hoffman, H. S., and Anday, E. K. 1986. Reflex augmentation of tap-elicited eyeblink: The effect of tone frequency and tap intensity. *Journal of Experimental Child Psychology* 41: 551–558.

DeCasper, A. J., and Fifer, W. P. 1980. Of human bonding: Newborns prefer their mothers' voices. *Science* 208: 1174–1176.

DeCasper, A. J., and Prescott, P. A. 1984. Human newborns' perception of male voices: Preference, discrimination, and reinforcing value. *Developmental Psychobiology* 17: 481–491.

DeCasper, A. J., and Spence, M. J. 1986. Prenatal maternal speech influences newborns' perception of speech sounds. *Infant Behavior and Development* 9: 133–150.

DeCasper, A. J., Maugais, R., Lecanuet, J. P., Granier-Deferre, C., and Busnel, M. C. 1986. Familiar and unfamiliar speech elicits different cardiac responses in human fetuses. Paper presented at the International Society for Developmental Psychobiology, Annapolis, Maryland.

Eimas, P. D., Sequeland, E. R., Jusczyk, P., and Vigorito, J. 1971. Speech perception in infants. *Science* 171:303–306.

Fifer, W. P. 1987. Personal communication.

Geschwind, N., and Behan, P. 1982. Left handedness: Association with immune disease, migraine, and developmental learning disorders. *Proceedings of the National Academy of Sciences* (U.S.A.) 79:5097–5100.

Gottlieb. G., and Krasnegor, N. A. eds. 1985. *Measurement of audition and vision in the first year of postnatal life: A methodological overview*. Norwood, N.J.: Ablex.

Hoffman, H. S., and Ison, J. R. 1980. Reflex modification of startle: I. Some empirical findings and their implications for how the nervous system processes sensory input. *Psychological Review* 87:175–189.

Hoffman, H. S., and Stitt, C. L. 1980a. Augmentation of the airpuff elicited eyeblink by concurrent visual and acoustic input. *Bulletin of the Psychonomic Society* 15:115–117.

Hoffman, H. S., and Stitt, C. L. 1980b Inhibition of the glabella reflex by monaural and binaural stimulation. *Journal of Experimental Psychology: Human Perception and Performance* 6:769–776.

Hoffman, H. S., Cohen, M. E., and Stitt, C. L. 1981. Acoustic augmentation and inhibition of the human eyeblink. *Journal of Experimental Psychology: Human Perception and Performance* 7:1357–1362.

Hoffman, H. S., Cohen, M. E., and English, L. M. 1985. Reflex modification by acoustic signals in newborn infants and in adults. *Journal of Experimental Child Psychology* 39:562–579.

Jusczyk, P. W. 1985. The high amplitude sucking technique. In Gilbert Gottlieb and Norman A. Krasnegor, eds., *Measurement of audition and vision in the first year of postnatal life: A methodological overview.* Norwood, N.J.: Ablex.

Jusczyk, P. W., Pisoni, D. P., Reed, M. A., Fernald, A., and Myers, M. 1983. Infants' discrimination of the duration of rapid spectrum change in non-speech signals. *Science* 222:175–177.

Kolata, G. 1984. Learning in the womb. *Science* 225:302–303.

Krasnegor, N. A., Blass, E. M., Hofer, M. A., and Smotherman, W. P., eds. 1987. *Perinatal development: a psychobiological perspective.* Orlando, Fla.: Academic Press.

Kuhl, P. K. 1985. Methods in the study of infant speech perception. In Gilbert Gottlieb and Norman A. Krasnegor, eds., *Measurement of audition and vision in the first year of postnatal life: A methodological overview.* Norwood, N.J.: Ablex.

Kuhl, P. K., and Meltzoff, A. N. 1982. The bimodal perception of speech in infancy. *Science* 218:1138–1141.

Kuhl, P. K., and Meltzoff, A. N. 1984. Infants' recognition of cross-modal correspondence for speech: Is it based on physics or phonetics? *Journal of the Acoustical Society of America* 76:580.

Lecanuet, J. P., Busnel, M. C., DeCasper, A. J., Granier-Deferre, C., and Maugais, R. 1986. Fetal perception of speech stimuli. Paper presented at the meeting of the International Society for Developmental Psychobiology, Annapolis, Maryland.

Miller, J. L., and Eimas, P. D. 1979. Organization in infant speech perception. *Canadian Journal of Psychology* 33:353–367.

Querleu, D., Renard, K., and Crepin, G. 1981. Perception auditive et reactive foetale aux stimulations sonores. *Journal de gynocologie obstetrique et biologie de la reproduction* 10:307–314.

Ray, W. S. 1934. A preliminary study of fetal conditioning. *Child Development* 3:173–177.

Sameroff, A. J., and Cavanaugh, P. J. 1979. Learning in infancy: A developmental perspective. In J. D. Osofsky, ed., *Handbook of infant development.* New York: Wiley.

Sherman, G. F., Galaburda, A. M., and Geschwind, N. 1983. Ectopic neurons in the brain of the auto-immune mouse: A neuropathological model of dyslexia? *Society for Neuroscience Abstracts* 9:939.

Sherman, G. F., Galaburda, A. M., and Geschwind, N. 1985. Ectopic neurons in the brain of the auto-immune mouse: A neuropathologic model of dyslexia. *Proceedings of the National Academy of Sciences* (U.S.A.) 82:8072–8074.

Smith, S. D., Kimberling, W. J., Pennington, B. F., and Lubs, H. A. 1983. Specific reading disability: Identification of an inherited form through linkage analysis. *Science* 219:1345–1347.

Smotherman, W. P., and Robinson, S. R. 1985a. Novel and aversive chemosensory stimuli: Discrimination by the rat fetus in utero. *Society for Neuroscience Abstracts* 11:837.

Smotherman, W. P., and Robinson, S. R. 1985b. The rat fetus in its environment: Behavioral adjustments to novel, familiar, aversive, and conditioned stimuli presented in utero. *Behavioral Neuroscience* 99:521–530.

Smotherman, S. P., and Robinson, S. R. 1987. Psychobiology of fetal experience in the rat. In Norman A. Krasnegor, Elliott M. Blass, Myron A. Hofer, and William P. Smotherman eds., *Perinatal development: A psychobiological perspective.* Orlando, Fla.: Academic Press.

Spelt, D. K. 1948. The conditioning of the human fetus in utero. *Journal of Experimental Psychology* 38:338–344.

Stickrod, G. 1981. In utero injection of rat fetuses. *Physiology and Behavior* 28:5–7.

Stickrod, G., Kimble, D. P., and Smotherman, W. P. 1982a. In utero taste/odor aversion conditioning in the rat. *Physiology and Behavior* 28:5–7.

Stickrod, G., Kimble, D. P., and Smotherman, W. P. 1982b. Met-5-enkephalin effects on associations formed in utero. *Peptides* 3:881–883.

Editor's Comments

We know that language arises from a set of genetically determined linguistic dispositions (the initial state) followed by an epigenetic fixation of parameters that reflects the particular linguistic environment to which the young human is exposed at critical periods of development (see Mehler in this volume). (The brain machinery underlying this process is likewise formulated and actualized during development. Brain related genes number in the thousands or perhaps in tens of thousands, and only a few have been located and characterized. Epigenetic regulation of neural ontogenesis is beginning to be better understood, and some aspects of it are treated in the chapters by Rakic, Dudai, Crossin and Edelman, and McEwen in this volume.)

The development of language from the initial state likely calls for certain preconditions to be in place. For instance, for language to begin to take hold, it may be necessary to have already well established sensory and perceptual structures such as hearing (in the case of ordinary infants) or vision (in the case of deaf babies; see Bellugi et al. in this volume), each with its own initial state and developmental schedule. Language thus defined is deeper than hearing or vision because it can rely on either hearing or vision in its expression.

Although it is possible that the fixation of parameters has something to do with the establishment in the brain of the fine structure of auditory or visual-association cortices during the late prenatal period and first decade of life, it is difficult to conceive that the *stuff* of language is identical to the stuff of auditory or visual function. Thus, while the deep structure of language appears to rely on whatever cortex maps relevant linguistic objects of the external world, it may itself be represented at an altogether different level of brain anatomy, the nature of which is at this time unknown. I am tempted to think that the stuff of language does not have a brain localization in the ordinary neuropsychological sense of the word, but that rather it is represented at the level of brain genes as a set of developmental and maintenance rules that command auditory, visual, somesthetic, and maybe other neural circuitries to connect and interact (hence behave) in specific, particularly human ways.

Damage to the utilized cortices, whether developmental or acquired, results in language disturbances only insofar as the stuff of language cannot occupy (or has not already redundantly occupied) another system, or another part of the same system, that can silently take over language tasks.

A question of significant interest to the participants of the conference upon which this volume is based was, what sort of alterations can affect perisylvian cortices in ways that the stuff of the deep structure of language is no longer expressed normally in these brain areas, with the result that language itself becomes abnormal?

The suggestion of the present chapter—that interference with the development of the perceptual and neural structures that serve as preconditions for the development of language, e.g., hearing, vision, somæsthesia, etc., constitutes a significant handicap to language development—must be checked empirically. In the clinics, for instance, one can see examples of normal or abnormal language function with abnormal or normal hearing. Infants growing up in a sound-free environment acquire language at the proper time and to its full power (see Bellugi et al. in this volume). Evidently, then, some types of alterations in prerequisite systems interfere, while others do not. After reading the developmental literature, one is tempted to conclude that partial injury to one or more of these systems during development is more of a hurdle to language acquisition than complete loss of some of them.

Anomalies in reading acquisition must first be studied at the initial state of reading acquisition. If at that initial state more fundamental sensory preconditions with earlier developmental schedules, e.g., auditory or visual perception, are found to be anomalous, then and only then they must be studied at their own initial states. This process should then be carried back until no other abnormality in some precondition can be demonstrated.

I do not mean to imply that the presence of hearing or visual abnormalities in a very young infant or fetus might not augur for dyslexia in its future, but chances are that it will not. In other words, only some abnormal perceptual-processing functions and accompanying neural substrates may predispose to dyslexia, and there is no way of predicting in advance. Nonetheless, the retrograde research proposed here is still apt to require the development of experimental techniques and paradigms for investigating the relevant preconditions in very young subjects. The present chapter encourages researchers to develop these approaches.

Chapter 8

Language at the Initial State

Jacques Mehler

Introduction

Most psychologists tend to accept, albeit tacitly, that the mind is un-interestingly void for many weeks, months, or even years after birth if it exists at all. To some extent such a belief is compatible with common sense, folk psychology and the dominant philosophical theories of the past few centuries. Adults are often impressed by the fact that a newborn infant sleeps most of the time, that is, it is inexpressive and remote. However, one can also be surprised by its curious gaze, responsive behavior, and the determined constancy with which it pursues its aims and interests. A single observer is often astonished by the ease with which his or her own impressions can change from one moment to the next. Professional observers like pediatricians and personnel of the caring professions have noticed and often reported that the infant is capable of processing stimuli, scanning its environment, and to some extent responding specifically to some of the stimulating configurations in the environment. Unfortunately, the work of pediatricians and those in the helping professions, the baby-watchers for short, has seldom been scientifically rigorous and well controlled enough to induce a change in the beliefs held by most parents and scientists. Beliefs were largely elaborated in the absence of objective observation, and generally the empiricists carried the day.

Empiricism changed psychology by establishing behaviorism and constructivism. Generations of students were almost exclusively taught these viewpoints. At the same time some philosophers and psychologists held positions closer to nativism and rationalism. They presented arguments that at times were as compelling and logical as the ones being put forward today. Yet at times nativists were as concerned with factual data as the empiricists. It is only in the last two or three decades that nativism has succeeded in taking on a "new look." To a large extent this is due to results from research into the initial state and to evidence arising from work in linguistics. The rapidity of this change can be attributed to two causes. The advent of computers and of computer science made it clear how difficult it is to explain growth and learning without some underlying structure to uphold and sustain such processes. Is it not strange to talk about learning or the acquisition of some ability in the absence of a learning device? But if we recognize such a device, the behaviors that it can acquire must surely depend to a large extent on its structure. And if this is so for any physical device, how could it be any different for the aptitudes of the human mind?

The growing awareness of the shortcomings of the learning systems that psychologists had proposed to account for the acquisition of language, logic, and other aptitudes was a further motive for change. Indeed, most of us are now persuaded that the learning systems proposed allow organisms to acquire notions that can be organized into conjectures to be evaluated in terms of the surrounding evidence. In brief, we reach a paradoxical state of affairs pointed out by Fodor (1975): Organisms should be capable of acquiring only those notions they already have in some form or other. In this sense, learning systems are modified versions of nativism in the extreme.

In addition, Chomsky (1957, 1965, 1966) argued very convincingly that complex systems like those underlying grammatical competence cannot be learned. He argued that language competence derives from universal innate structures, Universal Grammar, in conjunction with specialized processes by means of which the organism converges towards the grammar of the language to which it is exposed. Language is supposed to have biological underpinnings and is unique to the human species. In short, language, psychologists are told, should be studied like any other structure-function pair that results from some specialized biological system.

The above arguments, among others, promoted a change in attitude. Psychology became interested in the mind at birth. At first psychologists expected that their methods would provide a straightforward characterization of the mind at the initial state (IS). They imagined that with the progress of their empirical endeavors they would be able to ground philosophical theories in empirical science. This may turn out to have been a partially reasonable expectation. However, as Chomsky (1980) and others have pointed out, studies on the neonate can provide only a fairly impoverished estimate of the abilities of the mind at the IS. In fact, studies may fail to uncover a capacity or aptitude because of methodological shortcomings, because the aptitude under observation needs some environmental trigger to set it in motion, or because maturational processes necessary to prepare the machinery have not yet come to term. Thus, all in all, studies of neonates can at best provide a positive evaluation of the capacities detected, although many other capacities may remain without being positively identified. We hope that with time there will be fairly good convergence between the IS that is posited by formal modeling and the IS uncovered by empirical investigations of the organisms at birth.

The study of a faculty or an aptitude must be undertaken at several levels for a good understanding to ensue. Consider language and language use, for instance. Linguists describe Universal Grammar, the grammar of each language, and some of the more abstract formal properties of natural and artificial languages. In addition to this formal perspective many other empirical investigations are necessary to provide data that constrain the possible models. For instance, Chomsky (1986, 1988) stated ways in which natural languages may or may not be acquired. Furthermore, he also advocated that the characteristics of the language acquisition device be taken into consideration when deciding issues about competing grammars. Linguists need data from many different natural languages in order to understand how abstract parameters must be formulated to account for the range of variation observed. Likewise, psychologists try to explain how language is perceived and understood, produced and remembered, acquired and at times lost.

Moreover, linguists and psychologists alike learn a great deal about language by considering its biological foundations. For example, although higher vertebrates and humans share many abilities, they do not share linguistic capacity. Furthermore, language seems to have a cortical organization regarded by many neuropsychologists as specific. Brain lesions often result in selective loss of language capacity. The study of language, like that of any other biologically based aptitude, requires the joint efforts of formalists, functionalists, and neuroscientists to uncover how this ability functions. My position favoring a naturalistic approach to the study of language should not be understood to imply that the only procedure is to analyze the underlying machine responsible for the function. On the contrary, I am arguing that the study of the formal and functional aspects of language is necessary to improve theories of performance. Nevertheless, paying attention to the biological foundations of this faculty provides theoretical constraints that insure that our endeavors will be fruitful in the end. This is also, I believe, the message of investigators such as Lennenberg (1967) and Chomsky (1965).

In contrast to the stance described above, experimental psychology has often displayed a total neglect of biology if not an outright indifference to it. Skinner (1957), one of the major figures in psychology, was both true to this school of thought and to his beliefs when he argued that the term *CNS* (ordinarily central nervous system) was best taken to mean conceptual nervous system. As he stated, "the causes to be sought in the nervous system are, therefore, of limited usefulness in the prediction and control of specific behavior" (1953, pp. 28–29), and "the use of the nervous system as a fictional explanation of behavior was a common practice even before Descartes, and it is now much more widely current than is generally realized" (1938, p. 4). Such an extreme position is not wise and may impoverish the cognitive enterprise.[1] So rather than pushing this or that model of the mind, let us start by inspecting the evidence that research on human infancy has uncovered. These data may shed new light on an old debate.

Methods and Procedures

In the pages that follow I will review some experimental studies of linguistic dispositions in the human infant. We have selected linguistic dispositions to illustrate one of several areas of neonate competence that have been explored. Readers interested in other aptitudes can consult Mehler and Fox 1984.

Two of the first modern attempts to explore the behavior of newborn infants were carried out by André-Thomas (1960) for the auditory domain and by E. Gibson and her co-workers for the visual domain. André-Thomas showed that very young infants can locate a sound as well as recognize its mother's voice. As we shall see further on, these observations were later corroborated by several teams using more sophisticated techniques and controls. In collaboration with Walk, Gibson reported that six-month-old infants avoid a visual cliff (Walk and Gibson 1961). Infants will explore a virtual edge that separates an area on which they are crawling from an area that is much deeper but is covered by a sheet of plexiglass, which ensures that the infants will not fall off the "cliff." Of course, the two parts differ in depth only if the perceiver can use depth cues to elaborate three-dimensional space. Walk and Gibson reported that infants tend to stop at the visual edge as if they had inferred that the edge corresponded to a potentially dangerous discontinuity.

These first studies were immediately followed by a number of others, many of which were carried out by T. G. Bower (1979, 1977). Pioneering studies have the virtue of recruiting a variety of scientists into the new field of investigation. One consequence of these early studies was to encourage good methodologists to come into an area of research where they were much needed. Many methods were thus developed for exploring the perceptual and cognitive abilities of the very young in accordance with age. Two of these have met with the greatest amount of success: nonnutritive sucking and operant head turning. In nonnutritive sucking, the pressure the infant applies to a blind nipple and the rate of sucking are recorded (see Siqueland and De lucia 1969; Eimas et al. 1971; Mills and Meluish 1974; Mehler et al. 1976; and also Krasnegor, this volume). First, during a period called the baseline these measures are noted for a few minutes. Second, during the habituation phase the connection between sucking and the delivery of a reinforcing stimulus is established. During habituation sucking rate generally increases significantly, at least for a few minutes. After this initial increase, sucking rates drop for most infants, as if they had habituated to the reinforcing stimulus (or become "bored" by it). If the decrease meets a preestablished criterion, the reinforcing stimulus may then be modified during the subsequent test phase. Generally, two groups of subjects are tested. One, the experimental group, receives a different reinforcing stimulus during the habituation and test phases. The other, the control group, receives the same stimulus during both phases of the experiment. The results of the experimental and control groups can thus be compared to assess whether the sucking rates for the two groups differ in the beginning of the test phase and also whether the sucking rates before and after the shift differ from each other.

A modification of the high-amplitude sucking technique, described above, has been developed by Mehler, Lambertz, Jusczyk and Amiel-Tison (1986) for use with stimuli that last more than a few seconds. The sucking response in this procedure is noncontingent. It is used as an indication of activation rather than as the operant that secures reinforcement. This altered procedure uncovers whether infants have a preference for one type of stimulus over another. For instance, two groups of infants are each subjected to different kinds of continuous speech while sucking is measured. After reaching some criterion each group is split into two subgroups. The reinforcing stimulus is then changed from one kind of speech to another for the experimental subgroup, but not for the control subgroup.

The second major method mentioned above was developed by Moore, Wilson, and Thompson (1976). As described by Kuhl in the operant head-turn technique

> the infant is conditioned to turn her/his head toward a loudspeaker when the repetition of a single stimulus (the "background") is changed to the repetition of a new stimulus (the "comparison"). These are called "Change" trials. If the infant

produces a head-turn at the appropriate time, s/he is reinforced with a visual stimulus. On an equivalent number of "Control" trials, no change in the sound occurs, but the infant is monitored for head-turn responses. Performance is measured by comparing the number of head-turn responses on Change vs. Control trials. If the infant produces significantly more head-turn responses on Change trials, we infer that the infant can discriminate two stimuli. (1985 p. 237)

The nonnutritive sucking technique is widely used by laboratories studying infants that are a few hours to a few months of age; the head-turn technique is largely used by laboratories studying infants that are over four months old. It would be very useful to have a set of experiments comparing how the same aptitude and the same stimuli are evaluated when head turn and nonnutritive sucking are used to test populations of the same age. However, such a study is not available at this time.

Other methods used to study neonates are based either on measurements of behavioral indices (e.g., limb tremor, the orienting response, respiration, and eye fixation) or physiological indices (such as evoked potentials). Methods must be selected according to the age of the subjects and the aptitude under exploration. Some excellent reviews of the pros and cons of these methods can be found in Aslin, Pisoni, and Jusczyk 1983; Eimas 1975; and Kuhl 1985.

Many of the procedures used in testing infants rely on the habituation of some sort of response (visual, auditory, or other). The behavior of neonates in such habituation paradigms is not yet fully understood and is itself the object of numerous studies. For some investigators habituation involves fatigue or satiation of peripheral detectors. For others it involves subcortical processes only. Still other investigators argue that habituation is essentially based on cortical processes. Graham, Leavitt, Strock, and Brown (1978) reported the case of an anencephalic infant tested at two months of age using the orienting response to a speech sound (an attention-related change in heart rate). Initially, a typical decrease in heart rate indicated an orienting response to sound. After some trials, however, there was a return to a normal heart rate, which indicated that the orienting response had habituated. The finding by Graham et al. suggests that cortical activity is not necessary for obtaining a habituation to sound. On the basis of several studies Bronson (1974, 1982) has argued that habituation to visual stimuli in infants is probably measuring retinal adaptation, because the cortex is very immature at birth, while subcortical structures are much more mature. Furthermore, properties best processed by the subcortical structures are by and large the ones responsible for infants' behaviors.

The evidence advanced by Bronson was fairly widely accepted. Yet Slater, Morrison, and Rose (1983) showed that three-day-old infants who have habituated to a visual stimulus presented monocularly will recover equally well when the test item is presented to the same eye or to the contralateral one. Slater et al. used a cross and a circle in one experiment and green and red circles in another. The authors concluded that habituation cannot be attributed to retinal adaptation as Bronson suggested. Rather, it must involve more central processes like, say, memory.

The evidence reviewed suggests that all three processes (peripheral, subcortical, and cortical) play a role in learning and habituation by neonates. Experimenters interested in developmental neuropsychology should determine the extent to which these different structures contribute to observed behavior. If we are to understand the nature of cognitive change, we must also determine changes in information processing during growth to establish the functional architecture that accounts for observed behaviors at each age and for each test. The result may provide the means for establishing an interesting link between cognitive structures and their biological substrate. Psycholinguists would greatly welcome such a link, which would complement a number of approaches for gaining some insight into the way in which aptitudes and faculties are represented in the brain.

Aptitudes at the Initial State

The IS can be and has to some extent been explored largely with the methods described above. These methods are best adapted to the study of peripheral capacities, perceptual processing in particular. At the moment the investigation of the more central properties of the mind at the IS is only beginning.[2] Given the focus of this paper, I have chosen to concentrate on speech only. Speech is only the tip of the linguistic iceberg, yet the study of speech might help us to uncover properties that pertain to central cognitive processes.

The Atoms of Speech

Among the properties of the IS that prepare humans to acquire natural language, none has appeared as important as the ability to classify speech sounds into their constituents, as all speakers do. Eimas et al. (1971) explored the ability of very young infants, generally one month old, to distinguish minimally differing phonemes like /p/ and /b/, or /t/ and /d/. In experiments that have become classics in the field Eimas

(1974, 1975) and Eimas and Miller (1980) showed that very young infants can distinguish any two phonemes that differ by only one distinctive feature, e.g., voicing or place of articulation. Furthermore, the distinctions that infants make correspond to the ones adults use to delimit speech categories. The boundary between two adult categories corresponds to the one functionally employed by one-month-old infants. On balance, the results of the experiments carried out since the early seventies support the view that very young infants are capable of making all the phonetic distinctions that adults can make. This is one of the main results of the last decade or two of research on very young infants' linguistic dispositions.

However, the conclusion drawn in the previous paragraph is stated in a manner that is unfair to infants who can also spontaneously discriminate sounds that some adults consider alike. Indeed, many adults cannot distinguish speech sounds that their native language fails to use contrastively. Consider the syllables /ra/ and /la/, which can constitute different lexical entries in many languages. Speakers of English and French hear these syllables as different, and so do the infants tested by Eimas (1975). However, most Japanese speakers consider them to sound alike, because their initial phonemes are never used contrastively in Japanese, which uses mostly the /l/ sound (Miyawaki et al. 1975; Goto 1971; McKain, Best and Strange 1980). As we shall see below, young babies can discriminate phonemes not discriminated by adults.

One of the first researchers to explore empirically whether infants can discriminate speech contrasts that adults cannot was Trehub (1976), who showed that infants discriminate contrasts used in Czech syllables but not in English syllables, although English adults do not distinguish these same syllables. Werker et al. (1981) and Werker and Tees (1984) contributed further to our understanding of this issue by showing that only after ten to twelve months of language exposure do infants start losing their ability to distinguish nonpertinent contrasts. They showed that up until the eighth month infants discriminate foreign contrasts as well as contrasts used in the caretakers' language. Thereafter there is a decrease in the infants' ability to make the relevant discriminative response. By the age of twelve months babies tend to ignore the foreign contrasts altogether.

On the basis of the results presented so far we can say that all the distinctive features that can be used contrastively in any natural language are available at birth. Furthermore, infants converge towards a phonological system after selective pressure ensures preservation of just those contrasts used in the target language. This process of convergence is almost over before the babies start speaking. The outcome of this growth into the native language is the construction of a system of categories used to classify all speech sounds relevant to the target language. The evidence thus suggests that babies may lose a part of their capacity to use phonetic distinctions because of their experience with speech. This observation is compatible with the view that much learning may be established by selecting a subset of states within a larger envelope of potential ones (Changeux and Danchin 1974; Mehler 1974; Strange and Jenkins 1978).

Linguists, phonologists, and informed laymen may be able to use their know-how to classify sounds outside of their native language. However, such an ability is certainly not available to the uninformed native speaker under normal circumstances. The speaker of English can be made to notice the difference between two syllables that differ in tone or even the distinction between the vowels in the French words *tu* and *tout*. Interestingly, adult English speakers do not usually pay any attention to these distinctions, and they only learn to make them very slowly with coaching. This is very different from what the infant does, and this difference is to note. Nonetheless, I am not suggesting that we know at this time how to explain the difference between infant and adult performance. It is tempting to hypothesize that the foreign speaker learns to distinguish unfamiliar contrasts with procedures such as those Kluender, Diehl, and Killeen (1987) described for the Japanese quail. In contrast, babies use a different system, which remains available for some years only. Afterwards the well known difficulties encountered when learning a foreign language as an adult emerge.

In the above paragraph I presented evidence that the infant can make all the relevant segmental distinctions. In addition, Bertoncini and Mehler (1981) showed that infants can also distinguish between syllables that differ from each other only by the order of the segments they contain (e.g., [pat] versus [tap]) rather than by the segments they contain (e.g., [pat] versus [bat]). Nevertheless, this is not the case when the sequence is not a well-formed syllable but rather a series of segments (e.g. [pst] versus [tsp]). This result suggests that syllables can be discriminated from each other on the basis of a physical difference that is insufficient to allow babies to discriminate an identical difference in a nonsyllabic environment. On the basis of the behavior of very young infants Bertoncini and Mehler (1981) concluded that the syllable is a level of representation at which the speech signal is stored and then analyzed. Furthermore, the syllable is recognized and presumably categorized on the basis of information that may be stored within the first few milliseconds. Indeed, Bertoncini et al. (1987) showed that only the first twenty or so milliseconds are necessary for recognizing the first consonant and vowel. Infants and adults are capable of establishing the phonetic categories corresponding to the syllable from which the short segments were spliced. Last but not least, infants are able to distinguish syllabic sequences that differ only in the position of stress (Jusczyk and Thompson 1978).

The above reported results suggest that the infant segments speech in order to obtain a representation. The distinctions that it can make between two such representations are determined by the phonological contrasts allowed in natural languages. Furthermore, these results suggest that language universals are based on the untutored perceptual and discriminative aptitudes of the infant at the IS.

Speech stimuli, unlike most other stimuli, encode objects in the world and eventually also thoughts in our heads. The *raison d'être* of a noise is itself; in contrast, that of an utterance is to convey meaning. Meaning is encoded into speech by means of arbitrary segments and is ordered into fixed sequences. Thus, when we hear a noise, say that of a motorcycle, it is easy to discriminate it from another similar noise for a few seconds; thereafter, a large category of noises are considered equivalent to it. With speech, however, if one hears a word, say *elephant*, it will be possible to discriminate it from another speech sound for weeks or even years. The reason is trivial. Speech is a vehicle for representing; after a few seconds only the representation of what was heard remains; and the message quality itself deteriorates. The representation is twofold: it specifies the meaning and some of the properties of speech sounds. The dictum according to which we always remember in our own words should be borne in mind here. The language user retrieves the representation of utterances, while the formal characteristics drift away. What about infants? Do they at an early age remember a speech noise as a series of conventional segments, or do they code noises? This question remains to be answered. However, some data can be brought to bear on the issue.

Miller and Eimas (1979) showed that an infant is sensitive to phonemes not only because of its discriminative behavior but also because of its long-term representations. They presented subjects with two syllables during habituation and two other syllables during the test. The training and test syllables contained the same segments but in different order, or they differed in one segment only, either the consonant or the vowel. Infants discriminated all conditions equally well. The authors concluded that the infant uses phonetic segments to represent speech in long-term memory. This conclusion is very similar to the one that was independently reached by Kuhl (1980) and Hillenbrand (1984). Each of these investigators used a fixed order of stimuli throughout the experiment. Bertoncini et al. (1988) used a variant of the technique with a random ordering of items to address the same basic problem. They presented subjects with four syllables during habituation (e.g., /bi/, /si/, /li/, /mi/) and added an additional one during the test (e.g., /di/ or /da/). If the infant reacted to the test syllable it must have compared the novel syllable to each of the four training ones. These authors showed that the infant behaves differently at four days and at two months of age. The younger infants act as if they preserved information about the vowel in long term memory. They do not react to the addition of a syllable that differs only by a stop consonant from one of the training ones. However, if the change involves a vowel, they do react to the test. The older infants react to all the conditions in which a new syllable is added, even if the novel syllable differs from one of the earlier ones by just a stop consonant. It thus appears that there is a developmental change in the representation of speech during the first month of life.

The results just reported are of interest because they indicate that it is already possible to raise interesting questions concerning the way in which the infant represents and commits speech items to memory. Certainly, if the child tries to formulate phonological generalizations, it has to do so on the basis of long-term storage of speech sounds rather than on the basis of the inputs themselves. These studies suggest that important developmental changes take place very early in life. A reasonable question to ask, then, is whether at that early age there are already ways of detecting deviance in the coding of speech sounds due to family traits or dyslexia.

The Special Status of Speech
In this section I will present data to relate the above findings to speech. For many theoreticians speech is processed in a special way, different from that used for other acoustic stimuli.

Speech is a specifically human aptitude. No other animal acquires a complex linguistic system that it then uses to communicate, encode its environment, and ensure cultural transmission. Speech, however, is only a peripheral aspect of the linguistic system, and it could well be that it is not specifically human. Birds, for instance, use a sophisticated system of songs that in some respects may seem a little bit like speech. Furthermore, scientists acknowledge that most human traits are the consequence of a lengthy process of evolution. Thus, it may be that speech exists in an implicit state in other species. Evidence for the continuity is rather weak, and so we may as well ignore it. However, the suggestion that speech is special, that there is a mode for processing the speech signal that is different from the ordinary acoustic mode, has not received overwhelming empirical support either.

Rather than examining this issue once again, I will present evidence suggesting that there are human dispositions for speech acquisition that function within a linguistic framework. Those dispositions are most likely part and parcel of human nature.

It is natural to ask whether there are dispositions at the initial state ensuring that a specific phonological speech system will emerge without special training or coaching. Is there any evidence that the initial state is geared to operate on speech in a special manner, or at least single out speechlike stimuli from other acoustic input?

A very young infant prefers to listen to its own mother's speech rather than to that of unknown speakers. Mills and Meluish (1974) reported that babies only a few weeks old suck more vigorously and for longer periods of time for their own mothers' voices than for the unknown voice of other babies' mothers. Unfortunately, in Mills and Meluish's study the voices had not been prerecorded and the mothers were present in the room while the test was being carried out. Yet the same pattern of results was also observed by several other teams. Mehler, Bertoncini, and Barrière (1978) explored the ability of infants under two-months of age to distinguish the voices of their own mothers from those of other mothers. They reported that infants suck more to listen to their own mothers, provided that the recordings are of properly intonated speech. When infants are presented with recordings of mothers reading lists of words, neither preferences for nor discriminative responses to the mothers' voices are observed. This result suggests that an infant can recognize its mother's voice provided it is motivated by properly intonated speech. If not, it will react identically to its mother and a stranger. DeCasper and Fifer (1980) have observed similar results in infants barely a few hours old at the time of testing. By and large, these results show that an infant only a few hours old can already individuate a speaker and that an infant a few weeks old prefers its mother's voice to another voice if the speech conforms to the prosodic rules of the language. Establishing speaker invariance is one of the aptitudes of very young infants.

To evaluate whether speech is special, let us consider another set of results. One kind of evidence often adduced in this context is that speechlike stimuli are processed in the left hemisphere, while other acoustic stimuli are processed by the right hemisphere or equally by both hemispheres. A method often used to test this hypothesis is the dichotic-listening technique. It is a well-known fact that speech stimuli presented simultaneously to both ears tend to be processed better by the right than the left ear. This right-ear advantage (REA) is generally attributed to the more exhaustive processing of speech stimuli by the left hemisphere. Other acoustic stimuli usually do not show an

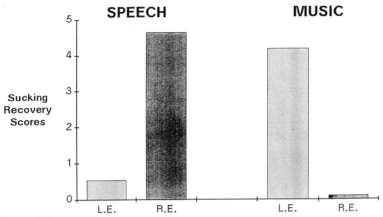

Figure 8.1
Sucking recovery scores (average of the first two postshift minutes minus average of the last two preshift minutes) as a function of the ear receiving the change (left ear or right ear) in the speech and music conditions.

ear advantage or may show a left-ear advantage (LEA). A question that is often asked is whether REA is a consequence of language learning or whether it is an indicator of structures in the nervous system that make language learning possible in the first place.

Functional asymmetry is difficult to study in very young infants. However, some researchers have approached it using several different methods. Entus (1977) and Vargha-Khadem and Corballis (1979), for instance, used the nonnutritive sucking technique and found an interaction. Pursuing the same problem, Bertoncini et al. (in press) employed the sucking technique with four-day-old infants and found a greater recovery of sucking when a linguistic change occurred in the right ear and a musical change in the left ear (see figure 8.1). Likewise, Best, Hoffman, and Glanville (1982), used the orienting response and showed that there is a clear LEA for musical stimuli at birth, but a REA for speech appears after two months of life. Segalowitz and Chapman (1980) used limb tremor as an indicator and observed greater tremor suppression in the right limb when speech was presented and greater tremor suppression in the left limb when music was presented. In short, the evidence favors specialization of the left hemisphere for processing speechlike stimuli at birth or very shortly thereafter. Confirmation of these results and their interpretation would constitute one of the stronger arguments favoring a biological basis for speech processing and consequently a strong innate component in language processing.

The proponents of the speech-is-special hypothesis have often couched their views in terms of the intimate relation that exists between speech perception and speech production. This relation can be clearly illustrated very reliably with the McGurk effect (McGurk and MacDonald 1976). This effect is the compromise in perception of nonconvergent visual and auditory stimuli. The acoustic and visual information listeners receive is usually congruent. Yet it is possible to present incongruent information by showing subjects the image of a mouth making one syllable accompanied by a sound track of another syllable. Under these conditions subjects report hearing a compromise of the visual and acoustic stimuli they have received. Are young infants also subject to this type of effect? Infants have recently been studied to evaluate the extent to which their perception of speech is related to motor or visual interaction.

MacKain et al. (1983) and Kuhl and Meltzoff (1984) have shown that very young infants will look more at a screen that displays a mouth moving congruently with a sound than to a screen displaying an incongruent movement. However, this preference for cross-modal correspondence operates only when the screen is placed in the infant's right visual field rather than left visual field in the experiment reported by McKain et al. (1983), but not in that reported by Kuhl and Meltzoff (1984). Subjects in the experiments by MacKain et al. were 5 to 6 months old, while those studied by Kuhl and Meltzoff were 4 to 4½ months old.

In short, even at a very early age, infants represent speech intermodally and perhaps make better matches of sound and sight in the right visual field than in the left. They also show a preference for speech produced by a familiar speaker rather than an unknown speaker. Furthermore, they behave differently for naturally intonated speech than for a monotone list of words. All in all, infants process speech as if it were different from other acoustic stimuli.

Speech as a Natural Object

In this section we shall present further evidence suggesting that the infant's processing of speech is special. At birth infants do not speak, and presumably, they do not know what a natural language is. Consequently, they ignore the fact that the adults around them speak English, French, Chinese, or whatever. However, as we saw above, before starting to speak, the newborn begins a process of converging towards the phonology of its caretaker's language. We know that infants learn to speak shortly after age two. We can thus assume that this is a reasonable estimate of the time this process requires to come to term. The fact remains, however, that we do not know how the infant succeeds in arriving at a system as complex as the phonological system of natural language, regardless of the time required.

Let us simply try to represent the magnitude of the problems facing the newborn infant. It comes into a world full of different signals. There are street noises, hospital-equipment noises, exclamations from enraptured parents and grandparents, and so forth. In addition, the infant hears the utterances of the people around. These utterances are punctuated by noises, interruptions, other utterances pronounced at the same time, the telephone, and what have you. The question is, How does the infant proceed to establish an equivalence class of informative stimuli in its attempt to establish the phonological regularities, rules, and constraints of the language? When the infant is surrounded by speakers of two languages, it is amazing that delays in speech acquisition have not been reported or have been only minimal. One disposition that might be of some use to the infant in its endeavor to acquire a language relates to the notion of natural language. If the infant is not somehow predisposed to find phonological regularities in the utterances it hears, its task would be insurmountably difficult. The task is not an easy one even if there is such a disposition, but it may be a manageable one. Infants probably inspect their acoustic environment expecting to find language and utterances that belong to it. To test this hypothesis we carried out the experiments reported below (see Mehler et al. 1988).

Four-day-old infants who listen to a recording of speech behave differently according to the linguistic nature of the utterances. Indeed, when the utterances belong to the parental language, in our case French, we observed a higher number of sucks than when the utterances were from another language, Russian. The recorded utterances were those of a bilingual speaker who was equally proficient in both languages. We also observed that switching presentations from the foreign language to the parental language results in a significant increase in sucking rate in comparison with control subjects. The switch from French to Russian utterances does not result in an increase in sucking. This asymmetry in discrimination may seem paradoxical at first. However, let us consider the following facts. When French infants go from French to Russian, they go from a "preferred" to a "non-preferred" stimulus, while the control group continues to listen to the preferred language.[4] After the change the sucking rate in both groups is high, though not for the same reasons. One group remains high because of the intrinsic nature of the stimulus, French for French infants, while the other group increases its sucking because it notices a change in stimulation. In contrast, the infants who go from Russian to French go from a non-preferred to a preferred

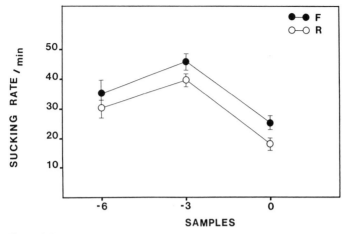

Figure 8.2
The change in sucking rate for the last three blocks of three consecutive samples during the first phase of experiment 1 for the infants who heard French (F) and the infants who heard Russian (R). The bars above and below each point indicate the standard error of the mean.

language, while the controls continue listening to a nonpreferred set of utterances. Both groups behave very differently during the test phase. Controls suck at low rates because they hear a nonpreferred stimulus, while experimental subjects experience two factors that result in an increase in sucking rate: a change in stimulation and going from a nonpreferred to a preferred set of stimuli. Thus, French babies have somehow learned to behave differently to utterances that belong to the language of their parents by the time they are four days old (see figures 8.2 to 8.3).

The results described above are all the more important when we consider that infants of foreign mothers born in Paris suck in response to French the way French infants suck in response to Russian (Mehler et al. 1988). Therefore, the preference of infants of French mothers for French is due to acquisition rather than to some intrinsic property of the French language not present in Russian. Ideally, these experiments should be carried out in Russian with babies of monolingual Russian mothers; we are currently attempting to get a collaboration going. In the meantime, in conjunction with Peter Jusczyk at the University of Oregon, my colleagues and I have pursued a study with American infants. Two-month-old infants are presented English and Italian utterances also recorded by bilingual speakers. We have found that two-month-old infants discern the switch from Italian to English

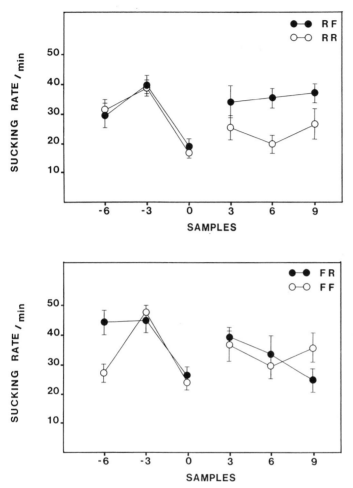

Figure 8.3
The top panel displays the sucking rates of the infants who heard Russian during the first phase of experiment 1. Group RF heard French during the second phase while group RR heard Russian. The comparable data for subjects who heard French during the first phase are shown in the bottom panel. Group FR heard Russian during the second phase while group FF continued to hear French. The bars above and below each point indicate the standard error of the mean.

and from English to Italian. No preference for English is apparent in the data. Furthermore, the infants did not discriminate French from Russian or Russian from French when we tested them using the same tape as the one used in Paris. Infants tested in Paris do not discriminate the switch from Italian to English and English to Italian. All these results indicate that it is necessary to have experience with one language before it can be discriminated from a foreign one. Two foreign languages are not discriminated from one another by very young infants.

What the results suggest is that the very young infant can extract characteristic properties of the parental language. Furthermore, once infants have determined these properties, they can infer whether new utterances belong to the parental language. This ability must be based on some specialized mechanism than operates on language stimuli, classifies them, and organizes new items in relation to those that have already been processed. Capacities like these were unsuspected even a few years ago. They oblige cognitive scientists like Gleitman (1981) and Gleitman and Wanner (1982) to reevaluate the nature of the mind at the IS and the mechanisms for learning that characterize it. We shall now turn our attention to those issues.

The Nature of the Initial State and Learning
The IS is difficult to define because it is a figment of the imagination whose usefulness depends on its consequences. The IS is the state of mind before it has had any commerce with the environment but after maturational processes have been completed. Naturally, the mind at birth may be composed of different ISs for each faculty. Thus, at birth, one IS may already be operational while another is not, because its neurological basis has not yet fully matured.

A definition of the IS implicitly presupposes that maturation and interaction with the environment are serially organized, that maturation takes place first, and only after this process is completed is there any interaction with the environment. That is almost certainly not the case for most faculties that have been explored in any detail. Indeed, before a system is fully mature it generally starts interacting with its milieu. This may not be a problem if it can be shown that the course of maturation is more or less unaffected by behaviors and by the nature of the interactions of the system during development. It is an empirical issue to determine which systems, if any, have a neurological structure that changes because of interaction with the environment.

The positions that scientists adopt concerning maturation serve to reveal their philosophical stance. Consider, for example, Piaget, who maintained that since constructivism accounts for the emergence of every cognitive competence of the organism, the notion of maturation can be dropped or avoided without any theoretical loss.

In contrast, many of those working within the paradigm postulating an IS that converges to a stable state, maintain that the course of maturation is minimally affected by early behavior. Such simplification makes it possible to understand how information is extracted and how inductive inference is carried out without worrying about the interaction between information types and nervous structures.

Within such a paradigm we still have to explain the results reported above, and in particular, we have to reply to a very frequently raised argument in connection with those results. Indeed, many scientists argue that the linguistic dispositions found in neonates are to be expected because the infant has had ample opportunity prior to birth to extract information about the acoustic environment into which it will be born. This may be right to some extent (Lecanuet et al. 1987). Consider the infant's preference for the caretaker's language. Even if we accept that the infant is exposed to the sentences that its mother utters during the last few months of pregnancy, it seems difficult to accept that this is a sufficient explanation for the way in which the infant makes phonetic and prosodic classifications, judges syllables, and characterizes the sound pattern of the parental language. Once the infant has constructed such a rule-governed system, it can classify new utterances according to whether they belong to the parental language, but it cannot separate the utterances of two unknown languages. Suppose that the infant required two months rather than two days to learn to distinguish utterances in the native language from those in a foreign language. The facts would remain equally mysterious and remarkable at the present state of our knowledge about how learning takes place. Furthermore, there is a sense in which the facts are even more surprising, since they imply that the infant is capable of mapping a distorted and filtered message onto previously classified utterance types.

Be this as it may, the most recent results obtained in our laboratory, which I present in a very preliminary fashion, show that the infant under twelve hours of age does not respond differentially to French and Russian utterances as do four-day-olds. Indeed, at that age there is no preference during the first phase of the experiment. Many factors could be invoked to explain such a preliminary result, and no doubt more empirical work is necessary before we jump to any hasty conclusion.

I would like to conclude this section with a speculative account of language acquisition that places this kind of achievement close to the learning mechanisms invoked by Gould and Marler (1987). They argue: "Learning is often thought of as the alternative to instinct, which is the information passed genetically from one generation to the next. Most of us think the ability to learn is the hallmark of intelligence. The difference between learning and instinct is said to distinguish human beings from "lower" animals such as insects. Introspection, that deceptively convincing authority, leads one to conclude that learning, unlike instinct, usually involves conscious decisions concerning when and what to learn" (p. 62). The authors proceed to argue that learning and instinct should be viewed as intimately related systems. Insects are capable of learning some very complicated tasks, while learning in humans is more often than not innately guided. They argue also that almost all animals are preprogrammed to learn "particular things in particular ways."

The work on the human infant has served to demonstrate that what Gould and Marler say about most animals applies equally well to the human species. The fact of the matter remains that the exact mechanisms that enable man to acquire many aptitudes in very short lapses of time remain mysterious.

Conclusion

The years to come will most certainly contribute data to complement our knowledge about systems that learn. In this paper I have tried to demonstrate that the human infant is already equipped to acquire language in ways that are at least determined by its biological makeup. How and how much the infant learns about speech and language remains an open issue. However, it is already apparent that the members of the human species are designed to acquire language in ways that are both specific and efficient. It is only when the genetic program fails that most problems arise. As with all genetic programs, the program for language acquisition unfolds in environments. What determines the effect of an environment is something that still has to be explored in much greater detail.

Before finishing this chapter it will be useful to relate my stance to movements currently quite popular in cognitive science. I am, of course, referring to the much publicized parallel-distributed-processing (PDP) models presented by McClelland and Rumelhart (1985), Elman and Sejnowski among others. (See the chapters by Churchland and Sejnowski and by Seidenberg and McClelland in this volume.)

PDP models have been created by exploring processes like the ones used in lexical access, category membership, and stabilization through attractors. Their implementation on desk-top computers will help to discipline some of the claims that learning theorists have been making, because many systems stabilize on some structures rather than on others. Though many psychologists have been converted to the belief that PDP models have the ability to learn without relying on rules, many psychologists are challenging this viewpoint with detailed analyses of the claims made. The extent to which PDP models might find application in speech acquisition is still unknown. It might be worthwhile to use such systems to understand the way in which the newborn infant can and does classify inputs.

It is interesting to understand what kinds of hardware can implement procedures demonstrably at work in behaviors typical of the human species. However, the procedures themselves generally need to be understood before we can rate the suitability of the mechanical implementations being proposed. In this chapter I have presented work aimed at uncovering the specificity of the procedures that allow the human infant access to language. My colleagues and I have discovered and presented some behavioral patterns that in our view deserve further study. We have not, however, presented any hypotheses as to the mechanisms underlying the behaviors discovered. It remains for future research to identify the mechanisms that sustain species-specific behaviors, some of which we have tried to characterize in the above paragraphs.

Does the research so far described contain any lessons that may help clarify the questions in special areas like reading acquisition and dyslexia? Of course, any data that increases our understanding of growth, the functioning of cognitive devices, and the impact of the environment on the IS may eventually help us to understand changes in behaviors like those described in the neuropsychological literature. However, the distance separating the levels at which the developmental psycholinguist and the reading expert are working is so huge that it is premature, to say the least, to connect these two domains at this time. There may be a time when knowledge of speech acquisition will clarify aspects of the acquisition of a phoneme-grapheme transcription system.

Notes

I would like to thank Al Galaburda and Peter Jusczyk for their help and advice on this chapter. I am grateful to Centre National de la Recherche Scientifique (Action Thématique Programmée, Procéssus cognitifs en jeu dans la production et la compréhension du langage) and the Fondation pour la Recherche Médicale for their generous support of the work reported here.

1. Unfortunately, such a position is still held in one version or another. For instance, efforts to detach neuropsychology from the broader domain of the brain sciences may be, despite disclaimers, a remnant of behaviorism even when it is couched in more modern cognitive psychology. Consider also the indifference to biology of many of the new trends in cognitive science. Should it not be argued that such neglect of an important part of the evidence will end up marginalizing cognitive science.

2. If we believe Fodor (1983), this hiatus between peripheral and central capacities is typical of the study of mind in general and not only of the IS:

> I am not suggesting that the reason why there is no serious psychology of central cognitive processes is the same as the reason why there is no serious philosophy of scientific confirmation. Both exemplify the significance of global factors in the fixation of belief, and nobody begins to understand how such factors have their effects. In this respect, cognitive science hasn't even *started*; we are literally no farther advanced than we were in the darkest days of behaviorism (though we are, no doubt, in some beneficent respects more disillusioned). If someone—a Dreyfus, for example—were to ask us why we should even suppose that the digital computer is a plausible mechanism for the simulation of global cognitive processes, the answering silence would be deafening. (p. 129)

Thus, the reader should not be surprised that the focus of my presentation is mostly on the results that have been gathered on the infant's dispositions for processing. That is where the data are.

3. Infants prefer noisebands to pure tones. They react best to sounds in the 1,003–3,000 Hz frequency range, which corresponds exactly to the range covering most of the speech signal. This result leads Eisenberg (1976) to speculate that "differential tuning to the carrier frequencies of language may be built in during intrauterine life" (p. 122). For some time it was unknown whether the reactivity for this range reflected psychophysical parameters or whether the behavior resulted, let us say, from a preference. Schneider, Trehub, and Bull (1979) used the head-turn technique to explore this question. They conditioned infants to turn their heads to a tone. Once infants had learned to do this, acuity to changes in stimuli of different pitches was measured. It was shown that infants are more sensitive to sounds higher in frequency than those within the speech range. Nonetheless, preference for pitches in the speech range was once again observed.

4. By "preferred" I mean a stimulus that all other things being equal, activates the infant to a greater extent than other stimuli.

5. I personally believe that the case of adequate information being available to the fetus is greatly overrated. However, for the sake of the argument presented here, it seems fair to take fiction for fact.

References

André-Thomas, C., and Autgaerden, S. 1960. *Locomotion from prenatal to postnatal life.* London: Heinemann.

Aslin, R. N., Pisoni, D. B., and Jusczyk, P. 1983. Auditory development and speech perception in infancy. In M. Haith and J. Campos, eds., *Carmichael's handbook of child psychology: Infancy and developmental psychobiology.* New York: Wiley.

Bertoncini, J, Bijeljac-Babic, R., Blumstein, S., and Mehler, J. 1987. Discrimination in neonates of very short CV's. *Journal of the Acoustical Society of America* 82:31–37.

Bertoncini, J., Bijeljac-Babic, R., Jusczyk, P. W., Kennedy, L., and Mehler, J. 1988. *Journal of Experimental Psychology: General.* 117 (1): 21–33.

Bertoncini, J., and Mehler, J. 1981. Syllables as units in infant speech perception. *Infant Behavior and Development* 4:247–260.

Bertoncini, J., Morais, J., Bijeljac-Babic, R., McAdams, S:., Peretz, I., and Mehler, J. In press. Dichotic perception and laterality in neonates. *Brain and Language.*

Best, C. T., Hoffman, H., Glanville, B. B. 1982. Development of infant ear asymmetries for speech and music. *Perception and Psychophysics* 31 (1):75–85.

Bower, T. G. R. 1977. *A primer of infant development.* San Francisco: W. H. Freeman.

Bower, T. G. R. 1979. *Human development.* San Francisco: W. H. Freeman.

Bronson, G. 1974. The postnatal growth of visual capacity. *Child Development* 45:873–890.

Bronson, G. 1982. *The scanning patterns of human infants.* Norwood, N. J.: Ablex Publishing Co.

Changeux, J. P., and Danchin, A. 1974. Apprendre par stabilisation sélective des synapses au coûrs du développement. In Morin, E., and Piattelli-Palmarini, M., eds., *L'Unité de l'homme.* Paris: Le Seuil.

Chomsky, N. 1957. *Syntactic structure.* The Hague: Mouton.

Chomsky, N. 1965. *Aspects of a theory of syntax.* Cambridge: MIT Press.

Chomsky, N. 1966. *Language and mind.* New York: Harcourt, Brace, and Johanovich.

Chomsky, N. 1980. The linguistic approach. In Piatelli-Palmarini, M., ed., *Language and learning: The debate between Jean Piaget and Noam Chomsky.* Cambridge: Harvard University Press.

Chomsky, N. 1986. *Knowledge of language.* New York: Praeger Publishers.

Chomsky, N. 1988. *Language and problems of knowledge.* Cambridge: MIT Press.

DeCasper, A. J., and Fifer, W. P. 1980. Of human bonding: Newborns prefer their mother's voices. *Science* 208:1174–1176.

Eimas, P. D. 1974. Auditory and linguistic processing of cues for place of articulation by infants. *Perception and Psychophysics* 16:513–521.

Eimas, P. D. 1975. Auditory and phonetic coding of the cues for speech: Discrimination of the (r-l) distinction by young infants. *Perception and Psychophysics* 18(5):341–347.

Eimas, P. D., and Miller, J. L. 1980. Contextual effects in infant speech perception. *Science* 209:1140–1141.

Eimas, P. D., Siqueland, E. R., Jusczyk, P. W., and Vigorito, J. 1971. Speech perception in infants. *Science* 171:303–306.

Eisenberg, R. 1976. *Auditory competence in early life.* Baltimore: University Park Press.

Elman, J. L., and Zipser, D. 1987. Learning and the hidden structure of speech. Technical report. Psychology Department, University of California, San Diego.

Entus, A. K. 1977. Hemispheric asymmetry in processing of dichotically presented speech and nonspeech stimuli by infants. In S. J. Segalowitz and F. A. Gruber, eds., *Language Development and neurological theory.* New York: Academic Press.

Fodor, J. A. 1975. *The language of thought.* New York: Crowell.

Fodor, J. A., and Pylyshyn, Z. W. 1988. Connectionism and cognitive architecture: A critical analysis. *Cognition* 28:3–71.

Gleitman, L. R. 1981. Maturational determinants of language growth. *Cognition* 10:103–114.

Gletiman, L. R., and Wanner, E. 1982. Language acquisition: The state of the state of the art. In E. Wanner and L. R. Gleitman, eds., *Language acquisition: State of the art*. New York: Cambridge University Press.

Goto, H. 1971. Auditory perception by normal Japanese adults of the sounds "L" and "R." *Neuropsychologia* 9:317–323.

Gould, J. L., and Marler, P. 1987. Learning by instinct. *Scientific American* 256(1):62–73.

Graham, F. K., Leavitt, L. A., Strock, B. D., and Brown, J. W. 1978. Preconscious carac orienting in a human anencephalic infant. *Science* 199:322–324.

Hillenbrand, J. 1984. Speech perception by infants: Categorization based on nasal consonant place of articulation. *Journal of the Acoustical Society of America* 75:1613–1622.

Jusczyk, P. W. 1977. Perception of syllable-final stop consonants by two-month old infants. *Perception and Psychophysics* 21:450–454.

Jusczyk, P. W., Derrah, C. 1987. Representation of speech sounds by young infants. *Developmental Psychology* 23:648–654.

Jusczyk, P. W., Halsted, N., and Mehler, J. In preparation. Factors underlying the young infant's capacity to distinguish one language from another.

Jusczyk, P. W., and Thompson, E. 1978. Perception of a phonetic contrast in multi-syllabic utterances by 2-month-old infants. *Perception and Psychophysics* 223:105–109.

Kluender, K. R., Diehl, R. L., and Killeen, P. R. 1987. Japanese quail can learn phonetic categories. *Science* 237:1195–1197.

Kuhl, P. K. 1980. Perceptual constancy for speech-sound categories in early infancy. In G. Yeni-Komshian, J. Kavanagh, and C. Ferguson, eds., *Child phonology*, vol. 2, *Perception*. New York: Academic Press.

Kulh, P. K. 1985. Methods in the study of infant speech perception. In G. Gottlieb and N. Krasnegor, eds., *Measurement of audition and vision in the first year of postnatal life: A methodological overview*. Norwood, N.J.: Ablex Publishing Co.

Kuhl, P. K., and Meltzoff, A. N. 1982. The bimodal perception of speech in infancy. *Science* 218:1138–1141.

Lachter, J., and Bever, T. G. 1988. The relation between linguistic structure and associative theories of language learning—A constructive critique of some connectionist learning models. *Cognition* 28:195–247.

Lecanuet, J. P., Granier-Deferre, C., De Casper, A. J., Mavgeais, R., Andrieu, A. J., and Busnel, M. C. 1987. Perception et discrimination foetales de stimuli langagiers mise en évidence à partir de la reactivité cardiaque: Résultats préliminaires. *Comptes rendus de l'Académie des sciences de Paris* 305 (3):161–164.

MacKain, K. S., Best, C. T., and Strange, W. 1980. Native language effects on the perception of liquids. *Journal of the Acoustical Society of America* 27:527.

MacKain, K., Studdert-Kennedy, M., Spieker, S., and Stern, D. 1983. Infant intermodal speech perception is a left-hemisphere function. *Science* 219:1347–1349.

McClelland, J. L., and Elman, J. L. 1986. The TRACE model of speech perception. *Cognitive Psychology* 1:1–86.

McClelland, J. L., and Rumelhart, D. E. 1985. Distributed memory and the representation of general and specific information. *Journal of Experimental Psychology: General* 114:159–188.

McGurk, H., and McDonald, J. 1976. Hearing lips and seeing voices. *Nature* 88:746–748.

McGurk, H., Turnure, C., and Creighton, S. 1977. *Child Development* 48:138–143.

Mehler, J. 1974. Connaître par desapprentissage. In *L'Unité de l'homme*, E. Morin and M. Piattelli-Palmarini, eds., Paris: Le Seuil.

Mehler, J., Barrière, M., and Jassik-Gerschenfeld, D. 1976. Reconnaissance de la voix maternelle par le nourrisson. *La Recherche* 7:786–788.

Mehler, J., Bertoncini, J., and Barrière, M. 1978. Infant perception of mother's voice. *Perception* 7:491–497.

Mehler, J., and Fox, R., eds. 1984. *Neonate cognition: Beyond the buzzing, blooming confusion.* Hillsdale, N.J.: L. Erlbaum.

Mehler, J., Lambertz, G., Jusczyk, P. W., and Amiel-Tison, C. 1986. Discrimination de la langue maternelle par le nouveau-né. *Comptes Rendus de l'Académie des Sciences de Paris* 303 (3):15.

Mehler, J., Juszcyk, P. W., Lambertz, G., Amiel-Tison, C., and Bertoncini, J. 1988. A precursor of language acquisition in young infants. *Cognition* 29:143–178.

Miller, J. L., and Eimas, P. 1979. Organization in infant speech perception. *Canadian Journal of Psychology* 33:353–365.

Mills, M., and Meluish, E. 1974. Recognition of mother's voice in early infancy. *Nature* 252:123–124.

Miyawaki, K., Strange, W., Verbrugge, R., Liberman, A. M., Jenkins, J. J., and Fujimura, O. 1975. An effect of linguistic experience: The discrimination of (r) and (l) by native speakers of Japanese and English. *Perception and Psychophysics* 18 (5): 331–340.

Molfese, D. L., and Molfese, V. J. 1979. Hemisphere and stimulus differences as reflected in the cortical response of newborn infants to speech stimuli. *Developmental Psychology* 15:501–511.

Moore, J. M., Wilson, W. R., and Thompson, G. 1976. Visual reinforcement of head-turn responses in infants under 12 months of age. *Journal of Speech and Hearing Disorders* 41:328–335.

Pinker, S., and Prince, A. 1988. On language and connectionism: Analysis of a parallel distributed processing model of language acquisition. *Cognition* 28:73–193.

Schneider, B. A., Trehub, S. E., and Bull, D. 1979. The development of basic auditory processes in infants. *Canadian Journal of Psychology* 33:306–319.

Segalowitz, S. J., and Chapman, J. S. 1980. Cerebral asymmetry for speech in neonates: A behavioral measure. *Brain and Language* 9:281–288.

Siqueland, E. R., and De Lucia, C. A. 1969. Visual reinforcement of nonnutritive sucking in human infants. *Science* 165:1144–1146.

Skinner, B. F. 1938. *The behavior of organisms.* Englewood Cliffs: Prentice-Hall.

Skinner, B. F. 1953. *Science and human behavior.* N.Y.: Macmillan Press.

Skinner, B. F. 1957. *Verbal behavior.* New York: Appleton-Century-Crofts.

Slater, A., Morrison, V., and Rose, D. 1983. Locus of habituation in the human newborn. *Perception* 12:593–598.

Strange, W., and Jenkins, J. J. 1978. The role of linguistic experience on the perception of speech. In R. D. Walk and H. L. Pick, eds., *Perception and experience.* New York: Plenum.

Trehub, S. E. 1976. The discrimination of foreign speech contrasts by infants and adults. *Child Development* 47:466–472.

Trehub, S. E., and Rabinovitch, M. S. 1972. Auditory-linguistic sensitivity in early childhood. *Developmental Psychology* 6:74–77.

Vargha-Khadem, F., and Corballis, M. 1979. Cerebral asymmetry in infants. *Brain and Language* 8:1–9.

Walk, R. D., and Gibson, E. J. 1961. A comparative and analytical study of visual depth perception. *Psychological Monographs* 75:15.

Weir, C. 1981. Validation of the auditory cradle with sound and tactile stimuli. *British Journal of Audiology* 15:61–65.

Werker, J. F., Gilbert, J. H. V., Humphrey, K., and Tees, R. C. 1981. Developmental aspects of cross-language speech perception. *Child Development* 2:349–355.

Werker, J. F., and Logan, J. S. 1985. Cross-language evidence for three factors in speech perception. *Perception and Psychophysics* 37(1):35–44.

Werker, J. F., and Tees, R. C. 1984. Phonemic and phonetic factors in adult cross-language speech perception. *Journal of the Acoustical Society of America* 75(6):1866–1878.

Editor's Comments

The main motivation for the research presented here is to help specify what about language is innate and what is acquired after exposure, however early, to the environment of a *particular* language. The innate aspects of language, or the linguistic dispositions of the organism, reflect, of course, the history of the species. These innate aspects form a phylogenetic record of sorts that determines a set of possibilities, "an envelope," within which acquisition of a particular language must take place by mechanisms totally opaque.

Is there a similar distinction between innate and acquired structures at the level of anatomy, or of hardware? The answer to this question must be a resounding yes. We as a species inherit a disposition to build a standard model of the specifically human brain. Immediately after conception this disposition begins to be expressed. Equally soon environmental forces modify the standard pattern of the fetus's brain, making it uniquely individual.

What constitutes the environment? A gene codes for a protein, which becomes part of the environment of another gene in the same genome. The ultimate anatomy of the brain results not merely from the separate products of individual genes but also from epigenetic interactions among gene products and their chemical and physical effects, acting in specific spatial and temporal sequences (see Crossin and Edelman in this volume). Wherein lies the distinction between innate and acquired? In talking of what is acquired, are we referring to epigenetic interactions arising from factors outside the genome itself? In that case, at what point in the ontogenesis of the brain does this external environment begin to play a modulating role? This is an especially puzzling question in view of the fact that from the outset the mother constitutes a part of that chemical and physical external environment.

Ascertaining that a child has at the beginning normal linguistic dispositions and a prescribed tendency to build a brain that can support normal language development presupposes normal subsequent interactions with the environment. As stated on this chapter, the innate dispositions themselves are figments of the imagination.

Attempts to teach human language to apes have failed probably because the appropriate initial state is not present. Or have we failed to find an environment appropriate to the expression of a disposition normally hidden from view? On the other hand perhaps it is possible to alter an environment so that innate dispositions for a logical system of rules will be expressed anomalously or so that logical systems that lack innate dispositions, e.g., anomalous grammar, will be expressed.

Is the problem in developmental dyslexia one of an abnormal initial state or one of an abnormal environment? This is a central research question about so-called developmental *learning* disorders, whose label wrongly implies that it has been *determined* that the problem is one of acquisition rather than one of innate disposition. In fact it seems more likely to me that the anomaly is present instead in the initial state. Thus, one can surmise that a deaf individual who acquires normal skills in American Sign Language, for instance, illustrates normal initial linguistic dispositions expressed in an extraordinary way (see the paper by Bellugi et al. in this volume). An altogether anomalous auditory environment is not by itself capable of changing the extent to which the linguistic disposition can be expressed or the time course of language acquisition. Can any distortion of the language environment, beneficial or deleterious, change the linguistic disposition of the brain? I suspect not. The continual improvement of methods for addressing very early language acquisition will hopefully lead to research on infants at risk for developmental dyslexia and to at least partial answers to these questions.

Although the human capacity for language is coded in the genes, it seems reasonable to propose that the brain must be complex enough before language acquisition can begin. We discover that some knowledge about the language is already in place only a few hours or days after birth, which means that the brain is complex enough at that time or earlier. How do babies born prematurely fare in acquiring language? The precarious state of health characteristic of these infants presents enormous barriers to answering this question, which is important for determining how early the appropriate complexity emerges. An intuitively guided answer is that it is unlikely that the initial brain state for language acquisition is present much before the infant is exposed to a language signal of a relatively good quality, i.e., much before birth. If that is so, developmental brain research should support the notions that the linguistically ready brain contains all of its long circuits and most of its short circuits in place and that the process of language acquisition involves maturation (probably by selection, stabilization, and reinforcement) of the synaptic and receptor architectures associated with these neural networks.

Chapter 9

Neural Representation and Neural Computation

Patricia Smith Churchland and Terrence J. Sejnowski

The types of representation and the style of computation in the brain appear to be very different from the symbolic expressions and logical inferences that are used in sentence-logic models of cognition. In this chapter we explore the consequences that brain-style processing may have on theories of cognition. Connectionist models are used as examples to illustrate neural representation and computation in the pronouncing of English text and in the extracting of shape parameters from shaded images. Levels of analysis are not independent in connectionist models, and the dependencies between levels provide an opportunity to coevolve theories at all levels. This is a radical departure from the a priori, introspection-based strategy that has characterized most previous work in epistemology.

1 How Do We Represent the World?

The central epistemological question, from Plato on, is this: How is representation of a world by a self possible? So far as we can tell, there is a reality existing external to ourselves, and it appears that we do come to represent that reality, and sometimes even to know how its initial appearance to our senses differs from how it actually is. How is this accomplished, and how is knowledge possible? How is science itself possible?

The dominant philosophical tradition has been to try to resolve the epistemological puzzles by invoking only intuition and logic to figure out such things as the organization of knowledge, the nature of the "mirroring" of the outer world by the inner world, and the roles of reason and inference in the generation of internal models of reality. Epistemology thus pursued was the product of "pure reason," not of empirical investigation, and thus epistemological theories were believed to delimit the necessary conditions, the absolute foundations, and the incontrovertible presuppositions of human knowledge. For this a priori task—a task of reflective understanding and pure reason—empirical observations by psychologists and neurobiologists are typically considered irrelevant, or at least incapable of effecting any significant correction of the a priori conclusions. Plato, Descartes, and Kant are some of the major historical figures in that tradition; some contemporary figures are Chisholm (1966), Strawson (1966), Davidson (1974), and McGinn (1982). It is safe to say that most philosophers still espouse the a priori strategy to some nontrivial extent.

In a recent departure from this venerable tradition of a priori philosophy, some philosophers have argued that epistemology itself must be informed by the psychological and neurobiological data that bear upon how in fact we represent and model the world. First articulated in a systematic and powerful way by Quine (1960),[1] this new "naturalism" has begun to seem more in keeping with evolutionary and biological science and to promise more testable and less speculative answers.

If, as it seems, acquiring knowledge is an essentially biological phenomenon, in the straightforward sense that it is something our brains do, then there is no reason to expect that brains should have evolved to have a priori knowledge of the true nature of things: not of fire, not of light, not of the heart and the blood, and certainly not of knowledge or of its own microstructure and microfunction. There are, undoubtedly, innate dispositions to behave in certain ways, to believe certain things, and to organize data in certain ways, but innateness is no guarantee of truth, and it is the truth that a priori reflections are presumed to reveal. Innate beliefs and cognitive structure cannot be assumed to be either optimal or true, because all evolution "cares" about is that the internal models enable the species to survive. Satisfying is good enough. It is left for science to care about the truth (or perhaps empirical adequacy), and the theories science generates may well show the inadequacies of our innately specified models of external reality. Even more dramatically, they may show the inadequacy of our model of our internal reality—of the nature of our selves.

The a priori insights of the great philosophers should be understood, therefore, not as the absolute truth about how the mind-brain must be, but as articulations of the *assumptions* that live deep in our collective *conception* of ourselves. As assumptions, however, they may be misconceived and empirically unsound, or at least they may be open to revision in the light of scientific progress. The possibility of such revision does not entail that the assumptions are ludicrous or useless. On the contrary, they may well be very important elements in the theoretical scaffolding as neurobiology and psychology inch their way toward empirically adequate theories of mind-brain function. The methodological point is that in science we cannot proceed with no theoretical framework, so even intuitive folk theory is better than nothing as the scientific enterprise gets underway.

In addition to asking how the self can know about the external reality, Kant asked, How is representation of a *self* by a knowing self possible? One of his important ideas was that the nature of the internal world of the self is no more unmediated or *given* than is knowledge of the external world of physical objects in space and time. A modern version of this insight says: just as the inner thoughts and experiences may represent but not *resemble* the outer reality, so the inner thoughts may represent but not resemble the inner reality of which they are the representation. This idea, taken with Quine's naturalism, implies that if we want to know how we represent the world—the external world of colored, moving objects, and the internal world of thoughts, consciousness, motives, and dreams—the scientific approach is likely to be the most rewarding. Inner knowledge, like outer knowledge, is conceptually and theoretically mediated—it is the result of complex information processing. Whether our intuitive understanding of the nature of our inner world is at all adequate is an empirical question, not an a priori one.

If empirical results are relevant to our understanding of how the mind-brain represents, it is also entirely possible that scientific progress on this frontier will be as revolutionary as it has been in astronomy, physics, chemistry, biology, and geology. With this observation comes the recognition that it may reconfigure our current assumptions about knowledge, consciousness, representation, and the self at least as much as Copernicus and Darwin reconfigured our dearest assumptions about the nature of the universe and our place in it. Our intuitive assumptions and even what seems phenomenologically obvious may be misconceived and may thus undergo reconfiguration as a new theory emerges from psychology and neurobiology.

Philosophers—and sometimes psychologists and occasionally even neuroscientists—generally make one of two responses to the naturalists' conception of the status of our self-understanding:

> (1) Philosophy is an a priori discipline, and the fundamental conceptual truths about the nature of the mind, of knowledge, of reason, etc. will come only from a priori investigations. In this way philosophy sets the bounds for science—indeed, the bounds of sense, as Strawson (1966) would put it. In a more extreme vein, some existentialist philosophers would claim that the naturalistic approach is itself symptomatic of a civilizational neurosis: the infatuation with science. On this view, the scientific approach to human nature is deeply irrational. Mandt (1986, p.

274) describes the existentialist criticism as follows: "That scientific modes of thought have become paradigmatic indicates the degree to which traditional modes of human life and experience have disintegrated, plunging civilization into a nihilistic abyss."
(2) Even if a naturalistic approach is useful for some aspects of the nature of knowledge and representation, the neurosciences in particular are largely irrelevant to the enterprise. Neuroscience may be fascinating enough in its own right, but for a variety of reasons it is irrelevant to answering the questions we care about concerning cognition, representation, intelligent behavior, learning, consciousness, and so forth. Psychology and linguistics might actually be useful in informing us about such matters, but neurobiology is just off the book.

2   Why Is Neurobiology Dismissed as Irrelevant to Understanding How the Mind Works?

2.1   The Traditional Problem
In its traditional guise, the mind-body problem can be stated thus: Are mental phenomena (experiences, beliefs, desires, etc.) actually phenomena of a physical brain? Dualists have answered no to this question. On the dualist's view, mental phenomena inhere in a special, nonphysical substance: the mind (also referred to as the soul or the spirit). The mind, on the dualist's theory, is the ghost in the machine; it is composed not of physical material obeying physical laws but of soul-stuff, or "spooky" stuff, and it operates according to principles unique to spooky stuff.

The most renowned of the substance dualists are Plato and Descartes and, more recently, J. C. Eccles (1977) and Richard Swinburne (1986). Because dualists believe the mind to be a wholly separate kind of stuff or entity, they expect that it can be understood only in its own terms. At most, neuroscience can shed light on the *interaction* between mind and body, but not on the nature of the mind itself. Dualists consequently see psychology as essentially independent of neurobiology, which, after all, is devoted to finding out how the *physical* stuff of the nervous system works. It might be thought a bonus of dualism that it implies that to understand the mind we do not have to know much about the brain.

Materialism answers the mind-body question (Are mental states actually states of the physical brain?) in the affirmative. The predominant arguments for materialism draw upon the spectacular failure of dualism to cohere with the rest of ongoing science. And as physics, molecular biology, evolutionary biology, and neuroscience have progressed, this failure has become more rather than less marked. In short, the weight of empirical evidence is against the existence of special soul-stuff (spooky stuff). (For a more thorough discussion of the failure of substance dualism, see P. S. Churchland 1986). Proponents of materialism include Hobbes (in the seventeenth century), B. F. Skinner (1957, 1976), J. J. C. Smart (1959), W. V. O. Quine (1960), D. C. Dennett (1978), and P. M. Churchland (1988).

Despite the general commitment to materialism, there are significant differences among materialists in addressing the central question of how best to explain psychological states. Strict behaviorists, such as Skinner, thought that explanations would take the form of stimulus-response profiles *exclusively*. Supporting this empirical hypothesis with a philosophical theory, philosophical behaviorists claimed that the mental terminology itself could be analyzed into sheerly physicalistic language about dispositions to behave. (For discussion, see P. M. Churchland 1988.) Curiously, perhaps, the behaviorists (both empirical and philosophical) share with the dualists the conviction that it is not necessary to understand the workings of the brain in order to explain intelligent behavior. On the behaviorists' research ideology, again we have a bonus: in order to explain behavior, *we do not have to know anything about the brain.*

In contrast to behaviorism, identity theorists (Smart 1959; Enc 1983) claimed that mental states, such as visual perceptions, pains, beliefs, and drives, were in fact identical to states of the brain, though it would of course be up to neuroscience to discover precisely what brain sites were in fact identical to what mental states. On the research ideology advocated by these materialists, explanation of behavior will have to refer to inner representations and hence to what the brain is doing.

2.2   The Contemporary Problem: Theory Dualism

Many philosophers who are materialists to the extent that they doubt the existence of soul-stuff nonetheless believe that psychology ought to be essentially autonomous from neuroscience, and that neuroscience will not contribute significantly to our understanding of perception, language use, thinking, problem solving, and (more generally) cognition. Thus, the mind-body problem in its contemporary guise is this: Can we get a *unified* science of the mind-brain? Will psychological theory reduce to neuroscience?

A widespread view (which we call theory dualism) answers no to the above question. typically, three sorts of reasons are offered:

· *Neuroscience is too hard.* The brain is too complex; there are too many neurons and too many connections, and it is a hopeless task to suppose we can ever understand complex higher functions in terms of the dynamics and organization of neurons.

· *The argument from multiple instantiability.* Psychological states are functional states and as such can be implemented (instantiated) in diverse machines (Putnam 1967; Fodor 1975; Pylyshyn 1984). Therefore, no particular psychological state, such as believing that the earth is round or that $2 + 2 = 4$, can be identified with exactly this or that machine state. So no functional (cognitive) process can be reduced to the behavior of particular neuronal systems.

· *Psychological states have intentionality.* That is, they are identified in terms of their semantic content; they are "about" other things; they represent things; they have logical relations to one another. We can think about objects in their absence, and even of nonexistent objects. For example, if someone has the belief that Mars is warmer than Venus, then that psychological state is specified as the state it is in terms of the sentence "Mars is warmer than Venus," which has a specific meaning (its content) and which is logically related to other sentences. It is a belief *about* Mars and Venus, but it is not caused by Mars or Venus. Someone might have this belief because he was told or because he deduced it from other things he knew. In cognitive generalizations states are related semantically and logically, whereas in neurobiological generalizations states can only be *causally* related. Neurobiological explanations cannot be sensitive to the logical relations between the contents of cognitive states, or to meaning or "aboutness." They respond only to *causal* properties. Neurobiology, therefore, cannot do justice to cognition, and thus no reduction is possible.

2.3   What Is Wrong with Theory Dualism?
In opposition to theory dualists, reductionists think we ought to strive for an integration of psychological and neurobiological theory. Obviously, a crucial element in the discussion concerns what is meant by "reduction"; hence, part of what must first be achieved is a proper account of what sort of business intertheoretic reduction is.

Roughly, the account is this: Reductions are *explanations* of phenomena described by one theory in terms of the phenomena described by a more basic theory. Reductions typically involve the coevolution of theories over time, and as they coevolve, one theory is normally revised, corrected and modified by its coevolutionary cohort theory at the other level. This revisionary interaction can, and usually does, go both ways: from the more basic to the less basic theory and vice versa. It is important to emphasize the modification to theories as they co-evolve because sometimes the modification is radical and entails massive reconfiguration of the very categories used to describe the phenomena. In such an event, the very data to be explained may come to be redescribed under pressure from the evolving theories. Examples of categories that have undergone varying degrees of revision, from the minor to the radical, include impetus, caloric, gene, neuron, electricity, instinct, life, and very recently, excitability (in neurons) (Schaffner 1976; P. M. Churchland 1979; Hooker 1981).

Because reductionism is frequently misunderstood, it is necessary to be explicit about what is *not* meant. First, seeking reductions of macro-level theory to micro-level theory does not imply that one must first know everything about the elements of the micro theory before research at the macro level can be usefully undertaken. Quite the reverse is advocated—research should proceed at all levels of the system, and coevolution of theory may enhance progress at all levels. Data from one level *constrain* theorizing at that level and at other levels. Additionally, the reduction of theories does *not* mean that the reduced phenomena somehow disappear or are discredited. The theory of optics was reduced to the theory of electromagnetic radiation, but light itself did not disappear, nor did it become disreputable to study light at the macro level. Nor was the reduced theory cast out as useless or discredited; on the contrary, it was and continues to be useful for addressing phenomena at a higher level of description. As for the phenomenon, it is what it is, and it continues to be whatever it is as theories are reduced or abandoned. Whether a category is ultimately rejected or revised depends on its scientific integrity, and that is, of course, determined empirically. (Fore more detail on inter-theoretic reduction, see P. S. Churchland 1986.)

Given this brief account of reduction as a backdrop, an outline of how the reductionist answers the theory dualist goes as follows:

· Neuroscience *is* hard, but with many new techniques now available, an impressive body of data is available to constrain our theories, and much data are very suggestive as to how neural networks function. (See Sejnowski and Churchland, in press.) We have begun to see the shape of neurobiological answers to functional questions, such as how information is stored, how networks learn, and how networks of neurons represent.

· High-level states are multiply instantiable. So what? If in any given species we can show that particular functional states are identical to specific neuronal configurations (for example, that being in REM sleep is having a specified neuronal state, or that one type of learning involves changing synaptic weights according to a Hebb rule), that will be sufficient to declare a reduction relative to that domain (Richardson 1979; Enc 1983; P. S. Churchland 1986; section 3 below). Very pure philosophers who cannot bring themselves to call these perfectly respectable domain-relative explanations "reductions" are really just digging in on who gets to use the word.

Moreover, it should be emphasized that the explanation of high-level cognitive phenomena will not be achieved directly in terms of phenomena at the lowest level of nervous-system organization, such as synapses and individual neurons. Rather, the explanation will refer to properties at higher structural levels, such as networks or systems. Functional properties of networks and systems will be explained by reference to properties at the next level down, and so on. What we envision is a chain of explanations linking higher to next-lower levels, and so on down the ladder of structural levels. (See Sejnowski and Churchland, in press.) Aspects of individual variation at the synaptic and cellular levels are probably invisible at the systems level, where similarity of larger-scale emergent properties, such as position in a high-dimensional parameter space, is critical in identifying similarity of information-processing function (Sejnowski, Koch, and Churchland 1988).

A theory of how states in a nervous system represent or model the world will need to be set in the context of the evolution and development of nervous systems and will try to explain the interactive role of neural states in the ongoing neuro-cognitive economy of the system. Nervous systems do not represent all aspects of the physical environment; they selectively represent information a species needs, given its environmental niche and its way of life. Nervous systems are programmed to respond to certain selected features, and within limits they learn other features through experience by encountering examples and generalizing. Cognitive neuroscience is now beginning to understand how this is done (Livingstone 1988; Goldman-Rakic 1988; Kelso, Ganong, and Brown 1986). Although the task is difficult, it now seems reasonable to assume that the "aboutness" or "meaningfulness" of representational states is not a spooky relation but a neurobiological relation. As we come to understand more about the dynamical properties of networks, we may ultimately be able to generate a theory of how human language is learned and represented by our sort of nervous system, and thence to explain language-dependent kinds of meaning.

Because this answer is highly cryptic and because intentionality has often seemed forever beyond the reach of neurobiology, the next section will focus on intentionality: the theory dualist's motivation, and the reductionist's strategy.

3 Levels, Intentionality, and the Sentence-Logic Model of the Mind

3.1 Sentential Attitudes and the Computer Metaphor
Two deep and interrelated assumptions concerning the nature of cognition drive the third antireductionist argument:

· Cognition essentially involves representations and computations. Representations are, in general, symbolic structures, and computations are, in general, rules (such as rules of logic) for manipulating those symbolic structures.

· A good model for understanding mind-brain functions is the computer—that is, a machine based on the same logical foundations as a Turing machine and on the von Neumann architecture form for a digital computer. Such machines are ideally suited for the manipulation of symbols according to rules. The computer metaphor suggests that the mind-brain, at the information-processing level, can be understood as a kind of digital computer; the problem for cognitive psychology is to determine the program that our brains run.

The motivating vision here is that cognition is to be modeled largely on language and logical reasoning; having a thought is, functionally speaking, having a sentence in the head, and thinking is, functionally speaking, doing logic, or at least running on procedures very like logic. Put this baldly, it may seem faintly ridiculous, but the theory is supported quite plausibly by the observation that beliefs, thoughts, hopes, desires, and so forth are essential in the explanation of cognition, and that such states are irreducibly semantic because they are identified in virtue of their content sentences. That is, such states are always and essentially beliefs that p, thoughts that p, or desires that p, where for p we substitute the appropriate sentence, such as "Nixon was a Russian spy" or "Custard is made with milk." Such cognitive states—the so-called sentential attitudes—are the states they are in virtue of the sentences that specify what they are about. Moreover, a content sentence stands in specific logical and semantic relations to other sentences. The state transitions are determined by semantic and logical relations between the content sentences, not by casual relations among states neurobiologically described. Thus, cognitive states have *meaning* (i.e., content, or intentionality), and it might be argued that it is precisely in virtue of their meaningfulness that they play the role in cognition that they do.

The fundamental conception is, accordingly, well and truly rooted in folk psychology, the body of concepts and everyday lore by means of which we routinely explain one another's behavior by invoking sentential attitudes (Stich 1983; P. M. Churchland 1988)—e.g., Smith paid for the vase because he believed that his son had dropped it and he feared that the store owner would be angry. In these sorts of intentional explanations, the basic unit of representation is the sentence, and state transitions are accomplished through the following rules: deductive inference, inductive inference, and assorted other rules.

Extending the framework of folk psychology to get an encompassing account of cognition in general, this approach takes it that thinking, problem solving, language use, perception, and so forth will be understood as we determine the sequence of sentences corresponding to the steps in a given information-processing task; i.e., as we understand the mechanics of sentence crunching. According to this research paradigm, known as sententialism, it is the task of cognitive science to figure out what programs the brain runs, and neuroscience can then check these top-down hypotheses against the wetware to see if they are generally possible. (See especially Fodor 1975, Fodor 1981, and Pylyshyn 1984.)

3.2   *Is Cognition Mainly Symbol Manipulation in the Language of Thought?*

Although this view concerning the nature of cognition and the research strategy for studying cognition may be appealing (where much of the appeal is derived from the comfortable place found for folk psychology), it suffers from major defects. Many of these defects have been discussed in detail by Anderson and Hinton (1981), by P. S. Churchland (1986), and in various chapters of McClelland and Rumelhart 1986. A summary will call them to mind:

> · Many cognitive tasks, such as visual recognition and answering simple true-or-false questions, can be accomplished in about half a second. Given what we know about conduction velocities and synaptic delays in neurons, this allows about 5 milliseconds per computational step, which means that there is time for only about 100 steps. For a sequential program run on a conventional

computer, 100 steps is not going to get us remotely close to task completion. Feldman and Ballard (1982) call this the hundred-step rule.

· Anatomically and physiologically, the brain is a parallel system, not a sequential von Neumann machine. The neural architecture is highly interconnected. Neurons such as Purkinje cells may have upwards of 80,000 input connections, and neurons in cerebral cortex can have upwards of 10,000 output connections (Anderson and Hinton 1981; Pellionisz and Llinas 1982, Sejnowski 1986).

· However information is stored in nervous systems, it appears to be radically unlike information storage in a digital computer, where storage and processing are separated and items are stored in memory according to addressable *locations*. In nervous systems, information seems to be stored in the connections between the same neurons that process the information. There does not appear to be a distinct storage location for each piece of stored information, and information is content addressable rather than location addressable. Information storage is probably at least somewhat distributed rather than punctate, since memories tend to be degraded with damage to the system rather than selectively wiped out one by one.

· A task may fall gracefully to one architecture and not to another. Certain kinds of tasks, such as numerical calculation, fall gracefully to a von Neumann architecture, but others, such as learning or associative memory, do not. Things we humans find effortless (such as facial recognition and visual perception) are tasks which artificial intelligence has great difficulty simulating on a von Neumann architecture, whereas things we find "effortful" (such as simple proofs in the propositional calculus or mathematical calculations) are straightforward for a digital computer (Anderson and Hinton 1981; Rumelhart, Hinton, and McClelland 1986). This suggests that the computational style of nervous systems may be very unlike that suited to von Neumann architectures.

· The hardware-software analogy fails for many reasons, the most prominent of which are that nervous systems are plastic and that neurons continually change as we grow and learn. Related, perhaps, is the observation that nervous systems degrade gracefully and are relatively fault tolerant. A von Neumann machine is rigid and fault intolerant, and a breakdown of one tiny component disrupts the machine's performance.

· The analogy between levels of description in a conventional computer (such as the hardware/software distinction) and levels of explanation in nervous systems may well be profoundly misleading. Exactly how many levels of organization we need to postulate in order to understand nervous-system function is an empirical question, and it may turn out that there are many levels between the molecular and the behavioral. In nervous systems we may already discern as distinct descriptive levels the molecule, the membrane, the cell, the circuit, networks, maps, brain systems, and several levels of behavior (from the reflexive to the highest levels of cognition). Other levels may come to be described as more is discovered about the nature of nervous systems. As is discussed below, the properties at one level may constrain the kind of properties realizable at another level.

· Nonverbal animals and infraverbal humans present a major problem for the sentence-logic theory of cognition: How is their cognition accomplished? On the sentence-logic theory of cognition, either their cognition resembles the human variety (and hence involves symbol manipulation according to rules, and a language of thought replete with a substantial conceptual repertoire) or their cognitive processes are entirely different from the usual human ones. Neither alternative is remotely credible. The first lacks any evidence. At best, its defense is circular; it helps to save the theory. The second alternative entails a radical discontinuity in evolution—sufficiently radical that language-of-thought cognition is a bolt from the blue. This implies that evolutionary biology and developmental neurobiology are mistaken in some fundamental respects. Since neither alternative can be taken seriously, the hypothesis itself has diminished credibility.

If cognition, then, is *not*, in general, to be understood on the sentence-logic model, the pressing questions then are these: How *does* the brain represent? How do nervous systems model the external world of objects in motion and the internal world of the nervous system itself? And when representations do stand in semantic and logical relations to one another, how is this achieved by neural networks? How is the semantic and logical structure of language—as we both comprehend and speak—represented in the brain? According to the rejected model, we postulate an internal organization—a language of thought—with the very same structure and organization as language. But if that model is rejected, what do we replace it with?

These are, of course, *the* central questions, and getting answers will not be easy. But the difficulty should not make the language-of-thought hypothesis more appealing. In certain respects, the current scientific state of a general theory of representation is analogous to the science of embryology in the nineteenth century. The development of highly structured, complex, fully formed organisms from eggs and sperm is a profoundly amazing thing. Faced with this mystery, some scientists concluded that the only way to explain the emergence of a fully structured organism at birth was to assume that the structure was already there. Hence the homuncular theory of reproduction, which claimed that a miniature but complete human already exists in the sperm and merely expands during its tenure in the womb.

We now know that there *is* structure in the sperm (and the egg)— not in the form of a miniature, fully structured organism, but mainly in the form of DNA—a molecule that looks not at *all* like a fully formed human. Thus, the structure of the cause does not resemble the structure of the effect. Accordingly, the homuncular theorists were right in supposing that the highly structured neonate does not come from *nothing*, but they were wrong in looking for a structural resemblance between cause and effect. It was, of course, terribly hard to imagine the nature of the structural organization that enables development yet in no way resembles the final product. Only through molecular biology and detailed work in embryology have we begun to understand how one kind of structure can, through intermediate mechanisms, yield another, very different kind of structure.

The parallel with cognitive neurobiology is this: the neuronal processes underlying cognition have a structure of some kind, but almost certainly it will not, in general, look anything like the semantic/logic structure visible in overt language. The organizational principles of nervous systems are what permit highly complex, structured patterns of behavior, for it is certain that the behavioral structure does not emerge magically from neuronal chaos. As things stand, it is very hard to imagine what those organizational principles could look like, and, just as in genetics and embryology, we can find answers only by framing hypotheses and doing experiments.

Instead of starting from the old sentence-logic model, we model information processing in terms of *the trajectory of a complex nonlinear dynamical system in a very high-dimensional space.* This structure does not resemble sentences arrayed in logical sequences, but it is potentially rich enough and complex enough to yield behavior capable of supporting semantic and logical relationships. We shall now explore what representing looks like in a particular class of nonlinear dynamical systems called connectionist models.

4   Representation in Connectionist Models

As the name implies, a connectionist model is characterized by connections and differential strengths of connection between processing units. Processing units are meant to be rather like neurons, and communicate with one another by signals (such as firing rate) that are numerical rather than symbolic. Connectionist models are designed to perform a task by specifying the architecture: the number of units, their arrangement in layers and columns, the patterns of connectivity, and the weight or strength of each connection (figures 9.1 and 9.2). These models have close ties with the computational level on which the task is specified, and with the implementation level on which the task is physically instantiated (Marr 1982). This species of network models should properly be considered a class of algorithms specified at various levels of organization—in some cases at the small-circuit level, in other cases at the system level. Both the task description and the neural embodiment are, however, crucially important in constraining the class of networks that will be explored. On the one hand, the networks have to be powerful enough to match human performance of the computational tasks, and on the other hand they have to be built from the available materials. In the case of the brain, that means neurons and synapses; in the case of network models, that means neuronlike processing units and synapselike weights.

Digital computers are used to simulate neural networks, and the network models that can be simulated on current machines are tiny in comparison with the number of synapses and neurons in the mam-

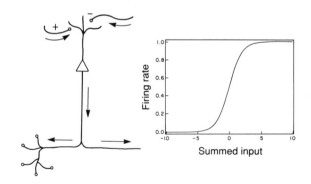

Figure 9.1
Left: schematic model of a neuronlike processing unit that receives synapselike inputs from other processing units. Right: nonlinear sigmoid-shaped transformation between summed inputs and the output "firing rate" of a processing unit. The output is a continuous value between 0 and 1.

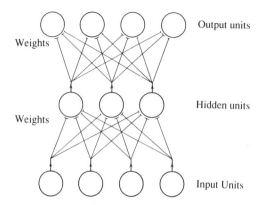

Figure 9.2
Schematic model of a three-layered network. Each input unit makes connections with each of the hidden units on the middle layer, which in turn projects to each of the output units. This is a feedforward architecture in which information provided as an input vector flows through the network, one layer at a time, to produce an output vector. More complex architectures allow feedback connections from an upper to a lower layer and lateral interactions between units within a layer.

malian brain. The networks that have been constructed should be understood, therefore, as small parts of a more complex processing system whose general configuration has not yet been worked out, rather than as simulations of a whole system. To avoid misunderstanding, it should be emphasized that connectionist models cannot yet support a full cognitive system. To begin to reach that goal will require both a computing technology capable of supporting more detailed simulations and a more complete specification of the nervous system.

Granting these limitations, we may nonetheless be able to catch a glimpse of what representations might look like within the parallel-style architecture of the brain by taking a look inside a connectionist network. The place to look is in the dynamics of the system; that is, in the patterns of activity generated by the system of interconnected units. This approach has its roots in the work of previous generations of researchers—primarily the gestalt school of psychology and D. O. Hebb (1949), who developed many ideas about learning and representation in neural assemblies. Only recently, however, has sufficient computer power been available to explore the consequences of these ideas by direct simulation, since the dynamics of massively parallel nonlinear networks is highly computation intensive. Parallel-network models are now being used to explore many different aspects of perception and cognition (McClelland and Rumelhart 1986; Feldman and

Ballard 1982; *Cognitive Science,* volume 9, special issue) but in this chapter we shall focus on two representative examples. The first is NETtalk, perhaps the most complex network model yet constructed, which learns to convert English text to speech sounds (Sejnowski and Rosenberg 1987, 1988). The second is a network model that computes surface curvatures of an object from its gray-level input image. NETtalk will be used primarily to illustrate two things: how a network can learn to perform a very complex task without symbols and without rules to manipulate symbols, and the differences between local and distributed representations.

Connectionist models can be applied on a large scale to model whole brain systems or on a smaller scale to model particular brain circuits. NETtalk is on a large scale, since the problem of pronunciation is constrained mainly by the abstract cognitive considerations and since its solution in the brain must involve a number of systems, including the visual system, the motor-articulatory system, and the language areas. The second example is more directly related to smaller brain circuits used in visual processing; the representational organization achieved by the network model can be related to the known representational organization in visual cortex.

In the models reviewed here, the processing units sum the inputs from connections with other processing units, each input weighted by the strength of the connection. The output of each processing unit is a real number that is a nonlinear function of the linearly summed inputs. The output is small when the inputs are below threshold, and it increases rapidly as the total input becomes more positive. Roughly, the activity level can be considered the sum of the postsynaptic potentials in a neuron, and the output can be considered its firing rate (figure 9.1).

4.1   Speech Processing: Text to Speech
In the simplest NETtalk system there are three layers of processing units.[2] The first level receives as input letters in a word; the final layer yields the elementary speech sounds, or phonemes (table 9.1); and an intervening layer of "hidden units," which is fully connected with the input and output layers, performs the transformation of letter to sounds (figure 9.3). On the input layer, there is *local representation* with respect to letters because single units are used to represent single letters of the alphabet. Notice, however, that the representation could be construed as *distributed* with respect to *words,* inasmuch as each word is represented as a pattern of activity among the input units. Similarly, each phoneme is represented by a pattern of activity among the output units, and phonemic representation is therefore

Table 9.1
Symbols for phonemes used in NETtalk

Symbol	Phoneme	Symbol	Phoneme
/a/	father	/D/	this
/b/	bet	/E/	bet
/c/	bought	/G/	sing
/d/	debt	/I/	bit
/e/	bake	/J/	gin
/f/	fin	/K/	sexual
/g/	guess	/L/	bottle
/h/	head	/M/	absym
/i/	Pete	/N/	button
/k/	Ken	/O/	boy
/l/	let	/Q/	quest
/m/	met	/R/	bird
/n/	net	/S/	shin
/o/	boat	/T/	thin
/p/	pet	/U/	book
/r/	red	/W/	bout
/s/	sit	/X/	excess
/t/	test	/Y/	cute
/u/	lute	/Z/	leisure
/v/	vest	/@/	bat
/w/	wet	/!/	Nazi
/x/	about	/#/	examine
/y/	yet	/*/	one
/z/	zoo	/\/	logic
/A/	bite	/^/	but
/C/	chin		

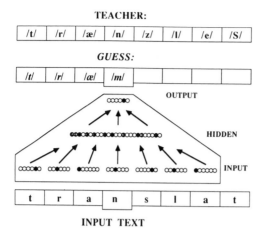

TEACHER:

/t/	/r/	/æ/	/n/	/z/	/l/	/e/	/S/

GUESS:

/t/	/r/	/œ/	/m/				

OUTPUT

HIDDEN

INPUT

t	r	a	n	s	l	a	t

INPUT TEXT

Figure 9.3
Schematic drawing of the NETtalk network architecture. A window of letters in an English text is fed to an array of 203 input units arranged in 7 groups of 29 units each. Information from these units is transformed by an intermediate layer of 80 hidden units to produce a pattern of activity in 26 output units. The connections in the network are specified by a total of 18,629 weight parameters (including a variable threshold for each unit). During the training, information about the desired output provided by the teacher is compared with the actual output of the network, and the weights in the network are changed slightly so as to reduce the error.

distributed. But each output unit is coded for a particular *distinctive feature* of the speech sound, such as whether the phoneme was voiced, and consequently each unit is local with respect to distinctive features.

NETtalk has 309 processing units and 18,629 connection strengths (weights) that must be specified. The network does not have any initial or built-in organization for processing the input or (more exactly) mapping letters onto sounds. All the structure emerges during the training period. The values of the weights are determined by using the "back-propagation" learning algorithm developed by Rumelhart, Hinton, and Williams (1986). (For reviews of network learning algorithms, see Hinton 1988 and Sejnowski 1988.) The strategy exploits the calculated error between the *actual* values of the processing units in the output layer and the *desired* values, which is provided by a training signal. The resulting error signal is propagated from the output layer backward to the input layer and used to adjust each weight in the network. The network learns, as the weights are changed, to minimize the mean squared error over the training set of words. Thus, the system can be characterized as following a path in weight space (the space of all possible weights) until it finds a minimum (fig-

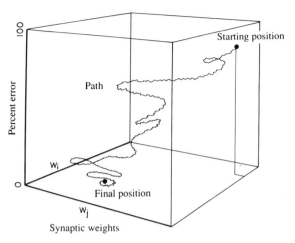

Figure 9.4
Schematic drawing of a path following in weight space as the network finds a minimum of the average error over the set of training patterns. Only two weights out of many thousands are shown. The learning algorithm only ensures convergence to a local minimum, which is often a good solution. Typically, many sets of weights are good solutions, so the network is likely to find one of them from a random starting position in weight space. The learning time can be reduced by starting the network near a good solution; for example, the pattern of connections can be limited to a geometry that reduces the number of variable weights that must be searched by gradient descent.

ure 9.4). The important point to be illustrated, therefore, is this: The network processes information by nonlinear dynamics, not by manipulating symbols and accessing rules. It learns by gradient descent in a complex interactive system, not by generating new rules (Hinton and Sejnowski 1986).

The issue that we want to focus on next is the structural organization that is "discovered" by the network, in virtue of which it succeeds in converting letters to phonemes and manages to pronounce, with few errors, the many irregularities of English. If there are no rules in the network, how is the transformation accomplished? Since a trained network can generalize quite well to new words, some knowledge about the pattern of English pronunciation must be contained inside the network. Although a representational organization was imposed on the input and output layers, the network had to create new, internal representations in the hidden layer of processing units. How did the network organize its "knowledge"? To be more accurate, how did the equivalence class of networks organize its knowledge? (Each time the network was started from a random set of weights, a different network was generated.)

The answers were not immediately available, because a network does not leave explanation of its travels through weight space, nor does it provide a decoding scheme when it reaches a resting place. Even so, some progress was made by measuring the activity pattern among the hidden units for specific inputs. In a sense, this test mimics at the modeling level what neurophysiologists do at the cellular level when they record the activity of a single neuron to try to find the effective stimulus that makes it respond. NETtalk is a fortunate "preparation," inasmuch as the number of processing units is relatively small, and it is possible to determine the activity patterns of all the units for all possible input patterns. These measurements, despite the relatively small network, did create a staggering amount of data, and then the puzzle was this: How does one find the order in all this data?

For each set of input letters, there is a pattern of activity among the hidden units (figure 9.5). The first step in the analysis of the activity of the hidden units was to compute the average level of activity for each letter-to-sound correspondence. For example, all words with the letter *c* in the middle position yielding the hard-*c* sound /k/ were presented to the network, and the average level of activity was calculated. Typically, about 15 of the 80 hidden units were very highly activated, and the rest of the hidden units had little or no activity. This procedure was repeated for each of the 79 letter-to-sound correspondences. The result was 79 vectors, each vector pointing in a different direction in the 80-dimensional space of average hidden-unit activities. The next step was to explore the relationship among the vectors in this space by cluster analysis. It is useful to conceive of each vector as the internal code that is used to represent a specific letter-to-sound correspondence; consequently, those vectors that clustered close together would have similar codes.

Remarkably, all the vectors for vowel sounds clustered together, indicating that they were represented in the network by patterns of activity in units that were distinct from those representing the consonants (which were themselves clustered together). (See figure 9.6.) Within the vowels, all the letter-to-sound correspondences that used the letter *a* were clustered together, as were the vectors of *e, i, o, u* and the relevant instances of *y*. This was a very robust organizational scheme that occurred in all the networks that were analyzed, differences in starting weights notwithstanding. The coding scheme for consonants was more variable from network to network, but as a general rule the clustering was based more on similarities in sounds than on letters. Thus, the labial stops /p/ and /b/ were very close together in the space of hidden-unit activities, as

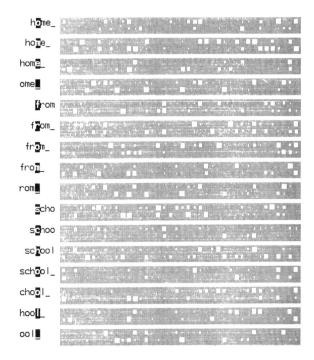

Figure 9.5
Levels of activation in the layer of hidden units for a variety of words. The input string
in the window of seven letters is shown to the left, with the target letter emphasized.
The output from the network is the phoneme that corresponds to the target letter. The
transformation is accomplished by 80 hidden units, whose activity levels are shown to
the right in two rows of 40 units each. The area of each white square is proportional to
the activity level. Most units have little or no activity for a given input, but a few are
highly activated.

were all the letter-to-sound correspondences that result in the hard-*c*
sound /k/.

Other statistical techniques, such as factor analysis and multidimensional scaling, are also being applied to the network, and activity patterns from individual inputs, rather than averages over classes,
are also being studied (Rosenberg 1988). These statistical techniques
are providing us with a detailed description of the representation for
single inputs as well as classes of input-output pairs.

Several aspects of NETtalk's organization should be emphasized:

· The representational organization visible in the trained-up network is not programmed or coded into the network; it is found
by the network. In a sense it "programs" itself, by virtue of being
connected in the manner described and having weights changed

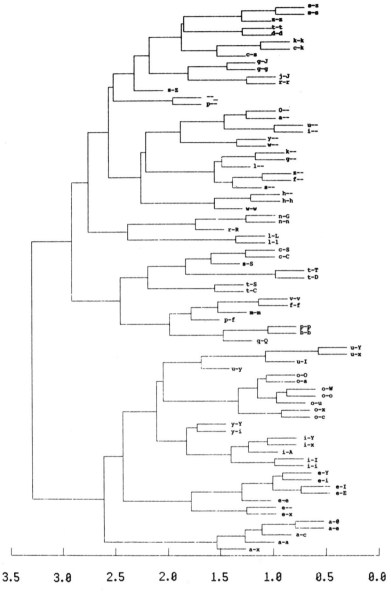

Figure 9.6
Hierarchical clustering of hidden units for letter-to-sound correspondences. The vectors of average hidden unit activity for each correspondence ('*l-p*' for letter *l* and phoneme *p*) were successively merging from right to left in the binary tree. The scale at the bottom indicates the Euclidean instance between the clusters. (From Sejnowski and Rosenberg 1987.)

by experience according to the learning algorithm. The dynamical properties of this sort of system are such that the network will settle into the displayed organization.

· The network's representation for letter-to-sound correspondences is neither local nor completely distributed; it is somewhere in between. The point is, each unit participates in more than one correspondence, and so the representation is not local, but since it does not participate in all correspondences, the representation is not completely distributed either.

· The representation is a property of the collection of hidden units, and does not resemble sentence-logic organization.

· The organization is structured, which suggests that emergent subordinate and superordinate relations might be a general principle of network organization that could be used as input for other networks assigned other tasks if NETtalk were embedded in a larger system of networks.

· General properties of the hierarchical organization of letter-to-sound correspondences emerged only at the level of groups of units. This organization was invariant across all the networks created from the same sample of English words, even where the processing units in distinct networks had specialized for a different aspect of the problem.

· Different networks created by starting from different initial conditions all achieved about the same level of performance, but the detailed response properties of the individual units in the networks differed greatly. Nonetheless, all the networks had similar functional clusterings for letter-to-sound correspondences (figure 9.6). This suggests that single neurons code information relative to other neurons in small groups or assemblies (Hebb 1949).

The representational organization in NETtalk may illustrate important principles concerning network computation and representation, but what do they tell us about neural representations? Some of the principles uncovered might be generally applicable to a wide class of tasks, but it would be surprising if the details of the model bore any significant resemblance to the way reading skills are represented in the human nervous system. NETtalk is more of a demonstration of certain network capacities and properties than a faithful model of some subsystem of the brain, and it may be a long time before data concerning the human neurobiology of reading become available. Nevertheless, the same network techniques that were used to explore the language domain can be applied to problems in other domains, such as vision, where much more is known about the anatomy and the physiology.

4.2 *Visual Processing: Computing Surface Curvature from Shaded Images*

The general constraints from brain architecture touched on in section 3 should be supplemented, wherever possible, by more detailed constraints from brain physiology and anatomy. Building models of real neural networks is a difficult task, however, because essential knowledge about the style of computation in the brain is not yet available (Sejnowski 1986). Not only is the fine detail (such as the connectivity patterns in neurons in cerebral cortex) not known, but even global-level knowledge specifying the flow of information through different parts of the brain during normal function is limited. Even if more neurophysiological neuroanatomical detail were available, current computing technology would put rather severe limits on how much detail could be captured in a simulation. Nevertheless, the same type of network model used in NETtalk could be useful in understanding how information is coded within small networks confined to cortical columns. The processing units in this model will be identified with neurons in the visual cortex.

Ever since Hubel and Wiesel (1962) first reported that single neurons in the cat visual cortex respond better to oriented bars of lights and to dark/light edges than to spots of light, it has been generally assumed, or at least widely hoped, that the function of these neurons is to detect boundaries of objects in the world. In general, the inference from a cell's response profile to its function in the wider information-processing economy is intuitively very plausible, and if we are to have any hope of understanding neural representations we need to start in an area—such as visual cortex—where it is possible to build on an impressive body of existing data. The trouble is, however, that many functions are consistent with the particular response properties of a neuronal population. That a cell responds optimally to an oriented bar of light is compatible with its having lots of functions other than detecting object boundaries, though the hypothesis that it serves to detect boundaries does tend to remain intuitively compelling. To see that our intuitions might really mislead us as we try to infer function from response profiles, it would be useful if we could demonstrate this point concretely. In what follows we shall show how the same response properties could in fact serve in the processing of visual information about the regions of a surface between boundaries rather than about the boundaries themselves.

Boundaries of objects are relatively rare in images, yet the preponderance of cells in visual cortex respond preferentially to oriented bars and slits. If we assume that all those cells are detecting boundaries, then it is puzzling that there should be so many cells whose sole function is to detect boundaries when there are not many boundaries to detect. It would, therefore, seem wasteful if, of all the neurons with oriented fields, only a small fraction carried useful information about a particular image. Within their boundaries, most objects have shaded or textured surfaces that will partially activate these neurons. The problem, accordingly, is this: Can the information contained in a population of partially activated cortical neurons be used to compute useful information about the three-dimensional surfaces between the boundaries of objects in the image?

One of the primary properties of a surface is its curvature. Some surfaces, such as the top of a table, are flat and have no intrinsic curvature. Other surfaces, such as cylinders and spheres, are curved, and around each point on a surface the degree of curvature can be characterized by the direction along the surface of maximum and minimum curvature. It can be shown that these directions are always at right angles to each other, and the values are called the *principal curvatures* (Hilbert and Cohn-Vossen 1952). The principal curvatures and the orientation of the axes provide a complete description of the local curvature.

One problem with extracting the principal curvatures from an image is that the gray-level shading depends on many factors, such as the direction of illumination, the reflectance of the surface, and the orientation of the surface relative to the viewer. Somehow our visual system is able to separate these variables and to extract information about the shape of an object independent of these other variables. Pentland (1984) has shown that a significant amount of information about the curvature of a surface is available locally. Can a network model be constructed that can extract this information from shaded images?

Until recently it was not obvious how to begin to construct such a network, but network learning algorithms (see above) provide us with a powerful method for creating a network by giving it examples of the task at hand. The learning algorithm is being used in this instance simply as a design tool to see whether some network can be found that performs the task. Many examples of simple surfaces (elliptic paraboloids) were generated and presented to the network. A set of weights was indeed found with this procedure that, independent of the direction of illumination, extracted the principal curvatures of three-dimensional surfaces and the direction of maximum curvature from shaded images (Lehky and Sejnowski 1987).

The input to the network is from an array of on-center and off-center receptive fields similar to those of cells in the lateral geniculate nucleus. The output layer is a population of units that conjointly represent the curvatures and the broadly tuned direction of maximum curvature. The units of the intermediate layer, which are needed to perform the transformation, have oriented receptive fields similar to those of simple cells in the visual cortex of cats and monkeys that respond optimally to oriented bars and edges (figure 9.7). It is important to emphasize that these properties of the hidden units were not put into the network directly but emerged during training. The system "chose" these properties because they are useful in performing a particular task. Interestingly, the output units, which were required to code information about the principal curvatures and principal orientations of surfaces, had properties, when probed with bars of light, that were similar to those of a class of complex cells that are end-stopped (Lehky and Sejnowski 1988). The surprising thing, given the plausible receptive-field-to-function inference rule, is that the function of the units in the network is not to detect bounding contours, but to extract curvature information from shaded images.

What the shape-from-shading network demonstrates is that we cannot directly infer function from receptive-field properties. In the trained-up network, the hidden units represent an intermediate transformation for a computational task quite different from the one that has been customarily ascribed to simple cells in visual cortex— they are used to determine shape from shading not to detect boundaries. It turns out, however, that the hidden units have *receptive fields similar to those of simple cells in visual cortex*. Therefore, bars and edges as receptive-field properties do not necessarily mean that the cell's function is to detect bars and edges in objects; it might be to detect curvature and shape, as it is in the network model, or perhaps some other surface property such as texture. The general implication is that there is no way of determining the function of each hidden unit in the network simply by "recording" the receptive-field properties of the unit. This, in turn, implies that, despite its surface intuitive plausibility, the receptive-field-to-function inference rule is untenable.

The function of a unit is revealed only when its *outputs*—its "projective field" (Lehky and Sejnowski 1988)—are also examined. It is the projective field of a unit that provides the additional information needed to interpret the unit's computational role in the network. In the network model the projective filed could be examined directly, but in real neural networks it can only be inferred indirectly by examining the next stage of processing. Whether or not curvature is directly represented in visual cortex, for example, can be tested by designing experiments with images of curved surfaces.

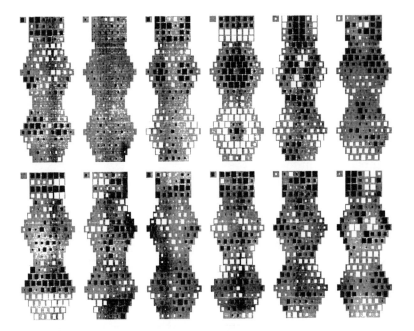

Figure 9.7
Hinton diagrams showing the connection strengths in a network that computes the principal curvatures and direction of minimum curvature from shaded images in a small patch of the visual field corresponding roughly to the area represented in a cortical column. There are 12 hidden units, which receive connections from the 122 inputs and project to each of the 23 output units. The diagram shows each of the connection strengths to and from the hidden units. Each weight is represented by one square, the area of which is proportional to the magnitude of the weight. The color is white if the weight is excitatory and black if it is inhibitory. The inputs are two hexagonal arrays of 61 processing units each. Each input unit has a concentric on-center (top) or off-surround (bottom) receptive field similar to those of principal cells in the lateral geniculate nucleus. The output consists of 24 units that conjointly represent the direction of maximum curvature (six columns) and principal curvature (four rows: two for each principal curvature.) Each of the 12 hidden units is represented in the diagram in a way that reveals all the connections to and from the unit. Within each of the 12 gray background regions, the weights from the inputs are shown on the bottom, and the weights to the output layer are shown above. To the left of each hidden unit, the lone square gives the threshold of the unit, which was also allowed to vary. Note that there emerged two different types of hidden units as revealed by the "projective field." The six units in the bottom row and the fourth and fifth from the left in the top row were mainly responsible for providing information about the direction of minimum curvature, while others were responsible for computing the signs and magnitudes of the two principal curvatures. The curvature-selective units could be further classified as convexity detectors (top row, third from left) or elongation filters (top row, second and sixth from left).

4.3 Next-Generation Networks

NETtalk and the shape-from-shading network are important examples because they yield clues to how the nervous system can embody models of various domains of the world. Parallel-network modeling is still in a pioneering stage of development. There are bound to be many snags and hitches, and many problems yet undreamt of will have to be solved. At this stage, the representational structure of networks has not yet been explored in detail, nor is it known how well the performance of network models will scale with the number of neurons and the difficulty of the task. (That is, will representations and computations in a cortical column with 200,000 neurons be similar to those in a model network comprising only a few hundred processing units?)

Moreover, taken literally as a model of functioning neurons, back-propagation is biologically implausible, inasmuch as error signals cannot literally be propagated back down the very same axon the signal came up. Taken as a *systems-level* algorithm, however, back-propagation may have a realization using feedback projections that do map onto neural hardware. Even squarely facing these cautionary considerations, the important thing is that something with this sort of character at least lets us see what representational structure— good, meaty, usable structure—could *look like* in a neuronal network.

Temporal chaining of sequences of representations is probably a prominent feature of many kinds of behavior, and it may turn out to be particularly important for language acquisition and use. It is conceivable that structured sequences—long, temporally extended sequences—are the elements of an abstract sort of neural state space that enable humans to use language. Sereno (1986) has suggested something along these lines, pointing out that DNA, as a spatially extended sequence of nucleotides, allows for encoding; by analogy, one may envision that the development of mechanisms for generating temporally extended sequences of neuronal (abstract) structures may allow for a kind of structured behavior (i.e., language) that short sequences do not allow for. (See also MacKay 1987; Dehaene et al. 1987.)

One promising strategy will be to try first to unscramble the more fundamental kinds of representing accomplished by nervous systems, shelving until later the problem of complex representations such as linguistic representations. To solve such problems, the solutions discovered for simpler representations may be crucial. At the most basic level, there appears to be an isomorphism between cell responses and external events (for example, cells in visual cortex responding to bars of light moving in a specific direction). At higher levels the receptive-field properties change (Allman et al. 1985; Andersen 1987), and it may be that the lower-level isomorphism gives way to more complicated and dynamic network effects. Motivation, planning, and other factors may, at this level, have roles in how a representation is generated. At still higher levels, still other principles may be operative. Once we understand the nature of representing in early sensory processing, as we have indeed begun to do, and go on to address the nature of representations at more and more abstract levels, we may finally be able to address how learning a language yields another kind of representation, and how symbols can be represented in neural networks. Whatever the basic principles of language representation, they are not likely to be utterly unrelated to the way or ways that the nervous system generates visual representations or auditory representations, or represents spatial maps and motor planning. (On semantic relations in connectionist models, see Hinton 1981, 1986.)

5   Dogmas and Dreams: Boole, Ramón y Cajal, and Marr

The connectionist models discussed are valuable for the glimpse of representational and computational space that they provide, for it is exactly such glimpses that free us from the bonds of the intuitive conceptions of representation as language-like and computation as logic-like. They thus free us from what Hofstadter (1982) called the *Boolean dream*, where all cognition is symbol-manipulation according to the rules of logic.

Equally important, they also free us from what we call the *Neurobiologists' dream* (perhaps, with all due respect, it might be called Cajal's dream), which is really the faith that the answers we seek will be manifest once the fine-grain details of each neuron (its morphology, physiology, and connections) are revealed. These models also teach the tremendously important lesson that *system properties are not accessible at the single-unit level*. In a system, what we need to know is how the elements in large sets of elements interact over time. Until we have new physiological techniques for supplying data of that sort, building network models is a method of first resort. To be really useful, a model must be biologically constrained. However, exactly which biological properties are crucial to a model's utility and which can be safely ignored until later are matters that can be decided only by hunches until a mature theory is in place. Such "bottom-up" constraints are crucial, since computational space is immensely vast, too vast for us to be lucky enough to light on the correct theory simply from the engineering bench. Moreover, the brain's solutions to the problems of vision, motor control, and so forth may be far more powerful, more beautiful, and even more simple than what we engineer into existence. This is the point of Orgel's Second Rule: Nature is more ingenious than we are. And we stand to miss all that power and ingenuity unless we attend to neurobiological plausibility. The point is, *evolution has already done it,* so why not learn how that stupendous machine, our brain, actually works?

This observation allows us to awake from *Marr's dream* of three levels of explanation: the computational level of abstract problem analysis, the level of the algorithm, and the level of physical implementation of the computation. In Marr's view, a higher level was independent of the levels below it, and hence computational problems could be analyzed independently of an understanding of the algorithm that executes the computation, and the algorithmic problem could be solved independently of an understanding of the physical implementation. Marr's assessment of the relations between levels has been reevaluated, and the dependence of higher levels on lower levels has come to be recognized.

The matter of the interdependence of levels marks a major conceptual difference between Marr and the current generation of connectionists. Network models are not independent of either the computational level or the implementational level; they depend in important ways on constraints from all levels of analysis. Network models show how knowledge of brain architecture can contribute to the devising of likely and powerful algorithms that can be efficiently implemented in the architecture of the nervous system and may alter even how we construe the computational problems.

On the heels of the insight that the use of constraints from higher up and lower down matters tremendously, the notion that there are basically three levels of analysis also begins to look questionable. If we examine more closely how the three levels of analysis are meant to map onto the organization of the nervous system, the answer is far from straightforward.

To begin with, the idea that there is essentially one single implementational level is an oversimplification. Depending on the fineness of grain, research techniques reveal structural organization at many strata; the biochemical level; then the levels of the membrane, the single cell, and the circuit; and perhaps yet other levels, such as brain subsystems, brain systems, brain maps, and the whole central nervous system. But notice that at each structurally specified stratum we can raise the functional question, What does it contribute to the wider, functional business of the brain?

This range of structural organization implies, therefore, that the oversimplification with respect to implementation has a companion oversimplification with respect to computational descriptions. And indeed, on reflection it does seem most unlikely that a single type of computational description can do justice to the computational niche of diverse structural organization. On the contrary, one would expect distinct task descriptions corresponding to distinct structural levels. But if there is a ramifying of task specifications to match the ramified structural organization, this diversity will probably be reflected in the ramification of the *algorithms* that characterize how a task is accomplished. And this, in turn, means that the notion of *the* algorithmic levels is as oversimplified as the notion of *the* implementation level.

Similar algorithms were used to specify the network models in NETtalk and the shape-from-shading network, but they have a quite different status in these two examples. On this perspective of the levels of organization, NETtalk is a network relevant to the *systems* level, whereas the shape-from-shading network is relevant to the *circuit* level. Since the networks are meant to reflect principles at entirely different levels of organization, their implementations will also be at different scales in the nervous system. Other computational principles may be found to apply to the single cell or to neural maps.

Once we look at them closely, Marr's three *levels of analysis* and the brain's *levels of organization* do not appear to mesh in a very useful or satisfying manner. So poor is the fit that it may be doubted whether levels of analysis, *as conceived by Marr*, have much methodological significance. Accordingly, in light of the flaws with the notion of *independence*, and in light of the flaws with the *tripartite* character of the conception of levels, it seems that Marr's dream, inspiring though it was for a time, must be left behind.

The vision that inspires network modeling is essentially and inescapably interdisciplinary. Unless we explicitly theorize above the level of the single cell, we will never find the key to the order and the systematicity hidden in the blinding minutiae of the neuropil. Unless our theorizing is geared to mesh with the neurobiological data, we risk wasting our time exploring some impossibly remote, if temporarily fashionable, corner of computational space. Additionally, without the constraints from psychology, ethology, and linguistics to specify more exactly the parameters of the large-scale capacities of nervous systems, our conception of the functions for which we need explanation will be so woolly and tangled as to effectively smother progress.

Consequently, cross-disciplinary research, combining constraints from psychology, neurology, neurophysiology, linguistics, and computer modeling, is the best hope for the coevolution that could ultimately yield a unified, integrated science of the mind-brain. It has to be admitted, however, that this vision is itself a dream. From within the dream we cannot yet reliably discern what are the flaws that will impede progress, what crucial elements are missing, or at which points the vague if tantalizing hunches might be replaced by palpable results.

Notes

1. An earlier exploration of these ideas is to be found in Kenneth Craik's book *The nature of explanation* (Cambridge University Press, 1943).
2. NETtalk networks can differ in how input letters and output phonemes are represented, and in the number and arrangement of hidden units.

References

Allman, J., F. Miezin, and E. McGuniness. 1985. Stimulus specific responses from beyond the classic receptive field. *Annual Review of Neuroscience* 8:407–430.

Andersen, R. A. 1987. The role of posterior parietal cortex in spatial perception and visual-motor integration. In *Handbook of Physiology*, vol. 5, *The Nervous System*, ed. V. B. Mountcastle, F. Plum, and S. R. Geiger.

Anderson, J. A., and G. E. Hinton. 1981. Models of information processing in the brain. In Hinton and Anderson 1981.

Chisholm, R. M. 1966. *Theory of knowledge*. Englewood Cliffs, N.J.: Prentice-Hall.

Churchland, P. M. 1979. *Scientific realism and the plasticity of mind*. Cambridge: Cambridge University Press.

Churchland, P. M. 1988. *Matter and consciousness*. Revised edition. Cambridge: MIT Press.

Churchland, P. S. 1986. *Neurophilosophy: Toward a unified science of the mind-brain*. Cambridge: MIT Press.

Davidson, D. 1974. On the very idea of a conceptual scheme. *Proceedings and addresses of the American Philosophical Association* 47:5–20.

Dehaene, S., J. -P. Changeux, and J.-P. Nadal. 1987. Neural networks that learn temporal sequences by selection. *Proceedings of the National Academy of Sciences* 84:2727–2731.

Dennett, D. C. 1978. *Brainstorms: Philosophical essays on mind and psychology*. Cambridge: MIT Press.

Eccles, J. C. 1977. Part 2 of K. Popper and J. C. Eccles, *The self and its brain*. Berlin: Springer-Verlag.

Enc, B. 1983. In defense of the identity theory. *Journal of Philosophy* 80:279–298.

Feldman, J. A., and F. H. Ballard. 1982. Connectionist models and their properties. *Cognitive Science* 6:205–254.

Fodor, J. A. 1975. *The language of thought*. New York: Crowell. Paperback edition: Cambridge: MIT Press, 1979.

Fodor, J. A. 1981. *Representations*. Cambridge: MIT Press.

Goldman-Rakic, P. S. 1987. Circuitry of primate prefrontal cortex and regulation of behavior by representational memory. In *Handbook of Physiology*, vol. 5, *The Nervous System*, ed. V. B. Mountcastle, F. Plum, and S. R. Geiger.

Hebb, D. O. 1949. *Organization of behavior*. New York: Wiley.

Hilbert, J., and S. Cohn-Vossen. 1952. *Geometry and the imagination*. New York: Chelsea.

Hinton, G. E. 1981. Implementing semantic networks in parallel hardware. In Hinton and Anderson 1981.

Hinton, G. E. 1986. Learning distributed representations of concepts. In *Proceedings of the eight annual conference of the Cognitive Science Society.* Hillsdale, N.J.: Erlbaum.

Hinton, G. E. 1989. Connectionist learning procedures. *Artificial Intelligence,* forthcoming.

Hinton, E. E., and J. A. Anderson, eds. 1981. *Parallel models of associative memory.* Hillsdale, N.J.: Erlbaum.

Hinton, G. E., and T. J. Sejnowski. 1986. Learning and relearning in Boltzmann machines. In McClelland and Rumelhart 1986.

Hofstadter, D. R. 1982. Artificial intelligence: Subcognition as computation. Technical Report No. 132, Computer Science Department, Indiana University.

Hooker, C. A. 1981. Toward a general theory of reduction. Part I: Historical and scientific setting. Part II: Identity in reduction. Part III: Cross-categorical reduction. *Dialogue* 20:38–59, 201–236, 496–529.

Hubel, D. H., and T. N. Wiesel. 1962. Receptive fields, binocular interaction and functional architecture in cat's visual cortex. *Journal of Physiology* 160:106–154.

Kelso, S. R., A. H. Ganong, and T. H. Brown. 1986. Hebbian synapses in hippocampus. *Proceedings of the National Academy of Sciences* 83:5326–5330.

Lehky, S., and T. J. Sejnowski. 1987. Extracting 3-D curvatures from images using a neural model. *Society for Neuroscience Abstracts* 13:1451.

Lehky, S., and T. J. Sejnowski. 1988. Neural network model for the representation of surface curvature from images of shaded surfaces. In *Organizing principles of sensory processing,* ed. J. Lund. Oxford University Press.

Livingstone, M. S. 1988. Art, illusion, and the visual system. *Scientific American* 258:78–85.

McClelland, J. L., and D. E. Rumelhart. 1986. *Parallel distributed processing: Explorations in the microstructure of cognition.* Cambridge: MIT Press.

McGinn, C. 1982. *The character of mind.* Oxford: Oxford University Press.

MacKay, D. 1987.*The organization and perception of action.* Berlin: Springer-Verlag.

Mandt, A. J. 1986. The triumph of philosophical pluralism? Notes on the transformation of academic philosophy. *Proceedings and Addresses of the American Philosophical Association* 60:265–277.

Marr, D. 1982. *Vision.* San Francisco: Freeman.

Pellionisz, A., and R. Llinás. 1982. Space-time representation in the brain: The cerebellum as a predictive space-time metric tensor. *Neuroscience* 7:2249–2970.

Pentland, A. P. 1984. Local shading analysis. *IEEE Transactions: Pattern Analysis and Machine Intelligence* 6:170–187.

Putnam, H. 1967. The nature of mental states. In *Arts, mind, and religion,* ed. W. H. Capitan and D. D. Merrill, University of Pittsburgh Press. Reprinted in H. Putnam, *Mind, language, and reality,* vol. 2 of *Philosophical Papers.* Cambridge University Press, 1975.

Pylyshyn, Z. 1984. *Computation and cognition.* Cambridge: MIT Press.

Quine, W. V. O. 1960. *Word and object.* Cambridge: MIT Press.

Richardson, R. 1979. Functionalism and reductionism. *Philosophy of Science* 46:533–558.

Rosenberg, C. R. 1988. Ph. D. thesis, Princeton University.

Rumelhart, D. E., G. E. Hinton, and J. L. McClelland. 1986. A general framework for parallel distributed processing. In Rumelhart and McClelland 1986.

Rumelhart, D. E., G. E. Hinton, and R. J. Williams. 1986. Learning internal representations by error propagation. In McClelland and Rumelhart 1986.

Schaffner, K. F. 1976. Reductionism in biology: Prospects and problems. In *PSA proceedings 1974*, ed. R. S. Cohen, C. A. Hooker, A. C. Michalos, and J. W. Van Evra. Dordrecht: Reidel.

Sejnowski, T. J. 1986. Open questions about computation in cerebral cortex. In McClelland and Rumelhart 1986.

Sejnowski, T. J. 1988. Neural network learning algorithms. In *Neural Computers*, ed. R. Eckmiller and C. von der Malsberg. Berlin: Springer-Verlag.

Sejnowski, T. J., and P. S. Churchland. In press. Brain and Cognition. In *Foundations of Cognitive Science*, ed. M. I. Posner. Cambridge: MIT Press.

Sejnowski, T. J., and C. R. Rosenberg. 1987. Parallel networks that learn to pronounce English text. *Complex Systems* 1:145–168.

Sejnowski, T. J., and C. R. Rosenberg. 1988. Learning and representation in connectionist models. In *Perspective in memory research and training*, ed. M. Gazzaniga. Cambridge: MIT Press.

Sejnowski, T. J., C. Koch, and P. S. Churchland. 1988. Computational neuroscience. *Science*.

Sereno, M. 1986. A program for the neurobiology of mind. *Inquiry* 29:217–240.

Skinner, B. F. 1957. *Verbal behavior.* New York: Appleton-Century-Crofts.

Skinner, B. F. 1976. *About behaviorism.* New York: Knopf.

Smart, J. J. C. 1959. Sensations and brain processes. *Philosophical Review* 68:141–156.

Stich, S. P. 1983. *From folk psychology to cognitive science: The case against belief.* Cambridge: MIT Press.

Strawson, P. F. 1966. *The bounds of sense: An essay on Kant's "Critique of pure reason."* London: Methuen.

Swinburne, R. 1986. *The evolution of the soul.* Oxford: Oxford University Press.

Editor's Comments

The chapters by Dudai and by Seidenberg and McClelland in this volume usefully complement the present chapter. Paired associative learning has now been studied in simple nervous systems at the cellular and molecular levels, and we are beginning to clarify the actual neural mechanisms of synaptic weighting (by potassium-channel phosphorylation and new protein synthesis, for instance) that lead to representation and computation in these learning paradigms. In their simplest form parallel-distributed-processing (PDP) models such as those illustrated in the present chapter and associative learning in simple animals have several features in common and offer a measure of reality to the vision that the Churchland and Sejnowski outline. Furthermore, efforts of the type presently considered constitute viable examples of the second half of a coherent reductionist research program (like that of C. A. Hooker) that aims to match functional decomposition (the work of neuroscience) to causal recomposition (the work of engineering). In other words, after brain changes down to the molecular level have been established to correlate with higher-order behaviors, it is crucial to model those changes in an attempt to recreate the behavior and thus establish a causal relationship between the levels.

In spite of its obvious value, from which I do not wish to detract, research on associative learning that uses simple animals and PDP models does not adequately address the question of sentential and logical thinking, a central concept for explaining innate linguistic dispositions that is raised by various serious disciplines and is amply illustrated throughout this volume. It is well established in invertebrate-memory research that the nature of a given behavior is determined in part by environmentally induced molecular cascades— which are in fact shared across functionally, ontogenetically, and phylogenetically distinct systems—and also by the higher-level architectures in which the molecular events occur (see Dudai in this volume). The building of those higher-order architectures is in large part under genetic control, and the outcome of gene actions is the generation of *inhomogeneous* structures (unlike those in PDP models) that contain varying types and numbers of neurons, connections, synapses, receptors, and other membrane and genomic characteristics. These characteristics at the initial state before any environmentally mediated learning has taken place (see Mehler in this volume) can presumably limit the type of learning that is possible by a given network and can even specify hierarchical representations and computational devices that at higher levels appear to be sentential and logical.

The persuasive arguments that attribute crucial roles to sentential and logical structures for the acquisition and performance of language are not incompatible, in my view, with the idea that PDP brain architectures are involved in paired associative learning (although at some point these architectures must be sequentially linked, and this cannot but undermine the concept of PDP at the level of cognitive theory).

From Dudai (this volume) we learn that the environment influences genomic regulation of both innate and learned behaviors, albeit to different extents. From Crossin and Edelman (this volume) we learn that the building of predetermined anatomies and of anatomies under marked environmental regulation employ identical molecular mechanisms, albeit in unequal proportions. And we know that genomic coding for structural and functional proteins can be highly conserved onto- and phylogenetically. It is possible, therefore, that adaptive pairings of some stimuli and responses by mechanisms similar or identical to those acting during ordinary paired associative learning but acting on a phylogenetic time scale, rather than in an ontogenetic one, can lead by natural selection to permanent changes in the genome. These permanent genomic changes could in turn support relatively hardwired weightings of neuronal assemblies down to the molecular level already expressed in the initial state. In other words, real neural networks may already be phylogenetically selected for the types of response properties they will express during learning. Furthermore, there is no reason why these types of selected structures cannot support representational and computational hierarchies that translate at higher levels into sentential or logical thinking. This would have the added advantages that these structures need not be learned ontogenetically, that they can be passed from generation to generation, and that all the members of the species have them. Again, it is the burden of neuroscientists and engineers adequately to describe and model the appropriate levels of implementation and thus demonstrate the emergence of sentential and logical structures in PDP models.

As suggested by the present chapter potential discoveries made with PDP models may offer a solution to another problem presented by sentential and logical thinking, that having to do with its ontogenetic development and phylogenetic evolution. The search for sentential and logical structures in other animals and some aspects of them in very young children has not borne fruit. This leads to the unwanted conclusion that their ontogenesis and evolution are discontinuous, i.e., they appear *de novo* in mature humans. However, this need not be the only conclusion if we extrapolate from the observations in the present chapter that unlike the Boolean dream, representations hidden in the units of PDP models need not be languagelike nor computations logiclike. Thus, it is quite possible that neuronal assemblies in other animals and at younger human environmental stages are not discontinuous with those in mature humans at the level of representation and computation hidden in the units, but not at higher levels of description. Only when discontinuities described at higher levels actually propagate to discoverable discontinuities at levels closer to the genome do evolutionary biologists begin to fret.

Sentence-logic arguments against PDP models are in my view resolvable. But other issues relevant to the brain present immediate challenges, albeit to empirical work rather than to a priori considerations. The procedures that can be carried out by a connected network depend in part on the physical properties of the system. One of the most obvious differences between computer networks and brain networks is illustrated by the processing time of the two systems: the biological machinery functions at a much slower time rate. This difference may be significant enough to determine that altogether different algorithms are being used.

Another property of neuronal assemblies involves a characteristic that would appear to interfere with the functioning of PDP models as currently structured. In PDP models units belonging to the same layer cannot be connected, while in real brains they in fact are. Thus, for instance, auditory input from the thalamus reaches via one synapse various subdivisions of the temporal auditory cortex, e.g., areas KA, paAr, paAc, paAlt, Tpt. These areas are in turn densely interconnected. Area KA, for example, sends projections to paAr, paAc, paAlt, etc., and receives projections from each of the latter. True, the neurons sending projections, which lie mainly in layers iii or v, are not the same neurons that receive them, which lie in layers iv and i respectively, but there is interlaminar connectivity via short circuit neurons. The solution of the problem may lie in a detailed knowledge of the connectional architecture, down to specific synaptic architectures, but present PDP models suggest that laminar interactions in the cortex represent added layers rather than interactions within layers and that parallel systems may be present down to compartments of single neurons (see Dudai in this volume).

In addition, PDP models may provide a practical means for testing hypotheses on abnormal behavior. Thus, for instance, acquired disorders of cognition involve predominantly the loss of processing units and connections, while developmental problems may involve both the loss and addition of units and connections. Attempts are currently under way to model these changes, and the results are promising. In addition to changes in the numbers of units, pathologically altered weights and weighting mechanisms, such as the loss of a particular portion of the chemical repertoire or the loss of the signals that regulate it, might be modeled for their functional consequences.

Chapter 10

Visual Word Recognition and Pronunciation: A Computational Model of Acquisition, Skilled Performance, and Dyslexia

Mark S. Seidenberg and James L. McClelland

Word recognition is an integral part of reading and may be the single most extensively studied topic in cognitive psychology. Aside from its obvious importance to the reading process, the topic has generated interest for several reasons: because learning to recognize words is among the first tasks beginning readers confront, because failure to acquire age-appropriate reading skills is typically associated with deficits in word processing, and because the study of word recognition impairments following brain injury has provided important evidence concerning the neuropsychological bases of complex behavior. The main characteristics of word processing in reading are known as a result of extensive study (for reviews see papers in Coltheart 1987a and Besner, Waller, and MacKinnon 1985). Primary among those characteristics is the fact that for skilled readers the process is very rapid and largely unconscious. The picture that has emerged is that lexical processing yields access to several types of information in a rapid and efficient manner. Readers are typically aware of the results of lexical processing, not the manner in which it occurs. One of the goals of research on visual word recognition has been to use experimental methods to unpack these largely unconscious processes. In this paper we present an overview of a new computational model of visual word recognition, the acquisition of word recognition skills, and the breakdown of these skills in dyslexia.

Scope of the Problem

The problem to be addressed is this: The lexical processor operates so as to rapidly yield several types of information associated with a given word; the skilled reader is able to discriminate an input string from thousands of other vocabulary items within a fraction of a second. What knowledge supports processing of this kind, and how does the child acquire it?

According to the hypothesis-testing view that has dominated reading research for many years, rapid word identification is possible because of information provided by the *literal* context in which a word occurs (see Henderson 1982 for review). Words appear in meaningful contexts; information provided by the context, in conjunction with knowledge of the language and general world knowledge, allows the reader to formulate hypotheses concerning the identity of subsequent words. At any given point in a sentence, the range of likely continuations is thought to be limited, so that less information needs to be extracted from the word itself, and this facilitates recognition. In Kenneth Goodman's phrase, reading is a "psycholinguistic guessing game" (Goodman 1967); the skilled reader is the person able to use contextual information in an efficient manner to facilitate recognition.

Questions concerning the scope of contextual effects on word recognition and the mechanisms responsible for such effects continue to be the focus of considerable attention and debate (see McClelland 1987 and Tanenhaus, Dell, and Carlson 1988). However, studies of children's reading have suggested that differences in the use of contextual information in recognizing words are not the primary source of differences in reading skill (Stanovich 1986). Other knowledge plays a critical role in word processing, specifically, the reader's knowledge of the lexicon itself. Rapid word recognition is possible because readers exploit information concerning the structure and distribution of word-forms in the language. A theory of recognition must characterize the relevant aspects of lexical structure, their representation in memory, and their use in decoding. This information represents the *virtual* context for word recognition, and is at least as important as the information provided by the literal context. The interactive-activation model of McClelland and Rumelhart (1981) was an attempt at characterizing readers' knowledge of the lexicon and its use in decoding, and the present model can be seen as its successor.

What Is to Be Learned
In acquiring word recognition skills, children must come to understand at least two basic characteristics of written English. First there is the alphabetic principle (Rozin and Gleitman 1977), the fact that in an alphabetic orthography there are systematic correspondences between the spoken and written forms of words. Beginning readers already possess large oral vocabularies; their initial problem is to learn how unfamiliar written forms map onto known spoken forms. The scope of this problem is determined by facts about the writing system. The alphabetic system for writing English is a code for representing spoken language; units in the writing system—letters and letter pat-

terns—largely correspond to speech units such as phonemes. However, the correspondence between the written and spoken codes is notoriously complex; many correspondences are inconsistent (e.g., *-ave* is usually pronounced as in *gave, save*, and *cave*, but there is also *have*) or wholly arbitrary (e.g., *-olo-* in *colonel, -ps* in *corps*).

A second aspect of the writing system the child must learn about concerns the distribution of letter patterns in the lexicon. Only some combinations of letters are possible, and the combinations differ in frequency. These facts about the distribution of letter patterns give written English its characteristic redundancy. Many aspects of orthographic redundancy derive from the fact that the writing system is primarily (though not exclusively) a cipher for spoken language. For example, the fact that letters *gp* never appear in word-initial position derives from a phonotactic constraint on the occurrence of the corresponding phonemes. Of the many possible combinations of 26 letters, only a small percentage yield letter strings that are permissible words in English. An even smaller percentage are realized as actual words in the lexicon. These constraints on the forms of written words may play an important role in the recognition process. The reader must discriminate the input string from other words in his or her vocabulary, a task that might be facilitated by knowledge of the letter combinations that are permissible or realized.

In sum, the child's problem is to learn how English is represented in written form. This task might be facilitated by the systematic aspects of the writing system, i.e., the constraints on possible letter sequences and the correspondences between spelling and sound. However, there are barriers to using these types of information. Facts about orthographic redundancy cannot be utilized until the child is familiar with a large number of words. Acquiring useful generalizations about spelling-sound correspondences is inhibited by the fact that many words have irregular correspondences and the fact that these words are overrepresented among the items the child learns to read first (*give, have, some, does, gone*, etc.). The child must nonetheless learn to use knowledge of the orthography in a manner that supports the recognition of words within a fraction of a second.

Our model addresses the acquisition and use of these two types of information: orthographic redundancy and orthographic-phonological correspondences. The model is realized within the connectionist framework being applied to many problems in perception and cognition (see Rumelhart and McClelland 1986; McClelland and Rumelhart 1986a). The model provides an account of how orthographic redundancy and orthographic-phonological correspondences are utilized in recognition and pronunciation. On this account, learning to read words involves learning facts about the distribution of letter patterns in the lexicon and the correspondences between orthography and phonology. This knowledge can be represented in the terms of the weights on the connections in a distributed memory network that consists of simple processing units. Learning involves modifying the weights through experience in reading and pronouncing words. We will argue that this connectionist approach is ideally suited to accounting for word recognition because of the nature of the task, which is largely determined by characteristics of the orthography.

The model gives a detailed account of a range of empirical issues of continuing interest to reading researchers, including differences between words in terms of processing difficulty, differences between readers in terms of word recognition skill, transitions from beginning to skilled reading, the role of phonology in reading, and differences between silent reading and reading aloud. The model also provides an account of certain forms of dyslexia that are observed developmentally and as a consequence of brain injury.

Overview of the Model

The model represents part of a more general theory of lexical processing. The goal is an integrated theory that accounts for several aspects of lexical processing, including access of meaning and pronunciation from print, access of meaning and spelling from speech, and access of spelling and pronunciation from meaning. The implemented model is concerned with how readers perceive letter strings and pronounce them aloud. Here we given an overview of the model; details are provided in Seidenberg and McClelland, in press. The model, which has the general form illustrated in figure 10.1, consists of a network of interconnected processing units. There are 400 units used to code letter strings, 200 hidden units, and 460 units used to code phonemic output. The distributed representation used for coding letter strings is similar to one described by Hinton, McClelland, and Rumelhart (1986). The scheme for coding phonological output, which also makes use of distributed representations, is described by McClelland and Rumelhart (1986b). The main feature of these representations is that a given letter or phoneme in a word is represented by a pattern of activation across a set of nodes, rather than by a single node. The network is a feed-forward system with complete connectivity from input units to hidden units, and from hidden units to output units. Each connection carries a weight that governs the forward spread of activation through the system. Weights on the connections are initially arbitrary and modified during a learning phase using the

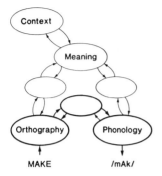

Figure 10.1
A general framework for lexical processing. The implemented model is outlined in bold.

back-propagation algorithm of Rumelhart, Hinton, and Williams (1986).

The system takes letter strings as input, and produces two kinds of output: a pattern of activation across the phonological units, and a re-creation of the input pattern across the orthographic nodes. The former can be thought of as the node's computation of the phonological code for a letter string. The latter can be thought of as a computation of an orthographic code that provides an index of the familiarity of the letter string. These codes provide the basis for performing tasks such as naming and lexical decision, as discussed below.

The model was trained on a set of 2,897 monosyllabic English words, a large proportion of the monosyllabic words in the language. The training procedure worked as follows. On each trial the model was given a stimulus pair consisting of a letter string and its pronunciation. The letter string was presented to the model, and the output—a pattern of activation across the phonological nodes and a re-creation of the letter string across the orthographic nodes—was computed using a simple spreading activation procedure, in which the activation of a unit is a function of the sum of the weighted activations along the lines coming into it. The model was initially configured with small random weights on the connections between units. The goal of training was to find a set of weights that enabled the model to produce optimal orthographic and phonological output for any input word, that is, output that closely approximated correct orthographic and phonological patterns. The patterns of activation actually produced by a given input can be compared to those that would be produced if the model performed perfectly. We characterize the differences between expected and obtained orthographic output in terms of error scores, which are the squared differences between actual and obtained output summed over all of the orthographic units; we derive a similar error score for phonological output. These error terms have two functions. First, they provide measures of the model's performance; error scores for words vary as a function of amount of training and as a function of lexical variables such as orthographic redundancy, orthographic-phonological regularity, and frequency. Second, the error scores were utilized in the learning algorithm, which was used to modify the weights on connections, as described by Seidenberg and McClelland (in press).

The model, then, produces output specifying the orthographic and phonological codes of the input string. These codes are then used in performing tasks such as naming and lexical decision. We characterize the model's performance in terms of error scores calculated for different types of words after different amounts of training and relate these to human performance on these tasks.

Before presenting the results of the simulations in more detail, we shall review the empirical phenomena it addresses. We shall then describe how various aspects of the model's performance relate to human performance. Finally, we shall consider some of the model's implications concerning acquired and developmental dyslexia.

Empirical Phenomena

Words vary in terms of their orthographic properties and in terms of orthographic-phonological correspondences. A large number of studies have investigated the effects of these aspects of word structure on recognition latencies. Five types of words are of primary interest.

- *Regular words* contain spelling patterns that recur in a large number of words, always with the same pronunciation. *Must*, for example, contains the spelling pattern *-ust*; all monosyllabic words that end in this pattern rhyme (*just*, *dust*, etc.). The pool of words sharing this spelling pattern are termed neighbors (Glushko 1979). These words can be pronounced by grapheme-phoneme correpondence rules, such as those proposed by Venezky (1970).
- *Exception words* contain common spelling patterns that are given irregular pronunciations. For example, *-ave* is usually pronounced as in *gave* and *save*, but has an irregular pronunciation in the exception word *have*. In terms of orthographic structure, regular and exception words are similar: both contain spelling

patterns that recur in many words. However, exception words have irregular pronunciations; they cannot be pronounced by rule.

· *Regular inconsistent words* (Glushko 1979) are complements of the exceptions. A word such as *gave* is regular in the sense of containing a common spelling pattern that is given a regular pronunciation in a large pool of words; however, it is inconsistent because there is a similarly-spelled exception word (i.e., *have*). Thus, regular inconsistent words have an exception word in their neighborhoods. These words can also be pronounced by rule.

· *Homographs* are words such as *wind, lead,* and *bass* that contain common spelling patterns having two pronunciations, each of which is a word in the language.

· Finally, there are words such as *aisle* and *once.* In contrast to the other classes of words, these items (which Seidenberg et al. [1984] term *strange*) contain unusual spelling patterns that do not recur in a large number of words; hence their neighborhoods are small. Like exception words, they cannot be pronounced by rule.

These types represent clear cases that have been useful in empirical and theoretical work. It should be noted that there are many intermediate cases. For example, a word such as *soap* has an unusual spelling (it is the only monosyllabic word ending in -*oap*), but according to the Venezky (1970) rules, its pronunciation is regular. A spelling pattern such as -*own* has two pronunciations, but in contrast to a pattern such as -*ave*, both pronunciations occur in many words. Empirical research in this area has tended to utilize the clear cases as a way to discover general processing principles. An explicit computational model, however, should be able to account for the entire range of cases.

Contrasts between these types of words have provided a way to investigate the factors that influence word recognition. The comparison between regular and exception words provides information about the computation of the phonological code. These words are similar in terms of orthographic factors; both contain common spelling patterns, and they can be equated in terms of other factors such as length and frequency. Differences between the words in terms of processing difficulty must be attributed to the one dimension along which they differ, namely, regularity of spelling-sound correspondences. The regularity factor might be expected to influence performance of a task such as naming, which requires articulatory output. However, a difference between regular and exception words on a silent reading task such as lexical decision would indicate that readers had computed the phonological code even where overt articulation was not required.

Hence, the contrast between these words provides a way of diagnosing access of this information.

The contrast between regular inconsistent words such as *gave* and regular words such as *must* has been thought to provide a way to test the claim that spelling-sound correspondence rules are used in reading words (Glushko 1979; Henderson 1982). Spelling-sound rules (e.g., a rule governing the pronunciation of *-ave* or a rule that lengthens a vowel when it is followed by a consonant and terminal *e*) correctly specify the pronunciations of regular inconsistent words. However, Glushko (1979) found longer naming latencies for regular inconsistent words than regular words. This result—which indicated that the pronunciation of *gave* was somehow influenced by the irregular *have*—is difficult to reconcile with the rule account. As with exception words, a difference between regular and regular inconsistent words on a silent reading task would indicate that phonological information has been computed.

Homographs provide another basis for distinguishing between orthographic and phonological effects in word recognition. These words are unremarkable from the point of view of orthography; they contain common spelling patterns. Like the spelling patterns in exception and regular inconsistent words, they are associated with two (or more) pronunciations. However, in a homograph both pronunciations yield actual words. Finally, the strange words such as *aisle* provide a way to investigate effects of orthographic redundancy. If the frequency with which a spelling pattern occurs in the lexicon influences processing, strange words should differ from regular words. Moreover, because the strange words contain unusual spelling patterns, their pronunciations may also be difficult to derive.

A large number of studies examining the recognition of such words have yielded a fairly precise set of results, which will be summarized briefly. There are two main findings. First, even among skilled readers of the language, words differ in terms of processing difficulty. Second, different results obtain when the task is lexical decision (a silent reading task) than when the stimuli are named aloud (a pronunciation task).

Naming Aloud
In regard to the effects of irregular spelling-sound correspondences, exception words produce longer naming latencies than regular words only when the stimuli are relatively low in frequency (Andrews 1982; Seidenberg et al. 1984; Seidenberg 1985a; Waters and Seidenberg 1985; Taraban and McClelland 1987). For a large pool of higher-frequency words, irregular spelling-sound correspondences have no

Table 10.1
Mean naming latencies (in msec) from Seidenberg 1985a, experiment 1

| Word type | Example | Subject group | | | |
		Fastest	Medium	Slowest	All
High frequency, regular	Nine	475	523	621	540 (0.4)
High frequency, exception	Lose	475	517	631	541 (0.9)
Difference		0	−6	+10	+3
Low frequency, regular	Mode	500	530	641	556 (2.3)
Low frequency, exception	Deaf	502	562	685	583 (5.1)
Difference		+2	+32	+44	+17

Standard errors in parentheses.

effect on naming latencies. A typical result (from Seidenberg 1985a) is presented in table 10.1.

Although Glushko (1979) found longer naming latencies for regular inconsistent words compared to regular words, later studies have qualified these results. Seidenberg et al. (1984) found that Glushko's results were due in part to repetition of matched regular inconsistent and exception word pairs; for example, the stimuli included *none*, *bone*, *done*, *gone*, and *lone*; *love*, *prove*, *cove*, and *shove*; etc. These repetitions result in priming effects that artifactually increase the magnitude of the regular inconsistent effect (see also Meyer, Schvaneveldt, and Ruddy 1974). Intralist priming will also produce an exception effect for higher frequency words (Treiman, Freyd, and Baron 1984; Taraban and McClelland 1987). When Seidenberg et al. (1984) presented each spelling pattern only once, longer latencies for regular inconsistent words were only obtained for words in the lower frequency range. In an experiment with a larger set of stimuli that also controlled for repetition of spelling patterns, Taraban and McClelland (1987) failed to obtain a statistically significant regular-inconsistent effect for either high or low frequency words. These results suggest that the mere presence of an exception-word neighbor is not sufficient to slow naming latencies for regular inconsistent words, an issue we consider again below.

Effects of the orthographically irregular, strange words also depend on frequency (Seidenberg et al. 1984; Waters and Seidenberg 1985). For higher-frequency words, naming latencies are similar for regular and strange words. For lower-frequency words, however, naming latencies for strange words are the longest of all word classes, including exceptions. Finally, homographs also produce longer naming latencies than regular words (Seidenberg et al. 1984); the effects of frequency have not been investigated with this word class.

In sum, the naming results indicate that for a large pool of high-frequency words, factors such as orthographic redundancy and regularity of orthographic-phonological correpondences have little discernible effect on processing. This pool of words is likely to be quite large because of the type-token facts about English (Seidenberg 1985a). A relatively small number of word types account for a large number of the tokens that a reader encounters. In the Kucera and Francis (1967) count, for example, the 133 most frequent words in the corpus account for about half of the total number of tokens. Hence, a small number of words recur with very high frequency, and these are the words for which the structural vriables have little effect. More-over, Seidenberg (1985a) found that the size of this pool varies as a function of reading skill. Faster readers recognize a larger pool of items without interference from irregular spelling or spelling-sound correspondences. In effect, they treat more words as though they were high-frequency items (see table 10.1).

For lower-frequency, more slowly recognized words, naming latencies depend on structural properties that reflect characteristics of written English. The words with common spelling patterns and regular pronunciations yield the best performance; words with common spelling patterns but irregular pronunciations (exceptions) yield somewhat poorer performance; and strange words, which have irregular spellings and pronunciations, produce the longest latencies and most errors. Note that the fact that effects of word structure are modulated by frequency may go some way towards explaining the inconsistent results of previous studies, most of which failed to consider this factor.

Lexcial Decision
The lexical decision task provides important information because it does not require articulatory output. It might be the case that phonological information is accessed only when overt pronunciation is required. As in naming, the effects of the structural variables on lexical decisions are limited to lower-frequency words (Waters and Seidenberg 1985; Seidenberg et al. 1984). For higher-frequency words, all of the word types yield similar lexical decision latencies and numbers of errors. The pattern of results for lower-frequency words in lexcial-decision studies differs in important ways from that obtained in naming. In many lexical-decision experiments orthographic-phonological regularity yielded no effects, yet in other experiments it did (see Henderson 1982 and Seidenberg 1985b for reviews). These inconsistent effects have been interpreted as indicating that the recognition of words in silent reading involves both "direct" (visually based) and

"mediated" (phonologically based) processes. Where there were no phonology effects, it was inferred that recognition is direct; where there were such effects, it was thought to be mediated. This interpretation of the lexical-decision results was consistent with the dual-route model. In contrast, the consistent effects of phonological regularity in naming were thought to be a consequence of the task, which requires computation of the phonological code.

While this account has the virtue of reconciling inconsistent experimental results, it did not explain the factors that determined which recognition process would be used in any given case. Note that the inconsistent results that led to this view involved the same types of stimuli (regular and exception words) used in different experiments. Hence, it cannot be the case that direct access is used for one type of word (e.g., exceptions) and mediated access for the other (e.g., regular).

Waters and Seidenberg (1985) provide an alternative account of these seemingly inconsistent results. Their evidence suggests that lexical-decision results depend on the types of words and nonwords included in a stimulus set. Consider first the exception effect. When the stimuli in an experiment contain only regular words, exception words, and pronounceable nonwords, there is no exception effect for lower-frequency words, in contrast to the results in naming (Waters and Seidenberg 1985). Under these conditions the effects of irregular spelling-sound correspondences obtained with the naming task are eliminated.

Consider now an experiment in which the subject sees regular words, exception words, strange words, and pronounceable nonwords. Again, there are no effects of word type among the higher-frequency items. However, for lower-frequency items, an exception effect now obtains (Waters and Seidenberg 1985). That is, with the same regular and exception words and even the same subjects used in the study mentioned in the previous paragraph, exception words produced longer lexical decision latencies than regular words. Strange words produced the longest latencies of all three types. In effect, when regular, exception, and strange words are included in the stimulus set, the results mimic those obtained in naming. The Waters and Seidenberg results for lower frequency words are summarized in table 10.2.

Thus, phonological effects in the lexical decision task depend upon the composition of the stimuli in the experiment. This factor explains the seemingly inconsistent results of previous lexical decision studies. Importantly, the results on the naming task are not affected by this factor; there are robust exception effects for lower-frequency

Table 10.2
Lexical decision and naming latencies (in msec) as a function of presence or absence of strange words

Word Type	Lexical decision task		Naming task	
	Include str	Exclude str	Include str	Exclude str
LF, regular	606	647	518	549
LF, exception	632	643	559	580
Difference	+26	−4	+41	+31

"Include str" = stimuli included strange words; "Exclude str" = stimuli did not include strange words. "LF" = low frequency.

words whether or not strange words are included (Waters and Seidenberg, 1985).

Three aspects of these results are important. First, the effects of structural variables are limited to lower-frequency words. Second, there are the differences between naming and lexical decision, particularly the fact that the properties of the stimulus set influence only the latter. Finally, the results indicate that both orthographic redundancy and orthographic-phonological correspondences influence recognition. The orthographically irregular strange words produced longer latencies than regular or exception words in both tasks. In contrast, effects of orthographic-phonological regularity were robust in naming but depended on the presence of strange words in lexical decision. Moreover, the latencies for exception words were intermediate between those of regular and strange words.

Developmental Trends
Studies of children's acquisition of word-recognition skills (e.g., Backman et al. 1984; Barron 1981) have addressed the question of how children reach the steady state observed in adults; they have also sought to identify the bases of failures to acquire age-appropriate reading skills and specific reading disability (dyslexia). Children in the earliest stages of learning to read typically recognize words by "sounding out," that is, they attempt to derive the pronunciation of a written word and match it to a known phonological form. However, word recognition processes rapidly change during the first few years of schooling. The study by Backman et al. (1984) examined the acquisition of the naming skill. Children named written regular, exception, and regular inconsistent words and nonwords derived from these items; the stimuli also included a fourth type of word, termed *ambiguous*. These words (e.g., *love*, *town*) include spelling patterns associated with two or more pronunciations, each of which occurs in

many words (e.g., *love, glove, shove, cove, dove, rove; town, clown, brown, flown, known, blown*). All of the stimuli were words that are high-frequency items in adult vocabularies. The subjects were children in grades 2, 3, 4 and high school reading at or above age-appropriate levels ("good readers") and children in grades 3 and 4 reading below age-appropriate levels ("poor readers"). Some of the main results from the study are presented in figure 10.2. Differences between word classes were manifested in number of mispronunciation errors.

The developmental trend exhibited in these data is clear: younger, less-skilled readers have more difficulty with the words associated with multiple pronunciations (exception, regular inconsistent, ambiguous); they show larger regularity effects. As children acquire reading skills, the differences between word classes are eliminated. The less-skilled readers have weaker knowledge of spelling-sound correspondences; this lack of knowledge is a liability when words have irregular, inconsistent, or ambiguous spelling-sound correspondences. Older children and adults are able to compute the pronunciations of high-frequency exemplars of all word classes about equally well; differences between word classes persist only for lower-frequency items. In effect, the unskilled readers' performance in nam-

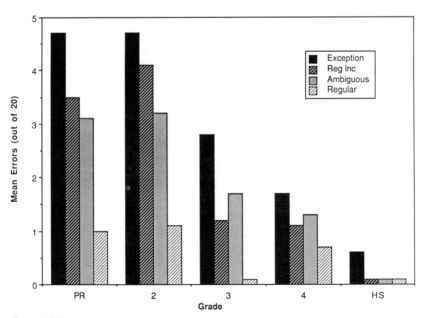

Figure 10.2
Results of the Backman et al. 1984 naming study. PR = poor readers in grades 3 and 4; HS = high school students.

ing higher-frequency words is similar to that of skilled readers in naming of lower-frequency words. At the same time that children are achieving the ability to name different types of words equally well, their knowledge of spelling-sound correspondences is expanding, as evidenced by the older readers' superior performance in reading nonwords.

It is known that acquiring knowledge of spelling-sound correspondences is a key component of learning to read; disorders in phonological analysis skills are thought to be a primary source of reading disability, and children who are backward readers (Backman et al. 1984) or developmental dyslexics (Seidenberg et al. 1986) exhibit relatively poor performance in naming words and nonwords aloud (see Jorm 1983 and Stanovich 1986 for reviews). One of the primary developmental trends observed in studies such as Backman et al. 1984 is that although children acquiring age-expected reading skills initially have more difficulty naming higher-frequency exception words (and other items containing spelling patterns associated with multiple pronunciations) than regular words, this deficit is eliminated by about grade 5 (10 years of age). During the first few years of instruction children learn to name common exception words as efficiently as regular words. Even among skilled adult readers, however, lower-frequency exception words continue to produce longer naming latencies and more errors than lower-frequency regular words. Note that the differences between good and poor younger readers in terms of the number of words read without interference from irregular spelling-sound correspondences are seen at a higher level of performance in skilled readers (Seidenberg 1985a). In both groups the number of words in this pool is related to reading skill. In the model these effects simply derive from the amount of training experience.

Both poor readers who are reading below age-expected levels and children who have been diagnosed as developmental dyslexics fail to show this improvement in naming higher-frequency exception words. For example, the naming performance of the poor readers in grades 3 and 4 in the study of Backman et al. was like that of good readers in grade 2. Both the younger and poorer readers made more errors on exception words and other items containing spelling patterns associated with multiple pronunciations.

Simulations

The network was trained on a list of 2,897 monosyllabic words. The list included all of the uninflected, monosyllabic words from Kucera and Francis 1967 plus additional words not appearing in that corpus minus a few foreign words, acronyms, and abbreviations. Stimuli ranged in length from three to seven letters and in frequency from 0 to 69,971 on the Kucera and Francis (1967) count. The primary data reported below concern the performance of the model on a subset of 240 words after varying amounts of training. Of these words 192 were used in a behavioral study by Taraban and McClelland (1987). These included 24 words from each of four categories created by crossing the factors of frequency (high and low) and type (exception and regular inconsistent). Each of these words was paired with a regular word matched in terms of frequency, initial phoneme, and length. The test items also include 24 high-frequency and 24 low-frequency strange words similar to those used in the experiments of Seidenberg et al. (1984) and Waters and Seidenberg (1985). Examples of the test stimuli are given in table 10.3.

The learning phase consisted of a series of epochs. For each epoch a subset of the 2,897 items were probabilistically selected for learning trials on the basis of their frequencies; 450 to 550 items were presented per epoch. Connection weights were modified according to the learn-

Table 10.3
Examples of stimuli used in simulations and experiments

Type	High frequency	Low frequency
Exception	*come*	*gross*
	done	*pint*
	foot	*pear*
	are	*spook*
Regular control	*came*	*grape*
	dark	*peel*
	fact	*pump*
	out	*stunt*
Regular inconsistent	*base*	*brood*
	catch	*cove*
	cool	*harm*
	dear	*rave*
Regular inconsistent control	*bird*	*brisk*
	clean	*cope*
	corn	*hide*
	dust	*reef*
Strange	*sign*	*aisle*
	film	*debt*
	jazz	*myth*
	corps	*soap*

ing procedure described by Seidenberg and McClelland (in press). Data are presented for 250 learning epochs. The performance of the model on all 2,897 items was tested after 5 epochs, after 5 additional epochs, and after subsequent intervals of 10 epochs. The main results concern the 240 test items. The dependent measures in these analyses are the orthographic and phonological error terms for each item after a given number of learning epochs. These data will be related to results from behavioral studies by Taraban and McClelland (1987), Seidenberg et al. (1984), Waters and Seidenberg (1985) and others. Results for orthographic and phonological output will be considered separately.

Results

Orthographic-phonological regularity and naming   We assume that overt naming involves three cascaded processes. The phonological code for the input letter string must be computed; the computed phonological code must be translated into a set of articulatory-motor commands; and the articulatory motor code must be executed, resulting in the overt response. Only the first of these processes is implemented in our model. In practice, the phonological output computed by the model is closely related to observed naming latencies.

A word is named by recoding the computed phonological output into a set of articulatory-motor commands, which are then executed. Differences in naming latencies primarily derive from differences in the quality of the computed phonological output. Informally, a word that the model "knows" well produces phonological output that more clearly specifies its articulatory-motor program than a word that is known less well. Thus, naming latencies are a function of phonological error scores, which index differences between observed and expected output.

Differences in naming latencies could also be associated with the execution of the compiled articulatory-motor programs. The distributions of phonemes in high- and low-frequency words differ; some phonemes and phoneme sequences occur more often in high-frequency words than low-frequency words, and vice versa. Phonemes also differ in terms of ease of articulation (Locke 1972); higher-frequency words may contain more of the phonemes that are easier to pronounce, or it may be that the phonemes characteristic of high-frequency words are easier to pronounce because they are used more often. Thus, naming latencies could differ for high- and low-frequency words not because frequency influences the computation of phonological output or the translation of this output into an articulatory code but because words in the two groups contain phonemes that differ in terms of ease of articulation. We will ignore this aspect of the naming process for two reasons. First, we have not implemented procedures for producing articulatory output. More importantly, existing studies indicate that the lexical variables of interest—frequency, orthographic-phonological regularity, orthographic redundancy, syllabic structure, etc.—have their primary effects on the computation of phonological output. These effects obtain even when articulatory factors are carefully controlled (see Theios and Muise 1977; McRae, Jared, and Seidenberg, in press).

To illustrate, consider a pair of high- and low-frequency homophones such as *main* and *mane*. The model is trained to produce the same phonological output for both words. After a sufficient amount of training, both words produce output that resembles the correct phonological output more closely than it resembles the phonological output for any other string of phonemes. Thus, the model produces the correct phonological codes of both words, from which pronunciations are assumed to be derived. Because they differ in frequency, however, *main* produces a smaller error score than *mane*; in general, the model performs better on words to which it has been exposed more often. It will be easier, then, to compile the pronunciation of the high-frequency item than the low-frequency item, resulting in faster naming latencies for *main* (McRae, Jared, and Seidenberg, in press). Because the words involve the same pronunciation, the same articulatory-motor program is used to produce overt responses. Hence, if the words are named after a one-second delay, the compilation stage will have been completed, and they should produce identical naming latencies, which they do (McRae, Jared, et al., in press). If the words had differed in terms of ease of articulation, latency differences would be observed in both immediate and delayed naming (Balota and Chumbley 1985).

Exception effects   Figure 10.3 presents the results of the simulation for the exception words and matched regular-word controls. Each data point represents the average phonological error score for the 24 items of each type used in the Taraban and McClelland (1987) experiments. The learning sequence is characterized by the following trends. Training reduces the error scores for all words in an approximately logarithmic manner. Throughout training, there are frequency effects; the model performs better on words to which it is exposed more often. Note that although the test stimuli are dichotomized into high- and low-frequency groups, frequency is actually a continuous variable, and it has continuous effects in the model. Early in training, there are large regularity effects for both high- and low-frequency items; in

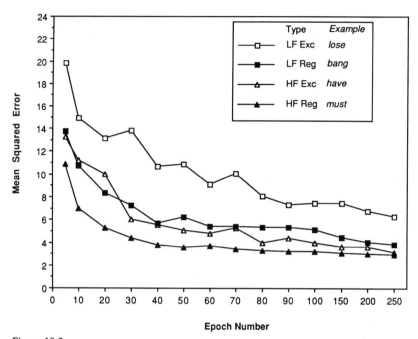

Figure 10.3
Mean phonological error scores for the stimuli used by Taraban and McClelland (1987).

both frequency classes, regular words produce smaller error terms than exception words. Additional training reduces the exception effect for higher-frequency words to the point where it is eliminated by epoch 250. However, the regularity effect for lower-frequency words remains.

These results relate to behavioral data in the following way. The performance of the model early in training captures a main feature of children's performance early in the acquisition of naming skills. Children in grades 2 to 4 have more difficulty pronouncing exception words than regular words, even when the words are the highest-frequency items in their vocabularies (Backman et al. 1984; Waters, Bruck, et al. 1985). As children acquire reading skills, the exception effect for higher-frequency items is eliminated. By the time children have acquired approximately grade-5 reading skills, they are able to name common exception words as well as regular words. Naming latencies continue to improve with additional experience; however, even among skilled adults there is an interaction between frequency and regularity, because there is a difference between regular and exception words only for relatively infrequent items (Seidenberg et al. 1984; Taraban and McClelland 1987).

The model captures the basic insight that naming performance depends on word structure and familiarity. It also provides a simple account of the differences among skilled adult readers observed by Seidenberg (1985a). That study showed that adults who are good readers nonetheless differ slightly in naming speed. For the fastest readers there was no regularity effect for even for words that occur with low frequency in standard corpora such as Kucera and Francis (1967). The model suggests that the basis for this individual difference is simply the number of times a word is encountered. Skilled readers may read more often, increasing the number of exposures to "low-frequency" items. As in the model, additional exposure tends to decrease the magnitude of the exception effect. It should be noted that word frequencies are unvarying in the model; the probability that a word is sampled on every epoch is determined by its Kucera and Francis frequency, which is fixed. For skilled readers the effect of experience is to move some words from "low" to "high" frequency status, with a resulting decline in the magnitude of the exception effect for such items. In effect, the standard estimates of frequency are not valid for these readers. With additional training, the magnitude of the lower-frequency exception effect in the model would also continue to decrease.

Regular inconsistent effects   In a well-known study Glushko (1979) reported longer naming latencies for regular inconsistent words such as *gave* compared to regular words such as *must*. As noted above, this effect has not proven to be robust. Seidenberg et al. (1984) obtained a small effect only for lower-frequency words, whereas Taraban and McClelland (1987) did not. The simulation results, presented in figure 10.4, suggest a reason for these inconsistent results. After 250 training epochs, error scores for higher-frequency, regular inconsistent words do not differ from the scores for matched regular words. In the lower-frequency range regular inconsistent words produce larger error scores than regular words, but the difference is very small. These effects may be too small to detect reliably in naming experiments. At best they should be limited to lower-frequency words, as in the Seidenberg et al. 1984 experiment. They should also be larger for less-skilled readers, because the lower-frequency, regular inconsistent effect is larger with fewer training epochs.[1]

Figure 10.5 provides a comparison between the results of the Taraban and McClelland 1987 naming study and the simulation using the same words. Difference scores were obtained by subtracting means for regular words from the means for matched exception and regular,

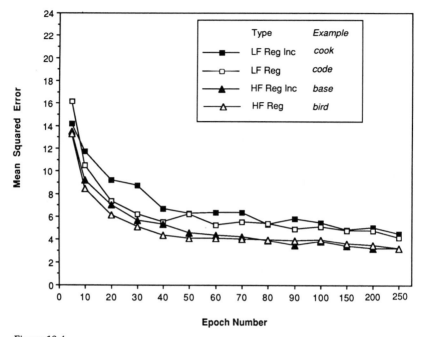

Figure 10.4
The model's performance on regular inconsistent and regular words used in the Tara-ban and McClelland 1987 study.

inconsistent words, respectively. As the graphs indicate, the simula-tion and naming data closely agree.

Strange words Figure 10.6 shows the data for the strange words, which contain unusual spelling patterns, compared to regular words of similar frequency and length (these regular words were also used as controls for the regular inconsistent items). The results are similar to those obtained with other types of words. Throughout the course of learning the model performs better on higher-frequency words than on the lower-frequency words. During the early epochs there is also a main effect of word type; the model performs more poorly on strange words than regular. By 250 epochs, the difference between high-frequency regular and strange words is nearly eliminated, while the difference between low-frequency regular and strange words remains.

The data from skilled human readers also yield this interaction. The 48 strange items used in the simulation have not been employed in any behavioral study, ruling out direct comparisons using the same

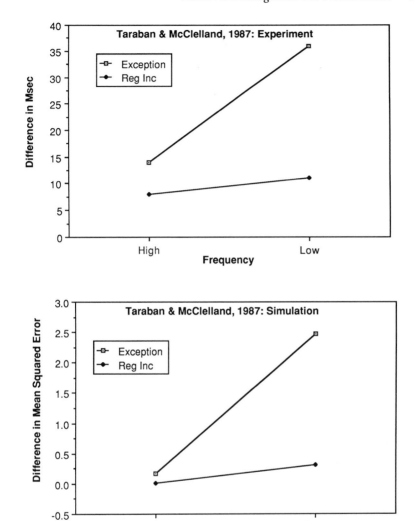

Figure 10.5
Results of the Taraban and McClelland 1987 study: experiment (upper graph) and simulation (lower graph).

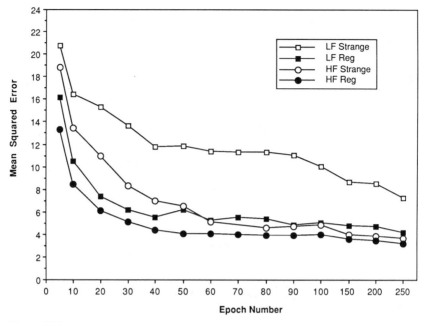

Figure 10.6
The model's performance on strange words. There were 24 items of each type.

items. However, Waters and Seidenberg (1985) used very similar words in a naming study. Figure 10.7 summarizes the Waters and Seidenberg (1985) data and the model's performance on the same items. In the simulation, there are no differences among exception, strange, and regular high-frequency words; in the lower-frequency range strange items produce the highest error scores, followed by exception and then regular words. Waters and Seidenberg (1985) also found no differences among naming latencies for the three types of higher-frequency words and in the lower-frequency range the same order of relative difficulty: strange > exception > regular.

Generalizations to novel stimuli   After training, the model has encoded facts about orthographic-phonological correspondences in the weights on the connections from hidden units to phonological-output units. Although the model performs best on the training stimuli, it will compute pronunciations for novel stimuli. In this respect it simulates the performance of subjects asked to pronounce nonwords such as *rone* or *bist*. The model was tested on a set of nonwords derived from the exception words used in the above analysis (table 10.4). For example, *mave* was derived from *have*. These nonwords can

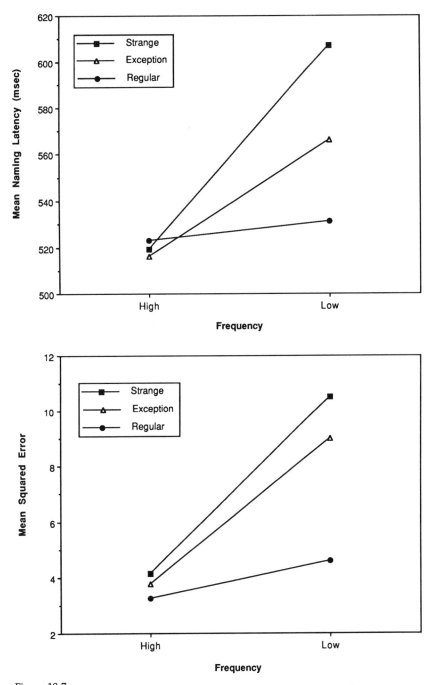

Figure 10.7
Results of the Waters and Seidenberg 1985 study: experiment (upper graph) and simulation (lower graph).

Table 10.4
Examples of stimuli used in nonword simulations

Type	Example	Pronunciation	Status of pronunciation
Exception words and derived nonwords			
HF word	*have*	/hav/	correct exception
	have	/hAv/	regularization error
LF word	*lose*	/lUz/	correct exception
	lose	/lOz/	regularization error
HF nonword	*bave*	/bAv/	regular pronunciation
	bave	/bav/	"exception" pronunciation
LF nonword	*yose*	/yOz/	regular pronunciation
	yose	/yUz/	"exception" pronunciation
Regular words and derived nonwords			
HF word	*came*	/kAm/	correct regular
	came	/kam/	incorrect regular
LF word	*deed*	/dEd/	correct regular
	deed	/ded/	incorrect regular
HF nonword	*pame*	/pAm/	regular pronunciation
	pame	/pam/	incorrect regular
LF nonword	*meed*	/mEd/	regular pronunciation
	meed	/med/	incorrect regular

Pronunciation key: a = *a* in *bat*; A = *ai* in *bait*; e = *e* in *bet*; E = *ee* in *beet*; O = *o* in *rope*; U = *oo* in *boot*. HF = high frequency; LF = low frequency.

be pronounced in two ways, either by analogy to the exception word (*mave* pronounced to rhyme with *have*) or by analogy to regular inconsistent word (*mave* rhymed with *gave*). Using the weights from 250 epochs, the model was tested to determine which pronunciation would be preferred. For each item, two phonological error scores were calculated: one using the regular pronunciation as target and one using the exception pronunciation as target. We calculated analogous scores for alternative pronunciations of the exception words themselves, e.g., *have* pronounced correctly and pronounced to rhyme with *gave*. This regularization error is sometimes produced by young children and by surface dyslexics (Patterson et al., 1985). Finally, we examined the pronunciations of regular words and nonwords derived from them. Here the alternatives were the "regular" pronunciation (*came* pronounced correctly; *pame* rhymed with *came*) or a plausible incorrect pronunciation (*came* or *pame* pronounced with a short *a*).

Figure 10.8 presents the mean error scores for the alternative pronunciations of exception words and derived nonwords. For words (upper graph), the correct exceptional pronunciations produce much smaller error scores than the incorrect, regularized pronunciations. Thus, the model's output resembles the patterns associated with the correct pronunciations rather than the regularized pronunciations. This occurs even though the model is exposed to many more words containing the regular pronunciation; that is, it computes correct output for *have* even though it is trained on *gave*, *save*, *pave*, *rave*, etc.

The opposite pattern obtains with the nonword stimuli derived from these words (figure 10.8, lower graph). Here the regular pronunciations are preferred to the pronunciations derived from the matched exception words. Note, however, that the difference between the two pronunciations is much smaller than in the corresponding word data, which suggests that the pronunciation of *mave* is influenced by the fact that the model has been trained on *have*.

Figure 10.9 presents the error scores for the regular prouncations of nonwords derived from regular and exception words. The error scores are larger for nonwords such as *mave* (derived from an exception word) than *pame* (derived from a regular word). The results again indicate that the pronunciation of novel stimuli such as *mave* is affected by the fact that the model has been trained on both *have* and regular words such as *gave*.

In sum, spelling patterns such as *-ave* are associated with two pronunciations in the lexicon. The model produces output corresponding to the correct pronunciations of exception words such as *have* and regular inconsistent words such as *gave*. As noted above, regular inconsistent words are little affected by training on the corresponding exception word. When presented with novel stimuli containing these ambiguous spelling patterns, the model produces output that corresponds more closely to the regularized pronunciation; however, this output is affected by the fact that the model has been trained on exemplars of both pronunciations. In effect, the model has encoded the fact that *-ave* is typically pronounced as in *gave*; however, its knowledge of exception words such as *have* also influences the computed output.

We have not completed the analysis of the model's performance on novel stimuli. It appears, however, that it produces plausible output. Nonwords containing common spelling patterns with regular pronunciations (e.g., *nust*, *bine*) produce output that specifies a particular

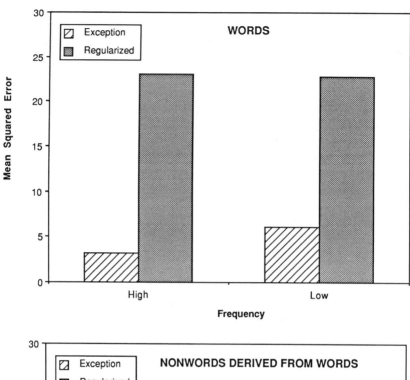

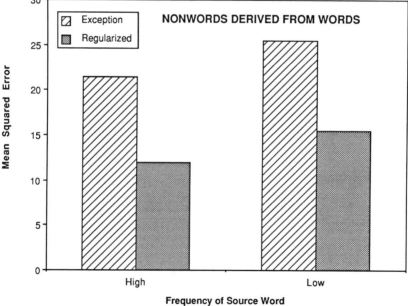

Figure 10.8
The model's performance on exception words (top graph) and derived nonwords (bottom graph) from Taraban and McClelland 1987. "Exception" pronunciations of nonwords rhymed with exception words (e.g., *mave* is pronounced like *have*); "regularized" pronunciations of nonwords rhymed with regular, inconsistent words (e.g., *mave* is pronounced like *gave*).

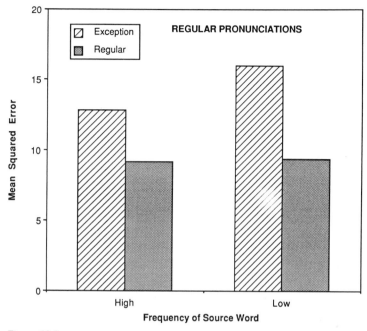

Figure 10.9
Error scores for regular pronunciations of regular and exception nonwords.

pronunciation. Some of these items actually produce smaller error scores than rare words containing unusual spelling patterns (e.g., *tryst, fugue*), leading to the prediction that they should be easier to pronounce. Other nonwords (e.g., those containing unusual spelling patterns or patterns associated with multiple pronunciations) produce output that does not clearly specify a single pronunciation. When human subjects are required to pronounce such nonwords, they may rely on other strategies for formulating a response, such as using explicit analogies to known words or pronunciation rules. In effect, when the computed output is ambiguous, subjects who are nonetheless required to respond may employ other strategies.

Summary of the naming simulations   The model captures basic facts about naming and the acquisition of the naming skill. Both human subjects and the model compute the pronunciations of different types of higher-frequency words about equally well. For less common words, irregular and inconsistent spelling-sound correspondences produce longer naming latencies and larger phonological error scores than regular words. The worst case is that of the strange items, which contain unusual spelling patterns. The exception words fare somewhat better, because they contain spelling patterns that recurred in other training stimuli. The model produces the correct output, but with a higher error score than words whose pronunciations are entirely regular. During the learning process the model goes through intermediate stages that closely correspond to the behavior of children learning to read. Finally, the model also performs well in terms of the pronunciation of novel stimuli.

The model simulates a range of empirical phenomena concerning the pronunciations of words and nonwords. Why the model yields this performance can be understood in terms of the effects of training on the set of weights. The values of the weights reflect the aggregate effects of many individual learning trials using the items in the training set. In effect, learning results in the re-creation of significant aspects of the structure of written English within the network. Because the entire set of weights is used in computing the phonological codes for all words, and because all the weights are updated on every learning trial, there is a sense in which the output for a given word is a function of training on all words in the set. Differences between words derive from facts about the writing system distilled during the learning phase. For a given item the magnitude of the effect of training on other words varies as a function of their similarity to the item. For words the main influence on the phonological output is the number of times the model was exposed to the word itself. Number of times the model was exposed to closely related words (e.g., similarly spelled items) exerts secondary effects; there are also small effects due to exposure to other words.

Orthographic Output and Lexical Decision

We turn now to the other type of output computed by the model. Orthographic output represents the retention or recycling of information about the literal form of the input. We assume that this information is relevant to visual-perceptual aspects of reading that have been widely studied by psychologists, including the word-superiority effect (Wheeler 1970; Reicher 1969) and other tachistoscopic-recognition phenomena such as feature-integration errors (Treisman and Schmidt 1982; Seidenberg 1987). This part of the model addresses the phonemena that motivated the interactive-activation model of McClelland and Rumelhart (1981). The computed orthographic code also may play an important role in some forms of deep dyslexia in which patients access semantic information but are unable to report the identities of words. Orthographic output also plays a critical role in the task that has been most widely employed in studies of word recognition, lexical decision. We shall first describe the computed orthographic output for different types of words and then present an account of the lexical-decision task.

The orthographic output for regular and exception words can be described simply: there are effects of frequency and amount of training but not of word class. The model performs better on high-frequency words than on low-frequency words, and error scores again decrease in an approximately logarithmic manner. However, at no stage in training are there consistent differences between regular and exception words. The absence of any effect of word class confirms the assumption that the regular and exception words differ only in regard to orthographic-phonological regularity, not in regard to orthographic redundancy. The data comparing the orthographic output for regular inconsistent and regular words show a similar pattern: approximately logarithmic learning curves, an effect of frequency, and no effect of word type. Strange words act somewhat differently, however. Again, there were overall effects of frequency, and the model's performance improved with additional training. Through the first 50 epochs the model performs poorly on both high- and low-frequency strange words. Through the next 200 epochs error scores for the high-frequency strange items gradually approached those for high-frequency regular words. But the lower-frequency strange items show much smaller gains: even after 250 epochs they produce the largest error scores. In sum, the regular, regular inconsistent, and exception words act alike in terms of orthographic redundancy; for these items, there are effects of frequency and experience, but not of word class. The strange words differ from the others in terms of orthographic redundancy, as Waters and Seidenberg (1985) suggested. Performance on the higher-frequency strange items improves to the point where they produce output that differs only slightly from that of the regular words; the lower-frequency strange items yield the poorest performance.

When considering both the orthographic and phonological data, one can see that the effects of both orthographic-phonological regularity and orthographic redundancy are largely restricted to words that occur relatively rarely in the language. Whereas lower-frequency exception words produce larger phonological error scores than lower-frequency regular words, these items do not differ in terms of orthographic output. Lower-frequency strange words produce the poorest performance in terms of orthography, because the computation of orthographic output is affected by facts about orthographic redundancy. These words also produce the poorest performance in terms of phonology, because they contain unusual spelling patterns with idiosyncratic pronunciations.

It follows from this analysis that if subjects were able to perform a word-recognition task by addressing only the orthographic output, the results would differ from those obtained with naming. Specifically, there should be no effects of irregular spelling-sound correspondences on such a task, only effects of orthographic redundancy. The lexical-decision task, to which we now turn, yields results consistent with this analysis.

Lexical decisions   A number of studies have examined the effects of orthographic redundancy and orthographic-phonological correspondences on lexical decisions. The task requires subjects to decide whether a string of letters is a word or not. The key finding from this literature is that subjects' criteria for making this decision vary depending on the kind of stimuli included in an experiment. The model provides a simple account of these varying decision criteria. Recall the Waters and Seidenberg (1985) results discussed above (table 10.2). The naming task produced the familiar frequency-regularity interaction: for higher-frequency stimuli, regular and exception words produced similar naming latencies; for lower frequency stimuli, exception words produced longer latencies than regular. This result obtained whether the stimulus set included strange words or not. In the lexical-decision task the exception effect for lower-frequency words depended upon the presence of strange words in the stimulus list. When the strange words were deleted, no effect of phonological regularity obtained.

Waters and Seidenberg (1985) proposed the following account of these results. When the stimuli consist of regular and exception words and pronounceable nonwords, subjects base their decisions on the results of orthographic analyses. Because the decisions are based on orthographic information, no effects of phonological regularity obtain. Including the strange stimuli increases the difficulty of word/nonword discrimination, however. Subjects are asked to respond "word" when they see an item with an unfamiliar spelling pattern such as *tryst* and to respond "nonword" when they encounter stimuli that contain common spelling patterns but are nonetheless not words (e.g., *rone*). Making this discrimination on the basis of orthographic information is difficult, so subjects change their response strategy: they use phonological information as an additional basis for their decisions. In effect, the subject responds "word" if the stimulus has a familiar pronunciation, and "nonword" if it does not. Under these conditions, the task is much like naming: it requires computing the phonological code. Thus, results are similar to those in naming, with a regularity effect for lower-frequency words.

Subjects thus vary the criteria by which lexical decisions are made. In contrast, subjects cannot vary their response strategies when the task is to name words aloud. The task does not involve discriminating between words and nonwords; rather, it requires the subject to produce the correct pronunciation, which cannot be accomplished until the phonological code has been computed. The empirical results agree with this analysis; as Waters and Seidenberg (1985) observed, effects of phonological regularity in the naming task do not depend upon the inclusion of strange words.

Consider now how the model accounts for this pattern of results. After the model has been trained, it can be tested on familiar words and on nonwords. These items produce orthographic output, which can be summarized in terms of error scores. In general, the error scores are smaller for words than nonwords; the model performs better on familiar stimuli. However, the magnitudes of these scores vary as a function of factors such as orthographic redundancy and length. The word and nonword stimuli in an experiment will yield distributions of orthographic error scores. If the word stimuli include regular and exception words (items that do not differ in terms of their orthographic properties) and pronounceable nonwords such as *rone* or *bist*, the word and nonword distributions will overlap very little. Lexical decisions can be modeled as the establishment of decision criteria that operate on the orthographic-error scores. As in a signal detection paradigm, the subject can establish a decision criterion such that scores below the cutoff are judged words and those above it, nonwords. Latencies should be a function of distance from the cutoff; words producing very small error scores and nonwords producing very large error scores should yield faster responses than stimuli whose scores are closer to the cutoff. Given these distributions, response criteria can be established that yield low error rates in the range observed in actual experiments.

The effect of including strange items in the stimulus set is to yield distributions of word and nonword scores with greater overlap; many of the lower-frequency strange items produce error scores as high or higher than those for nonwords. Low-frequency strange words such as *tryst* or *fugue* have been encountered very rarely, and they contain spelling patterns that do not recur in other items. Nonwords such as *bist* or *rone* are also encountered very rarely (typically never), but they contain spelling pattern that recur in many other words. In many experiments the nonwords are also somewhat shorter than the word stimuli, which will tend to produce smaller error scores. Hence, the error scores for some lower-frequency strange words will be larger than those for some nonwords.

Thus, when strange words are included in the stimulus set, subjects can no longer establish response criteria that yield acceptably low error rates. Lexical decisions cannot be based on the discriminibility of words and nonwords in terms of orthographic output. Under these circumstances, subjects must utilize other information in making their decisions. One strategy that subjects apparently use is to consult the results of phonological processing, i.e., phonological output. If subjects begin to consult phonological output, their response latencies should be like those obtained in the naming task, which is also based on this output. The empirical prediction, then, is quite clear: if the strange words are excluded, responses are based on orthographic output, with no difference between regular and exception words, only a frequency effect. If strange words are included, blocking responses based on orthographic output alone, there should be longer latencies for lower-frequency exception words than for lower-frequency regular words, because this pattern is observed in the phonological output, which now provides the basis for making the lexical decision. These are exactly the outcomes observed in the Waters and Seidenberg (1985) experiments.

We tested the model on the Waters and Seidenberg word and nonword stimuli, using the weights from 250 learning epochs. Figure 10.10 (top) presents the data for the condition in which the stimuli consist of high- and low-frequency regular and exception words. Figure 10.10 (middle) shows the corresponding data for the nonword stimuli. The distributions of orthographic-error scores are such that a decision criterion can be established that yields a low error rate similar to that observed in the actual experiment. Since the regular and exception words do not differ in terms of orthographic output, no regularity effect is observed. Figure 10.10 (bottom) presents the data for regular, exception, and strange items. There is considerable overlap between the word and nonword distributions, which makes it impossible to establish a decision criterion that yields a low error rate. Under these circumstances, we argue, subjects begin to look to phonological output. Decision latencies now exhibit the pattern associated with the naming task, longer latencies for lower-frequency exception words than regular words.

In sum, the model provides a simple account of observed differences between lexical decision and naming performance. The naming task requires the subject to compute the phonological code for a word. Under most conditions the lexical-decision task can be performed on the basis of the output of orthographic analysis. In these

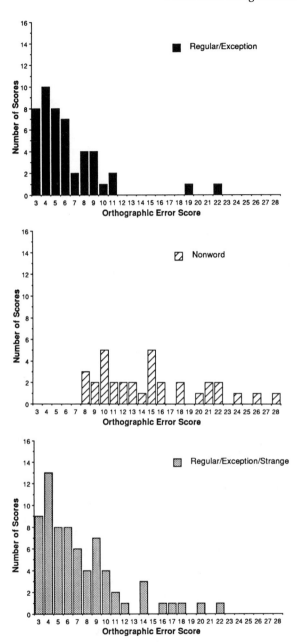

Figure 10.10
Simulation of the Waters and Seidenberg 1985 studies. Orthographic error scores for regular and exception words (top graph); pronounceable nonwords (middle graph); regular, exception and strange words (bottom graph).

cases naming produces effects of phonological regularity for lower-frequency words, but lexical decision does not. Strange words produce longer latencies on both tasks, in lexical decision because they contain unusual spelling patterns and in naming because they are difficult to pronounce. However, if the stimuli in a lexical-decision experiment include very wordlike nonwords and very nonwordlike words, subjects base their decisions on computed phonological codes. Under these conditions lexical decision results are like those obtained in naming, because both responses are based on the same information.

This model of the lexical-decision process will account for other findings in the literature, including the frequency blocking effects observed by Gordon (1983) and Glanzer and Ehrenreich (1979), and the orthographic and phonological priming effects studied by Meyer, Schvaneveldt, and Ruddy (1974), Hillinger (1980), and others (see Seidenberg and McClelland, in press).

Homographs Further evidence in support of this analysis of lexical decision and naming is provided by the data for homographs, words like *wind* or *lead* with two pronunciations, each of which corresponds to a different word in English. Seidenberg et al. (1984) found that homographs produce longer naming latencies than regular words; however, latencies for the two types of words did not differ on the lexical-decision task. The corpus used in training the model included 11 homographs. Each homograph was presented with both correct pronunciations: on one trial, for example, the model was given the feedback that the correct pronunciation of *lead* rhymes with *bead*; on another trail it was given the feedback that the pronunciation rhymes with *dead*. The orthographic output of the homographs did not differ from that of regular words matched in terms of frequency and length. However, homographs produce very large phonological-error scores compared to regular words. This occurs, of course, because the model has been exposed to two pronunciations of these words. In the naming task longer latencies result because subjects must choose between two computed pronunciations. Note that a very similar account applies to the naming of strange words (such as *gauge* or *caste*), whose pronunciations are not known with certainty (as discussed above). Readers may encode different pronunciations on different encounters; that is what it means to say that they are uncertain about their pronunciations. Consideration of two different pronunciations for such words makes them effectively act like homographs, yielding long naming latencies. Because only one pronunciation is actually correct, they also produce many errors.

Dyslexia

We have seen that the model provides an account of a broad range of phenomena related to visual word recognition and naming. (The model also accounts for a number of additional phenomena we have not described; see Seidenberg and McClelland, in press, for details). As a learning model, it also speaks to the issue of how these skills are acquired; moreover, it provides an interesting perspective on the kinds of impairments characteristic of developmental and acquired dylsexias. Developmental dyslexia can be seen as a failure to acquire the knowledge that underlies word recognition and naming. Acquired dyslexias naturally correspond to impairments following damage to the normal system. The model clearly suggests a number of possible sources of processing impairment, which we are in the process of fully exploring. In this section we shall summarize our initial efforts, which have focused on naming impairments. We chose this focus for two reasons. First, it is known that acquiring knowledge of spelling-sound correspondences is a key component of learning to read. Disorders in phonological-analysis skills are thought to be a primary source of reading disability, and children who are backward readers (Backman et al. 1984) or developmental dyslexics (Seidenberg et al. 1986) perform relatively poorly in naming words and nonwords aloud. Second, much of the research on various types of acquired dyslexia has been concerned with overt naming. Disorders such as phonological and surface dyslexia (Patterson 1981) are largely associated with different kinds of naming errors. Hence, naming disorders seemed a good place to start.

Training with Fewer Hidden Units
Consider first the results of an experiment in which we retrained the model with half as many hidden units, 100 instead of 200. In all other respects the training procedure was the same as before. The model was initialized with small random weights on the connections between units; the weights were modified during a training phase using the back-propagation learning algorithm. Figure 10.11 gives the mean phonological-error scores for regular and exception words in the test set described above using 100 hidden units. The figure can be compared to the results for the same stimuli using 200 hidden units (presented in figure 10.3). Two main results can be observed. First, from epochs 10 to 250, training with fewer hidden units yields poorer performance for all word types. High-frequency regular words, for example, asymptote at a mean squared error of about 4.8 in the 100-unit model and at about 3 in the 200-unit model; other words yield similar

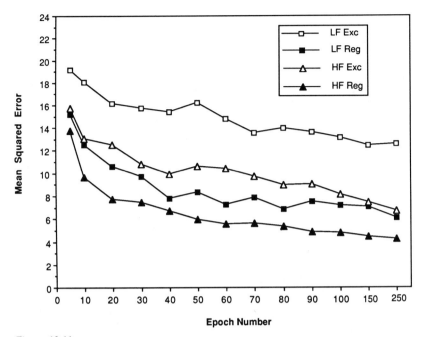

Figure 10.11
The model's performance on regular and exception words from Taraban and Mc-Clelland 1987; 100 hidden units.

results. Second, exception words produce significantly poorer output than regular words in both the high- and low-frequency ranges in the 100-unit model even after 250 epochs of training; in the 200-unit model, exception words produce larger error scores only in the lower-frequency range.

As previously noted, one of the primary developmental trends observed in studies such as Backman et al. (1984) is that younger children and poorer readers show larger regularity effects; that is, they perform worse on exception words (and other items with inconsistent spelling-sound correspondences) than on regular words. For most children, this difference between word classes is eliminated for the most common words in their vocabularies by about grade 5. Even among skilled adult readers, however, exception words continue to produce longer naming latencies and more errors than regular words in the lower-frequency range.

Both poor readers who are reading below age-expected levels and children who have been diagnosed as developmental dyslexics fail to show this improvement in naming higher-frequency exception words. We obtained similar results by eliminating half the hidden units. Like the dyslexic child, the model showed large exception effects for both high- and low-frequency words; similar results were observed for regular, inconsistent and strange words. With 200 hidden units the phonological output for regular inconsistent words did not differ from that for regular words in both high- and low-frequency ranges. With 100 hidden units, lower-frequency regular inconsistent words produced larger error scores than matched regular words. Similarly, training with 200 hidden units eventually produced similar output for high-frequency regular and strange items, but larger error scores for lower-frequency strange items in comparison with regular items. With 100 hidden units the model performs poorest on high- and low-frequency strange words; unlike the 200-unit data, scores for the high-frequency strange words did not converge on those for higher-frequency regular words.

Eliminating half the hidden units, then, produces a general decrement in performance; more importantly, *higher* frequency words produce the patterns associated with *lower* frequency words in the 200-unit simulation, i.e., larger error scores for exception and strange words in comparison to regular words. Even with fewer hidden units the model continues to encode generalizations about the correspondences between spelling and pronunciation; error scores are smaller for regular words than for other types. However, it performs more poorly on words whose pronunciations are not entirely regular. Apparently, including fewer hidden units makes it more difficult to encode item-specific information about pronunciation. Note also that because of this limitation the difference between high-frequency regular and exception words probably would not be completely eliminated with additional training.

These results capture a key feature of the data obtained in studies of dyslexic readers. These children continue to perform poorly in naming even higher-frequency exception words. At the same time, their performance shows that they have learned some generalizations about spelling-sound correspondences; for example, they are able to pronounce many nonwords correctly (Seidenberg et al. 1986). One of the main hallmarks of learning to read English is acquiring knowledge of spelling-sound regularities. Dyslexic readers achieve some success in this regard but cope poorly with the irregular cases. The model performs in a similar manner with too few hidden units; with the resources available it is able to capture crude generalizations about regularity but at the expense of the exception words. The main implication of the simulation, of course, is that children who are not achieving age-expected reading skills may be limited in the computational resources they have available for the task. There is also another important implication. Apparently, the architecture of the model determines in an important way its ability to behave like humans. If there are too few units, the model can learn generalizations about the regularities in the writing system; however, it does not have the capacity to encode enough of the word-specific information relevant to exception words to perform as well as people. With a sufficient number of units, it is able to cope with both regular and irregular cases, although not equally well on all items. The important point is that human performance seems to reflect rather subtle constraints concerning computational resources. The idea that impaired performance might result from dedicating too few resources to a task is one that could be pursued in future research.

Lesioning the Model

We turn now to a brief discussion of some forms of dyslexia observed following brain injury. Numerous studies have shown that brain injury often results in selective impairment of word-recognition and naming processes (see papers in Patterson, Marshall, and Coltheart 1985 for reviews). Case studies of these acquired forms of dyslexia have provided important clues to the brain bases of reading behavior, as well as a source of evidence bearing on the development of theories of reading. Much of what we know about these patients concerns their impaired performance in reading words aloud. Since our model provides an account of the types of knowledge and processes used in naming, it is reasonable to ask whether damage to this system would yield performance similar to that of different types of dyslexic patients. In this section we describe some experiments that address this question; this work is described in greater detail in Patterson, Seidenberg, and McClelland (in press). We should stress the preliminary nature of these investigations. We present them here primarily to suggest that the model provides an interesting and potentially illuminating perspective on acquired dyslexias.

There are many different ways the model could be "lesioned," possibly yielding very different types of impaired performance. Our initial investigations focused on the main types of errors characteristic of surface (Marshall and Newcombe 1973; Patterson, Marshall, and Coltheart 1985) and phonological (Beauvois and Derouesné 1979; Shallice and Warrington 1975) dyslexias. We were interested in these types of dyslexia because they have been seen as providing evidence for a class of reading models very different from ours (the dual-route model of Coltheart [1978] and variations thereon). We should acknowledge from the outset that categories such as surface and phonological dyslexia are based on characteristic patterns of errors, and it is widely acknowledged that a given error pattern could arise from more than one type of pathology. Indeed, the performance of patients within each of these categories varies considerably. These observations suggest that it is unlikely that each type of dyslexia is associated with a unique type of damage.

Since it will probably take quite a while to examine all of the implications of the model concerning reading impairments, we began these investigations with a simpler question: Could the model be damaged in such a way as to produce the main types of errors characteristic of surface and phonological dyslexias? If the model simply cannot produce these types of errors, it would indicate that some rethinking was in order; if the model can produce these types of errors, it would provide a source of evidence corroborating the studies of normals and would motivate detailed studies of more subtle aspects of dyslexic performance (concerning, for example, the proportions of errors of different types or particular words that yield errors).

The basic characteristics of these forms of dyslexia are as follows. Differences among patients can be observed by examining their abilities to read regular and exception words and nonwords. Surface dyslexics are able to name regular words and nonwords but show impairments in naming words with irregular or inconsistent spelling-sound correspondences. They make a disproportionate number of errors on the latter types of words, producing characteristic mispronunciations such as *have* → /hAv/, *pint* → /pint/, and *flood* → /flOd/. The first two of these errors are regularization errors; the patient pronounces the word as it would be pronounced if the spelling-sound correspondence were in fact regular. The third example represents another common type of error, in which the pronunciation is phonologically related to the correct pronunciation but is not a strict regularization. In contrast, phonological dyslexics correctly name regular and exception words, but show an impairment in reading nonwords. In some dramatic cases the patient reads words correctly and, when confronted with a nonword such as *nust,* either makes no response (other than "I don't know") or produces a lexicalized response (e.g., *nust* → /must/, or *pind* → /pink/). That is, they respond by naming a word that is orthographically and phonologically similar to the nonword target. In terms of dual-route models of reading (Patterson et al. 1985), surface dyslexia is thought to derive from impairment of the "addressed" or "lexical" naming mechanism, whereas phonological dyslexia derives from impairment of the "assembled" or "sublexical" mechanism. Clearly, since our model admits only one naming route (in the terminology of the earlier model, it suggests that all pronunciations are "assembled"), it would be a challenge to show that it could produce these distinct patterns of impairment. Presumably these different patterns could be a consequence of damage to different components of the network rather than distinct pronunciation "routes."

According to the standard interpretation of surface dyslexia (within the dual-route model), exception words are read by accessing representations of their pronunciations stored in a phonological lexicon. Errors result because the entries for some words have been damaged. The patient then uses another type of knowledge (rules governing spelling-sound correspondences) to pronounce the exception word, resulting in a regularization error or other systematic mispronunciation. Our model differs from the dual-route conception in two respects. First, there is no phonological lexicon in which the pronunciations of words are stored; rather, pronunciations are computed on the basis of knowledge of spelling-sound correlations encoded by the weights on connections. Second, there are no separate rules governing spelling-sound correspondences. Our hypothesis is that the impaired performance of at least some surface dyslexics results from damage to the lexical network that leaves the processing of regular words and nonwords relatively intact but results in errors on exception words. The basic idea is that the regular spelling-sound correspondences are more robustly encoded by the network than the irregular ones. Damage to the system (e.g., loss of units or connections) is expected to affect performance on all types of stimuli but with greater impact on the exceptions. This produces the characteristic types of errors.

Patterson, Seidenberg, and McClelland (in press) examined this possibility in the following way. We take the weights that were created after 250 epochs of training; these are the weights that provide the basis for our simulations of skilled performance. We can then damage the system in different ways and retest the model's performance on different types of items. As before, we characterize the model's performance on a given word by calculating error scores that index the fit between the computed phonological output and the correct patterns associated with different pronunciations. For example, we compare the computed output for *have* to the pattern for the correct pronunciation /hav/, the regularized pronunciation /hAv/, and other potential pronunciations. In the undamaged mode the best fit to the computed output is almost invariably the correct phonological code. The errors characteristic of surface dyslexia correspond to cases in which the best fit is provided by something other than the correct pronunciation. A regularization error, for example, corresponds to the case in which the best fit to the computed output is provided by the regularized pronunciation.

The main result of these damage simulations can be summarized as follows. We examined several types of damage to the network, including eliminating connections from input units to hidden units, eliminating connections from hidden units to phonological output units, and eliminating the output from hidden units. We also varied the degree of damage (that is, the proportion of connections eliminated). In all cases damage had a bigger impact on exception words and nonwords than on regular words. Although performance on regular words declines as a consequence of damage (i.e., they produce larger error scores), it is rarely the case that the best fit to the computed output is something other than the regular pronunciation. Exception words fare differently. For a significant proportion of these items (the exact proprtion depends on the degree of damage), the best fit to the computed output is not the correct, exceptional pronunciation. In most of these cases the best fit is provided by the regularized pronunciation; for a word such as *deaf*, for example, the computed output more closely approximates /dEf/ than /def/. In other cases the best fit is provided by a pronunciation that is systematically related to the correct one but is not a strict regularization. For example, the output for *pint* might correspond to the pronunciation of *pant*.

The simulations indicate that damage to the model can produce the types of errors characteristic of surface dyslexia. This demonstration is suggestive insofar as it appears that accounting for these errors does not require appeal to separate lexical and nonlexical naming mechanisms. To move beyond this demonstration it will be necessary to consider more detailed aspects of surface dyslexics' performance, aspects concerning, for example, the proportions of errors of different types, the latencies of naming responses, and performance on other types of words and on nonwords. This will require addressing the very important differences among patients who have been classified as surface dyslexics. For example, though both were considered to be surface dyslexics, the patients studied by Bub, Cancelliere, and Kertesz (1985) and Shallice, Warrington, and McCarthy (1983) performed in very different ways. The patient studied by Bub et al. made a large number of regularization errors, with a larger proportion of errors among lower-frequency words than among high-frequency words. Moreover her latencies did not differ greatly from those of normal subjects. The patient studied by Shallice et al. produced many errors that were not regularizations, and the errors were not frequency sensitive. It seems unlikely that such different patterns of performance could derive from a common source.

Similar issues arise in connection with phonological dyslexia. We have observed that damage to the system can produce lexicalization errors. We damage the system and test the model's performance on nonwords such as *nust*. In the undamaged state the model produces plausible output for many regular nonwords, with the best fit to the computed output provided by the correct phonological code. A lexicalization error results when the best fit to the output computed by the damaged system is an orthographically and phonologically similar word. The output for *nust*, for example, is closer to /must/ than to /nust/. Damage to the model can produce a number of these errors, but it remains to be determined whether we can obtain a pattern of performance that closely fits the profiles of phonological dyslexic patients.

In sum, because the model in its undamaged mode closely simulates a broad range of behaviors, we expected that damage to the system would produce impaired performance of a recognizable sort. Our preliminary experiments indicate that this is indeed the case. Obviously many questions remain to be addressed, and it is a daunting challenge to accommodate the entire range of phenomena associated with the acquired dyslexias.

Conclusions

We have described a model of lexical processing that illustrates how systematic, "rule-governed" behavior can emerge from a network of simple processing units. According to this account, lexical processing involves computing several types of information—orthographic, phonological, and semantic—in parallel. We have described the computation of the orthographic and phonological codes in some detail and have shown that the model provides a quantitative account of various behavioral phenomena. The model accounts for differences among words in terms of processing difficulty, differences in reading skill, and the course of acquisition and points to some plausible bases for acquired and developmental forms of dyslexia. We characterized lexical decision and naming in terms of how the computed codes are utilized in making these types of responses. A task such as naming focuses on the use of one type of code, phonology; a task such as lexical decision may involve all of the codes. The same types of knowledge representations and processes are involved in the computation of all three codes (although the implemented model is restricted to orthography and phonology). Knowledge is represented by the weights on connections between units. These weights are primarily determined by the nature of the English orthography that acts as input, in conjunction with feedback during the learning phase. Our claim is that representing knowledge of the orthography in this way is felicitous because of the quasiregular nature of the system; the characteristics of English orthography are more congruent with this type of knowledge representation than with the kinds of pronunciation rules that have previously been proposed. The computation of the orthographic code is affected by the distribution of letter patterns in the lexicon; computation of the phonological code is affected by correlations between orthography and phonology.

The model differs from previous accounts in several respects. First, it makes quantitative, testable predictions about the processing of individual words as well as general types of words. This is simply a consequence of the explicit nature of the knowledge representations and processes, which had to be achieved in order to develop a working simulation model. Second, it differs from previous accounts in terms of the types of knowledge and processes underlying performance. In contrast to the dual-route model, there are no rules specifying the regular spelling-sound correspondences of the language, and there is no phonological lexicon in which the pronunciations of all words are listed. All items—regular and irregular, word and nonword—are pronounced using the knowledge encoded by a single set of connections. The main assumption of the dual-route model is that separate mechanisms are required to account for the capacity to name exception words and nonwords. Exception words cannot be pronounced by rule, only by consulting a stored lexical entry; hence one route is termed "lexical" or "addressed" phonology. Nonwords do not have lexical entries; hence, they can only be pronounced by rule. Accordingly, the second route is termed the "nonlexical" or "subword" process. One of the main contributions of the network model is that it demonstrates that pronunciation of exception words and nonwords can be accomplished by a single mechanism employing weighted connections between units. Our model also differs from proposals by Glushko (1979) and Brown (1987) in that there are no lexical nodes representing individual words and no feedback from neighbors. In fact, phonological output is computed on a single, forward pass through the network, giving the model a very different character from these other accounts, in which behavioral phenomena result from complex interactions among partially activated words and letters.

The model reflects a very basic change in perspective on issues concerning word recognition. The models described by Coltheart (1987b), Monsell (1987), and others contain multiple lexicons, including separate orthographic lexicons used in reading and writing and separate phonological lexicons used in listening and speaking. Research within this framework has focused on questions concerning what has been termed lexical access: how the entries for different codes are accessed in reading, the order in which they are accessed, and how access of one code affects access of other codes.

Our model departs from these precursors in a fundamental way: lexical memory does not consist of entries for individual words; there are no logogens (Morton 1969, this volume). Knowledge of words is embedded in a set of weights on connections between processing units encoding letters, phonemes, and the correlations between them. The spellings, pronunciations, and meanings of words are not listed in separate stores; hence, lexical processing does not involve accessing these stored codes. Rather, these codes are computed from the input string using the knowledge stored in the network structure, which results in the activation of distributed representations. Thus, the notion of lexical access does not play a central role in our model, because it is not congruent with the model's representational and processing assumptions.

The view that lexical processing involves *activation* of different types of information rather than *access* to stored lexical codes represents more than a change in terminology. The access view suggests that there is a moment in time at which a letter string is identified as a particular word, which provides immediate access to stored representations of its meanings. In our model, information simply accrues over time, and it would be arbitrary to designate a particular point in this process as the moment of "lexical access." More generally, access to a lexical code is an all-or-none phenomenon, whereas our framework sanctions the notion of partial or graded activation of lexical codes. In an activation model with distributed representations a code is represented as a pattern of activation across a set of nodes. The activations of the nodes can differ in strength. These conceptions raise different questions and generate different empirical predictions. For example, within the access framework it is meaningful to ask how many of the meanings of an ambiguous word are accessed; Swinney (1979) and Onifer and Swinney (1981) has proposed that lexical access make all the meanings of an ambiguous word available. In contrast, the activation approach suggests that meanings may be activated with different strengths; moreover, a network with distributed representations, such as ours, affords the possibility of partial activation of meaning (see Kawamoto 1987; McClelland and Kawamoto 1986; McClelland and Rumelhart 1985; Hinton and Sejnowski 1986). The latter view is consistent with behavioral evidence that different aspects of the meaning of a word—or different meanings entirely—are activated in different contexts (Barsalou 1982; Schwanenflugel and Shoben 1985; Tabossi 1988).

Similarly, within the lexical-access framework the well-studied question of phonological mediation concerned whether the phonological code was accessed before or after the semantic code ("prelexically" or "postlexically"). In our framework, phonology is one of several codes computed in parallel, and the primary question concerns how knowledge of the orthography affects this computation. Since the computation of the phonological code is orthogonal to the computation of meaning, questions as to whether frequency effects in naming are due to lexical access or production (Balota and Chumbley 1985; McCann and Besner 1987) do not arise.

In sum, the notion of lexical access carries with it a concern with certain types of theoretical questions. The primary questions concern the number of lexicons, how they are organized and linked, and whether it is orthographic or phonological information that provides access to meaning. The primary processing mechanism is search through one or more ordered lists. In our model the codes are distributed; they are computed on the basis of three orthogonal processes; and the primary processing mechanism is spread of activation. The primary theoretical questions concern the properties of these computations, which are determined by the properties of the writing system that are picked up by the learning algorithm on the basis of experience.

In its present state the model is limited in many respects. It deals only with monosyllabic words; there is no mechanism for actually pronouncing a word based on the computed phonological output; there is neither representation of meaning nor consideration of how contextual information could influence processing; we do not have a solid account of the acquired dyslexias (see Seidenberg and Mc-Clelland, in press, and Seidenberg, in press, for discussion). These are important limitations, and they mean that the model is by no means a complete account of lexical processing in reading. We see the model as having succeeded in addressing a number of basic issues that have preoccupied reading researchers for some time and hope that it represents a step toward developing a genuinely explanatory account of these important phenomena.

Notes

This research was supported by the National Science Foundation (BNS 8609729), Office of Naval Research (N00014-86-G-0146), Natural Science and Engineering Research

Council (A7924), Quebec Ministry of Education (FCAR EQ-2074), and National Institutes of Health (HD-22271). McClelland was also supported by an NIH career development award (MH00385). We thank Karalyn Patterson, who has collaborated on studies of the implications of the model for acquired forms of dyslexia (Patterson, Seidenberg, and McClelland, in press) and is primarily responsible for the experiments on surface and phonological dyslexia. We should also acknowledge the important work by Sejnowski and Rosenberg (1986), whose NETtalk model was the first application of the algorithm of Rumelhart, Hinton, and Williams (1986) to the problem of learning the spelling-sound correspondences of English. Sejnowski and Rosenberg recognized that this knowledge could be represented within a parallel distributed network rather than as a set of pronunciation rules. Our goal was to explore the adequacy of this approach by developing a model that could be related to a broad range of behavioral phenomena.

1. There is another factor that probably contributed to the inconsistent results in studies comparing regular, inconsistent and regular words. Brown (1987) has noted that the number of times a spelling pattern occurs with a given pronunciation influences naming latency. For example, -*ust* is pronounced /ust/ in a certain number of words, which may differ from the number of times -*ist* is pronounced /ist/. Tests of the effects of the inconsistency of a spelling-sound pattern are valid only if this factor is controlled. Specifically, the number of times a regular, inconsistent pattern is assigned the regular pronunciation (e.g., -*ave* is pronounced /Av/) should be equal to the number of times the spelling pattern in a regular word is assigned the regular pronunciation (e.g., -*ust* is pronounced /ust/). With the stimuli equated in this way, any naming-latency differences could be safely attributed to the inconsistency factor. Studies of regular, inconsistent words did not in fact equate the stimuli in this way. When the stimuli are equated in this way, there is a small but reliable consistency effect for lower-frequency words (Seidenberg and McClelland, in press).

References

Andrews, S. 1982. Phonological recoding: Is the regularity effect consistent? *Memory and Cognition* 10:565–575.

Backman, J., Bruck, M., Hebert, M., and Seidenberg, M. 1984. Acquisition and use of spelling-sound information in reading. *Journal of Experimental Child Psychology* 38:114–133.

Balota, D. A., and Chumbley, J. I. 1985. The locus of the word frequency effect in the pronunciation task: Lexical access and/or production? *Journal of Memory and Language* 24:89–106.

Barron, R. W. 1981. Reading skill and reading strategies. In A. M. Lesgold and C. A. Perfetti, eds., *Interactive processes in reading*. Hillsdale, N.J.: Erlbaum.

Barsalou, L. W. 1982. Context-independent and context-dependent information in concepts. *Memory and Cognition* 10:82–93.

Beauvois, M. F., and Derouesné, J. 1979. Phonological alexia: Three dissociations. *Journal of Neurology, Neurosurgery, and Psychiatry* 42:1115–1124.

Besner, D., Waller, T. G., and MacKinnon, G. E. 1985. *Reading research: Advances in theory and practice*. Vol. 5. New York: Academic Press.

Brown, G. D. A. 1987. Resolving inconsistency: A computational model of word naming. *Journal of Memory and Language* 26:1–23.

Bub, D., Cancelliere, A., and Kertesz, A. 1985. Whole-word and analytic translation of spelling to sound in a non-semantic reader. In K. E. Patterson, J. C. Marshall, and M. Coltheart, eds., *Surface dyslexia*. London: Erlbaum.

Coltheart, M. 1978. Lexical access in simple reading tasks. In G. Underwood, ed., *Strategies of information processing*. New York: Academic Press.

Coltheart, M., ed. 1987a. *Attention and Performance*. Vol. 12, *Reading*. London: Erlbaum.

Coltheart, M. 1987b. Functional architecture of the language-processing system. In M. Coltheart, G. Sartori, and R. Job, eds., *The cognitive neuropsychology of language*. London: Erlbaum.

Glanzer, M., and Ehrenreich, S. L. 1979. Structure and search of the internal lexicon. *Journal of Verbal Learning and Verbal Behavior* 18:381–398.

Glushko, R. J. 1979. The organization and activation of orthographic knowledge in reading aloud. *Journal of Experimental Psychology: Human Perception and Performance* 5:674–691.

Goodman, K. S. 1967. Reading: A psycholinguistic guessing game. *Journal of the Reading Specialist* 6:126–135.

Gordon, B. 1983. Lexical access and lexical decision: Mechanisms of frequency sensitivity. *Journal of Verbal Learning and Verbal Behavior* 22:24–44.

Henderson, L. 1982. *Orthography and word recognition in reading*. London: Academic Press.

Hillinger, M. L. 1980. Priming effects with phonemically similar words: The encoding-bias hypothesis reconsidered. *Memory and Cognition* 8:115–123.

Hinton, G. E., McClelland, J. L., and Rumelhart, D. E. 1986. Distributed representations. In D. E. Rumelhart and J. L. McClelland, eds., *Parallel distributed processing: Explorations in the microstructure of cognition*, vol. 1. Cambridge: MIT Press.

Hinton, G. E., and Sejnowski, T. J. 1986. Learning and relearning in Boltzman machines. In D. E. Rumelhart and J. L. McClelland, eds., *Parallel distributed processing: Explorations in the microstructure of cognition*, vol. 1. Cambridge: MIT Press.

Jorm, A. F. 1983. *The psychology of reading and spelling disabilities*. London: Routledge and Kegan Paul.

Kawamoto, A. 1988. Interactive processes in lexical ambiguity resolution. In S. Small, G. Cottrell, and M. K. Tanenhaus, eds. *Lexical ambiguity resolution: Computational, linguistic, and psychological perspectives*. New York: Morgan Kauffman.

Kucera, H., and Francis, W. N. 1967. *Computational analysis of present-day American English*. Providence: Brown University Press.

Locke, J. L. 1972. Ease of articulation. *Journal of Speech and Hearing Research* 15:194–200.

McCann, R. S., and Besner, D. 1987. Reading pseudohomophones: Implications for models of pronunciation assembly and the locus of word-frequency effects in naming. *Journal of Experimental Psychology: Human Perception and Performance* 13:14–24.

McClelland, J. L. 1987. The case for interactionism in language processing. In M. Coltheart, ed., *Attention and Performance*, vol. 12, *Reading*. London: Erlbaum.

McClelland, J. L., and Kawamoto, A. 1986. Mechanisms of sentence processing: Assigning roles to constituents. In J. L. McClelland and D. E. Rumelhart, eds., *Parallel distributed processing: Explorations in the microstructure of cognition*, vol. 2. Cambridge: MIT Press.

McClelland, J. L., and Rumelhart, D. E. 1981. An interactive activation model of context effects in letter perception: Part 1. An account of basic findings. *Psychological Review* 88:375–407.

McClelland, J. L., and Rumelhart, D. E. 1985. Distributed memory and the representation of general and specific information. *Journal of Experimental Psychology: General* 114:159–188.

McClelland, J. L., and Rumelhart, D. E., eds. 1986a. *Parallel distributed processing: Explorations in the microstructure of cognition*, vol. 2. Cambridge: MIT Press.

McClelland, J. L., and Rumelhart, D. E. 1986b. A distributed model of human learning and memory. In J. L. McClelland and D. E. Rumelhart, eds., *Parallel distributed processing: Explorations in the microstructure of cognition*, vol. 2. Cambridge: MIT Press.

McRae, K., Jared, D., and Seidenberg, M. S. In press. On the roles of frequency and lexical access in word naming. *Journal of Memory and Language*.

Marshall, J. C., and Newcombe, F. 1973. Patterns of paralexia: A psycholinguistic approach. *Journal of Psycholinguistic Research* 2:175–199.

Meyer, D. E., Schvaneveldt, R. W., and Ruddy, M. G. 1974. Functions of graphemic and phonemic codes in visual word recognition. *Memory and Cognition*, 2:309–321.

Monsell, S. 1987. On the relation between lexical input and output pathways for speech. In D. A. Allport, D. G. MacKay, W. Prinz, and E. Scheerer eds., *Language perception and production: Relationships among listening, speaking, reading, and writing*. London: Academic Press.

Morton, J. 1969. Interaction of information in word recognition. *Psychological Review* 76:165–178.

Onifer, W., and Swinney, D. 1981. Accessing lexical ambiguities during sentence comprehension: Effects of frequency, meaning, and contextual bias. *Memory and Cognition* 9:225–236.

Patterson, K. E. 1981. Neuropsychological approaches to the study of reading. *British Journal of Psychology* 72:151–174.

Patterson, K., Marshall, J. C., and Coltheart, M. 1985. *Surface dyslexia*. London: Erlbaum.

Patterson, K. E., Seidenberg, M. S., and McClelland, J. L. In press. Reading acquisition and dyslexia: A connectionist perspective. In P. Morris, ed., *Connectionism: The Oxford Symposium*. Oxford University Press.

Reicher, G. M. 1969. Perceptual recognition as a function of meaningfulness of stimulus material. *Journal of Experimental Psychology* 81:274–280.

Rozin, P., and Gleitman, L. 1977. The structure and acquisition of reading, II: The reading process and the acquisition of the alphabetic principle. In A. Reber and D. Scarborough, eds., *Toward a psychology of reading*. Hillsdale, N.J.: Erlbaum.

Rumelhart, D. E., Hinton, G. E., and Williams, R. J. 1986. Learning internal representations by error propagation. In D. E. Rumelhart and J. L. McClelland, eds., *Parallel distributed processing: Explorations in the microstructure of cognition*, vol. 1. Cambridge: MIT Press.

Rumelhart, D. E., and McClelland, J. L., eds. 1986. *Parallel distributed processing: Explorations in the microstructure of cognition*, vol. 1. Cambridge: MIT Press.

Schwanenflugel, P. J., and Shoben, E. J. 1985. The influence of sentence constraint on the scope of facilitation for upcoming words. *Journal of Memory and Language* 24:232–252.

Seidenberg, M. S. 1985a. The time course of phonological code activation in two writing systems. *Cognition* 19:1–30.

Seidenberg, M. S. 1985b. The time course of information activation and utilization in visual word recognition. In D. Besner, T. Waller, and G. E. MacKinnon, eds., *Reading research: Advances in theory and practice*, vol. 5. New York: Academic Press.

Seidenberg, M. S. 1987. Sublexical structures in visual word recognition: Access units or orthographic redundancy? In M. Coltheart, ed., *Attention and Performance*, vol. 12, *Reading*. Hillsdale, N.J.: Erlbaum.

Seidenberg, M. S. In press. Reading complex words. In G. Carlson and M. K. Tanenhaus, eds., *Language comprehension and linguistic theory*. Amsterdam: Reidel.

Seidenberg, M. S., Bruck, M., Fornarolo, G., and Backman, J. 1986. Word recognition skills of poor and disabled readers: Do they necessarily differ? *Applied Psycholinguistics* 6:161–180.

Seidenberg, M. S., and McClelland, J. L. In press. A distributed, developmental model of visual word recognition and pronunciation. *Psychological Review.*

Seidenberg, M. S., Waters, G. S., Barnes, M. A., and Tannenhaus, M. K. 1984. When does irregular spelling or pronunciation influence word recognition? *Journal of Verbal Learning and Verbal Behavior* 23:383–404.

Shallice, T., and Warrington, E. 1975. Word recognition in a phonemic dyslexic patient. *Quarterly Journal of Experimental Psychology* 27:189–199.

Shallice, T., Warrington, E., and McCarthy, R. 1983. Reading without semantics. *Quarterly Journal of Experimental Psychology* 35A:111–138.

Stanovich, K. E. 1986. Matthew effects in reading: Some consequences of individual differences in the acquisition of literacy. *Reading Research Quarterly* 21:360–407.

Swinney, D. A. 1979. Lexical access during sentence comprehension: (Re)consideration of context effects. *Journal of Verbal Learning and Verbal Behavior* 18:645–659.

Tabossi, P. 1988. Effects of context on the immediate interpretation of unambiguous nouns. *Journal of Experimental Psychology: Learning, Memory, and Cognition* 14:153–162.

Tanenhaus, M. K., Dell, G., and Carlson, G. 1988. Context effects in lexical processing: A Connectionist approach to modularity. In J. Garfield, ed., *Modularity in knowledge representation and nautral language processing.* Cambridge: MIT Press.

Taraban, R., and McClelland, J. L. 1987. Conspiracy effects in word recognition. *Journal of Memory and Language* 26:608–631.

Theios, J., and Musie, J. G. 1977. The word identification process in reading. In N. J. Castellan, Jr., D. B. Pisoni, and G. R. Potts, eds., *Cognitive theory,* vol. 2. Hillsdale, N.J.: Erlbaum.

Treiman, R., Freyd, J., and Baron, J. 1984. Phonological recoding and use of spelling-sound rules in reading of sentences. *Journal of Verbal Learning and Verbal Behavior* 22:682–700.

Teisman, A., and Schmidt, H. 1982. Illusory conjunctions in the perception of objects. *Cognitive Psychology* 14:107–141.

Venezky, R. 1970. *The structure of English orthography.* The Hague: Mouton.

Waters, G. S., Bruck, M., and Seidenberg, M. S. 1985. Do children use similar processes to read and spell words? *Journal of Experimental Child Psychology* 39:511–530.

Waters, G. S., and Seidenberg, M. S. 1985. Spelling-sound effects in reading: Time course and decision criteria. *Memory and Cognition* 13:557–572.

Wheeler, D. D. 1970. Process in word recognition. *Cognitive Psychology* 1:59–85.

Editor's Comments

The chapters by Dudai and by Churchland and Sejnowski in this volume complement the present chapter. Parallel-distributed-processing (PDP) models based on paired associated learning, such as those depicted here, are capable of pronouncing English words of many types and successfully completing lexical decision tasks. For me, the most informative and remarkable aspect of this exercise is that the computer outputs closely resemble humans' performances with real language, at least at the level of single words. (This would not be at all obvious were it not for the fact that experimental linguists have been able to specify a great deal of these data for both normal subjects and individuals with developmental and acquired language disturbances.) However, it remains to be seen what will happen when the models are made to perform at levels involving more than single words, at levels where only sentential and logical theories can explain the empirical data.

To neurologists the discovery that "lesioned" machines can produce errors that resemble those made by our patients is truly awesome. It might be argued that because of the nature of the task, the resemblance will break down in one of a limited number of ways (see Morton in this volume). On the other hand, it is astounding that the nature of the implementation hardware, whether cut and dry silicone chips or wet and sinewy neural networks, does not appear to be very important in this respect.

Two simulations of pathological states are presented here. One considers the effects of developmental anomaly by incomplete development (in the simulation the number of hidden units is intentionally diminished). Several of the difficulties encountered by the device thus altered resemble those met by developmental dyslexics. The other considers the effects of damaged connections. This time the device performs similarly to patients with acquired dyslexia.

A third possibility needs to be simulated: a device with increased numbers of processing units or connections. This may turn out to be a fair characterization of at least part of the neural substrate underlying developmental dyslexia (see Sherman et al. and Galaburda et al. in this volume). Excessive numbers of processing units may lead to difficulty with generalization and sluggish or inadequate emergence of rules from the learning period. Excessive numbers of connections at the initial state may lead to nonrandom initial weighting and subsequent interference with appropriate experience-based weighting. As connections may play a role in the sequential linking of separate

PDP devices, anomalous connections might conceivably lead to what at the cognitive level may look like abnormal sentence and logic architectures, a fair characterization of the performances of some developmental dyslexics.

Chapter 11

Aphasia in Men and Women

Hanna Damasio, Daniel Tranel, Jon Spradling, and Randall Alliger

Introduction

There is a vast body of research in neuropsychology and neurobiology relating to psychological performance, neuroanatomical structure, and neural function. A theory recently advanced by Geschwind and Galaburda (1985) on the development of cerebral dominance supports the general notion that gender-related neuroendocrine differences could lead to different morphogenesis and physiology. Notwithstanding, the fact that structural and functional differences between the brains of boys and girls had been suggested as early as the 1960s (Lansdell 1962, 1964; Lansdell and Urbach 1965), the research community received with surprise the claims made by some investigators that somehow women do not become aphasic as often as men (McGlone 1977) and that aphasia in women is more often of the Broca type and rarely if ever of the Wernicke type (Kimura 1980, 1983). At first glance the claims appear extravagant indeed. Most neurologists and neuropsychologists have cared for women with aphasia, both fluent and nonfluent. Yet perhaps clinical impressions have been deceptive and women are in fact in a minority, or though aphasic, their aphasias were out of step with their lesions, or their aphasias were simply different from those of men in neuropsychological profile or recovery pattern.

The subjects used in the McGlone and Kimura studies had lesions caused by several different neuropathological processes (stroke, primary and secondary tumors of the central nervous system, etc.), and the localization of lesions was based on different methods with varied sensitivity and precision. Furthermore, some of the patients used in the McGlone study were also included in the Kimura study. Harasymiw and Halper (1981) found no significant difference between gender groups but did note that women tended to have more Broca aphasia. Studies by other investigators revealed the opposite trend; women have more fluent aphasias (Burst et al. 1976; De Renzi et al.

1980), or they failed to identify any difference at all (Kertesz and Sheppard 1981; Kertesz and Banke 1986).

Here we report the preliminary results of a study that addresses the relation of gender to the neuroanatomical characteristics of aphasia-causing lesions, and to the neuropsychological characterization of the aphasias. The study was conducted on a large population of patients who became aphasic following lesions of a single neuropathological type, stroke. It draws on a database of independently conducted neuroanatomical analyses (based on computerized X-ray tomography and magnetic resonance tomography) and standardized neuropsychological assessments. Our goal was to provide a more powerful test of the hypothesis that there are gender-related differences in the development of aphasia.

The specific questions taken up in this first report are as follows: (1*a*) Do males and females develop aphasia following lesions in the language-related areas of the left hemisphere? (1*b*) Do males and females develop aphasia with lesions in the right hemisphere in areas homologous to the language-related areas of the left? (1*c*) Is there a difference between aphasic males and aphasic females regarding the severity of their neuropsychological deficits?

We also wanted to explore the possibility of differences in site of damage as a function of gender. This could conceivably influence the interpretation of the results obtained from the analyses described immediately above. To explore this issue, we investigated the following two questions: (2*a*) Is the distribution of lesion locations different in males and females? (2*b*) Are the sizes of lesions in a given region different in males and females?

And finally, we addressed the issue of recovery: (3) Is there a difference in outcome of neuropsychological deficits in males and females when location of lesions is the same?

Method

Design

An overview of the general design used in this study is helpful in characterizing our approach to the questions posed in the introduction. There are three main data sources: a set of anatomical variables; a set of neuropsychological variables; and several demographic variables. There are two main epochs of data collection: acute and periacute, defined as 0 to 10 days after the stroke, and chronic, defined as 3 to 12 months after onset of aphasia. Combining these epochs with the hemispheric side of lesion yields four main subject groups: left-acute, left-chronic, right-acute, and right-chronic. These groups are dealt with independently, and no direct comparisons should be made between the acute and chronic data sets. We did use a within-subject comparison to address the recovery question, but in this case a special subgroup drawn from the acute and chronic left hemisphere groups was formed.

Subject Selection
Subjects were selected from a pool of 307 patients with cerebrovascular accidents who have been intensively studied in our department as part of an ongoing program project dedicated to the study of neural substrates of complex behavior and cognition. Subjects entered into this research program are identified in two ways: all patients with *any* neuropsychological deficits studied in the Department of Neurology, regardless of the neuroanatomical correlate of the deficit, and all patients with computerized-tomography (CT) or magnetic-resonance (MR) scans that show a focal vascular lesion in the cerebrum, regardless of neuropsychological correlate. Subject selection thus independently takes into account disturbed cognition and disturbed neuroanatomy. All patients in the project have been studied in the acute and/or the chronic stage with a complete set of standardized neuropsychological techniques. Core neuroanatomical and neuropsychological studies of the subjects thus inducted into the study proceed independently, as the investigators in charge of each line of data collection did not have access to data in the other set.

In addition to the specifications mentioned above, all patients in the research pool met the following criteria: eight or more years of education; native English speakers; no history of mental retardation; no history of significant head trauma, alcohol or drug use, or psychiatric illness; no developmental learning disability.

To be selected for the current study, patients had to have a single infarct in the left hemisphere in an area related to language function or in a homologous area of the right hemisphere. Only cases with unilateral lesions were selected. Patients also had to be fully right-handed, i.e., they had to score +100 on the Oldfield-Geschwind handedness questionnaire. This latter criterion was adopted because of our desire to keep the power of our analyses focused on issues of gender.

Neuroanatomical Studies
CT and MR images of patients inducted into the program project are obtained at the same epochs at which core neuropsychological studies are carried out. Detailed analysis of these images aimed at deter-

mining the involvement of cortical and subcortical cerebral structures is performed using a standard method (Damasio 1988; Damasio and Damasio 1989). The investigator performing the neuroanatomical analysis only has available information about the date of the stroke and the date of the CT or MR scan. The identification of all image transparencies is masked by a research assistant, and the subjects are identified by a code number.

In the anatomical analysis damage seen on CT or MR images is assigned to predefined areas of interest, a total of 60 in each hemisphere. The researcher estimated the amount of involvement of each area and assigned a value of 1 (less than 25 percent involvement of the total area), 2 (between 25 and 75 percent involvement), or 3 (greater than 75 percent involvement). The value 0 corresponds to no involvement.

For the purposes of this study our analysis focused on those regions about which there is a current consensus regarding their link to language and speech processing. The following 16 areas were considered (numbered areas are in Brodmann's nomenclature): (1) Broca's area, defined as areas 44 and 45; (2) the region superior to Broca's area, defined as areas 8 and 6; (3) the region posterior to Broca's area, defined as area 6; (4) the anterior periventricular region; (5) the caudate nucleus; (6) the lenticular nucleus; (7) the anterior limb of the internal capsule; (8) the insula; (9) the auditory cortex (areas 41 and 42); (10) posterior area 22 (Wernicke's area); (11) area 37; (12) areas 20 and 21; (13) anterior area 22; (14) the angular gyrus (area 40); (15) the supramarginal gyrus (area 39); and (16) the posterior periventricular region. All patients who showed a lesion in any of these regions in the left hemisphere were entered into the study. The same procedure was applied to subjects with right hemisphere lesions. These 16 areas were further consolidated into 8 regions: (1) Broca's area, (2) the region surrounding Broca's area (including original 2, 3, and 4), (3) the basal ganglia (including original 5, 6, and 7), (4) the insula, (5) Wernicke's region (including original 9 and 10), (6) the posterior temproal (including original 11 and 12), (7) the anterior temporal (original 13), and (8) the parietal (including original 14, 15, and 16). Rating the extent of involvement in the consolidated cells was obtained by weighting the different components used in forming each cell and using these weights as factors in determining the extent of involvement. This consolidation process maintains a high degree of anatomical specificity and at the same time allows the application of multivariate statistical techniques described below. It should be noted that this process was applied separately to each of the four distinct groups of patients, i.e., acute left-hemisphere (95 subjects), chronic left-hemisphere (64 subjects), acute right-hemisphere (39 subjects), and chronic right-hemisphere (27 subjects). The acute and chronic groups in each hemisphere only overlapped partially in the chronic state, and a few subjects in the chronic group had not been seen during the acute episode.

Neuropsychological Studies

All patients seen as part of our program project are routinely studied with detailed neuropsychological tests that probe the areas of speech and language, complex visual behavior, memory, and executive control. These studies are performed during both the acute or periacute period and the chronic stage (at least 3 months after onset).

Rather than using traditional syndromatic classifications of aphasias (e.g., Broca's, Wernicke's) to group the neuropsychological data, for this study we analyzed the information according to 10 dimensions of speech and language, described below. Also, to retain the largest possible number of subjects for the statistical analyses and to bring the neuropsychological data into the same scale as that used for the anatomical information, we reduced the neuropsychological data using a rating system. Thus, rather than using raw or percentile scores on particular tests, which necessitates prorating and deleting subjects that do not have complete data sets, we used a rating scale system that preserves some magnitude information while also allowing a composite evaluation of a particular patient's performance.

The ten dimensions of speech and language were: fluency; articulation, melodic contour, paraphasias, visual naming, repetition, aural comprehension, reading comprehension, writing, and verbal-associative fluency. For each of these, the patient's level of performance was rated on a four-point scale: $0 =$ intact; $1 =$ mild impairment; $2 =$ moderate impairment; $3 =$ severe impairment. Ratings were based on information from the following sources: audiotapes of the patient's speech, descriptions in the neuropsychological assessment protocols, and results of various subtests of the Multilingual Aphasia Examination (MAE; Benton 1976) and the Boston Diagnostic Aphasia Examination (BDAE; Goodglass and Kaplan 1972). Ratings of fluency, articulation, melodic contour, and presence of paraphasias were adapted to the structure used to rate these characteristics in the BDAE. The ratings were based on information from audiotapes of structured interviews, descriptions of the Cookie Theft picture, and descriptions in the patient's files. Ratings of visual naming were based on results of the visual naming test of the MAE. Repetition was evaluated with the sentence repetition tests from both the MAE and the BDAE. Aural comprehension and reading comprehension were evaluated with the tests of aural comprehension and reading comprehension of words and phrases from the MAE, the Token Test (MAE). The test of reading comprehension of sentences and paragraphs was from the BDAE. Writing was evaluated with tests of writing to copy, to dictation, and spontaneously from the MAE and the BDAE. Verbal associative fluency was measured with the MAE controlled oral word-association test. Ratings were made for as many of the variables, and for as many of the patients, as possible. When the rater could not generate a rating because of missing or insufficient data, the item was recorded as having missed data.

For each patient two sets of ratings were generated whenever possible: one corresponding to the acute phase, and one to the chronic. These periods coincide with those used for the neuroanatomical studies.

Data Quantification and Analysis

Questions 1a and 1b   The question of whether there are gender-related differences in how likely one is to develop aphasia following a left- or right-hemisphere lesion was addressed by noting the frequency with which males and females developed aphasic disturbances following lesions in the left or right hemisphere in the sample.

Question 1c   We utilized several statistical probes to address the question of whether there are gender-related differences in the severity of speech and language disturbances that follow left-hemisphere lesions. We first conducted a series of *t*-tests on the 10 neuropsychological variables, using gender as the grouping variable. Thus, males were compared to females on the various speech and language parameters. Note that this set of analyses is aimed only at the left-hemisphere group. Also, the t-tests were conducted separately on the acute and chronic data sets.

The next procedure was a stepwise-regression analysis. For this, each of the 10 neuropsychological variables was analyzed separately. For each measure the following independent variables were included as candidates for the regression equation: age, gender, education, and the eight anatomical variables. The variable-selection process involved a forward entry procedure: variables already included in the model were analyzed for removal before another variable is tested for entry. The level of significance for factor entry and exit was set at .15. This rather liberal significance level was selected in order to allow a reasonably high chance for gender to enter the model as one of the factors. Thus, if a factor accounted for enough variance in the dependent measure to be considered significant at the .15 level, the factor was entered into the regression model. Note that the procedure is stepwise, so that each factor is entered into the model in the order of the degree of variance for which it accounted from the most and to the least. The incremental amount of variance accounted for is given as a partial R^2. Factor entry was discontinued when no candidate met the criterion of the .15 level of significance.

The third statistical probe utilized two sets of regression analyses. The stepwise procedure yielded an overall R^2 for a model from the factors that were identified in the regression as significant at the .15 level (without gender). We then conducted a second regression using the same set of factors plus gender. An overall R^2 is again generated. By subtracting the first R^2 from the second one, the degree of variance that gender accounts for is ascertained. Note that this is a statistically liberal procedure that provides direct evidence regarding the degree to which gender can account for variance in the 10 neuropsychological measures.

Question 2   To investigate gender-related anatomical differences, we compared males to females on each of the eight neuroanatomical variables delineated above using the Wilcoxon rank sum test (a nonparametric counterpart to the *t*-test). This test was used because in several instances the sample size was insufficient for using the parametric *t*-test. This set of comparisons was conducted for each hemisphere, and for each data epoch, yielding four sets. Note that in these comparisons only subjects with a lesion in a particular anatomical region are included in the analysis for that region. For example, to compare males and females on the involvement of Broca's area we included only subjects with some degree of involvement of Broca's area in the statistical comparison.

Question 3   The final question addressed in this study concerns the issue of whether there are gender-related differences in recovery from aphasia. To explore this issue, we selected from our left-hemisphere group all subjects who had both acute and chronic neuropsychological information and a chronic CT or MR scan. We compared subgroups of patients with lesions in similar locations, using nine anatomical cells that were mutually exclusive, i.e., a patient could be in only one cell. Each of these subgroups was further divided into high (more than 25 percent) or low (less than 25 percent) involvement. We then compared males to females by calculating the average change in score for each neuropsychological variable as a function of gender. In this comparison we dropped any subject who had either 0 or 1 as an acute value on that particular variable, as this would not allow ample room for recovery effects to become manifest.

Results

Demographic Characteristics of the Patient Sample

Our final group of patients included 100 left-hemisphere cases and 49 right-hemisphere cases. The demographic breakdown of these two groups is presented in table 11.1 as a function of gender, age, and education. The males and females, and the left- and right-hemisphere groups, are very similar in terms of average age and level of education. We statistically compared males and females on age and education using *t*-tests within the left- and right-hemisphere groups. All differences were nonsignificant. These demographic characteristics are very typical of our research subject pool as a whole.

The Appearance of Aphasia with Left- or Right-Hemisphere Lesions

Not surprisingly, all patients in our sample with left-hemisphere lesions developed aphasia, and no patient developed aphasia as a result of a right-hemisphere lesion.

Although we did not use traditional classification systems, every patient in the left-hemisphere group met the core definition of aphasia in the sense of having an "acquired disturbance in the comprehension and formulation of verbal messages." We must thus conclude that in our sample *both* males and females developed aphasia if they had lesions in the language-related areas of the left hemisphere.

Some of the right-hemisphere cases showed deficits in articulation and prosody, but none had a set of defects that meets the core defini-

Table 11.1
Demographic characteristics of the sample

	Age	Education
Left-hemisphere group		
Males (N = 58)	$\overline{X}$ = 56.5	$\overline{X}$ = 11.9
	S.D. = 14.6	S.D. = 2.5
Females (N = 42)	$\overline{X}$ = 56.0	$\overline{X}$ = 11.6
	S.D. = 16.3	S.D. = 1.6
Right-hemisphere group		
Males (N = 32)	$\overline{X}$ = 55.6	$\overline{X}$ = 11.1
	S.D. = 15.3	S.D. = 2.5
Females (N = 17)	$\overline{X}$ = 62.5	$\overline{X}$ = 10.7
	S.D. = 11.2	S.D. = 3.8

Table 11.2
Independent *t*-tests for neuropsychological differences between acute male and female patients with left-hemisphere lesions

Neuropsychological variable	Males (N = 54)		Females (N = 41)		
	X̄	S.D.	X̄	S.D.	*t*[a]
Fluency	1.06	1.34	1.46	1.25	−1.52
Articulation	0.89	1.22	1.29	1.12	−1.65
Melodic contour	0.89	1.24	1.12	1.10	−0.95
Paraphasias	2.19	0.93	1.95	0.97	1.19
Visual naming	2.30	1.18	2.56	1.03	−1.15
Sentence repetition	2.28	1.19	2.24	1.16	0.14
Aural comprehension	2.37	0.98	2.24	0.97	0.63
Reading comprehension	2.22	1.11	2.12	1.05	0.45
Writing	2.52	0.93	2.54	0.90	−0.10
Verbal-associative fluency	2.83	0.69	2.76	0.80	0.50

a. All *ps* > .10.

tion of aphasia. Again, there were no differences between males and females in terms of the absence of aphasia following a right-hemisphere lesion.

The Severity of Speech and Language Disturbances Following Left-Hemisphere Lesions
Table 11.2 (acute stage) and table 11.3 (chronic stage) present the *t*-test results for the 10 speech and language variables, comparing males to females.

None of the *t*-tests were significant. In the acute data set some of the largest male-female differences occurred on the variables of fluency, articulation, melodic contour, and visual naming (all of these variables showed more severe impairments for females); males on the other hand had more paraphasias. In the chronic data set females continued to show slightly worse articulation and melodic contour. The absence of significant t-tests, however, warrants the conclusion that there are no significant gender-related differences in the severity of speech and language deficits following left-hemisphere lesions in either the acute or chronic phase.

The results of the stepwise-regression analyses (presented in tables 11.4 and 11.5 for the acute and chronic data sets, respectively) support this conclusion. Using the liberal .15 significance level, gender enters the model in only *one* instance (acute-visual naming), and in that instance it is only the fourth factor entered. Thus, for none of the 10 neuropsychological variables does gender account for an appre-

Table 11.3
Independent *t*-tests for neuropsychological differences between chronic
male and female patients with left-hemisphere lesions

Neuropsychological variable	Males (N = 36)		Females (N = 28)		t^a
	$\overline{X}$	S.D.	$\overline{X}$	S.D.	
Fluency	0.53	1.03	0.46	0.74	0.28
Articulation	0.36	0.72	0.39	0.83	−0.16
Melodic contour	0.33	0.72	0.43	0.79	−0.50
Paraphasias	1.22	1.02	1.00	0.98	0.88
Visual naming	1.11	1.32	1.21	1.34	−0.31
Sentence repetition	1.50	1.32	1.36	1.37	0.42
Aural comprehension	1.31	1.67	1.14	1.11	0.56
Reading comprehension	1.06	1.17	0.96	0.96	0.33
Writing	1.36	1.25	0.93	1.07	1.46
Verbal-associative fluency	2.03	1.30	1.96	1.29	0.20

a. All *ps* > .10.

ciable amount of variance. This outcome is true in both the acute and chronic data sets. Instead, the factors that lead in model entry are the anatomical variables, as these tables indicate. In the acute data set, for example, anatomical variables had the highest partial R^2 for eight of the neuropsychological measures. In the chronic data set anatomical variables also dominate the first and second place position. The stepwise-regression analyses clearly point to the anatomical variables as the factors that account for appreciable amounts of variance in the neuropsychological parameters. In contrast, the stepwise regressions do not indicate any significant role for gender.

As mentioned before, one additional statistical probe was employed in an effort to reveal to what extent gender had any relationship to the 10 neuropsychological parameters. The results of this procedure, which involved a subtraction method to determine the exact amount of R^2 that gender contributes to each neuropsychological variable, are presented in table 11.6. Note that in the best instance (only once) gender accounts for about 5 percent of the variance; in the majority of cases, the amount is less than 1 percent. Again, the evidence argues against the notion that there are gender-related differences in the severity of speech and language disturbances associated with left-hemisphere lesions.

The Distribution of Lesions and Degrees of Involvement
The results of the tests comparing males and females on the degree of involvement of each anatomical area are presented in tables 11.7 to

Table 11.4
Stepwise regression analyses for neuropsychological measures in acute patients with left-hemisphere lesions ($N = 87$)

Neuropsychological variable	Statistically significant variables ($p < .15$), partial R^2 in parentheses							
Fluency	peri-Broca (.27)	area 37+ (.04)	anterior 22 (.02)					
Articulation	basal ganglia (.37)	peri-Broca (.08)	insula (.03)					
Melodic contour	basal ganglia (.29)	peri-Broca (.10)	anterior 22 (.02)					
Paraphasias	Wernicke's (.23)	age (.02)	basal ganglia (.02)					
Visual naming	insula (.17)	parietal (.08)	peri-Broca (.05)	gender (.05)	education (.03)	anterior 22 (.03)	basal ganglia (.02)	age (.02)
Sentence repetition	Wernicke's (.12)	peri-Broca (.07)	parietal (.02)	age (.02)				
Aural comprehension	insula (.13)	parietal (.08)	Broca's (.08)	age (.05)				
Reading comprehension	insula (.17)	parietal (.14)	education (.06)	Broca's (.05)	age (.03)			
Writing	insula (.12)	parietal (.12)	peri-Broca (.08)	age (.03)	education (.02)			
Verbal-associative fluency	parietal (.09)	age (.05)	area 37+ (.03)	Broca's (.03)				

Table 11.5
Stepwise regression analyses for neuropsychological measures in chronic patients with left-hemisphere lesions ($N = 54$)

Neuropsychological variable	Statistically significant variables ($p < .15$), partial R^2 in parentheses					
Fluency	peri-Broca (.34)	Wernicke's (.07)	basal ganglia (.07)	Broca's (.02)		
Articulation	peri-Broca (.13)	Broca's (.05)	basal ganglia (.05)			
Melodic contour	basal ganglia (.22)	peri-Broca (.11)	Wernicke's (.05)			
Paraphasias	Wernicke's (.22)	insula (.07)	education (.05)			
Visual naming	peri-Broca (.18)	area 37 + (.11)	education (.05)	anterior 22 (.04)	parietal (.03)	age (.03)
Sentence repetition	Wernicke's (.44)	peri-Broca (.08)	education (.04)	area 37 + (.04)		
Aural comprehension	peri-Broca (.16)	education (.07)	parietal (.05)	insula (.04)	age (.04)	anterior 22 (.03)
Reading comprehension	area 37 + (.15)	age (.10)	peri-Broca (.10)	education (.09)		
Writing	peri-Broca (.19)	Wernicke's (.14)	education (.11)			
Verbal-associative fluency	education (.17)	insula (.16)	parietal (.05)	Broca's (.03)	area 37 + (.03)	

Table 11.6
Additional variance explained by adding gender to stepwise
regression models of left-hemisphere patients

Neuropsychological variable	Acute (N = 87)	Chronic (N = 54)
Fluency	0.0088	0.0001
Articulation	0.0022	0.0016
Melodic contour	0.0001	0.0051
Paraphasias	0.0001	0.0050
Visual naming	0.0520	0.0003
Sentence repetition	0.0134	0.0052
Aural comprehension	0.0010	0.0007
Reading comprehension	0.0062	0.0029
Writing	0.0134	0.0120
Verbal-associative fluency	0.0003	0.0029

Table 11.7
Wilcoxon rank-sum tests for anatomical differences between acute male and
female patients with left-hemisphere lesions

Anatomical area	Males			Females			t^a
	N	$\overline{X}$	S.D.	N	$\overline{X}$	S.D.	
Broca's	18	1.89	0.68	14	1.93	0.47	−0.24
peri-Broca	26	1.73	0.78	24	1.62	0.77	0.52
Basal ganglia	14	2.00	0.88	19	1.68	0.75	1.05
Insula	31	2.20	0.83	22	1.91	0.75	1.31
Wernicke's	31	2.20	0.75	11	2.00	0.63	0.84
Area 37+	16	2.16	0.72	8	1.75	0.46	1.34
Anterior 22	15	2.00	0.76	6	1.67	0.52	0.94
Parietal	31	1.61	0.62	10	1.60	0.70	0.13

a. All ps > .10.

11.10. As can be surmised from the tables, very few of the male-
female differences are statistically significant. One can notice, however, a tendency for females to have relatively more involvement in
the anterior areas. This pattern is most clearly evident in the chronic
data sets, which probably contain the most reliable anatomical information (images of stable lesions). In the chronic, left-hemisphere
group, for example, females have greater involvement than males of
Broca's area, the peri-Broca area, the basal ganglia, and the insula. In
contrast, males have larger lesions, although not significantly so, in
the more posterior areas, such as Wernicke's area and the parietal
region.

Table 11.8
Wilcoxon rank-sum tests for anatomical differences between chronic male and female patients with left-hemisphere lesions

Anatomical area	Males			Females			
	N	$\overline{X}$	S.D.	N	$\overline{X}$	S.D.	t
Broca's	11	1.73	0.65	11	1.91	0.70	−0.61
Peri-Broca	19	1.63	0.60	13	2.08	0.64	−1.99[a]
Basal ganglia	8	1.75	0.89	10	1.80	0.79	−0.19
Insula	16	2.19	0.75	14	1.86	0.77	1.19
Wernicke's	16	2.19	0.75	6	2.17	0.98	−0.04
Area 37+	13	1.62	0.51	5	2.00	0.00	—
Anterior 22	6	2.17	0.75	5	1.60	0.55	1.37
Parietal	20	1.65	0.75	10	1.50	0.53	0.36

a. $p = .056$.
— = no value generated.

Table 11.9
Wilcoxon rank-sum tests for anatomical differences between acute male and female patients with right-hemisphere lesions

Anatomical area	Males			Females			
	N	$\overline{X}$	S.D.	N	$\overline{X}$	S.D.	t
Broca's	13	1.85	0.55	5	2.00	0.71	−0.46
Peri-Broca	17	1.76	0.75	8	1.75	0.89	0.12
Basal ganglia	15	1.73	0.80	11	2.18	0.87	−1.34
Insula	19	2.37	0.76	10	2.40	0.70	−0.02
Wernicke's	16	2.56	0.51	6	1.83	0.41	3.01[a]
Area 37+	9	1.89	0.60	2	1.00	0.00	—
Anterior 22	11	2.10	0.83	1	1.00	0.00	—
Parietal	17	1.82	0.64	6	1.33	0.52	1.72

a. $p < .01$.
— = no value generated.

Table 11.10
Wilcoxon rank-sum tests for anatomical differences between chronic male and female patients with right-hemisphere lesions

Anatomical area	Males			Females			
	N	$\overline{X}$	S.D.	N	$\overline{X}$	S.D.	t
Broca's	5	1.60	0.55	2	1.00	0.00	—
Peri-Broca	7	2.00	1.00	5	1.20	0.45	1.71
Basal ganglia	9	1.67	0.87	4	2.75	0.50	−2.30[a]
Insula	12	2.17	0.83	3	2.33	0.58	−0.22
Wernicke's	11	1.21	1.27	2	2.00	0.00	—
Area 37 +	—	—	—	—	—	—	—
Anterior 22	6	2.17	0.75	1	1.00	0.00	—
Parietal	12	1.92	0.51	3	1.67	0.58	0.73

a. $p < .05$.
— = no value generated.

Table 11.11
Frequency of anterior and posterior lesions in left-hemisphere patients as a function of epoch and gender

	Acute[a]		Chronic[b]	
	Males	Females	Males	Females
Anterior only	13	17	10	10
Posterior only	23	6	14	7

a. $\chi^2 (1, N = 59) = 8.024; p = .005$.
b. $\chi^2 (1, N = 41) = 1.172; p = .279$.

Our next probe was to determine whether there might be gender-related differences in lesion location. The first step in this process was to redefine the anatomical areas as anterior only and posterior only. The anterior-only group included all cases with lesions exclusively in Broca's area (1), the regions surrounding Broca's area (2), or the basal ganglia (3). The lesion could, however, extend into the insula (4). The posterior-only group, on the other hand, included all cases with lesions exclusively in Wernicke's region (5), the posterior temporal (6), or the parietal (8). Here too the lesion could extend into the insula (4). We purposefully excluded all cases with involvement in both anterior (1–3) *and* posterior (5, 6, and 8) areas. This procedure eliminated most of the subjects in the right-hemisphere groups, leaving only 16 cases in the acute right-hemisphere group and 10 in the chronic group. Hence, our analysis of anterior versus posterior distribution of lesions was confined to the left-hemisphere groups.

A frequency count was conducted for the two left-hemisphere groups, and the results are presented as function of gender, epoch, and the anterior-posterior dichotomy in table 11.11. A chi-square test on the acute data was significant ($\chi^2[1, 59] = 8.02$; $p = .005$). This reflected the posterior skew for males and the anterior skew for females. The same pattern was found in the chronic data, although the chi-square is not significant. It would appear reasonable to state, then, that in our sample of patients with lesions in their left hemisphere, males more often had posteriorly situated lesions, while females, on the other hand, more frequently suffered anteriorly centered lesions.

We had some concern that our conclusion regarding the gender-related difference in lesion location might be confounded with effects of age, since some data indicate that age affects lesion location (Eslinger and Damasio 1981). To explore this possibility, we conducted a logistic regression analysis of the frequency data in Table 11.11, using age and gender as the two predictor variables. Both the main effect of age and the effect of age and sex interaction were nonsignificant; hence, we can conclude that the gender-related lesion distribution evident in our data is not attributable to age.

Recovery
The final issue we sought to explore was the question of whether there are gender-related differences in the extent to which subjects with left-hemisphere lesions recover from their initial aphasic deficits. As described above, we used 9 anatomical cells, divided into high and low degrees of involvement, and 10 neuropsychological variables. This design yields 180 potential cells; of these, 23, all of which were high-involvement areas, contained at least 2 or more subjects of each gender. In 15 of the 23 comparisons the males and females differed in their average degree of recovery (or change of score) by 0.5 units or more. There were several smaller male-female differences, but we considered these too small to be of practical significance. In 7 cases the advantage favored males; in 8 instances the females showed greater recovery. Obviously, our conclusions must be cautious because of the small number of subjects. Nevertheless, our recovery data do not support the conclusion that there are systematic gender-related differences in recovery from aphasia.

Discussion

The salient findings in this preliminary study are that both males and females develop aphasia with lesions in language-related areas of the left hemisphere but not with lesions in homologous areas of the right hemisphere and that if lesions are in the same location, males and females develop similar deficits in speech and language. At first glance, then, one can conclude that there is really no difference between the genders as far as aphasia is concerned. However, our results do point to possible gender-related differences in several instances, even though these differences are not statistically significant.

We found that females tended to have more severe deficits in variables such as fluency, articulation, melodic contour, and visual naming, whereas men's deficits were more severe in the categories of paraphasic errors, sentence repetition, aural comprehension, and reading comprehension. Since several defects in the former set are associated with Broca aphasias, and several defects in the latter set with Wernicke aphasia, it is reasonable to suggest that females show a greater tendency to have symptoms of the Broca type, and males symptoms of the Wernicke type. This finding is in keeping with Kimura's early results but is at odds with data from other investigators (Brust et al. 1976; De Renzi et al. 1980).

The interpretation of these findings, however, is an entirely different matter. Both Kimura and McGlone either ascribed the gender disparity to differences in brain organization or actually used the findings to deduce that the brains of men and women are different in language-related function. We believe that our findings permit a reasonable alternative explanation. Our data show that females more often have anterior strokes and that males more often have posterior strokes. Because of this anatomical distribution we should expect more Broca-type symptoms in women and more Wernicke symptoms in men. The neuropsychological difference can be accommodated without the need to postulate a difference in brain organization. One can also look at our data to determine what might account for the neuropsychological defects. On the basis of the regression analyses it is evident that the determinant of each deficit was first and foremost the site of lesion. Gender accounts for very little of the variance (5 percent in one instance, but most of the time less than 1 percent). This indicates that it is the site of damage that determines the type neuropsychological deficit rather than gender, a hypothesis that De Renzi and collaborators (1980) raised in their study.

The fact that in our sample females more often had anterior strokes rather than posterior strokes is intriguing. It has been suggested that Broca aphasia and, presumably, anterior lesions occur more often in a younger population and that Wernicke aphasia, which is linked to posterior lesions, occurs more often in older subjects (Kertesz et al.

1977; Obler et al. 1978; Eslinger and Damasio 1981). This raises the question that posterior strokes might be more common among older patients (Eslinger and Damasio 1981). However, recent studies do not seem to support such age-related stroke differences (Habib et al. 1987). We also did not find any effects of age on lesion location.

We have considered that our findings might be due to a selection bias, and this possibility cannot be discounted. A serial study of all strokes admitted to a given unit over a long period of time may clarify the issue, and we are presently conducting such a survey.

An alternative explanation relates to the branching of the Sylvian vessels, which may be different in males and females. Such a variation, combined with different endocrine-controlled hemodynamic conditions, might account for a slightly different overall distribution of cerebrovascular lesions in males and females. To our knowledge, no one has yet studied possible gender-related differences in the branching pattern of the Sylvian vessels, especially the takeoff angles and the calibers of frontal branches. We do know that there is marked variability in the branching pattern of those vessels, and it might be that independent and early branching is more common in females.

A final question relates to the pattern of recovery in males and females with the same type of lesion. Basso et al. (1982) suggested that females had a tendency to recover more in oral expression than their male counterparts. Recovery of comprehension did not show this difference. In our sample in the few cells in which we could make the appropriate comparisons, we could not detect any systematic tendency for either females or males to recover more but our final analysis must await further collection of data.

Let us return to the original point of debate: that females, because they have a different brain organization, are less susceptible to aphasia than males. Our findings indicate that even if males and females have a different organization of the neural substrates for language, these differences are not strong enough to protect females from becoming aphasic when a lesion involves the appropriate brain structures.

Note

This research was supported by NINDS grant PO1 NS19632.

References

Basso, A., E. Capitani, and S. Moraschini. 1982. Sex differences in recovery from aphasia. *Cortex* 18:469–475.

Benton, A. L. 1976. *Multilingual aphasia examination.* Iowa City: Department of Neurology, University of Iowa.

Brust, J. C. M., S. Q. Shafer, R. W. Richter, B. Brunn. 1976. Aphasia in acute stroke. *Stroke* 7:167–174.

Damasio, H. 1989. Neuroimaging contributions to the understanding of aphasia. In *Handbook of neuropsychology,* ed. F. Boller and J. Grafman. Elsevier.

Damasio, H., and Damasio, A., 1989. *Lesion analysis in neuropsychology.* New York: Oxford University Press.

De Renzi, E., P. Faglioni, and P. Ferrari. 1980. The influence of sex and age on the incidence and type of aphasia. *Cortex* 16:627–630.

Eslinger, P. J., and A. R. Damasio. 1981. Age and type of aphasia in patients with stroke. *Journal of Neurology, Neurosurgery, and Psychiatry* 44:377–381.

Geschwind, N., and A. M. Galaburda. 1985. Cerebral lateralization. *Archives of Neurology* 42:428–459, 521–552, 634–654.

Goodglass, H., and E. Kaplan. 1972. *The assessment of aphasia and related disorders.* Philadelphia: Lea and Febiger. Rev. ed., 1983.

Habib, M., A. Ali-Cherif, and M. Poncet. 1987. Age-related changes in aphasia type and stroke location. *Brain and Language* 31:245–251.

Harasymiw, S. J., and A. Halper. 1981. Sex, age, and aphasia type. *Brain and Language* 12:190–198.

Kertesz, A., D. Lesk, and P. McCabe. 1977. Isotopic localization of infarcts in aphasia. *Archives of Neurology* 34:590–601.

Kertesz, A., and A. Sheppard. 1981. The epidemiology of aphasic and cognitive impairment in stroke: Age, sex, aphasia type and laterality differences. *Brain* 104:117–128.

Kertesz, A., and T. Benke. 1986. The sexual mystique of intrahemispheric language organization. Paper presented at the Academy of Aphasia in Nashville.

Kimura, D. 1980. Sex differences in intrahemispheric organization of speech. *The Behavioral and Brain Sciences* 3:240–241.

Kimura, D. 1987. Sex differences, human brain organization. In *Encyclopedia of Neurosciences,* ed. G. Adelman Boston: Birkhauser, 1084–1085.

Kimura, D. 1983. Sex differences in cerebral organization for speech and praxic functions. *Canadian Journal of Psychology* 37:19–35.

Lansdell, H. 1962. A sex difference in effect of temporal-lobe neurosurgery on design preference. *Nature* 194:852–854.

Lansdell, H. 1964. Sex differences in hemispheric asymmetries of the human brain. *Nature* 203:550.

Lansdell, H., and N. Urbach. 1965. Sex differences in personality measures related to size and side of temporal lobe ablations. *Proceedings of American Psychological Association* 73:113–114.

McGlone, J. 1977. Sex differences in the cerebral organization of verbal functions in patients with unilateral brain lesions. *Brain* 100:775–793.

Obler, L. K., M. L. Albert, H. Goodglass, and D. F. Benson, 1978. Aphasia type and aging. *Brain and Language* 6:318–322.

Vignolo, L. A., and E. Boccardi, and L. Caverni. 1986. Unexpected CT-scan findings in global aphasia. *Cortex* 22:55–69.

Editor's Comments

There is abundant interest in both the lay and scientific literatures in sex differences in mental function. Other than what is obvious about the organization of the brain for sexual function and related behaviors (about which there is a fair amount of data from neurobiology to sociology), it is difficult to believe that significant sex differences exist in cognitive capacity, at least on the surface. If we assume, then, that at the level of practical application men's and women's cognitive capacities have evolved to comparable strength, does this mean that there are no differences at a deeper level that might reflect the existence of different neural substrates? In other words, men and women perform the same cognitive tasks equally well on the average. But do they perform them in exactly the same manner, i.e., using the same mental processes and relying on identical neural substrates? The profound differences between the sexes in genetic and epigenetic makeup that lead to brain development—Y-chromosome related genes, hormonal differences before birth and after puberty, and sociocultural differences—provoke the thought that the neural mechanisms underlying cognitive behaviors are apt to develop, be maintained, and function differently.

There are at least two ways in which potential differences between the sexes in neural organization and cognitive architecture may be interesting, even though there is little practical difference. One concerns the question of whether the different genes and epigenetic factors of males and females are capable of building identical networks of neurons with identical functional capacities. Or do males and females build different networks that can support indistinguishable functions. The second interest concerns the particular responses of the two machineries to particular forms of neuropsychological testing, to acquired injury, and to factors that interfere with normal development. The present chapter addresses some of the difficulties in judging the effects of injury on male and female brains and illustrates the importance of assessing the exact location and size of the lesions before gender comparisons are made.

The chapters by Marshall and Morton in this volume address important issues on how applicable lesion-related data are to interests in architecture and the development of functional capacities. They complement the present paper and help the reader make the transition between sex differences in acquired disorders and sex differences in developmental disorders, such as dyslexia.

We learn from the present paper that males and females with acquired lesions do not differ significantly in the incidence of aphasia.

It suggests that some of the reported differences may be spurious because location and size of lesions are not detailed enough.

From the point of view of cerebral lateralization, these results may indicate that males and females are identically lateralized in anatomy and function. However, significant differences in anatomical asymmetry might be compatible with similar and even paradoxical differences in functional lateralization between the sexes. Thus, Geschwind and Galaburda have suggested that on the average the female brain is anatomically more asymmetrical (usually to the left), and that of the male brain is less asymmetrical in either direction (see figure 11.1 and Sherman et al. in this volume). This hypothesis, together with some assumptions based on the available anatomical and funtional data, may lead to a model of cerebral lateralization that can account for most of the behavioral findings, even those that appear paradoxical at first.

The assumptions of the model are that the intact male brain is on the average less effective in language function and is anatomically less asymmetric, interhemispherically more connected and intrahemispherically less connected. On the other hand, the intact female brain is on the average more effective in language functioning, anatomically more asymmetric, intrahemispherically more connected, and interhemispherically less connected.

The model as stated makes the following physiological predictions. Dichotic and tachistoscopic studies attempting to isolate the hemispheres should demonstrate linguistic asymmetry in both the female and male brains. The functional capacity of the right side will appear

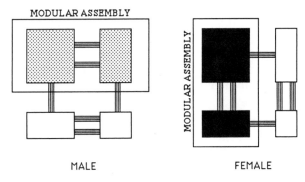

Figure 11.1
Hypothetical models of male and female neural organization for language function. In the male the neuronal assemblies are less asymmetrical and more bilaterally interconnected. In the female the assemblies are more asymmetrical and more ipsilaterally interconnected. Moreover, the intact male brain is less efficient (stippled), and the female's more efficient (black).

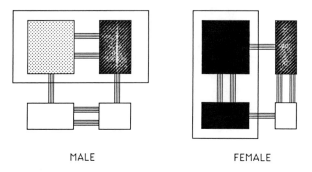

MALE   FEMALE

Figure 11.2
Hypothetical male and female brains with right-hemisphere damage (hatched). In both cases the major portion of the language substrate is preserved, and no aphasia ensues.

greater in the female brain than in the male brain, because the right-side component of the female brain is less connected and dependent on callosal information, and stimuli arriving in the right hemisphere can be checked against additional right-hemisphere information via its relatively superior intrahemispheric connectivity. Conversely, the functional capacity of the right side of the male brain should appear to be inferior to that of the female brain, because it is more connected with, and dependent on, its left-hemisphere component, which is not tapped by the test, and is less well connected to other parts of the right hemisphere.

Therefore, the greater anatomical asymmetry of the type proposed in this model paradoxically results in greater nondominant functional capacity, as assessed by hemispheric physiological studies. In fact, this prediction is to a large extent verified by tachistoscopic and dichotic studies in adult men and women. These studies have led to claims that women are less lateralized for language function. It is therefore possible that women are not less lateralized but are simply better with their nondominant hemispheres within the constraints of unilateral hemispheric testing.

The model also predicts the effects of injury to language-related neuronal assemblies on language function. Right hemisphere damage should spare language in the female and male brains, because in both the dominant portion of the system, which is of comparable size, remains undamaged (figure 11.2). However, the sparing of function may be only partial or inconsistent in the male brain, because the uninjured portion is less efficient and has diminished access to uninvolved ipsilateral neuronal assemblies. One may therefore expect qualitative differences between the female and male brains in the nature of the preserved, nonaphasic language.

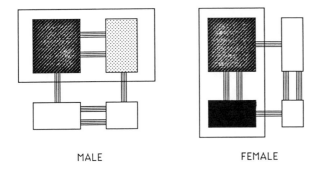

MALE   FEMALE

Figure 11.3
Hypothetical male and female brains with left-hemisphere damage (hatched). In both cases the major portion of the language substrate is injured, and aphasia ensues.

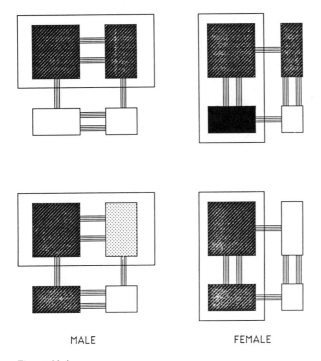

MALE   FEMALE

Figure 11.4
Hypothetical male and female brains with bilateral damage (top). In this situation women may exhibit superior recovery. Hypothetical male and female brains with large left-hemispheric damage (bottom). In this situation men may exhibit superior recovery.

Left-hemisphere damage should lead to aphasia in both the female and male brains, because the dominant portion of the assembly, approximately of equal size in the two cases, is destroyed (figure 11.3). Small left-hemisphere lesions in the female brain should do less damage functionally, because a smaller proportion of the efficient, extended left-hemisphere network would be affected. On the other hand, damage within a larger area of the left hemisphere of the male brain may produce at least some symptoms because of the more extended left-hemisphere network. Thus, small left-hemisphere lesions may be associated with frank aphasia less often in women than in men, yet some linguistic abnormalities more difficult to detect may appear more often in women with lesions in atypical areas.

Recovery should occur predominantly with preserved contralateral structures in the male brain and with preserved ipsilateral structures in the female brain. Thus, bilateral damage should be more serious in the male brain and less likely to result in recovery (figure 11.4, top), while extensive left-hemisphere damage should be more serious and less likely to result in recovery in the female brain (figure 11.4, bottom).

Of course, complicated as it may already seem, the present model does not even begin to take into consideration possible sex differences in plasticity and regrowth of tissue after injury or the potential enlisting of other, nonlinguistic areas for the completion of language tasks. It does, however, serve to illustrate the probability that functional lateralization, the effect of injury, the recovery of function, and developmental language disorders depend not only on the degree of anatomical asymmetry but also on the exact sizes, efficiencies, and connectional networks of the relevant neuronal assemblies within and between the hemispheres of the brain.

Chapter 12

Language Processing and Familial Handedness

Thomas G. Bever, Caroline Carrithers,
Wayne Cowart, and David J. Townsend

The hand that rocks the cradle rules the world.
—W. R. Wallace

A common belief is that all normal people process language in the same way. This presupposition underlies the search for a single set of mechanisms for sentence processing. Another common belief is that there is a normal neurological configuration for language, at least among right-handed people. This notion underlies the belief that cerebral asymmetries in right-handers reveal that language function is predominantly dependent upon particular areas in the left hemisphere. The research reported in this chapter challenges some aspects of these beliefs. We review a number of studies suggesting that right-handers may fall into two groups that differ markedly in their relative dependence on structural and conceptual information during language processing. The differences are linked to a familial trait, left-handedness. Right-handers with no left-handed family members (RHF) depend relatively more on grammatical relations between words; right-handers with left-handed family members (LHF) depend more on the conceptual information of individual words. On our view, familial left-handedness may signal a heritable trait that alters the developmental processes determining the cerebral organization of language. At the end of this paper we shall briefly speculate on how the neurological differences in linguistic organization might arise and how they might result in different language-processing styles.

Classical clinical evidence suggests that language function is more dependent on certain areas in the left hemisphere than the right, even among most left-handed people (Broca 1961; Luria 1947; Russell and Espir 1961). Yet some facts indicate that left-handedness is associated with a different neurological representation for linguistic ability. For example, left-handers with left-hemisphere damage relatively often suffer no aphasia at all and show higher incidence of recovery from aphasia (Luria 1947; Russell and Espir 1961; Hecaen and Albert 1978).

Furthermore, mental abilities in left-handers have often been reported to vary more than in right-handers. For example, left-handers have a relatively high incidence of language disabilities and also have a higher incidence of mathematical precocity (Benbow and Benbow 1984).

Previous research has occasionally suggested that familial left-handedness in right-handers is also associated with an exceptional neurological organization of cognitive abilities. For example, Luria (1947) noted that left-hemisphere wounds cause major aphasia in right-handers with left-handed family members less often than in right-handers with only right-handed relatives; like left-handers, LHF right-handers recover more quickly than RHF right-handers from aphasia caused by left-hemisphere damage; LHF right-handers also show aphasia more often in response to wounds to the right hemisphere. Consistent with this, Joanette et al. (1983) report that minor right-hemisphere lesions result in subtle language disturbances in LHF right-handed patients more often than in RHF right-handed patients. Furthermore, LHF right-handers have a higher incidence of dyslexia than do RHF right-handers (Orton 1925; Gordon 1980, 1983) and a higher incidence of mathematical precocity (Benbow and Benbow 1984; Benbow 1986).

The preceding surveys suggest that familial left-handedness is associated with a less-concentrated representation for language in the left-hemisphere. Some experimental studies suggest this as well. For example, in right-handers, verbal tasks interfere with rhythmic tapping by the right hand more than by the left hand, an effect that presumably reflects the competition for left-hemisphere resources between language processing and right-hand activity. This left-right asymmetry is smaller in LHF right-handers (Kee, Bathurst, and Hellige 1983). Furthermore, verbal-intelligence test scores correlate positively with right-ear dominance in a dichotic words task for RHF right-handers, while the verbal scores correlate negatively with right-ear dominance for LHF right-handers (Kraft 1983). Finally, RHF right-handers also show a much stronger hemispheric asymmetry than LHF right-handers in event-related brain potentials during silent reading (Kutas, VanPetten and Besson 1988). Such results suggest at the least that familial left-handedness is a phenotypic marker of a neurological organization for language and cognition different from that in purely right-handed families.[1] (See also the papers by McKeever and his colleagues listed in the bibliography.)

Geschwind and Galaburda (1987) present a theory of the development of cerebral lateralization that might predict the neurological structure of LHF right-handers to be different from that of RHF right-handers. They note that in a standard anatomical pattern, certain structures in the language areas of the left hemisphere are larger than the corresponding structures of the right hemisphere. However, they estimate that about 35 percent of the population has "anomalous dominance," in which certain areas in the right hemisphere are unusually large compared to the standard, asymmetrical case. Anomalous dominance occurs in most left handers, but in an additional 25 percent of right-handers as well. Left-handers reveal most clearly that these anomalous anatomical patterns are associated with various behavioral phenomena, including dyslexia, other learning disorders, and special nonlinguistic talents. Geschwind and Galaburda (1987) also find that left-handedness is associated with an increased frequency of autoimmune disorders (Geschwind and Behan 1982, 1984; Benbow 1986; Searlman and Fugagli 1987).

The coincidence of autoimmune and allergic disorders with left-handedness is startling. Geschwind and Galaburda review evidence that one developmental cause of these disorders may be high activity of fetal testosterone. They further claim that normal hemisphere development can be inhibited by high testosterone activity at certain points in fetal cerebral growth. Since the structures that influence left-hemisphere dominance develop early (by hypothesis), high testosterone activity will often result in both autoimmune disorders and anomalous cortical representations for language. Furthermore, they suggest that the mechanisms underlying explicit handedness develop later and are less vulnerable to high testosterone activity. Thus, anomalous cerebral dominance for language will occur more often than explicit left-handedness.

On this view, familial left-handedness may be a phenotypic marker of the genetic substrate for high testosterone activity during gestation. Even when it does not result in overt left-handedness, it may result in distinct cortical representations for higher cognitive functions. This hypothesis predicts that even among right-handers few should be a strong statistical relations among autoimmune disorders, linguistic performance, and familial left-handedness. Relatively few data have been collected from normal right-handed people to determine the effects of familial left-handedness on them. We started our investigation of the relationship with a simple questionnaire of about 400 undergraduates at the University of Rochester. We found that 49 percent of LHF right-handed undergraduates report having some kind of allergy, while only 15 percent of RHF right-handed undergraduates do.[*2] Furthermore, the average verbal SAT score for RHF right-handed subjects is 16 points higher than that of LHF right-handed subjects, (while the math SAT score is lower by about the same amount).[3] In addition, over the last decade we have frequently noticed that LHF right-handers respond to language stimuli in experiments differently from RHF right-handers (summarized in Bever 1983; see also Bever, Carrithers, and Townsend 1987). Such preliminary results indicate that there may be qualitative differences in language behavior that distinguish linguistically normal LHF and RHF right-handers.

How might styles of language behavior differ? Language behavior involves the exploitation of two kinds of knowledge: the structural system; which concerns syntactic, semantic, and phonological knowledge, and the conceptual system, which includes knowledge of the reference of words and conceptual knowledge of the world. Variation in language behavior might arise if different individuals can exploit these two kinds of knowledge to different degrees. In several studies we have found that utilization of syntactic structure during sentence processing is one dimension along which individuals can differ (Gerken and Bever 1986; Townsend et al. 1987). Since familial left-handedness has been associated with difficulties on specific language tasks, we developed the working hypothesis that LHF right-handers are less sensitive to grammatical structure than RHF right-handers, and LHF right-handers are more sensitive to conceptual and referential information than RHF right-handers. This hypothesis is presented with preliminary supporting data in Bever, Carrithers, and Townsend 1987.

Experimental Studies

In the research reported here, we attended directly to handedness background, using it as the basis for differentiating two groups of right-handed subjects matched on other variables such as age, sex, and verbal ability. The RHF subjects reported only right-handers in their family, while the LHF subjects reported at least one left-hander (the family included siblings, parents, uncles and aunts, and grandparents).[4]

Our first goal was to find out if the sensitivity to grammatical structures differs in RHF and LHF right-handers. We tested this by studying subjects' sensitivity during comprehension to two levels of structural constraints: the dominance relations between main and subordinate clauses and the thematic relation between phrases in canonical and noncanonical phrase order.

Subordinate and Main Clauses

There is considerable evidence that the clause is an important organizing unit in ongoing comprehension (Bever 1970; Fodor et al. 1974). Words in clauses are immediately segregated together and provide a framework for recoding into semantic propositions. Typically, a sentence involves both main and subordinate clauses. The intuitive and formal role of a subordinate clause is to modify the meaning of a main clause. Nonetheless, the relation between a main and a subordinate clause is a structural one, not a lexical or semantic one. For example, the three sentences below use the same words (except for the conjunctions *though* and *but*) and have the same meaning. But only in (1a) is the second clause subordinate to the first.[5]

(1a) Main-subordinate: Harry called up Bill, though he didn't want to.

(1b) Main-main: Harry called up Bill, but he didn't want to.

(1c) Subordinate-main: Though Harry called up Bill, he didn't want to.

The fact that the difference between main-main structures and main-subordinate structures does not necessarily involve a difference in meaning makes processing sensitivity to the main/subordinate clause distinction a useful probe of sensitivity to pure structure. Cowart (1987) found that RHF right-handed subjects read the beginning of final subordinate clauses more slowly than the beginning of main clauses, while LHF right-handers do not. This is consistent with the view that RHF right-handers are more immediately sensitive to the increased processing load associated with a subordinate clause. The following two studies suggest that RHF right-handed subjects are more sensitive to the main/subordinate distinction than LHF right-handed subjects.

Meaning Probes

A marked initial subordinate clause is always followed ultimately by a main clause that dominates it, but an initial main clause can stand alone. For example, the first clause in (1c) must be followed by the second clause; this is not true of (1a) and (1b). There are many well-known linguistic properties associated with this difference (Bever and Langendoen 1973; Ross 1967; Reinhart 1983). For example, a pronoun can occur in an initial subordinate clause with its antecedent in a later clause, but a pronoun cannot take an antecedent in a following subordinate clause;[6] initial subordinate clauses may be shortened by deletion, but initial main clauses may not be, and so on. In each case, it appears that information can be missing from a marked initial subordinate clause because the listener knows that there will follow a main clause that will provide the missing information. An initial main clause may stand alone, so there is no guarantee that an additional clause will follow (Bever 1970). This difference explains the tolerance for linguistically degraded initial subordinate clauses. This difference also has a behavioral implication: during comprehension, initial main clauses can be recoded into a semantic form immediately, while initial subordinate clauses are temporarily retained in linguistic form attendant on subsequent integration with their main clauses (Townsend and Bever 1978; Bever et al. 1980).

We studied the form in which listeners immediately represent a clause, with a phrase-matching technique used in laboratory studies of language processing (Townsend and Bever 1978). In this experimental task a listener hears a word sequence that is part of a sentence, followed by a single probe phrase, as in (2):

(2) Sentence fragment   Tone   Probe phrase

   Though Harry called up Bill yesterday—beep—talk on phone.

The listener must quickly respond verbally whether the probe phrase[1] was related to the meaning of the just-heard sequence or not. In our study, the critical sentence fragments were both subordinate and main clauses.[7]

The overall prediction was that phrase probes would be recognized more quickly after a main clause than after a subordinate clause. This follows from the hypothesis that a main clause can immediately be processed for meaning, while a lower-level representation of a subordinate clause must be retained, so that it can be integrated with the ultimate main clause (Townsend and Bever 1978; Bever et al. 1980). This should facilitate recognition of a semantically related phrase after a main clause, in comparison with a phrase after a subordinate clause. The main-clause facilitated recognition in the study but only for RHF right-handed listeners: they responded more quickly to main-clause probes than to subordinate-clause probes (figure 12.1),[*] a response pattern different from that of LHF right-handed listeners,[*] whose latencies were the same for both kinds of clauses. This result is consistent with the hypothesis that RHF right-handed subjects are more sensitive than LHF right-handers to the main-clause/subordinate-clause distinction.

Word-by-Word Reading and Pronominal Anaphora

The next study involved the role of the syntactic relation between clauses in processing pronouns. The experimental materials were two-clause sentences with a pronoun (*they, he, she*) in the subject position of the second clause and a potential antecedent in the first

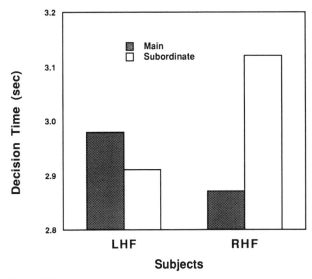

Figure 12.1
Time to decide that a phrase corresponds in meaning to the content of a just-heard main or subordinate clause sentence-fragment (Bever, Carrithers, and Townsend 1989).

clause. The potential antecedent could or could not actually serve as an antecedent according to whether it agreed with the pronoun in gender and number. The first clause was either subordinate to the second clause or the two clauses were main clauses, as in (3).[8]

(3) Samples of materials in pronoun reading time study

(a) Subordinate clause with antecedent present (or absent)
Even though *the librarian* (the librarians) made an awful lot of noise, *she* kept on working on her own material.

(b) Main clause with antecedent present (or absent)
The librarian (the librarians) made an awful lot of noise, but *she* kept on working on her own material.

Reading a pronoun and the material following it should be facilitated if the pronoun has a readily available antecedent. An initial subordinate clause must be integrated within its following main clause, while an initial main clause can be encoded as a distinct unit. This difference involves a higher degree of syntactic integration between clauses in the comprehension of subordinate-main constructions than of main-main constructions. Hence, the presence of an available antecedent should facilitate pronoun integration more strongly in subordinate-main constructions than main-main constructions for those subjects

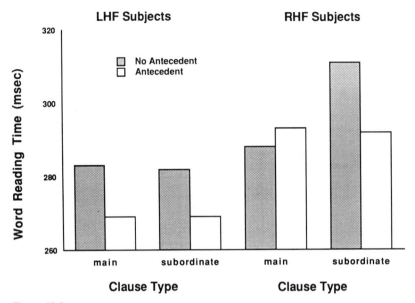

Figure 12.2
Word reading time for the three words following a pronoun in a final main clause, as a function of whether there is an antecedent in the initial clause and whether the initial clause is main or subordinate (Cowart 1988).

who immediately process an initial subordinate clause in a way that looks ahead to the coming main clause.

Subjects read sentences in a self-paced, cumulative, word-by-word task. Every time the subject pushes a button, the next word appears on a computer screen in its correct location. We averaged the reading time on the three words following the pronoun as a measure of the effect of the presence or absence of an antecedent. RHF right-handed subjects read the words following the pronoun faster when an antecedent was present, but only in subordinate-main constructions, not in main-main constructions* (figure 12.2). LHF right-handed subjects, however, were equally helped by the antecedent in subordinate-main and main-main structures. The difference of construction type on the effect of the antecedent is significantly larger for RHF right-handed subjects than for LHF right-handed subjects.*[9] It appears that RHF right-handed subjects encode potential antecedents in a way that makes them available for the following main clause only if they occur in an initial subordinate clause. LHF right-handed subjects retain potential antecedents in initial clauses with equal accessability, regardless of clause type.

The preceding two experiments support the hypothesis that comprehension processes in RHF right-handers are relatively sensitive to the difference between main and subordinate clauses. They immediately encode an initial main clause in a form that makes its meaning more quickly accessible than that of an initial subordinate clause. They encode an initial subordinate clause in a form that prepares it for integration with the following main clause. LHF right-handers do not encode initial subordinate clauses in a form different from initial main clauses. In sum, RHF right-handers may be relatively sensitive to structural relations between clauses within a sentence.

Canonical and Noncanonical Assignment of Thematic Roles
Let us now turn to a study of RHF and LHF right-handers' relative sensitivity to structures within clauses. In English the canonical phrase order of noun phrase, verb, noun phrase conveys the basic thematic relations agent, predicate, patient. Agent status is assigned to the initial noun phrase and patient status to the second noun phrase, as in (4a) and (4b). There is considerable evidence that during comprehension, people attempt to assign thematic relations based on this standard word order: for example, noncanonical word orders, as in (4c) and (4d), can be relatively hard to understand (McMahon 1963; Bever 1970; Slobin and Bever 1982; Carrithers 1988).[10]

(4a) John hit Sam.

(4b) It's John who hit Sam.

(4c) Sam was hit by John.

(4d) It's Sam who John hit.

The next study explores sensitivity to canonical word order in two ways: with noncanonical sentence constructions such as the passive and with particular verbs that assign noncanonical thematic relations to subject and object phrases. In each case, we found that RHF right-handers are more sensitive than LHF right-handers to canonical/noncanonical order manipulation.

We used a self-paced word-by-word reading task similar to that employed by Aaronson and Scarborough (1976): every time the subject presses a button on a computer keyboard, the next word appears in the same location on a video screen, wiping out the previous word. The experimental materials included sentences with the canonical agent-verb-patient order (active constructions) and those without that order (passive sentences). These sentences were semantically reversible; that is, the subject and object could be exchanged, and the result would be a sensible sentence.[11]

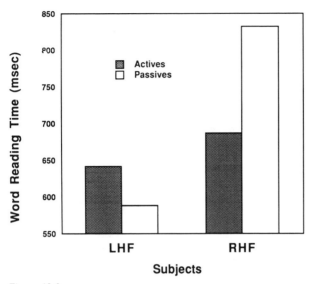

Figure 12.3
Final word reading time for active and passive sentences (see Carrithers 1988).

We used reading time on the last word of each sentence as a measure of its difficulty, scoring responses for each subject only when he correctly answered a subsequent comprehension question. The results showed that RHF readers are more sensitive to the difference between active and passive word order than LHF readers (figure 12.3).* RHF right-handed subjects spent a longer time on the last word of passive constructions than on active constructions.* LHF right-handed subjects did not show any differences as a function of word order.[12]

Canonical and Noncanonical Verbs
In this study we used two types of verbs to explore whether RHF readers are relatively sensitive to structural information conveyed by single words, as well as to variations in word order. One type of verb was a simple transitive verb such as *hit, see,* or *love.* These verbs maintain a canonical identity between grammatical object and thematic patient: in (5a) *Sam* is the direct object of *hit,* and Sam is the thematic patient (the one affected by the action). (The asterisk indicates peculiar or ungrammatical English.)

(5a) John hit Sam easily

(5b) John scared Sam easily

(5c) Sam scared easily for John

(5d) *Sam hits easily for John

The second type of verb inverts that relation, e.g., *scare, upset,* or *please* (Postal 1971; Carrithers 1988; Belleti and Rizzi 1988). Intuitively, the grammatical object of this second class of verb is the thematic agent of an intransitive form of the verb. Thus, the object of (5b) can become the apparent subject, as in (5c), a variation that cannot occur with standard transitive verbs, hence the ungrammaticality of (5d). This and other facts suggest that the apparent direct object of such verbs is thematically an experiencer or agent. This violates the usual confluence of grammatical and thematic object. The distinction between simple transitive and inverse thematic verbs is reflected differently in different linguistic theories. But, however it is correctly represented, it is a structural property, not a conceptual one: the fact that the object of *scare* is the experiencer is a grammatical fact, not a conceptual fact about the activity of scaring or being scared. We expected thematically inverse verbs to be comprehended more slowly than simple transitives, just because they violate the canonical relation between syntactic and thematic relations. In fact, final words of sentences with thematically inverse verbs were read more slowly than those of sentences with normal transitive verbs.* This difference was larger for RHF right-handers than for LHF right-handers (figure 12.4).*

Lexical-Conceptual Sensitivity
The preceding studies all suggest that RHF right-handers are more immediately sensitive than LHF right-handers to syntactic structures during processing. This confirms the first working hypothesis—that comprehension processes in RHF right-handers are more dependent on grammatical information than in LHF right-handers. We now turn to the complementary hypothesis, that LHF right-handers are more sensitive to conceptual information in words. Words are the interface in memory between structural and conceptual information. So we predicted that LHF right-handers would be more sensitive to individual word presentation and to nonlinguistic conceptual information that relates words to each other. The following studies suggest that LHF right-handers may indeed be more sensitive to word-based conceptual information.

Subject-Paced Reading Time for Individual Words
On our view, LHF right-handers access individual words during comprehension more readily than do RHF right-handers. This explains a

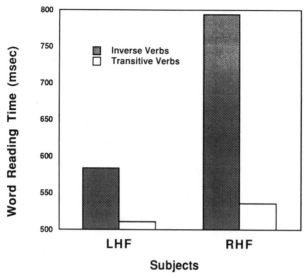

Figure 12.4
Final word reading time for sentences with transitive verbs ("hit") and thematically inverse verbs ("scare"). (See Carrithers 1988.)

surprising result found in the preceding study of self-paced, word-by-word reading: the average reading times per word were 21 percent slower for RHF right-handers than for LHF right-handers.* On our interpretation, forcing an RHF right-hander to read on a word-by-word basis interferes with the usual comprehension process in a way that does not hold for the LHF right-handed reader.[13] This hypothesis predicts that RHF right-handed readers should read faster when a whole clause is presented at a single time, since the minimal unit of syntactic structure is the clause (Bever et al. 1973, 1980). We tested this by having a new group of subjects read sentences in a clause-by-clause self-paced task.[14] As predicted, mean clause reading time for RHF right-handed subjects was faster by 15 percent than for the LHF right-handers.*

Auditory Word Segregation
It was important to test the hypothesis that separate word access is easier for LHF right-handers than for RHF right-handers in the auditory mode. To do this, we specially recorded a set of short essays, so that in some cases all the closed-class function words were presented to one ear while the content words were presented to the other ear. Even when the function and content words were segregated by ear, they were presented in the correct order for grammatical sentences.

The words were presented slowly, about one per second. This slow word-by-word presentation was used to exaggerate any disruption in comprehension when combined with segregating the content from the function words in different ears. Each auditorily presented essay was followed by written content questions.[15] RHF right-handers performed better on the questions when all the words in the essay were presented to the same ear.* Conversely, LHF right-handers performed better when the content and function words were segregated in separate ears (figure 12.5).*

This further supports the idea that LHF right-handers approach language comprehension first in terms of accessing individual words. Segregating the content and function words to different ears actually makes the comprehension task easier for them because it simplifies the acoustic isolation of each word. Conversely, such segregation makes the comprehension task harder for RHF right-handers, because it interferes with their normal mode of processing.

The Effects of Associative and Semantic Priming on Lexical Decision
The preceding two studies are consistent with the view that LHF right-handers benefit from individual word presentation during comprehension more than RHF right-handers, but the studies do not bear

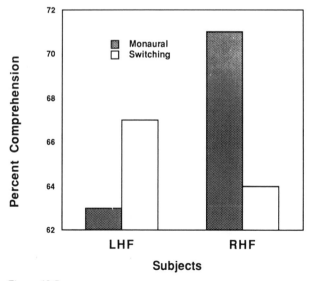

Figure 12.5
Postauditory written essay-comprehension score as a function of whether the essay was presented monaurally or with the function words heard in one ear and the content words heard in the other ear (Iverson and Bever 1989).

on the kind of lexical information that LHF right-handers access. We noted above that RHF right-handers are more sensitive to the structural information borne by certain verbs. So LHF right-handers must be accessing nonstructural, lexically borne information.

It is difficult to test for access of lexically based conceptual information during ongoing sentence comprehension, as the buildup of a representation of the conceptual information conveyed by the entire sentence may obscure the effects of individual words. Hence, we started our investigation of the hypothesis that LHF right-handers initially access nonlinguistic information in individual words, with a standard single-word experimental task: deciding that a sequence of letters is a word. This process can be affected by preceding words, and the amount of time it takes to make the lexical decision is often used to probe for the extent to which a word is primed by different kinds of contexts. For example, a critical word (e.g., lily) can be preceded by a word in the same semantic category (e.g., rose) or by a word that is highly associated with it (e.g., frog). A semantic prime is linguistically related to the critical word because they are defined as in the same semantic category. Associatively related words are related conceptually. Hence, we can use the amount of each kind of priming to tap the extent to which a subject arrives at the two kinds of lexical representation: associative priming taps a conceptual representation of the relation between the words in the world, whereas category priming taps a linguistic representation of their relation.

Various studies have found that both kinds of primes can have small facilitating effects on lexical-decision time (Lupker 1984), though there are some differences in the literature on this point (Fischler 1977a, 1977b). We designed a study with sets of semantic and associative prime words, along with unrelated control prime words. On each trial, a subject first fixates on a central target ('+'), then a prime word appears for 0.75 second, followed by the probe letter sequence. In the cases of interest, the letter sequence is a word. The amount of priming occasioned by the prime word is indicated by how much faster the probe word is recognized following a related prime than following an unrelated control (table 12.1).[16]

Table 12.1
Lexical decision materials

	Prime	Probe
Category prime	ROSE	LILY
Unrelated control	DOG	LILY
Associate prime	POND	LILY
Unrelated control	DOG	LILY

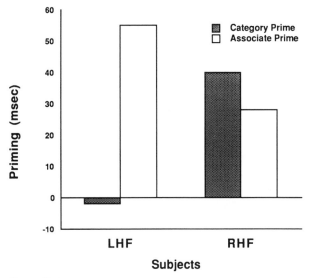

Figure 12.6
Amount of lexical-decision (LD) priming for semantic category and associative primers. Priming score is (LD preceded by unrelated word) – (LD preceded by a priming word). (Burgess and Beves 1989)

We contrasted LHF with RHF right-handers, using both kinds of priming. The results show a strong interaction between familial handedness and the kind of priming relation* (figure 12.6). LHF right-handers show more category priming than associative priming.* These results suggest further that LHF right-handers access conceptual information in individual words more directly than grammatical information, whereas RHF right-handers access grammatically encoded information more readily than conceptual information.

Utterance Length and Grammaticality in Young Children
These experiments all point in the same direction: right-handed people from right-handed families are more sensitive to syntactic structure than are right-handed people from families with left-handers. It also appears that they deal with single-word tasks less well. These generalizations invite speculation about individual differences in language development. In particular, we might expect that RHF right-handed children would typically show earlier syntactic development than LHF right-handed children. We subjected this hypothesis to a preliminary test by examining the speech of 43 two-year-old children who participated in another study (Gerken 1987).[17] The mean age of the two groups was the same (26 months) and the pro-

portion of females was within 4 percent. The RHF right-handed children actually showed a lower mean length of utterance than LHF right-handed children.* The mean length of utterance includes both grammatical ("I do that") and ungrammatical ("Me do that") utterances. To assess children's sensitivity to grammatical structures, we calculated the percentage of each child's multiword utterance types that were well-formed sentences an adult could use in isolation. Overall, RHF right-handed children produce a higher proportion of such utterances than LHF right-handed children.* The higher grammaticality rating of RHF right-handers was not due to the fact that LHF right-handed children had higher MLUs (and therefore a bigger chance of producing errors). The superior performance of RHF right-handed children occurred throughout the MLU range of the children. Thus, at the very young age studied here, it appeared that RHF right-handed children use fewer words per utterance but do so more grammatically.

Discussion

Our working hypotheses have received initial confirmation: RHF right-handers emphasize grammatical information and LHF right-handers emphasize other lexical information during language processing. There are a number of implications of such a difference.

The Distinct Operation of Linguistic Subsystems
In recent years it has been argued that the capacity to learn language is based on innate, skill-specific mechanisms. These mechanisms are most easily viewed as modules, distinct processing systems each with its own capacity and characteristics (Fodor 1983). For example, the mental representation of structural knowledge about language is distinct from the representation of lexical reference. The corresponding biological hypothesis is that there are distinct physiological mechanisms underlying the two kinds of knowledge. There are very few biological sources of data that confirm such a hypothesis. Most notably, the ways in which language is normally acquired and breaks down in aphasia have been argued to reveal the existence of linguistic subsystems. For example, anomias of specific kinds can occur without loss of grammatical capacity, and grammatical functioning can be lost without apparent loss of individual word denotations. Correspondingly, the acquisition of specific word denotations appears to occur parallel to, but distinct from, the acquisition of grammatical systems.

Systematic heritable variation offers a third kind of data confirming the hypothesis that there are distinct genetic mechanisms underlying a skill. For example, the quantal nature of inherited defects of color vision was strong evidence for the existence of different kinds of color receptors. Heritable differences in the capacity to taste different chemicals is evidence for specific taste receptors. We may have found a difference between people who lay particular stress on structure in language processing and others who assign relatively greater weight to lexical information. The critical role of familial handedness in separating these groups suggests strongly that the difference in processing styles is biologically mediated. Confirmation of the heritability of this difference will support a polymorphic hypothesis about the biological basis for language. In particular, our results lend validity to the claim that grammatical mechanisms are neurologically distinct from referential mechanisms.

In psycholinguistics there is an ongoing debate between modularists and interactionists over the extent to which grammatical structure is processed independently of other kinds of knowledge (see papers in Garfield 1987). The role of referential knowledge in syntactic processing is a central topic in this controversy: interactionists claim that conceptual knowledge can guide immediate syntactic decisions; modularists argue that the two kinds of information are initially processed independently. Our research is aimed at demonstrating that there is heritable variation in the extent to which comprehension emphasizes one or the other of these kinds of linguistic knowledge. If our preliminary results are confirmed, it will demonstrate that the modular theory is correct, at least insofar as it claims that the two kinds of information can be behaviorally isolated as a function of a familial trait.

Individual Differences
A less important but serious implication of this research concerns the interpretation of many current lines of research on language processing: our research suggests that familial handedness is not merely a source of noise in the data; it is a *systematic* source of variability that bears directly on many of the controversial issues in the field. About 50 percent of right-handers have left-handed family members. Hence, many weak experimental effects of structure or referential knowledge may be obscured by chance variation of familial handedness in experimental subjects. This is not a happy fact for the field, but it must be recognized and attended to in future research.

These results may also shed some light on individual differences in style of language acquisition. Numerous authors have noted that children have different approaches to learning a first language. Some invoke such distinctions as analytic versus holistic learners or word versus phrase learners (Bloom 1973; Nelson 1973; Peters 1983; Bates et al. 1988). We have found evidence that one contributing factor to such individual differences in linguistic style is the handedness of the child's family. Our preliminary analysis of the speech of young children suggests that LHF right-handed children may approach language behavior initially as a problem of mastering the words, while RHF right-handed children may focus initially on the acquisition of grammatical relations.

In our experiments RHF right-handers are clearly more immediately sensitive to grammatical structures than LHF right-handers. But it is less clear what typifies the language processing of LHF right-handers, or even whether a single characteristic pattern exists. We have reported evidence that LHF right-handers can access individual words during sentence comprehension better than RHF right-handers and that their sentence processing benefits when words are segregated for them. But LHF right-handers are not sensitive to all lexical information as such. The generalization that is supported by our results is that RHF right-handers are more sensitive to linguistic information in individual words (thematic-role structure, semantic category), while LHF right-handers are more sensitive to conceptual information. That is, during comprehension, LHF right-handers may access representations of lexical referents more immediately than RHF right-handers. This possibility has interesting implications for the apparent distribution of aphasias in response to left-hemisphere damage. For example, it may be that LHF right-handed patients with left-hemisphere damage are better able to mask loss of grammatical capacity by relying on their already well-developed lexical-referential strategies for language behavior. Conversely, LHF right-handed patients may show an apparent aphasia from right-hemisphere damage because it impairs access to their usual lexically based processing strategies (Kolk and van Grunsven 1985; Kolk 1987).

Underlying Mechanisms
We have noted that there are two major systems of knowledge involved in language behavior: grammatical structures and referential knowledge. We now turn to some speculations about why the LHF right-handers are relatively more sensitive to referential knowledge in language-processing style. One hypothesis is based on neurological distribution of the two kinds of language systems. Suppose that the neurological substrate for grammatical structures is always limited to a particular hemisphere, regardless of the overall growth or balance between the hemispheres. This would explain why almost

everybody shows evidence of some left-hemisphere control of language, even when there is also some right-hemisphere control. Suppose further that the lexical-reference system can be neurologically represented more variably and is represented more widely when the two hemispheres have equal potential. Recent evidence has suggested that the right hemisphere does access some lexical information (Chiarello 1985; Burgess and Simpson 1988). This hypothesis might explain the frequent report that people with familial left-handedness have a relatively widespread neurological implementation of language. On this view, it is lexical-referential knowledge that is widespread.

A difference in the extent to which lexical knowledge is neurologically widespread would explain why LHF right-handers are relatively sensitive to lexical and conceptual information during sentence comprehension. If such information is neurologically represented throughout the brain, there can be more points of contact between language and other kinds of knowledge of the world. Conversely, a small, localized area for lexical-referential knowledge in RHF right-handers would be more exclusively controlled by linguistic processes. Thus, tasks that are facilitated by independent access to lexical-referential information will be better performed by LHF right-handers.

There is an alternative, maturational account of the relative dependence of LHF right-handers on lexical-referential information that does not necessarily involve the right hemisphere. The maturational hypothesis follows Geschwind and Galaburda's theories quite closely: in LHF fetuses all cortical growth is slowed during the period when the left hemisphere would otherwise grow more rapidly. Suppose the neurological basis for the lexical-referential system is within the left hemisphere but normally matures later than the grammatical system. This would result in a difference between LHFs and RHFs in the maturation of the neurological basis for lexical and grammatical knowledge during the first few years: LHF children would have relatively more developed lexical-referential systems. Such a difference would influence the young LHF child to access linguistic knowledge with more dependence on that system.

We have extrapolated our causal speculations about the basis of the effects of familial handedness on right-handers from Geschwind and Galaburda's (1987) recent theories of the developmental basis for left-handedness. There are other views on this, most notably, that the source of handedness is genetic (Annett 1985; McManus 1985). On Annett's view, right-handedness results from a dominant genetic structure that causes a shift to the right from equipotentiality (and a related shift to the left hemisphere for higher functions like language). Annett suggests that the developmental mechanism for the expression of the genetic structure actually involves *suppression* of the right hemisphere. On one view, the right-shift gene may express this suppressive effect developmentally via increased fetal-testosterone activity (Geschwind and Galaburda offer this as a potential interpretation of the right-shift theory). In any case, Annett (1985) notes that since about a third of all right-handers should have a double signal for right-hemisphere suppression, familial handedness may have effects on cerebral organization among right-handers. Thus, the right-shift hypothesis for dominance is at least consistent with our findings.

So much for speculations about mechanisms. Whatever its basis turns out to be, we believe that the heterogenous studies reviewed here are initial indicators of an effect of familial handedness on language processes. This brief review is intended to alert cognitive scientists and neurologists interested in the study of language behavior to a subject variable that may affect their work and theories: RHF right-handers show significantly more sensitivity to syntactic structure than do LHF right-handers, while LHF right-handers show more ready access to individual words and conceptual relations between words.

There is much to do. First, we have not systematically explored the interaction of handedness background with sex, though we have controlled for this in most of our research. Second, we have not studied left-handers themselves, simply because it is much more difficult to find and match them for sex, handedness background, and manifest verbal ability. There are also important questions about the impact of the immediacy of familial left-handedness. We do not know to what extent LHF right-handers whose nearest left-handed relative is a grandparent or an aunt or uncle are different from RHF right-handers. If the effect of familial handedness is basically genetic, then the size of the LHF/RHF differences should correlate with the extent and closeness of left-handers in LHF families.

A Cautionary Note on Neophrenology
We conclude this report by emphasizing the preliminary, statistical, and experimental nature of our findings. Clearly, there are many factors that influence an individual's neurological organization and behavioral style. We may have isolated an effect of one of them, using laboratory techniques that reveal small but significant differences in performance on specially constructed tasks. But we do not yet under-

stand the true nature of these effects, we do not have a general theory of how they interact with other factors, and we have no idea how they are expressed in ordinary contexts.

The scientific and popular literature today is littered with neophrenologic studies that focus on alleged individual differences between 'right-brained' and 'left-brained' individuals. Even relatively conservative scholars sometimes link the kinds of differences we are reporting to talents for different professions. We, on the other hand, are more impressed by the enormous organizational resilience of the human brain and the remarkable cognitive similarities among people, despite occasional extreme anatomical differences. The kinds of studies we have carried out do not demonstrate that there are two right-handed talents that could provide the basis for assessing a person's functional capacity. Rather, our specialized experimental techniques show that there can be different processing styles underlying the same manifest abilities. This result may provide helpful insights for understanding the multiple nature of the relations between brain, knowledge, and behavior, but it leads to no obvious prescriptions for pedagogy or any other practical concern. Human behavior is the product of many factors, among which the organization of the neonate brain is just one.

Notes

1. There are numerous reports of nonlinguistic effects of familial left-handedness in right-handers, e.g., Deutsch 1983; Yeo and Cohen 1983; Burnett, Lane, and Dratt 1982; Tinkcom, Obrzut, and Poston 1983; Melamed and Arnett 1984; McKeever et al. 1983; Kraft 1983; Xintian, Minggao, Huikun, and Kuihe 1984; Bryden, Hecaen, and DeAgostini 1983. These studies are quite heterogenous, so we concentrate on those studies that we think potentially involve the role of grammatical relations and lexical knowledge in language comprehension.

2. Each of the experimental studies summarized here has been published elsewhere or is being prepared for separate publication with full experimental details and statistical analyses. Unless otherwise noted, every result marked in this paper with an asterisk (*) is statistically reliable at least at the $p < .05$ level. Almost all results are actually $p < .01$.

3. Subjects filled out a variant of the Edinburgh handedness questionnaire, used in all our research reported in this paper. In addition, they filled out a familial handedness questionnaire, which asks about the handedness of all family relations, including immediate family, grandparents, uncles and aunts: the questionnaire distinguishes blood relations from others; it also distinguishes the handedness categories of left, right, ambidextrous, and "right handed but switched from left." The allergy question on the survey was simply whether the subject had any allergies. Because of the association of left-handedness with mathematical ability, we note that University of Rochester undergraduates have a mean score of around 550 on the verbal SAT, and a mean of 625 on the math SAT.

4. Unless otherwise noted, all the studies reported in this chapter used this definition of *family* to differentiate familial handedness. With this criterion, about half of our self-reporting college undergraduates are classified as LHF. We counted only full biological relatives; any relative who was reported as "having been left-handed, but forced to become right-handed" was counted as left-handed, as were ambidextrous relatives. Geschwind and Galaburda usually discuss familial left-handedness only in relation to parents and siblings. This may explain why our LHF group is larger than Geschwind and Galaburda's estimate of the frequency of anomalous dominance among right-handers. In all the studies reported here, LHF and RHF groups did not differ in the strength of right-handedness according to the multi-item test, and every subject we used scored above 95 percent right-handed.

5. A simple structural demonstration that the sentence with *but* is not a main-subordinate construction is the fact that the second clause cannot be moved to the beginning of the structure: i.e., one cannot say, "But he didn't want to, Harry called up Bill," though one can say, "Though he didn't want to, Harry called up Bill."

6. The complete story is more complex. It is specified in terms of the structural relation 'c-command' to allow for cases such as "John told his mother that Bill left," for which many speakers accept two readings, including one in which *Bill* is the antecedent of *his*. See Reinhart 1983.

7. Bever, Carrithers, and Townsend 1989. There were 24 LHF and 24 RHF right-handed subjects, balanced for sex and verbal SAT scores (a mean of 575 in each group). The subjects were drawn from undergraduate subject pools at the University of Massachusetts and the Johns Hopkins University. In this study a subject was counted as LHF only if an immediate family member was left-handed; a subject was counted as RHF only if there were no left-handers in the entire family in as defined in footnote 2. Each sentence fragment was either a main clause or a subordinate clause produced by adding *if* or *though* to the main clause. We constructed experimental sets of 12 critical sequences with varying versions of each fragment in each set, as well as 12 fragments in which the probe phrase did not have a related meaning. The fragments ranged in length from 8 to 12 words. The stimuli were presented monaurally in blocks: there were significant differences according to the ear of presentation, but they involve complex interactions and present no clear picture.

8. Cowart 1987. The familial handedness of the subjects in this study was assessed in the same way as in the first study. The groups, however, were not balanced for sex or for general verbal ability (neither SAT nor ACT scores were consistently available). In the experiments, eight groups of subjects (four groups divided by materials and two groups divided by handedness background) read 24 two-clause sentences arrangd so that each sentence appeared once for each group. Subjects answered a content question after each trial. There were 50 subjects in all, 26 LHF and 24 RHF right-handers.

9. Subsequent work suggests that differences attributable to familial left-handedness may occur over a slightly smaller domain, just the two words following the pronoun (see Cowart, in preparation).

10. Note that the observation that there is a canonical sentence type in English does not provide a theoretical explanation for it. Various theories of sentence comprehension can embrace the observation but may offer different explanations of it.

11. Carrithers 1988. In each family-handed group there were 28 right-handed male subjects paired for SAT scores and drawn from the Columbia University undergraduate subject pool. Familial handedness was assessed by the conservative criteria described in footnote 7. Sentences were followed by a heterogenous set of comprehension questions. The actual sentences ranged in length from 12 to 18 words.

12. A word about theory and results is in order here. The effect of canonical word order was almost entirely due to sentences with verbs discussed in the next section. Thus, the active/passive difference was statistically significant by subject for RHF right-handers, but there was only a marginal difference by items. The active/passive difference was significantly larger for RHF right-handers than for LHF right-handers when the two groups were compared, but marginally so when items were compared. Recently Carrithers (1986, 1988) and Bever et al. (1988) have argued that the passive construction with transitive verbs should be easier to apprehend than actives with certain verbs, which may explain why Carrither's results varied so by verb.

13. We should note that the RHF right-handed readers were slightly better at answering the questions correctly. There was, however, no speed-versus-accuracy trade-off across subjects ($r = .04$). Overall accuracy was about 80 percent. In the cumulative word-by-word reading studies, the LHF and RHF reading rates are much more similar to each other. This may be because the accumulating series of words on the screen allows the RHF right-handed subjects to integrate larger units than a single word.

14. Srinivas and Bever, in preparation. Sixteen LHF and RHF right-handed subjects read 20 two-clause sentences presented on a standard computer screen and were asked to paraphrase each sentence right after reading it. Subjects were drawn from the University of Rochester undergraduate subject pool. Groups were balanced for verbal SAT score and were roughly balanced by sex.

15. Iverson and Bever 1989. There were 16 RHF and 16 LHF right-handed subjects balanced for sex and verbal SAT score. Subjects were drawn from the University of Rochester undergraduate subject pool. Each subject heard eight short essays, four monaurally and four with content and function words presented to different ears. The essays were about 40 words long and were recorded from a slow but natural reading of the essay, with content and function words recorded on different tracks of a tape recorder. The presentation rate was then electronically sped up to about 1.5 words per second. Monaural presentations mixed the two separate tracks. There were weak interaction effects of sex and which ear heard the content words, but further research is needed to assess these effects.

16. Burgess and Bever 1989. There were 17 LHF and 17 RHF right-handers balanced for sex and verbal SAT, drawn from the University of Rochester subject pool. There were 15 trials of each of four types (two with related primes and two with unrelated control primes). There were also 60 pronounceable nonword trials. The semantic primes were controlled to be low associates of their following probes.

17. Our examination is based on 43 children studied by Gerken (1987), ages 23 to 30 months, with a mean length of utterance (MLU) of 1.3 to 5.0. Only children who passed a pretest of their ability to imitate a three-word sentence were included in this study, so the population sample may be biased in a crucial way. We also excluded children who had a clear preference for the left hand. The mean MLU for RHF children was 2.6, while for LHF children it was 3.3; the proportion of structurally well-formed multiword sequences for RHF children was 59 percent, while for LHF children it was 47 percent. The group MLU differences we report are signifciant by chi-square tests, as are the grammaticality differences. We accept these results with caution, however, because of the possibility of subject bias and because we can not be sure of the children's ultimate handedness. By chance, almost all of the children were first-born offspring of highly verbal parents. Also, note that our measure of grammaticality counted as grammatical every sentence that *could* be grammatical in some context even if it was not grammatically or socially acceptable in the context of the child's use of it.

References

Aaronson, D., and Scarborough, H. 1976. Performance theories for sentence coding: Some quantitative evidence. *Journal of Experimental Psychology: Human Perception and Performance* 2:56–70.

Annett, M. 1983. Hand preference and skill in 115 children of two left-handed parents. *British Journal of Psychology* 74 (1): 17–32.

Annett, M. 1985. *Left, right hand and brain: The right shift theory.* Hillsdale, N.J.: Lawrence Erlbaum Associates.

Bates, E., Bretherton, I., and Snyder, L. 1988. *From first words to grammar: Individiual differences and dissociable mechanisms.* New York: Cambridge University Press.

Belleti and Rizzi, L. 1986. Psych-verbs and Th-theory. Lexicon Project Working Paper no. 13. Center for Cognitive Science, MIT.

Benbow, C. P. 1986. Physiological correlates of extreme intellectual precocity. *Neuropsychologia* 24 (5): 719–725.

Benbow, C. P., and Benbow, R. M. 1984. Biological correlates of high mathematical reasoning ability. In G. J. De Vries et al., eds., *Progress in brain research*, vol. 61. Amsterdam: Elsevier Science Publishers.

Benbow, C. P., and Stanley, J. C. 1980. Sex differences in mathematical ability: Fact or artifact? *Science* 210:1262–1264.

Benbow, C. P., and Stanley, J. C. 1983. Sex differences in mathematical reasoning ability: More facts. *Science* 222:1029–1031.

Bever, T. G. 1970. The cognitive basis for linguistic structures. In R. Hayes, ed., *Cognition and language development*, pp. 277–360. New York: Wiley and Sons.

Bever, T. G. 1983. Cerebral lateralization, cognitive asymmetry, and human consciousness. In E. Perecman, ed., *Cognitive processing in the right hemisphere*, pp. 19–39. New York: Academic Press.

Bever, T. G., Carrithers, C., and Townsend, D. 1987. A tale of two brains, or The sinistral quasimodularity of language. In *Proceedings of the Ninth Annual Cognitive Science Society Meetings*, pp. 764–773. Hillsdale, N.J.: Lawrence Erlbaum Associates.

Bever, T. G., Carrithers, C., and Townsend, D. 1989. Sensitivity to clause structure as a function of familial handedness. University of Rochester, Cognitive Sciences Technical Report no. 43.

Bever, T. B., Garrett, M. F., and Hurtig, R. 1973. The interaction of perceptual processes and ambiguous sentences. *Memory and Cognition* 1:277–386.

Bever, T. G., Kirk, R., and Lackner, J. 1970. An autonomic reflection of syntactic structure. *Neuropsychologia* 7:23–28.

Bever, T. G., and Langendoen, T. 1971. A dynamic model of the evolution of language. *Linguistic Inquiry* 2:433–463.

Bever, T. G., Straub, R. O., Terrace, H. S., and Townsend, D. S. 1980. The comparative study of serially integrated behavior in humans and animals. In P. Jusczyk and R. Klein, eds., *The nature of thought: Essays in honor of D. D. Hebb.* Hillsdale, N.J.: Lawrence Erlbaum Associates.

Bloom, L. 1973. *One word at a time.* The Hague: Mouton.

Bouma, A., VanStrien, J. W., Bekker, C., and Tjerkstra, A. 1984. Dichotic listening and tactual mental rotation in females as a function of familial sinistrality and strength of handedness. *Journal of Clinical Neuropsychology* 6 (2): 171–188.

Bradsahw-McNulty, G., Hicks, R. E., and Kinsbourne, M. 1984. Pathological left-handedness and familial sinistrality in relation to degree of mental retardation. *Brain and Cognition* 3 (4): 349–356.

Broca, P. 1961. Remarques sur le siège de la faculté de la parole articulée, suivies d'une observation d'aphémie. *Bulletin de la Société d'anatomie* (Paris) 36:330–357.

Brown, R. 1973. *A first language*. Cambridge: Harvard University Press.

Bryden, M. P., Hecaen, H., and DeAgostini, M. 1983. Patterns of cerebral organization. *Brain and Language* 20 (2): 249–262.

Burgess, C., and Bever, T. G. 1989. Lexical access and familial handedness. University of Rochester, Cognitive Science Technical Report no. 44.

Burgess, C., and Simpson, G. B., 1988. Neuropsychology of lexical ambiguity resolution. In Small, S. C., Cottrell, G. W., and Tonenhaus, M. K., eds., *Lexical ambiguity resolution*. San Mateo, Calif.: Morgan Kaufmann Publishers.

Burnett, S. A., Lane, D. M., and Dratt, L. M. 1982. Spatial ability and handedness. *Intelligence* 6 (1): 57–68.

Carrithers, C. 1986. The special status of non-canonical sequences. Ph.D. dissertation, Columbia University.

Carrithers, C. 1988. Canonical sentence structure and psych-ergative verbs. *Journal of Psycholinguist Research*.

Carrithers, C., Townsend, D. J., and Bever, T. G. 1988. Sentence-processing in listening and reading among college and school-age skilled and average readers. In R. Horowitz, and S. J. Sammuels, eds., *Comprehending spoken and printed language*. New York: Academic Press.

Channon, L. D. 1985. The relationship between laterality indices, inversion of the writing hand, and some demographic variables. *Australian Journal of Psychology* 37 (1): 89–96.

Chiarello, C. 1985. Hemisphere dynamics in lexical access: Automatic and controlled priming. *Brain and Language* 26:146–172.

Cowart, W. 1987. Relation to neurophysiological variation. *Proceedings of the Ninth Annual Conference of the Cognitive Science Society*, pp. 811–823. Hillsdale, N.J.: Lawrence Erlbaum Associates.

Cowart, W. 1988. Familial sinistrality and syntactic processing. In J. M. Williams and C. J. Long, eds., *Cognitive approaches to neuropsychology*, pp. 273–286. New York: Plenum.

Deutsch, D. 1983. The octave illusion in relation to handedness and familial handedness background. *Neuropsychologia* 21 (3): 289–293.

Fischler, I. 1977a. Associative facilitation without expectancy in a lexical decision task. *Journal of Experimental Psychology: Human Perception and Performance* 3:18–26.

Fischler, I. 1977b. Semantic facilitation without association in a lexical decision task. *Memory and Cognition* 5:335–339.

Fodor, J. A. 1983. *The modularity of mind*. Cambridge: MIT Press.

Fodor, J., Bever, T. G., and Garrett, M. 1974. *The psychology of language*. New York: McGraw Hill.

Garfield, J., ed. 1987. *Modularity in knowledge representation and natural language understanding*. Cambridge: MIT Press.

Gerken, L. A. 1987. Telegraphic speaking does not imply telegraphic listening. *Papers and Reports on Child Language Development* 26:38–46.

Gerken, L. A., and Bever, T. G. 1986. Linguistic intuitions are the result of interactions between perceptual processes and linguistic universals. *Cognitive Science* 10:457–476.

Geschwind, N., and Behan, P. 1982. Left-handedness: Association with immune disease, migraine, and developmental learning disorder. *Proceedings of the National Academy of Sciences* (U.S.A.) 79:5097–5100.

Geschwind, N., and Behan, P. 1984. Laterality, hormones, and immunity. In N. Geschwind and A. Galaburda, eds., *Cerebral dominance: The biological foundations*. Cambridge: Harvard University Press.

Geschwind, N., and Galaburda, A. M. 1987. *Cerebral lateralization.* Cambridge: MIT Press.

Gordon, H. W. 1980. Cognitive asymmetry in dyslexic families. *Neuropsychologia* 18:645–656.

Gordon, H. W. 1982. Learning disabled are cognitively right. In M. Kinsbourne, ed., *Topics in learning disabilities* 3:29–39. Rockville, Md.: Aspen Systems Corp.

Healy, J. M., and Aram, D. M. 1986. Hyperlexia and dyslexia: A family study. *Annals of Dyslexia* 36:237–252.

Hécaen, H., and Albert, M. 1978. *Human neuropsychology.* New York: Wiley.

Iverson, P., and Bever, T. G. 1989. Auditory lexical segregation, comprehension, and familial handedness. University of Rochester, Cognitive Science Technical Report no. 45.

Joanette, Y., Lecours, A. R., Lepage, Y., and Lamoureux, M. 1983. Language in right-handers with right hemisphere lesions: A preliminary study including anatomical, genetic, and social factors. *Brain and Language* 20:217–248.

Kee, D. W., Bathurst, K., and Hellige, J. B. 1983. Lateralized interference of repetitive finger tapping: Influence of familial handedness, cognitive load, and verbal production. *Neuropsychologia* 21 (6): 617–624.

Kennedy, A., and Murray, W. S. 1984. Inspection times for words in syntactically ambiguous sentences under three presentation conditions. *Journal of Experimental Psychology: Human Perception and Performance* 10:833–849.

Koff, E., Naeser, M. A., Piendiadz, J. M., and Foundas, A. L. 1986. Computed tomographic scan hemisphereic asymmetries in right- and left-handed male and female subjects. *Archives of Neurology* 43 (5): 487–491.

Kolk, H. 1987. A theory of grammatical impairment in aphasia. In G. Kempsen, ed., *Natural language generation.* Dordrecht: Martinus Nijhoff Publishers.

Kolk, H. H. J., and van Grunsven, M. M. F. 1985. Agrammatism as a variable phenomenon. *Cognitive Neuropsychology* 2:347–384.

Kraft, R. H. 1983. The effect of sex, laterality, and familial handedness on intellectual abilities. *Neuropsychologia* 21 (1): 79–89.

Kutas, M., Van Petten, C., and Besson, M. 1988. Event-related potential asymmetries during the reading of sentences. *Electroencephalography and Clinical Neurophysiology* 69:218–233.

Lupker, S. J. 1984. Semantic priming without association: A second look. *Journal of Verbal Learning and Verbal Behavior* 23:709–733.

Luria, A. R. 1947. *Traumatic aphasia: Its syndrome, psychopathology, and treatment* (Russian). Moscow: Academy of Medical Sciences. Translation, The Hague: Mouton, 1970.

McKeever, W. F., and Hoff, A. L. 1982. Familial sinistrality, sex, and laterality differences in naming and lexical decision latencies of right-handers. *Brain and Language* 17 (2): 225–239.

McKeever, W. F. 1983. Interacting sex and familial sinistrality characteristics influence both language lateralization and spatial ability in right handers. *Neuropsychologia* 21 (6): 661–668.

McKeever, W. F., Nolan, D. R., Diehl, J. A., and Seitz, K. S. 1984. Handedness and language laterality: Discrimination of handedness groups on the dichotic consonant-vowel task. *Cortex* 20 (4): 509–523.

McLaughlin, J. P. 1986. Aesthetic preference and lateral preferences. *Neuropsychologia* 24 (4): 587–590.

McMahon, L. 1963. Grammatical analysis as part of understanding a sentence. Ph.D. dissertation, Harvard University.

McManus, I. C. 1985. *Handedness, language dominance, and aphasia: A genetic model.* Psychological Medicine Monograph, supplement 8. New York: Cambridge University Press.

Melamed, L. E., and Arnett, W. B. 1984. The effect of familial sinistrality on perceptual learning. *Neuropsychologia* 22 (4): 495–502.

Minggao, L., Xintian, L., Huikun, G., and Xiaoqin, W. 1984. A study of hand preference in children. *Information on Psychological Sciences* 2:1–7.

Nelson, K. 1973. Structure and strategy in learning to talk. *Monographs of the Society for Research in Child Development* 38.

Orton, S. T. 1925. "Word-blindness" in school children. *Arch. Neurol. psychiat.* 14:581–615.

Peters, A. 1983. *The units of languge acquisition.* Cambridge: Cambridge University Press.

Postal, P. 1971. *Cross-over phenomena.* New York: Holt, Rinehart, and Winston.

Pringle, G. F., Anderson, S. W., and Jaffe, J. 1985. Speed of color naming and degree of familial sinistrality: Correlation in girls, no correlation in boys. *Journal of Communication Disorders* 18 (1): 59–62.

Reinhart, T. 1983. *Anaphora and semantic interpretation.* Chicago: University of Chicago Press.

Ross, J. R. 1967. Constraints on varibles in syntax. Ph.D. dissertation, MIT. Published as *Infinite syntax* (Norwood, N.J.: Ablex Publishing Corp., 1986).

Russell, W. R., and Expir, M. L. E. 1961. *Traumatic aphasia.* Oxford: Oxford University Press.

Searleman, A., and Fugagli, J. 1987. Suspected autoimmune disorders and left-handedness: Evidence from individuals with diabetes, Crohn's disease, and ulcerative colitis. *Neuropsychologia* 25:367–374.

Searleman, A., Herrmann, D. J., and Coventry, A. K. 1984. Cognitive abilities and left-handedness: An interaction between familial sinistrality and strength of handedness. *Intelligence* 8 (4): 295–304.

Slobin, D. I. 1966. Grammatical transformations and sentence comprehension in childhood and adulthood. *Journal of Verbal Learning and Verbal Behavior* 5:219–227.

Slobin, D. I., and Bever, T. G. 1982. Children use canonical sentence schemas in sentence perception. *Cognition* 12:229–265.

Spiegler, B. J., and Yeni-Komshian, G. H. 1983. Incidence of left-handed writing in a college population with reference to family patterns of hand preference. *Neuropsychologia* 21 (6): 651–659.

Srinivas, K., and Bever, T. G. In preparation. Lexical and decompositional representations of idioms.

Tan, L. E. 1983. Handedness in two generations. *Perceptual and Motor Skills* 56 (3): 867–874.

Tinkcom, M., Obrzut, J. E., and Poston, C. S. 1983. Spatial lateralization: The relationship among sex, handedness, and familial sinistrality. *Neuropsychologia* 21 (6): 683–686.

Townsend, D. J., and Bever, T. G. 1978. Interclausal relations and clausal processing. *Journal of Verbal Learning and Verbal Behavior* 17:509–521.

Townsend, D. J., Carrithers, C., and Bever, T. G. 1987. Listening and reading processes in college- and middle-school-age readers. In R. Horowitz, and S. J. Samuels, eds., *Comprehending oral and written language,* pp. 217–242. San Diego: Academic Press.

Xintian, L., Minggao, L., Huikun, G., and Kuihe, J. 1984. Experimental study on grasping with left or right hand by 6 months to 3-year-old children. *Acta Psychologica Sinica* 16 (2): 214–222.

Yeo, R. A., and Cohen, D. B. 1983. Familial sinistrality and sex differences in cognitive abilities. *Cortex* 19 (1): 125–130.

Editor's Comments

Heretofore both biology and psychology have concentrated on extracting from their observations and experiments those characteristics that are universal among living organisms, e.g., DNA, the simple reflex, memory. More recently neurobiologists and psychologists are beginning to address the issue of individual differences and are trying to discover universal principles underlying the generation of diversity, as evidenced by several chapters in this volume. The present chapter looks at functional diversity in language processing as constrained by biological factors such as hand preference. What emerges is a remarkable set of preliminary data on the effects that family handedness in right-handers have on the extent to which the latter rely on structural or conceptual-lexical knowledge during language processing. Specifically, those right-handers with left-handed family histories (LHF) rely more heavily on conceptual-lexical factors, while right-handers with a right-handed family history (RHF) rely more on structural information.

Right- and left-handers differ in the anatomy of language-relevant cortical regions, a fact that has not yet been checked for RHF and LHF right-handers. Right-handers more often than left-handers tend to show the expected population distribution of Sylvian-fissure asymmetry, which is about 65 percent with longer left sides, about 25 percent symmetrical, and about 10 percent with longer right sides. Left-handers instead show a substantial and significant increase in the frequency of symmetrical Sylvian fissures (up to 66 percent of all cases). Symmetry of the Sylvian fissures reflects to a great extent symmetry of the planum temporale, a language-related area on the temporal lobe. And symmetry of the planum temporale in turn reflects greater development of the right planum temporale in comparison to those brains in which the planum temporale is leftward asymmetrical. Related work shows that compared to asymmetrical equivalents, symmetrical brain regions contain more neurons and greater densities of more diffuse interhemispheric connections than asymmetrical brain regions (see Sherman et al. and Galaburda et al. in this volume). These anatomical facts, together with the observation that the right planum varies in size to a much greater extent than the left, support the speculation of Bever et al. that left-hemisphere linguistic activities may be comparable among RHF right-handers and LHF right-handers (and perhaps right- and left-handers?), while right-hemispheric nonlinguistic contributions to language function may vary more and be more important in individuals with atypical cerebral dominance. Whether the functional and anatomical findings of the present chapter appear equally well in left-hander and right-hander comparisons as in comparisons of RHF and LHF right-handed subjects remains an empirical issue, as the authors warn. But it does appear that handedness plays a role in both anatomical and functional architectures related to language.

An interesting set of questions arising from this research is whether the described processing biases of RHF and LHF right-handers lies along a continuum and whether there are extremes of this continuum that constitute developmentally pathological states. Are there individuals who must rely so much on one strategy or the other that situations in which the required strategy is not adequate lead to failure? One such situation may be reading, for which only a limited amount of conceptual-lexical information is available and reliance on structure is important to extract meaning efficiently. When learning to read, small children (who by adult standards have only a limited knowledge of the world) have a greater need to rely on structural aspects of language than later on when world knowledge increases. Either absolute or relative increases in the need to rely on structural knowledge might, therefore, lead to disorders of reading acquisition and reading competence.

Many dyslexia experts have raised the issue of grammatical abnormalities in developmental dyslexics. My co-workers and I have learned that functional and anatomical lateralization is so altered in this population that there are excess anomalous patterns of asymmetry. A tempting hypothesis stemming from these observations is that some dyslexics rely exceptionally on conceptual-lexical knowledge for extracting meaning from print, which tends to favor those with advanced structural skills. Hence, their reading acquisition is slow and improves only insofar as they become more efficient with experience at extracting the maximum lexical knowledge from texts. Any interference with the process of deriving contextual information from texts should lead to a reading disability. Thus far the brains of severely dyslexic individuals have shown absence of asymmetry and another anatomical difference as well: male brains studied show multiple instances of laminar disorganization and many ectopic neurons (together termed *microdysgenesis*) in the perisylvian cortex of both hemispheres, but more on the left. The perisylvian cortex contains language-relevant areas. What we are witnessing in the most severe dyslexics may thus be a relatively physiological difficulty in using structural information, which is related to the lack of asymmetry, coupled with sluggishness in deriving lexical knowledge from print, which is related to the microdysgenesis. This hypothesis is speculative in that we cannot as yet assess the effects of microdysgenesis on language processes and we do not have a clear understanding of the relationship between linguistic capacities and cerebral asymmetry (as opposed to handedness). To confirm or reject this hypothesis, we need to isolate the two anatomical findings in dyslexic populations. High resolution neuroimaging coupled with cognitive assessment remains the most promising for progress in this regard.

Chapter 13

Reflections on Visual Recognition

Antonio R. Damasio

Neuropsychologic and Psychophysiologic Findings in Subjects with Acquired Defects in Visual Recognition

Patients with focal brain damage involving the visual system or the limbic system may develop remarkably selective disorders in visual recognition. The most commonly encountered of these disorders compromises reading and is exemplified by those cases of pure alexia that can be accounted for as an agnosia for visuoverbal stimuli. Other commonly found disturbances involve the recognition of objects (visual-object agnosia) or faces (prosopagnosia). In this chapter we shall concentrate on the neuropsychologic and neuroanatomical characterization of object and face recognition and briefly sketch a model that can account for visual recognition. The fact that both of these disorders combined or in relative isolation are often not associated with alexia provides indirect clues about the neural and cognitive underpinnings of the reading process.

Isolated Disorders of Face Recognition
Defects in the recognition of face identity, generally known as prosopagnosia, can appear in relative isolation (pure prosopagnosia) or as part of an amnesic syndrome. In pure prosopagnosia, recognition defects are confined to the visual modality. Patients fail to recognize previously familiar faces but can promptly identify the voices of the same people when they speak, i.e., there is patent access through nonvisual channels to memories that confer specific identity to familiar stimuli. Patients have no difficulty categorically recognizing faces as faces, and they can recognize face subcomponents. All forms of generic recongition operate at the "basic-object level" (in the sense given to the term by Rosch et al. [1976]). Most of them can identify the meaning of facial expressions, assign gender to faces, and even estimate age (Tranel, Damasio, and Damasio 1988).

In the few subjects in which the recognition of facial expressions is impaired, the problem occurs only with static expressions, like those shown in photographs, but not when the expressions occur in a real setting with movement. That is, these patients can recognize an expression of surprise or a smile if they actually watch it develop over time.

In a well specified context patients can occasionally recognize a face on the basis of a telltale fragment. One of my patients systematically "recognized" any man with his hair parted in the middle as her husband and any young woman with a darkened upper tooth as her daughter. Those relatives had those salient facial features. The patient's accuracy ranged between complete success to complete failure according to context. Intelligent prosopagnosics can recognize persons well known to them by characteristic postures and movements (stoops, velocity of gait, and shape of gestures). Obviously, they are recognizing unique identities not on the basis of faces but rather on the basis of other visual cues, such as motion. In a context with other adjuvant clues their chance of success is considerable but without such contextual help these secondary systems of recognition are not as effective as faces can be for unique recognition of identities.

Prosopagnosics have impaired appreciation of texture (Newcombe 1979) and of color perception (Meadows 1974; Damasio et al. 1980). Visual acuity is normal, but prosopagnosics may have partial field cuts for form vision, especially in the upper quadrants (Damasio 1985a). Sensitivity to spatial contrasts is normal (Rizzo et al. 1986). Stereopsis is normal (Damasio et al. 1980; Rizzo and Damasio 1985), and so are the scan paths with which they inspect faces (Rizzo et al. 1987).

Most pure prosopagnosics perform normally in facial discrimination tasks in which they are asked to match unfamiliar and differently lit photographs of faces but not requested to recognize any of them (Benton 1980; Tzavaras et al. 1970; Benton and Van Allen 1972). They can distinguish figure from ground, and they can sketch the contours of figures shown in photographs, diagrams, or real models. They can also detect motion. Furthermore, they can localize and attend to stimuli in space. Unlike patients with Balint syndrome, they experience vision in appropriate perspective, i.e., their verbal descriptions of their visual field correspond to what the observer sees (Benton 1980; Damasio 1985b). It is noteworthy that the visually disturbed Balint patients can recognize previously known faces when the stimuli are presented in a way that compensates for the perceptual weakness (Meier and French 1965; Damasio 1985a).

Last but not least, prosopagnosic patients can often read, although some do so more slowly than before the onset of prosopagnosia. This is certainly a powerful indication that at least in part the neural underpinnings of reading are segregated from those of nonverbal object recognition.

Prosopagnosics have difficulty in recognizing more than just faces. Patients also fail to recognize other previously recognized visual stimuli if one requests that they recognize them as particular objects. Typical examples include their own cars, houses, and familiar landmarks, e.g., buildings. The least impaired of all prosopagnosics I have had a chance to study in nearly 20 years cannot recognize either faces or buildings (when looking at her house in a photograph or in reality, she has no idea that it is indeed her house), although she can recognize personal effects. DeRenzi (1986) has noted that one prosopagnosic could recognize personal effects and even his own handwriting. I believe that such recognition relies on a particular strategy that prosopagnosics are able to carry out but that is of limited use in recognizing unique faces. The strategy can be successful for personal effects, e.g., a wallet with a salient feature that allows recognition in a relatively forced-choice situation.

Most patients with prosopagnosia also have some difficulty in recognizing selected categories of objects at the categorical level, that is, objects they are asked to recognize not as unique examplars but rather as members of a conceptual category. (The difficulty applies to certain animals, makes of cars, articles of clothing, food ingredients, and musical instruments; see Pallis 1955; Faust 1955; Bornstein 1963; Lhermitte et al. 1972; Damasio et al. 1982.)

Subjects who fail to recognize an entire stimulus may recognize correctly a part of the stimulus, which may be independently meaningful. This happens even when the identity attributed to the fragment conflicts with the identity of the whole (Damasio, Welsh, and Damasio 1986). Given a set of object drawings that can be decomposed in fragments with independent meanings, i.e., meanings that semantically conflict with the meaning of the global frame, prosopagnosics are superior at recognizing the fragments rather than global frames. Their worst performances occur when local fragments manifestly clash in semantic terms with the global frame. The prosopagnosic's difficulty is one of relating parts to a coherent whole, whatever part he happens to be drawn to and to recognize correctly. In sum, prosopagnosics fail to recognize unique, familiar faces; other unique and familiar visual stimuli; and some examples of nonunique visual stimuli.

The size and membership of the categories to which stimuli belong is another important factor influencing recognition. When stimuli belong to categories made up of many different but physically similar members, prosopagnosics have greater difficulties with recognition.

An illustration is animals in the cat family (tigers, cats, panthers) or physically similar plants or physically similar car makes. Using Rosch's nomenclature as a framework (Rosch et al. 1976) in which stimuli are classified as superordinate, a basic object, or subordinate according to their degree of uniqueness, I can say that the patients are normal at the superordinate and basic-object levels, i.e., they can recognize an animal or vehicle as such but fail to recognize objects at the subordinate level, the level of familiar and unique human faces. Their recognition is better at basic-object and superordinate levels, though even here it is partially disturbed.

An illustration of the importance of situation and context in recognition is illustrated by the fact that for most of us there is no need to recognize anything but the prototypical elephant, yet a zoo keeper needs to and does learn to recognize the several individual elephants he deals with. Among botanical species, fruits, vegetables, flowers, and some trees share so many features and dimensions that correct recognition is often impaired in visual agnosics, even when they are compared to controls, whose performance in those categories is not flawless either.

However, there may be other factors at play. The functional role of the stimulus appears critical. Clearly, the well-defined and relatively specific function of many carpentry tools and kitchen utensils contrasts with the more general function of faces, animals, or fruits. Warrington and Shallice (1984) have argued that the better recognition of the former items by visual agnosics is due to the clear-cut functional role of the stimuli. I concur on the importance of function, although I believe that even with such stimuli other factors influence performance. For instance, the sensory mapping of the result of use of the item is no less crucial, I believe.

One aspect of the disordered recognition profile of these patients that must be stressed is that in no case does one ever see a complete wipeout of recognition for a given category. This is a strong indication that the ability to recognize is linked to the physical characteristics of the stimulus (its properties, operations, relationships, and the movement and affective processing that it invokes in the perceiver), not to the concept that defines the category it belongs to and least of all to the name of the category.

Visual-Object Agnosia

Recognition defects for nonfacial stimuli, an extremely rare condition, is the only one that can be called true visual-object agnosia, because it occurs in the absence of prosopagnosia. Hécaen and de Ajuriaguerra (1956) provided a good description of the condition in a patient whose condition was unfortunately not appropriate for reliable anatomical analysis. On the basis of suggestions raised by that case and on the basis of my own cases and of a recent report (Feinberg et al. 1986), I believe such instances are related to unilateral lesions of the left hemisphere that involve the lateral visual cortices in occipitotemporal and occipitoparietal regions.

Nonconscious "Recognition" of Visual Stimuli by Agnosics
Under certain laboratory conditions, prosopagnosics can "recognize" familiar faces, but they do so without being aware that they do. For instance, in psychophysiological experiments, the amplitude of skin-conductance responses to familiar faces is dramatically larger than the responses to unfamiliar faces (Tranel and Damasio 1985; Bauer 1984). The responses generated by the autonomic nervous system of these subjects discriminate familiar from unfamiliar faces, which indicates that these patients possess and access knowledge of these faces, although they can not bring such knowledge into consciousness.

In recent studies Daniel Tranel and I have shown that these findings can also be obtained with nonfacial stimuli, including previously familiar buildings, cars, and even personal effects (Tranel and Damasio 1987). This is unequivocal evidence that patients with visual agnosia covertly discriminate the familiar from unfamiliar, but that the recognition process stops short of activating the information at a level accessible to consciousness.

The study of eye movements (scan paths) used by prosopagnosics to perceive familiar versus unfamiliar faces provides comparable evidence. The perception of unfamiliar faces generates predictable scan paths similar to those produced by normal individuals, while the inspection of familiar faces generates less predictable scan paths (Rizzo et al. 1986). These findings seem to indicate that these patients can access, again without being aware, the internal schemata of the unique faces they have learned.

Partial Face-Recognition Defects
Some patients with focal lesions of the visual system have less pervasive defects of recognition. Most of those patients have unilateral lesions (Damasio, Welsh, and Damasio 1987). Patients with right-sided lesions tend to have a slow approach to recognition. They often correctly recognize faces and objects that they are extremely well acquainted with but frequently make errors on those items with which they are less familiar. In my experience they are less likely to produce "don't know" responses than bilateral agnosics. On the other hand, patients with left occipital lesions tend to give quicker but incorrect

responses that are in the semantic vicinity of the approximate response. Patients with right-sided lesions appear to approach the stimulus on the basis of local fragments and to use the fragments to guide a deliberate search for the identity. The strategy often works but not always. Patients with left-hemisphere lesions appear rapidly to grasp the general identification of the subject, to the point of correctly detecting the subject's geographic and professional placement, but they may fail in the final assignation of specific identity.

Neuroanatomical Findings in Subjects with Acquired Defects of Visual Recognition

The brain damage that causes pure prosopagnosia is located in the inferior sector of the occipitotemporal region. It undercuts or directly destroys the medial and ventral surfaces of these cortices, although in some cases the lateral cortices are also involved (Damasio 1985a). The lesions invariably disconnect or destroy association cortices and largely spare the primary cortices. Brodmann's fields 18 and 19 and a fraction of higher-order cortices in cytoarchitectonic fields 37, 36, and 35 may be compromised.

The characteristic lesions in pure prosopagnosia are occipitotemporal and *not* occipitoparietal, i.e., not superior occipital and parietal. Even when the lesion trespasses into the occipitoparietal cortices, it still significantly destroys the occipitotemporal region. Lesions located exclusively in the occipitoparietal region do not cause prosopagnosia. By contrast, occipitoparietal lesions cause disturbances of visuospatial processing, stereopsis, and detection of motion. As noted above, patients with such lesions can recognize faces and even read when the stimuli are presented in the workable sector of their visual fields, although many are unable to recognize the meaning of symbolic movements (Damasio et al. 1982; Damasio 1985a).

Findings from both human and nonhuman studies reveal that within the classic areas 18 and 19 there are several functional territories specialized in mapping form, texture, stereopsis, color, and motion (Damasio 1985a; Van Essen and Maunsell 1983; Allman et al. 1985). The subareas are probably grouped in two major functional and anatomical streams. One is dedicated to the analysis of the physical structure of entities (color, texture, shape) and the other is related to the movement and position of entities in space (Ungerleider and Mishkin 1982; Damasio et al. 1982). In humans, that functional separation corresponds to the inferior and superior occipital regions, and it is clear that pure prosopagnosia is related to a disorder of the former (Damasio 1985a).

The lesions found in amnesic patients with defects in facial recognition spare the early visual association cortices, i.e., areas 17, 18, and 19. Damage occurs in the hippocampus proper, the entorhinal cortex, the amygdala, and higher-order temporal cortices located in areas 20, 21, 37, 35, 36, 38. Those areas are part of a system of processors that receive projections from the early association cortices in the inferior occipital and posterior temporal regions. In turn, those areas project to the hippocampus via the entorhinal cortex (Van Hoesen and Pandya 1975a, 1975b). Finally, all of these areas project back to points where their feeding projection originated. There is thus an intricate system of feedforward and feedback interlocking. The lesions found in amnesics with facial-recognition defects compromise the same processing system but at anatomical points rostral to the ones disrupted in the cases of pure prosopagnosia.

Mapping of Faces and Mapping of Objects

The picture that emerges from the many types of impairments of visual recognition that different lesions can cause is that different categories of entities (objects or faces) and different conditions of entities are cognitively represented in multiple ways. Recognizing the category an entity belongs to and recognizing its uniqueness depend on matching the target stimulus with a certain number of those multiple representations. If the entities belong to different categories, then different representations have different recognition weights, and success or failure of recognition must depend on access to the representation best suited for each given condition of recognition. From a physiopathological standpoint, compromised access can result from deficient progress of the inadequate perceptual build-up (due to partial destruction of functional regions or inadequate interconnection of regions) or from actual loss of critical information (due to sizable destruction of functional regions).

Critical Representations

The information critical for mapping a face so that it can later be recognized as unique must include: (*a*) facial expression, (*b*) the physical structure of the face, (*c*) the scan paths needed to perceive (*a*) and (*b*), (*d*) characteristic contexts of the face, (*e*) the participation of the face in unique episodes, and (*f*) the perceiver's affective reactions to interactions with the face.

The information critical for mapping a nonface entity includes: (*a*) properties of the physical structure of the object; (*b*) characteristic spatial relationships such as typical positioning and movements of the object in space; (c) operations of the object; (d) the outcome of such operations; (e) movements of the perceiver required to map (a), (b), and (c); (f) frequent primary relationships of the object, including typical relationships with humans and in particular with the hand, mouth, or body (for instance, a manipulable tool or a musical instrument has a prefered relationship with the hand or hands and is held in a typical posture in relation to the body; the relationships of a building and of a manipulable tool to a perceiver's body are of an entirely different nature and their sensory mappings must be different); (g) frequent secondary relationships; (h) participation in unique episodes; and (i) the perceiver's affective reaction to interaction with the object.

Other factors that play a role in learning and recognizing visual stimuli are the magnitude of exposure to the stimulus; the epoch in development at which learning occurs; the recognition level required socially by the stimulus; and the level at which recognition is sought.

The Multiplicity of Representations

The dissociations noted in face agnosia indicate unequivocally that entities generate a multiplicity of representations in the brain, each of which can lead to recognition. The identity of a given person can be recovered from the configuration of a face, from typical postures of a body, from the timbre of a voice, or from a tell-tale context. Objects too generate multiple representations.

Owing to the rich anatomical and physiological specialization within subregions of the visual association cortices, recording the varied stimuli generated by diverse entities cannot possibly occur in a single anatomical site. It must occur at different sites across multiple sensory and motor sytems, as required by the combination of diverse external signals and interactions with the perceiver. The categorization of external stimuli is thus governed by signals that emanate from external entities, by the degree of shared physical structure of those signals, and by their combinatorial arrangements. The clustering of representations in categories is naturally caused by their closeness or distance along given, intrinsically physical or relational dimensions. This results from the fact that the brain is competitively organized and probably records signals next to or overlapping with previous signals that share similar features and dimensions.

The range of representations required for each type of stimulus is varied, and so is the cognitive and neural mapping. This is also true of each unique stimulus. The reasons for this are that different stimuli have varied frequencies of occurrence in the universe; perceivers have various degrees of exposure to the stimuli, which is independent of their frequency of occurrences; and the stimuli themselves have different physical characteristics, operations, and meanings.

A Model of Facial Recognition

I view the goal of facial learning as the construction of a representation of a face that retains some part of the physical uniqueness of the face. Activating memories uniquely pertinent to the possessor of that face depends on recording physical uniqueness.

Differences among faces are limited to minimal variations in the shape and planar orientation of their components and in relational arrangements assumed by those components, i.e., the facial configuration. The ability to learn a new face relies on recording some of those differences.

Two processes must follow the establishment of a facial representation in order to permit facial recognition. First the brain must secure a representation that is relatively stable, though modifiable (an ensemble of partial records generated by a face and probabilistically available upon re-presentation so that the brain may recognize that face). Second, the brain must establish probabilistic, reliable linkages between face records and other records pertinent to the possessor of the face. Recognition cannot take place without this second step, because of a distinctive feature of my model: the records of the physical structures of a face, which are obtained on the basis of its visual characteristics, do *not* contain information on the identity of the face (Damasio et al. 1982). Face records per se, it is important to note, are insufficient for conscious recognition of that face. Although their activation may lead to autonomic, nonconscious respones, it does not produce an experience of familiarity. For familiarity and recognition to take place, face records must promote the coactivation of other nonfacial records pertinent to the possessor of the face. Those nonfacial records are both nonverbal (e.g., visual, auditory, somatic, motor, olfactory of visceral) and verbal. What type of records they are depends on what has been learned in association with the given face. The name of the possessor of the face is a part of many records linked to a face, but it is not necessary for recognition (Damasio et al. 1982). This feature of the model is central to my view of cognitive and neural organization and pertains to other stimuli as well. The sensory records of a stimulus serve as an interface to other stimuli but do not contain the information required for its identification. The comprehensive achievement of the highest level of recognition requires a neural process that is parallel, sequential, and, most important, recursive, and whose results are nonlinear. Neuroanatomically, such operations require a rich interlocking of feedforward and feedback projections (Damasio 1989).

The Process of Recognition
Drawing on traditional information-processing models of brain function, theorists have conceived the process of consciously identifying a stimulus as stepwise and sequential, with the stimulus of interest being transferred through a cascade of progressively more refined neural stations and somehow gathering an ever increasing amount of correlated information so that a comprehensive internal representation emerges in consciousness. This accords, at least superficially, with some facts of neuroanatomy and neurophysiology; namely, sensory systems do project forward into the anterior temporal and anterior frontal cortices, where integration is assumed to occur, and neurons do respond in more complex fashion and with larger receptive fields the farther away they are from the sensory portals of the brain. The consequences of the focal cerebral lesions in humans described above, however, have led me to a different view (Damasio 1989). In my view, the whole repository of direct representations of the external world must be mapped in the more posterior and "earlier" association cortices, closer to the primary sensory cortices. Progressively more anterior cortices hold knowledge about those representations, namely, about the way the separate representations of different properties, operations, or relationships of a given real object are bound together or about how separate objects are bound in time or space (Damasio et al. 1982; Damasio et al. 1985a; Damasio et al. 1985b). From this view, the fact that an ensemble of neurons responds to a number of different properties means not that neurons in that given group actually map the representations of all those properties themselves but rather that the neurons have received inputs from other neuron ensembles that do represent those properties. When higher-order neurons project back to neuron ensembles that once fired upon them during feedforward activity, the system is capable of reconstituting representations in an approximation of the way they occurred in previous experiences. In short, I believe that as neuronal units are farther removed from the primary and early association cortices, they represent reality less concretely and more in an abstract indical form. Those progressively more abstract units constitute a routing system for knowledge activation. By projecting back to other pertinent units, they coevoke real associations between properties of objects and thus attempt to replicate the original experiences that led to learning.

This view of the organization of a system capable of recognition was inspired by data on human lesions and developed to accommodate such data. But it accommodates neurophysiological data and neuroanatomical data on feedforward and feedback connectional systems.

In short, the model requires divergent units that map the physical properties of surfaces at different scales and several orders of convergent zones that know about activity in divergent units (convergent zones are distributed within association cortices of both visual and nonvisual modalities; they project back into the previous feeding level).

The elementary processes of face categorization (recognition of faces as faces or of facial expressions) can be performed with the first order of convergent zones. Further categorization (recognition of membership in an ethnic group) or recognition of unique identity depends on the higher-order convergent zones.

In this system knowledge is distributed at multiple levels and in various modes. The early units of the system represent concrete physical structure (e.g., features of entities) or some type of operation. Intermediate units represent knowledge about those concrete representations, knowledge whose binding can define entities with given features. Higher-order units know about all previous units and about their coincident activation in time. They are thus suited to bind knowledge about the relations among entities in given events (see Damasio 1989).

Note

Supported by NINDS grant PO1 NS19632.

References

Allman, J., F. Miezin, E. McGuinnes. 1985. Stimulus specific respones from beyond the classical receptive field: Neurophysiological mechanisms for local-global comparisons in visual neurons. *Annual Review of Neuroscience* 8:407–430.

Assal, G. 1969. Régression des troubles de la reconnaissance des physionomies et de la mémoire topographique chez un malade operé d'un hematome intracérébral parieto-temporal droit. *Revue Neurologique* 121:184–185.

Bauer, R. M. 1984. Autonomic recognition of names and faces in prosopagnosia: A neurophysiological application of the Guilty Knowledge Test. *Neuropsychologia* 22:457–469.

Baylis, G. C., E. T. Rolls, and C. M. Leonard. 1985. Selectivity between faces in the responses of a population of neurons in the cortex in the superior temporal sulcus of the monkey. *Brain Research* 342:91–102.

Benton, A. L. 1980. The neuropsychology of facial recognition. *American Psychologist* 35:176–186.

372   *Antonio R. Damasio*

Benton, A. L., and M. W. Van Allen. 1972. Prosopagnosia and facial discrimination. *Journal of Neurological Sciences* 15:167–172.

Bornstein, B. 1963. Prosopagnosia. In *Problems of Dynamic Neurology*, ed. L. Halpren. Jerusalem: Hadassah Medical.

Bruce, C., R. Desimone, and C. G. Gross. 1981. Visual properties of neurons in a polysensory area in superior temporal sulcus of the macaque. *Journal of Neurophysiology* 46:369–384.

Corkin, S. 1984. Lasting consequences of bilateral medial temporal lobectomy: Clinical course and experimental findings in H.M. *Seminars in Neurology* 4:249–259.

Damasio, A. R. 1985a. Disorders of complex visual processing. In *Principles of Behavioral Neurology*, ed. M. M. Mesulam, Contemporary Neurology Series, Philadelphia: F. A. Davis.

Damasio, A. R. 1985b. Prosopagnosia. *Trends in Neurosciences* 8 (3): 132–135.

Damasio, A. R. 1989. Multiregional retroactivation: A systems level model for some neural substrates of cognition. *Cognition*, in press.

Damasio, A. R., H. Damasio, and G. W. Van Hoesen. 1982. Prosopagnosia: Anatomical basis and behavioral mechanisms. *Neurology* 32:331–41.

Damasio, A. R., P. J. Eslinger, H. Damasio, G. W. Van Hoesen, and S. Cornell. 1985a. Multimodal amnesic syndrome following bilateral temporal and basal forebrain damage: The case of patient D. R. B. *Archives of Neurology* 42:252–259.

Damasio, A. R., N. Graff-Radford, P. Eslinger, H. Damasio, and N. Kassell. 1985b. Amnesia following basal forebrain lesions. *Archives of Neurology* 42:263–271.

Damasio, A. R., K. Welsh, and H. Damasio. 1986. Mechanisms of recognition impairment associated with occipitotemporal damage. *Society for Neuroscience* 12 (1): 21.

Damasio, A. R., K. Welsh, and H. Damasio. 1987. The neural substrate of visual recognition impairments. *Neurology* 37:129.

Damasio, A. R., T. Yamada, H. Damasio, J. Corbett, and J. McKee. 1980. Central achromatopsia: Behavioral, anatomic, and physiologic aspects. *Neurology* 30:1064–1071.

DeRenzi, E. 1986. Prosopagnosia in two patients with CT scan evidence of damage confined to the right hemisphere. *Neuropsychologia* 24 (3): 385–389.

Desimone, R., T. D. Albright, C. G. Gross, and C. Bruce. 1984. Stimulus-selective responses of inferior temporal neurons in the macaque. *Journal of Neuroscience* 4:2051–2062.

Faust, C. 1955. *Die zerebralen Herdstorungen bei Hinterhauptsverletzungen und ihr Beurteilung*. Stuttgart: Thieme.

Feinberg, T. E., L. Rothi, and K. Heilman. 1986. Multimodal agnosia after unilateral left hemisphere lesion. *Neurology* 36:864–867.

Gazzaniga, M. S., and C. S. Smylie. 1983. Facial recognition and brain asymmetries: Clues to underlying mechanisms. *Annals of Neurology* 13:537–540.

Gross, C. G., C. E. Rocha-Miranda, and D. B. Bender. 1972. Visual properties of neurons in inferotemporal cortex of the macaque. *Journal of Neurophysiology* 35:96–111.

Hécaen, H., and de Ajuriaguerra, J. 1956. Agnosie visuelle pour les objets inanimés par lésion unilatérale gauche. *Revue neurologique* 94:222–233.

Kendrick, K. M., and B. A. Baldwin. 1987. Cells in temporal cortex of conscious sheep can respond preferentially to the sight of faces. *Science* 236:448–450.

Landis, T., J. L. Cummings, L. Christen, J. E. Bogen, and H.-G. Imhof. 1986. Are unilateral right posterior cerebral lesions sufficient to cause prosopagnosia? Clinical and radiological findings in six additional patients. *Cortex* 22:243–252.

Leonard, C. M., E. T. Rolls, F. A. W. Wilson, and G. C. Baylis. 1985. Neurons in the amygdala of the monkey with responses selective for faces. *Behavioural Brain Research* 15:159–176.

Levy, J., G. Trevarthen, and R. W. Sperry. 1972. Perception of bilateral chimeric figures following hemispheric disconnection. *Brain* 95:61–78.

Lhermitte, J., F. Chain, R. Escourolle, B. Ducarne, and B. Pillon. 1972. Étude anatomo-clinque d'un cas de prosopagnosie. *Revue Neurologique* (Paris) 126:329–346.

Meadows, J. C. 1974. The anatomical basis of prosopagnosia. *Journal of Neurology, Neurosurgery, and Psychiatry* 34:489–501.

Meier, M. J., and L. A. French. 1965. Lateralized deficits in complex visual discrimination and bilateral transfer of reminiscence following unilateral temporal lobectomy. *Neuropsychologia* 3:261–272.

Nardelli, E., F. Buonanno, G. Coccia, A. Fiaschi, H. Terzian, and N. Rizzuto. 1982. Prosopagnosia: Report of four cases. *European Neurology* 21:289–297.

Newcombe, F. 1979. The processing of visual information in prosopagnosia and acquired dyslexia: Functional versus physiological interpretation. In *Research in psychology and medicine*, vol. 1, ed. D. J. Osborne, M. M. Gruneberg, and J. R. Eiser. London: Academic Press.

Overman, W. H., and R. W. Doty. 1982. Hemispheric specialization displayed by man but not macaques for analysis of faces. *Neuropsychologia* 20:113–128.

Pallis, C. A. 1955. Impaired identification of faces and places with agnosia for colours. *Journal of Neurology, Neurosurgery, and Psychiatry* 18:218–224.

Perrett, D. I., E. T. Rolls, and W. Caan. 1982. Visual neurons responsive to faces in the monkey temporal cortex. *Experimental Brain Research* 47:329–342.

Rizzo, M., and H. Damasio. 1985. Impairment of stereopsis with focal brain lesions. *Annals of Neurology* 18 (1): 147.

Rizzo, M. R., J. Corbett, H. Thompson, A. Damasio. 1986. Spatial contrast sensitivity in prosopagnosia. *Neurology* 36 (9): 1254–1256.

Rizzo, M., R. Hurtig, and A. R. Damasio. 1987. The role of scanpaths in facial recognition and learning. *Annals of Neurology* 22:41–45.

Rolls, E. T., G. C. Baylis, and C. M. Leonard. 1985. Role of low and high spatial frequencies in the face-selective responses of neurons in the cortex in the superior temporal sulcus in the monkey. *Vision Research* 25:1021–1035.

Rosch, E., C. Mervis, W. Gray, D. Johnson, and P. Boyes-Braem, 1976. Basic objects in natural categories. *Cognitive Psychology* 8:382–439.

Rosenfeld, S. A., and G. W. Van Hoesen. 1979. Face recognition in the rhesus monkey. *Neuropsychologia* 17:503–509.

Scoville, W. B., and B. Milner. 1957. Loss of recent memory after bilateral hippocampal lesions. *Journal of Neurology, Neurosurgery, and Psychiatry* 20:11–21.

Sperry, R., E. Zaidel, and D. Zaidel. 1979. Self recognition and social awareness in the deconnected minor hemisphere. *Neuropsychologia* 17:153–166.

Tranel, D., and A. Damasio. 1985. Knowledge without awareness: An autonomic index of recognition of prosopagnosics. *Science* 228 (21): 1453–1454.

Tranel, D., and A. Damasio. 1987. Autonomic (covert) discrimination of familiar stimuli in patients with visual agnosia. *Neurology* 37:129.

Tranel, D., A. Damasio, and H. Damasio. 1988. Intact recognition of facial expression, gender, and age in patients with impaired recognition of face identity. *Neurology* 38:690–696.

Tzavaras, A., H. Hecaen, and H. Le Bras. 1970. Le probleme de la specificité du deficit de la reconnaissance du visage humain lors des lesions hemispheriques unilaterales. *Neuropsychologia* 8:403–416.

Ungerleider, L. G., and M. Mishkin. 1982. Two cortical visual systems. In *The analysis of visual behavior*, ed. D. J. Ingle, R. J. W. Mansfield, and M. A. Goodale. Cambridge: MIT Press.

Van Essen, D. C., and J. H. R. Maunsell. 1983. Hierarchical organization and function streams in the visual cortex. *Trends in Neurosciences* 6:370–375.

Van Hoesen, G. W., and D. N. Pandya. 1975a. Some connections of the entorhinal (area 28) and perirhinal (area 35) cortices of the rhesus monkey: I. Temporal lobe afferents. *Brain Research* 95:1–24.

Van Hoesen, G. W., and D. N. Pandya. 1975b. Some connections of the entorhinal (area 28) and perirhinal (area 35) cortices of the rhesus monkey: III. Efferent connections. *Brain Research* 95:39–59.

Warrington, E. K., and T. Shallice. 1984. Category specific semantic impairments. *Brain* 107:829–854.

Whitely, A. M., and E. K. Warrington. 1977. Prosopagnosia: A clinical, psychological, and anatomical study of three patients. *Journal of Neurology, Neurosurgery, and Psychiatry* 40:395–403.

Wilbrand, H. 1892. Ein Fall von Seelenblindheit und Hemianopsie mit Sectionsbefund. *Deutsche Z. nervenheik.* 2:361–387.

Editor's Comments

In search of a clearer understanding of the relationship between brain and mind, researchers for over a century have systematically carried out attempts to relate loss of cognitive or emotional function to specific changes in the brain anatomy after injury. Such efforts have led to extremely useful information regarding, on the one hand, the discrete brain organization for certain functional capacities and representations and, on the other, the complex and often expansive nature of the circuitries that connect functionally related neural substrates. The widespread distribution of these connected, discrete loci reflects partly the physically separate nature of the sensory substrates involved in the perception of real-world objects (e.g., bells have shapes, sounds, and vibrations), partly the fact that objects in the real world can be linked to movement and action (e.g., bells can be held and shaken), partly associations between objects and emotionally laden memories (e.g., wedding bells and church bells tolling for the dead), and partly the purpose of having object representation participate in mental processes that may be distant from the representation itself (e.g., creating a sentence with the word *bell* in it or deriving a mathematical function for the bell-shaped curve).

Brains are composed of genes and other intrinsic and extrinsic molecules, synapses, small circuits, distributed networks, connections to other systems (like the immune and endocrine systems), and perhaps links to other brains (by pheromones and other such far-reaching chemical connections). Thus, the first problem to be solved has to do with the question of how changes in behavior after brain injury or developmental disorders correspond to changes at different levels of anatomical description. In other words, when brain injury results in the loss of a previously acquired capacity or in the partial degradation of the representation of an object, does this loss or degradation reflect changes taking place at the molecular level, at the level of microcircuits, at the level of intra- or interhemispheric connections, or at the level of organismal or interpersonal connections?

With our improving capability to describe behavior and the brain at several levels at once and accurately to measure changes in functional and physical states, it may be possible to detect how mechanisms and processes map onto each other. A fastidiously chronological approach is crucial, since changes occurring at one level tend to propagate (often quite rapidly) to other levels and thus potentially to obscure the level at which physical change is relevant to the observed behaviors. For instance, withholding light from the retinal photoreceptors of one eye during critical developmental stages produces changes in receptor architecture, the organization of retinal microcircuits, and the connectional and cellular organization of the nearby visual thalamus and the more distant visual cortex, as well as changes in visual perception. In the mature state damage to the behaviorally relevant architecture of a neuronal circuit propagates rapidly to the lowest levels of gene regulation and expression, and the molecular events that follow may merely reflect behaviorally mute attempts at repairing the physical damage. Attributing changes in behavior to changes at one or another physical level, and thus addressing the issue of the physical representation of mind, depends at least in part on the ability to detect change and sequences of change.

Moreover, detection of behavioral and anatomical changes depends on methods of detection, as well as on the brain mechanisms and mental processes that ultimately explain change. Thus, the documentation of functional change and anatomical disruption carries more weight than the absence of such demonstrations. For example, demonstration of change may fail because the injured structure may be irrelevant to the functional capacity under study, because repair occurs at an anatomical level different from that under observation, or because overall function is not sufficiently degraded and the patient can still complete the task. Preservation of overall function does not necessarily imply redundancy of processes and multiplicity of brain representations; rather, it may reflect the useful availability of several strategies for solving particular cognitive problems. Such processes may help some patients escape prosopagnosia and others to "recover" from disabling childhood reading difficulties.

Chapter 14

The Neural Origin of Developmental Dyslexia: Implications for Medicine, Neurology, and Cognition

Albert M. Galaburda, Glenn D. Rosen, and Gordon F. Sherman

Introduction

Developmental dyslexia refers to unexpected difficulty in learning to read, which usually translates into acquisition that is somewhere in between slow and effortful on the one hand and slow, effortful, incomplete, and anomalous on the other (Critchley 1964; Vellutino 1979). The difficulty is unexpected only in that there are no commonly recognized impediments to learning in general (e.g., significant physical limitations, general intellectual inadequacies, general attentional disorders, significant emotional disturbances, and absent or significantly aberrant environmental stimuli).

Pathogenetic Considerations

"Unexpected" does not at all speak to as yet unknown physical, cognitive, attentional, emotional, or cultural limitations that may apply specifically to the task of reading acquisition. Developmental dyslexia may in principle reflect alterations in any or all of these factors, as long as they are relatively specific to reading. I say "relatively specific" because by and large dyslexics exhibit a limited degree of alteration in other, related cognitive behaviors (Vellutino 1979; Birch 1962; Vogel 1975; also see Bertelson and De Gelder in this volume), but this does not change my overall argument.

Perhaps the observation that most pointedly indicates the likely noncultural nature of the pathogenesis of the disorder is its heritability (DeFries and Decker 1982; Smith, Kimberling, et al. 1983; Smith, Pennington, et al. 1983). Clearly, cultural predispositions to reading problems are conceivable in isolated cultural niches, but none have been observed. Moreover, dyslexia is found in widely different cultures and social strata. So on epidemiologic grounds the cultural environment, characterized, for instance, by the language to be read and the educational system, is not likely to play a significant role in the pathogenesis of dyslexia, although it is known that the cultural environment can have profound effects on the severity and consequences of its expression.

All of the other possible factors (specific physical, cognitive, attentional, and emotional characteristics) can be hereditary either through direct genomic effects or through heritable forms of epigenetic regulation of the relevant genomic activity. In other words, a family may be predisposed to developmental dyslexia because genes that code for the specific brain substrates supporting the altered cognitive capacities are abnormal or because environmental factors—whether extrinsic or intrinsic to the brain or to the individual—that can modify the expression of those genes are present in successive generations. For instance, some environmental toxins, infectious agents, and aberrant intrauterine hormonal or metabolic milieux, each of which may be present in successive generations, could lead to unusual brains (Friede 1975). Again, epidemiological research should help to restrict the possible pathogenetic role of each of these factors, but none to date is conclusive in this regard. To my knowledge no specific toxin or other extrinsic noxious effect has been identified, and genomic aberrations or intrinsic environmental anomalies, dated mostly in the fetal and immediately postnatal period, have only been hinted at without adequate proof (Smith, Pennington, et al. 1983; Geschwind and Galaburda 1985).

We have failed to pinpoint pathogenetic factors on the basis of epidemiology alone. Since one of the important possibilities is anomalous anatomical structures caused by genetic or epigenetic disturbances, the next step involves physically examining the brain. These efforts have been productive in other developmental and acquired conditions, and in fact, anatomical findings, coupled with neurobiological data on normal anatomy and development, can be useful for pointing to pathogenesis. For instance, finding noncommunicating hydrocephalus in a newborn may lead to examination of the aqueduct of Sylvius, the discovery of gliosis, and the implication of inflammatory processes in etiology of the hydrocephalus (Blackwood et al. 1958; Friede 1975).

Various lines of reasoning, beginning with the observation that the behavioral profile in dyslexia is relatively restricted to linguistic and closely related cognitive capacities, suggested that the level of anatomical analysis most likely to produce findings was that of neuronal assemblies, rather than molecular and cellular levels of analysis on the one hand and the whole brain on the other. Sufficient data were available from molecular neurobiological approaches to the study of learning and memory to show that molecular reactions were shared by widely different systems involved in different cognitive activities and therefore to suggest that molecular-level errors would likely be expressed in many systems and lead to more general cognitive disturbances (Kandel and Schwartz 1982 and Dudai in this volume). Such molecular mechanisms are more likely in primary attention deficits accompanied with widespread intellectual difficulties than in developmental dyslexia. Alternatively, by presently altogether unknown mechanisms, generalized molecular errors could produce localized cognitive deficits, because different systems depended differently on the altered molecular event, a far less parsimonious interpretation.

Cellular-level errors are also more likely to lead to relatively widespread cognitive abnormalities, since no specific neuronal type characterizes areas of the brain that support language and reading or areas supporting the cognitive functions occasionally seen to be altered in conjunction with the reading disorder. Involvement at the level of the whole brain by factors acting primarily at that level (e.g., widespread physical injury or meningoencephalitis) should also lead to more widespread cognitive dysfunction.

Anatomical Findings

Anatomical approaches to the study of developmental dyslexia were suggested in our laboratory by considerations similar to those described above. Our research approach was set at the level of cellular architectonics, which attends to the three-dimensional arrangement of large groups of neurons presumably comprising distinct neural networks and their connectional interrelationships in experimental animal models. We particularly concentrated on cortical and subcortical areas known to support linguistic capacities, since the behavioral disorder in developmental dyslexia is primarily linguistic. To exclude physical anomalies specific to more basic auditory and visual behaviors, we also examined neuronal assemblies associated with the auditory and visual functions.

The behavioral literature also suggested that dyslexics exhibited disturbances in cerebral dominance (cf. Hier et al. 1978; Haslam et al. 1981). So it seemed advisable also to search for oddities in the manifestation of anatomical asymmetry of the language regions, since patterns of architectonic asymmetry were already known for neurologically intact populations (Geschwind and Galaburda 1985; Galaburda, LeMay, et al. 1978; Galaburda, Sanides, et al. 1978; Galaburda 1980; Eidelberg and Galaburda 1982, 1984).

Architectonic Microdysgenesis
Five male dyslexic brains were entirely sectioned in thicknesses of 35 μm, and the cerebrocortical cytoarchitecture of every 20th section was examined (Galaburda, Sherman, et al. 1985). It was possible to recognize all previously described cerebrocortical areas in their appropriate topographic locations, but all of the brains showed focal areas of cellular disorganization, labeled *microdysgenesis*. They consisted of nests of subpial, ectopic neurons (abnormal placement) and of focally disorganized, dysplastic cortical layering (abnormal architecture). Several of these had associated disorganized bundles of fibers and small blood vessels. Rarely, the areas of dysplasia and ectopia led to frank disruption of the contour of the pial surface to form a brain wart or microgyria (Friede 1975; MacBride and Kemper 1982; Ranke 1905). More often, the cellular disturbances were small and focal, each measuring 700 to 1000 μm in diameter, and numbered between 30 and 150 per brain.

The distribution of these anomalies was bihemispheric in all the brains, but they were more numerous in the left hemisphere. They primarily affected the perisylvian cortices, particularly the frontal and temporal opercula, but isolated foci could be seen in other areas of the cerebral convexity and the sagittal plane as well. There was no particular involvement of the primary auditory and visual neural substrates, although one case showed architectonic distortions in the medial geniculate nuclei (Galaburda and Eidelberg 1982).

Small foci of abnormally placed neurons and focally distorted cortical lamination are occasionally found in routine autopsy studies (Veith and Schwindt 1976; Morel and Wildi 1952). Thus, the percentage of brains with anomalies depends on the level of detail at which the analysis is carried out and the source of the specimens, and it ranges between 3 and 30 percent in the literature. Our own studies of normative specimens, prepared and analyzed identically to the dyslexic brains, disclosed four foci distributed among three out of ten brains (Kaufmann and Galaburda 1988).

These types of abnormalities are thought to reflect disorders of late neuronal migration taking place at, around, or shortly after, the middle of gestation (MacBride and Kemper 1982; Dvorák and Feit 1977; Dvorák et al. 1978; Bertrand and Gruner 1955; Grcevic and Robert 1961; Crome 1952; and Caviness et al. in this volume). They are seen in association with several congenital toxic, vascular, and infectious insults (Martin and Norman 1967; Christensen and Melchior

1967; Hicks 1953; Slotnick and Brent 1966), and they can be produced experimentally in animals by similar mechanisms of cortical injury during comparable developmental stages (Dvorák and Feit 1977; Dvorák et al. 1978; Sato et al. 1982). In related studies of rodent models of these types of cortical anomaly (see Sherman et al. in this volume), we have showed that the events involved in the formation of ectopias and dysplasias lead not only to neurons' being displaced to abnormal locations and in abnormal arrangements but also to an increase in the total numbers of neurons present in the vicinity of the focal abnormalities. Moreover, a preliminary research finding is that local and interhemispheric connectivity appears increased in the region of focal abnormality (Galaburda et al. 1987).

We have argued that the uniform prevalence of large numbers of ectopic and dysplastic foci in male dyslexic brains represents a significant association with the behavioral phenotype and may reflect congenital focal injury (Galaburda, Sherman, et al. 1985b). Below we further consider whether a tendency to suffer certain types of injury can be inherited.

One brain of a dyslexic woman showed focal laminar disorganization because of localized neuronal loss and gliosis, rather than as a result of displaced or disorganized neurons. Many of the microscars were densely myelinated, which suggested that the original damage took place before the second year of life and as early as the late prenatal period. The number of focal lesions in this case was comparable to that of dysplastic and ectopic foci in the male brains, and their distribution was likewise primarily in the left hemisphere and the perisylvian areas. The implications of these findings are obscure at this time, and any hypothesis will have to await the study of additional female brains.

Asymmetry in the Brain
It is now well accepted that some regions of the cerebral cortex are asymmetrical in size between the hemispheres (Geschwind and Galaburda 1985). Some of these asymmetries have been demonstrated at several levels from gross anatomical, through architectonic, to neurochemical and may involve cortical as well as subcortical regions, since the grey matter contains cell somata and the white matter connecting fiber bundles. One of the most striking of these asymmetries is visible in a gross cortical landmark known as the planum temporale (Geschwind and Levitsky 1968). This region, found on the supratemporal plane just posterior to the transverse auditory gyrus of Heschl, is much more often larger on the left side than on the right. We have reanalyzed the distribution of planum temporale asymmetry in the

brains reported by Geschwind and Levitsky (1968) and have found a bimodal curve that shows a large peak in the leftward asymmetrical range tapering down to the symmetrical range and again peaking slightly in the extreme rightward asymmetrical range. The areas under the respective parts of the curve show that 75 percent of the brains are asymmetrical toward the left, 15 percent symmetrical (less than 10 percent difference between the sides), and 10 percent asymmetrical toward the right, with most of the latter showing extreme rightward asymmetry (Galaburda et al. 1987).

Thus far all reports of radiologically determined brain asymmetry involving either the planum temporale or the length of the occipital poles state that the asymmetry distribution differs in dyslexic populations, because of increased numbers of symmetrical brains, increased numbers with reverse asymmetry (right greater), or both (Hier et al.1978; Haslam et al. 1981). Our own autopsy studies of five male and one female dyslexic brains in which the planum temporale was available for full measurement have shown symmetry in each case (Galaburda, Sherman, et al. 1985). Since the proportion of brains that are symmetrical in the planum temporale range approximately from 15 to 25 percent in published reports of normative studies, we have argued that the consistent presence of symmetry and unexpected asymmetry in the dyslexic brains is significantly associated with the behavioral phenotype (Galaburda, Sherman, et al. 1985). These distributions still hold even if corrections are made for the fact that some of the dyslexic individuals whose brains were studied were left-handed (in normative left-handed studies the proportions of symmetrical brains hovers at around 50 to 60 percent; Hochberg and LeMay 1975).

The received belief is that language is lateralized to the left, lateralized to the right, or shared between the two sides in proportions varying according to the individual's laterality bias. One implication of this belief is that there is an approximately constant amount of language substrate to be distributed between the hemispheres according to laterality. Our anatomical findings falsify this prediction. We find that the total amount of language substrate in a particular language area varies with degree of asymmetry (Galaburda et al. 1987; also see Sherman et al. in this volume). Brains that are increasingly symmetrical in the planum temporale have more total planum cortex than those that are asymmetrical, and in the latter cases, as the asymmetry increases, the total amount of planum cortex continues to decrease. Furthermore, the diminution in total planum cortex with increasing asymmetry results primarily from diminution in one side, the right side in most cases. Related studies of rat visual cortex have showed that with increasing asymmetry of architectonic area there appears to be a diminution in the total number of neurons pertaining to that area but no significant changes in the architectonic pattern per se (Galaburda, Aboitz, et al. 1985; also see Sherman et al. in this volume). Moreover, other related studies have showed that in the symmetrical cases, with the increase in the number of neurons there is an increase in the density of interhemispheric connections, in comparison with the asymmetrical cases (Rosen et al. 1987; also see Sherman et al. in this volume). We must conclude, therefore, that the brains of dyslexics have increased numbers of neurons and connections in the symmetrical language areas studied.

To summarize, male dyslexic brains have revealed an unexpectedly uniform absence of left-right asymmetry in the language area and focal dysgenesis referrable to midgestation in at least part of the left cortical areas ordinarily involved in language function, but possibly having more widespread cytoarchitectonic and connectional repercussions. A single dyslexic female brain showed planum temporale symmetry and multiple small areas of actual scarring (gliosis and loss of neurons) predominantly in the left-hemisphere perisylvian cortex attributable to damage occurring some time between late in gestation and two years of age. Both types of changes in the male brains are associated with increased numbers of neurons and connections and qualitatively different patterns of cellular architecture and connections. We tentatively conclude that excessive neurons and connections organized into anomalous three-dimensional architectures may represent a significant pathogenetic factor behind dyslexia and that language-area symmetry and early damage to the left hemisphere, albeit focal and subtle, represent risk factors.

Further Epidemiologic Studies

Since absence of standard brain asymmetry of the language areas and the presence of microdysgenesis or early scarring in the cerebral cortex characterize the dyslexic brains studied thus far, is there any evidence to help pinpoint possible developmental triggers for such changes? Furthermore, can those triggers be inherited or otherwise present in successive generations? In the case of symmetry and asymmetry, there is a fair amount of data to support the claim that cerebral dominance and presumed associated brain asymmetries are partly under direct genetic control (see Habib and Galaburda 1987). Epigenetic regulation of the expression of these genetic traits is also possible and is the subject of extensive discussion elsewhere (Geschwind and Galaburda 1985). This leaves the inheritance of focal injury to the developing brain to be discussed.

There is little evidence that the neurons and connections comprising neural networks underlying specific cognitive capacities, such as language, all share any particular, genetically dictated characteristic. The ability to make language areas out of auditory cortices in hearing individuals or out of parieto-occipital cortices in congenitally deaf-mute individuals merely on the basis of peripheral influences shows that the ordinary language areas are probably not genetically determined (Damasio et al. 1986; Bellugi et al. in this volume). On the other hand, the explanation for the heritability of focally directed damage to language-related areas of the brain may come from clinical epidemiologic studies that have linked anomalous cerebral dominance (left handedness and ambidexterity) to learning disability (including dyslexia) and certain disorders of immune function (including allergies and autoimmunity) that tend to run in families (Geschwind and Behan 1982, 1984; Geschwind 1984; Schachter and Galaburda 1986). A comparable link between similar brain anomalies, learning disturbances, and autoimmunity and allergy has been demonstrated in certain inbred strains of mice (see Sherman, Rosen, and Galaburda in this volume).

Although much more information is needed, we have a possible pathogenetic link to the brain anomalies. For instance, it has been shown that pregnant mothers with the autoimmune condition known as systemic lupus erythematosus—which in fact is one of the disorders associated with increased incidence of dyslexia (Lahita 1988)—carry antibodies that can damage fetal heart tissue after crossing the placenta (Scott et al. 1983). Although there are several other examples of immune-based injury to fetal tissues (see Galaburda 1986), it still remains to be shown that injury can take place in the fetal brain via similar mechanisms. Preliminary evidence from the laboratory of one of our collaborators has showed that pregnant rabbits inoculated with autotoxic antibodies give birth to animals with marked cerebral dysmorphism, including holotelencephaly (also see Slotnick and Brent 1966). Some of our current efforts in the laboratory are aimed at discovering evidence for immune injury in the developing brains of immune-defective mice with resulting learning disorders and anomalies in cerebral dominance (see Sherman, Rosen, and Galaburda in this volume).

Thus, the heritable mechanism for immune-based early focal brain injury that this line of research is apt to demonstrate relates to the inheritance of a tendency to develop immune disorders, some of which can in turn produce the observed damage. The focal nature of the damage by the proposed mechanism may implicate locally expressed antigens restricted to language-related neural systems, but as previously stated, there is no evidence to date that specific antigens are peculiar to linguistic and related neural networks at any time of development. Yet more widely expressed antigens may be targets with focal consequences for as yet unspecified reasons. For example, focal effects despite widespread expression of target antigens may be explained by, for instance, an intervening vascular mechanism. Thus, damage to blood vessels does not ordinarily lead to tissue injury in the total field of perfusion of the affected vessel because there are collateral perfusion channels. So early vascular damage by circulating autotoxic antibodies could result in relatively focal damage. Moreover, autoimmune and allergic disorders very often make blood vessels their targets of injury (Blackwood et al. 1958). Clearly, these speculations come very early in the research program, but they are ultimately amenable to empirical testing.

Future Research

Future research on dyslexia and the brain should include additional epidemiological studies, which would help narrow the range of etiological mechanisms and also identify biological markers for dyslexia. Additional work must be done to better specify the nature of the cognitive disorder and the changes affecting the three-dimensional neural substrates underlying the altered cognitive structures. As neuroscience endeavors to describe at lower and lower levels possibly altered components of the malfunctioning neural system, efforts should be made to reconstruct these findings in models designed to test their possibly causal role in dyslexia. Finally, actual genetic and epigenetic triggers and mechanisms involved in the production of anomalous brain architectures need to be tested in experimental neuropathological models along lines guided by findings of epidemiologic research.

References

Bertrand, I., Gruner, J. 1955. The status of verrucosus of the cerebral cortex. *Journal of Neuropathology and Experimental Neurology* 14:331–347.

Birch, H. G. 1962. Dyslexia and maturation of visual function." In *Reading Disability*, ed. J. Mahoney. Baltimore: Johns Hopkins University Press.

Blackwood, W., McMenemey, W. H., Meyer, A., Norman, R. M., and Russell, D. S. 1958. *Greenfield's Neuropathology*. London: Edward Arnold.

Christensen, E., and Melchior, J. 1967. *Cerebral palsy—A clinical and neuropathological study*. London: William Heinemann Medical Books.

Critchley, M. 1964. *Developmental dyslexia*. London: William Heinemann Medical Books.

Crome, L. 1952. Microgyria. *Journal of Pathology and Bacteriology* 64:479–495.

Damasio, A., Bellugi, U., Damasio, H., Poizner, H., and Gilder, J. V. 1986. Sign language aphasia during left-hemisphere Amytal injection. *Nature* 322:363–365.

DeFries, J. C., and Decker, S. N. 1982. Genetic aspects of reading disability: A family study. In *Reading disorders: Varieties and treatments*, ed. R. N. Malatesha and P. G. Aaron. New York: Academic Press.

Dvořák, K., and Feit, J. 1977. Migration of neuroblasts through partial necrosis of the cerebral cortex in newborn rats—Contribution to the problems of morphological development and developmental period of cerebral microgyria. *Acta Neuropathologica* (Berlin) 38:203–212.

Dvořák, K., Feit, J., and Juránková, Z. 1978. Experimentally induced focal microgyria and status verrucosus deformis in rat—Pathogenesis and interrelation histological and autoradiographical study. *Acta Neurologica* (Berlin) 44:121–129.

Eidelberg, D., and Galaburda, A. M. 1982. Symmetry and asymmetry in the human posterior thalamus, Part I: Cytoarchitectonic analysis in normals. *Archives of Neurology* 39:325–332.

Eidelberg, D., and Galaburda, A. M. 1984. Inferior parietal lobule: Divergent architectonic asymmetries in the human brain. *Archives of Neurology* 41:843–852.

Friede, R. L. 1975. *Developmental neuropathology*. Pp. 57–61. New York: Springer.

Galaburda, A. M. 1980. La région de Broca: Observations anatomiques faires un siècle après la mort de son découvreur. *Revue Neurologique* 136:609–616.

Galaburda, A. M. 1986. Research problems concerning some acquired and developmental neurobehavioral disorders. In *Neuroimmunology: Crossroads between behavior and disease*, ed. C. W. Cotman, A. M. Galaburda, B. S. McEwen, and D. M. Schneider. New York: Raven Press.

Galaburda, A. M., Aboitiz, F., Rosen, G. D., and Sherman, G. F. 1985. Histologic asymmetries in the rat's primary visual cortex: Implications for mechanisms of cerebral asymmetry. *Cortex* 22:151–160.

Galaburda, A. M., Corsiglía, J., Rosen, G. D., and Sherman, G. F. 1987. Planum temporale asymmetry: Reappraisal since Geschwind and Levitsky. *Neuropsychologia* 25:853–868.

Galaburda, A. M., and Eidelberg, D. 1982. Symmetry and asymmetry in the human posterior thalamus, Part II: Thalamic lesions in a case of developmental dyslexia. *Archives of Neurology* 39:333–336.

Galaburda, A. M., LeMay, M., Kemper, T. L., and Geschwind, N. 1978. Right-left asymmetries in the brain. *Science* 199:852–856.

Galaburda, A. M., Sanides, F., and Geschwind, N. 1978. Human brain: Cytoarchitectonic left-right asymmetries in the temporal speech region. *Archives of Neurology* 35:812–817.

Galaburda, A. M., Sherman, G. F., Rosen, G. D., Aboitiz, F., and Geschwind, N. 1985. Developmental dyslexia: Four consecutive patients with cortical anomalies. *Annals of Neurology* 18:222–223.

Geschwind, N. 1984. Immunological associations of Cerebral Dominance. In *Neuroimmunology*, ed. P. O. Behan and F. Spreafico, Serono Symposia Publications, vol. 12, pp. 451–461. New York: Raven Press.

Geschwind, N., and Behan, P. 1982. Left-handedness: Association with immune disease, migraine, and developmental learning disorder. *Proceedings of the National Academy of Sciences* (USA) 79:5097–5100.

Geschwind, N., and Behan, P. 1984. Laterality, hormones and immunity. In *Cerebral lateralization: Biological mechanisms, associations, and pathology,* ed. N. Geschwind and A. M. Galaburda. Cambridge: MIT Press.

Geschwind, N., and Galaburda, A. M. 1985. Cerebral lateralization: Biological mechanisms, association, and pathology. *Archives of Neurology* 42:428–462, 521–556, 634–654.

Geschwind, N., and Levitsky, W. 1968. Human brain: Left-right asymmetries in temporal speech region. *Science* 161:186–187.

Grcevic, N., and Robert, F. 1961. Verrucose dysplasia of the cerebral cortex. *Journal of Neuropathology and Experimental Neurology* 20:399–411.

Habib, M., and Galaburda, A. M. 1986. Determinants biologues de la dominance cérébrale. *Revue Neurologique* 142:869–894.

Haslam, R. H. A., Dalby, J. T., Johns, R. D., and Rademaker, A. W. 1981. Cerebral asymmetry in developmental dyslexia. *Archives of Neurology* 38:679–682.

Hicks, S. P. 1953. Developmental malformations produced by radiation: A timetable of development. *American Journal of Roentgenology* 2:272–293.

Hier, D. B., LeMay, M., Rosenberger, P. B., and Perlo, V. P. 1978. Developmental dyslexia: Evidence for a subgroup with a reversal cerebral asymmetry. *Archives of Neurology* 35:90–92.

Hochberg, F. H., and LeMay, M. 1975. Arteriographic correlates of handedness. *Neurology* 25:218–222.

Kandel, E. R., and Schwartz, J. H. 1982. Molecular biology of learning: Modulation of transmitter release. *Science* 218:433–443.

Kaufmann, W. E., and Galaburda, A. M. 1989. Cerebrocortical microdysgenesis in neurologically normal subjects: A histopathologic study. *Neurology* 39:238–244.

Lahita, R. G. 1988. Systemic lupus erythematosus: Learning disability of the male offspring of female patients and relationship to laterality. *Psychoneuroendocrinology* 13:385–396.

MacBride, M. C., and Kemper, T. L. 1982. Pathogenesis of four-layered microgyric cortex in man. *Acta Neuropathologica* (Berlin) 57:93–98.

Martin, J. K., and Norman, R. M. 1967. Maple syrup urine disease in an infant with microgyria. *Developmental Medicine and Child Neurology* 9:152–159.

Morel, F., and Wildi, E. 1952. Dysgénésie nodulaire disséminée de l'écorce frontale. *Revue Neurologique* 87:251–270.

Ranke, O. 1905. Status corticus verucosus deformis. *Zeitschrift fur die gesamte Neurologie und Psychiatrie* 28:635.

Rosen, G. D., Sherman, G. F., and Galaburda, A. M. 1987. Neocortical symmetry and asymmetry in the rat: Different patterns of collosal connections. *Society for Neuroscience Abstracts* 13:44.

Sato, H., Sato, N., Tamaki, N., and Matsumoto, S. 1982. Experimentally induced cranial meningocele and cerebral microgyria. *Brain Development* 4:73–75.

Schachter, S. C., and Galaburda, A. M. 1986. Development and biological associations of cerebral dominance: Review and possible biological mechanisms. *Journal of the American Academy of Child Psychiatry* 25:741–750.

Scott, J. S., Maddison, P. J., Taylor, P. V., Esscher, E., Scott, O., and Skinner, R. P. 1983. Connective tissue disease, antibodies, ribonucleoprotein, and congenital heart block. *New England Journal of Medicine* 309:209–212.

Slotnick, V., and Brent, R. L. 1966. The production of congentical malformations using tissue antisera. *Journal of Immunology* 96:606–610.

Smith, S. D., Kimberling, W. J., Pennington, B. F., and Lubs, H. A. 1983. Specific reading disability: Identification of an inherited form through linkage analysis. *Science* 219:1345–1347.

Smith, S. D., Pennington, B. F., Kimberling, W. J., and Lubs, H. A. 1983. A genetic analysis of specific reading disability. In *Genetic aspects of speech and language disorders*, ed. C. L. Ludlow and J. A. Cooper, pp. 169–178. New York: Academic Press.

Veith, G., and Schwindt, W. 1976. Pathologisch-anatomischer Beitrag zum Problem "Nichtsesshaftigkeit." *Fortschritte der Neurologie, Psychiatrie, und iher Grenzgebiete* 44:1–21.

Vellutino, F. R. 1979. *Dyslexia: Theory and research*. Cambridge: MIT Press.

Vogel, S. A. 1975. *Syntactic abilities in normal and dyslexic children*. Baltimore: University Park Press.

Chapter 15

Animal Models of Developmental Dyslexia: Brain Lateralization and Cortical Pathology

Gordon F. Sherman, Glenn D. Rosen, and Albert M. Galaburda

Introduction

Two distinct anatomic differences exist between the brains of male dyslexics and normal readers studied at autopsy: focal cortical dysplasias and ectopias (microdysgenesis) and symmetry in a typically asymmetric language region (Galaburda and Kemper 1979; Galaburda et al. 1985b; Galaburda et al., this volume). Five male dyslexic brains have been examined, and every case has shown some degree of cerebrocortical microdysgenesis. These anomalies of cortical architecture consist of collections of neurons in layer I (ectopias), associated laminar and columnar disorganization (dysplasia), and occasional distortion of the pial contour in the form of cortical nodules (verrucous dysplasia) or fused, small gyri (microgyria). The characteristic appearance and location of the neuropathology suggest that the anomalies arise during the late migrational to early postmigrational stage (weeks 20 to 24) of fetal corticogenesis (McBride and Kemper 1982). The prevalence, location, and severity of the cortical changes differ greatly from those seen in a sample of 10 identically processed normal brains (Kaufmann and Galaburda 1989) and from other reports in the literature (Morel and Wildi 1952; for a review see Kemper 1984).

The other significant finding in the dyslexic brains is the consistent absence of the expected leftward asymmetry of the language-relevant cortical area known as the planum temporale, which is replaced by symmetry, a finding seen in only 16 to 24 percent of normal brains (Geschwind and Levitsky 1968; Galaburda et al. 1987b; Galaburda et al., this volume).

We considered in the previous chapter possible genetic and epigenetic factors linking the two types of anatomical findings to the dyslexic brain. Using epidemiologic studies, we also discussed possible pathogenetic events that trigger the developmental reorganization of the affected areas of the cerebral cortex. Our central hypothesis is that an immunological interaction between mother and fetus disrupts the normal mechanism of neuronal migration and thus leads to the observed cortical dysgenesis (Sherman et al. 1988). The triggering event may also modify patterns of cerebral asymmetry, which are otherwise loosely genetically encoded (see Geschwind and Galaburda 1987). The anomalies of architecture and asymmetry may be accompanied by changes in the number of neurons (and perhaps in neuronal types) and significantly altered patterns of connectivity, which may in turn account for the cognitive difficulties seen in dyslexia.

The program of research employing experimental animals seeks to model the two cardinal findings in the dyslexic brains: the alteration in the pattern of cerebral asymmetry, and the disturbance of neuronal migration and assembly leading to focal microdysgenesis of the cerebral cortex. The rat tends to be both behaviorally and anatomically asymmetric (Denenberg 1981; Diamond et al. 1975, 1981). It is being used in our laboratory to study development and variation in anatomic asymmetry. The epidemiological links among anomalous cerebral dominance, developmental dyslexia, and disorders of the immune system (Geschwind and Behan 1982; also see Galaburda et al. in this volume) suggested to us that genetically immune-disordered mice might constitute a useful model of immunopathological-neuropathological interactions during corticogenesis. The results from these two lines of inquiry will be detailed in this chapter.

Mechanisms of Anatomic Asymmetry

The first goal of this research has been to specify the differences that exist between brain areas that are symmetric (as in the dyslexic situation) and asymmetric, in search of organizational differences in anatomy that may affect differences in cognitive capacity. Toward this goal, we have begun to characterize in both humans and animals the relationships between (1) substrate size and degree of substrate asymmetry, (2) histological features (neuron numbers and packing densities) and degree of substrate asymmetry, and (3) patterns of interhemispheric connectivity and degree of substrate asymmetry.

Substrate Size and Asymmetry

Symmetric substrates of equal size may result from an increase in the size of the normally small side, a decrease in the large side, or a decrease in the large side and an increase in the small side. In the first possibility the total substrate (left plus right) is greater in the symmetric than in the asymmetric case, whereas the opposite is true in the second case; in the third possibility the total brain substrate does not change in relation to changes in degree of substrate asymmetry (see figure 15.1). In order to discriminate among these alternatives, we compared the total area (right + left) of the planum temporale in brains according to degree of asymmetry of the planum.

We examined the same 100 human brains studied by Geschwind and Levitsky (1968) but measured the total left and the right planum areas instead of the outside planum length, as done in the earlier study. Like Geschwind and Levitsky we found a leftward asymmetry in 63 percent of the brains, a rightward bias in 21 percent, and no bias (symmetry) in 16 percent (Galaburda et al. 1987b). When we plotted the total planum area against a directionless coefficient of planum asymmetry ($|R - L|/[(R + L)(0.5)]$), a significant negative correlation was found ($r = -.530$; $t = 6.19$; d.f. $= 98$; $p < .001$), which indicated that as asymmetry increased, the total planum area decreased. Furthermore, the area of the smaller of the two plana significantly predicted asymmetry ($r = -.831$; $t = 14.79$; d.f. $= 98$; $p < .001$), whereas there was no correlation between the larger planum area and the degree of asymmetry ($r = -.065$; $t = 0.64$; n.s.), which indicates that differences in degree of asymmetry result predominantly from a change in the size of one side. Thus, two large sides are characteristic of planum symmetry, whereas one large and one small side characterize asymmetry.

Histology and Substrate Asymmetry
There are only two possible parameters that involve neurons in three-dimensional space and determine architectonic volume: cell-packing density and number of cells. Either increased cell-packing density or decreased number of cells acting alone diminishes volume, and the opposite changes increase volume. Hence there are only three possibilities that can explain volume differences between asymmetric and symmetric brain regions: a difference in the number of cells without any change in cell-packing density, a change in cell-packing density with no difference in the number of cells, or a combination of changes in cell-packing density and the number of cells (see figure 15.2).

These possibilities were investigated in the primary visual cortex (area 17) of the rat. We first determined whether the negative correlation between total substrate size and degree of asymmetry held true for the visual cortex of the rat, as it did for the human planum temporale. We measured the volume of area 17 and found an inverse relationship between total volume of area 17 and the coefficient of

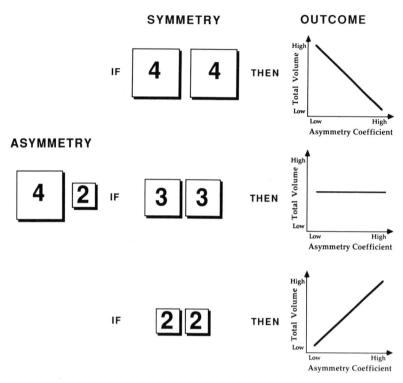

Figure 15.1
Schematic illustrations of the three hypothetical possibilities comparing an asymmetric brain region to a symmetric region. The symmetric brain can be made up of two large sides (top), two small sides (bottom), or two medium-sized sides (middle). Each of these possibilities carries with them predictable outcomes based on the comparison of the total (right + left) area (or volume) of a region to the asymmetry coefficient $[(R - L)/(0.5(R+L))]$. Thus, when the symmetric brain region is made up of two large sides, one would expect a negative correlation between these two variables, whereas a positive correlation is predicted if symmetric brain regions are composed of two smaller sides. In the case of the medium-sized symmetric brain region there is no change in total volume with changes in asymmetry coefficient.

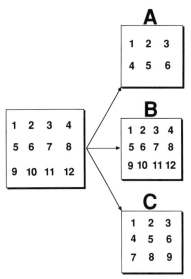

Figure 15.2
A schematic diagram demonstrating the three hypothetical possibilities of histological differences between the two sides of an asymmetric brain region. (*A*) Changes could occur in the number of cells with no changes in cell-packing density; (*B*) changes could occur in both cell-packing density and cell number; or (*C*) changes could occur in cell-packing density with no changes in cell number.

asymmetry ($|R - L|/[(R + L)(0.5)]$; $r = -.489$; $t = 2.31$; d.f. = 17; $p < .05$). The small side was inversely related to degree of asymmetry ($r = -.609$; $t = 3.17$; d.f. = 17; $p < .05$), whereas the large side was not ($r = -.347$; $t = 1.52$; d.f. = 17; n.s.). Thus, the relationship between substrate size and substrate asymmetry could now be seen in two species and at two levels of analysis, the architectonic level and the gross level. With this established, we proceeded to test the three possible alternatives outlined above.

Neuronal counts within area 17 did not disclose a relationship between cell-packing density and volume asymmetry ($r = -.085$; $t = .35$; d.f. = 17; n.s.). We therefore concluded that volume asymmetry was related to side differences in total cell numbers (Galaburda et al. 1985b). Accordingly, symmetric and asymmetric substrates contain different numbers of neurons; symmetric substrates have more.

That side differences in cell-packing density do not play a major role in asymmetry is not surprising. For example, we have seen particularly in asymmetric cortical areas in humans that side-volume differences can be quite large, up to 700 percent. For changes in cell-packing density to account for this degree of volume difference there would have to be major architectonic differences between the sides, which would make recognizing and assigning homology to the bilateral regions impossible. Ongoing studies show that side differences in numbers of neurons are present in a subcortical region as well (Williams and Rakic 1988).

Connectivity and Substrate Asymmetry

It has long been speculated that the mechanism of cerebral dominance lies in callosal connectivity (Weiskrantz 1977). Witelson (1985) demonstrated a difference in the midsagittal area of the corpus callosum between left- and right-handers: left-handers, whose brains are more likely to be symmetric (Hochberg and LeMay 1975), had larger midsagittal corpus callosum areas than did their right-handed counterparts.

It has been argued that the dominant hemisphere exerts control over its homologue through the corpus callosum. By this reasoning, one might expect that the larger, dominant brain area, which has more cells than its smaller homologue, sends more projections across the corpus callosum. A lack of such callosal asymmetry, and therefore a potential for competition and unresolved dominance, might exist when substrates are symmetric, and this possibility has in fact been suggested to take place in dyslexia (Orton 1937). Alternatively, symmetric and asymmetric substrates may differ qualitatively, as well as quantitatively, in their patterns of interhemispheric connectivity.

We investigated this question by examining the pattern of axonal terminal degeneration in eight 90-day-old Wistar rats with nearly complete section of the corpus callosum, with minimal extracallosal involvement.[1] One week following surgery the animals were perfused transcardially, and each brain was processed using a modification of the Fink-Heimer silver method (Fink and Heimer 1967). Adjacent sections were stained with cresylechtviolett for Nissl substance and therefore cytoarchitecture.

The first stage of quantification was performed using an image acquisition and analysis system. Optical images from slides were captured using a video camera attached to a stereomicroscope and interfaced to a digitizing device. Dark-field images were digitized from the series of sections silver-stained for terminal axonal degeneration, and light-field images were digitized from the Nissl series.

The somatosensory-somatomotor cortex (SM; areas 3, 1, and 2) and parts of the visual cortex (VIS; areas 17 and 18a) were parceled on the Nissl-stained sections, and these demarcated areas were electronically overlayed with the adjacent silver-stained sections to trace the area borders of the former onto the latter. The average density of silver stain (defined as the sum of the gray-level value for each pixel within the appropriate architectonic border, divided by the total number of pixels within the border) was determined for VIS and SM for each animal. In addition, the directionless asymmetry coefficient (δ) was computed for each region ($\delta = |R - L|/[(R + L)(0.5)]$), as well as the asymmetry coefficient of VIS and SM combined ($\delta_{TOT} = (\delta_{VIS} + \delta_{SM})/2$).

An inverse relationship was present between δ_{VIS} and δ_{TOT} and the average terminal axonal density of these areas. Thus, δ_{VIS} was significantly correlated with the average density of VIS ($r = -.776$; $t = 2.68$; d.f. $= 6$; $p < .05$), and δ_{TOT} was negatively correlated with the average density of TOT ($r = -.731$; $t = 2.62$; d.f. $= 6$; $p < .05$). However, there was no significant correlation between δ_{SM} and the average density of SM. This indicated that some substrates tended to have denser callosal terminations when symmetric than when asymmetric.

Because callosal projections in the mature rat (and in other mature mammals that have been studied) are segregated into columns of terminations (Cipolloni and Peters, 1979), this result—that symmetric brain regions can have a greater density of callosal terminations than asymmetric ones—suggested a number of possible interpretations: there could be more columns of termination in symmetric regions; there could be comparable numbers but denser columns in the symmetric regions; or there could be fewer but broader columns of termination (in essence, more diffuse terminations) in symmetric regions (see figure 15.3).

Each of these alternatives carries certain predictable outcomes. For example, if symmetric brain regions have more columns than their asymmetric counterparts, a negative correlation between the number of columns and the degree of asymmetry should be seen. On the other hand, a positive correlation should be seen if symmetric regions have fewer columns. Finally, if the number of columns are the same, albeit denser in the symmetric cases, no correlation should be present between δ and the number of columns.

We counted the number of discrete columns of callosal terminations in each brain and found a positive correlation between the number of callosal columns and δ_{TOT} ($r = .714$; $t = 2.50$; d.f. $= 6$; $p < .05$) and δ_{SM} ($r = .771$; $t = 2.97$; d.f. $= 6$; $p < .05$), which indicates that the number of columns increases as architectonic asymmetry increases (Rosen et al. 1987).

Witelson (1985) reported that the brains of left-handers have more extensive corpora callosa, which may reflect the fact that their brains are more symmetrical (Hochberg and LeMay 1975). However, this

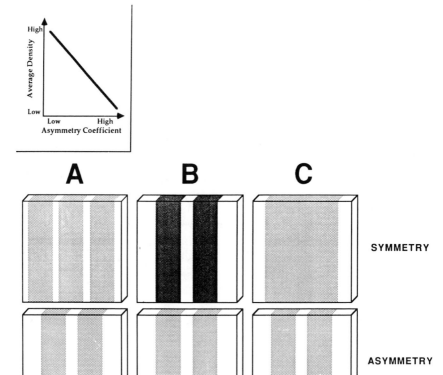

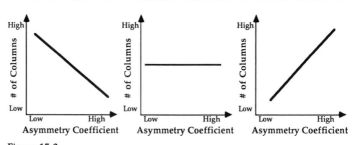

Figure 15.3
Three possible outcomes of the finding of an inverse relationship between volume asymmetry and average optical density (inset). (A) Symmetric brains could have more columns of terminations than asymmetric brains; this would also produce a negative correlation between number of columns and asymmetry coefficient. (B) Symmetric brains could have the same number of columns of terminations as asymmetric brains, but the density within the columns would be greater in the former; in this case there would be no correlation between the number of columns and the asymmetry coefficient. (C) Finally, there could be fewer columns of terminations in the symmetric brain, but they would occupy a greater portion of the area. In this case, a negative correlation would be found between the volumetric asymmetry coefficient and the number of columns of terminations. A combination of increased density of projections and more diffuse projections would also fit the right lowermost curve.

study did not distinguish the two possibilities of greater numbers of fibers and lesser density of fibers in the symmetric cases. Our results are compatible with the first possibility, that more symmetric brains have relatively greater numbers of callosal fibers. Moreover, the overall pattern of callosal terminations is more diffuse (less columnar) in symmetric brains, which is an additional difference between symmetric to asymmetric brains. Thus, if the detailed architecture of cells and connections, as well as their numbers, matter to functional capacity, symmetric and asymmetric brains may differ in functional capacity, cognitive styles, and other functional characteristics in addition to functional lateralization (see Churchland and Sejnowski in this volume).

The differences in the pattern and number of callosal terminations between symmetric and asymmetric cortical regions may be considered in the light of the ontogeny of callosal connectivity. During early development callosal cells of origin are diffusely represented throughout the cerebral cortex (Ivy et al. 1979; Innocenti and Clarke 1983; Wise and Jones 1976), but as the brain matures, these cells are seen only in discrete laminar and columnar locations (Jacobson and Trojanowski 1974). Likewise, at the earlier stage of development of axonal terminations of callosal cells the fibers are diffusely placed beneath the cortex until they penetrate and terminate in discrete bundles within the cortical plate (Zaborsky and Wolff, 1982). It is thought that this progressive restriction of callosal cells of origin and terminations is likely to be the result of cell death and axonal pruning or axonal rerouting (Ivy et al. 1979).

The lesser average density of callosal terminals in the more asymmetric brain regions suggests that the volume diminishes less rapidly than the numbers of callosal terminals, which in turn means that cell loss is less severe than callosal fiber loss. One developmental hypothesis to explain this finding suggests that some of the fibers may be withdrawn from the callosum and rerouted within the ipsilateral hemisphere during ontogenesis. If so, callosal fibers would be lost, but the cells providing those fibers would be preserved in intrahemisphere assemblies (also see the comments on the paper by H. Damasio et al. in this volume).

To summarize, there are a number of anatomic differences between asymmetric and symmetric brains. At the gross morphometric level, symmetric substrates are larger than asymmeric substrates. The increased volume in the symmetric substrate reflects a failure to develop a small side and can be explained by an excess of neurons. Finally, the pattern of callosal connections differs between animals with symmetric and asymmetric brain regions; the latter have an ontogenetically more mature pattern characterized by more discrete columns of termination. What remains unanswered at present is the crucial question of how the development of asymmetric and symmetric substrates differs. Are brain regions symmetric or asymmetric from the start, that is, at the level of germinal zones during the time of cell proliferation, or do later genetic or epigenetic factors regulating the number of cells assigned to specific architectonic areas play a role in the formation of symmetry or asymmetry? The answer to this question has profound implications for the mechanisms producing specialized cortical areas, regulating symmetric and asymmetric neural networks, and generating anomaly and deviation, such as that seen in developmental dyslexia.

Mechanisms of Cortical Anomaly

Mice with Immune Disorders

Stimulated by the findings of Geschwind and Behan (1982), which showed relations among left-handedness, developmental dyslexia, and autoimmune and allergic disorders, we investigated whether genetically inbred strains of mice with immune disorders exhibited neuronal migration abnormalities in the neocortex similar to those seen in male dyslexics. The brains from three strains of mice (New Zealand Black [NZB/BlNJ], BXSB/Mp, and MRL/1) that spontaneously develop autoimmune disorders were examined. The immunologic characteristics of each of these strains have been extensively studied, and although there are many shared features among them, each strain develops its own unique constellation of immune disorders. NZB mice develop an autoimmune disease characterized by the presence of autoantibodies and abnormalities of stem cells, macrophages, and T and B lymphocytes. The mice develop hemolytic anemia and die prematurely at ages of about 16 to 17 months. The BXSB strain develops an immune disease characterized by the development of autoantibodies, proliferation of B lymphocytes, and immune complex glomerulonephritis. BXSB males are more severely affected than females and die much younger. The sex difference in the BXSB strain, unlike that seen in the NZB/W hybrid strain, is not under the control of sex hormones but instead appears to be determined by genes located on the Y chromosome (Theofilopoulos and Dixon 1981). The MRL/1 strain develops autoantibodies and experiences proliferation of T lymphocytes and enlargement of the lymph nodes and spleen. Death occurs from immune-complex glomerulonephritis. MRL females are more severely affected than males. The recessive gene lpr

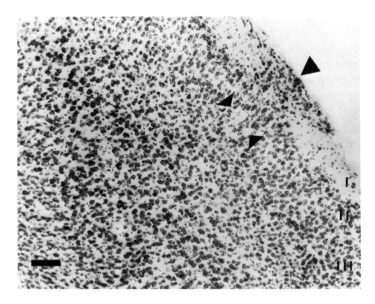

Figure 15.4
Ectopic collection of neurons in layer I (large arrowhead) and underlying dysplasia (small arrowheads) in the motor cortex of the autoimmune mouse brain (bar = 50 μm).

has been implicated in the expression of the disorder in the MRL strain (for a review see Talal 1983).

Cerebrocortical Anomalies
We have now examined serial histological sections of over 100 brains of autoimmune (NZB, BXSB, and MRL) and control (DBA/2, C57BL/6, and NZW) mice and have reported that NZB and BXSB mice, but not the MRL mice, showed cerebrocortical microdysgenesis (Sherman et al. 1985; Sherman et al. 1987). The anomalies mainly consisted of single collections of ectopic neurons in layer I, often with dysplasia of the underlying cortical laminae (figure 15.4). On rare occasions we saw more striking abnormalities of cortical layering (including neuron-free areas) in the full thickness of the cortical plate. At the light-microscopic level the anomalies were similar in appearance to those seen in the male dyslexic brain.

About 25 to 30 percent of the NZB and BXSB mice showed brain anomalies. In addition, about 24 percent of the offspring of crosses between the BXSB and NZB strains had anomalies. Only a small number of mice in the control and MRL strains showed cortical ectopias, although many MRL mice developed severe hydrocephalus.

Anomalies were unilateral in 87 percent of the cases in the NZB and BXSB strains. Typically, only one ectopic nest was seen in each affected brain, although 25 percent of the affected brains of the BXSB strain revealed multiple ectopias. Fully 85 percent of the anomalies seen in NZB mice were present in the sensorimotor cortices, whereas 80 percent of those in the BXSB mice were in the frontal/motor cortices (χ^2 = 22.55, d.f. = 1, $p < .001$). An asymmetry bias was present in the NZB and BXSB strains when the anomalies were analyzed for architectonic location. Thus, 76 percent of the anomalies in the frontal/motor cortices were seen in the left hemisphere (χ^2 = 5.76; d.f. = 1, $p < .02$), while 53 percent of the anomalies in the sensorimotor cortex were in the right hemisphere (χ^2 = n.s.). The lateral bias between the two regions was statistically significant (χ^2 = 3.87, d.f. = 1, $p < .05$). In addition, about twice as many male as female mice had anomalies (χ^2 = 5.97, d.f. = 1, $p < .02$), and a recent analysis has revealed that each litter has at least one member with an abnormal brain.

Other investigators have shown that the neocortex and caudate putamen are 11 to 14 percent smaller in volume in 4-to-6-month-old NZB mice than in the outbred CFW control strain and that a 21 percent decrease in the packing density of cholinergic cells is present in the basal-forebrain region of NZB mice (Zilles 1985). Recently, abnormalities of neuronal migration were reported in the hippocampus of NZB mice (Nowakowski 1986; Nowakowski and Sekiguchi 1987). We have confirmed this finding in our own material.

Brain Reorganization

Injury occurring during the time of neuronal migration and shortly thereafter, in addition to producing the type of focal dysgenesis described in dyslexics and mice with immune disorders, may be capable of significantly reorganizing the cortex through local and distant effects on the number and type of neurons and connections. We have seen an example of substantial reorganization of interhemispheric afferents to an area of cortical dysgenesis (Galaburda et al. 1987a). Specifically, a spontaneously occurring area of microgyria with ectopic neurons, fused molecular layers, and abnormal lamination was seen in the auditory cortex of a rat that had undergone callosal section and later staining for degenerating axon terminals. The abnormal cortex exhibited diffuse, dense, and distorted callosal terminations affecting all cortical layers, a pattern that is different from that normally seen in this region. The analogous microscopic appearance and developmental time frame of the cortical abnormalities in male dyslexics, mice with immune disorders, and rats suggest that abnormal connectivity may be a general feature of these forms of microdysgenesis, which may in turn affect functional capacity.

Behavioral Associations

NZB mice show difficulties in learning an active avoidance response (Nandy et al. 1983) and do not do as well as control mice on learning tasks involving passive avoidance (Spencer and Lal 1983). The next step was to examine the relationship between brain pathology and learning difficulties in the autoimmune strains. In collaboration with Victor H. Denenberg we tested NZB and BXSB mice (with and without ectopias) and DBA control mice on a variety of behavioral tasks. These included tests of water escape, water discrimination, paw preference, rotational swim asymmetry, and unilateral neglect. Strain differences were present for many of the tasks, but more importantly, the tasks of water escape and discrimination revealed a behavioral difference between animals with and without ectopias for the first time. Water discrimination was performed faster by BXSB mice without ectopias than those with ectopias ($F[1, 21] = 10.55; p < .01$). In contrast, water escape was performed better by mice with ectopias ($F[1, 21] = 4.29; p < .051$). NZB mice, however, did not show these differences. We are using additional tests and are testing more mice to support these initial findings.

Conclusions

It is clear that biological similarities between humans and other species make possible the study of general principles of brain organization and pathology through animal models. In this research project we are attempting to discover the pathogenetic mechanisms involved in a specifically human learning disability by studying asymmetries in rats and abnormalities in neuronal migration in mice with immune disorders. The rat model has shown that symmetric brain substrates are larger in total volume and contain more neurons than their asymmetric counterparts. Furthermore, the connectional pattern of symmetric substrates is more diffuse than that of asymmetric brains.

The links among left-handedness, autoimmune disease, and learning disabilities in humans led to the discovery that mice with immune-disorders develop brain anomalies and behavioral problems. We have speculated that in male dyslexics and autoimmune mice, abnormal immunologic processes during gestation (acting either directly on neural or glial antigens involved in neuronal migration or indirectly on cerebral blood vessels nourishing these structures) produce a disruption in the normal course of migration that results in focal neuronal displacement and abnormal regulation of neuron and axon numbers, with resultant behavioral consequences (Sherman et al. 1987; Sherman et al. 1988; see also Galaburda et al. in this volume).

Note

Suported in part by NIH grants 19819 and 20806 and by grants from the Orton Dyslexia Society and Carl J. Herzog Foundation.

1. The results of this experiment are reported in preliminary form here. Since the time of submission, a more complete analysis has yielded additional information, which, while somewhat different from that reported here, does not change the overall results.

References

Cippolloni, P. B., and A. Peters. 1979. The bilaminar and banded distribution of the callosal terminals in the posterior neocortex of the rat. *Brain Research* 176:33–47.

Denenberg, V. H. 1981. Hemispheric laterality in animals and the effects of early experience. *Behavioral and Brain Sciences* 4:1–49.

Diamond, M. C., R. E. Johnson, and C. A. Ingham. 1975. Morphological changes in the young, adult, and aging rat cerebral cortex, hippocampus, and diencephalon. *Behavioral Biology* 14:163–174.

Diamond, M. C., D. Young, S. S. Singh, and R. E. Johnson. 1981. Age-related morphologic differences in the rat cerebral cortex and hippocampus: Male-female, right-left. *Experimental Neurology* 81:1–13.

Fink, R. P., and L. Heimer. 1967. Two methods for selective silver impregnation of degenerating axons and their synaptic endings in the central nervous system. *Brain Research* 4:369–374.

Galaburda, A. M., F. Aboitiz, G. D. Rosen, and G. F. Sherman. 1985a. Histological asymmetry in the primary visual cortex of the rat: Implications for mechanisms of cerebral asymmetry. *Cortex* 22:151–160.

Galaburda, A. M., J. Corsiglia, G. D. Rosen, and G. F. Sherman. 1987b. Planum temporale asymmetry, reappraisal since Geschwind and Levitsky. *Neuropsychologia* 25:853–868.

Galaburda, A. M., and T. L. Kemper. 1979. Cytoarchitectonic abnormalities in developmental dyslexia: A case study. *Annals of Neurology* 6:94–100.

Galaburda, A. M., G. D. Rosen, and G. F. Sherman. 1987a. Connectional anomaly in association with cerebral microgyria in the rat. *Society for Neuroscience Abstracts* 13:1601.

Galaburda, A. M., G. F. Sherman, G. D. Rosen, F. Aboitiz, and N. Geschwind. 1985b. Developmental dyslexia: Four consecutive cases with cortical anomalies. *Annals of Neurology* 18:222–233.

Geschwind, N., and P. O. Behan. 1982. Left-handedness: Association with immune disease, migraine, and developmental learning disorder. *Proceedings of the National Academy of Sciences* (USA) 79:5097–5100.

Geschwind, N., and A. M. Galaburda. 1987. *Cerebral lateralization: Biological mechanisms, associations, and pathology.* Cambridge: MIT Press.

Geschwind, N., and W. Levitsky. 1968. Human brain: Left-right asymmetries in temporal speech region. *Science* 161:186–187.

Hochberg, F. H., and LeMay, M. 1975. Arteroigraphic correlates of handedness. *Neurology* 25:218–222.

Innocenti, G. M., and S. Clarke. 1983. Multiple sets of visual cortical neurons projecting transitorily through the corpus callosum. *Neuroscience Letters* 41:27–32.

Ivy, G. O., R. M. Akers, and H. P. Killackey. 1979. Differential distribution of callosal projections in the neonatal and adult rat. *Brain Research* 195:607–617.

Jacobson, S., and J. Q. Trojanowski. 1974. The cells of origin of the corpus callosum in the rat, cat, and rhesus monkey. *Brain Research* 74:149–155.

Kaufmann, W. E., and A. M. Galaburda. 1989. Cerebrocortical microdysgenesis in normal human brains. *Neurology* 39:238–244.

Kemper, T. L. 1984. Asymmetrical lesions in dyslexia. In N. Geschwind and A. M. Galaburda, eds., *Cerebral dominance: The biological foundations*. Cambridge: Harvard University Press.

McBride, M. C., and T. L. Kemper. 1982. Pathogenesis of four-layered microgyric cortex in man. *Acta Neuropathologica* 57:93–98.

Morel, F., and E. Wildi. 1952. Dysgénésie nodulaire disséminée de l'écorce frontale. *Revue Neurologique* (Paris) 87:251–270.

Nandy, K., H. Lal, M. Bennet, and D. Bennett. 1983. Correlation between a learning disorder and elevated brain-reactive antibodies in aged C57BL/6 and young NZB mice. *Life Sciences* 33:1499–1503.

Nowakowski, R. S. 1986. Abnormalities in neuronal migration in the hippocampal formation of the NZB/BINJ mouse. *Society for Neuroscience Abstracts* 12:317.

Nowakowski, R. S., and M. Sekiguchi. 1987. Abnormalities of granule cell dendrites and axons in the dentate gyrus of the NZB/BINJ mouse. *Society for Neuroscience Abstracts* 13:1117.

Orton, S. T. 1937. *Reading, writing, and speech problems in children*. New York: W. W. Norton Company.

Rosen, G. D., G. F. Sherman, and A. M. Galaburda. 1987. Neocortical symmetry and asymmetry in the rat: Different patterns of callosal connections. *Society for Neuroscience Abstracts* 13:44.

Sherman, G. F., A. M. Galaburda, P. O. Behan, and G. D. Rosen. 1987. Neuroanatomical anomalies in autoimmune mice. *Acta Neuropathologica* 74:239–242.

Sherman, G. F., A. M. Galaburda, and N. Geschwind. 1985. Cortical anomalies in brains of New Zealand mice: A neuropathological model of dyslexia? *Proceedings of the National Academy of Sciences* (USA) 82:8072–8074.

Sherman, G. F., G. D. Rosen, and A. M. Galaburda. 1988. Neocortical anomalies in autoimmune mice: A model for the develomental neuropathology seen in the dyslexic brain. In H. Lal and B. Reisberg, eds., *Autoimmunity: Its role in Alzheimer's disease and other behavioral disorders*. In press.

Spencer, D. G., and H. Lal. 1986. Specific behavioral impairments in association tasks with an autoimmune mouse. *Society for Neuroscience Abstracts* 12:96.

Talal, N. 1983. Immune response disorders. in H. L. Foster, J. D. Small, and J. G. Fox, eds., *The mouse in biomedical research*, vol. 3. New York: Academic Press.

Theofilopoulos, A. N. and F. J. Dixon 1981. Etiopathogenesis of murine SLE. *Immunological Reviews* 55:179–216.

Williams, R. W., and P. Rakic. 1988. Elimination of neurons from the rhesus monkey's lateral geniculate nucleus during development. *Journal of Comparative Neurology* 272:424–436.

Weiskrantz, L. 1977. On the role of cerebral commissures in animals. In I. S. Russell, M. W. van Hof, and G. Berlucchi, eds., *Structure and function of cerebral commissures.* Baltimore: University Park Press.

Wise, S. P., and E. G. Jones. 1976. The organization and postnatal development of the commissural projection of the rat somatic sensory cortex. *Journal of Comparative Neurology* 168:313–344.

Witelson, S. F. 1985. The brain connection: The corpus callosum is larger in left-handers. *Science* 229:665–668.

Zaborsky, L., and J. R. Wolff. 1982. Distributional patterns and individual variation of callosal connections in the albino rat. *Anatomy and Embryology* 165:213–232.

Zilles, K. 1985. Morphological studies on brain structures of the NZB mouse: An animal model for the aging human brain? In J. Traber and W. H. Gispen, eds., *Senile dementia of the Alzheimer type.* Berlin: Springer-Verlag.

Chapter 16

Abnormal Neuronal Patterns and Disorders of Neocortical Development

Verne S. Caviness, Jr., Jean-Paul Misson, and Jean-François Gadisseux

The neocortex, the dominant cortical structure of the cerebral hemispheres, plays a central role in higher functions of man. Abnormalities in neocortical function have been implicated in autism and the principal developmental disorders of childhood associated with impairment of cognition, language, and motor control. Some of these disorders are associated with abnormalities in the architectonic pattern of the neocortex. The present chapter inquires into the pathophysiologic mechanisms acting during development and giving rise to abnormal neocortical architectonic patterns.

The architectonic character of the neocortex is similar in all mammalian species (Brodmann 1909; Bailey and von Bonin 1951; Caviness 1975). The structure is composed of six concentric layers. The most superficial layer, layer i, is plexiform. It is composed principally of dendrites and axons although it does include sparsely scattered neuronal somata. It is bounded superficially by the limiting glial membrane and the leptomeninges. Five subjacent layers are each dominated by the somata of a principal neuronal class: small and medium pyramidal cells in layers ii and iii, stellate cells in layer iv, large pyramidal cells in layer v, and polymorphic cells in layer vi. The six layers are continuous through the multiple cytoarchitectonic fields of the neocortex, but there is substantial laminar variation from architectonic field to field. This variation reflects, in part, differences from field to field in the numbers, size and form, and packing density of the principal neuronal classes. Other neuronal classes, interneurons in particular, and afferent axons are also among the cellular elements contributing to an overall laminar appearance in the various neocortical architectonic fields.

The laminar architectonic pattern of the neocortex emerges through a histogenetic sequence that begins with cytogenesis. The neurons of the neocortex are generated in an epithelium bordering the ventricular cavities deep within the cerebral hemispheres (His 1889; Schaper

1897) and referred to as the ventricular zone (VZ; Boulder Committee 1970). When its final mitosis is completed in the VZ, the young neuron must ascend over an extended migration to its destination within the cortex (Sidman and Rakic 1973). Once in position the young neuron elaborates its dendritic and axonal processes, enlarges rapidly, and engages in synaptic contact with other neurons (Astrom 1967; Morest 1969). The synaptic connections formed between the young cell and others may be both within and remote from the cortical region where its soma is located.

These histogenetic processes may be disrupted by a wide variety of heritable, metabolic, and acquired pathophysiologic processes (Rakic 1975; Evrard, Gadisseux, and Lyon 1982; Caviness and Williams 1984; Barth 1987). Some, though not all, of these processes modify the laminar pattern of the neocortex. Central to our concern here are the pathologic processes that modify patterns of neuronal movement during cortical histogenesis. Such processes lead to anomalous positions of different classes of cortical neurons relative to one another, which results in a disarray of neocortical laminae.

The extent and severity of malformation resulting from disorders affecting neocortical histogenesis vary. At one extreme are abnormalities mostly restricted to the neocortex. Clinically important examples have been identified by the analyses of Galaburda and Kemper (1979) as significantly correlated with mild to moderate disturbances of language and cognition. At the other extreme, malformation may severely extend to several structures of the central nervous system, including the neocortex. Severe and generalized malformation often results in fetal death or only brief postnatal survival.

The Early Events of Neocortical Histogenesis

One objective of this chapter is to formulate hypotheses relating to pathophysiologic mechanisms that might underlie developmental malformations of the cerebral cortex. An understanding of the cellular events of neuronal migration and the relation of these cellular events to cortical histogenesis is essential to this objective. Neuronal migration is among the most complex of the cellular processes that serve neocortical histogenesis. Neuronal migration is quite extended in time. It involves several classes of cells, and these classes execute their maneuvers under critical time constraints. Specific cellular encounters and transformations are required. All must occur within the constraints of a complex cellular geometry that is continuously changing through the migratory epoch. Under conditions of normal development these mechanisms appear to be subject to certain amount of error. Despite these complexities, the cellular mechanisms of migration possess a robustness that assures the overall success of cortical and neocortical histogenesis under widely varying conditions of development.

Stratification

At the outset of neocortical histogenesis, the cerebral wall is composed principally of the VZ (figure 16.1). A narrow plexiform marginal zone (MZ) lies between the VZ and the external limiting membrane. After neuronal migrations are initiated, the laminate cortical anlage emerges and expands within the MZ at the surface of the cerebral wall. The intermediate zone (IZ), which intervenes between the VZ and MZ, expands with the entry of multiple axon systems (Marin-Padilla 1978; Marin-Padilla and Marin-Padilla 1982). Conspicuous among these axonal systems and lying superficially in the IZ is the external sagittal stratum (ESS). The ESS, which includes axons of the thalamocortical projection, is a useful landmark in that it defines the inferior limits of the developing neocortex in the nonconvoluted rodent cerebrum (Crandall and Caviness 1984) and the inner border of the corona radiata in the convoluted cerebrum of larger mammals (Kostovic and Rakic 1984).

From early in cortical histogenesis, differentiating postmigratory neurons become distributed throughout a broad field that extends inward from the cortical plate deeply into the IZ. The inferior limit of this zone of postmigratory cells lying deep to the cortical plate is referred to as the subplate. This zone extends inward to the ESS. It corresponds to the entire postnatal corona radiata in large mammals (for research on cats see Luskin and Shatz 1985; for research on man see Sims et al. 1987). The portion of the subplate immediately below the cortical plate is the anlage of layers v and vi. The inferior limit of these layers within the subplate is demarcated in the rodent cerebrum by the ESS, but not in the cerebrum of larger mammals.

Neurogenesis

Our starting point for neocortical histogenesis is neuron replication. Neocortical neurons are formed over an extended period of time that in man and other large mammals spans the second half of the first trimester and the whole second trimester of gestation (Rakic and Sidman 1968; Rakic 1974; Kadhim, Gadisseux, and Evrard 1987; Sidman and Rakic 1982). In the smaller brain of the rodent cell generation continues through most of the second half of intrauterine life (Angev-

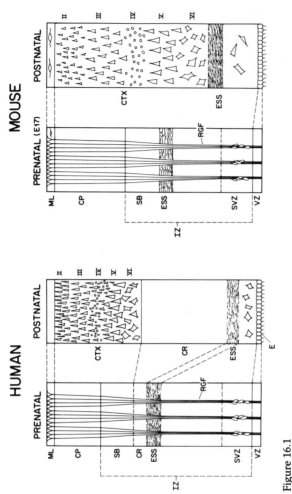

Figure 16.1
Comparative stratification of the human and murine cerebral wall with corresponding strata at pre-natal and postnatal stages of development. *Prenatal* refers to the late stages of neuronal migration, while *postnatal* refers to the postmigratory stages. The represented prenatal strata include the molec-ular layer (ML); the cortical plate (CP); the intermediate zone (IZ), which includes the subplate (SB), the corona radiata (CR), the external sagittal stratum (ESS), and the subventricular zone (SVZ); and the ventricular zone (VZ). Additional postnatal structures are the cortex (CTX) with its cellular layers ii to vi and the ependyma (E). Fascicles of radial glial fibers (RGF) are present in the prenatal period.

ine and Sidman 1961; Berry and Rogers 1965; Shimada and Langman 1970; Caviness and Sidman 1973; Raedler and Raedler 1978).

The multiple classes of neocortical neurons are generated in a set sequence in which the cells that inhabit the deepest cortical layer are formed first and those of layer ii are formed last (Angevine and Sidman 1961). The intermitotic neuronal precursor is attached by junctional complexes near the ventricular surface to the centrally directed processes of adjacent cells (Hinds and Ruffett 1971). It is radially elongated and has its nuclei at the abventricular pole. The DNA synthesis (S) phase proceeds while the cell is maximally elongated with its nucleus in the outer third of the epithelium. During the mitotic (M) phase the cell appears to be nearly spherical and contracted at the ventricular margin. It is intermediate in length during the gap 1 (G1) and gap 2 (G2) phases (Sauer 1935a, 1935b; Seymour and Berry 1975).

Neuronal Migration

Neurogenesis largely overlaps the period of neuronal migration. Migration continues through a somewhat longer cycle into the earliest weeks of the third trimester of gestation in man and two to three days beyond birth in rodents (Angevine and Sidman 1961; Berry and Rogers 1965; Sidman and Rakic 1982). After its terminal division the postmitotic neuron becomes a freely motile element. It then finds its way across the dense tangle of cell processes of the IZ to reach its destined position in the cortex. As development proceeds, the distance intervening between the centrally located generative epithelium and the developing cortex at the cerebral surface rapidly increases. Dramatic and complex changes occur in the structure of the cerebral wall (Marin-Padilla 1971; Caviness 1982). Thus, the earliest postmitotic cells move centrifugally into the narrow nonstratified MZ. They come to rest in regular tangential register at the interface of the superficial plexiform zone and the subjacent intermediate or migratory zone. There they form the primary histogenetic cortical lamina, which is referred to as the cortical plate (CP).

A central hypothesis of current developmental neurobiology is that the migrating cell finds its way in its complex, extended journey by climbing the radially ascending process of a specialized glial cell, the radial glial cell (Rakic 1971, 1972). The young neuron is observed to remain closely attached to the surface of the glial cell until it reaches the plexiform zone at the outer cerebral wall. During migration the neuron is small and simple in configuration, with only tapered ascending and descending radial processes extending from the cell soma. As the leading process of the cell encounters the plexiform zone and its migration terminates, the cell appears to become readily detachable from the glial surface. It rapidly elaborates apical and basal dendritic processes. In so doing, it becomes fixed in position with respect to cells that preceded it in migration or migrated at the same time. After the cell becomes fixed in position, it is bypassed by subsequently arriving cells. In this way the earliest formed cells come to occupy the deepest levels of the cortex, while cells generated successively later come to inhabit progressively more superficial layers (Angevine and Sidman 1961; Rakic 1974; Caviness 1982).

The Radial Glial Cell

In subsequent sections of this chapter we shall develop the hypothesis that pathologic processes acting upon radial glial cells or the relation of these cells migrating neurons is at the origin of malformations like abnormalities of neocortical laminar patterns. These considerations require that we review the developmental history of radial cells.

Radial glial cells emerge as a differentiated population of the VZ long before the first neocortical neurons become postmitotic (Edwards et al. 1986; Misson et al. 1988b). In the murine cerebrum these elements may be identified by selective monoclonal antibodies RC1 and RC2 from as early as embryonic days 9 or 10 (figure 16.2; Edwards et al. 1986; Misson et al. 1988a; Misson et al. 1988b). In the human brain the cell may be stained from as early as the first trimester with antibodies against the glial intermediate filament anti-GFAP (Antanitus, Choi, and Lapham 1976; Choi and Lapham 1978; Choi 1986) and from as early as the late second timester with antibody RC1 (figure 16.3).

A bipolar radial configuration is characteristic of the radial-cell form throughout the entire neural tube from the earliest phases of development of the central nervous system (Schmechel and Rakic 1979; Edwards et al. 1986). The bipolar form remains conspicuous in the forebrain, and the radial-glial form is thought to serve as the guide for migrating neurons destined for the neocortex (Rakic 1971, 1972). Monopolar forms, cells with one or more ascending but no descending radial process, are thought to be derived from the bipolar population (Schmechel and Rakic 1979; Eckenhoff and Rakic 1984; Edwards et al. 1986). The monopolar forms appear throughout the central nervous system and in certain structures are also thought to serve as guides to neuronal migrations. A well-studied example is the Bergmann glial cell, which is thought to guide the migratory descent of

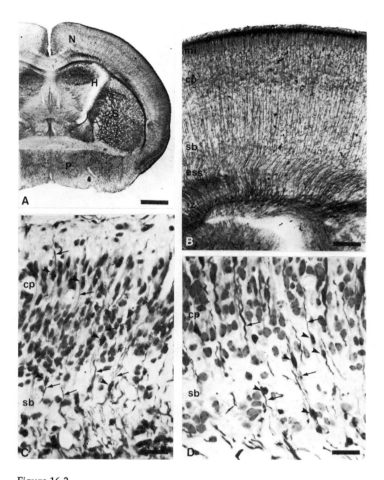

Figure 16.2
Radial glial fibers stained selectively with monoclonal antibody RC2 in a general view
of the developing murine forebrain (*A*) and at higher magnification in the neocortex
(*B–D*). The radial fibers are darkly stained. Other cellular elements are unstained. (*A*)
When the forebrain is sectioned in the coronal plane, the radial alignment of the fibers
is readily evident in the neocortex (N). Other section planes would be necessary to
demonstrate their radial alignment in the striatum (S), hippocampal formation (H), and
preoptic region (P). In (*B*) glial fiber fascicles are sharply deflected in transition from IZ
through ESS and into SB. More distal ascent is more uniformly radial in the area of
neocortex shown. The size of glial fascicles is reduced in stepwise fashion in their
ascent through the successive strata of the cerebral wall. (*A*) and (*B*) are of P1; 50-μm
sections; bar = 600 μm (*A*), 1,300 μm (*B*). (*C*) Migrating neurons (arrowheads) are
marked autoradiographically. (*D*) Neurons migrating in close apposition to radial glial
fibers are indicated by arrowheads. (*C*) embryonic day 16; (*D*) embryonic day 17; 2 μm
sections counterstained with toluidine blue and embedded in plastic; bar = 25 μm (*C*),
20 μm (*D*).

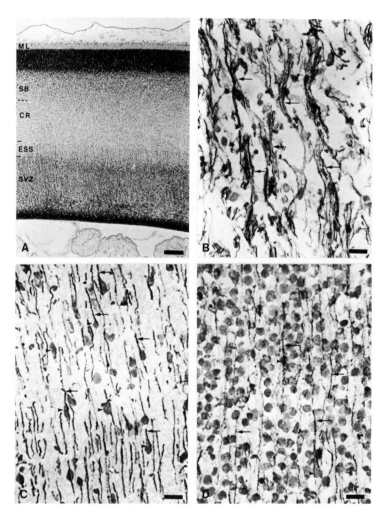

Figure 16.3
The human cerebral wall at 16 weeks (A) and 20 weeks (B, C, D) of gestation. (A) Stratification. Paraffin-embedded, 35-μm section; cresyl-violet stain; bar = 300 μm. Fascicles of radial glial fibers (arrows), stained selectively with monoclonal antibody RC1, become successively smaller with ascent through the IZ (B), the CR (C) and the CP (D). Migrating neurons are marked with arrowheads. (B) to (D) are cryostat-cut, 10-μm sections; toluidine-blue counterstain; bar = 15 μm.

the granule cells of the cerebellar cortex (Rakic and Sidman 1973; de Blas 1984; Benjelloun-Touimi et al. 1985).

The soma of the cerebral bipolar radial glial cell may be located within the VZ or more superficially within the SVZ or IZ. A centrally directed process attaches at the ventricular margin to the basal processes of other cells of the ventricular zone. The ascending process crosses the wall of the neural tube and becomes integral with the limiting glial membrane at the cerebral surface. The bipolar radial glial cells increase dramatically in number throughout neocortical histogenesis (Schmechel and Rakic 1979; Levitt and Rakic 1980). The radial cells subsequently disappear from the cerebral wall by transformation, it is thought, into fibrous and protoplasmic astrocytes. Throughout the course of cell migrations the bipolar radial glial cells are mitotically active and serve as a progenitor pool for other radial glial cells (Levitt, Cooper, and Rakic 1981, 1983; Misson et al. 1988a; Misson et al. 1988b).

Radial glial cells come to form a complex multicellular architectural system (Levitt and Rakic 1980) with specific structural features that vary according to cerebral region, depth in the cerebral wall, and stage of cortical development (Gadisseux and Evrard 1985; Edwards et al. 1987). Thus, the radial, descending processes of these cells appear from light micrographs virtually to saturate the interstices between the neuronal precursors of the ventricular epithelium. The ascending processes of the radial glial cells are gathered into fascicles as they cross the IZ. At different stages of development the fascicles break up into single fibers as they cross the cortex. This occurs stepwise through sequential strata. An initial drop in fascicle size occurs at the inferior margin of the ESS in rodents and at the lower margin of the corona radiata of convoluted cerebra in human specimens. A further reduction occurs at the level of the anlage of layer vi of the neocortex of the mouse. A final spreading of fibers is observed at the lower margin of the cortical plate in both the primate and murine brain. Relatively late in the migratory epoch as the supragranular layers are being assembled, fascicles are fully reduced to single fibers as they cross the cortical plate (Gadisseux and Evrard 1985).

As it migrates across the IZ, the young neuron appears to be applied to the perimeter of the compact glial fiber fascicles and is thus in contact with the multiple radial glial fibers that compose the fascicle. Within the cortical sector of its migration, however, the young cell appears to penetrate among and separate the multiple fibers of the fascicle it is ascending. In this way the migrating neuron may contribute to the progressive defasciculation of the fiber fascicles within the cortex (Gadisseux and Evrard 1985). It is of note that defasciculation in the rodent is initiated within the external sagittal stratum that abuts the inferior margin of the cortex. As noted earlier, in the primate brain the ESS lies central to the corona radiata, deep within the cerebral wall. Defasciculation occurs principally within the cortex and therefore outside the ESS in the primate brain.

Experimental Studies of Neocortical Neuron Migration
The central hypothesis emerging from anatomic and cytologic study of neuronal migration in the intact developing forebrain is, as we have stated, that migrating neurons are guided in their ascent by radial glial fibers. Experimental analyses must test the hypothesis that attachment to glial fibers is necessary for neuron migration. If the hypothesis holds, experimental study will be required to unravel the molecular mechanisms that regulate this interaction between neurons and glial cells. Experimental models must also be developed for further study of the pathophysiologic processes that disrupt neuronal migration in man and animals. Experimental studies of cerebral neuronal migration conducted thus far and motivated by these general objectives include analyses in both the intact animal and in tissue-culture systems.

Experimental Studies in the Intact Animal
If applied as neuronal migrations are proceeding, a variety of teratogenic agents, including antimetabolites and x-rays, will disrupt neocortical histogenesis (Hicks, D'Amato, and Lowe 1963; Johnston and Coyle 1979; Kameyama and Hoshino 1986; Brent, Beckmann, and Jensh 1986). Neurons in the mitotic cycle are preferentially destroyed. If injury is inflicted at late stages of cortical histogenesis, the correspondingly late-formed, principally supragranular layers are not formed. If formed prior to injury, the infragranular layers will be formed and will achieve their essential cytoarchitectonic character. If injury occurs early, formation of even the infragranular layers will be aborted. If cells do migrate, their disposition in the cortex will not be an orderly laminate one. Following such manipulations many neurons may fail to migrate and may instead remain stranded at a subcortical level of the cerebral wall.

Ethyl alcohol, among the teratogenic agents employed in rodents, appears to impair neuron generation, migration, and differentiation if the fetus is exposed throughout gestation to extremely high doses (Clarren et al. 1978; Wisniewski et al. 1983; Miller 1986, 1987). Migrations of neurons destined for the supragranular layers have been interrupted, though not migrations of earlier-formed cells. The cells normally destined for supragranular layers are selectively interrupted in their ascent at the level of the ESS and the lower margin of the cortex. As noted above, this level of the cerebral wall is the level where the glial fiber fascicles begin to break up into smaller fascicles.

Experimental studies in the intact animal are ambiguous about the role of the radial glial cell in neuronal migration. Injury to the forebrain occurring in the course of cortical histogenesis provokes transformation of radial glial cells into astrocytes (see figure 10C below; Bignami and Dahl 1976; Roessmann and Gambetti 1986; Eriksdotter-Nillson et al. 1986; Powers et al. 1988). Thus, a breakdown in migratory mechanisms occurring after injury might reflect transformation of, or damage to, the radial glial cells, which makes the radial cell system unable to support migrations. A disruption of migration occurring after injury might also reflect direct neuronal injury that renders the postmigratory cell incompetent to migrate.

Lesions largely restricted to the murine cerebral cortex, delivered by a cold probe applied to the surface of the skull in the terminal stages of cortical histogenesis, may disrupt local neuronal migration only incompletely (Dvorák and Feit 1977; Dvorák et al. 1978). Despite causing substantial local tissue disruption and scarring, the lesions appeared not to prevent the ascent of all neurons destined for the supragranular layers. Some late-migrating cells were observed to achieve their destined relative positions and to generate recognizable layers ii and iii. Migrations proceeded more completely where cortical damage was incomplete and where radial alignment of pyramidal-cell apical dendrites, revealed by Golgi impregnations, was relatively preserved. Although such injury was expected to damage or lead to the transformation of radial glia, this was not overtly demonstrated to have occurred by the methods employed. These studies raise the possibility that there are surfaces favorable for neuron migration within damaged sectors of cortex. These surfaces must serve as alternatives to radial fiber surfaces when these latter are damaged or transformed by cortical injury. Such alternative surfaces have not been specifically identified but may be dendritic, astrocytic, or even pericytic surfaces.

The robustness and flexibility of the mechanisms of migration implied by the experiments reviewed in the foregoing paragraph are explicitly demonstrated by a series of transplant experiments performed in the developing ferret by McConnell (1985, 1986). Neurons of a donor animal were labeled *in vivo* at the time of their terminal mitosis. This was done after tissue dissociation either by intrauterine exposure to tritiated thymidine or incubation in a medium containing true blue. The neurons dissociated from the occipital region included neurons destined for layers ii and iii or for layer v. The labeled dissociated cells were reintroduced by injection into or near the ventricular zone of neonatal animals. In the neonatal host animal, neurons destined for layers ii and iii were undergoing their migrations.

In isochronic experiments, that is, when the injected postmitotic cells were those normally destined for layers ii and iii, the majority of the transplanted cells appeared to migrate normally and to achieve appropriate positions in layers ii and iii of the host animal (McConnell 1985). A relatively small percentage, less than 10 percent, appeared to remain stranded in the region of the ventricular zone of the adult animal. In heterochronic experiments, that is, experiments in which the introduced cells were those normally destined for layer v, migrations occurred, but the resulting pattern of cell distribution was abnormal (McConnell 1986). Many cells normally destined for layer v continued upward fully to the cortical plate-molecular layer interface. They ultimately became incorporated heterotopically into layers ii and iii along with cells of the host animal that were migrating with the transplanted cells. Other transplanted cells took up positions normal for their cell class in subjacent cortical layers. A large number (estimated at 75 percent) failed to migrate at all and instead remained in the periventricular region of the adult animal.

The experiments of McConnell reviewed above allow, we suggest, the following principal interpretations. First, they suggest that the point of encounter between the postmitotic neuron and the radial glial fiber may not be critical to the success of neuron migration. It cannot be assumed that all neurons introduced experimentally that migrated to the cortex made their contact with the radial fiber within the VZ itself. Many may have been delivered by the injection at variable depths in the IZ. Second, the studies imply that neuronal migration delivers the migrating cell by design to the interface of the cortical plate and the plexiform zone. It does this in both the isochronic and heterochronic experimental conditions. If cells migrate at all, they appear to ascend fully to that interface. Heterochronically migrating cells did not terminate their upward movement at layer v even though under normal circumstances layer v would have been the cortical depth appropriate to this class of cells. Admittedly, in the heterochronic experiment a number of cells did end up at cortical levels subjacent to layers ii and iii, but this deeper cortical position appeared not to be a preferred alternative. That is, as with cells normally destined for supragranular layers but exposed *in utero* to high levels of alcohol, these cells appear to have become arrested in their ascent in the depths of the cortex where glial fiber fascicles become reduced in size. Migration might have terminated at deeper positions in the cortex as a result of a failure of the migratory mechanism itself. Such termination may not reflect a positional choice dictated by cell class and made by the cell itself.

In Vitro Experimental Studies
After tissue dissociation the radial glial cells of the cerebral wall are not induced to form elongate, migration-supporting fibers but rather transform rapidly into astrocytes (A. Pearlman, personal communication). Early stages of migrating neurons defined as a cohort by 3H-thymidine autoradiography appear to proceed in embryonic cerebral slice preparations (Hemmendinger and Caviness 1988). It has not been established that migrations proceed along the surfaces of radial glial fibers in these slice preparations.

In vitro models of neuronal migration based upon the cerebellar granule cell have thus far been more informative. First, dissociated glial cells thought to be Bergmann glial cells and maintained in microwell culture have been observed to construct extended glial fiber fascicles, or cables. These cables appear to be a preferred substrate for granule-cell movements (Hatten and Liem 1981; Hatten, Liem, and Mason 1984; Hatten 1985; Hatten, Liem, and Mason 1986). The dissociated granule cell appears able to migrate along the cables only during a narrow developmental time window corresponding approxiately to the time the postmitotic cell would have executed its migrations in the intact animal (Trenkner, Smith, and Segil 1984). The cells subsequently tend to cluster in stationary fashion around glial somata (Hatten and Liem 1981). Migratory movements along the cables are bidirectional; the individual cell may reverse its direction of movement along a cable. Cells coming from opposite directions along the same cable are able to bypass each other (Hatten 1985).

Second, the molecular mechanisms that appear to implement granule cell migration are becoming clarified in experimental systems. Two general molecular mechanisms are currently under study. These are cell adhesion and the action of proteolytic enzymes.

Let us first consider cell adhesion. Granule cell migration along the radial fibers appears to depend upon adhesive cellular interactions. Cell-to-cell adhesion appears to be mediated by multiple glycoproteins synthesized either by glial cells or by neurons. A current list of candidate ligands synthesized by glial cells includes cytotactin (Chuong, Crossin, and Edleman 1987; Crossin, Chuong, and Edelman 1985; Crossin et al. 1986; Grumet et al. 1985) and laminen (Selak, Foidart, and Moonen 1985). Those synthesized by neurons include astrotactin (Edmondson et al. 1988) and NgCAM (Chuong, Crossin, and Edelman 1987). These macromolecules may mediate glial-to-glial or glial-to-neuron adhesion or interactions between neurons, glial cells, and the proteoglycans that saturate the interstices around the migrating cells. Adhesion mediated by these substances appears to be selective. For instance, FAB fragments of monoclonal antibodies against these several antigens interfere selectively with cellular migration along the fibers. This phenomenon has been demonstrated for antiastrotactin in cerebellar microwell culture systems (Edmondson and Hatten 1987; Hatten et al. 1987) and for antibodies against NgCAM and cytotactin in cerebellar cortical slice preparations (Chuong, Crossin, and Edelman 1987; Crossin, Chuong, and Edelman 1985).

AntiNgCAM and anticytotactin appear to have differential effects upon the migration of granule cells according to the location of the cell. Thus, antiNgCAM preferentially blocks the movement of postmitotic cells from the external granule layer into the molecular layer. This antibody has relatively less effect upon the migratory excursion through the transmolecular layer. Anticytotactin, by contrast, exerts its principal effect after the cell has cleared the external granule cell layer and while it is crossing the molecular layer. Since these several antibodies have different effects, the complete migratory excursion of the cell may include a sequence of separate cellular events. For example, initiating migration may require specific cellular conformational changes, including an outgrowth of the migratory process. Continuation of migration through the molecular layer may be further mediated by a different and perhaps selective set of ligands.

Now let us consider proteolysis. The advance of the migrating neuron through the tangle of processes that impinge upon it and the radial fibers contacted by the migrating cell may require the action of proteolytic enzymes. Such enzymes might either be carried by the young neuron or activated in the surround by substances excreted by the neuron. Attention has thus far focused upon the action of the serine protease plasmin (Moonen, Grau-Wagemans, and Selak 1982) and the serine proteases inhibited by the glia-derived neurite promoting factor (GdNPF; Lindner et al. 1986). An activating factor for plasmin as well as GdNPF may be largely derived from glial cells. Substances that inhibit these enzymes cause only a partial block in migration.

Disorders of Neuronal Migration in Man and Animals

The neuropathology of the developing cerebrum of man and animals presents an extended range of abnormalities of neocortical patterns (figure 16.4). Relatively few of these patterns have been approximated

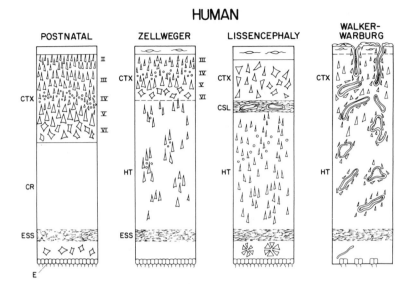

Figure 16.4
Stratification of the normal postnatal human cerebral wall compared to that of the malformations associated with the Zellweger syndrome, classic lissencephaly, and the Walker-Warburg malformation. HT in the three malformations refers to the zone of heterotopic neurons within the corona radiata. The heterotopic zone is separated from the cortex by a cell-sparse zone (CSL) in lissencephaly. Other abbreviations are listed in the caption for figure 16.1.

by experimental manipulations, and the pathogenesis of none of them has been clarified, certainly not in terms of cellular events and molecular regulation. In this section we shall review the architectonic features of a selected series of such neocortical developmental malformations. The malformations presented have been selected with two principal objectives in mind. First, plausible hypotheses about the development of such malformations enlarges our understanding of the cellular events underlying the development of the normal cortical pattern. Toward this first objective we will initiate the series with a description of a cerebral teratoma, a malformation that dramatically illustrates the robustness of the cellular mechanisms that create conditions necessary for neocortical histogenesis. Other malformations selected for presentation suggest in a way complementary to experimental work already discussed that the mechanisms of migration vary with depth in the cerebral wall and that surfaces other than radial glial fibers may be competent to support neuronal migration once the cell has entered the cortex.

A second objective of the present review of neocortical malformations is to explore plausible, though entirely hypothetical, pathogenetic mechanisms for the discussed and certain related neocortical malformations. The arguments rest largely on extrapolations from normal cytologic and experimental analyses reviewed above. We will consider disorders of three classes in terms of cellular pathogenesis: those in which the glial fiber system appears to have been the attack point of disease, disorders that appear to reflect aberrations of neuron-glia interaction in the course of migration, and an architectonic anomaly similar to that associated with certain examples of dyslexia, in which superficial cortical injury appears to activate neuronal movements through zones that do not contain radial glial fibers.

A Cerebral Teratoma

The essential conditions for elementary neocortical histogenesis through neuronal migration appear to have been achieved in a cerebral teratoma (Landrieu et al. 1981). Removed from the cerebral hemisphere of a child shortly after birth, the teratoma included neuroectodermal tissue, stratified epithelium, glandular and enteric epithelium, as well as muscle cartilage and bone. A neuroectodermal mass projected via a stalk into a cavity lined by connective tissue.

The center of the mass contained a lumen bounded by ciliated, pseudostratified epithelium with a large number of mitotic cells concentrated at its luminal margins. Surrounding this "generative" epithelium in concentric fashion were two zones with architectonic features reminiscent of the intermediate zone and the immature neocortex of the developing cerebral wall. The intermediate zone contained fusiform, radially aligned cellular elements similar to the migrating cells of the normal developing cerebral wall. The cortical zone included a cortical plate bracketed above and below by fibrous strata containing scattered neuronal somata. The postmigratory neurons lying most superficially in the cortical plate were the least differentiated, whereas those more deeply situated were larger and more differentiated (figure 16.5). Nomarski optics allowed one to visualize radially aligned, presumably glial fibers spanning the full width of the cortical zone and the intermediate or migratory zone. In the outer third of the cortical plate the somata of neurons were arranged into radial columns separated from each other by intervals containing cellular processes. The plexiform zone was intercalated between the neuronal somata of the cortical plate and the investing mesothelial envelope.

The architectonic features of the teratomatous neural structure were unquestionably neocortical. Despite isolation, the cellular elements normally involved in migration appear to have supported mi-

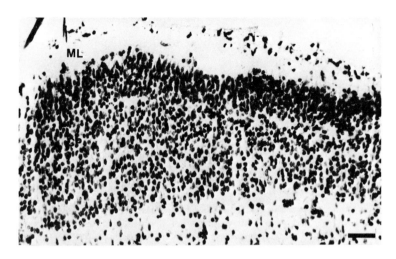

Figure 16.5
"Cortical plate" formed within an intracerebral teratoma. Cells at the interface of the molecular layer and the cortical plate are smaller and more darkly stained than those in the depths of the cortical plate, which suggests that those superficially located are the more recently formed. Paraffin embedded, 10-μm sections; cresyl violet stain; bar = 25 μm. (Adapted from Landrieux et al. 1981.)

gration very much as they do in the normal developing cerebral wall. They thus appear to migrate in a radially centrifugal pattern from the germinal epithelium out to an investing plexiform zone. As in the normal developing cerebral wall, radially aligned glial fibers in the teratoma presumably implemented this migration. Even in the isolation of the teratoma, the mechanisms of migration appear to have allowed an outward radial order within the "cortical plate" in the cell-generation sequence. This is inferred from the deep to superficial maturation gradient of neurons within the cortical plate of the teratoma. By implication, migrating neurons in this teratoma were able to bypass their predecessors in their ascent along the guiding glial fibers as in the normally developing brain.

Aborted Migration in the Normal Animal
Neurons that fail to complete their migrations have been recognized in the normal adult animal. For example, subcortical Purkinje cells have been impregnated by the Golgi method in otherwise normal cerebella (Lafarga, Berciano, and Blanco 1986). Though less well known, the phenomena may also occur in the cerebrum. Cells that have not migrated from the periventricular region have also been provisionally identified in general cell stains by McConnell (1985) in the normal adult ferret. Furthermore, large neurons with pyriform or poly-

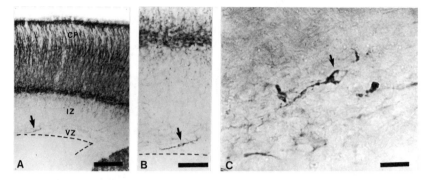

Figure 16.6
Neurons located heterotopically in close relation to the murine lateral ventricle at postnatal day 1 (P1). Neuronal somata and dendrites are selectively stained with a monoclonal antibody against MAP2. Other tissue elements are unstained. (*A*) The cerebral wall in coronal section. A large heterotopic neuron is marked by the arrow. The same neuron is presented at higher magnification in (*B*). (C) Another example of a heterotopic neuron. Vibratome cut, 50-μm sections; bar = 400 μm (*A*), 100 μm (*B*), and 20 μm (*C*).

morphic somata and elaborate, richly differentiated dendritic arbors are clearly presented in the ventricular zone of perinatal mice by staining with a polyclonal antibody against MAP2 (figure 16.6).

There is no reason to suggest that the failure of neurons to migrate in normal animals reflects the effects of an otherwise unsuspected pathologic event. It is more plausible to infer from aborted migration that neurons produced in the ventricular zone of the normal animal vary in their competence or opportunity to execute the maneuvers required by migration. Importantly, the periventricular locus of the neurons in question suggests that these cells never initiated their migrations. The phenomenon thus resembles the effects of antiNgCAM in tissue slices of the developing cerebellar cortex. Possibly, the neurons in question have been unable to achieve the conformational changes required to initiate migration. Alternatively, they have been unable to gain access to the glial fiber system because of local encumbrances exerted by neighboring cells.

Heterotopias and Ectopias
A wide range of developmental disorders, many of obscure etiology but including both heritable and acquired conditions, give rise to neocortical malformations characterized by abnormal position of the principal neuron classes (Caviness and Williams 1984). One encounters malformations in which neurons have failed to initiate or failed to complete migrations and lie in "heterotopic" position somewhere

along the presumed migratory path. Heterotopia may be highly focal or relatively generalized in distribution throughout the hemispheres. The cells may be arrested in positions at variable depths within the cerebral wall. For example, in malformations described by Dooling and Richardson (1980) and Gadisseux et al. (unpublished) migration arrested between the VZ and ESS. In lissencephaly and in the Walker-Warburg malformation, described below, neuronal arrest occurs in the corona radiata between the ESS and the cortical plate. One also encounters malformations in which neurons have migrated beyond the normal limits of the cortical plate to establish "ectopias" in the molecular layer or even more distally in the arachnoidal compartment.

Heterotopia
The presence of heterotopia suggests that a pathologic process acts to disrupt migration without destroying large numbers of neurons. Plausibly, the system of radial glial fibers is the attack point of the pathologic process in this circumstance. We suggest that the glial system may be affected in two different ways. The radial fibers might be frankly destroyed by a pathologic process. Alternatively, as a consequence of cerebral injury radial cells might be transformed to astrocytic forms and cease to support neuronal migrations across the cerebral wall. As we shall consider with regard to ectopia, the transformed astrocytes may enable neuronal migration within the cortex itself, if not at subcortical levels.

These two classes of disruption of the radial glial fiber system may be plausibly viewed to underlie the two human malformations: classic lissencephaly (Bielschowsky 1923; Chrome 1956; Stewart, Richman, and Caviness 1975) and the Walker-Warburg malformation (Evrard, Gadisseux, and Lyon 1982; Williams et al. 1984). Neuronal heterotopias occupy a wide subcortical field within the cerebral wall in both classic lissencephaly and the Walker-Warburg malformation. In both malformations the true cortex is represented by a relatively small population of superficially located neurons having the cytologic features of neurons normal to neocortical layers v and vi. Thus, in both lissencephaly and the Walker-Warburg malformation the earliest generated neurons appear to have completed their migrations prior to the activation of the pathologic process. In both disorders the cerebral surface is agyric or contains only a few broad gyri ("pachygyria").

Lissencephaly
In lissencephaly (figure 16.7A) gyral and cytoarchitectonic anomalies are congruent. The extent of the distribution of the architectonic abnormality within the hemispheres approximates the distal territories

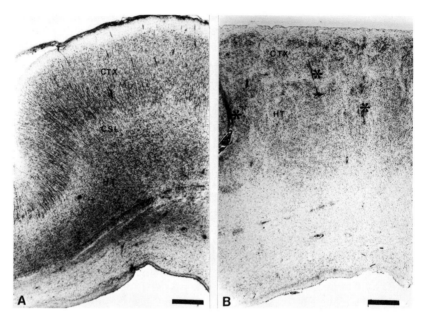

Figure 16.7
Heterotopic neurons in the corona radiata in cerebral malformations. (*A*) Lissence-phaly. The incompletely formed cortex (CTX) separated from the field of heterotopic neurons (HT) by a cell sparse zone (CSL). (*B*) The Walker-Warburg malformation. The field of heterotopic neurons, continuing from the incompletely formed cortex into the corona radiata is broken up by columns of glial tissue (*). The leptomeninges and cortex are unified by dense cicatrix. (*A*) and (*B*): paraffin-embedded, 35-μm sections; cresyl-violet stain; bar = 500 μm.

of perfusion of the major cerebral arteries (Stewart et al. 1975). Corti-cal regions corresponding to proximal arterial territories, by contrast, are usually normal in terms of their gyral configurations and their architectonic patterns and include the orbitofrontal and medial corti-cal regions. The leptomeninges are normal.

The wide heterotopic zone is richly populated by apparently healthy neurons. The dominant neuronal classes are those normally predominant in the granular and supragranular neocortical layers. Characteristically interposed between the heterotopic and true corti-cal zones is a cell-sparse zone. Fiber stains may show consolidation of axons along this plane, but the cell-sparse zone contains a few neu-ronal somata, includes fibrous astrocytes, and shows an increased density of small vascular channels. Thus, the histologic pattern sug-gests that tissue necrosis has occurred in a restricted laminar zone between the true cortex and the heterotopic neuronal field. We hy-pothesize that migrations are interrupted because the glial fibers have been transected at this zone of tissue necrosis, while subjacent neurons are left stranded but relatively undamaged.

The specific pathophysiologic process that gives rise to this malformation has not been elucidated. It occurs spontaneously but also runs in families as a component of a more general malformation affecting multiple organ systems (Miller 1963; Dieker et al. 1969). Thus, it is probable that multiple specific disorders acting during the second trimester when cerebral migrations are proceeding vigorously may reproduce this classic architectonic picture. For those specimens in which the region of cortical malformation approximates that of the distal arterial fields, we have previously suggested that the causative pathophysiologic event is transient vascular hypoperfusion (Stewart et al. 1975). No direct evidence supports this hypothesis.

Walker-Warburg Malformation

The topography, histopathology, and neocortical architectonic anomaly associated with the Walker-Warburg malformation differ substantially from those of classic lissencephaly (figure 16.7B; Chan et al. 1980; Williams et al. 1984; Bordarier, Aicardi, and Goutieres 1984). The Walker-Warburg malformation involves the entire cerebral hemisphere and is not restricted, as in certain examples of classic lissencephaly, to the distal fields of arterial perfusion. In contrast to classic lissencephaly, there is extensive proliferation of collagenous tissue and other mesenchymal elements in the leptomeningeal compartment and of dense mesenchymal, glial adhesions at the surface of the brain, which completely obliterate the subarachnoid space and lead to hydrocephalus. Furthermore, mesenchymal elements proliferate substantially around penetrating vascular channels, and this results in a pattern of scarring that interdigitates deeply into the cerebral substance. Broad bands of proliferated astroglial fibers continuing from the zones of mesenchymal proliferation extend in an irregular radial fashion even more deeply into the cerebral wall. These zones of glial proliferation span the true cortex and the subcortical heterotopic zone. Again in contrast to classic lissencephaly, there is no discrete laminar cell-sparse zone between true cortex and the heterotopic zones. Instead, the two zones make up a cellular continuum in which the normal radial alignment of neurons has been dramatically deflected or interrupted for substantial distances.

The meningeal and glial reactions of this malformation, so extensive in the cerebrum, appear virtually throughout the brain. The meningeal reaction is associated with anomalies of fiber and cell patterns in the cerebellum and the axial nervous system. In these regions, as in the cerebrum, the disorder of architectonic patterns reaches a maximum at the surface. The overall histopathologic pattern suggests the effects of a cicatrizing process acting over an extended period of development. We infer from the extent that cerebral neuronal migrations have been disturbed that the process must begin in the early second trimester, when neocortical migrations are underway. It must continue into the third trimester, when it disrupts cerebellar cortical histogenesis.

A self-limiting meningoencephalitis of moderate to low virulence might plausibly excite such a histopathologic reaction. Transformation of radial glial cells into reactive astrocytes in response to an infectious process might be the mechanism that leads to disruption of neuronal migration and the associated deformations of neuronal patterns. In a single reported case a similar histopathologic and architectonic anomaly has been associated with serologically documented intrauterine infection by an enterovirus. It is of interest that this rare malformation is more prevalent among siblings and has a tendency to occur in consecutive pregnancies. It has not been encountered in consecutive generations. Thus, although family associations are characteristic of the disorder, this may reflect heightened vulnerability to a teratogenic process rather than transmission by an autosomal recessive gene. Though unusual, such patterns of "horizontal" transmission of viral agents from mother to multiple offspring in the course of several pregnancies has been seen in experimental animals.

Ectopia
Ectopic neurons occupy positions superficial to cortical layers ii and iii. They may lie within the molecular layer or even outside the cerebrum as components of neuroglial masses actually within the leptomeninges. One assumes the ectopic neurons reach these positions by ascending surfaces other than those of radial glial fibers. A heterogeneous group of cerebral malformations may be associated with neuronal ectopia. For example, typical examples of this anomalous neuronal pattern have been observed in association with the fetal alcohol syndrome (Clarren et al. 1978; Wisniewski et al. 1983), but the phenomenon is probably not specific to any teratogen. Typically, the anomaly is associated with what appears to be relatively mild injury to the most superficial part of the developing cortex, the interface of mesenchymal membranes and the molecular layer (figure 16.8A; Caviness, Evrard, and Lyon 1978). At points where damage occurs, a mesenchymal, neuroglial scar forms. Young neurons approaching or already in position at the most superficial level of the cortex where the injury occurs are presumably dissociated from tissue constraints as a consequence of the destructive effects of the pathologic process

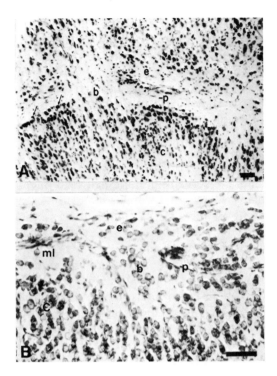

Figure 16.8
Neocortical ectopias in a human brain (A) and in the brain of the murine *dr^sst* mutant
(B). Ectopias (e) located in the extracerebral compartment are linked by a neuroglial
bridge (b) to the neocortex (c). Limited segments of pia (p) overlie the molecular layer
(ml), which is reduced in width. Arrows in (A) mark the interface of the molecular
layer and neocortical layer ii, where disruption is less marked. (A) and (B): paraffin-
embedded, 10-μm sections; cresyl-violet stain. Bar = 120 μm (A) and 65 μm (B). ((A)
is adapted from Caviness and Rakic 1978; (B) from Wahlsten and Caviness,
unpublished.)

on the tissue rather like the tissue dissociation that precedes the transfer of neurons to *in vitro* culture. Apparently the pathologically dissociated neurons are able to resume their migrations after the injury and to advance beyond the limits of the central nervous system to establish substantial colonies of neuronal cells in the subarachnoid compartment. The phenomenon may be essentially the same as that seen in the experiments of Dvorak and Feit (1977), in which neurons continue their migratory ascent after injury to nearly the full thickness of the cortex.

This ectopic pattern underscores the critical roles that the molecular layer and the glial pial membrane serve in limiting neuronal migration under normal circumstances. Also, it illustrates the readiness of the young neuron to continue its movements along surfaces other than radial glial fiber surfaces once constraining forces are disrupted.

The Dreher-Shaker short-tail (dr^{sst}) mutation gives rise to a complex brain malformation affecting the cerebrum, brain stem, and cerebellum (figure 16.8B; Caviness and Rakic 1978). An initiating event appears to be an entrapment of brain stem and cerebellum resulting from volume mismatch between the neural and osseous structures of the posterior cranial fossa (Wahlsten and Caviness, unpublished). In the terminal week of gestation an aqueductocele expands from the retrocollicular recess of the ventricular system. Typically, the degree of expansion causes the mass to herniate through the lambdoidal suture conjunction. The mass also entraps and destroys the cerebellum to a variable degree. The amount of neuronal ectopia in relation to meningeal scarring and damage to the neocortical molecular layer varies over the cerebral convexities. The cerebral ectopia in this mutant is virtually identical in distribution and pattern to those described above in human malformations. This effect on the neocortical architectonic pattern in dr^{sst} is seen only in the neonatal period as neuronal migrations to the most superficial cortical layers are being completed. The toxic and inflammatory effects of the hemorrhagic meningitis associated with the destructive malformation of the posterior fossa may plausibly disrupt the mesenchymal, neuroglial barrier over the cerebrum and may thereby allow the ectopias to form.

Disordered Cell Ascent along the Radial-Fiber Surface
The malformations presented in previous sections illustrate the consequences of disorders that strike the glial-fiber system relatively selectively. In the present section we shall turn to a spectrum of cortical malformations in which, we hypothesize, the abnormal interaction of postmitotic neurons and radial glial fiber results in arrest of neuronal ascent. Despite these disorders the integrity of the glial-fiber system

appears to be maintained. Two disorders transmitted by autosomal recessive inheritance have been selected to represent this class of disturbances.

The Reeler Mutation
The reeler (*rl*) mutation in mice is associated with a systematic inversion in relative position of the principal neuron classes in cerebral-cortical formations (figure 16.9; Caviness 1976; Caviness and Rakic 1978). Similar abnormalities of neuronal pattern also occur in the cerebellum (Mariani et al. 1977; Wilson, Sotelo, and Caviness 1981; Goffinet et al. 1984). In addition, there are anomalies of axon trajectories in the axial nervous system especially affecting the retinotectal and retinogeniculate projections (Frost et al. 1986). Neocortical neurons of various classes are formed normally in the VZ. Radial glial fibers grouped in fascicles span the cerebral wall. Postmitotic neurons closely applied to the surface of radial glial fibers migrate normally across the IZ (Pinto-Lord, Evrard, and Caviness 1982). As the young neuron ascends athrough the external sagittal stratum and into the lower margin of the developing cortex, upward progression along the surface of the glial fiber appears to be blocked. The obstruction appears to be caused by other neurons that have migrated earlier. These are still extensively applied to the surface of radial glial fibers after they have ceased to move and have begun to grow and differentiate (Pinto-Lord, Evrard, and Caviness 1982).

It is of note that the transcortical segments of the radial glial fibers in the reeler animal remain tightly fasciculated throughout the migratory epoch, in contrast to those in the normal animal (Gadisseux and Evrard 1985). Young cells cannot penetrate the bundles and separate the fibers from each other, as they appear to do in the normal cortex. Plausibly, surface properties of the migrating neurons or the radial fibers augment glial-glial or neuronal-glial adhesivity and impede further cellular movement. The molecular derangement in the mutant appears to affect all migrating cells in virtually all cortical structures. It may affect patterns of fasciculation of certain axonal systems as well.

Zellweger Malformation
Though associated with heterotopia, the anomalous neuronal pattern associated with the Zellweger malformation in man (Bowen et al. 1964) differs substantially from that of lissencephaly and the Walker-Warburg malformation mentioned above (figure 16.10A; Volpe and Adams 1972; Evrard et al. 1978). In the Zellweger malformation the abnormality in the cerebral gyral pattern is more restricted. This gyral

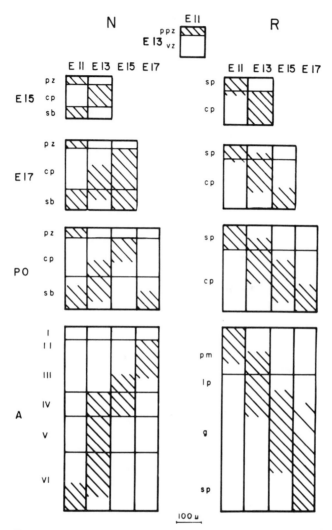

Figure 16.9

The distribution of 3H-thymidine labeled cohorts of neurons at graded developmental ages in normal (N) and reeler (R) mutant mice. The ages at which cohorts were labeled embryonic day 11 to 17 are presented on the horizontal axis, while the ages at which neuron cohorts were mapped embryonic day 15 to postnatal day 0 and as adults) is presented on the vertical axis. Cohorts that undergo terminal division at the same time in normal and reeler littermates include neurons of the same classes and migrate at the same time. In the cortex of the normal animal successively formed cohorts adopt innermost positions but in the reeler cortex they adopt outermost positions (adapted from Caviness 1982).

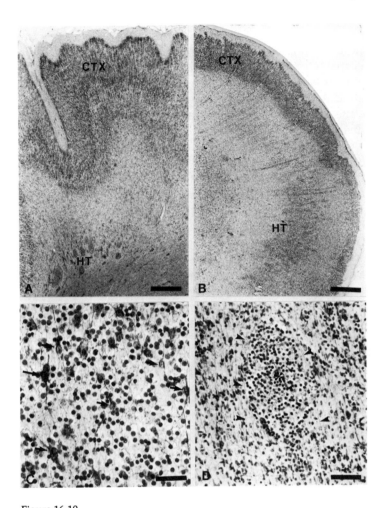

Figure 16.10
The cerebral wall in the Zellweger malformation in the first year of postnatal life (*A*) and at 20 weeks of gestational age, (*B–D*). A wide field of heterotopic neurons extends inward from the cortex through the corona radiata. Small cells with round to oval nuclei form cylindrical aggregates extending through the subcortical heterotopic field (*B, D*). Multipolar astrocytes and astrocytic cells with ascending radial processes characteristic of transitional forms between astrocytes (arrows) and radial glial cells are abundant among the subcortical heterotopic neurons (*C*); radial glial fibers (arrowheads) ascending through the corona radiata appear to course around, rather than through, the cylindrical cellular aggregates (*). (*A*) and (*B*): GFAP cresyl-violet stain; bar = 750 μm (*A*) and (*B*), 25 μm (*C*), and 55 μm (*D*).

anomaly, which is restricted to the centrosylvian regions, is bilaterally symmetrical (Evrard et al. 1978). Gyri of the parasylvian region are smaller, and those higher along the central convexity are wider, than their counterparts in the normal brain. Anomalies of neuronal pattern approximately underlie the gyral anomalies. In contrast to the cortical patterns associated with lissencephaly and the Walker-Warburg malformation, the cortex in the Zellweger malformation explicitly retains the five principal neuronal layers.

A large contingent of neurons is distributed in heterotopic fashion throughout all levels of the cortex, even deep into the subcortical white matter. Among neurons in heterotopic position are cells of all neuron classes, that is, cells that were destined for all the neocortical layers. Thus, the cell pattern suggests that neuronal migration is impeded but not interrupted in this disorder. In specimens recovered from abortuses 14 and 20 to 24 weeks of gestational age, there appears to be a tendency for migrations to arrest superficially in the developing corona radiata, near the transition to the inferior zone of the cortical anlage (figure 16.10B–D; Powers et al. 1988). Although only a limited proportion of neurons are affected, the heterotopic population includes cells that undergo their migrations throughout the entire migratory epoch.

The disorder is transmitted by autosomal recessive inheritance (Bowen et al. 1964). It is associated with a profound reduction in the number of cellular peroxisomes and an impairment of virtually all peroxisomal functions (Goldfischer et al. 1973; Moser et al. 1984; Vamecq et al. 1986). These include multiple catalytic reactions, in particular the enzymatic degradation of very long fatty-acid chains and of phytanic acid. The amino acid pipicholic acid is present in high concentrations in the blood. There is also defective synthesis of plasmalogen, a complex lipid structure integral to cellular membranes. One or more of these molecular anomalies may directly or indirectly affect the surface properties of glial cells and neurons in a way that makes postmigratory elements not readily displaced from the surface of radial glial fibers by later migrating cells.

Prospectus

The experimental and neuropathological studies reviewed in the foregoing sections focus attention upon two general themes for future inquiry. These themes are both of critical importance to our understanding of the biological and molecular cell processes of normal and abnormal cortical histogenesis.

Preferred Surfaces for Neuronal Migration
The current position of research is that the surface of the radial glial fiber is an obligate corridor for cell migration from the ventricular zone to the cortex. Under pathological circumstances, however, other as yet unidentified substrates appear competent to guide neuronal migration across the cortex and even beyond. Slice preparations maintained *in vitro* may afford more direct tests of the obligate role of the glial fibers along the initial migratory trajectory through the subcortical portion of the cerebral wall. Electron microscopy may identify the substrates that support migration across the cortex in pathological conditions. A difference in guidance requirements between subcortical and intracortical migration, if it exists, could have several explanations. The explanation might lie, for example, in differences in patterns of deployment of suitable surfaces to support migration. Alternately, transformations may occur in the properties of the young neuron itself as it enters the cortex. These changes may allow the migrating neuron to accept different classes of surfaces for migration or perhaps to be directed in its movements by a wider range of tropic cues.

Neuronal Migration: A Sequence of Specific Biological Processes
The organization of the radial fiber system varies with the cerebral architectonic strata of the developing cerebral wall. Specifically, the pattern of fiber fasciculation changes sequentially with ascent through the VZ, IZ, subplate, and the successive strata of the cortical anlage. Under conditions of normal development and even more dramatically under certain experimental and pathological conditions, arrest of migration appears to occur selectively within restricted planes corresponding more or less to zones of transition in the organization of fiber fascicles. In particular, arrest appears to occur where the postmitotic cell should exit the VZ and gain access to the fascicle system and in the lower zone of the cortex where the fascicles break up in crossing the ESS and anlage of the infragranular layers. For reasons reviewed above, arrest at the level of the VZ may reflect failures of complex conformational changes occurring in the postmitotic neuron that are essential to migration. Whatever the specific pathologic process or its molecular mechanisms, arrest occurring at the inferior margins of the cortex may reflect an intrinsically elevated resistance to cell movement at planes of transition. Obviously, variations in resistance to migration might be mechanical. They might relate to cell or ambient-process conformation or to resistance to the sheer inherent in the reciprocal adhesivity of apposed cellular surfaces. Apropos, the molecular mechanisms that direct the migrating cell to penetrate the

fiber fascicles and presumably to contribute to the process of defasciculation may contribute also to the maneuvers of cells in the depths of the developing cortex under normal and pathological conditions.

Note

The authors thank Ms. Virginia Tosney for her tireless effort in preparing the manuscript. This work was supported by NIH grant R01 NS12005 (V. S. C), a Frank Boas Scholarship (J. P. M.), a NATO Research Fellowship (J. P. M.), a grant from the Foundation Princess Marie-Christine (J. F. G., J. P. M.), and the Charles A. King Trust Research Fellowship (J. P. M.).

References

Angevine, J. B., Jr., and R. L. Sidman. 1961. Autoradiographic study of cell migration during histogenesis of cerebral cortex in the mouse. *Nature* 192:766–768.

Antanitus, D. S., B. H. Choi, and L. W. Lapham. 1976. Demonstration of glial fibrillary acidic protein in the cerebrum of the human fetus by indirect immunofluorescence. *Brain Research* 103:613–616.

Astrom, K.-E. 1967. On the early development of the isocortex in fetal sheep. In *Progress in brain research*, ed. C. G. Bernhard and J. P. Schade. Amsterdam: Elsevier.

Bailey, P., and G. von Bonin. 1951. *The isocortex of man.* Urbana: University of Illinois Press.

Barth, P. G., 1987. Disorders of neuronal migration. *Canadian Journal of Neurological Sciences* 14:1–16.

Benjelloun-Touimi, S., C. M. Jacque, P. Derer, F. De Vitry, R. Maunoury, and P. Dupouey. 1985. Evidence that mouse astrocytes may be derived from the radial glia: An immunohistochemical study of the cerebellum in the normal and reeler mouse. *Journal of Neuroimmunology* 9:87–97.

Berry, M., and A. W. Rogers. 1965. The migration of neuroblasts in the developing cerebral cortex. *Journal of Anatomy* 99:691–709.

Bielschowsky, M. 1923. Über die Oberflachengestaltung des Grosshirnmantels bei Mikrogyrie und bei normaler Entwicklung. *Journal für Psychologie und Neurologie* 30:29–76.

Bignami, A., and D. Dahl. 1976. The astroglial response to stabbing: Immunoflourescence studies with antibodies to astrocyte-specific protein (GFA) in mammalian and submammalian vertebrates. *Neuropathology and Applied Neurobiology* 2:99–111.

Bordarier, C., J. Aicardi, and F. Goutieres. 1984. Congenital hydrocephalus and eye abnormalities with severe developmental brain defects: Warburg's syndrome. *Annals of Neurology* 16:60–65.

Boulder Committee. 1970. Embryonic vertebrate central nervous system: Revised terminology. *Anatomical Record* 166:257–262.

Bowen, P., C. S. N. Lee, H. Zellweger, and R. Lindenberg. 1964. A familial syndrome of multiple congenital defects. *Bulletin of the Johns Hopkins Hospital* 114:402–414.

Brent, R. L., D. A. Beckmann, and R. P. Jensh. 1986. The relationship of animal experiments in predicting the effects on intrauterine radiation effects in the human. In *Radiation risks to the developing nervous system*, ed. H. Kreigel, W. Schmahl, G. B. Gerber, and F. G. Stieve. Stuttgart: Gustav Fischer Verlag.

Brodmann, K. 1909. *Vergleichende Localisationslehre der Grosshirnrinde in ihren Prinzipien dargestellt auf Grund des Zellenbaues*. Leipzig: J. A. Barth.

Caviness, V. S., Jr. 1975. Architectonic map of neocortex of the normal mouse. *Journal of Comparative Neurology* 164:247–264.

Caviness, V. S., Jr. 1976. Patterns of cell and fiber distribution in the neocortex of the reeler mutant mouse. *Journal of Comparative Neurology* 170:435–448.

Caviness, V. S., Jr. 1982. Neocortical histogenesis in normal and reeler mice: A developmental study based upon [3H]thymidine autoradiography. *Developmental Brain Research* 4:293–302.

Caviness, V. S., Jr., P. Evrard, and G. Lyon. 1978. Radial neuronal assemblies, ectopia and necrosis of developing cortex: A case analysis. *Acta Neuropathologica* (Berlin) 41:67–72.

Caviness, V. S., Jr., and P. Rakic. 1978. Mechanism of cortical development: A view from mutations in mice. In *Annual review of neuroscience*, ed. M. W. Cowan, Z. W. Hall, and E. R. Kandel. Palo Alto: Annual Reviews.

Caviness, V. S., Jr., and R. L. Sidman. 1973. Time of origin of corresponding cell classes in the cerebral cortex of normal and reeler mutant mice: An autoradiographic analysis. *Journal of Comparative Neurology* 148:141–152.

Caviness, V. S., Jr., and R. S. Williams. 1984. Cellular patterns in developmental malformations of neocortex: Neuron-Glial interactions. In *The developing brain and its disorders*, ed. M. Arima, Y. Suzuki, and H. Yabuuchi. Tokyo: University of Tokyo Press.

Chan, C. C., P. R. Egbert, M. K. Herrick, and H. Urich. 1980. Oculocerebral malformations. *Archives of Neurology* 37:104–108.

Choi, B. H., 1986. Glial fibrillary acidic protein in radial glia of early human fetal cerebrum: A light and electron microscopic immunoperoxidase study. *Journal of Neuropathology and Experimental Neurology* 45:408–418.

Choi, B. H., and L. W. Lapham. 1978. Radial glia in the human fetal cerebrum: A combined Golgi immunoflurescence and electron microscopy study. *Brain Research* 148:295–311.

Chrome, L. 1956. Pachygyria. *Journal of Pathology and Bacteriology* 71:335–352.

Chuong, C.-M., K. L. Crossin, and G. M. Edelman. 1987. Sequential expression and differential function of multiple adhesion molecules during the formation of cerebellar cortical layers. *Journal of Cell Biology* 104:331–342.

Clarren, S. K., E. C. Alvord, Jr., S. M. Sumi, A. P. Streissguth, and D. W. Smith. 1978. Brain malformations related to prenatal exposure to ethanol. *Journal of Pediatrics* 92:64–67.

Crandall, J. E., and V. S. Caviness. Jr. 1984. Axon strata of the cerebral wall in embryonic mice. *Developmental Brain Research* 14:185–195.

Crossin, K. L., C.-M. Chuong, and G. M. Edelman. 1985. Expression sequences of cell adhesion molecules. *Developmental Biology* 82:6942–6946.

Crossin, K. L., S. Hoffman, M. Grumet, J.-P. Thiery, and G. M. Edelman. 1986. Site-restricted expression of cytotactin during development of the chicken embryo. *Journal of Cell Biology* 102:1917–1930.

De Blas, A. L. 1984. Monoclonal antibodies to specific astroglial and neuronal antigens reveal the cytoarchitecture of the Bergmann glia fibers in the cerebullum. *Journal of Neuroscience* 4:265–273.

Dieker, H., R. H. Edwards, G. ZuRhein, S. M. Chou, H. A. Hartman, and J. M. Opitz. 1969. The lissencephaly syndrome. In *Birth defects*, Original Article Series, vol. 5, no. 2. Baltimore: Wiliams and Wilkins.

Dooling, E. C., and E. P. Richardson. 1980. A case of adult microcephaly. *Archives of Neurology* 37:688–692.

Dvorák, K., and J. Feit. 1977. Migration of neuroblasts through partial necrosis of the cerebral cortex in newborn rats: Contribution to the problem of morphological development and developmental period of cerebral microgyria. *Acta Neuropathologica* (Berlin) 38:203–212.

Dvorák, K., J. Feit, and Z. Jurankova. 1978. Experimentally induced focal microgyria and status verrucosus deformis in rats—Pathogenesis and interrelation. *Acta Neuropathologica* (Berlin) 44:121–129.

Eckenhoff, M. F., and P. Rakic. 1984. Radial organization of the hippocampal dentate gyrus: A golgi, ultrastructural and immunocytochemical analysis in the developing rhesus monkey. *Journal of Comparative Neurology* 223:1–21.

Edmondson, J. C., R. K. H. Liem, J. E. Kuster, and M. E. Hatten. 1988. Astrotactin: A novel neuronal cell surface antigen that mediates neuron-astroglial interactions in cerebellar microcultures. *Journal of Cell Biology* 106:505–517.

Edwards, M., M. Yamamoto, G. Schwarting, and V. S. Caviness, Jr. 1986. Development of radial glia in the mouse: An immunohistochemical study with a cell-class specific monoclonal antibody. *Society for Neuroscience Abstracts* 12:182.

Eriksdotter-Nillson, M., G. Jonsson, D. Dahl, and H. Bjorklund. 1986. Astroglial development in microcephalic rat brain after fetal methylazoxymethanol treatment. *International Journal of Developmental Neuroscience* 4:353–362.

Evrard, P., V. S. Caviness, Jr., J. Prats-Vinas, and G. Lyon. 1978. The mechanism of arrest of neuronal migration in the Zellweger malformation: An hypothesis based upon cytoarchitectonic analysis. *Acta Neuropathologica* (Berlin) 41:109–117.

Evrard, P., J.-F. Gadisseux, and G. Lyon. 1982. Les malformations du systeme nerveux central. In *La naissance du cerveau,* ed. P. Royer. Paris: Lafayette.

Frost, D. O., M. A. Edwards, G. M. Sachs, and V. S. Caviness, Jr. 1986. Retinotectal projection in reeler mutant mice: Relationships among axon trajectories, arborization patterns and cytoarchitecture. *Journal of Comparative Neurology* 28:109–120.

Gadisseux, J.-F., and P. Evrard. 1985. Glial-neuronal relationship in the developing central nervous system. *Developmental Neuroscience* 7:12–32.

Galaburda, A. M., and T. L. Kemper. 1979. Cytoarchitectonic abnormalities in developmental dyslexia: A case study. *Annals of Neurology* 60:94–100.

Goffinet, A. M., K.-F. So, M. Yamamoto, M. Edwards, and V. S. Caviness, Jr. 1984. Architectonic and hodological organization of the cerebellum in reeler mutant mice. *Developmental Brain Research* 16:263–276.

Goldfischer, S., C. L. Moore, A. B. Johnson, A. J. Spiro, M. P. Valsamis, H. K. Wisniewski, R. H. Ritch, W. T. Norton, I. Rapin, and L. M. Gartner. 1973. Peroxysomal and mitochondrial defects in the cerebro-hepato-renal syndrome. *Science* 182:62–64.

Grumet, M., S. Hoffman, K. L. Crossin, and G. M. Edelman. 1985. Cytotactin, an extracellular matrix protein of neural and non-neural tissues that mediates glia-neuron interaction. *Developmental Biology* 82:8075–8079.

Hatten, M. E. 1985. Neuronal regulation of astroglial morphology and proliferation in vitro. *Journal of Cell Biology* 100:384–396.

Hatten, M. E., and R. K. H. Liem. 1981. Astroglial cells provide a template for the positioning of developing cerebellar neurons in vitro. *Journal of Cell Biology* 90:622–630.

Hatten, M. E., R. K. Liem, and C. A. Mason. 1984. Two forms of cerebellar glial cells interact differently with neurons in vitro. *Journal of Cell Biology* 98:193–204.

Hatten, M. E., R. K. H. Liem, and C. A. Mason. 1986. Weaver mouse cerebellar granule neurons fail to migrate on wild-type astroglial processes in vitro. *Journal of Neuroscience* 6:2676:2683.

Hemmendinger, L. M., and V. S. Caviness, Jr. 1988. Cellular migration in developing cerebral wall explants *in vitro*. *Developmental Brain Research* 38:291–295.

Hicks, S., C. J. D'Amato, and M. J. Lowe. 1963. Low dose radiation of the developing brain. *Science* 141:903–905.

Hinds, J. W., and T. L. Ruffett. 1971. Cell proliferation in the neural tube: An electron microscopic and Golgi analysis in the mouse cerebral vesicle. *Zeitschrift für Zellforschung und mikroskopische Anatomie* (Berlin) 115:226–264.

His, W. 1889. Die Neuroblasten und deren Entstehung im Embryonalen Marke. *Abhandlungen der mathematisch physischen klasse der Sachsischen Akademie der Wissenschaften* 15:313–372.

Johnston, M. V., and J. T. Coyle. 1979. Histological and neurocheical effects of fetal treatment with methyl-azoxy-methanol acetate on rat neocortex in adulthood. *Brain Research* 170:135–155.

Kadhim, H., J.-F. Gaidsseux, and P. Evrard. 1988. Topographical and cytological evolution of the glial phase during prenatal development of the human brain: Histochemical and electron microscopic study. *Journal of Neuropathology and Experimental Neurology* 47:166–188.

Kameyama, Y., and K. Hoshino. 1986. Sensitive phases of CNS development. In *Radiation risks to the developing nervous system*, ed. H. Kriegel, W. Schmahl, G. B. Gerber, and F. G. Stieve. Stuttgart: Gustav Fischer Verlag.

Kostovic, I., and P. Rakic. 1984. Development of prestriate visual projections in the monkey and human fetal cerebrum revealed by transient cholinesterase staining. *Journal of Neuroscience* 4:25–42.

Lafarga, M., M. T. Berciano, and M. Blanco. 1986. Ectopic Purkinje cells in the cerebellar white matter of normal adult rodents: A Golgi study. *Acta Anatomica* 127:53–58.

Landrieu, P., A. Goffinet, V. S. Caviness, Jr., and G. Lyon. 1981. Formation of "neocortex" in a congenital human teratoma. *Acta Neuropathologica* (Berlin) 55:35–38.

Levitt, P., M. L. Cooper, and P. Rakic. 1981. Coexistence of neuronal and glial precursor cells in the cerebral ventricular zone of the fetal monkey: An ultrastructural immunoperoxidase analysis. *Journal of Neuroscience* 1:27–39.

Levitt, P., M. L. Cooper, and P. Rakic. 1983. Early divergence and changing proportions of neuronal and glial precursor cells in the primate cerebral ventricular zone. *Developmental Biology* 96:472–484.

Levitt, P., and P. Rakic. 1980. Imunoperoxidase localization of glial fibrillary acidic protein in radial glial cells and astrocytes of the developing rhesus monkey brain. *Journal of Comparative Neurology* 193:815–840.

Lindner, J., J. Guenther, H. Nick, G. Zinser, H. Antonicek, M. Schachner, and D. Monard. 1986. Modulation of granule cell migration by a glia-derived protein. *Proceedings of the National Academy of Science* (USA) 83:4568–4571.

Luskin, M. B., and C. J. Shatz. 1985. Studies of the earliest generated cells of the cat's visual cortex: Cogeneration of subplate and marginal zones. *Journal of Neuroscience* 5:1062–1075.

Mariani, J., F. Crepel, K. Mikoshiba, J. P. Changeux, and C. Sotelo. 1977. Anatomical, physiological, and biochemical studies of the cerebellum from reeler mutant mouse. *Philosophical Transactions of the Royal Society of London* 281:1–28.

Marin-Padilla, M. 1971. Early prenatal ontogenesis of the cerebral cortex (neocortex) of the cat (felis domestica), A Golgi study: I. The primordial neocortical organization. *Zeitschrift für Anatomie und Entwicklung—Geschichte* 134:117–145.

Marin-Padilla, M. 1978. Dual origin of the mammalian neocortex and evolution of the cortical plate. *Anatomy and Embryology* 152:109–126.

Marin-Padilla, M., and T. M. Marin-Padilla. 1982. Origin, prenatal development, and structural organization of layer I of the human cerebral (motor) cortex: A Golgi study. *Anatomy and Embryology* 164:161–206.

McConnell, S. K. 1985. Migration and differentiation of cerebral cortical neurons after transplantation into the brains of ferrets. *Science* 229:1268–1271.

McConnell, S. K. 1986. Fate of visual cortical neurons after heterochronic transplantation. *Society for Neuroscience Abstracts* 12:1371.

Miller, J. Q. 1963. Lissencephaly in two siblings. *Neurology* 13:841–850.

Miller, M. W. 1986. Effects of alcohol on the generation and migration of cerebral cortical neurons. *Science* 233:1308–1311.

Miller, M. W. 1987. Effect of prenatal exposure to alcohol on the distribution and time of origin of corticospinal neurons in the rat. *Journal of Comparative Neurology* 257:372–382.

Misson, J.-P., M. A. Edwards, M. Yamamoto, and V. S. Caviness, Jr. 1988a. Mitotic cycling of radial glial cells of the fetal murine cerebral wall: A combined autoradiographic and immunohistochemical study. *Developmental Brain Research* 466:183–90.

Misson, J.-P., M. Yamamoto, M. Edwards, G. Schwarting, and V. S. Caviness, Jr. 1988b. Identification of radial glial cells within the developing murine CNS based upon a new histochemical marker. *Developmental Brain Research*, in press.

Moonen, G., M. P. Grau-Wagemans, and I. Selak. 1982. Plasminogen activator-plasmin system and neuronal migration. *Nature* 298:753–755.

Morest, D. K. 1969. The differentiation of cerebral dendrites: A study of the post-migratory neuroblast in the medial nucleus of the trapezoid body. *Zeitschrift für Anatomie und Entwicklungs—Geschcichte* (Berlin) 128:271–289.

Moser, H. W., A. E. Moser, I. Singh, and B. P. O'Neill. 1984. Adrenoleukodystrophy survey of 303 cases: Biochemistry, diagnosis, and therapy. *Annals of Neurology* 16:628–641.

Pinto-Lord, M. C., P. Evrard, and V. S. Caviness, Jr. 1982. Obstructed neuronal migration along radial glial fibers in the neocortex of the reeler mouse: A Golgi-EM analysis. *Developmental Brain Research* 4:379–393.

Powers, J. M., R. C. Tummons, V. S. Cainvess, Jr., A. B. Moser, and H. W. Moser. 1988. Structural and chemical alterations in the cerebral maldevelopment of fetal cerebro-hepato-renal (Zellweger) syndrome. *Journal of Neuropathology and Experimental Neurology*, in press.

Raedler, E., and A. Raedler. 1978. Autoradiographic study of early neurogenesis in rat neocortex. *Anatomy and Embryology* 154:267–284.

Rakic, P. 1971. Neuron-glia relationship during granule cell migration in developing cerebellar cortex: A Golgi and electromicroscopic study in Macacus rhesus. *Journal of Comparative Neurology* 141:283–312.

Rakic, P. 1972. Mode of cell migration to the superficial layers of fetal monkey neocortex. *Journal of Comparative Neurology* 145:61–84.

Rakic, P. 1974. Neurons in rhesus monkey visual cortex: Systematic relation between time of origin and eventual disposition. *Science* 183:425–427.

Rakic, P. 1975. Cell migration and neuronal ectopias in the brain. *Birth Defects* 11:95–129.

Rakic, P., and R. L. Sidman. 1968. Supravital DNA synthesis in the developing human and mouse brain. *Journal of Neuropathology and Experimental Neurology* 27:246–276.

Rakic, P., and R. L. Sidman. 1973. Weaver mutant mouse cerebellum: Defective neuronal migration secondary to abnormality of Bergmann glia. *Proceedings of the National Academy of Science* (USA) 70:240–244.

Roessmann, U., and P. Gambetti. 1986.·Pathological reaction of astrocytes in perinatal brain injury. *Acta Neuropathologica* (Berlin) 70:302–307.

Sauer, F. C. 1935a. Mitosis in the neural tube. *Journal of Comparative Neurology* 62:377–405.

Sauer, F. C. 1935b. The cellular structure of the neural tube. *Journal of Comparative Neurology* 63:13–23.

Schaper, A. 1897. Die fruhesten Differenzierungsvorgange im central nerven system. *Archiv für Entwicklungsmechanik der Organismen* 5:115–152.

Schmechel, D. E., and P. Rakic. 1979. A Golgi study of radial glial cells in developing monkey telencephalon: Morphogenesis and transformation into astrocytes. *Anatomy and Embryology* 156:115–152.

Selak, I., J. M. Foidart, and G. Moonen. 1985. Laminin promotes cerebellar granule cells migration in vitro and is synthesized by cultured astrocytes. *Developmental Neuroscience* 7:278–285.

Seymour, R. M., and M. Berry. 1975. Scanning and transmission electron microscope studies of interkinetic nuclear migration in the cerebral vesicles of the rat. *Journal of Comparative Neurology* 160:105–126.

Shimada, M., and J. Langman. 1970. Cell proliferation, migration, and differentiation in the cerebral cortex of the golden hamster. *Journal of Comparative Neurology* 139:227–244.

Sidman, R. L., and P. Rakic. 1973. Neuronal migration, with special reference to developing human brain: A review. *Brain Research* 62:1–35.

Sidman, R. L., and P. Rakic. 1982. Development of the human central nervous system. In *Histology and histopathology of the nervous system*, ed. W. Haymaker and R. D. Adams. Springfield: Charles C. Thomas.

Sims, K., J. E. Crandall, K. Kosik, and R. Williams. 1988. Microtubule-associated protein 2 (MAP2) immunoreactivity in human fetal neocortex. *Developmental Brain Research* 449:192–200.

Stewart, R. M., D. P. Richman, and V. S. Caviness, Jr. 1975. Lissencephaly and pachygria: An architectonic and topographical analysis. *Acta Neuropathologica* (Berlin) 31:1–12.

Trenkner, E., D. Smith, and N. Segil. 1984. Is cerebellar granule cell migration regulated by an internal clock? *Journal of Neuroscience* 4:2850–2855.

Vamecq, J., J. P. Draye, F. van Hoof, J.-P. Misson, P. Evrard, G. Verellen, H. J. Eyssen, J. V. Eldere, R. B. H. Schutgens, R. J. A. Wanders, and S. L. Goldfischer. 1986. Multiple peroxisomal enzymatic deficiency disorders: A comparative biochemical and morphologic study of Zellweger cerebrohepatorenal syndrome and neonatal adrenoleukodystrophy. *American Journal of Pathology* 125:524–535.

Volpe, J. J., and R. D. Adams. 1972. Cerebro-hepato-renal syndrome of Zellweger: An inherited disorder of neuronal migration. *Acta Neuropathologica* (Berlin) 20:175–198.

Williams, R. S., C. N. Swisher, M. Jennings, M. Ambler, and V. S. Caviness, Jr. 1984. Cerebro-ocular dysgenesis (Walker-Warburg syndrome): Neuropathologic and etiologic analysis. *Neurology* 34:1531–1541.

Wilson, L., C. Sotelo, and V. S. Caviness, Jr. 1981. Heterologous synapses upon Purkinje cells in the cerebellum of the reeler mutant mouse: An experimental light and electron microscopic study. *Brain Research* 213:63–82.

Wisniewski, K., M. Dambska, J. H. Sher, and Q. Qazi. 1983. A clinical neuropathological study of the fetal alcohol syndrome. *Neuropediatrics* 14:197–201.

Editor's Comments

A useful distinction is made in cognitive psychology between initial states and the subsequent expression of cognitive capacities (see Mehler in this volume). It is very clear that the human inherits innate dispositions, or universals, present as part of the evolutionary record, the phylogeny, at the initial state but before exposure to the personal environment. These dispositions are expressed in a particular manner after the personal history, the ontogeny, begins to unfold. Thus, humans have a disposition for learning a human language, though not a particular human language; other animals, lacking these dispositions, do not achieve the ability to use a language characteristically human irrespective of the environmental stimulus.

We learn from various lines of research that the innate functional dispositions are exceedingly robust. An eminently human language emerges in a remarkable variety of normal environments, i.e., in every known human society and in every historical period, and after marked deviation from standard environmental interaction, e.g., among the deaf, the blind, the severely culturally deprived, and Russian babies raised by bilinguals in Spanish and French (see Bellugi et al. in this volume).

Is the brain machinery that supports the innate dispositions for human behaviors like language also an expression of innate anatomical dispositions? Much of the evidence reviewed in this chapter seems to support this view. Thus, transplanted neurons tend to go to the right places, and mutant mouse strains, organize their neuronal assemblies in a remarkably normal fashion against terrible odds.

How is this innateness coded in the genes, stably maintained, and passed from generation to generation for thousands, if not tens of thousands of years. Interesting inroads into some of these questions are being made (see Crossin and Edelman in this volume).

However, we also learn from the present chapter, that brains can exhibit a remarkable amount of structural variety, as it is possible to physiologically and pathologically alter and moderate each developmental step from cytogenesis to histogenesis. Moreover, this variety is evident in the anatomy of the brain already in the fetal period, before the infant has been significantly exposed to its cultural environment. At least at the levels of cytoarchitecture, brain asymmetry, and patterns of neuronal connectivity, brains differ often markedly before, say, language acquisition has truly had a chance to get going (see Sherman, Rosen, and Galaburda in this volume). Is this sufficient evidence that the initial state, i.e., the set of dispositions devoid of expression, is represented in the nervous system even before cyto-

and histogenesis, that is, closer to the level of the genes themselves? Or can the anatomical structure of cell groups and connections change substantially without attendant change in functional capacity? The wing, for instance, has an intrinsic disposition for flight. This disposition is shared by the wing of a bat, the wing of different types of birds, and even the wing of an airplane. Can the macrostructure of the human brain change as much without changing its disposition for, let us say, human language. Clearly, the shape of the wing is represented in the genomic blueprint of the bat and the bird and in the blueprint in the airplane factory, for that matter. It appears on first inspection that even with enormous variation in the blueprint itself there can still be a flying wing. We must conclude, therefore, that the architecture of brain structures from genes to hemispheres may be capable of great structural variation without changing the functional dispositions of the final product. This is a very disturbing conclusion if we are interested in finding out how functional dispositions are represented at the level of material substance.

To say that the structure of the brain can change enormously without making it incapable of its phylogenetically determined behavioral imperative does not mean that no amount of anatomical change can have this effect. Once again, we know that nonhuman animals do not have the capacity for anything remotely resembling human language. Moreover, we know that under some pathological states in the human the linguistic capacity is not fully expressed or is expressed only anomalously. Among several possibilities this may mean that the innate capacity was not there to start with, as in Down's syndrome, infantile autism, developmental dyslexia, and other serious developmental neurological conditions leading to mental retardation. Only some of these conditions are known or suspected to have initial genetic anomalies; the rest have clearly identifiable nongenetic causes, e.g., viral infections and exposures to toxins (which, of course, can also lead to genetic injury).

Additional clues to the relationship between language acquisition and the acquisition in stages of the mature brain structure may indeed come from the study of a variety of developmental brain anomalies such as those described in the present chapter. For example, children with Down's syndrome, whose brains have a deficient number of (late-generated) interneurons, appear to develop normally linguistically, albeit somewhat slowly, until they reach a less than mature stage, and then their development stops. Dyslexics, I have argued, achieve normal cell and connectional architectures that are subsequently disrupted and reorganized into cellular and connectional architectures that are anomalous (exuberant rather than impoverished).

Their syntax and phonology too appear to be anomalous rather than simply impoverished. Autistic children, who evidence disruption of brain structures known to undergo histogenesis later than those involved in Down's syndrome and dyslexia, namely the hippocampus and cerebellum, appear to acquire normal language, which later becomes bizarre. There may indeed be initial states for each stage of language acquisition. A clearer understanding of the developmental stages and mechanisms of the brain will be useful for etablishing the appropriate relationships between brain and language. It is a pity that the innate dispositions of rodents do not include language.

Chapter 17

Competitive Interactions during Neuronal and Synaptic Development

Pasko Rakic

For many years the prevailing view was that the establishment of synaptic connections is determined exclusively by membrane-bound recognition molecules distributed differentially on each neuron and its processes. This consensus grew from the pioneering work elegantly formulated in the chemoaffinity theory by Sperry (1963). The essence of this idea is that pre- and postsynaptic elements bear specific labels that provide lock-and-key type recognition between growing axons and their targets. One important implication of this hypothesis is that instruction for the entire repertoire of neuronal connections within the brain is prespecified in a genetic program in some respects similar to the encoding of amino acid sequences of the proteins in the cell genome. The outcome of this precisely run developmental process was thought to be hard wired in synaptic circuitry and predictable to its finest detail. The expectation was that a full understanding of the mechanisms underlying neural development from the simplest to the most complex brain can be reached by simply unraveling the molecular mechanisms of gene control. In the past few years this simple version of the chemoaffinity theory has been abandoned by many developmental neurobiologists and even by some of its early proponents. The modern version of the chemoaffinity theory also involves competitive interactions, the outcome of which can be influenced by a variety of environmental factors, including functional activity (e.g., Easter et al. 1985).

Obviously, the basic organization of the brain cannot be achieved without precise genetic instruction. In fact, early developmental events, the establishment of basic cell lineages, and the fundamental blueprint of the nervous system in any species must be carried out by precise, intrinsic information and rigidly preprogrammed building of its components expressed through the differentiation of individual cells. There is considerable progress now being made in this exciting research area, and I believe that many critical developmental events can adequately be explained by noncompetitive interactions among participating elements. However, accumulated evidence in the various subfields of developmental neurobiology has revealed that most of the proposed models of the molecular mechanisms underlying synaptogenesis appear to be too narrow and do not apply to every aspect of neural development, especially not to the types of cell interaction that occur at later stages of structural and functional brain maturation. In particular, the view that every single detail of synaptic connectivity observed in the adult vertebrate brain is prespecified and immutably hard-wired cannot be reconciled with numerous experimental data in laboratory animals and with the known consequences of pre- and postnatal brain injuries in humans.

The upshot of recent research in developmental neurobiology and neuronal plasticity is that the final organization of synaptic circuits at least in the complex vertebrate brain does not follow a precise and rigid antigen-antibody type of molecular fitting but rather occurs in a piecemeal fashion that involves complex, competitive interactions among heterogeneous cells (Easter et al. 1985; Changeux and Dunchin 1976; Rakic 1979; Edelman 1987; Edelman and Finkel 1984; Purves 1988). Competitive interactions in developmental neurobiology are usually defined as those cellular events in which two or more neurons or their processes require some resource (e.g., trophic factor, membrane surface of adjacent cells, electrical stimulation) that is available in a limited quantity. Specific neuron types or their processes that are deprived of a sufficient amount of an essential resource either diminish in size, withdraw from the target region, or degenerate. In the broad sense of this definition all phenomena of neural structural plasticity, including the consequences of brain lesion in adults, can be considered to be the result of competitive interactions. For example, when one input to a given neuron or structure is removed, this makes some resource of the target cells available for use by the other inputs, which then can enlarge and expand into the vacated space. However, such competition, often referred to as "reactive synaptogenesis" (Nieto-Sampedro and Cotman 1987), is artificially induced and may not have any role in normal development. In this presentation I shall focus exclusively on competitive interactions that occur naturally during normal development as an essential step in the formation of neuronal connections.

Knowledge of the rules, sequences, and principles involved in these complex interactions is essential for understanding both normal and pathological development of the nervous system. Research in this area can be conducted with a variety of methods at the molecular, subcellular, cellular, multicellular, and systemic levels (figure 17.1). Among well-documented epigenetic factors are diffusible agents

Genetic endowment   Levels of analysis   Epigenetic factors

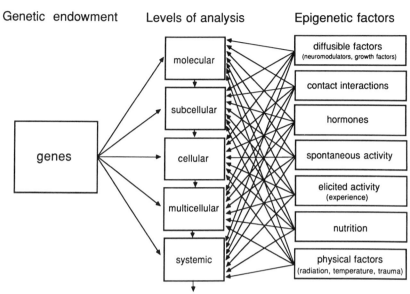

Figure 17.1
A diagrammatic representation of how various epigenetic factors (right column) that
have an effect on the output of genetic endowment (left) can be assessed at different
levels of analysis (middle column). While the genetic regulation of brain development
at each level may be examined selectively and directly (e.g., in single gene mutations),
epigenetic factors, which usually affect several levels, make meaningful analysis a formidable task. For this reason the present review is concerned only with selected types
of contact interactions at the multicellular level within the primate visual system.

(e.g., neurotransmitters and growth factors), contact interactions,
hormones, spontaneous or elicited electrical activity, nutrition, and
various physical forces (e.g., trauma, irradiation, and temperature).
The important fact is that certain phases of these interactions can be
influenced by the external environment. This fact is highly relevant to
developmental neuropathology in general and has some direct implications for understanding reading disorders, including the pathogenesis of developmental dyslexia. Unfortunately, study of cellular
interactions within the large mammalian cerebrum poses considerable logistic problems. For example, any physical or chemical manipulation of the developing brain may induce complex structural and
molecular changes to many classes of interacting neurons and their
membranes, second messenger molecules, and RNA and DNA in
both pre- and postsynaptic elements involved in the formation of connections. Unraveling, or even sorting out these alterations in multi-
neuronal structures is a technically formidable task. At present most
of the evidence for competitive interaction comes from anatomical

and cytological studies and ablation experiments in the developing brain. The present article will deal only with the principle of competitive contact interaction at the multicellular level.

The findings from my research that are probably most relevant to the competitive interaction and human developmental disorders discussed in this symposium are: many neuronal classes and their projections are more numerous in the developing brain than in the normal adult; developing axons can reach their proper targets by alternative routes; inputs from two or more sources that project to separate territories of a single structure are often initially intermixed; synapses in most areas are also initially overproduced and more widespread than in the adult; elimination of supernumerary neurons, axons, and synapses depends in many instances on competition and is not intracellularly programmed; environmental influences, including functional activity, may act more powerfully at the elimination phase than at the production phase.

Although the molecular mechanisms of these complex cellular events are not understood, study of these developmental events reveals the dynamic nature of neural development and synaptogenesis, delineates critical and vulnerable phases, unravels the relative contributions of genetic and epigenetic factors in the formation of synaptic circuits, and sheds some light on the pathogenesis of certain neurological disorders. Instead of reviewing the extensive literature on this subject, I shall limit myself to a series of studies on the normal and experimentally altered visual system. Although many laboratories have contributed to this rapidly growing field, I shall base my presentation mostly on the work on rhesus monkeys in my laboratory.

Neurons and Their Connections Initially Overproduced

It is well established that with few exceptions most structures in the higher vertebrate brain have a larger number of neurons during the developmental phase than in adulthood (for review see Hamburger and Oppenheim 1982; Williams and Herrup 1988). Furthermore, in most cases where it was possible to provide accurate counts, axons, dendrites, dendritic spines, and synapses were also found to be more numerous during a specific phase of development (Easter et al. 1985; Cowan et al. 1987). It is not within the scope of this article to review the evidence, the precise timetable of these events or the magnitude of overproduction of neural elements in various visual structures. Here, I will use examples from our own work on the development of the binocular visual system in rhesus monkeys to make the general point that perhaps the most important role of neuronal overproduction may be to provide the structural and molecular basis for selectivity.

Although precise data are not available for every part of the visual system in the rhesus monkey, wherever an adequate quantitative analysis has been performed, significant overproduction has been found. Furthermore, this overproduction always occurs during a well-delineated stage in development. Thus, retinal ganglion cells and optic axons are at midgestation more than twice as numerous as they are in the adult animal (Rakic and Riley 1983a), while the lateral geniculate nucleus contains an approximately 35 percent surplus of neurons at the end of the first two months (Williams and Rakic 1988). Judging from the density and distribution of pyknotic (degenerating) cells in the fetal visual cortex, there is also substantial overproduction of neurons in the primary visual cortex during the second half of pregnancy in this species (Williams, Ryder, and Rakic 1987). Overproduction extends beyond the neurons; dendrites, dendritic spines, and synapses are also created in excess. For example, during infancy there is a prolonged phase when the number of synapses in the primary visual cortex exceeds the adult level by about 50 percent (Rakic et al. 1986; Bourgeois, Jastreboff, and Rakic 1989). As discussed below, the number, pattern of distribution, and type of surviving elements (neurons, axons, and synapses) can be significantly modified at critical stages by the removal of the neurons with which they have a synaptic or trophic relationship.

Axons Can Find Targets Using Alternative Pathways

Most axons grow in an orderly and stereotypic manner using a well-defined substrate to reach their appropriate targets. However, in both normal and experimentally perturbed situations, an axon can also reach its correct target by an alternative route. For example, axons from the eyes implanted in an ectopic position within the amphibian nervous system can find their way to the appropriate target by unusual and totally foreign routes (Constantine-Paton and Capranica 1975; Harris 1986). To illustrate a similar event in a normal situation within the mammalian brain, I shall again use an example from our own work in the primate visual system. In order to determine whether the tips of growing retinal axons (called growth cones) follow a well-defined route on their way to the brain, we reconstructed a part of the optic nerve from a series of over 500 electron microscopic sections. The results revealed that during embryonic development, optic axons enroute to their targets in the thalamus do not retain a particular set of immediate neighbors (Williams and Rakic 1985). The progressive loss of neighbors seems to be the consequence of the non-selective behavior of growing axons. Within a relatively short trajectory a given growth cone may lose all of its initial axonal neighbors. Thus, an axon can reach its appropriate target by more than one route and can follow a different set of neighbors. We concluded that even with detailed knowledge of the order of axonal growth and axon distribution at the exit from the eye cup we cannot predict the order of point-to-point connectivity eventually achieved by their growth into the optic tract or within the target structure neurons in the lateral geniculate nucleus. These data collectively suggest that the pathway for each axon may not be precisely prescribed at the level of individual axons. Rather, growing axons may interact with the adjacent cellular milieu, which in turn changes its properties in response to contact with the axon. More simply, individual axons do not follow immutable, prespecified pathways; rather, they create their own pathways. Such pathways, eventually leading to functionally appropriate targets, can be created only by responsive cellular elements. There are, I believe no blueprints for pathways before or without axons; the axons themselves establish their own paths.

Phase of Overlapping Connections

In many instances initial connections are more widespread and less selective than in the mature brain. This also can be illustrated in the developing visual system of animals with binocular vision. The concept that formation of retinofugal binocular connections proceeds from a diffuse to a segregated phase was originally revealed by the finding that radioactive tracers injected into a single eye of monkey embryos before midgestation equally label both lateral geniculate nuclei equally (Rakic 1976). This simple observation showed that initially there is a total overlap of the projections originating from the two eyes and that therefore, at least half of the retinal axons initially do not project to the proper target neuron in the lateral geniculate nucleus. Axons and their growth cones apparently cannot distinguish between subpopulations of geniculate neurons serving the left or right eye, even though neurogenesis of the lateral geniculate nucleus is completed about four weeks earlier (Rakic 1977a). To understand the significance of this finding, one should recall that until that time it was assumed that axons were attracted and eventually attached to their proper targets exclusively by receptor molecules embedded in the plasma membrane of pre- and postsynaptic sites. Now, the situation appears to be more complex. As will be discussed below, formation of synaptic connections also involves segregation that depends on competitive interaction among heterogeneous cell classes. The segregation phase, during which axonal terminals originating from the left and right eyes become restricted to separate layers of the lateral geniculate nucleus, occurs during the third quarter of gestation and is completed three weeks before birth (Rakic 1977b). A similar progression in the formation of retinogeniculate connections has subsequently been shown in other mammalian orders with binocular vision (for reviews see Casagrande and Brunso-Bechtold 1985 and Rakic 1986).

The biphasic mode of development, which proceeds from more diffuse to sharply defined terminal fields, has also been shown to exist in nonvisual structures in a variety of mammalian species (Easter et al. 1985; Goldman-Rakic 1981; Mihailoff et al. 1984). In each case terminal fields initially more widely spread become restricted as input from another source becomes engaged in competition. For example, corticostriatal projections terminate in a diffuse manner before they retract from the territories that eventually become occupied by afferent systems that form later (Goldman-Rakic 1981). It should be underscored that corticostriatal projections normally have a slight contralateral component, which can be enhanced by removing competitive ipsilateral corticostriatal input at the appropriate age (Goldman 1978). These examples reveal that the formation of neuronal connections is achieved through dynamic cellular interactions that involve at least two well defined steps. In the first step one structure projects to the target structure without regard to its specific location. In the second phase these dynamic cellular interactions sort out and connect more selective sets of neurons. As will be discussed below, several mechanisms may be involved in the sorting-out process.

Synapses Initially More Numerous and Widespread

So far we have been dealing with the initial steps of axon guidance and axon search for target structures. These axons subsequently form synaptic junctions with individual neurons. In most structures of the vertebrate brain for which we have reasonably accurate quantitative data, both the density of synapses and their total number is higher in one stage of development than in the adult state. Furthermore, during the over-production phase, supernumerary synapses are usually more diffusely distributed than later in life. In particular, in the visual system of both man and the rhesus monkey it has been demonstrated that synapses are more numerous during infancy than in adulthood (O'Kusky and Collonier 1982; Bourgeois and Rakic 1983; Rakic et al. 1986; Huttenlocker and de Courten 1987). Elimination of synapses also involves the rearrangement of connections, and these changes are considered to be the result of competition for some trophic factors on target cells, as has been postulated for the peripheral nervous system (Purves 1986, 1988).

We found that in the rhesus monkey visual cortex the overproduction phase develops at identical rates and exists simultaneously in all layers of the visual, somatosensory, motor, and prefrontal areas (figure 17.2). This isochronic course of synaptogenesis in anatomically and functionally diverse regions indicates that the establishment of cell-to-cell communication in this structure may be orchestrated by a single genetic or humoral signal (Rakic et al. 1986). This finding stands in contrast to the traditional view of hierarchical development of cortical regions and provides new insight into the maturation of cortical functions.

Since the phase of synaptic overproduction in the cortex extends beyond infancy, it may provide the opportunity for competition among various intracortical connections. The capacity to perform various sensory and motor tasks coincides with the time when synaptic density reaches its peak, which suggests that a critical mass of cortical synapses is essential for cognitive functions to emerge (Goldman-Rakic 1987). However, the full maturation of such functions may depend upon the elimination of excess synapses that occurs during adolescence. Correlative analysis of this structural-functional relationship provides new insight into cognitive maturation and may enhance our understanding of cognitive developmental disorders such as developmental dyslexia.

Understanding the role of synaptic overproduction in the development of binocular vision at the cellular and molecular level is, however, still rather vague. It seems that a simple and straightforward explanation will not suffice to explain this complex phenomenon. For example, contrary to our expectation, the phase of ocular-dominance formation, which begins during the last three weeks of gestation and continues during the first two postnatal months, is characterized by an increase rather than decrease in synaptic density. Furthermore, we recently found that premature visual stimulation in infant monkeys delivered before term does not affect the rate of synaptic accretion or the size, typology, and laminar distribution of synapses (Bourgeois, Jastreboff, and Rakic 1989). Rather, these morphological parameters develop according to the time of conception and are not influenced by the time of birth. These results suggest that visual stimulation in infancy may affect the visual cortex predominantly through strengthening, modifying, and eliminating synapses already formed rather

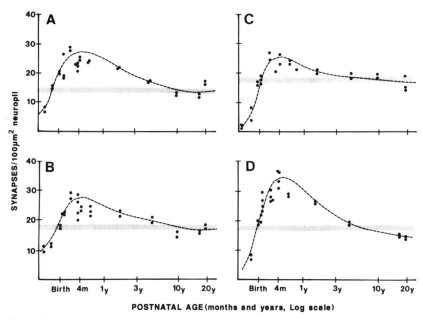

Figure 17.2
Histograms of the density of synapses per 100 square microns of neuropil in the primary somatosensory (A), primary motor (B), prefrontal (C), and primary visual (D) cortices at various ages. Each black dot represents the value obtained from an uninterrupted electron microscopic probe consisting of about 100 photographs across the entire depth of the cortex. The stippled horizontal stripe denotes the average synaptic density in the adult monkey for each area. Age in months (m) and years (y) is presented on a logarithmic scale in order to fit the entire life span of the monkey onto a single graph (from Rakic et al. 1986).

than by regulating the rate of their production (see the later section on the role of activity).

Competition in Elimination

Studies in a variety of mammalian species support the hypothesis that competitive interactions between two or more populations of neurons early in development play a significant role in selective elimination of the initial axons and later on in the patterned distribution of their synapses. In most instances the balance between the overproduction and elimination of neurons and axons may ultimately determine the size of a given pathway or the extent of territories devoted to a given terminal field. Again, the initial studies and perhaps the best documented examples of neuronal competition in the central nervous system are developmental analyses of the binocular visual system

(Guillery 1972; Rakic 1976, 1977b, 1981; Hubel et al. 1977; Shatz 1983; Casagrande and Brunso-Bechtold 1985).

Theoretically, the elimination of axons could occur with or without their competition for specific postsynaptic space on neurons in the lateral geniculate nuclei. For example, it seems reasonable that the elimination of supernumerary axons should start after the emergence of membrane receptors on the appropriate neurons. This could lead to a simple recognition of the target by axons with matching molecules. However, several lines of evidence indicate that competition between two or more axonal populations for targets plays an important role in this process. The first evidence in favor of competition came from the finding that segregation of axons in the lateral geniculate nucleus of the monkey does not result in regularly alternating inputs to the ipsi- and contralateral layers. Rather, adjacent layers II and III on both sides receive ipsilateral input. One can argue that magnocellular layers I and II and parvocellular layers III through VI receive physiologically different sets of retinal axons (Y-like and X-like respectively), and that therefore, segregation in each subset occurs independently. Nevertheless, the reverse order of input from the left and right eyes that takes place between layers II and III cannot be explained by competition between two inputs without some local information generated within neurons of the lateral geniculate nuclei (Rakic 1981, 1986).

Further evidence that the process of segregation involves selective rather than random loss of excess axons comes from the results of monocular enucleation performed on embryos before they enter the stage of major axon elimination. Autoradiographic analysis of the projections from the remaining eye after birth reveals that retinofugal axons can be found throughout the lateral geniculate nuclei, even within inappropriate territories (Rakic 1981). The initial interpretation of these results was that in the absence of competition, diffusely distributed axon terminals from a single eye remain at their initial sites. We subsequently discovered that such animals retain 30 to 40 percent of the supernumerary embryonic axons. This indicates that their survival depends on the availability of specific synaptic targets in the lateral geniculate nucleus, normally occupied by fibers from the contralateral eye (Rakic and Riley 1983b). Enlargement of the terminal projections of the remaining eye is, therefore, to a large extent due to the retention of the axons that would normally lose in the competitive struggle (Rakic 1981). The role of competition in the process of elimination is further supported by the results of early monocular enucleation in mice, which rescues mostly ganglion cells that project to inappropriate territories (Godement et al. 1984; Jacobs et al. 1984).

However, it should be pointed out that competition also plays a significant role in the rearrangement of terminal fields, including extension or withdrawal of the terminal branching emanating from surviving axons (Sretavan and Shatz 1984). These two types of competitive interactions are the most obvious and perhaps the best documented, but they are by no means the only types that occur during development. For example, in cats where axons of X-like and Y-like neurons are intermixed, there is also strong evidence of competitive interactions for available space among them (Sherman and Spear 1985). Thus, several diverse lines of evidence indicate that supernumerary and widespread projections in the retinogeniculate system are eliminated through several types of competitive interactions.

The Role of Functional Activity in Synaptogenesis

There is little doubt that during development neuronal circuits can be changed in response to induced or spontaneous electrical activity. Perhaps the best known examples come from study of the peripheral nervous system. Experimental perturbations in this system that increase or decrease neural activity affect the magnitude and pattern of synapse elimination at the neuromuscular junction (Benoit and Changeux 1975; Thompson 1985). Although details of the mechanisms involved in competition are still controversial (see, e.g., Callaway et al. 1987), there is little disagreement that it occurs. The initiation of neuronal activity may be spontaneous or evoked, but its presence contributes to the selection process by favoring some synapses and helping the elimination of others.

In the central nervous system initial developmental events such as cell proliferation, neuronal migration, and the outgrowth of axons may orderly proceed in the absence of activity-dependent cues. In contrast, the later phases of development that includes the elimination of neurons, axons, and synapses and the shaping of the final circuits or topographical maps may be regulated by the state of electrical activity within the system. The theory of competitive elimination, reminiscent of Darwinian selection of the fittest, contributes to the specification of synaptic connectivity. The Darwinian scheme has been used to model various aspects of development and learning (Changeux and Danchin 1976; Edelman and Finkel 1984; Edelman 1987). Direct and unambiguous examples can again be drawn from the development of binocular connections, including a celebrated case in which monocular eye deprivation resulted in enlargement of the ocular dominance columns subserving the functional eye (Hubel et al. 1977). More recently it was shown that binocular connections fail to withdraw to appropriate territories after blockade of electrical activity by tetrodotoxin, which prevents the influx of sodium ions across the membrane (Dubin, Stark, and Archer 1986; Stryker and Harris 1986).

Although the phenomenon of competitive elimination is well established, we are still ignorant about the cellular and molecular mechanisms underlying these changes. Competitive elimination of synapses is the focus of intense research both in developmental neurobiology and in the neurobiology of learning, and progress can be expected in the near future. It is presently generally agreed that a qualitative or quantitative change in synapse architecture must involve gene expression (Changeux and Konishi 1987). These changes may arise by genomic rearrangement or by several other mechanisms that include third messengers, but the most common mechanism of activity-dependent regulation of development seems to occur at the level of gene transcription. Although detailed molecular processes are the focus of interest, the basic problem remains that of finding out how synaptic connections adjust their structural and functional properties in response to initial spontaneous or elicited activity.

Neuronal activity can be generated within the nervous system in the form of the spontaneous firing of nerve cells. This activity can occur before birth and may not be related to or induced by the external environment. Nevertheless, one nerve cell can influence the development of another nerve cell by the pattern, sequence, and timing of electrical impulses (for reviews for the visual system see Barlow 1975; Wiesel 1982). Perhaps a more relevant point for the study of developmental dyslexia is that electrical activity usually occurs in response to stimulation from the environment. In this respect, orchestration of the firing of nerve cells may be equated with sensory experience (Blakemore and Van Sluyters 1975; Singer et al. 1981; Fregnac and Imbert 1984; Manstronade 1983). Again, the effect of both spontaneous and environmentally induced activity in neural connections had been demonstrated in the visual system, where it can best be tested and measured (Hubel et al. 1977; Wiesel 1982; Schmidt and Teiman 1985). The study of mechanisms involved in activity-dependent competition is important because it reveals that the precise pattern of synaptic connectivity cannot be predicted even with full knowledge of the instruction contained in the cell genome. The responsiveness of the developing brain to environmental influences, including experience, may be the anatomical basis of diversity in human behavior, talent, and creativity (Goldman and Rakic 1979; Rakic 1988). A disturbance of the balance between these forces is perhaps the cause of many alterations of higher brain function in which neuropathologists cannot find any cellular abnormality.

Conclusions

Formation of neuronal connections was for a long time thought to be determined exclusively by cell-to-cell recognition between membrane-bound, specific labels distributed by rigid genetic intracellular programs. Although this may hold for the basic anatomical framework, in recent years it has become apparent that the establishment of final patterns of local neuronal circuits, particularly at later developmental stages, depends also on intercellular competitive interactions. Learning more about the rules and principles involved in these complex interactions *in vivo* is essential for understanding cellular and molecular mechanisms that control normal and pathological development of the nervous system. I have briefly reviewed what we presently know about these processes from analyses of normal and experimentally modified development in the binocular visual system of the rhesus monkey. Although the molecular mechanisms of complex cellular events underlying cellular competition are not fully understood, the results presented reveal the dynamic nature of neural differentiation and synaptogenesis, delineate critical and vulnerable developmental phases, and unravel the relative contributions of genetic and epigenetic factors in the formation and maintenance of synaptic circuits and in the pathogenesis of certain inherent neurological disorders.

At the end I should emphasize that the concept of competitive interaction is not a substitute for the chemoaffinity hypothesis and that it does not contradict or diminish the essential role of surface-mediated recognition among cells. Competitive interaction should be viewed as an additional cellular mechanism that has emerged and been elaborated during the course of evolution and has perhaps become most pronounced in primates (Easter et al. 1985). Perhaps the highest and most complex biological functions, such as reading or human thought, may be viewed as arising from the random generation of many alternatives developed by a selective process. One prediction based on recent advances is that when more facts are known, cell specificity will be seen in the light of highly dynamic changes that are regulated epigenetically. The studies that I have reviewed here are selective but nevertheless illustrate rather explicitly how new developmental mechanisms may emerge from the interplay between the functional, anatomical, and molecular approaches. At present the research on competitive interactions is primarily relevant to understanding normal development of the central nervous system. However, this research also has potential implications for understanding genetic and acquired brain malformations and for assessing and predicting recovery of function following brain damage in the fetus, infant, and child. This damage can occur at all levels of the neuraxis and at different stages of development, and it can be influenced by a variety of intrinsic and extrinsic factors. At this point in our industrial society we have to worry about new man-made agents and natural forces that played relatively minor roles in the past. I refer in particular here to exposure of the developing brain to new types of neuroactive drugs, large amounts of toxic chemicals from industrial waste, and ionizing radiation.

To summarize, there is growing evidence that brain development is a more dynamic and complex process than initially recognized. Competitive interaction among nerve cells is an important concept that has emerged during the last decade. It has become evident that the goal of developmental neurobiology should be not simply to try to figure out how genes build the neuronal circuits that underlie behavior but also to unravel mechanisms of competitive interactions or epigenetic nonprogrammatic functional relations (Stent 1981). Although this goal is extremely difficult and still elusive, it is coming conceptually and technically within our reach. If I were asked at this time to select some simple messages about this goal worth taking home, I would say: the basis is overproduction, the method is competitive interaction, the goal is selective elimination, and the benefit to the organism is immense diversity in synaptic patterns that goes beyond predictable genetic instruction.

References

Barlow, H. B. 1975. Visual experience and cortical development. *Nature* 258:199–204.

Benoit, P., and J.-P. Changeux. 1975. Consequences of tenotomy on the evolution of multiinnervation in developing rat soleus muscle. *Brain Research* 99:354–358.

Blakemore, C., and R. C. Van Sluyters. 1975. Innate and environmental factors in development of the kitten's visual cortex. *Journal of Physiology* 248:663–716.

Bourgeois, J.-P., and P. Rakic. 1983. Synaptogenesis in the primary visual cortex: Quantitative analysis in pre- and postnatal rhesus monkeys. *Society for Neuroscience Abstracts* 9:692.

Bourgeois, J.-P., P. Jastreboff, and P. Rakic. 1989. Synaptogenesis in visual cortex of normal and preterm monkeys: Evidence for intrinsic regulation of synaptic overproduction. *Proceedings of the National Academy of Sciences* (USA) 86:4297–4301.

Callaway, E. M., J. M. Soha, and D. C. Van Essen. 1987. Competition favoring inactive over active motor neurons during synapse elimination. *Nature* 328:422–426.

Casagrande, V. A., and J. K. Brunso-Bechtold. 1985. Critical events in lateral geniculate nucleus development. *Advances in Neurology Behavior and Development* 1:33–78.

Changeux, J.-P., and A. Danchin. 1976. Selective stabilization of developing synapses as a mechanism for the specialization of neural network. *Nature* 264:705–712.

Changeux, J.-P., and M. Konishi, eds. 1987. *The neural and molecular bases of learning.* Dahlem Konferenzen. New York: Wiley and Sons.

Constantine-Paton, M., and P. R. Capranica. 1975. Central projection of optic tract from translocated eyes in the leopard frog (*Rana pipiens*). *Science* 189:480–482.

Cowan, W. M., J. W. Fawcett, D. D. O'Leary, and B. B. Stanfield. 1984. Regressive events in neurogenesis. *Science* 225:1258–1265.

Dubin, M., L. A. Stark, and S. M. Archer. 1986. A role for action-potential activity in the development of neuronal connections in the kitten retinogeniculate pathway. *Journal of Neuroscience* 6:1021–1036.

Easter, S. S., Jr., D. Purves, P. Rakic, and N. C. Spitzer. 1985. The changing views of neuronal specificity. *Science* 230:507–511.

Edelman, G. M. 1987. *Neural darwinism.* New York: Basic Books.

Edelman, G. M., and L. J. Finkel. 1984. Neuronal group selection in the cerebral cortex. In *Dynamic aspects of neocortical function*, ed. G. M. Edelman, W. E. Gale, and W. M. Cowan. New York: Wiley and Sons.

Fregnac, Y., and M. Imbert. 1984. Development of neuronal selectivity in primary visual cortex of the cat. *Physiological Reviews* 64:325–434.

Godement, P., J. Salaün, and M. Imbert. 1984. Prenatal and postnatal development of retinogeniculate and retinocollicular projections in the mouse. *Journal of Comparative Neurology* 230:552–575.

Goldman, P. S. 1978. Neuronal plasticity in primate telencephalon: Anomalous crossed cortico-caudate projections induced by prenatal removal of frontal association. *Science* 202:768–776.

Goldman, P. S., and P. Rakic. 1979. Impact of the outside world upon the developing primate brain. Prospective from neurobiology. *Bulletin of Menninger Clinic* 43:20–28.

Goldman-Rakic, P. S. 1981. Prenatal formation of cortical input and development of cytoarchitectonic compartments in the neostriatum of rhesus monkey. *Journal of Neuroscience* 1:721–735.

Goldman-Rakic, P. S. 1987. Development of cortical circuitry and cognitive function. *Child Development* 58:601–622.

Guillery, R. W. 1972. Binocular competition in the control of geniculate cell growth. *Journal of Comparative Neurology* 144:117–130.

Hamburger, V., and R. W. Oppenheim. 1982. Naturally occurring neuronal death in vertebrates. *Neuroscience Communications* 1:39–55.

Harris, W. A. 1986. Homing behavior of axons in the embryonic vertebrate brain. *Nature* 320:266–269.

Hubel, D. H., T. N. Wiesel, and S. LeVay. 1977. Plasticity of ocular dominance columns in monkey striate cortex. *Philosophical Transactions of the Royal Society of London*, series B 278:377–409.

Huttenlocher, P. R., and C. de Courten. 1987. The development of synapses in striate cortex of man. *Human Neurobiology* 6:1–9.

Jacobs, D. S., V. H. Perry, and M. J. Hawken. 1984. The postnatal reduction of the uncrossed projection from the nasal retina in the cat. *Journal of Neuroscience* 4:2425–2433.

Mastronade, D. N. 1983. Correlated firing of cat retinal ganglion cells: I. Spontaneously active inputs to X and Y cells. *Journal of Neurophysiology* 49:303–324.

Mihailoff, G. A., C. E. Adams, and D. J. Woodward. 1984. An autoradiographic study of the postnatal development of sensorimotor and visual components of the corticopontine system. *Journal of Comparative Neurology* 227:116–127.

Nieto-Sampedro, M., and C. W. Cotman. 1987. Synaptic plasticity. In *Encyclopedia of neuroscience*, pp. 1166–1167. Boston: Birkhauser.

O'Kusky, J., and M. Colonnier. 1982. A laminar analysis of the number of neurons, glia and synapses in the visual cortex (area 17) of the adult macaque monkey. *Journal of Comparative Neurology* 210:278–290.

Purves, D. 1986. The trophic theory of neural development. *Trends in Neurosciences* 9:486–489.

Purves, D. 1988. *A trophic theory of neuroal organization.* Cambridge: Harvard University Press.

Rakic, P. 1976. Prenatal genesis of connections subserving ocular dominance in the rhesus monkey. *Nature* 261:467–471.

Rakic, P. 1977a. Genesis of the dorsal lateral geniculate nucleus in the rhesus monkey: Site and time of origin, kinetics of proliferation, routes of migration, and pattern of distribution of neurons. *Journal of Comparative Neurology* 176:23–52.

Rakic, P. 1977b. Prenatal development of the visual system in the rhesus monkey. *Philosophical Transactions of the Royal Society of London,* series B 278:245–260.

Rakic, P. 1979. Genetic and epigenetic determinants of local neuronal circuits in the mammalian central nervous system. In *The neurosciences: Fourth study program,* ed. F. O. Schmitt, and F. G. Worden. Cambridge: MIT Press.

Rakic, P. 1981. Development of visual centers in primate brain depends on binocular competition before birth. *Science* 214:928–931.

Rakic, P. 1986. Mechanisms of ocular dominance segregation in the lateral geniculate nucleus: Competitive elimination hypothesis. *Trends in Neurosciences* 9:11–15.

Rakic, P. 1988. Specification of cerebral cortical areas. *Science* 241:170–176.

Rakic, P., J.-P. Bourgeois, M. F. Eckenhoff, N. Zecevic, and P. S. Goldman-Rakic. 1986. Concurrent overproduction of synapses in diverse regions of the primate cerebral cortex. *Science* 232:232–235.

Rakic, P., and K. P. Riley. 1983a. Overproduction and elimination of retinal axons in the fetal rhesus monkey. *Science* 219:1441–1444.

Rakic, P., and K. P. Riley. 1983b. Regulation of axon number in primate optic nerve by binocular competition. *Nature* 305:135–137.

Schmidt, J. T., and D. L. Edwards. 1983. Activity sharpens the map during the regeneration of the retinotectal projection in goldfish. *Brain Research* 269:29–39.

Schmidt, J. T., and S. B. Teiman. 1985. Eye-specific segregation of optic afferents in mammals, fish, and frogs: The role of activity. *Cellular and Molecular Neurobiology* 5:5–34.

Shatz, C. J. 1983. Prenatal development of cat's retinogeniculate pathway. *Journal of Neuroscience* 3:482–399.

Sherman, S. M., and P. D. Spear. 1985. Organization of visual pathways in normal and visually deprived cats. *Physiological Reviews* 62:738–855.

Singer, W., B. Freeman, and J. Rauschecker. 1981. Restriction of visual experience to a single orientation affects the organization or orientation of columns in cat visual cortex: A study with deoxyglucose. *Experimental Brain Research* 41:199–215.

Sperry, R. W. 1963. Chemoaffinity in the orderly growth of nerve fiber patterns and connections. *Proceedings of the National Academy of Sciences* (USA) 50:703–710.

Sretavan, D. W., and C. J. Shatz. 1984. Prenatal development of individual retinogeniculate axons during the period of segregation. *Nature* 308:845–848.

Stent, G. S. 1981. Strength and weakness of the genetic approach to the development of the nervous system. *Annual Reviews of Neuroscience* 4:163–194.

Stryker, M. P., and W. A. Harris. 1986. Binocular impulse blockade prevents the formation of ocular dominance columns in cat visual cortex. *Journal of Neuroscience* 6:2117–2133.

Thompson, W. J. 1985. Activity and synapse elimination at the neuromuscular junction. *Cellular and Molecular Neurobiology* 5:167–182.

Wiesel, T. N. 1982. Postnatal development of the visual cortex and influence of environment. *Nature* 299:583–591.

Williams, R. W., and K. Herrup. 1988. Control of neuron number. *Annual Reviews of Neuroscience* 11:423–453.

Williams, R. W., and P. Rakic. 1985. Dispersion of growing axons within the optic nerve of the embryonic monkey. *Proceedings of the National Academy of Sciences* (USA) 82:3906–3910.

Williams, R. W., and P. Rakic. 1988. Elimination of neurons in the rhesus monkey's lateral geniculate nucleus during development. *Journal of Comparative Neurology* 272:424–436.

Williams, R. W., K. Ryder, and P. Rakic. 1987. Emergence of cytoarchitectonic differences between areas 17 and 18 in the developing rhesus monkey. *Society for Neuroscience Abstracts* 13:1044.

Editor's Comments

From the point of view of assemblies of neurons, axons, and synapses the present paper sketches and illustrates the most uniform and consistent of the themes running through the pages of this volume: The development of the brain (and the mind for that matter) proceeds according to innate dispositions blueprinted in the genetic code and in response to the specific requirements imposed by the personal environment. Actual, real-life brains and minds, therefore, reflect the inseparable diversities present within the species-specific gene pool and in individual environments. Moreover, anomalies of brain (and mind) architecture come about as the result of alterations in the genetic code or in e environment or in both.

The record of the outcome of phylogenetic interactions between organisms and their environments from primeval times until the present is kept in the genome as a blueprint of potential structures to be built during individual development. Within this blueprint of potentialities, ontogenetic interactions determine specific structures and further contribute to the genetic blueprints of the future.

The genome must be able to offer to the task of matching emergent structure and specific environment an adequate repertoire of neurons, axons, synapses, receptors, and the range of possibilities within which such elements can be assembled. Ontogenetic interactions will in turn determine the exact numbers and types of elements and architectures that will emerge from this range of possibilities.

It thus appears that an initial, genetically determined overproduction, followed by a partly environmentally determined ontogenetic curtailment (whether of neurons, axons, synapses, molecules, or patterns of connections) is the means by which actual brains arise from potential anatomies. It appears also that the curtailment takes place after competitive selection from among available neural elements and connectional patterns for the best fit with the personal environment.

The overproduction and subsequent partial removal of neural elements can be demonstrated at multiple brain loci (e.g., the retina, lateral geniculate nucleus, and visual cortex) as well as at several levels of anatomical expression (e.g., whole assemblies of neurons, individual neurons, axons, dendrites, synapses, receptor molecules, and gene activity). This process is indeed observed at much higher levels of analysis: cognitive architectures for vision and language emerge as specific instantiations from within a wider range of possibilities as a result of environmentally guided selective reduction occurring at multiple levels of representation.

It is important to keep in mind that genetic unfolding begins at the very instant of conception and continues throughout life and that ontogenetic environmental interactions range from simple maternal chemical effects on the zygote to the complex cultural influences on an infant learning a language. Moreover, the chronology of the unfolding offers the opportunity for linking observations at one level of analysis with those at other, very different levels.

The development of the brain typically proceeds from coarse to fine, from general to specific. The initial curtailment of possibilities determines that a subset of embryonic cells will make up the nervous system and no other system. These neurally committed cells will be subject to additional selection and segregation for building the separate components of the system.

Early differentiation is followed by large-scale cell proliferation, widespread cell and axonal migration, and finally maturation of neurons and connections. It appears that widely dispersed neuronal assemblies involving special types of neurons and long axons are laid down first. This is followed by the establishment of local circuits requiring different types of neurons and short axons. The subsequent steps involve the selection of specific patterns of synaptic organization with appropriate chemical characteristics.

In the human brain the bulk of selective curtailment takes place before birth. Neuronal migration is nearly complete by the middle of pregnancy. The establishment of long and local circuits and the neuronal and axonal attrition that accompanies it appears to be finished by the time of birth or shortly thereafter. These events possibly continue at a much-reduced scale into the first decade.

By the time the human infant is fully exposed to its linguistic environment, local and far reaching neural connections are mostly established, though synaptic and connectional architectures are not. It would appear, therefore, that established synaptic architectures are not required for the initial stages of learning a language. Rather, they may emerge as a result of initial learning. On the other hand, absence of long and short connections and a number of neurons or significant alterations in their patterns may be incompatible with ordinary language acquisition. The brain of the dyslexic maybe an example of this level of alteration (see the chapters by Galaburda, Rosen, and Sherman and by Sherman, Rosen, and Galaburda in this volume).

An interesting observation cited in the present paper is that synaptic pruning appears to occur synchronously in anatomically and functionally diverse areas of the brain. This observation is compatible with the finding that language development follows the same chronology in hearing and congenitally deaf babies, who presumably rely on different brain areas for language acquisition. However, the preceding stages of neuronal migration and neuronal attrition do not follow a comparably synchronous course. These findings, in addition to the chronological constraints cited above, suggest that the initial state of language acquisition might rest on patterns of cerebral connectivity laid down before birth, but the acquisition of a particular language may actively influence the establishment of specific patterns of synaptic architectures.

Chapter 18

The Role Hormones Acting on the Brain Play in Linking Nature and Nurture

Bruce S. McEwen

Introduction

Each somatic cell of the body contains the same complement of genetic information in the form of DNA, and yet cells and organs differ substantially in the gene products that they express and the structures and functions that they assume. Genomic activity does not stop when embryonic life is over. The expression of gene products specific and common to different tissues and organs begins early in development and continues throughout adult life into senescence. This genomic activity is controlled by signals coming from within the cell, from neighboring cells, and from other tissues and organs. The external environment has an important influence over these signals in that sensory input from light, cold and heat, and various experiences can affect genomic activity in target cells throughout the body (McEwen 1988a, 1988b).

One important class of chemical messengers is represented by the gonadal, adrenal, and thyroid hormones, which are secreted in response to hormones emanating from the pituitary gland, which in turn are regulated by the hypothalamus. The hormonal output of the hypothalamus is in turn subject to influences from higher brain centers through the action of emotions and thoughts, as well as influences from experiences and behavioral interactions. The endocrine products controlled by the nervous system feed back to the brain, as well as the rest of the body, to regulate specific cellular events. In the brain and pituitary gland, as in a thermostat, endocrine feedback controls hormone output. It also influences behavioral states and moods, which in turn can influence the types of sensory input and experiences that are particularly effective in triggering hormone output. Thus, hormones guide the activity of the nervous system through both a direct feedback loop and a longer, behaviorally mediated feedback loop (McEwen 1988a, 1988b). This idea of interaction is further highlighted by the fact that hormonal feedback to the brain alters brain structure and function through actions on genomic activity from early development, throughout adult life, and into senescence. A corollary to this is that individual differences in experience can have different effects on brain function, early experiences and hormone exposure altering the later response characteristics of the brain. The purpose of this chapter is to examine how the influences of hormones on the brain help to determine individual differences in behavior and brain function through their actions to alter gene expression. I use the term "nature" to refer to the genomic complement, which is linked to the environment by means of hormonal signals. "Nurture" refers to the environment.

Hormones and Gene Expression

How do we know that hormones affect genomic function in the brain? More than 25 years ago receptor sites were identified for steroid hormones, and we now know that these receptors are proteins with a steroid-recognition domain and a DNA-binding domain (McEwen 1988a). Binding of the hormone alters the conformation of the receptors and exposes the DNA-binding domain so that the receptor binds tightly to specific enhancer-like DNA elements located on nearby genes. These DNA elements are turned on or off by steroid exposure.

Such receptors are found in the brain. For each type of steroid hormone there are specific receptors with different neuroanatomical distribution (McEwen et al. 1979). Glucocorticoid receptors are concentrated in the hippocampus, and estrogen receptors are concentrated within the hypothalamus and preoptic area. Estrogen receptors in the hypothalamus are linked to the control of sexual behavior. In the female rats, estrogen implants in the basal hypothalamus induce feminine sexual behavior by a process that is temporally delayed and can be blocked by RNA and protein synthesis inhibitors. Neurons in the ventromedial nucleus of the hypothalamus (VMN) are believed to be the principal estrogen targets, since they show rapid changes in the size of the cell nucleus and nucleolus and in the diameter of cell somata after estrogen exposure (McEwen, Jones, and Pfaff 1987). Synaptic growth and rearrangement of synapses also result from estrogen actions (Carrer and Aoki 1982). Estrogen treatment induces increased output of 28S ribosomal RNA in VMN neurons and alters the pattern of newly synthesized proteins in VMN tissue (McEwen, Jones, and Pfaff 1987). All of this information about estrogen action in the VMN in inducing female sexual receptivity is consistent with the idea of a hormonally induced cascade of gene expressions in which early gene products lead to later steps in gene activation.

It would be a mistake to assume that steroid-hormone signals act alone in producing their genomic effects on neural tissue. Rather, steroid hormones and other neurotransmitters and hormones act in concert (McEwen 1988b). One mechanism by which this synergism occurs is via the steroid receptors themselves. This synergism is observed in the fact that drugs which mimic or block neurotransmitters modify the number of available estrogen and progestin receptor sites in the hypothalamus and pituitary. For example, VMN treatment of estrogen-primed female guinea pigs with the alpha-1 adrenergic blocking drug, prazosin, blocks sexual behavior, and also reduces the level of progestin receptors. The receptor change is specific for just the VMN among the brain regions examined. The mechanism for the decrease in receptors is unknown, but it may involve a postsynthetic modification of existing receptors such processes as by phosphorylation or dephosphorylation.

Another type of interaction between steroid hormones and other chemical messengers is also found in the basal hypothalamus. It too involves the estrogen estradiol. The ability of estradiol to regulate tyrosine hydroxylase (TH) gene transcription in an upward or downward direction is determined by the estrogen-induced release of an unidentified pituitary hormone that apparently acts synergistically with estradiol to determine that TH transcription is decreased (Blum et al. 1987).

The Classification of Hormone Effects on the Brain

The effects of hormones on the brain may be classified in various ways. One long-standing scheme distinguishes between activational and organization effects. The former are reversible effects occurring in the mature brain, and the latter are developmental effects that are largely irreversible. Recently, it has become evident that this scheme is too simplistic, and that there are other types of hormone effects that are not distinguished strictly on the basis of the stage of brain maturation during which they act. So I prefer the following classification.

Synaptic Plasticity

Here we have developmental effects occurring prior to the establishing of stable synaptic connections. However, these developmental effects can recur in damaged brain tissue when associated with collateral sprouting. Such regenerative influences of glucocorticoids, estrogens, and androgens have been described in several different regions of the central nervous system (CNS) (McEwen 1988b).

Neural Pathology

Another category of hormone action, opposite to the one above, leads to neural damage on prolonged or persistent exposure. In a sense, this is also a developmental effect, since it influences the aging process, albeit in a negative manner. Such actions are reported in female rodents and involve gonadal-steroid effects to terminate estrous cycling (Finch et al. 1984). There is also evidence that prolonged exposure to glucocorticoids causes neuronal loss in at least one brain structure, the hippocampus. This results in progressive loss of negative feedback control of glucocorticoid secretion, which in turn gives rise to progressively higher levels of circulating glucocorticoids (Sapolsky et al. 1986).

Activation

Hormones have activational effects, which are reversible actions that result from cyclical secretion. Cyclical hormone secretion is determined by the interplay between endogenous clocks and exogenous light-dark cycles and the seasons. These interactions cyclically activate neural circuits related to sexual activity, diurnal and nocturnal behavior, sleep, and locomotor activity. Examples in this category are the activation of female sexual behavior by estradiol secreted in the estrous cycle and the influences of diurnally secreted glucocorticoid on food intake, locomotor activity, and sleep.

Adaptation

Adaptational effects, like activation effects, are reversible. Yet they are produced by hormones secreted in response to behavioral signals that are not cyclical but rather fluctuate less predictably. For this reason I assign these effects to a separate category. The effects of stress-induced glucocorticoid secretion are adaptational. They assist the brain as well as the rest of the body in responding and adjusting to stressful experiences (McEwen and Brinton 1987). Besides protective effects, there are also the effects of behavioral signals on related behaviors, such as the role of aggression-induced androgen secretion in elevating sexual activity in birds and other seasonally breeding vertebrates. This category of hormone action points up the ability of the experiences of an animal to modify behavior, brain structure, and function through the endocrine system. It is one of the principal bases for examining the role that the endocrine system plays in individual differences in brain structure, function, behavior. The above-mentioned effects of aggression on androgen secretion and enhanced readiness for mating are reminiscent of the observations by the late

Daniel Lehrman (1964) of an unfolding sequence of behavioral and interdependent endocrine events that lead to sequences of behavior. Such chains of cause and effect also link events that are more separated in time than those that Lehrman first described.

Let us examine some chains of interactions between hormone effects on the brain and the development of group and individual differences.

Models of Hormone Action in Relation to Individual and Group Differences in Brain Structure and Function

Hormone secretion during development and in adult life is responsible for some of the important individual and group differences in brain function. The purpose of this section is to examine some model systems in which we can study these events. The important chains of cause and effect in these cases extend over months or years and connect the early developmental history of an organism with its adult function and its senescence.

Sex Differences

One of the most important group differences is based on sex. Brain sexual differentiation is a significant feature of male-female differences in brain function and behavior. Testosterone secreted by the tests early in development determines the masculine differentiation of the reproductive tract and of specific regions of the brain (Goy and McEwen 1980). Receptors for gonadal steroids, which enable the brain and reproductive tract to respond to testosterone and its metabolites, are elaborated concurrently with the onset of embryonic testicular activity. Operating via genomic activation, testosterone and its metabolites increase neurite outgrowth and alter formation of neural connections as they alter neurochemical features of the brain. The net result is that a male brain differs subtly from a female brain both in circuitry and in features of its functional neurochemistry. Sex differences in brain structure and function go beyond strictly reproductive processes and include sex differences in the lateralization of cerebral cortical thickness, in anatomical characteristics of the hippocampus (Diamond 1984), in the response properties of serotonergic receptors in the hypothalamus and midbrain (Fischette et al. 1983), and in cyclic AMP formation in the hippocampus induced by noradrenaline and vasoactive intestinal peptides (Harrelson and McEwen 1987). Knowing that such sex differences exist, we can appreciate that sex differences in behavior encompass spatial and verbal abilities, susceptibility to dyslexia, and to endogenous depressive illness. How these sex differences develop is undoubtedly a matter of complex interactions between the biological substrate and the environment. Here is an example of sex differences in behavior. In the first few hours after birth infant girls attend more to people in the nursery than do boys (Hittelman and Dickes 1979). Does this type of biological sex difference form an initial bias in a cascade of experiences and reactions and cause boys and girls to diverge in their postnatal development? Another example concerns the higher energy expenditure of juvenile males in comparison with females. This higher energy expenditure is evident in the rough-and-tumble play of juvenile rats, rhesus monkeys, and humans. Such a biological bias is undoubtedly a factor in the choice of playthings and modes of play (Meaney and Stewart 1981), and it leads to further choices and differential experiences as maturation proceeds (Goy and McEwen 1980).

Aging Effects
As noted above, lifetime exposure to gonadal and adrenal steroids has been shown to cause neural damage and alter physiological control mechanisms. Ovariectomy of female mice in midlife prolongs the chronological age at which ovarian grafts will show cyclic ovulation, which indicates that CNS control mechanisms continue to function properly (Finch et al. 1980). Conversely, induced persistent estrus, characterized by low-level estrogen secretion, causes hypothalamic damage even in young adult rodents, which permanently terminates cyclic ovulation (Brawer et al. 1980). Moreover, perinatal exposure to testosterone or estradiol in doses too low to defeminize sexual behavior or stop ovulation outright leads to the delayed anovulatory syndrome, a form of premature aging in which estrous cycling begins at puberty but disappears well before the age at which ovulation normally ceases (Harlan and Gorski 1978).

Steroid hormone secretion also leads to aging within the hippocampal region of the brain (Sapolsky et al. 1986). Loss of neurons in the hippocampus of rats during the second year of life is attenuated by adrenalectomy in middle age. Conversely, neuronal loss can be accelerated by treating young rats with glucocorticoids for 12 weeks. Moreover, neuronal loss due to hypoxia and application of excitatory amino acids is accelerated by excess glucocorticoids, which indicate that these hormones help determine the effect of other agents that can cause neural damage. Because the common elements linking hypoxia and excitotoxins are the excitatory amino acids and because excitation may kill cells by overwhelming their ability to generate ATP and to maintain ion gradients, it stands to reason that elevated glucocorticoids represent a more general risk factor in the conditions of life (i.e., stress and nutrition).

Glucocorticoids may be involved in neurodegenerative diseases (McEwen 1988). Because they exacerbate damage caused by excitotoxins and because the endogenous excitatory amino acid glutamate can cause neural damage, glucocorticoids may act synergistically with these endogenous substances to bring about neural damage. A recent speculative article has pointed to the similarities between brain lesions induced by excitatory amino acids and those occurring in the Alzheimer type of senile dementia (Maragos et al. 1987).

Developmental Influences
Prenatal and postnatal experiences modify the subsequent adult behavior of rats. It is conceivable that such developmental influences may alter susceptibility to destructive influences during aging. Prenatal, unpredictable stress of the mother increases the offspring's vulnerability to the effects of stressful stimuli and decreases habituation to such stimuli.

Experiments with newborn rats indicate that handling them as infants increases the binding capacity of hippocampal glucocorticoid receptors and at the same time increases the feedback of hippocampal glucocorticoid receptors for shutting off the stress response (Meaney and Aitken 1985; Meaney, Aitken, et al. 1985). It may be that the two results are linked, as there is evidence that glucocorticoids act at least in part on the hippocampus to shut off glucocorticoid secretion after stress. In that case, it is of particular interest to inquire how handling causes the glucocorticoid receptors to increase in numbers. Recent evidence points to an increase in thyroid function as a major factor (Meaney et al. 1987).

What are the consequences of having greater control over pituitary and adrenal function? One prediction is that rats with better control will age more slowly in terms of decline of hippocampal function and related behavioral capabilities. This prediction is supported by recent studies by Meaney et al. (1988).

Conclusions

What is the relevance of nature and nurture to the problem of developmental learning disabilities such as dyslexia? Insofar as such disabilities have a recognizable genetic trait (Smith et al. 1983), there is the question of the penetrance of the trait, i.e., how many carriers express the trait and at what stage of development is it expressed?

Clearly, penetrance is related to environmental control over the expression of a genetic trait: in some individuals the trait may be fully expressed, whereas in others it may not be expressed at all. On the other hand, dyslexia may also result from acquired environmental influences on an otherwise normal genetic substrate, e.g., accidents involving acquired autoimmunity or cerebrovascular injury that disrupt cortical development (see Galaburda et al. and Sherman et al. in this volume). In such cases the genome is also called upon to mediate developmental reorganization. Thus, in both inherited and acquired dyslexia environmental factors including hormones may contribute to the pathology underlying the disorder.

How might this happen? Sex hormones appear to play some role in that dyslexia is more prevalent in males than in females by a considerable ratio (Critchley 1970). In males testosterone may contribute to cerebral hemispheric specialization, and so restrict the ability of the other hemisphere to take over in the event of lateralized pathology in the language areas (Geschwind and Galaburda 1987). Alternatively, testosterone may increase autoimmunity, which is associated with many cases of dyslexia and which may contribute to abnormal cortical development (Geschwind and Behan 1982; Pennington et al. 1987).

Stress may also contribute, since prenatal and postnatal stress alter the output of both glucocorticoids and thyroid hormones and lead to alterations in the development of the hippocampus and the cerebral cortex of the types described above for the rat. Another aspect of stress involves the effects of separating offspring from parents or other abnormal parent-infant interactions. A key component of these effects is the secretion of and response to growth hormone. Prolonged separation of infants from the mother leads to loss of sensitivity to growth hormone in the brain and other tissues and gives rise to behavioral abnormalities as well as to reduced growth (Hofer 1981; Schanberg and Kuhn 1980; Kuhn et al. 1979). Curiously, effect of maternal deprivation on these parameters in rats can be overcome by tactile stimulation of the pups (Evoniuk et al. 1979). This type of treatment may have beneficial effects on the growth of premature human infants as well (Schanberg and Kuhn 1980).

Thus far none of the above-mentioned hormone effects, save those of testosterone, have been considered from the standpoint of their possible influence on the development of cerebral dominance and lateralization of cerebral function. Future studies in animal models of cerebral lateralization should thus consider the impact not only of sexual differentiation but also of perinatal stress acting through adrenal, thyroid, and growth-hormone secretion.

References

Blum, M., McEwen, B. S., and Roberts, J. 1987. Transcriptional analysis of tyrosine hydroxylase gene expression in the tuberoinfundibular dopaminergic neurons of the rat arcuate nucleus after estrogen treatment. *J. Biological Chemistry* 262:817–821.

Brawer, J., Schipper, H., and Naftolin, F. 1980. Ovary-dependent degeneration in the hypothalamic arcuate nucleus. *Endocrinology* 107:274–279.

Carrer, H., and Aoki, A. 1982. Ultrastructural changes in the hypothalamic ventromedial nucleus of ovariectomized rats after estrogen treatment. *Brain Research* 240:221–233.

Critchley, M. 1970. *The dyslexic child*. 2nd ed. Springfield, Ill.: Charles Thomas.

Diamond, M. 1984. Age, sex, and environmental influences. In *Biological substrates: Cerebral dominance*, ed. N. Geschwind and A. Galaburda. Cambridge: Harvard University Press.

Evoniuk, G., Kuhn, C., and Schanberg, S. 1979. The effect of tactile stimulation on serum growth hormone and tissue ornithine decarboxylase activity during maternal deprivation in rat pups. *Communications in Psychopharmacology* 3:363–370.

Finch, C., Felicio, L., Mobbs, C., and Nelson, J. 1984. Ovarian and steroidal influences on neuroendocrine aging processes in female rodents. *Endocrine Reviews* 5:467–497.

Fischette, C., Biegon, A., and McEwen, B. S. 1983. Sex differences in serotonin₁ binding in rat brain. *Science* 222:333–335.

Fride, E., Dan, Y., Feldon, J., Halevy, G., and Weinstock, M. 1986. Effects of prenatal stress on vulnerability to stress in prepubertal and adult rats. *Physiology and Behavior* 37:681–687.

Geschwind, N., and Behan, P. 1982. Left-handedness: Association with immune disease, migraine, and developmental learning disorder. *Proceedings of the National Academy of Sciences* (USA) 79:5097–5100.

Geschwind, N., and Galaburda, A. M. 1987. *Cerebral lateralization*, Cambridge: MIT Press.

Goy, R., and McEwen, B. S., eds. 1980. *Sexual differentiation of the brain*. Cambridge: MIT Press.

Harlan, R., and Gorski, R. 1978. Effects of postpubertal ovarian steroids on reproductive function and sexual differentiation of lightly androgenized rats. *Endocrinology* 102:1716–1724.

Harrelson, A., and McEwen, B. S. 1987. Gonadal steroid modulation of neurotransmitter-stimulated cAMP accumulation in the hippocampus of the rat. *Brain Research* 404:89–94.

Hittelman, J., and Dickes, R. 1979. Sex differences in neonatal eye contact time. *Merrill-Palmer Quarterly* 25:171–184.

Hofer, M. 1981. Parental contributions to the development of their offspring. In *Parental care in mammals*, ed. D. Gubernick and P. Klopfer. New York: Plenum Press.

Kuhn, C., Evoniuk, G., and Schanberg, S. 1979. Loss of tissue sensitivity to growth hormone during maternal deprivation in rats. *Life Science* 25:2089–2097.

Lehrman, D. S. 1964. The reproductive behavior of ring doves. *Scientific American* 211:48–54.

Maragos, W., Greenamyre, T., Penney, J., and Young, A. 1987. Glutamate dysfunction in Alzheimer's disease: An hypothesis. *Trends in Neurosciences* 10:65–68.

McEwen, B. S. 1988. Endocrine effects on the brain and their relationship to behavior. In *Basic neurochemistry*, ed. G. Siegel, W. Albers, B. Agranoff, and R. Katzman. Boston: Little Brown. In press.

McEwen, B. S. 1988b. Steroid hormones and the brain: linking "nature" and "nurture." *Neurochemical Research* 13:663–669.

McEwen, B. S. 1988c. Destructive hormonal influences on brain aging: The result of interacting modulators? In *New trends in aging research*, ed. G. Pepeu. Abano Terme, Italy: Fidia.

McEwen, B. S., and Brinton, R. E. 1987. Neuroendocrine aspects of adaptation. In *Progress in Brain Research*, vol. 72, ed. R. DeKloet and D. DeWied. Amsterdam: Elsevier Publishers.

McEwen, B. S., Davis, P., Parsons, B., and Pfaff, D. 1979. The brain target for steroid hormone action. *Annual Review of Neuroscience* 2:65–112.

McEwen, B. S., Jones, K., and Pfaff, D. W. 1987. Hormonal control of sexual behavior in the female rat: Molecular, cellular, and neurochemical studies. *Biology of Reproduction* 36:37–45.

Meaney, M., and Aitken, D. 1985. The effects of early, postnatal handling on hippocampal glucocorticoid receptor concentrations: Temporal parameters. *Developmental Brain Research* 22:301–304.

Meaney, M., Aitkens, D., Berkel, C., Bhatnagar, S., and Sapolsky, R. 1988. Effect of neonatal handling on age-related impairments associated with the hippocampus. *Science* 239:766–768.

Meaney, M., Aitken, D., Bodnoff, S., Iny, L., Tatarewicz, J., and Sapolsky, R. M. 1985. Early postnatal handling alters glucocorticoid receptor concentrations in selected brain regions. *Behavioral Neuroscience* 99:765–770.

Meaney, M., Aitken, D., and Sapolsky, R. M. 1987. Thyroid hormones influence the development of hippocampal glucocorticoid receptors in the rat: A mechanism for the effects of postnatal handling on the development of the adrenocortical stress response. *Neuroendocrinology* 45:278–283.

Meaney, M., and Stewart, J. 1981. Neonatal androgens influence the social play of prepubescent rats. *Hormones and Behavior* 15:197–213.

Pennington, B. F., Smith, S. D., Kimberling, W. J., Green, P. A., and Marshall, H. M. 1987. Left-handedness and immune disorders in familial dyslexia. *Arch. Neurol.* 44:634–639.

Sapolsky, R. M., Krey, L., and McEwen, B. S. 1986. The neuroendocrinology of stress and aging: The glucocorticoid cascade hypothesis. *Endocrine Review* 7:284–301.

Schanberg, S., and Kuhn, C. 1980. Maternal deprivation: An animal model of psychosocial dwarfism. In *Enzymes and neurotransmitters in mental disease*, ed. E. Usdin, T. Sourkes, and B. Youdim. New York: John Wiley and Sons.

Editor's Comments

Irrespective of the level at which cognitive functions like language, visual cognition, and memory are represented in the nervous system, the machinery that supports each of them must be built and maintained by biological interactions taking place at the molecular level. These interactions reflect information that is both coded in the genome and alterable by environmental meddling. This paper illustrates this point and considers some effects of hormones. What emerges is the overwhelmingly complex nature of the relationship between the organism and its environment throughout life.

First, McEwen makes it plain that the genomic blueprint passed along from generation to generation represents only a starting point. We may dispense with the notion that what is written in the genes is sacrosanct. We may also dispense with the equally oversimplified belief that abnormalities coded for in genes cannot be corrected, and I do not necessarily mean by the methods of genetic engineering. Once the nature of molecular interactions between genes and their environment is understood, perhaps gene expression will be amenable to manipulation by varying the physical and chemical environment at appropriate stages of development.

Second, McEwen points out that genetic and environmental interactions take place at every stage of the maturation of the organism. Hormones are as important in regulating gene expression when synapses (and other neural structures) are first being established as in subsequent developmental stages when they need to be maintained and modulated. Brain structures underlying sexual behavior are first established early in development, are changed at the onset of puberty, and are again modified during climacteric. Quite likely anatomical structures underlying nonsexual, cognitive behaviors and modifiable by sex steroids undergo comparable regulation during the life cycle. The emergence of cognitive capacities and the sex differences thereof during puberty may relate to these regulatory activities. The changes often observed among developmental dyslexics during the second decade may also be the result of neural restructuring by sex hormones, probably at the level of synaptic and receptor architecture rather than at higher levels involving long- and short-distance neural circuits. Sex differences in acquired disorders of later life, e.g., Alzheimer's disease, may reflect some of the toxic effects of circulating hormones.

The nature of hormone and brain interactions refuses to be pinned down to a manageable few general rules. There are immediate effects, as well as effects that restructure the brain in the long run. There are effects that appear to be constructive, as well as effects by the same hormone that break the system down. Both types of effects may be positive. From Rakic (this volume) we have learned that growth and development involve both destructive and constructive events. Thus, it is conceivable that even the obviously destructive effects of corticosteroids, are adaptive in that they act synergistically with excitatory neurotransmitters to remove poorly functioning neurons that do more damage to the functional integrity of the system by functioning partially than by not functioning at all. An example of system construction that has at least some negative functional consequences can be illustrated by the brain changes in developmental dyslexia and related animal models (see Galaburda et al. and Sherman et al. in this volume). Therefore, observations of anatomical remodeling must be considered in the light of observed functional consequences before they can be truly labeled as negative or positive.

Chapter 19

Adhesion Molecules in Pattern Formation and Neural Histogenesis

Kathryn L. Crossin and Gerald M. Edelman

Recent studies of cell-adhesion molecules (CAMs) and substrate-adhesion molecules (SAMs) suggest that many key events related to the formation of embryonic and neural patterns depend upon cell surface modulation. In this chapter we provide a short review of the evidence supporting this conslusion.

The generation of patterns in the embryo and the developing brain is a fundamental problem that has vexed biologists over the ages. What are the mechanisms that yield overall constancy among organisms of a species yet allow for the individual diversity upon which natural selection acts? To examine this fundamental problem, it is necessary to relate both developmental-genetic and mechanochemical factors at levels of organization from the gene and gene products, to cells, tissues, and organs, and ultimately back to the gene. In this brief survey we shall review the increasing evidence for the hypothesis that CAMs are excellent candidates for the genetic regulation of patterns in the development of the early embryo and of the brain. Although we do not touch directly upon functional disorders of the central nervous system (CNS), it is obvious that this regulation must be fundamental to such disorders as developmental dyslexia.

Regulative development consists of a number of parallel primary processes that are governed by complex interactions at the cell surface: cell division, cell movement, cell death, cell adhesion, and milieu-dependent differentiation (or embryonic induction). The interactions among these processes lead to morphogenesis and histogenesis in a series of epigenetic sequences. The epigenetic nature of these sequences points up an apparent paradox: although the genome itself cannot contain specific information about the exact position of a cell in time and space, morphogenesis is under genetic control. This paradox poses the key morphogenetic question: How can a one-dimensional genetic code specify a three-dimensional animal?

Embryonic induction occurs when groups of cells of different histories are brought together by means of morphogenetic movements, mutually interact, and thereby alter the fate of one or both groups of interacting cells (Jacobson 1966). Thus, the critical timing of gene expression associated with epigenetic sequences is intimately correlated with cell movements and the accumulation of groups of cells and must therefore involve regulatory control mechanisms ranging from the genes to tissues and back to the same or other genes.

All of these properties suggest that the molecular aspects of cell adhesion are likely to be involved in this regulatory control loop. The recent characterization of CAMs provides an opportunity to examine the role of adhesion in epigenetic sequences. The accumulated data prompt the hypothesis that CAMs act as regulators of morphogenetic movements (Edelman 1984a). They thus act as important links from the one-dimensional code that specifies these molecules to the three-dimensional collectives central to morphogenesis. While this hypothesis is far from confirmed and though the roles of such other molecules as substrate-adhesion molecules (including laminin, fibronectin, and collagens) must also be considered (Edelman and Thiery 1985), data on CAM expression sequences and on CAM perturbation indicate that these molecules have a particularly significant role in the formation of linked cells in collectives important in morphogenesis.

CAM Structure and Modulation

So far three CAMs of different specificity and structure have been isolated and characterized in detail (figure 19.1). Other CAMs have been described but their structures are not as well-known (for a review see Edelman 1986). The first two, the liver-cell adhesion molecule (L-CAM; Cunningham et al. 1984) and the neural-cell adhesion molecule (N-CAM; Hoffman et al. 1982; Edelman 1983), are called primary CAMs and appear early in embryogenesis upon derivatives of multiple germ layers. The third, the neuron-glia CAM (Ng-CAM; Grumet and Edelman 1984; Grumet et al. 1984b), is a secondary CAM that is not seen in early embryogenesis and that appears only on neuroectodermal derivatives, specifically, on postmitotic neurons (Thiery et al. 1985b).

All of the CAMs are glycoproteins synthesized by the cells on which they function. The evidence suggests that N-CAM and L-CAM are intrinsic membrane proteins; this appears to be true also of Ng-CAM but has not been as firmly established. N-CAM and probably L-CAM bind by homophilic mechanisms, i.e., the CAM on one cell binds to another identical CAM on an apposed cell. The two primary

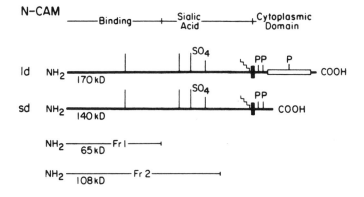

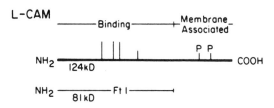

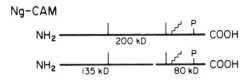

Figure 19.1

Diagrams of the linear chain structure of two primary CAMs (a neural-adhesion molecule [N-CAM] and a liver-adhesion molecule [L-CAM]) and of the secondary neuron-
glia adhesion molecule (Ng-CAM). N-CAM is composed of two chains that differ in the
size of their cytoplasmic domains. As indicated by the open bar at the COOH terminus,
the large-domain (ld) polypeptide contains approximately 250 more amino-acid resi-
dues in this region than does the small-domain (sd) polypeptide. The third and smallest (ssd) polypeptide is not shown. The thick vertical bar indicates the membrane-
spanning region. Below the chains are the fragments Fr1 and Fr2 derived by limited
proteolysis. As indicated by vertical lines, most of the carbohydrate is covalently attached in the middle domain at three sites and is sulfated, although the exact sulfation
site is unknown. Attached to these carbohydrates is polysialic acid. There are phosphorylation (P) sites as well in the COOH terminal domains. The diagonal staircases refer
to covalent attachment of palmitate. L-CAM yields one major proteolytic fragment (Ft1)
and has four attachment sites for carbohydrate (vertical lines) but lacks polysialic acid.
It is also phosphorylated in the COOH terminal region. Ng-CAM is shown as a major
Mr 200,000 chain. There are two components (Mr 135,000 and 80,000) that are probably
derived from a posttranslationally cleaved precursor. Each is related to the major Mr
200,000 chain (which may be the precursor), and the smaller is arranged as shown on
the basis of a known phosphorylation site.

CAMs show no binding specificity for each other. Ng-CAM on neurons may bind to glia by a heterophilic mechanism, but binds homophilically to itself on neurons.

It has been suggested (Edelman 1984a) that CAMs act to regulate binding by a series of mechanisms of cell surface modulation. Local cell-surface modulation is the alteration over time of the amount, position, distribution, or chemical properties of a particular kind of molecule at the cell surface (Edelman 1976). All of these mechanisms have been shown to occur for one CAM or another at different developmental times. Extensive examples of the first two forms of modulation are given below in a description of CAM expression sequences. An example of chemical modulation is seen in the so-called embryonic-to-adult (E-A) conversion of N-CAM (Rothbard et al. 1982; Hoffman et al. 1982). This is a gradual but large decrease during development of α-2-8-linked polysialic acid (Finne et al. 1983) at three sites present in the middle domain of the molecule (Crossin et al. 1984). In the microheterogeneous embryonic form of N-CAM, there are 30 g of sialic acid per 100 g of polypeptide. In the discrete adult forms this is reduced to 10 g per 100 g polypeptide. E-A conversion is seen in the brain, muscle (Rieger et al. 1985), and skin (Chuong and Edelman 1985a, 1985b). Recent studies suggest that N-CAM turns over at the cell surface and that the embryonic form is replaced by newly synthesized adult forms (Friedlander et al. 1985). Although the carbohydrate is not directly involved in binding, kinetic studies of CAM vesicle binding suggest that this E-A conversion results in a 4-fold increase in binding rates (Hoffman and Edelman 1983). It seems likely that the charged polysialic acid either modulates the conformation of the neighboring CAM-binding region or directly competes with homophilic binding from cell to cell by repulsion. Even more striking than the effects of E-A conversion is the dependency of homophilic binding on changes in CAM prevalence or surface density: a 2-fold increase in embryonic forms leads to an increase in binding rates of greater than 30-fold. These nonlinear dependencies suggest the possibility that at high surface densities N-CAM chains interact to form polyvalent multimers. Similar rate studies across a variety of vertebrate species suggest that the N-CAM-binding mechanism and specificity is conserved during evolution (Hoffman et al. 1984).

Such nonlinear binding effects and surface modulation are compatible with the notion that CAMs act as sensitive regulators of cell aggregation and cell motion. This notion has received support from experimentally disturbing CAM function *in vitro* and *in vivo*, the results of which will be described after considering CAM expression sequences.

CAM Expression Sequences

Correlations of time and place of expression of each CAM with sites of embryonic induction and with key events of histogenesis have been observed by means of immunocytochemistry. If the hypothesis that CAMs act as regulators of morphogenesis is correct, one would expect precise sequences of expression at important histogenetic sites. This is because the hypothesis puts a strong emphasis on the need for selective local control of CAM surface modulation to yield form. Here we shall review the observed gross sequences of expression in embryogenesis and two of the detailed microsequences occurring during brain and feather histogenesis.

A systematic examination of the spatiotemporal appearance of each of the CAMs during development (Edelman et al. 1983) shows a characteristic sequence of expression and definite restriction in fate maps (figure 19.2). The two primary CAMs characterized, N-CAM and L-CAM, are both present at low levels on the chick blastoderm before gastrulation. As gastrulation occurs in the chick and cells ingress through the primitive streak, the amount of detectable CAMs decreases (Thiery et al. 1982, 1984; Edelman et al. 1983; Crossin et al. 1985), which presumably reflects the fact that they have been decreased or masked. This phenomenon is seen particularly in mesoblast cells that ultimately give rise to the mesoderm.

After gastrulation and coincident with neural induction there is a marked change in the distribution of the two primary CAMs. An increase in immunofluorescent N-CAM staining appears in the region of the neural plate and groove as L-CAM staining disappears. In conjugate fashion L-CAM staining is enhanced in the surrounding somatic ectoderm as N-CAM staining slowly diminishes (see figure 19.2A). Placodes destined to build neural structures express both primary CAMs, but eventually lose L-CAM in the neural structures and show a complex modulation of N-CAM and L-CAM in the epithelial components, like the otic placode (Richardson et al. 1987). During its presence in the limb bud, the apical ectodermal ridge expresses both CAMs. Indeed, at all sites of secondary embryonic induction N-CAM, L-CAM, or both together undergo a series of prevalence modulations that follow two main rules (Crossin et al. 1985; Edelman 1985b, 1986). All epithelial-mesenchymal transformations show a modal transition of N→O→N, where N means expressing N-CAM, and O means either low or undetectable levels of the CAM (rule 1). Epithelial cells show other modal transitions, i.e. either NL→L or NL→N, where NL means expressing both CAMs and N or L means

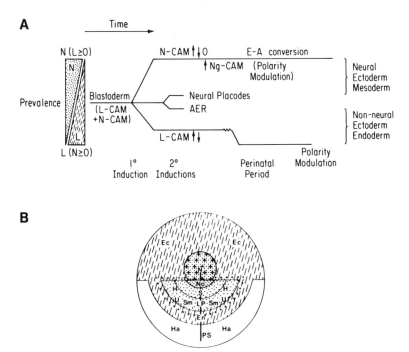

Figure 19.2

The major expression sequence and composite fate map of CAMs in the chick. The top schematic diagram (*A*) shows the temporal sequence of CAM expression during embryogenesis. Vertical wedges at the left refer to relative amounts of each CAM in the different parts of the embryo. Thus, the line referring to blastoderm indicates relatively large amounts of each CAM whereas that for neural ectoderm indicates major amounts of N-CAM but little or no L-CAM. After an initial differentiation event, N-CAM and L-CAM diverge in cellular distribution and are then modulated in prevalence within various regions of inductions or actually decrease greatly when mesenchyme appears or cell migration occurs. Note that placodes with both CAMs echo the events seen for neural induction. Just before the appearance of glia a secondary CAM (Ng-CAM) emerges. Unlike the other two CAMs, this CAM is not found in the fate map (*B*) before 3.5 days. In the perinatal period a series of epigenetic modulations occurs: E-A conversion for N-CAM and polar redistribution for L-CAM on tissues of 5-to-14-day embryos is mapped back onto the tissue precursor cells in the blastoderm. Areas expressing N-CAM are denoted by stippling; those with L-CAM by hatching; those with Ng-CAM by crosses. Additional regions of N-CAM staining in the 5-day embryo are shown by larger dots. In the early embryo, the borders of CAM expression overlap is more restricted: N-CAM disappears from somatic ectoderm and from endoderm, except for a population of cells in the lung. L-CAM is expressed on all ectodermal and endodermal epithelia but remains restricted in the mesoderm to epithelial derivatives of the urogenital system. The vertical bar represents the primitive streak (PS). Also indicated are intra- and extraembryonic ectoderm (Ec), endoderm (En), the nervous system (N), precordal and chordamesoderm (No), somite (S), smooth muscle (Sm), hemangioblastic area (Ha), urogenital region (U), lateral plate mesoderm (LP), and heart (H).

expressing either N-CAM or L-CAM (rule 2). The expression of CAMs in epigenetic sequences expressing these rules is map restricted: particular CAMs appear in an ordered pattern in a fate map of chick blastoderm (figure 19.2*B*).

At somewhat later periods the secondary CAM (Ng-CAM), which binds neurons to neurons and neurons to glia, appears in the CNS and peripheral nervous system (PNS; Grumet et al. 1984a; Grumet et al. 1984b; Thiery et al. 1985a; Thiery et al. 1985b; Daniloff et al. 1986a). Ng-CAM, which is present on neurons, is seen mainly on extending neurites in the CNS, except where cell bodies move on glia, at which times it is seen also on cell bodies. In the PNS it is distributed on both cell bodies and neurites. During the subsequent perinatal period N-CAM undergoes E-A conversion, Ng-CAM diminishes in myelinated areas of the CNS, and L-CAM is increasingly modulated in polarity in epithelial tissues. This is reflected, for example, by its presence on apicolateral portions of exocrine pancreatic cells.

Within this overall macrosequence of CAM expression there occur histogenetic events marked by cellular differentiation. These events are accompanied by microsequences consisting of specific CAM appearances and disappearances over limited tissue neighborhoods and shorter times. Two illuminating examples are (1) the feather both as it is periodically induced in the skin and as it forms a periodic set of structures within itself leading to a characteristic hierarchical pattern and (2) the nervous system as it forms its detailed connectivity.

CAM Expression and Perturbation of Morphology in the Feather

Perhaps the most dramatic example of the coordinated modulation of expression of the two primary CAMs is the feather. Examination of this periodic and hierarchically organized structure provides an opportunity to analyze the coupling of cell collectives in detail and to relate their interactions to cell differentiation events within a dimensionally well-organized appendage. Feathers are induced through the formation of dermal condensations of mesenchyme derived from the mesoderm. These condensations act on ectodermal cells to form placodes (Sengel 1976). Such placodes and condensations are eventually hexagonally close packed as feather induction proceeds in rows from medial to lateral aspects of the chicken skin. Within each induced placode a dermal papilla is subsequently formed as a result of a repeated cycle of inductive interactions between mesoderm and ectoderm. Subsequently there is a cellular proliferation of barb ridges (which fuse to form a rachis), followed by formation of the barbule

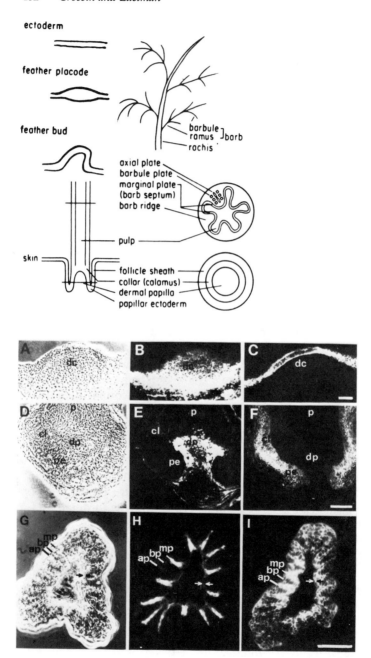

Figure 19.3
CAM expression in feather development. The diagram above shows successive stages and nomenclature in feather development. Below are comparisons of anti-N-CAM and

plate. This yields the basis for three levels of branching: rachis, ramis, and barbule (see figure 19.3).

At each of these levels is seen an extraordinary series of events involving L-CAM-linked collectives of cells adjoining N-CAM-linked collectives either by movement and adhesion or by cell division and adhesion (Chuong and Edelman 1985a, 1985b). L-CAM linked ectodermal cells are initially approached by CAM-negative mesenchyme cells moving into the vicinity. Just beneath the ectoderm the mesenchyme cells become N-CAM positive and accumulate in lens-shaped mesodermal condensations (figure 19.3 *A–C*). Later the L-CAM positive placode cells transiently express N-CAM. In the formation of the dermal papilla, N-CAM-positive mesodermal cells adjoin L-CAM-positive ectodermal cells. At this stage the ectodermal cells in the highly proliferative collar epithelium express both L-CAM and N-CAM (figure 19.3 *D–F*). Derivatives of these cells lose N-CAM while retaining L-CAM as they form barb ridges by division. In the valleys between the ridges, single or small numbers of basilar cells then express N-CAM while losing L-CAM (figure 19.3 *G–I*). This process extends cell by cell up each ridge and results in the formation of the N-CAM-positive marginal plate. The net result is a series of L-CAM linked barb ridges and N-CAM-linked marginal plates. As ridge cells organize into barbule plates linked by L-CAM, a similar process recurs: N-CAM is expressed in cells lying between each of the future barbules which results in yet another level of periodic expression of CAM couples. The net result is a series of cellular patterns in which cell collectives expressing L-CAM alternate with those expressing N-CAM at both the secondary barb level and the tertiary barbule level. Finally, after further growth of these structures and extension of the barb ridges into rami, the L-CAM positive cells keratinize, and the N-

anti-L-CAM fluorescence at some of these stages. A feather placode from the dorsal skin of a stage-33 embryo (*A*) shows anti-N-CAM fluorescence (*B*) and anti-L-CAM fluorescence (*C*). Feather follicles from the wing skin of a newly hatched chicken (*D*) show intense N-CAM staining in the dermal papilla (*E*) and L-CAM staining in the papillar ectoderm (*F*). The collar epithelium stains for both N-CAM and L-CAM. Feather filaments from the skin of the back of a stage-44 embryo (*G*) show staining for both N-CAM (*H*) and L-CAM (*I*). N-CAM staining occurs in marginal and axial plates, and strong L-CAM staining occurs in the barb-ridge epithelium. The distribution of the two CAMs thus has a periodic appearance. Arrows point to the basilar layer. Lower case letters indicate the axial plate (ap), barbule plate (bp), marginal plate (mp), dermal condensation (dc), dermal papilla (dp), papillar ectoderm (pe), and collar (cl). Bar = 50 μm.

CAM positive cells die without keratinization. This process produces alternate spaces between rami and between barbules and yields the characteristic feather morphology.

In this sequence of histogenetic CAM expression, one observes periodic CAM modulation, periodic and successive formation of L-CAM-linked and N-CAM-linked cell collectives (CAM couples), and a definite association of particular gene-expression events during cell differentiation with particular kinds of CAMs. The most dramatic example is the association of the gene expression of keratins only with L-CAM-containing cells. Throughout these sequences there is an intimate connection of the regulatory process of adhesion with the epigenetic sequences of the different primary processes that act as driving forces: morphogenetic movement for the original mesenchymal induction, mitosis for the formation of papillar ectoderm and barb ridges, and death for the N-CAM-linked collectives in the terminal period of feather formation. These findings have several important implications, for they raise the possibility that CAM function is causally important in inductive sequences, and they suggest that a series of local signals must be responsible for particular sequences of CAM expression.

This view is supported by experiments showing that CAMs play a key role in causal sequences during induction and histogenesis of the feather *in vitro*. (Gallin et al. 1986). Antibodies to L-CAM added to chicken skin explants altered the pattern of N-CAM-linked dermal condensation from a hexagonal symmetry to a pattern showing a tendency of feather placodes to fuse mediolaterally into stripes. Longerterm cultures with anti-L-CAM present showed formation of scalelike plates rather than the featherlike filament patterns seen in unperturbed controls. Thus, antibodies to one CAM in an inducing cell collective can alter patterns formed by cells in the other, induced cell collective. A computer model based on the notion that the antibody alters the signals sent to dermal condensations by epidermal cells reproduces this pattern of symmetry breaking (Gallin et al. 1986).

This example in a nonneural tissue provides a background for examining neural tissues as they express neuronal CAMs. The nervous system shows similar but additional features, including the expression of secondary CAMs and of SAMs.

Neuronal CAMs and Neural Histogenesis

As seen in the example of feather formation, one of the key structural events in embryogenesis is boundary formation, an event that appears to be strongly tied to the early differentiation rules found for the two well-characterized primary CAMs (Edelman 1985a, 1985b, 1986; Crossin et al. 1985). After neural induction and the exclusion of L-CAM from neural derivatives, a secondary CAM specific for neural derivatives, Ng-CAM, is expressed on postmitotic neurons that already display N-CAM. In the CNS, this CAM is seen mainly on extending neurites of stationary cells and in very slight amounts on cell somata. This represents a striking example of polarity modulation, i.e., unequal distribution of CAMs within the membrane of a single cell. But at just those sites and times at which neuronal migrations on radial glia take place, Ng-CAM is strongly expressed on somata and leading processes in addition to neurites (Thiery et al. 1985b; Daniloff et al. 1986a). Ng-CAM is not seen on glia in the CNS, but in the PNS, Ng-CAM and N-CAM are both present on Schwann cells and neurons. It is notable that when examined with immunocytochemical techniques, PNS neurons do not exhibit the polarity modulation of Ng-CAM seen in the CNS.

During development Ng-CAM shows a microsequence of appearances and disappearances that is closely correlated with the successive occurrences of histogenetic events at different neural locations (figure 19.4). The order of appearances is strict and reproducible from animal to animal, which suggests that local signals related to cellular maturation are responsible for the remarkable prevalence modulation of Ng-CAM at the neuronal-cell surface. Neither the mechanisms nor the signals for the additional polarity modulation of this molecule in the CNS are understood, but it is a reasonable conjecture that the cytoskeleton and axonal transport are involved.

Two additional modulation mechanisms are observed for N-CAM. One, discussed above, is the perinatal occurrence of E-A conversion (a loss of polysialic acid with concurrent changes in binding properties) of N-CAM in tracts. The other is that in neural crest cells, which form the PNS and other structures, N-CAM is lost or lowered on the surface of migrating crest cells and reappears at sites where ganglion formation occurs (Thiery et al. 1982, 1985a).

All of these sequences reveal coordinated local events of cell-surface modulation occurring during the formation of particular neural structures: prevalence modulation, polarity modulation, and chemical modulation (E-A conversion). Recent studies on the large-cytoplasmic-domain polypeptide of N-CAM (Mr 180,000) (Hemperly et al. 1986) indicate that N-CAM is expressed only in the nervous system (also see Murray et al. 1986b). This molecule (figure 19.1) differs from the small-cytoplasmic-domain chain (Mr 140,000) in having a large and different cytoplasmic domain that is 261 amino acids long (Hemperly et al. 1986). The large-domain chain is differentially ex-

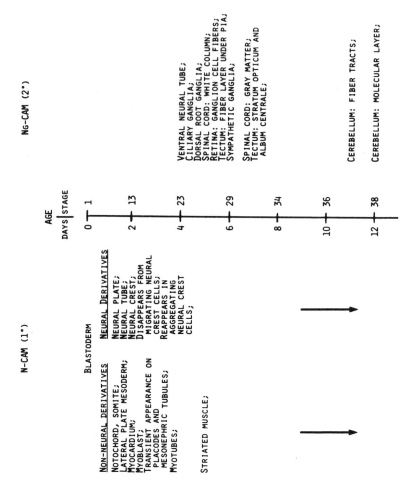

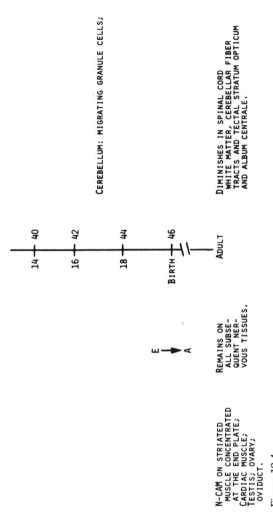

Figure 19.4

The expression sequence of two neuronal CAMS in the developing chick nervous system: N-CAM, a primary (1°) cell-adhesion molecule, appears in the blastoderm stage in both neural and nonneural derivatives. After birth it remains on all subsequent nervous tissues. Ng-CAM, a secondary (2°) adhesion molecule, appears later during embryogenesis and is first observed on the developing spinal cord (Thiery et al. 1985b; Daniloff et al. 1986a). The sequential appearance of Ng-CAM in the CNS and PNS regions is here summarized. In the adult Ng-CAM is limited to the unmyelinated CNS regions (tracts or laminae) and PNS (see Daniloff et al. 1986a).

pressed in certain layers during development of the cerebellum and retina (Williams et al. 1985; Pollerberg et al. 1985; Murray et al. 1986b). Alternative RNA splicing leads to coding for the larger cytoplasmic domain in the large-domain polypeptide (Murray et al. 1986a), which might interact differentially with the cytoskeleton or other proteins in the cortical region of the cell by mechanisms similar to those responsible for the polarity of Ng-CAM (Hemperly et al. 1986). An attractive hypothesis is that differential cell-surface modulation of the large- and small-domain chains could lead to altered patterns of cell interaction, migration, and layering. The adequate signal for this modulation would be one that controlled alternative splicing in a local tissue region.

SAMs in Embryogenesis and Neural Histogenesis

The evidence suggesting that CAMs play significant roles in embryogenesis and neural histogenesis by means of modulation and regulation prompts the idea that complementary functions may be exercised by substrate adhesion molecules. A newly discovered extracellular matrix protein, cytotactin, appears to have such a role.

Cytotactin was isolated from 14-day embryonic chicken brains as structurally related polypeptides of Mr 220,000, 200,000, and 190,000 (Grumet et al. 1985). These polypeptides were efficiently extracted in the absence of detergent and appeared to be disulfide-linked to form higher polymers. Cytotactin was involved in glia-neuron adhesion *in vitro* by a mechanism different from that of Ng-CAM, yet unlike Ng-CAM, it was absent from neurons. The molecule was synthesized in culture by glia and cells from smooth muscle, lung, and kidney. It was found at the surface of cultured glia in a cell-associated fibrillar pattern.

Although cytotactin was initially identified as a molecule that mediates glia-neuron interactions, preliminary immunohistochemical localization of the molecule suggested that it is an extracellular matrix protein with a widespread distribution that is, however, more restricted than either fibronectin or laminin. Analysis of the sequence of its expression showed that it is first present in the gastrulating chicken embryo (Crossin et al. 1986). It later appears in the basement membrane of the developing neural tube and notochord in a temporal sequence that begins in the cephalic regions and proceeds caudally. Between two and three days of development the molecule is present at high levels in the early neural-crest pathways surrounding the neural tube and somites, but in contrast to fibronectin and laminin, it was not found in the lateral plate mesoderm or ectoderm. At later times cytotactin is extensively distributed in the central nervous system, in lesser amounts in the peripheral nervous system, and in a number of nonneural sites, most prominently in all smooth muscles and in the basement membranes of lung and kidney. In the cerebellum it appears on glial endfeet, Bergmann glial fibers, and in extracellular spaces.

The findings raise the possibility that certain extracellular matrix proteins such as cytotactin contribute to pattern formation in embryogenesis as a result of their restricted spatiotemporally regulated expression at some sites but not at others. As discussed below, analyses of the role of cytotactin in supporting or modulating the migration of external granule cells support this idea and raise the possibility that mutual coordination and differential expression of CAMs and SAMs are major factors in regulating morphogenetic pattern (Chuong et al. 1987).

Perturbation of CAM and SAM Expression and Morphology

The hypothesis that CAMs may act as regulators of morphogenesis implies that CAM expression and maintenance of morphology are interdependent. As discussed above in the case of the feather, interfering with the expression of CAMs can lead to perturbation of subsequent morphology. Similar perturbations have been observed for neuronal CAMs and cytotactin. Conversely, in the PNS it has been shown that perturbing morphology by nerve compression or transection results in dramatic changes in CAM and SAM expression.

The evidence that CAM modulation is a major factor in embryogenesis is particularly compelling in the nervous system. It is striking that CAMs of different specificity play complementary or differential roles in altering various morphogenetic processes at different times and places. Different cellular systems have revealed functional differences for each CAM that reflect its relative amount (prevalence modulation) and cellular location (polarity modulation) (Hoffman et al. 1986).

Each of three cellular processes examined *in vitro* was found to be selectively inhibited only by antibodies to Ng-CAM at different sites (Hoffman et al. 1986). Both neurite fasciculation in cultured dorsal root ganglia and the migration of cerebellar granule cells were inhibited by anti-Ng-CAM. Antibodies to N-CAM inhibited the formation of histological layers in the retina. Quantitative immunoblotting showed the relative Ng-CAM/N-CAM ratios in comparable extracts of the brain, dorsal root ganglia, and retina to be respectively 0.32, 0.81, and 0.04. Thus, the relative ability of antibodies to Ng-CAM to inhibit interaction between cells in different neural tissues was strongly correlated with the local Ng-CAM/N-CAM ratio. During a culture of dorsal root ganglia in the presence of nerve growth factor (NGF), the Ng-CAM/N-CAM ratio rose to 4.95 in neurite outgrowths and to 1.99 in the ganglion proper, which shows that there is both polarity and prevalence modulation. These findings show that the degree to which a particular CAM influences a morphogenetic process depends upon the site, its amount relative to other CAMs, and the particular histogenetic process being mediated.

An excellent example of these principles and of the correlated effects of SAMs is seen in the cellular migration of external granule cells in the developing cerebellum. Recent studies (Hoffman et al. 1986; Chuong et al. 1987) indicate that antibodies to N-CAM have only slight effects on the migration of external granule cells in cerebellar slices *in vitro*. In contrast, antibodies to Ng-CAM arrested most cells in the external granular layer, and antibodies to cytotactin arrested most cells in the molecular layer. Time-course analyses combined with sequential addition of different antibodies in different orders showed that anti-Ng-CAM had a major effect in the early period of culture and a lesser effect in the second part of the culture period. Anticytotactin had essentially no effect at the earlier time but had major effects at a later period, which suggests that these molecules affect two temporally distinct processes of migration previously demonstrated in anatomical studies. The evidence suggests that Ng-CAM may play a role in both early and late events. Correlation of these effects with the spatiotemporal expression of these different molecules suggests a complex complementary scheme in which temporal expression, different binding roles, and different functional effects on interaction between neurons and Bergmann glia all are required for pattern formation in the cerebellar cortex.

All of the experiments above were done on *in vitro* preparations. Agarose implants containing anti-N-CAM placed in the tectum of *Xenopus laevis* caused severe distortion of *in vivo* map formation and regeneration (Fraser et al. 1984). The physiological alterations were accompanied by a sharp decrease in the density of axonal arbors in the region of the implant (Fraser et al. 1988). Perhaps the most striking aspect of this experiment was the return to a more normal map pattern as the local concentration of anti-N-CAM decreased in the tectum.

It is quite obvious from both the *in vitro* and *in vivo* studies that interfering with CAM binding function can alter morphology. To develop a consistent notion of the molecular regulation of neural morphogenesis, it is necessary to show that disruption of morphology or

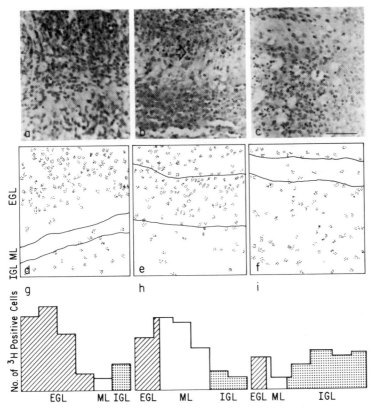

Figure 19.5
The effects of anti-Ng-CAM and anticytotactin on the migration of tritiated cerebellar granule cells. (*a–c*) Autoradiograms of paraffin sections of cerebellar explants that were pulse-labeled with tritiated thymidine for one hour and cultured for three days. (*d–f*) Tracings of (*a–c*) to highlight the silver grains and the relative thickness of the cortical layers. (*g–h*) Histograms of the number of tritiated cells versus distance along layers. Anti-Ng-CAM is indicated in (*a, d,* and *g*); anticytotactin in (*b, e,* and *h*); and a non-immune control in (*c, f, i*). The arrow in (*b*) points to granule cells in the ML piled up along the Bergmann glia. EGL designates the external granule layer; ML, the molecular layer; IGL, the internal granule layer. Bar = 50 μm. (See Chuong et al. 1987.)

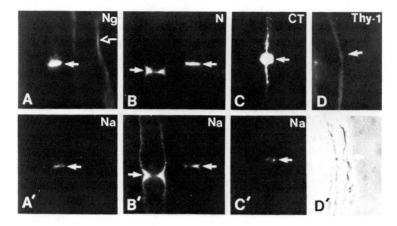

Figure 19.6
Colocalization of neuronal CAMs and cytotactin at the node of Ranvier. Ng-CAM (*A*), N-CAM (*B*), and cytotactin (*C*) were all seen to localize with the Na⁺ channel (*A'*, *B'*, *C"*), a marker for the node of Ranvier (closed arrows), made visible by fluorescent-bungarotoxin staining. In contrast, unmyelinated fibers were uniformly stained for Ng-CAM (open arrow in *A*) and N-CAM (not shown). Cytotactin was present in a spindle shaped pattern most densely at the node and decreasing approximately 5 to 20 microns away. Antibodies to the neuronal surface marker Thy-1 (*D*) uniformly stained the axon surface. This indicates that increased staining at the nodes was not an artifact of the exposed membrane. (*D'*) is the phase micrograph corresponding to (D). Bar = 10 μm. (See Rieger et al. 1986.)

of linked structures can lead to alterations of CAM expression, which would indicate that a control loop exists between the form maintained in tissues and CAM synthesis or modulation. This control loop can be seen most clearly in analyses of the role of CAMs in the PNS.

Pattern and Regeneration in the Periphery

After neural crest and other cells establish the PNS, CAMs and SAMs play key roles in later pattern formation. Because one can observe regenerative effects and defined manipulable interactions of cell types (Schwann cells, neurons, muscles), structures in the PNS provide an excellent opportunity to test the notion that interactions of cells in different tissues regulate CAM expression. For example, N-CAM, Ng-CAM, and cytotactin are highly concentrated at the nodes of Ranvier of the adult chicken and mouse (Rieger et al. 1986). In contrast, unmyelinated axonal fibers were uniformly stained at low levels by specific antibodies to both CAMs but not by antibodies to cytotactin (figure 19.6). Moreover, developmental analysis suggested that the interaction between neurons and Schwann cells (which displayed N-CAM and Ng-CAM) may play a role in establishing the one-dimensional periodic pattern of nodes. At embryonic day 14, before myelination had occurred, small-caliber fibers of chick embryos showed periodic, coincident accumulations of the two CAMs but not of cytotactin and only faint labeling in the axonal regions between accumulations. Cytotactin was found on Schwann cells and in connective tissue. By embryonic day 18, nodal accumulations of CAMs were first observed in a few medium- and large-caliber fibers. These findings are consistent with the hypothesis that surface modulation of neuronal CAMs mediated by signals shared between neurons and glia may be necessary for establishing and maintaining the nodes of Ranvier.

In view of the epigenetic nature of tissue formation and the existence of defined CAM-expression sequences, it is reasonable to suppose that CAM expression and modulation depend upon local signals that vary according to the state, composition, and integrity of the particular interacting cell collectives. Thus, CAMs (along with SAMs and cell-junctional molecules) may serve to stabilize tissue structures, and their modulation and expression should depend in turn upon local cellular interactions in the stabilized structure. A number of studies have shown that disrupted morphology or altered morphogenesis can actually lead to changes in CAM modulation patterns. For example, disturbing normal *in vivo* cell interaction during degeneration and regeneration has been shown to result in altered CAM expression and distribution (figure 19.7). N-CAM is present at the neuromuscular junction of striated muscles but is absent from the rest of the surface of the myofibril (figure 7A; Rieger et al. 1985). After the sciatic nerve is cut, the molecule appears diffusely at the cell surface and in the cytoplasm but returns to normal after regeneration (figure 7B, C; Rieger et al. 1985; Covault and Sanes 1985; Daniloff et al. 1986b). These experiments indicate that the early events of regeneration can be accompanied by altered CAM modulation. More recent experiments show that both crushing and cutting a nerve have widespread effects (Daniloff et al. 1986b). These range from altered anti-CAM staining in the motor neurons of the spinal cord on the affected side (figure 7 F, G) to modulatory changes in N-CAM and Ng-CAM within Schwann cells near the lesion (figure 7D, E).

CAM modulation has also been found to be disturbed in genetic diseases with altered morphology. As described above, N-CAM and Ng-CAM colocalize at nodes of Ranvier in peripheral myelinated nerves (Rieger et al. 1986). In two dysmyelinating mouse mutants,

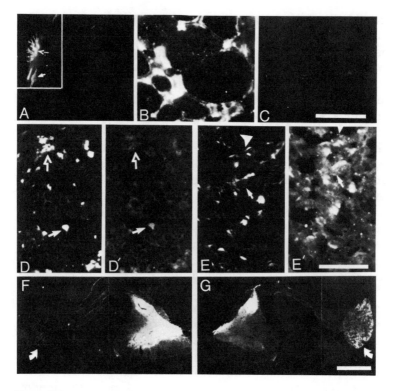

Figure 19.7
Changes in CAM expression throughout the neuromuscular system following nerve transection. Cross sections of chick gastrocnemius muscles stained with polyclonal anti-N-CAM (*A–C*) showed that the surface of muscle fibers were faintly labeled in normal chicken muscles (*A*). The inset shows a whole-mount preparation of normal adult teased muscled fibers (magnification = ×7). The muscle surface was faintly labeled with anti-N-CAM; a motor endplate (open arrow) and several mononucleated cells that are probably satellite cells (filled arrow) were intensely labeled. Ten days after the sciatic nerve was cut, a dramatic increase occurred in the intensity of N-CAM (*B*); a normal pattern was restored after 150 days (*C*). In cross sections of normal adult nerves, bundles of nonmyelinated axons (open arrow) and Schwann cells (filled arrow) were intensely stained for Ng-CAM (*D*). These cells also formed N-CAM positive regions (*D'*) within unstained donutlike structures, which represent the myelin sheath. Only Schwann cells and not fibers expressed S100 protein (not shown). In the distal stump 10 days after the nerve was cut, many abnormal spaces were seen in the nerve (arrowheads in *E* and *E'*). Ng-CAM staining was most intense in Schwann cells (filled arrow in *E*). The overall intensity of N-CAM staining (*E'*) was greater than in controls (*D'*). Although all components of the nerve appeared to express N-CAM at this time (*E'*), the S100 staining pattern indicated that most staining was associated with Schwann cells. (*F, G*): cross sections of the lowest lumbar segment of the spinal cord and DRG 20 days after cutting the sciatic nerve. On the experimental, lesioned side (*G*) the intensity of Ng-CAM staining decreased in the ventral horn (black arrow) and increased within the ganglia (white curved arrow) in comparison with the side contralateral to the lesion (*F*). Bar = 50 μm (*A–E*), 800 μm (*F–G*). (See Daniloff et al. 1986b).

trembler ($+/Tr$) and motor endplate disease (*med/med*), the distribution pattern of these molecules was found to be disrupted in the myelinated fibers. A recent study indicated that alterations in the amount of N-CAM are associated with a number of human myopathies (Walsh and Moore 1985). This is in accord with the observations of iterated CAM expression in muscle degeneration and regeneration. These failures of regulations have a counterpart in the central nervous system: in the mouse mutant *staggerer*, which shows connectional defects between Purkinje cells and parallel fibers in the cerebellum and extensive granule cell death, E-A conversion of N-CAM is greatly delayed in the cerebellum (Edelman and Chuong 1982). Accumulated data both from interventions and by examining disease states argue that an elaborate series of local morphology-dependent signals regulate CAM expression in various tissues. CAM-mediated adhesion must therefore be analyzed in a context-dependent fashion related to actual tissue and cell morphology. Although this makes analysis more difficult, the contextual combinations of mechanisms having important effects on morphogenesis are virtually limitless and free one from having to specify definite molecular cell addresses as the basis for neural morphogenesis (Sperry 1963; Edelman 1984b).

The Regulator Hypothesis: Mechanochemistry Linked to Developmental Genetics

We are now in a position to consider a theory that relates CAM and SAM expression to the development of form in the embryo and the developing brain. The evidence of the structure, function, and sequences of CAM expression and evidence from perturbation experiments suggest that these molecules play a major regulatory role in morphogenesis. This conclusion provides a basis for the regulator hypothesis (Edelman 1984a), which states that by means of cell-surface modulation CAMs are key regulators of morphogenetic motion, epithelial integrity, and mesenchymal condensation. The evidence suggests that the morphoregulatory genes affecting CAM expression act independently of and prior to the historegulatory genes controlling tissue-specific differentiation, since CAM expression in most induced areas initially precedes the expression of most cell-differentiation products. This is consistent with the observation that the expression of CAMs occurs in tissues of different types, as can be seen in a classical fate map (figure 19.2). As cell adhesion molecules are likely to be proteins specified by particular genes, their function provides a candidate mechanism for how the one-dimensional genetic code might regulate three-dimensional form. If this is one such mechanism, it would serve not only to link mechanochemistry to developmental genetics but would also provide a major mechanism of morphologic evolution.

A main action of CAMs is to attach cells in collectives and to regulate movement, and so a major part of their function is mechanochemical in nature. Although CAMs have a relatively small number of specificities, they are capable of a large number of alterations in their binding properties, which are graded and nonlinear. To relate this mechanochemical CAM function to CAM expression sequences and to the expression of other gene products concerned with cell differentiation, we must assume that chemical or mechanochemical signals act locally on cells in collectives. Altered pressure, tension, or flow in the vicinity of a collective of cells held together by a CAM of different specificity, acting together with chemical factors released by such collectives, could alter the expression or modulation of the CAMs at cell surfaces. Changing the temporal sequence of such expression would alter morphogenetic movements and lead to changes in specific form and pattern. We must therefore examine how such signals might effect morphoregulatory genes for CAMs and SAMs and historegulatory genes for tissues.

At the level of a given kind of cell and its descendants, CAM expression may be viewed as occuring in a cycle (figure 19.8). Traversals of the outer loop of this cycle lead either to switching on one or another of the CAM genes or to switching it off. We suggest that there is switching on and off of the same genes in the case of mesenchymal cells that contribute to dermal condensations and in the case of neural crest cells. Switching to a different CAM gene is suggested in the case of epithelia. The subsequent action of historegulatory genes (the inner loop of figure 19.8) is diagrammed as the result of signals arising in the new milieux that occur through CAM-dependent cell aggregation, motion, and tissue folding. If the expression of historegulatory genes alters cell motion, cell shape, or posttranslational events, this would alter the effects of subsequent traversals of the outer loop on morphogenesis. One key example directly affecting cells containing N-CAM is the expression of genes specifying the enzyme responsible for E-A conversion, an event that leads to changes in N-CAM binding rates.

Combination of the outer and inner loops of the cycle and the linkage of two such cycles by the formation of CAM couples (as in the feather) could lead to a rich set of mechanisms for altering the path of morphogenesis. When considering how two such cycles of different

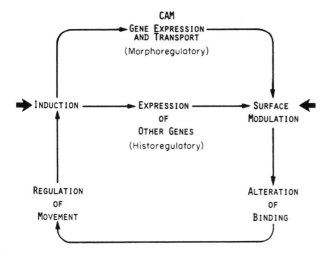

Figure 19.8
The proposed regulatory cycle. Early induction signals (heavy arrow at left) lead to CAM gene expression. Surface modulation (by prevalence changes, polar redistribution on the cell, or chemical change such as E-A conversion) alters binding rates of cells. This regulates morphogenetic movements, which in turn affect embryonic induction or milieu-dependent differentiation. These changes can again affect CAM gene expression as well as the expression of other genes for specific tissues. The heavy arrows at the left and right indicate possible as yet unknown signals for initiation of induction. These signals could result from global surface modulation as a result of CAM binding (right) or from a release of morphogens affecting induction (left). This representation of the regulator hypothesis expressly proposes that regulatory genes for CAMs and those for tissue-specific proteins are under separate temporal schedules of control. This is equivalent to saying that the outer loop of the cycle must be traversed at least once before the inner loop is engaged. Successive courses through this cycle would lead to epigenetic changes during morphogenesis and histogenesis.

CAMs might interact, we must consider the nature of the signals that activate morphoregulatory and historegulatory genes during induction. It remains unknown whether these signals are morphogens released by cells linked by a particular CAM (figure 19.8, left large arrow) or whether they are derived from mechanical alterations of the cell surface or cytoskeleton through global cell-surface modulation (figure 19.8, right large arrow).

According to the hypothesis CAMs are molecules that provide the linkage between the genes and the mechanochemical requirements of epigenetic sequences. Linked CAM cycles occurring in various contexts provide a potential solution to the problem of mechanochemical control during regulative development of patterns at levels ranging from gene to organ and back to gene. According to this view place in the embryo is not recognized by a microscopically assigned marker; it is established as a consequence of modulation and control. CAMs act as regulators of cellular mechanochemical events. Their expression, through control of morphoregulatory genes, links the one-dimensional genetic code to higher-order assemblages of cells and tissues. If this view is correct, the CAM-regulatory cycle provides a particularly elegant solution to the problem of mechanochemical control of pattern at several layers of organization (from genes and gene products, to cells, to tissues and organs, and back to the genes), a problem that is posed by the occurrence of epigenetic sequences both in regulatory development and in regeneration.

We expect that the nervous system should in general conform to the regulator hypothesis. This hypothesis makes CAMs and SAMs key structural determinants of anatomical constancy and variation in neural networks. The relation of CAM function to dynamic neuroanatomy in terms of interactive events at the molecular, cellular, and tissue levels should provide a fundamental basis for further developments within the emerging sciences of molecular embryology and molecular histology. Of particular interest is the possibility that the paths taken by neural growth cones and neurite outgrowth depend upon target-induced modulation of CAMs on the cell surfaces of pioneer neurons. Just a few changes in the path choices of a single neurite could greatly alter neural pattern. The general principles of signaling neurite paths may resemble those seen in embryonic induction systems like the feather (Gallin et al. 1986) but on a finer scale. In view of the extraordinarily local order of organization in neural tissue, the great number of opportunities to exchange chemical signals at the synaptic level, and the continued maturation of neural structure after birth as a result of behavior, it would not be surprising if additional CAMs and SAMs and new types of modulations were found to be special to neural tissue. It is already clear, for example, that the large-domain chain of N-CAM arises from an alteration of RNA splicing events that is specific to the nervous system. In view of the number of modulation mechanisms already known, their context-specific and epigenetic character, and the combinatorial possibilities, it would not require many more mechanisms to account for the remarkable complexity of neural structure. Present knowledge of the dynamic properties of modulation mechanisms and of the genetic control of CAMs and SAMs already provides an initial basis on which to improve our understanding both of the developmental constraints on neural evolution and of the somatic variability of individual neural networks. A growing understanding of these issues should cast light on the structural bases of functional disorders like dyslexia.

References

Bertolotti, R., U. Rutishauser, and G. M. Edelman. 1980. A cell surface molecule involved in aggregation of embryonic liver cells. *Proc. Natl. Acad. Sci.* (USA) 77:4831–4835.

Chuong, C.-M., K. L. Crossin, and G. M. Edelman. 1987. Sequential expression and differential function of multiple adhesion molecules during the formation of cerebellar cortical layers. *J. Cell Biol.* 104:331–342.

Chuong, C.-M., and G. M. Edelman. 1985a. Expression of cell adhesion molecules in embryonic induction: I. Morphogenesis of nestling feathers. *J. Cell Biol.* 101:1009–1026.

Chuong, C.-M., and G. M. Edelman. 1985b. Expression of cell adhesion molecules in embryonic induction: II. Morphogenesis of adult feathers. *J. Cell Biol.* 101:1027–1043.

Covault, J., and J. R. Sanes. 1985. Neural cell adhesion molecule (N-CAM) accumulates in denervated and paralyzed skeletal muscles. *Proc. Natl. Acad. Sci.* (USA) 82:4544–4548.

Crossin, K. L., C.-M. Chuong, and G. M. Edelman. 1985. Expression sequences of cell adhesion molecules. *Proc. Natl. Acad. Sci.* (USA) 82:6942–6946.

Crossin, K. L., G. M. Edelman, and B. A. Cunningham. 1984. Mapping of three carbohydrate attachment sites in embryonic and adult forms of the neural cell adhesion molecule. *J. Cell Biol.* 99:1848–1855.

Crossin, K. L., S. Hoffman, M. Grumet, J.-P. Thiery, and G. M. Edelman. 1986. Site-restricted expression of cytotactin during development of the chicken embryo. *J. Cell Biol.* 102:1917–1930.

Cunningham, B. A., S. Hoffman, U. Rutishauser, J. J. Hemperly, and G. M. Edelman. 1983. Molecular topography of the neural cell adhesion molecule N-CAM: Surface orientation and location of sialic acid-rich and binding regions. *Proc. Natl. Acad. Sci.* (USA) 80:3116–3120.

Cunningham, B. A., Y. Leutzinger, W. J. Gallin, B. C. Sorkin, and G. M. Edelman. 1984. Linear organization of the liver cell adhesion molecule L-CAM. *Proc. Natl. Acad. Sci.* (USA) 81:5787–5791.

Daniloff, J. K., C.-M. Chuong, G. Levi, and G. M. Edelman. 1986a. Differential distribution of cell adhesion molecules during histogenesis of the chick nervous system. *J. Neurosci.* 6:739–758.

Daniloff, J. K., G. Levi, M. Grumet, F. Rieger, and G. M. Edelman. 1986b. Altered expression of neuronal cell adhesion molecules induced by nerve injury and repair. *J. Cell Biol.* 103:929–945.

D'Eustachio, P., G. C. Owens, G. M. Edelman, and B. A. Cunningham. 1985. Chromosomal location of the gene encoding to the neural cell adhesion molecule (N-CAM) in the mouse. *Proc. Natl. Acad. Sci.* (USA) 82:7631–7635.

Edelman, G. M. 1976. Surface modulation in cell recognition and cell growth. *Science* (Washington, D.C.) 192:218–226.

Edelman, G. M. 1983. Cell adhesion molecules. *Science* 219:450–457.

Edelman, G. M. 1984a. Cell adhesion and morphogenesis: The regulator hypothesis. *Proc. Natl. Acad. Sci.* (USA) 81:1460–1464.

Edelman, G. M. 1984b. Modulation of cell adhesion during induction, histogenesis, and perinatal development of the nervous system. *Ann. Rev. Neurosci.* 7:339–377.

Edelman, G. M. 1985a. Cell adhesion and the molecular processes of morphogenesis. *Annu. Rev. Biochem.* 54:135–169.

Edelman, G. M. 1985b. Expression of cell adhesion molecules during embryogenesis and regeneration. *Exp. Cell Res.* 161:1–16.

Edelman, G. M. 1986. Cell adhesion molecules in the regulation of animal form and tissue pattern. *Ann. Rev. Cell Biol.* 2:81–116.

Edelman, G. M. and C.-M. Chuong. 1982. Embryonic to adult conversion of neural cell adhesion molecules in normal and *staggerer* mice. *Proc. Natl. Acad. Sci.* (USA) 79:7036–7040.

Edelman, G M., W. J. Gallin, A. Delouvee, B. A. Cunningham, and J.-P. Thiery. 1983. Early epochal maps of two different cell adhesion molecules. *Proc. Natl. Acad. Sci.* (USA) 80:4384–4388.

Edelman, G. M. and J.-P. Thiery, eds. 1985. *The cell in contact: Adhesions and junctions as morphogenetic determinants.* New York: Wiley.

Finne, J., U. Finne, H. Deagostini-Bazin, and C. Goridis. 1983. Occurrence of α2-8 linked polysialosyl units in a neural cell adhesion molecule. *Biochem. Biophys. Res. Commun.* 112:482–487.

Fraser, S. E., M. S. Carhart, B. A. Murray, C.-M. Chuong, and G. M. Edelman. 1988. Alterations in the *Xenopus* retinotectal projection by antibodies to *Xenopus* N-CAM. *Devel. Biol.* 129:217–230.

Fraser, S. E., B. A. Murray, C.-M. Chuong, and G. M. Edelman. 1984. Alteration of the retinotectal map in *Xenopus* by antibodies to neural cell adhesion molecules. *Proc. Natl. Acad. Sci.* (USA) 81:4222–4226.

Friedlander, D. R., R. Brackenbury, and G. M. Edelman. 1985. Conversion of embryonic forms of N-CAM *in vitro* results from *de novo* synthesis of adult forms. *J. Cell Biol.* 101:412–419.

Gallin, W. J., C.-M. Chuong, L. H. Finkel, and G. M. Edelman. 1986. Antibodies to L-CAM perturb inductive interactions and alter feather pattern and structure. *Proc. Natl. Acad. Sci.* (USA) 83:8235–8239.

Gallin, W. J., G. M. Edelman, and B. A. Cunningham. 1983. Characterization of L-CAM, a major cell adhesion molecule from embryonic liver cells. *Proc. Natl. Acad. Sci.* (USA) 80:1038–1042.

Grumet, M., and G. M. Edelman. 1984. Heterotypic binding between neuronal membrane vesicles and glial cells is mediated by a specific neuron-glial cell adhesion molecule. *J. Cell Biol.* 98:1746–1756.

Grumet, M., S. Hoffman, C.-M. Chuong, and G. M. Edelman. 1984a. Polypeptide components and binding functions of neuron-glia cell adhesion molecules. *Proc. Natl. Acad. Sci.* (USA) 81:7989–7993.

Grumet, M., S. Hoffman, K. L. Crossin, and G. M. Edelman. 1985. Cytotactin, an extracellular matrix protein of neural and non-neural tissues that mediates glia-neuron interaction. *Proc. Natl. Acad. Sci.* (USA) 82:8075–8079.

Grumet, M., S. Hoffman, and G. M. Edelman. 1984b. Two antigenically related neuronal CAMs of different specificities mediate neuron-neuron and neuron-glia adhesion. *Proc. Natl. Acad. Sci.* (USA) 81:267–271.

Hemperly, J. J., B. A. Murray, G. M. Edelman, and B. A. Cunningham. 1986. Sequence of a cDNA clone encoding the polysialic acid-rich and cytoplasmic domains of the neural cell adhesion molecule N-CAM. *Proc. Natl. Acad. Sci.* (USA) 83:3037–3041.

Hoffman, S., C.-M. Chuong, and G. M. Edelman. 1984. Evolutionary conservation of key structures and binding functions of neural cell adhesion molecules. *Proc. Natl. Acad. Sci.* (USA) 81:6881–6885.

Hoffman, S., and G. M. Edelman. 1983. Kinetics of homophilic binding by E and A forms of the neural cell adhesion molecule. *Proc. Natl. Acad. Sci.* (USA) 80:5762–5766.

Hoffman, S., D. R. Friedlander, C.-M. Chuong, M. Grumet, and G. M. Edelman. 1986. Differential contributions of Ng-CAM and N-CAM to cell adhesion in different neural regions. *J. Cell Biol.* 103:145–158.

Hoffman, S., B. C. Sorkin, P. C. White, R. Brackenbury, R. Mailhammer, U. Rutishauser, B. A. Cunningham, and G. M. Edelman. 1982. Chemical characterization of a neural cell adhesion molecule purified from embryonic brain membranes. *J. Biol. Chem.* 257:7720–7729.

Jacobson, A. 1966. Inductive processes in embryonic development. *Science* 152:25–34.

Murray, B. A., J. J. Hemperly, E. A. Prediger, G. M. Edelman, and B. A. Cunningham. 1986a. Alternatively spliced mRNAs code for different polypeptide chains of the chicken neural cell adhesion molecule (N-CAM). *J. Cell Biol.* 102:189–193.

Murray, B. A., G. C. Owens, E. A. Prediger, K. L. Crossin, B. A. Cunningham, and G. M. Edelman. 1986b. Cell surface modulation of the neuronal cell adhesion molecule resulting from alternative mRNA splicing in a tissue-specific developmental sequence. *J. Cell Biol.* 103:1431–1439.

Owens, G. C., G. M. Edelman, and B. A. Cunningham. 1987. Organization of the neural cell adhesion molecule (N-CAM) gene: Alternative exon usage as the basis for different membrane-associated domains. *Proc. Natl. Acad. Sci.* (USA) 84:294–298.

Pollerberg, E. G., R. Sadoul, C. Goridis, and M. Schachner. 1985. Selective expression of the 180-KD component of the neural cell adhesion molecule N-CAM during development. *J. Cell Biol.* 101:1921–1929.

Richardson, G. P., K. L. Crossin, C.-M. Chuong, and G. M. Edelman. 1987. Expression of cell adhesion molecules during embryonic induction. *Dev. Biol.* 119:217–230.

Rieger, F., J. K. Daniloff, M. Pincon-Raymond, K. L. Crossin, M. Grumet, and G. M. Edelman. 1986. Neuronal cell adhesion molecules and cytotactin colocalize at the node of Ranvier. *J. Cell Biol.* 103:379–391.

Rieger, F., M. Grumet, and G. M. Edelman. 1985. N-CAM at the vertebrate neuromuscular junction. *J. Cell Biol.* 101:285–293.

Rothbard, J. B., R. Brackenbury, B. A. Cunningham, and G. M. Edelman. 1982. Differences in the carbohydrate structures of neural cell adhesion molecules from adult and embryonic chicken brains. *J. Biol. Chem.* 257:11064–11069.

Sengel, P. 1976. *Morphogenesis of skin.* Cambridge: Cambridge Univ. Press.

Sperry, R. W. 1963. Chemoaffinity in the orderly growth of nerve fiber patterns and connections. *Proc. Natl. Acad. Sci.* (USA) 50:703–710.

Thiery, J.-P., J. C. Boucaut, and K. M. Yamada. 1985a. Cell migration in the vertebrate embryo. In *Molecular determinants of animal form*, ed. G. M. Edelman, pp. 167–93. New York: Liss.

Thiery, J.-P., A. Delouvee, W. J. Gallin, B. A. Cunningham, and G. M. Edelman. 1984. Ontogenetic expression of cell adhesion molecules: L-CAM is found in epithelia derived from the three primary germ layers. *Dev. Biol.* 102:61–78.

Thiery, J.-P., A. Delouvee, M. Grumet, and G. M. Edelman. 1985b. Initial appearance and regional distribution of the neuron-glia cell adhesion molecule in the chick embryo. *J. Cell Biol.* 100:442–456.

Thiery, J.-P., J.-L. Duband, U. Rutishauser, and G. M. Edelman. 1982. Cell adhesion molecules in early chick embryogenesis. *Proc. Natl. Acad. Sci.* (USA) 79:6737–6741.

Vakaet, L. 1985. Morphogenetic movements and fate maps in the avian blastoderm. In *Molecular determinants of animal form*, ed. G. M. Edelman. New York: Liss.

Walsh, F. S., and S. E. Moore. 1985. Expression of cell-adhesion molecule, N-CAM, in diseases of adult human skeletal-muscle. *Neurosci. Lett.* 59:73–78.

Williams, R. K., C. Goridis, and R. Akeson. 1985. Individual neural cell-types express immunologically distinct N-CAM forms. *J. Cell Biol.* 101:36–42.

Editor's Comments

This chapter offers a cellular and molecular perspective of some of the same issues raised by other authors in this volume. Yet it is not immediately obvious what the contribution of developmental molecular neurobiology to the study of reading problems might be. The molecular and cognitive levels of analysis are, after all, so far apart that the possibilities for linking changes at one level to changes at another appear vanishingly small. But at least the key words seem to be the same. Theories at both levels (and at all intervening levels) assign formative roles to genetically coded innate dispositions and to regulatory environmental factors in the building of anatomical (and functional) structures. Yet only molecular neurobiology offers the possibility of specifying the actual mechanisms of gene expression and their epigenetic regulation.

The ability to build specifically configured three-dimensional neural architectures, each processing unit of which attains appropriate size, shape, position in space, and connectional relationships, may be the exact mechanism by which morphogenetic genes establish weighted neural networks capable at their initial states to begin learning in a predefined orientation (see the chapters by Mehler, by Gleitman et al., and by Churchland and Sejnowski in this volume). In this scheme learning is conceived to act through different cytoregulatory genes that change the functional properties of processing elements and connections by changes in dendritic, synaptic, membrane characteristics at their already predefined three-dimensional loci.

This is the driving hypothesis of the research on mechanisms of cerebral asymmetry (see Sherman et al. in this volume). This line of research conceives differences in asymmetry, which reflect differences in the three-dimensional organization of neurons and connections, to have a direct impact on cognitive capacity at the initial state. Cerebral asymmetry appears to be at least partly under genetic control and partly under environmental influence; for example, handedness is to an extent a familial trait but can be changed by several environmental manipulations. It thus becomes relevant to understanding this biological characteristic to consider genetic and epigenetic molecular mechanisms that lead to differences in three-dimensional design. The present chapter offers hypotheses for the genetic modulation of molecular events that lead to collectives of neurons and for the feedback regulation of the genome by local epigenetic events, and hence for a molecular mechanism for the genetically based generation of three-dimensional patterns and environmental modifications of these predetermined forms.

The evidence presented here indicates that the information contained in the few genes that modulate the spatial and temporal expression of various forms of cell-adhesion and related molecules and the feedback regulation of genes arising locally from the cell collectives themselves are sufficient for the emergence of the somatic variability of neural networks. (An additional role in morphogenesis may be reserved for the actual signals involved in genomic activity and its feedback regulation from cell collectives, the nature of which is still obscure.) When perturbed at either genomic or peripheral loci, this information is distorted and anomalous three-dimensional neural architectures may emerge. Distinct and predictable consequences on the three-dimensional characteristics of the emerging structures may be expected according to the site and time of disruption. This means that systematic alterations in brain architecture can be expected from some genetic mutations as well as from environmental effects capable of producing local physicochemical change.

We are shown that antibodies raised against adhesion molecules are an epigenetic disturbance sufficient to disturb cell arrays, presumably through effects on motility, aggregation, and feedback regulation of morphogenetic genes. Irregular cell arrays that consist of misplaced cells and irregular connections, in addition to changes in numbers of neurons and axons, characterize some dyslexic brains and the brains of immunologically defective mouse strains (see Galaburda et al. and Sherman et al. in this volume). It is reasonable to conjecture that antibodies directed against cell-adhesion molecules may mediate these changes in architecture, especially since immunological abnormalities consistent with the presence of autotoxic antibodies have been described in both dyslexic populations and affected mice. Abnormal regulation of adhesion-molecule expression in these special cases may also arise from some other form of abnormal epigenetic activity, e.g., focal injury leading to physicochemical distortion, or it may even be the result of mutation in morphoregulatory genes in these dyslexic families and inbred mouse strains.

At this early date it is not possible to pinpoint molecular events leading to disturbances of cell migration and assembly of the type under consideration, but because of the remarkably focal nature of architectonic abnormalities, it would seem unlikely that the primary event originates either in morphoregulatory genes coding for cell adhesion or in its epigenetic regulation. Any such abnormality would produce widespread and perhaps diffuse abnormalities, since these molecules are widely, albeit regionally, expressed at each ontogenetic stage. In fact, mutant mice disclose generalized abnormalities of neuronal migration (see Caviness et al. in this volume), and frog retinas exposed to antibodies to CAMs become diffusely dysplastic. If ubiquitous neural and glial molecules implicated in the formation of three-dimensional neural arrays are involved in the focal abnormalities seen in a variety of neurodevelopmental disorders, including developmental dyslexia, the origin of their abnormal regulation is likely a focal mechanochemical event.

Chapter 20

Molecular Dissection of Complex Behaviors: Elementary Mechanistic Rules in Search of Content

Yadin Dudai

1 The Frame of Discussion

Days are hectic yet also quite rewarding for scientists engaged in studying the cellular and molecular bases of behavior. Ample information becomes available, sometimes at an almost alarming pace, on biochemical and biophysical events that take place in neurons when they receive or emit information. Researchers identify genes that code for neuronal constituents and direct the development of nervous systems. In some cases such information makes it possible to suggest how defects in genes and their products might contribute to a pathological phenotype. At least from the point of view of availability of new findings, the program of reductionist analysis of the structure and function of nervous systems, and hence of behaviors too, seems to have embarked upon a very promising avenue.

But precisely because so many novel findings are constantly streaming from laboratories into the scientific literature, and because the very powerful tools of neurochemistry, molecular biology, neurogenetics, neuroanatomy, and neurophysiology are sure to yield more and more data in the near future, the time is ripe to discuss the rationales, significance, and constraints of reductionist analyses of complex brain faculties and behaviors. The purpose of the present paper is to contribute to such a discussion by commenting briefly on some aspects of recent research in one branch of neurobiology.

A detailed, systematic discussion of reductionism in neurobiology far exceeds the scope of this paper (for a recent treatise, see Churchland 1986 and also Block 1980; for examples of reductionist, experimentalist points of view, see Barlow 1972; Kandel and Schwartz 1982; and Dudai 1989). I entertain here a very relaxed, pragmatist definition of reduction, which does not require a complete explanation of molar properties by molecular properties. Suffice it that the biological problem be reduced by at least one order of complexity (qualitatively defined) while at least some of the core characteristics of the complex phenomenon are preserved. Reductionist dissection of such highly complex phenomena as the mechanisms and functions of hemispheric specializations is still in its very early infancy (or better, in its early embryogenesis), and translating research objectives related to these brain functions into cellular and molecular terminology is still rare (but see this volume). In what follows, I shall confine my discussion to a complex behavioral phenomenon that can be partially reduced to the levels of molecular biology, biochemistry, biophysics, and cell biology. This phenomenon is learning and memory.

I should emphasize that this selected biological phenomenon is presented here only as an example, though as explained below, a very convenient one. I shall argue that some generalizations that emerge from the reductionist dissection of learning and memory apply to other complex neurobiological phenomena as well. By adhering to selected experimental systems, I will try to demonstrate that reductionist research strategies may result in concrete, testable models that attempt to explain both the specific and the universal biological mechanisms underlying a particular behavior. These mechanisms are capable of dictating the structural and operational properties of the biological system that executes the behavior and impose constraints on the system, yet by themselves they are not sufficient to explain the behavioral output. For the latter a knowledge of the global computational and representational properties of the neuronal system is required. I shall also mention in passing the great power of the reductionist approach in elucidating phylogenetic drives that mold behavior and in unraveling intricate connections between seemingly remote behavioral and physiological processes. In addition to their explanatory value these potential experimental results may also possess clinical significance.

2   The Choice of an Experimental System

Learning and memory, although considered to be among the highest mental faculties of the human brain, present a crucial experimental advantage: simple forms of learning can be clearly demonstrated in very simple organisms. Thus, whereas the phylogenetic rudiments of some other faculties of human brain are not easy to locate, nonassociative and associative learning are often surprisingly similar in very remote phylogenetic echelons. This tremendously facilitates some aspects of research, because it suggests that information obtained from the study of very simple systems is relevant to complex learning systems and might explain some of their basic properties, although it cannot be expected to explain all their properties. One would expect learning and memory, as any other property of the nervous system, to have evolved in phylogeny. Some mechanisms that enable mammalian brains to acquire, store, and retrieve novel information and to alter old information should therefore be based on cellular and molecular properties that already exist in very simple brains.

One could search for organisms that offer the experimentalist some practical advantages. Such a search often culminates in what appears to the outsider as a bizarre choice indeed. The urge to avoid delving into complex brains might lead to rather stupid organisms. This, by the way, is not unique to the field of learning research. Brain lesions in rodents serve as models for complex neurological disorders in humans; aberrations in tissue and cell cultures serve to illuminate malignancy in man; and cortical laterality, so often associated with speech and reasoning, the highest of all human faculties, is sometimes studied in animals that display neither rationality nor cognition.

Modern research on elementary learning and memory mechanisms has focused on invertebrates (this research is reviewed in Carew and Sahley 1986 and Dudai 1989). Mollusks are a representative example. They became experimental favorites because they have relatively simple nervous systems, their nerve cells are often very big and amenable to electrophysiological and biochemical analysis, and identified neuronal networks can be associated with identified behaviors. Other invertebrates have other experimental advantages. In this chapter I shall very briefly summarize some results obtained from the study of two systems, a mollusk, *Aplysia californica*, and an insect, *Drosophila melanogaster*. In each case I shall present the relevant experimental advantages and the major experimental findings, as well as general implications of these findings for learning and memory in other systems.

3 A Simple Network That Learns

Aplysia is a marine snail. Its behavioral repertoire is simple: most of the time the animal is quiescent or is slowly crawling towards sea weed and eating it. When the time comes, it copulates in a group-sex ritual and later lays eggs. Most of these behaviors do not require plasticity and can be accounted for by rigid innate responses.

Yet *Aplysia* can also learn from experience (as reviewed in Abrams 1985; Byrne 1985; Goelet et al. 1986; and Kandel and Schwartz 1982). This can be clearly demonstrated in its defensive reflexes. A frequently studied example is the gill-and-siphon withdrawal reflex.

Aplysia has an external respiratory organ, a gill, housed in a respiratory cavity called the mantle cavity. At its posterior end the mantle shelf forms a fleshy spout, the siphon. The siphon normally protrudes out of the mantle cavity. If one applies a weak to moderate tactile stimulus to the siphon or the mantle shelf, *Aplysia* exhibits a gill-and-siphon-withdrawal reflex, a two component reflex aimed at defending the precious gill.

The gill-and-siphon-withdrawal reflex is innate and resembles other defensive reflexes in *Aplysia*, such as tail withdrawal or inking. Nevertheless, the reflex can be modified nonassociatively and associatively by experience. For, example, the reflex can be habituated: repeated application of weak to moderate tactile stimuli to the same locus on the skin of the mantle or siphon results in a decreased withdrawal reflex, i.e., habituation. On the other hand, a noxious stimulus applied to the head or to the tail results in an enhanced subsequent gill and siphon withdrawal, i.e., sensitization. Both habituation and sensitization are nonassociative behavioral modifications, which can be found in all eukaryotes.

In addition to displaying primitive, nonassociative forms of learning, *Aplysia* is also capable of more advanced, associative forms of learning. Under certain experimental conditions *Aplysia*'s responses are not very different from those of a Pavlovian dog. Thus, a light tactile stimulus to the siphon, which normally hardly elicits a gill-and-siphon-withdrawal reflex, can be used as a conditioned stimulus (CS), and a strong electric shock to the tail can be used as an unconditioned stimulus (US). Specific temporal pairing of the CS and US markedly enhances subsequent reflex responses to the CS alone. This is classical conditioning, or more accurately, alpha conditioning. *Aplysia* is also capable of instrumental conditioning of its reflexes.

The nervous system of *Aplysia* consists of few ganglia and contains all together around 20,000 nerve cells. The neural circuit that controls the withdrawal of the gill and siphon is located in the abdominal ganglia, and part of its cellular components have been identified. There are more than a dozen identified central motor cells, which are activated by two populations of sensory neurons, each containing about 24 cells. One population innervates the siphon skin, the other the mantle shelf. The sensory neurons synapse onto interneurons and motor neurons. The motor neurons synapse directly onto the gill or siphon muscle.

It thus appears that even *Aplysia's* relatively simple reflexes involve a substantial number of neurons and connections. A great experimental advantage of the system, though, is the ability of the experimenter to depict schematically a portion of the network underlying the reflex as composed of modules, each containing only three components. These components are the sensory neuron, which receives stimuli from the mantle or siphon; the motor neuron, which innervates the contracting muscle; and a facilitatory interneuron, which synapses onto the presynaptic side of the synapse from the sensory neuron to the motor neuron and conveys information from other body parts, e.g. the tail or head.

The gill-and-siphon-withdrawal reflex of *Aplysia* has been extensively studied by Kandel, Schwartz, Castellucci, Carew, Klein, Siegelbaum, Abrams, and their colleagues, and work along similar lines on another defensive reflex, the tail-withdrawal reflex, has been conducted by Byrne, Walters, and their colleagues (this research is reviewed in Abrams 1985; Byrne 1985; Goelet et al. 1986; and Kandel and Schwartz 1982). Cellular analysis of the reflex revealed that short-term habituation is a homosynaptic process, in which the synapse from sensory to motor neuron is gradually inhibited from releasing transmitter upon arrival of a sensory signal from the skin. Sensitization of the reflex is partly due to presynaptic facilitation, a heterosynaptic process, which also involves the synapse from sensory to motor neuron. Here the amount of transmitter released by the sensory, presynaptic terminal onto the motor neuron is increased as a result of activity in a facilitatory pathway.

4   Reducing Learning to Molecular Cascades.

The gill-and-siphon-withdrawal behavior of *Aplysia* can be reduced to a molecular model. Kandel and Schwartz (1982) have suggested that the following molecular mechanism accounts for the presynaptic facilitation underlying sensitization: The sensitizing stimulus (a noxious stimulus applied to head or tail) releases a neurotransmitter from the interneuron into the presynaptic side of the synapse from sensory neuron to motor neuron. This neurotransmitter binds to specific receptors on the postsynaptic membrane, thereby activating adenylate cyclase, the enzyme that synthesizes cAMP. This initiates the cAMP cascade, one of the major ubiquitous second-messenger cascades in cells (for a review see Dudai 1987). CyclicAMP activates a cAMP-dependent protein kinase (cAMP-dPK), which phosphorylates substrate proteins. At least one of these is presumably associated with a specific type of K^+ channel (named the S channel, since it is phosphorylated in the presence of seratonin). Phosphorylation of the S channel results in channel closure. As a consequence of the reduction in the repolarizing K^+ current, later action potentials that invade the presynaptic terminal upon sensory stimulation last longer. This causes more Ca^{2+} to enter the terminal. Transmitter release is a function of Ca^{2+} concentration, and so more transmitter is subsequently released per impulse.

Several lines of evidence suggest that memory during the first minutes after training might be merely the increased activity of the cAMP cascade, which might result from persistent activation of adenylate cyclase or of cAMP-dPK. During the first hours after training, memory consolidates to a more stable and long-lasting form. Consolidation may involve protein synthesis and alteration of gene expression (Goelet et al. 1986). Cyclic AMP or other second messengers may serve as triggers for consolidation.

It is now clear that this cascade of events is not the only one activated in sensitization. In addition to closing the S channels, the neuromodulator(s) released from the facilitatory neuron can alter the availability of Ca^{2+} within the cell and enhance the mobilization of transmitter, a mechanism that probably involves activating a C-kinase cascade in concert with the cAMP cascade. This second, mobilizing component of facilitation comes into play mainly when the synapse is depressed (Klein et al. 1986).

A molecular model was also suggested for classical conditioning of the gill-and-siphon-withdrawal reflex in *Aplysia* (for reviews see Abrams 1985; Byrne 1985; and Goelet et al. 1986). Classical conditioning, it was suggested, is an elaboration of the mechanism of sensitization of the reflex. It results, according to the model, from amplification of the presynaptic facilitation by the temporally paired activity in the sensory neuron that mediates the CS and in the facilitatory interneuron that mediates the US. The following molecular mechanism was suggested to account for this activity-dependent facilitation (or modulation): the action potential that invades the sensory-neuron terminal leads to Ca^{2+} influx, and the firing of the interneuron leads to a neurotransmitter-induced increase in the level of cAMP in the same sensory-neuron terminal. A yet unknown mechanism, which might involve the adenylate cyclase complex, integrates the two stimuli, and if they converge within the appropriate time-window (e.g., CS initiated 0.5 sec prior to US), an enhanced activation of the cAMP cascade results, leading again to phosphorylation and closure of the S channel. Later impulses will therefore release more transmitter per impulse. A Ca^{2+}/calmodulin-stimulated adenylate cyclase was proposed as the site of convergence of the two stimuli: transmitter and Ca^{2+}. Other phosphorylation or receptor systems capable of simultaneous activation by both extracellular transmitter and intracellular Ca^{2+} will do as well (for a review see Dudai 1987).

Thus, in elementary mechanisms of both associative and nonassociative learning, modification of a K$^+$ channel by phosphorylation may play a crucial role. On the cellular level in this model, acquisition is suggested to be the elevated level of cAMP (possibly due to activation of the enzymatic complex that synthesizes the second messenger), and memory readout, at least during the immediate phase after acquisition, is the altered ion current due to the blocked, phosphorylated channel. This readout results in an altered probability of the reflex response, which is the behavioral manifestation of learning in this case.

Phosphorylation of ion channels resulting in long-lasting, modified excitability was implicated in elementary learning and short-term memory not only in *Aplysia* studies but also in other systems, including invertebrates (e.g., *Hermissenda*, Alkon 1984) and vertebrates (for a review see Dudai 1987). For the purpose of this discussion it is of interest to turn our attention to an additional system that allows an entirely different experimental approach. The system is the fruit fly, *Drosophila melanogaster*, and the approach is neurogenetics.

5 How Do Genes Code for Learning Mechanisms?

Whereas in studies of *Aplysia* and other invertebrates with relatively simple nervous systems one pursues a direct strategy and takes advantage of the ability to poke, dissect, or modify identified cells and connections, *Drosophila*, with its very compact brain of tiny cells, prohibits such a direct approach. Yet *Drosophila* has its own advantages: genes that can be analyzed and manipulated more easily than in any other eukaryote. The rationale for using this experimental advantage to study learning and memory is actually quite straightforward (for a review see Dudai 1988 and Quinn 1984). Genes must encode the macromolecular building blocks of biological learning systems, exactly as they code for any other component of the organism. By altering any of the appropriate genes separately, one can disrupt the ability of the organism to learn and remember. The degree of specificity of the behavioral effect depends on the role of the gene product in physiological functions besides learning. Genetic, electrophysiological, biochemical, and molecular-biological comparisons of mutant and normal organisms that differ in one gene only may unveil the identity of the affected gene product crucial for normal learning. Later on, molecular studies might be employed to isolate the gene itself, which would thus pave the way to its identification in other organisms as well.

To date researchers have isolated several single gene mutants of *Drosophila* that have defective learning and memory capabilities and yet develop and behave essentially normally (or at least their other phenotypic abnormalities can be clearly dissociated from the learning defects). These mutants are thus lesioned in genes whose products are strong candidates for macromolecular components of learning and memory systems. For our purposes, suffice it to briefly state only several main findings and conclusions.

To date four learning and memory mutants of *Drosophila* have been shown to affect various components of second messenger and phosphorylation cascades: two components of the cAMP cascade and two components possibly related to the cAMP cascade. The first isolated mutant, *dunce*, is lesioned in a structural gene for the enzyme cAMP-phosphodiesterase, which degrades cAMP. Only one form of the enzyme is lesioned by the mutation, leaving a large proportion of cAMP-phosphodiesterase activity intact. Another mutant, *rutabaga*, is lesioned in a subpopulation, or a functional state, of the enzyme that synthesized cAMP, namely, adenylate cyclase. A large proportion of total adenylate cyclase activity is likewise spared. The form of the enzyme affected in *rutabaga* is characterized by several kinetic and regulatory properties, the most prominent of which is activation by Ca^{2+}/calmodulin; such activation is completely abolished by the mutation. A third mutation, *Ddc*, lesions dopa-decarboxylase, an enzyme required for synthesizing aminergic neurotransmitters and neuromodulators. These amines often function by activating the cAMP cascade, although other phosphorylation cascades may also be involved. A fourth mutation, *turnip*, lesions a Ca^{2+}-phospholipid-activated protein kinase named C-kinase; here too defects exist in the activity of the adenylate cyclase complex, and they are probably secondary to the lesion in C-kinase.

As with the *Aplysia* results, the *Drosophila* results, taken together, implicate in elementary learning and memory processes second-messenger cascades, especially (yet not exclusively) the cAMP cascade. All *Drosophila* mutations tested so far behave abnormally in more than one type of learning paradigm, indicating that the affected biochemical processes are shared by different learning systems. Especially interesting is the observation that mutations affecting learning and memory also have effects on behaviors that till now were considered strictly innate. This occurs especially within the context of courtship. The love life of fruit flies, it appears, requires some experience. Without such experience the naive fly may waste its time courting a member of its own sex or an unresponsive mate. Indeed, it has been suggested that in *Drosophila* learning capacity may have evolved to improve courtship. Another interesting aspect of *Drosophila* behavior that seems to be related at least to some aspects of learning is the biological clock. Mutations that lengthen biological rhythms also disrupt some aspects of learning. It is not yet clear whether this is due to intimate involvement of a biological clock in some learning processes or alternatively to macromolecules that, in different contexts, take part in both clock-related actions and learning.

6   Some Reduced Properties of Biological Learning Systems

The studies of *Aplysia* and *Drosophila* exemplify concrete results obtained by adhering to a reductionistic strategy in the study of elementary learning and memory. I could have cited other, quite similar examples based on similar approaches, for example, studies of *Hermissenda, Limax, Pleurobranchaea* (reviewed in Carew and Sahley 1986), or studies of processes in mammalian brain that presumably take part in learning, like studies of long-term-potentiation (LTP) in the hippocampus (reviewed in Dudai 1989). What might these studies of elementary processes of behavioral plasticity tell us about learning and memory in general? Several conclusions might be considered.

- Physical alterations that underlie learning and memory can be localized. The data obtained from *Aplysia* and several other invertebrates and vertebrate systems demonstrate that elementary processes of learning and memory that contribute significantly to changes in the organism's behavior can be localized to individual cells or synapses.
- The nervous system utilizes in memory formation ubiquitous molecular cascades that are also employed for mere information transfer. Studies to date have not revealed novel types of macromolecules employed only for learning and memory. Mechanisms that serve as components of learning systems are shared by very many cellular processes (see Dudai 1988; Schwartz and Greenberg 1987). Novel macromolecules that function only in learning and memory might of course be detected in the future, but cellular learning systems can already be described without evoking unknown biochemistry and physiology.
- Similar types of biochemical mechanisms giving rise to neuronal plasticity may operate in different subcellular localities. The universality of certain molecular cascades in learning consists only of the use of these cascades in plastic manipulation of neuronal and network properties, not of the cellular loci at which plasticity takes place. *Aplysia* implicates mainly presynaptic events, LTP both presynaptic and postsynaptic events, and *Hermissenda* somatic events.

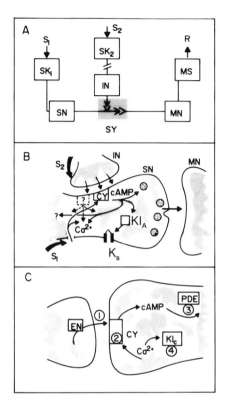

Figure 20.1

A schematic representation of some cellular and molecular aspects of two relatively simple learning systems. (*A*) A block diagram of a simplified neuronal module underlying a substantial portion of the gill-and-siphon-withdrawal reflex in *Aplysia*. A mechanical stimulation (S_1) of the siphon skin (SK_1) is transmitted by a sensory neuron (SN) to a motor neuron (MN) via a chemical synapse (SY). The motor neuron stimulates the gill muscle (MS), which leads to contraction and the withdrawal response (R). Repetitive, monotonous stimulation leads to decreased transmitter released at SY and hence to habituation. A noxious stimulation (S_2) applied to the head or tail (SK_2) modulates SY via an interneuron (IN), which leads to presynaptic facilitation and hence to sensitization. The system is also capable of associative learning: S_1 can serve as a CS, and S_2 as a US; their temporal pairing leads to activity-dependent presynaptic facilitation in SY and hence to increased R (a conditioned response). In this system, learning is alteration in the probability of a reflexive response; the description of the contribution of alterations in SY to behavioral modification makes sense because the role of the network components in the behavioral algorithm is known. Similar synaptic modulations can result in different behavioral alterations if incorporated into other networks. (*B*) A molecular model for part of the mechanisms underlying sensitization and associative learning in the gill-and-siphon-withdrawal reflex in *Aplysia*. CY, adenylate cyclase; KI_A, cAMP-dependent phosphorylation. S_2, S_2, SN, MN, and IN have the same meaning as in (*A*) above. Dotted vesicles represent quanta transmitter. Questions marks are yet unidentified processes. CY may serve as one of the integration sites for

• Molecular and cellular mechanisms are used by nervous systems to distinguish between transient information and information to be stored. If for learning, neurons use cascades that ubiquitously take part in inter- and intracellular communication, methods should exist to enable the cell to distinguish between signals that should not be remembered and information that should be stored. The invertebrate data mentioned above, as well as additional data, suggest two possible cellular mechanisms for differentiating between transient and persistent information. One is repetition. If the signal is repeated enough times, the cascade of molecular events initiated by this signal is repeatedly activated, and the level of appropriate intracellular messages is increased above a certain threshold, and this results in appropriate cellular modifications. Quantity is thus transformed into a qualitative alteration. A second mechanism is coincidence. By itself a signal does not increase the level of the appropriate intracellular molecular agents above the threshold, but coincidence of signals (e.g., transmitter and ions) leads to convergence of stimuli on a molecular cascade, and hence amplification and cellular modification result. Similar principles of repetition and coincidence function not only on the cellular level but also on the circuit and system level within the brain (Mishkin 1982 and Dudai 1989).

• Plastic modifications can be elicited in neurons by ubiquitous inter- and intracellular signals. As a first approximation individual neurons and connections in a learning system can be treated the same, regardless of whether they receive signals from sensory pathways or from interneurons mediating information from other brain regions. In other words, the source of teaching signals is irrelevant as far as learning processes in individual cells are concerned.

• Similar types of molecular and cellular mechanisms are shared by different learning systems, probably also at very different phylogenetic levels. In *Aplysia* similar second-messenger cascades

S_1 and S_2 in associative learning. Such a model already suggests heuristic molecular explanations for persistence, coincidence, temporal specificity, and the rudiments of parallel processing. Other model systems for elementary learning also implicate second-messenger-induced modifications of synaptic plasticity in learning, although the subcellular loci of the plastic alterations vary. (C) A drawing of a generalized synapse depicting the molecular lesions in *Drosophila* learning mutant. (1) Reduced level of aminergic transmitters (*Ddc*), (2) defective adenylate cyclase (*rutabaga*), (3) defective cAMP phosphodiesterase (*dunce*), (4) defective protein kinase C (*turnip*). EN, enzyme synthesizing aminergic transmitters; PDE, phosphodieterase; KI_C, protein kinase C.

operate in nonassociative and associative learning of different associative tasks (e.g., the gill-and-siphon-withdrawal and tail-withdrawal reflexes). Essentially similar types of mechanisms are revealed in *Hermissenda* and probably in the mammalian brain too. In *Drosophila* too second-messenger and phosphorylation systems are implicated in different associative tasks, and a single mutation affects very different learning situations. The assumption that learning and memory systems have elementary building blocks that have evolved and been conserved through evolution appears to be justified.

• There is no single, exclusive elementary learning and memory mechanism. In both *Aplysia* and *Drosophila*, as well as in other relatively simple systems, it is clear that different molecular cascades are recruited by teaching signals, very probably in the same cells. It seems that parallel processing starts in the brain on the cellular level. Such multiplicity may suggest that many information-mediating molecular cascades have the ability to store information. This multiplicity may have been established by a phylogenetic drive to ensure both information back-up and variation of interpretation of data in response to minor alterations in cellular milieu and incoming signals.

• Molecular and cellular mechanisms might suggest heuristic explanations for some behavioral laws of learning. The effects of persistence and causality have already been mentioned above in the context of repetition and coincidence as mechanisms that enable the distinction between transient and stored information. Results from various cellular systems suggest working hypotheses to explain in cellular and molecular terms additional behavioral characteristics of associative learning. One example is temporal specificity, i.e., the often observed inability of backward conditioning (US starting before CS) to evoke a conditioned response. *Aplysia* results suggest that temporal properties of the interaction of Ca^{2+} (or a Ca^{2+}-stimulated molecular cascade) and a neurotransmitter with the adenylate-cyclase system might account for the need for Ca^{2+} (the code of the CS in this model) to precede transmitter in its interaction with the enzyme. Molecular tests of this hypothesis are underway. Another example is the multiphasic nature of memory. Molecular and cellular models of memory indicate why a phase transition is required (i.e., the limited life-span of modified proteins) and suggest mechanisms for consolidation (e.g., intermolecular automodification, gene activation). Such models also suggest that dividing memory into two or three phases, e.g., short term and long term, is gross, and one should expect additional intervening phases.

• Elementary learning and memory capabilities have a genetic basis, and genetic lesions might result in quite specific learning and memory aberrations. These conclusions, which emerge from *Drosophila* studies, are not necessarily confined to fruit flies. It is of interest to note that genetic lesions similar to those detected in *Drosophila* learning mutants induce behavioral defects in humans too (see, e.g., Farfel and Friedman 1986).

• Already at the molecular level, complex mechanisms operate at optimal performance but not at peak performance. For example, the *dunce* mutation of *Drosophila* increases cAMP level yet leads to defective learning. A delicate optimal balance probably exists between the level of molecular signals that participate in elementary learning. This might explain why supersmart *Drosophila* mutants were not found (for a review see Dudai 1988). It might also predict that excelling in a certain capability can be accompanied by defects in other capabilities (see Gardner and Dudai 1985).

• Behaviors considered purely innate may have plastic components. Courtship in *Drosophila* is one example. The introduction of experience-dependent components in innate programs may hint at phylogenetic drives that have brought learning into existence.

• The same biochemical defect may have very different and seemingly unrelated effects on physiology and behavior. For example, mutations in the *per* locus of *Drosophila* affect various manifestations of circadian rhythms, courtship behavior, and some aspects of learning (Hall 1986). The mutation occurs in a gene that codes for a proteoglycan, whose physiological role is not yet known. Mutations in the *dnc* locus often affect fertility. This might result from the heterogeneous function of different transcripts of a complex gene.

7 What Reduction Might Miss

The points listed above illustrate the power of molecular and cellular approaches to behavior. Yet the limitations of these approaches should not be disregarded. There are three major issues in research on elementary learning mechanisms (for a comprehensive, general discussion of reductionism and the neurosciences see Churchland 1986). These issues are: establishing necessary versus sufficient conditions for learning and memory, explaining emergent system properties, and elucidating the representation of the behavioral output.

Necessary versus Sufficient Conditions for Learning
Most cellular and molecular studies of learning indicate mechanisms
that are necessary for learning and memory. Such studies suggest, for
example, that activation of second messenger cascades and subsequent posttranslational modification of substrate proteins are initial
steps in the acquisition and retention of a memory. Yet even if it could
be demonstrated that a biochemical modification leads to cellular alterations in isolated cells expected to contribute to the behavioral
modification, the data do not prove that this cellular modification is
sufficient to establish learning and memory in the behaving organism. As a matter of fact, only rarely has it been demonstrated that a
biochemical modification can account for a given behavioral alteration, and invariably it has not been proven that the same biochemical
modification indeed leads to altered behavior *in vivo*. Actually, it is
quite clear that several mechanisms function together in memory
formation.

Emergent System Properties
Complex memory systems display properties that cannot be accounted for solely by events that take place in subcellular compartments or isolated cells. For example, complex memories are often
characterized by completion (the ability to reconstruct a memory from
partial information) and graceful degradation (the immunity of a
memory to partial loss of its components) (for reviews see Hinton and
Anderson 1981; McClelland et al. 1986; Dudai 1989). To account for
such properties, one must invoke multicellular interactions and distributed representations. Local events occurring in individual cells
and connections still serve as a basis for distributed-system operations (Hinton and Anderson 1981; Hopfield 1982; McClelland et al.
1986; von der Malsberg and Bienenstock 1986; see also Hebb 1949).
Yet reducing the system into isolated elements would not explain how
overall information is represented. This issue is further addressed in
the next section.

Mechanisms and Constraints versus Content
To date, almost all studies of the cellular and molecular bases of learning and memory have been performed on systems of reflexive memories. In some of these cases we know part of the algorithm executed
by the neuronal system and hence the contribution of some network
components to behavioral output. From the experimenter's point of
view, the experimental approach is initially a top-down one: the overall behavioral output is given, and the search for the bottom-up operations of a rather simple biological system is performed within the

framework of the given behavior. For example, in the *Aplysia* gill-and-siphon-withdrawal reflex we know the general role of most of the major neuronal components (sensory neuron, motor neuron, interneuron) in executing the reflex. So an understanding of the plastic modification of specific components (e.g., a synapse from sensory to motor neuron) leads to concrete postulates of the contribution of these modifications to learning and memory. Without knowledge of the behavioral output of the network, knowledge of plastic modification in a specific synapse per se does not reveal how the organism's behavior is altered. When incorporated into other networks, similar cellular modifications would lead to entirely different behavioral outputs, which might or might not result in some forms of learning.

In other words, although reductionist research projects aimed at elucidating learning and memory result in intriguing data and in concrete, testable cellular and molecular models that portray elementary mechanisms of learning and memory and suggest structural and operational rules and constraints, these strategies per se do not explain the behavioral output. To do that, we need a knowledge of the representations encoded in the neuronal system and the computations performed on these representations.

8   What Reduction Might Offer

What can be inferred from molecular and cellular studies of simple learning and memory systems that is applicable to analysis of other complex behavioral phenomena? I shall consider several points.

- Elementary rules pertinent to complex behaviors may become unveiled in reduced preparations. Certain micro properties may reflect macro properties, and certain simple properties may reflect complex properties. This might be termed the *reflection principle*. It results not only from the integration of simple, micro properties in the emergent complexity in phylogenesis but also from functional constraints. Simple learning modules and simple learning systems share some operational rules with complex systems, because all are geared to solve problems of learning. This is a functionalist view that nevertheless considers hardware very relevant to the output. It bears practically on more than just learning in invertebrates. Suppose we can gain an understanding of single neurons and connections between few neurons, or better, the integrated activity of discrete groups of neurons, in a cortical area related to a complex behavior. In such a case, some firing characteristics, intercellular interactions, or responses that occur only in concert with the activity of other brain regions may shed light on specific response characteristics of the system, even though the operation of the system as a whole is far from being understood. Such reduced-brain preparations as cell cultures and slices, along with novel recording methods that enable real-time monitoring of the activity of many neurons with fine spatial and temporal resolution, may be valuable in this respect (Grinvald 1985).

• A simple system offers practical, experimental advantages even though it does not display all the functional characteristics of the more complex systems. As previously mentioned, learning and memory greatly facilitate the experimenter's task, since simple forms of learning can be traced to very simple organisms that lend themselves to experimental manipulations. Yet sometimes even if primitive forms of the behavior under study are not immediately apparent, rudimentary phylogenetic precedents of the complex faculty can serve as appropriate starting points for experimental study. Laterality in animals, for example, may manifest itself in physiological and behavioral specializations very different from those in man, yet our understanding of the ontogenesis and maintenance of cortical lateralization could benefit from investigations of such relatively simple systems (Bradshaw and Nettleton 1983; Denenberg 1981; Geschwind 1980; Sherman et al. 1985).

• Simple systems may be used to develop experimental tools for studying complex systems. Such tools may include enzyme and receptor assays, genetic probes, and antibodies for specific neuronal components.

• Abnormalities in physiological and behavioral phenomena of interest could be used to illuminate the normal process. This, of course, is well established not only in biochemistry and molecular biology (where the use of mutants and inhibitors is common and highly successful) but also in pathological studies of cognitive processes.

• Quite specific aberrations in complex behaviors may result from defects in ubiquitous neuronal components and operations rather than from defects unique to the system that executes the specific behavior. In other words, we may obtain important information on neurological disorders by characterizing nerve cells not necessarily related to the affected neurological function, or even by characterizing genetic, physiological, and biochemical properties of nonneuronal tissues. There is always a possibility that the molecular defect is widespread in many or all tissues but is manifested most strongly in specific brain centers. Even in *Drosophila*, mutations that cause rather specific learning and memory defects can be easily detected in tissues that have no relevance to memory. Pseudohypoparathyroidism in man, for example, is due to a molecular defect that manifests itself in many tissues, yet the major physiological manifestations are exhibited in specific tissues.

• Additional, apparently unrelated abnormalities in individuals deficient in the behavior of interest may shed light on that behavior, since these other abnormalities may expose shared molecular and cellular building blocks or elucidate the ontogenesis of the defect. A very interesting example emerges from the studies of Geschwind and his co-workers on dyslexia, stuttering, left-handedness, susceptibility to autoimmune disease, migraine, asthma, and myopia (Geschwind and Behan 1982). This cluster of symptoms may emerge from hormonal abnormalities during embryogenesis. Such correlations between behavioral and physiopathological characteristics may be of great predictive and diagnostic value.

In conclusion, cellular and molecular approaches seem to have great theoretical as well as practical relevance to the study of complex behaviors in general and of the pathology of such behaviors in particular. Nevertheless, even if complex brain faculties and behaviors finally succumb to the tools of cellular physiology and molecular biology, such complex phenomena are like Mondrian's trees: The observer can successively reduce them into their basics, extract their essences, and finally unravel abstract features that make the leaves leaves. Yet bottom-up reconstruction of a tree is possible on the basis of such information only if we know what a real tree looks like, or at least experience something similar to Mondrian's impressionistic image of it. Similarly, mechanistic rules of neurons and synapses are of great interest per se but make much better sense if we consider their integration into the detailed, functional neuronal network that underlies the behavior in question. Currently this is only rarely possible.

References

Abrams, T. W. 1985. Activity-dependent presynaptic facilitation: An associative mechanism in *Aplysia*. *Cell. Mol. Neurobiol.* 5:123–145.

Alkon, D. L. 1984. Calcium-mediated reduction of ionic currents: A biophysical memory trace. *Science* 226:1037–1045.

Barlow, H. B. 1972. Single units and sensation: A neuron doctrine for perceptual psychology? *Perception* 1:371–394.

Block, N., ed. 1980. *Readings in philosophy of psychology.* Vol. 1. Cambridge: MIT Press.

Bradshaw, J. L., and Nettleton, N. C. 1983. Human cerebral asymmetry. Englewood-Cliffs, N.J.: Prentice-Hall.

Byrne, J. H. 1985. Neural and molecular mechanisms underlying information storage in *Aplysia:* Implications for learning and memory. *Trends in Neurosci.* 9:478–482.

Carew, T. J., and Sahley, C. L. 1986. Invertebrate learning and memory: From behavior to molecules. *Ann. Rev. Neurosci.* 9:435–487.

Churchland, P. S. 1986. *Neurophilosophy.* Cambridge: MIT Press.

Dudai, Y. 1987. The cAMP cascade in the nervous system: Molecular sites of action and possible relevance to neuronal plasticity. *CRC Crit. Rev. Biochem.* 22:221–281.

Dudai, Y. 1988. Neurogenetic dissection of learning and short-term memory in *Drosophila. Ann. Rev. Neurosci.* 11:537–563.

Dudai, Y. 1989. *The neurobiology of memory.* Oxford: Oxford University Press, in press.

Farfel, Z., and Friedman, E. 1986. Mental deficiency in pseudohypoparathyroidism type I is associated with N_s-protein deficiency. *Ann. Int. Medicine* 105:197–199.

Gardner, H., and Dudai, Y. 1985. Biology and giftedness. *Items* 39:1–6.

Geschwind, N. 1980. Some comments on the neurology of language. In *Biological studies of mental processes*, ed. A. Caplan. Cambridge: MIT Press.

Geschwind, N., and Benhan, P. 1982. Left-handedness: Association with immune disease, migraine, and developmental learning disorders. *Proc. Natl. Acad. Sci.* (USA) 79:5907–5100.

Goelet, P., Castellucci, V. F., Schacher, S., and Kandel, E. R. 1986. The long and the short of long-term memory—A molecular framework. *Nature* 322:419–422.

Grinvald, A. 1985. Real-time optical mapping of neuronal activity: From single growth cones to the intact mammalian brain. *Ann. Rev. Neurosci.* 8:263–305.

Hall, J. 1986. Learning and rhythms in courting, mutant *Drosophila. Trends in Neurosci.* 9:414–418.

Hebb, D. O. 1949. *The organization of behavior: A neuropsychological theory.* New York: Wiley.

Hinton, G. E., Anderson, J. A., eds. 1981. Parallel models of associative memory. N.J.: Erlabaum.

Hopfield, J. J. 1982. Neural networks and physical systems with emergent collective properties. *Proc. Natl. Acad. Sci.* (USA) 79:2554–2558.

Kandel, E. R. and Schwartz, J. H. 1982. Molecular biology of learning: Modulation of transmitter release. *Science* 218:433–443.

Klein, M., Hochner, B., and Kandel, E. R. 1986. Facilitatory transmitters and cAMP can modulate accommodation as well as transmitter release in *Aplysia* sensory neurons: Evidence for parallel processing in a single cell. *Proc. Natl. Acad. Sci.* (USA) 83:7994–7998.

McClelland, J. L., Rumelhart, D. E., and Hinton, G. E. 1986. The appeal of parallel distributed systems. In *Parallel distributed processing*, vol. 1, ed. Rumelhart, D. E., and McClelland, J. L. Cambridge: MIT Press.

Mishkin, M. 1982. A memory system in the monkey. *Phil. Trans. Roy. Soc. Laud.*, Series B, 298:85–95.

Quinn, W. G. 1984. Work in invertebrates on the mechanisms underlying learning. In *Biology of learning*, ed. Marler, P. and Terrace, H. S., Berlin: Springer-Verlag.

Schwartz, J. H., and Greenberg, S. M. 1987. Molecular mechanisms for memory: Second-messenger induced modifications of protein kinases in nerve cells. *Ann. Rev. Neurosci.* 10:459–476.

Sherman, G. F., Galaburda, A. M., and Geschwind, N. 1985. Cortical anomalies in brains of New Zealand mice: A neuropathologic model of dyslexis? *Proc. Natl. Acad. Sci.* (USA) 82:8072–8074.

von der Malsburg, C., and Bienenstock, E. 1986. Statistical coding and short-term synaptic plasticity: A scheme for knowledge representation in the brain. In *Disordered systems and biological organization*, ed. E. Bienestock, F. Fogelman, and G. Weisbuch. Berlin: Springer-Verlag.

Editor's Comments

In a recent conference on reductionism and cognition the philosopher Paul M. Churchland praised reductionistic efforts as potentially leading to "better generalizations," "better coherence," and "fewer ad hoc explanations (also see Churchland and Sejnowski in this volume)." The present chapter offers several examples of the most productive approaches in contemporary, reductionistic behavioral research, outlines the types of biological generalizations that can be made, but is also careful to point out caveats.

Many objections have been raised to reductionist approaches. Some of those objecting have recently argued that a distinction must be drawn between what the brain does and how it does it. What the brain does, the behavior, can eventually be decomposed into behavioral modules and smaller functional units; how it does it can eventually be explained by anatomical changes that range down to molecular rearrangements. What it does can be explained in terms of the algorithms run; how it does it can be explained by describing changes in the machineries that run the algorithms.

It is not my intention in these comments to support or attack reductionist approaches, but it is important to remember that findings at the molecular level are devoid of functional meaning in the absence of knowledge about the behavior to be explained, as is amply emphasized in the present chapter. Moreover, despite occasionally perfect top-down correlations between simple behaviors and molecular changes, it is clear that molecular events cannot predict a specific behavior unless behavior at higher levels or even the next higher level of organization is specified. For instance, we are reminded that the cyclic-AMP cascade associated with gill retraction in *Aplysia* is employed in other innate and associative behaviors in this mollusk and indeed in several altogether different behaviors in species as distant as *Drosophila*.

The neural context in which these molecular events occur (i.e., the types, numbers, and connections of neurons involved) determine in large part the nature of the behavior. The architectural specificity of these higher-level structures is itself under molecular control that is partly genetic and partly epigenetic. These building mechanisms may also be shared to some extent by widely different species (see Crossin and Edelman and the comments to Churchland and Sejnowski in this volume).

The ultimate actual behaviors to result from molecular changes as they work their way up through molecular architectures, neurons, neuronal assemblies, a multipurpose brain, and a multisystem organism will be determined by ecological constraints that bear upon the behaving animal in its environment. It would be indeed fascinating, for instance, to discover fully the neural to molecular events that support reading. But *what* we read and *why* we read are even more important, and if the neural substrates do not suffice to explain what we read and why we read, alternative mechanisms must be sought.

Changes observed at the behavioral level can be shown to correlate perfectly with changes seen at the molecular level, but this does not mean that the molecular changes are causally related to the behavior. The philosopher Clifford A. Hooker has argued that no form of decomposition can possibly address questions of causality, which instead requires additional recomposition, a sort of scientific analysis followed by an engineering project. For instance, many of the molecular events observed to correlate with behavioral changes may be epiphenomena that do not lead to the function to be explained but instead reflect building and maintenance of the machineries required to support other, functionally relevant chemical changes that presently escape detection. Unless the reconstruction of the suspected molecular events alone leads to the expected behavior, a causal relation cannot be established.

Molecular events are shared by various functionally distinct systems and by different onto- and phylogenetic states, and distinct molecular events can result in comparable behaviors. Therefore, genetic lesions affecting a shared chemical reaction would not ordinarily produce focal or restricted cognitive disabilities but should rather disrupt function at all loci where the reaction is employed. Alternatively, a genetic disorder affecting a shared chemical reaction can result in altered behavior only in those systems that have neither alternative molecular strategies for the same behavior nor compensatory strategies at any other higher level up to the behavior itself. Moreover, the altered behavior might go unnoticed more easily in some systems rather than others missing the molecular reaction because of determinants present at higher levels.

A corollary hypothesis would be that the presence in a behavioral disorder of several abnormal cognitive functions would more likely implicate shared lower-level reactions, while a more discrete functional disturbance is more likely to implicate a higher-level alteration. For instance, primary disorders of attention in which abnormality is observed in several cognitive modalities should have a lower (possibly even molecular) level of explanation than developmental dyslexia, which is mainly language dysfunction. In partial support of this hypothesis is the observation that medications, which act at the molecular level, are markedly more useful in the former disorder than in the latter.

Contributors

Randall Alliger
Department of Preventive
Medicine
College of Medicine
University of Iowa
Iowa City, Iowa

Ursula Bellugi
Laboratory of Language and
Cognitive Sciences
Salk Institute for Biological
Studies
La Jolla, California

Paul Bertelson
Laboratoire de psychologie
expérimentale
Université libre de Bruxelles
Brussels

Thomas G. Bever
University of Rochester
Rochester, New York

Caroline Carrithers
Johns Hopkins University
Baltimore, Maryland

Verne S. Caviness, Jr.
Department of Neurology
Massachusetts General Hospital
Harvard Medical School
Boston, Massachusetts

Patricia Smith Churchland
Department of Philosophy
University of California,
San Diego
La Jolla, California

Wayne Cowart
Ohio State University
Columbus, Ohio

Kathryn L. Crossin
Rockefeller University
New York, New York

Antonio R. Damasio
Department of Neurology
College of Medicine
University of Iowa
Iowa City, Iowa

Hanna Damasio
Department of Neurology
College of Medicine
University of Iowa
Iowa City, Iowa

Béatrice De Gelder
Tilburg University
Tilburg, Netherlands

Yadin Dudai
Department of Neurobiology
Weizmann Institute of Science
Rehovot, Israel

Gerald M. Edelman
Rockefeller University
New York, New York

Angela Fok
University of Hong Kong
Salk Institute for Biological
Studies
La Jolla, California

Jean-François Gadisseux
Department of Pediatric
Neurology
Université catholique de
Louvain
Brussels

Albert M. Galaburda
Department of Neurology
Beth Israel Hospital
Harvard Medical School
Boston, Massachusetts

Henry Gleitman
Department of Psychology
University of Pennsylvania
Philadelphia, Pennsylvania

Lila Gleitman
Department of Psychology
University of Pennsylvania
Philadelphia, Pennsylvania

Edward S. Klima
University of California,
San Diego
Salk Institute for Biological
Studies
La Jolla, California

Norman A. Krasnegor
National Institute of Child
Health and Human
Development
Bethesda, Maryland

Barbara Landau
Department of Psychology
Columbia University
New York, New York

André Roch Lecours
Laboratoire Théophile-
Alajouanine
Centre de recherche du Centre
hospitalier
Côte-des-Neiges
Université de Montréal
Montreal, Quebec

James L. McClelland
Department of Psychology
Carnegie-Mellon University
Pittsburgh, Pennsylvania

Bruce S. McEwen
Laboratory of
Neuroendocrinology
Rockefeller University
New York, New York

John C. Marshall
Radcliffe Infirmary
Oxford

Jacques Mehler
Laboratoire de sciences et
psycholinguistique
Centre d'études des processus
cognitifs et du langage
Paris

Jean-Paul Misson
Department of Developmental
Anatomy and Pathology
Eunice Kennedy Shriver Center
Waltham, Massachusetts

John Morton
Cognitive Development Unit
Medical Research Council
London

Pasko Rakic
Section of Neuroanatomy
Yale University School of
Medicine
New Haven, Connecticut

Glenn D. Rosen
Department of Neurology
Beth Israel Hospital
Harvard Medical School
Boston, Massachusetts

Mark S. Seidenberg
Department of Psychology
McGill University
Montreal, Quebec

Terrence J. Sejnowski
Salk Institute for Biological
Studies
La Jolla, California

Gordon F. Sherman
Department of Neurology
Beth Israel Hospital
Harvard Medical School
Boston, Massachusetts

Jon Spradling
Department of Neurology
College of Medicine
University of Iowa
Iowa City, Iowa

David J. Townsend
Montclair State College
Montclair, New Jersey

Daniel Tranel
Department of Neurology
College of Medicine
University of Iowa
Iowa City, Iowa

Ovid Tzeng
University of California,
Riverside
Salk Institute for Biological
Studies
La Jolla, California

Eric Wanner
Russell Sage Foundation
New York, New York

Index